Heritage Signature® Auction #1136

FUN 2010 ORLANDO

Platinum Night

January 7, 2010 | Orlando, Florida

LOT VIEWING
Orange County Convention Center
North Concourse, Level 2
Room 220 D, E, F
9400 Universal Boulevard • Orlando, FL 32819

Monday, January 4, 2010 • 10:00 AM - 7:00 PM ET
Tuesday, January 5, 2010 • 8:00 AM - 7:00 PM ET
Wednesday, January 6, 2010 • 8:00 AM - 7:00 PM ET
Thursday, January 7, 2010 • 8:00 AM - 7:00 PM ET
Friday, January 8, 2010 • 8:00 AM - 7:00 PM ET
Saturday, January 9, 2010 • 8:00 AM - 6:00 PM ET

View Lots and Video Lot descriptions Online at HA.com/Coins

LIVE FLOOR BIDDING
Bid in person during the floor sessions.

LIVE TELEPHONE BIDDING *(floor sessions only)*
Phone bidding must be arranged on or before Tuesday, January 5, 2010, by 12:00 PM CT.
Client Service: 866-835-3243.

HERITAGE Live!™ BIDDING
Bid live from your location, anywhere in the world, during the Auction using our HERITAGE Live!™ program at HA.com/Live

INTERNET BIDDING
Internet absentee bidding ends at 10:00 PM CT the evening before each session. HA.com/Coins

FAX BIDDING
Fax bids must be received on or before Tuesday, January 5, 2010, by 12:00 PM CT. Fax: 214-409-1425

MAIL BIDDING
Mail bids must be received on or before Tuesday, January 5, 2010.

Please see "Choose Your Bidding Method" in the back of this catalog for specific details about each of these bidding methods.
This auction is subject to a 15% Buyer's Premium.
Extended Payment Terms available. See details in the back of this catalog.
Lots are sold at an approximate rate of 200 lots per hour, but it is not uncommon to sell 150 lots or 250 lots in any given hour.

LIVE AUCTION
SIGNATURE® FLOOR SESSIONS 1-5
(Floor, Telephone, HERITAGE Live!,™ Internet, Fax, and Mail)
Orange County Convention Center
North Concourse, Level 2 • Room 230 B
9400 Universal Boulevard • Orlando, FL 32819

SESSION 1 *(see separate catalog)*
Wednesday, January 6, 2010 • 7:00 PM ET • Lots 1–958

SESSION 2
THE BOCA COLLECTION, PART I *(see separate catalog)*
Thursday, January 7, 2010 • 6:30 PM ET • Lots 2001–2071

SESSION 3 - PLATINUM NIGHT
Thursday, January 7, 2010
Immediately following Session 2 (Approximately 7:00 PM)
Lots 2072–2646

SESSION 4 *(see separate catalog)*
Friday, January 8, 2010 • 12:00 PM ET • Lots 2647-3405

SESSION 5 *(see separate catalog)*
Friday, January 8, 2010 • 7:00 PM ET • Lots TBD

NON FLOOR/NON PHONE BIDDING SESSIONS 6-7
(HERITAGE Live!,™ Internet, Fax, and Mail only)

SESSION 6 *(see separate catalog)*
Saturday, January 9, 2010 • 2:00 PM CT • Lots 7001–8490

SESSION 7 *(see separate catalog)*
Sunday, January 10, 2010 • 2:00 PM CT • Lots 8491–10201

AUCTION RESULTS
Immediately available at HA.com/Coins

LOT SETTLEMENT AND PICK-UP
Room 220 D, E, F
Thursday, January 7, 2010 • 10:00 AM - 1:00 PM ET
Friday, January 8, 2010 • 10:00 AM - 1:00 PM ET
Saturday, January 9, 2010 • 10:00 AM - 1:00 PM ET
Sunday, January 10, 2010 • 9:00 AM - 12:00 PM ET

THIS AUCTION IS PRESENTED AND CATALOGED BY HERITAGE NUMISMATIC AUCTIONS, INC.

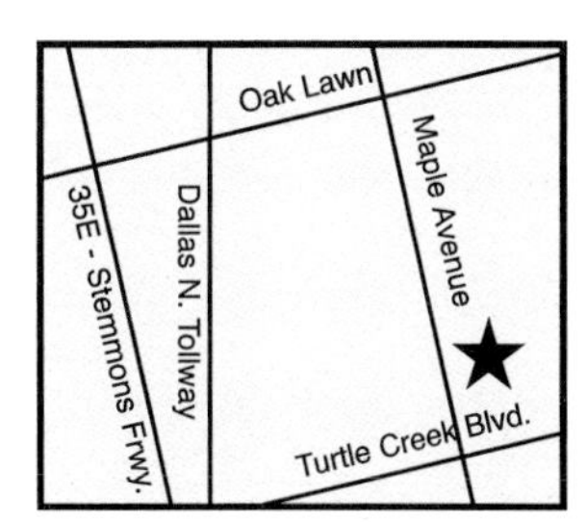

Heritage World Headquarters

HERITAGE HA.com
Auction Galleries

Home Office • 3500 Maple Avenue, 17th Floor • Dallas, Texas 75219
Design District Annex • 1518 Slocum Street • Dallas, Texas 75207
214.528.3500 | 800.872.6467 | 214.409.1425 (fax)
Direct Client Service Line: Toll Free 1.866.835.3243 • Email: Bid@HA.com

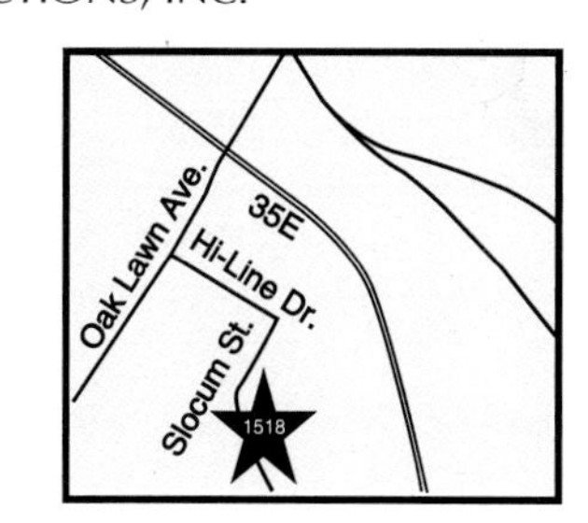

Heritage Design District Annex

FL licenses: Heritage Numismatic Auctions, Inc.: AB665; Currency Auctions of America: AB2218; FL Auctioneer licenses: Samuel Foose AU3244; Robert Korver AU2916; Mike Sadler AU3795; Shaunda Fry AU3915; Jacob Walker AU4031; Andrea Voss AU4034.

HERITAGE Live! Patent Pending

18259

DIRECTORY FOR DEPARTMENT SPECIALISTS AND SERVICES

COINS & CURRENCY

COINS – UNITED STATES

HA.com/Coins

Leo Frese, Ext. 1294
Leo@HA.com
David Mayfield, Ext. 1277
DavidM@HA.com
Jessica Aylmer, Ext. 1706
JessicaA@HA.com
Diedre Buchmoyer, Ext. 1794
DiedreB@HA.com
Win Callender, Ext. 1415
WinC@HA.com
Bert DeLaGarza, Ext. 1795
BertD@HA.com
Chris Dykstra, Ext. 1380
ChrisD@HA.com
Sam Foose, Ext. 1227
SamF@HA.com
Jason Friedman, Ext. 1582
JasonF@HA.com
Shaunda Fry, Ext. 1159
ShaundaF@HA.com
Jim Jelinski, Ext. 1257
JimJ@HA.com
Katherine Kurachek, Ext. 1389
KK@HA.com
Bob Marino, Ext. 1374
BobMarino@HA.com
Mike Sadler, Ext. 1332
MikeS@HA.com

RARE CURRENCY

HA.com/Currency

Len Glazer, Ext. 1390
Len@HA.com
Allen Mincho, Ext. 1327
Allen@HA.com
Dustin Johnston, Ext. 1302
Dustin@HA.com
Michael Moczalla, Ext. 1481
MichaelM@HA.com
Jason Friedman, Ext. 1582
JasonF@HA.com

U.S. COINS PRIVATE TREATY SALES

HA.com/Coins

Todd Imhof, Ext. 1313
Todd@HA.com

U.S. COINS PURCHASED

HA.com/Coins

Jim Stoutjesdyk, Ext. 1310
JimS@HA.com

WORLD & ANCIENT COINS

HA.com/WorldCoins

Warren Tucker, Ext. 1287
WTucker@HA.com
Cristiano Bierrenbach, Ext. 1661
CrisB@HA.com
Scott Cordry, Ext. 1369
ScottC@HA.com

COMICS & COMIC ART

HA.com/Comics

Ed Jaster, Ext. 1288
EdJ@HA.com
Lon Allen, Ext. 1261
LonA@HA.com
Barry Sandoval, Ext. 1377
BarryS@HA.com
Todd Hignite, Ext. 1790
ToddH@HA.com

FINE ART

AMERICAN & EUROPEAN PAINTINGS & SCULPTURE

HA.com/FineArt

Edmund P. Pillsbury, Ph.D., Ext. 1533
EPP@HA.com
Ed Jaster, Ext. 1288
EdJ@HA.com
Courtney Case, Ext. 1293
CourtneyC@HA.com
Marianne Berardi, Ph.D., Ext. 1506
MarianneB@HA.com
Ariana Hartsock, Ext. 1283
ArianaH@HA.com

ART OF THE AMERICAN WEST

HA.com/WesternArt

Michael Duty, Ext. 1712
MichaelD@HA.com

FURNITURE & DECORATIVE ART

HA.com/Decorative

Tim Rigdon, Ext. 1119
TimR@HA.com
Meredith Meuwly, Ext. 1631
MeredithM@HA.com
Nicholas Dawes, Ext. 1605
NickD@HA.com

ILLUSTRATION ART

HA.com/Illustration

Ed Jaster, Ext. 1288
EdJ@HA.com
Todd Hignite, Ext. 1790
ToddH@HA.com

MODERN & CONTEMPORARY ART

HA.com/Modern

Frank Hettig, Ext. 1157
FrankH@HA.com

SILVER & VERTU

HA.com/Silver

Tim Rigdon, Ext. 1119
TimR@HA.com

TEXAS ART

HA.com/TexasArt

Atlee Phillips, Ext. 1786
AtleeP@HA.com

20TH-CENTURY DESIGN

HA.com/Design

Christina Japp, Ext. 1247
CJapp@HA.com
Nicholas Dawes, Ext. 1605
NickD@HA.com

VINTAGE & CONTEMPORARY PHOTOGRAPHY

HA.com/ArtPhotography

Ed Jaster, Ext. 1288
EdJ@HA.com

HISTORICAL

AMERICAN INDIAN ART

HA.com/AmericanIndian

Delia Sullivan, Ext. 1343
DeliaS@HA.com

AMERICANA & POLITICAL

HA.com/Historical

Tom Slater, Ext. 1441
TomS@HA.com
Marsha Dixey, Ext. 1455
MarshaD@HA.com
John Hickey, Ext. 1264
JohnH@HA.com
Michael Riley, Ext. 1467
MichaelR@HA.com

CIVIL WAR AND ARMS & MILITARIA

HA.com/CivilWar

Dennis Lowe, Ext. 1182
DennisL@HA.com

HISTORICAL MANUSCRIPTS

HA.com/Manuscripts

Sandra Palomino, Ext. 1107
SandraP@HA.com

RARE BOOKS

HA.com/Books

James Gannon, Ext. 1609
JamesG@HA.com
Joe Fay, Ext. 1544
JoeF@HA.com

SPACE EXPLORATION

HA.com/Space

John Hickey, Ext. 1264
JohnH@HA.com
Michael Riley, Ext. 1467
MichaelR@HA.com

TEXANA

HA.com/Historical

Sandra Palomino, Ext. 1107
SandraP@HA.com

JEWELRY & TIMEPIECES

FINE JEWELRY

HA.com/Jewelry

Jill Burgum, Ext. 1697
JillB@HA.com

WATCHES & FINE TIMEPIECES

HA.com/Timepieces

Jim Wolf, Ext. 1659
JWolf@HA.com

MUSIC & ENTERTAINMENT MEMORABILIA

HA.com/Entertainment

Doug Norwine, Ext. 1452
DougN@HA.com
John Hickey, Ext. 1264
JohnH@HA.com
Garry Shrum, Ext. 1585
GarryS@HA.com
Jim Steele, Ext. 1328
JimSt@HA.com
Kristen Painter, Ext. 1149
KristenP@HA.com

NATURAL HISTORY

HA.com/NaturalHistory

David Herskowitz, Ext. 1610
DavidH@HA.com

RARE STAMPS

HA.com/Stamps

Harvey Bennett, Ext. 1185
HarveyB@HA.com
Steven Crippe, Ext. 1777
StevenC@HA.com

SPORTS COLLECTIBLES

HA.com/Sports

Chris Ivy, Ext. 1319
CIvy@HA.com
Peter Calderon, Ext. 1789
PeterC@HA.com
Mike Gutierrez, Ext. 1183
MikeG@HA.com
Lee Iskowitz, Ext. 1601
LeeI@HA.com
Mark Jordan, Ext. 1187
MarkJ@HA.com
Chris Nerat, Ext. 1615
ChrisN@HA.com
Jonathan Scheier, Ext. 1314
JonathanS@HA.com

VINTAGE MOVIE POSTERS

HA.com/MoviePosters

Grey Smith, Ext. 1367
GreySm@HA.com
Bruce Carteron, Ext. 1551
BruceC@HA.com
Isaiah Evans, Ext. 1201
IsaiahE@HA.com

TRUSTS & ESTATES

HA.com/Estates
Mark Prendergast, Ext. 1632
MPrendergast@HA.com

CORPORATE & INSTITUTIONAL COLLECTIONS/VENTURES

Jared Green, Ext. 1279
Jared@HA.com

AUCTION OPERATIONS

Norma Gonzalez, Ext. 1242
V.P. Auction Operations
Norma@HA.com

CREDIT DEPARTMENT

Marti Korver, Ext. 1248
Marti@HA.com
Eric Thomas, Ext. 1241
EricT@HA.com

MARKETING

Debbie Rexing, Ext. 1356
DebbieR@HA.com

MEDIA & PUBLIC RELATIONS

Noah Fleisher, Ext. 1143
NoahF@HA.com

HOUSTON OFFICE

Mark Prendergast
713-899-8364
MPrendergast@HA.com

CORPORATE OFFICERS

R. Steven Ivy, Co-Chairman
James L. Halperin, Co-Chairman
Gregory J. Rohan, President
Paul Minshull, Chief Operating Officer
Todd Imhof, Executive Vice President
Leo Frese, Vice President

Dear Platinum Night Bidder,

Welcome to another thrilling Platinum Night Auction, highlighted by the Olsen/Hawaii Five-O 1913 Liberty nickel, the 1927-D twenty out of the Ralph P. Muller Collection, one of only two known Bickford $10 pieces struck in gold, the Proof Sets of the Boca Collection, and hundreds of other significant rarities. The Platinum Night catalogs showcase the finest numismatic items available at Heritage's Official Auction at FUN 2010.

FUN 2010 contains the 'best-of-the-best' treasures from more than 575 consignors (750+ including NYINC), and especially from our anchor consignors:

- The Atherton Family Collection
- The Jerry Bagne Collection of Prooflike Commemoratives, Part Two
- The Big Sky Montana Collection
- The Boca Collection, Part I
- The Jay Brahin Collection
- The Chandler Collection, Part Two
- The Cherokee County Collection, Part One
- The Five Point Collection
- The Kiev Collection
- The Ralph P. Muller Collection
- The Snow White Collection

I invite you to read more about these collections in the main Signature® catalog and in the dedicated catalogs.

We consider every Platinum Night a very special event, and we have heard from hundreds of bidders that they feel the same way. These wonderful numismatic rarities are a thrill to inspect, and even more so to own after the very spirited competition that is also a Platinum Night tradition! Heritage held our first Platinum Night at FUN 2004, and since then they have a well-deserved reputation among the entire collecting community.

If you wish to stretch your budget to buy one of these special coins, please consider our Extended Payment Plan – the details can be found online at HA.com, or contact Eric Thomas at 214.409.1241 (e-mail EPP@HA.com).

We cordially invite you to attend FUN personally, and remind you to please stop by our bourse booth and introduce yourself – especially if you have never had the opportunity to attend the year's best attended convention. If you cannot join us in Orlando, remember that HERITAGE Live! (the unique bidding system at HA.com) allows you to personally and easily bid through the Internet at the live session. You really can directly participate in all of the excitement of the auction floor action from your kitchen table or from your hotel room, wherever in the world you are. However you participate, enjoy yourself, and good luck with your bidding! We thank the fine folks of FUN and the entire collecting community for your continued support; we never forget that serving the collector is the basis of our success.

Sincerely,

Greg Rohan
President

EARLY PROOF SETS

Splendid 1859 Silver-Minor Proof Set

2072 **1859 7-Piece Proof Set NGC.** In 1859 the Indian cent made its debut, the three cent silver piece had its design modified, the half dime had special "hollow stars," and the dime ended its design at Philadelphia.

1859 Cent PR65 Cameo. After a short production of Flying Eagle cents, the design of the still new small cent was changed to an Indian on the obverse, and a laurel wreath on the reverse. This lovely tan Gem Cameo proof has exceptional contrast with fully mirrored fields and frosty devices. Faint amber, blue, and iridescent toning adds to its eye appeal. Census: 7 in 65 Cameo, 6 finer (11/09).

1859 Three Cent Silver PR65. While the basic design of the three cent silver coins remained the same, slight modifications took place in 1854 and again in 1859. The initial design had a plain star on the obverse. From 1854 to 1858 the Type Two obverse had a double outline around the star. Beginning in 1859, and continuing to the end of the series in 1873, the Type Three obverse had a single outline around the star. This deeply toned piece is exceptional for its brilliant blue and iridescent presentation over fully mirrored proof surfaces. Census: 21 in 65, 11 finer (11/09).

1859 Half Dime PR64. The center of each star is hollow, meaning that it had to be raised in the actual die. The 1 in the date is boldly repunched below, while the 8, 5, and 9 a re each slightly repunched. This pleasing piece is attractively toned and shows excellent contrast between the mirrored fields and lustrous devices.

1859 Dime PR65 Cameo. Although it remained in production the following year on the West Coast, the Stars Obverse design ceased to exist after 1859 in Philadelphia. This Gem Cameo proof has gorgeous iridescent toning over fully mirrored fields and highly lustrous devices. Census: 8 in 65 Cameo, 17 finer (11/09).

1859 Quarter PR65. A lovely example, this Gem exhibits obvious cameo contrast, although the toning prevents such a designation from the grading service. This piece has fully mirrored fields that frame its satiny devices, all beneath moderate iridescent toning. Census: 15 in 65, 16 finer (11/09).

1859 Half Dollar PR65. A borderline cameo piece, this Gem proof half dollar has excellent field-device contrast with delicate iridescent toning on each side. It is a splendid piece that might have been assigned the Cameo designation on any other day. Census: 19 in 65, 7 finer (11/09).

1859 Dollar PR66 NGC. The majestic Seated Liberty silver dollar, the largest physical coin in this set, is also the highest graded piece, as it should be with its amazing aesthetic appeal. The surfaces are deeply mirrored and contrast nicely with the lustrous devices, all beneath delightful gold and iridescent toning. Census: 18 in 66, 4 finer (11/09).

UNITED STATES OF AMERICA
1884
ONE CENT
III
V
CENTS
ONE DIME
QUAR. DOL.
HALF DOL.
E PLURIBUS UNUM
In God we trust
ONE DOLLAR

Wonderful 1884 Proof Set, NGC Certified

2073 1884 7-Piece Proof Set NGC. Mint records indicate that 3,942 proofs of each minor denomination were struck in 1884, alongside 875 proofs of each silver denomination. Proof Trade dollars were officially discontinued the previous year, so this set includes a Morgan dollar as do most sets. There are 10 proof 1884 Trade dollars known, but those coins were made under speculative circumstances.

1884 Cent PR66★ Brown. A delightful Premium Gem proof, this piece has a blend of chestnut, sea-green, pale yellow, and light orange toning on the obverse, with deeper blue, violet, and lime-green on the reverse. The fields are nicely mirrored around frosty and boldly defined devices. NGC Census: 3 in 66★ Brown, 5 finer (12/09).

1884 Three Cent Nickel PR66 Cameo. The 1880s three cent pieces are infrequently found with such excellent contrast between the fields and devices, primarily because most of the proofs were poorly made with little mirrored surface. This piece is a wonderful exception. It is a fully brilliant Premium Gem proof with wisps of champagne toning. The fields are deeply mirrored and the sharply detailed devices are highly lustrous. NGC Census: 42 in PR66 Cameo, 18 finer (12/09).

1884 Five Cent PR63. This is the only piece in the present set that is below Gem quality, and its grade is the result of slightly subdued proof surfaces and minor spots. Both sides are sharply detailed with deep gold and iridescent toning.

1884 Dime PR65. Each of the silver coins in this 1884 proof set are nicely matched. This Gem proof has excellent contrast beneath its deep toning. The fields are fully mirrored around lustrous devices. The obverse exhibits deep heather and pale blue toning, while the reverse is deeper blue-green with peripheral light yellow.

1884 Quarter PR66. A stunning Premium Gem proof, this piece has fully mirrored fields and frosty devices beneath gorgeous emerald-green, cobalt-blue, and magenta toning. NGC Census: 36 in PR66, 18 finer (12/09).

1884 Half Dollar PR65. This boldly detailed Gem proof has mostly violet-gray and sea-green toning on each side with a splash of lighter silver on the reverse. Some contrast between the fields and devices remains evident beneath the toning. NGC Census: 30 in PR65, 19 finer (12/09).

1884 Morgan Dollar PR66. This beautiful Premium Gem proof is boldly struck with excellent field/device contrast. The obverse has violet, amber, pale blue, and light green toning, while the reverse is mostly sea-green and gold. NGC Census: 18 in PR66, 3 finer (12/09).(Total: 7 coins)

Desirable 1888 Silver-Minor Proof Set, NGC Certified

2074 1888 7-Piece Proof Set NGC. The proof production in 1888 included 4,582 examples of each minor denomination, 832 examples of the dime, quarter, and half dollar, and 833 Morgan dollars. We are unsure why the single extra proof Morgan was struck.

1888 Cent PR66★ Red and Brown. An amazing Indian cent, this Premium Gem proof has rich reddish-orange mint color, slightly subdued over time, with exceptional contrast. NGC Census: 1 in PR66★ Red and Brown, none finer (12/09).

1888 Three Cent Nickel PR65. Splashes of pale gold toning appear over the light gray surfaces of this Gem proof. All of the design elements are boldly detailed.

1888 Nickel PR63. Sharp design details confirm the proof status of this piece. The obverse has light gold toning with a few flecks, while the reverse has rainbow toning.

1888 Dime PR66. A lovely Premium Gem proof with outstanding iridescent toning and impressive design definition. A splash of light silver brilliance is evident on the obverse. NGC Census: 24 in PR66, 7 finer (12/09).

1888 Quarter PR64. The obverse of this attractive proof has a circle of light silver brilliance with violet and sea-green toning. The reverse is similar but slightly darker.

1888 Half Dollar PR66. A delightful Premium Gem, this piece has light contrast with considerable brilliant silver on the obverse, accented by rainbow toning. The reverse has violet and sea-green around central brilliance. NGC Census: 17 in PR66, 6 finer (12/09).

1888 Morgan Dollar PR64. An exceptional Choice proof with full cameo contrast beneath the toning, although it is not designated as a Cameo proof. This piece is deeply toned with sea-green and gold on each side, the reverse with additional violet and light silver brilliance.

Important Complete 1900 Proof Set PCGS
Cent Through Double Eagle
Sold as individual lots.

2075 1900 Cent PR65 Red and Brown PCGS. Close to a full Red designation, since the peach-red and honey-gold color has minimally mellowed over the past century. Intricately struck and flashy with the expected infrequent minuscule carbon. Neither side has any contact marks, and the eye appeal is obvious.

2076 1900 Nickel PR65 PCGS. Delicately toned in pastel gold and slate shades. The strike is bold except for the incompleteness on the left ear of corn that is characteristic of the series. One minute fleck beneath the hair bun and a hint of gray patina near the mouth, but otherwise a pleasing proof type coin.

2077 1900 Proof Dime PCGS Genuine. The PCGS number ending in .91 indicates Questionable Color as the reason, or perhaps one of the reasons, that PCGS deemed this coin not gradable. In our opinion, this proof coin shows no wear but has dull surfaces from dipping. Nonetheless, it is well struck and devoid of abrasions.

2078 1900 Quarter PR63 PCGS. A fully struck turn-of-the-century proof type coin. Mostly brilliant, although the obverse margin is golden-brown and the reverse border is gunmetal-gray, sun-gold, and plum-red. The portrait and eagle exhibit mild cameo contrast. One small granular area is noted near obverse star 13.

2079 1900 Half Dollar PR63 Cameo PCGS. Blushes of peach-red and electric-blue invigorate the peripheries of this otherwise brilliant Select proof. White-on-black contrast is impressive on both sides, and approaches a Deep Cameo designation. The glassy fields display a few trivial hairlines, visible only when inspected beneath a lens.

2080 1900 Morgan Dollar PR65 Cameo PCGS. A gleaming Gem proof with substantial field-to-device contrast. While the icy devices are silver-white, the fields take on a golden tint that adds splashes of deeper crimson color close to the squared rims. Outstanding visual appeal for this turn-of-the-century proof issue. Population: 8 in 65 Cameo, 4 finer (11/09).

2081 1900 Quarter Eagle PR66 Deep Cameo PCGS. At 205 proofs, the 1900 quarter eagle issue was the first of its denomination to exceed the 200 mark for pieces produced, with the next year's mintage of 223 examples the only other one to surpass that total in the Liberty series. This Deep Cameo specimen is outstandingly contrasted with stunning eye appeal. The yellow-gold mirrors turn nearly "black" at certain angles, bringing out the best of the cameo effect. Decisively detailed devices are thickly frosted, particularly on Liberty's portrait. Amazing eye appeal with few distractions. Population: 12 in 66 Deep Cameo, 5 finer (11/09).

2082 1900 Half Eagle PR65 Deep Cameo PCGS. As the highest-mintage proof Liberty half eagle issue (230 pieces struck), the 1900 is well known for its availability, though its total population is comparable to that of the significantly lower-mintage 1901 issue. Also interesting to note is that compared to 46 pieces not awarded any sort of contrast designation, PCGS has graded only 11 Deep Cameo specimens of this issue (11/09). This Gem ranks highly among them, as evidenced by the population of just two coins in PR65 Deep Cameo with only one Deep Cameo coin finer. Smooth "black" fields offer virtually perfect contrast with the textured yellow-gold of the devices. Only a hint of cloudiness is visible below Liberty's hair bun.

2083 1900 Eagle PR65 Deep Cameo PCGS. At 120 pieces struck, the 1900 has the distinction of being the highest-mintage Liberty eagle proof issue, though all is not as it appears; standing in direct contrast to the mintage is Walter Breen's assertion, found in his *Proof Coin Encyclopedia*, that the date is "[l]ess often seen than its mintage suggests, and might legitimately be called rare." With recourse to contemporary certified population data, this assertion is ratified, if by a slim margin; the number of PCGS certification instances for the 1900 across all contrast designations is lower than that of the 1903, 1904, or 1907, all of which have smaller proof mintages.

More specifically, PCGS has 37 certification events in its *Population Report*, as of (11/09), with seven Deep Cameo coins, three Cameo pieces, and the rest not designated as either. This Gem Deep Cameo specimen is one of three so graded, with only three numerically finer Deep Cameo pieces certified by the same service.

This specimen offers gleaming yellow-gold fields which show only mild traces of orange-peel texture, which appear mostly around the upper obverse stars. The boldly frosted portrait and eagle have pale, icy color which contrasts dramatically with the fields, which are "black" at most angles. Close examination reveals only a handful of minuscule contact marks in the fields, though these minor flaws preclude an even finer designation.

2084 1900 Double Eagle PR65 Cameo PCGS. The 1900 double eagle proof issue is unusual among the year's gold proofs in that it was not the highest-mintage proof issue of its denomination up to that time; in 1896, Philadelphia coined 128 proofs, versus just 124 specimens for 1900. Still, the high mintage does not equate to widespread accessibility. Garrett and Guth, in their *Encyclopedia of U.S. Gold Coins*, state that "Although the number of coins known for this date is relatively high for a Proof Liberty Head double eagle, many are impaired or otherwise damaged. There are probably around 50 examples known in all levels of preservation."

While this issue was struck before the brilliant-proof watershed year of 1902, strongly contrasted coins are rarely found. Garrett and Guth hedge, claiming "The 1900 double eagle is seen with and without cameo devices." Such an assertion is meaningless without hard numbers, however, and a quick check of the PCGS *Population Report* reveals that out of 51 certification events as of (11/09), just 13 of those resulted in a Cameo or Deep Cameo grade.

This is the finest of seven Cameo examples certified by PCGS, though there are also five Deep Cameo coins at the same grade level, as well as a PR66 coin without any contrast designation. The contrast level is decidedly on the upper end of the Cameo scale, though ultimately it falls just short of the next level. Powerful yellow-gold mirrors show only occasional cloudy elements, though a small planchet flaw is noted near Liberty's chin. Still, this is a pleasingly preserved and undeniably appealing Gem that commands respect as a high-end proof gold survivor.

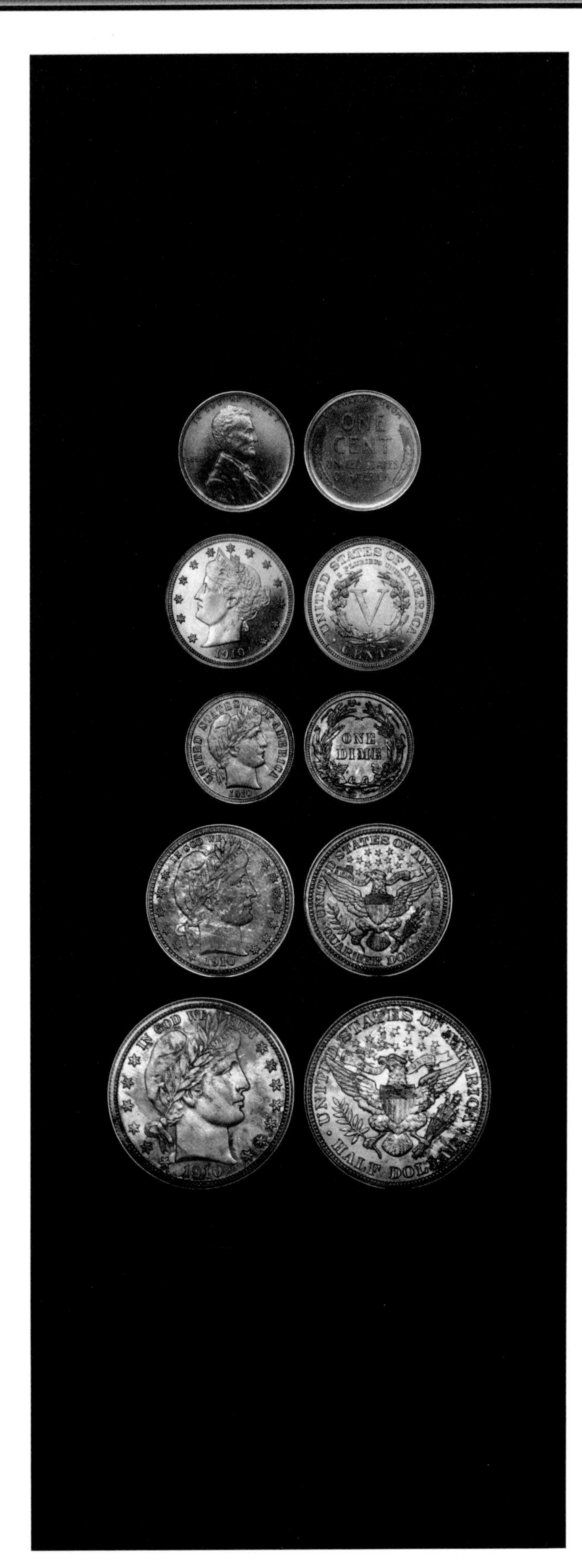

Exceptional 1910 Proof Set, PR65 to PR68 Cent Through Half Dollar

2085 **Five Piece 1910 Proof Set PR65 to PR68 NGC.** This important set includes:

1910 cent PR65 Red and Brown NGC. Magnificently toned in swaths of cherry-red, orange-gold, and powder-blue. Satiny and exactingly struck with nary a trace of contact. Carbon is virtually impossible to locate. Matte proof Lincoln cents are underappreciated, especially those with exceptionally attractive toning.

1910 nickel PR66 NGC. Medium honey-gold toning bathes this needle-sharp and prominently mirrored Premium Gem. A minuscule gray spot at 7:30 on the reverse, but otherwise immaculate.

1910 dime PR67 NGC. A deep blanket of lavender and cobalt-blue dominates the obverse, while the reverse exhibits moderately lighter shades of ocean-blue and canary-gold. The strike is unimprovable, and the surfaces appear undisturbed beneath the patina. A mere 551 proofs were released, and high grade survivors are rarities. Census: 12 in 67, 4 finer without a Cameo designation (11/09).

1910 quarter PR67 NGC. Richly variegated plum-red, magenta, and electric-blue consumes the obverse. Deep gunmetal-blue occupies the reverse. Both sides are immaculate. The strike is unusually sharp, even on the fletchings and right shield corner. A prize for the connoisseur of originally patinated silver proofs. As with the proof 1910 dime and half dollar, a mere 551 pieces were produced. Census: 23 in 67, 10 finer without a Cameo designation (11/09).

1910 half dollar PR68 NGC. Iridescently toned in peach-gold, powder-blue, slate-gray, and apple-green. The remarkably preserved fields are flashy, and the motifs are fully impressed save for the knuckles on the right (facing) claw. Extraordinary quality for this low mintage proof date. Census: 7 in 68, 2 in 68 Cameo, none finer (11/09).(Total: 5 coins)

GOLD DOLLARS

Spectacular 1854 Type Two Gold Dollar, MS66

2086 1854 Type Two MS66 PCGS. CAC. The 1854 Type Two gold dollars have a well-deserved reputation as among the most difficult U.S. gold type coins to acquire in problem-free high grade. The entire series has a checkered and interesting history. In the first place, the U.S. Mint came very late to the party: The one dollar denomination had been produced by the Bechtler family of Rutherford Country, North Carolina, beginning in 1831, but only in 1849 did Congress authorize a federal issue. The Type One coins, made from 1849-1854, were too small. The Type Two coins, introduced in midyear 1854, were larger in diameter, but to compensate for the fixed alloy and gold content, they were also thinner. Compounding the trouble were the high-relief design and the placement of the high points of each side in direct opposition, so that full strikes were virtually unheard of, die clashes were common, and weak strikes were the norm.

Another peculiarity of coin series of this era is a phenomenon known as Longacre doubling, named after Mint Engraver James B. Longacre. According to the fifth edition, volume I of *Cherrypickers' Guide:*

> "This term was coined by J.T. Stanton as an easy way to describe the doubling that is typical on many coins designed by James Barton Longacre. These include Indian Head cents, nickel three-cent pieces, Shield nickels, and many gold issues. We're certain many readers have seen this doubling before; almost all of the letters are doubled, with the secondary image appearing on both sides of the letters. Some specialists believe this is from the shoulder of the punch penetrating the die, causing the secondary step. Others feel it was an intentional design on Longacre's part, to help the metal flow into the tight crevices of the die. Although this doubling is evident on many of the coins that Longacre designed, it is not seen on all his coins. This would likely remove the theory that the secondary or 'stepped' image was planned to help with metal flow."

While this spectacular Premium Gem shows the Longacre doubling around many of the obverse devices, there is no sign of die clashing. Even more unusual, the strike is full in all areas, a requirement for the grade but one seldom indeed seen. There are no obvious abrasions on either side, and deep mint luster complements the enormous appeal. Expect runaway bidding on this one. Population: 10 in 66, 2 finer (11/09).(#7531)

Low Mintage, Rare 1855-D Gold Dollar, AU58

2087 1855-D AU58 NGC. Variety 7-J. The scant mintage of 1,811 pieces and its very low survival rate makes the 1855-D gold dollar rare in all grades. NGC and PCGS have certified a little over 90 coins in all levels of preservation, a number of which are likely resubmissions. A mere 10 of these are Mint State, none finer than MS64.

The near-Mint State example in the present offering is therefore the highest grade that is likely to be encountered by most collectors. Rich orange-gold coloration splashed with powder-blue and lilac occupies both sides, each of which displays considerable luster and is minimally abraded. A well directed strike imparts strong definition to the design elements, including all of the letters in LIBERTY. Only the 8 in the date reveals the usual strike weakness. Census: 14 in 58, 6 finer (11/09).(#7534)

Boldly Struck 1856-S Type Two Gold Dollar MS63 Tied for Finest Graded at PCGS

2088 1856-S Type Two MS63 PCGS. The 1856-S gold dollar is an interesting issue of the Type Two subtype, struck at a time when the other mints making 1856-dated gold dollars—Philadelphia and Dahlonega—were already producing coins of the Type Three design. Breen writes, "The 1856 S dies were shipped west in 1855 before [Mint Director James Ross] Snowden's decision to redesign the obv." It was 1857 before San Francisco struck S-mint Type Three gold dollars.

As a result, the 1856-S issue is something of an anomaly, as the only S-mint Type Two gold dollar, the only 1856-dated Type Two, and the rarest of the six Type Two issues, which also include the 1854 and 1855 Philadelphia issues and the 1855 coins from Charlotte, Dahlonega, and New Orleans. All of the 1856-S gold dollars show repunching on the mintmark, despite some separate listings in various references. Later die states, diagnosed by die cracks or shattering, show less of the mintmark repunching due to die wear.

This is an especially well produced example that shows strong strike details in the centers of both sides. No die clash marks are present in the fields, which exhibit the often-seen semiprooflike finish. Each side is covered with rich reddish-orange patina. In MS63 this piece is one of only a half-dozen so graded at PCGS, and there are none finer (11/09). NGC has certified four pieces in MS64.

This coin would make a marvelous type coin for collectors seeking "something out of the ordinary" for that challenging Type Two spot in a gold type set.(#7536)

Enchanting 1867 Gold Dollar MS67 ★ Prooflike

2089 1867 MS67 ★ Prooflike NGC. The 1867 gold dollar, coming from a mintage of 5,200 circulation strikes, is rare in any level of preservation. NGC and PCGS have certified about 125 pieces in all grades. NGC has assigned only seven coins the Prooflike designation and has given the Star to only three examples—an MS66 and an MS67 nonprooflike and the present Superb Gem Prooflike.

Yellow-gold surfaces are splashed with apricot on the obverse. The design elements are exquisitely impressed and their frosty texture yields a good degree of contrast with the fields irrespective of the angle of observation. Clash marks are visible on both sides, but neither reveals post-strike impairments. The reverse is rotated a few degrees. All in all, this piece generates enchanting eye appeal.(#77566)

Delightful 1881 Gold Dollar, MS68

2090 1881 MS68 PCGS. CAC. Gold dollars of 1881 were apparently saved in large quantities at the time of issue, as evident from the several hundred Mint State examples certified by PCGS and NGC. Jeff Garrett and Ron Guth (2006) point to a famous hoard of 54 1881 gold coins sold to Paramount Rare Coins by Leo Lindheim, a well-known Cleveland collector and numismatic writer. Of these, 46 are reported to be circulation strikes and eight proofs.

The brassy-gold surfaces of this MS68 example display frosty, exquisitely struck design motifs that stand out against partially reflective fields. Close examination reveals immaculate preservation. These attributes add up to the most delightful eye appeal, aptly recognized by the CAC green label. Population: 38 in 68, 0 finer (11/09).(#7582)

PROOF GOLD DOLLAR

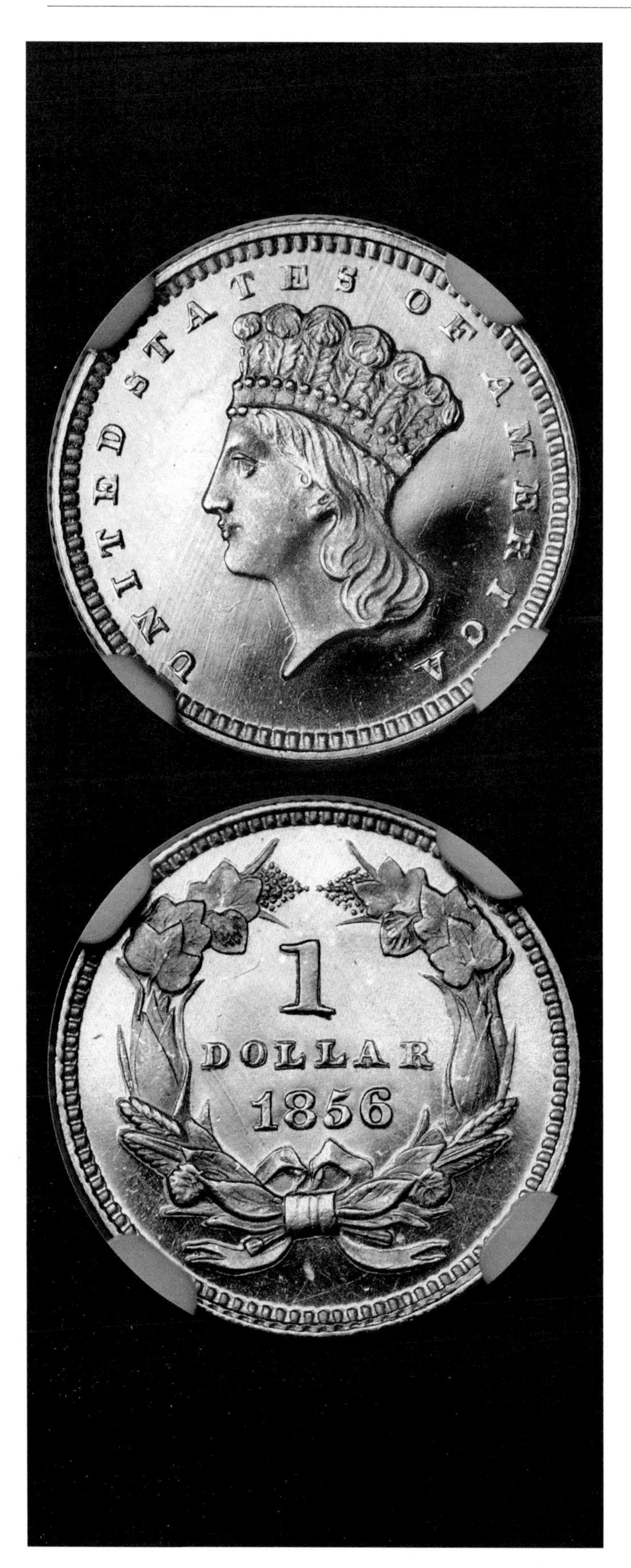

Glittering 1856 Gold Dollar, PR66 ★ Ultra Cameo

2091 1856 Slanted 5 PR66 ★ Ultra Cameo NGC. A variety of reasons makes this 1856 Type Three proof gold dollar one of the most important pieces in the present sale. The quality is exceptional with amazing cameo contrast between the fully and deeply mirrored fields and frosty devices, with rich lemon-yellow color and excellent rose toning highlights. As a major rarity in proof, there are only an estimated eight to 10 known examples, and this piece is the finest of all. It is a first year of issue type coin representing the third and final gold dollar design change. The strike is extraordinary and the aesthetic appeal is second to none.

The following roster of proof 1856 gold dollars presents just eight apparently distinctive specimens, with four others that may or may not be duplicates:

1. **PR66 ★ Ultra Cameo NGC**. Bowers and Merena (7/2002), lot 677. **The present specimen.**

2. **PR66 Cameo NGC**. Lorin G. Parmelee (New York Coin & Stamp Co. 1890), lot 1267; William H. Woodin, lot 856; F.C.C. Boyd; World's Greatest Collection (Numismatic Gallery, 1/1946), lot 11; Memorable Collection (Numismatic Gallery, 3/1948), lot 11; Thomas Melish (Abe Kosoff, 4/1956), lot 1750; John Jay Pittman (David Akers, 10/1997), lot 872; Bowers and Merena (3/2003), lot 2043.

3. **PR65 Ultra Cameo NGC** Superior (5/2004), lot 2252

4. **PR65 Deep Cameo.** Smithsonian Institution.

5. **PR65 PCGS** Stack's (4/1978), lot 769; Superior (1/1993), lot 1266; Heritage (1/2007), lot 3364; Heritage (8/1996), lot 8125.

6. **PR64 PCGS**. Stickney Collection (Henry Chapman, 1907); Clapp Collection (1942); Eliasberg Collection; Bowers 10/1982: 31; Connoisseur Sale (Superior, 1/1989), lot 259; Ed Trompeter; Superior 2/1992: 2; Bowers and Merena (1/1995), lot 1145.

7. **PR64 PCGS**. Bowers and Ruddy (12/27/1971); Harry W. Bass, Jr. Collection (Bowers and Merena, 5/2000), lot 28.

8. **Proof**. Wayte Raymond; private collection since 1938; David Akers; Auction '85 (Paramount, 7/1985), lot 1367; Harry W. Bass, Jr. Core Collection.

A. **Proof.** Charles Jay (Stack's, 10/1967), lot 217; Stack's (12/1994), lot 1162

B. **Proof.** R.C.W. Brock; University of Pennsylvania; Philip H. Ward, Jr. (Stack's, 4/1964), lot 1603

C. **Proof.** Major Lenox R. Lohr (Stack's, 10/1956), lot 967.

D. **Proof**. Brock; Morgan; ANS.(#97606)

1806/5 Capped Bust Right Quarter Eagle, AU58 7x6 Stars, BD-2 Rare Overdate of Previously Used Die

2092 1806/5 7x6 Stars AU58 NGC. Breen-6123, BD-2, High R.5. The year 1806 was the penultimate date for the Capped Bust Right type, which was retired in favor of John Reich's Capped Bust Left design after the 1807 coinage. Two die varieties are known for the date, both from overdated dies. The present coin is a representative of the less available BD-2 variety, characterized by the 7x6 arrangement of the obverse stars. From a tiny original mintage of 480 coins, the BD-2 die marriage is quite rare today. Experts estimate only 25-35 examples are known in all grades. In *Early U.S. Gold Coin Varieties,* John Dannreuther calls the issue "one of the rarest of the early quarter eagles," with only the 1796 No Stars BD-1, 1797 BD-1, and the 1804 13 Star Reverse quarter eagles more difficult to locate. Considering both leading grading services, a total of eight examples have been certified in AU58, with eight finer (11/09).

In their *Encyclopedia of U.S. Gold Coins 1795-1933,* Jeff Garrett and Ron Guth explain the unusual circumstances of the 1806/5 striking:

> "The 1806/5 overdate represents one of the rare instances when a die that had already been used to strike coins in one year was softened, overdated, rehardened, and then used to strike even more coins. Most other overdates occur on unused dies from previous years."

Perhaps the overdated obverse die failed quickly, accounting for the limited mintage.

The present coin is sharply struck, with bright, semiprooflike fields. Only slight, even wear is noted on the highest points of the design. A prominent die crack is visible through the top of LI in LIBERTY and a few adjustment marks are evident on the reverse center. (#7655)

MS61 Certified 1807 Quarter Eagle, BD-1

2093 1807 MS61 PCGS. Breen-6124. BD-1, R.3. The obverse stars are arranged seven and six, with the flag atop the 1 in the date solidly over Liberty's hair curl. Prominent arcing lathe lines are evident on Liberty's neck, and between hair strands. The obverse die was only used for this single marriage of 1807, totaling 6,812 strikes. On the reverse the stars between the clouds and eagle are large, UNITED is high, there are 13 arrows, and there are five berries. The reverse die saw extensive use on 1805, 1806, and 1807 quarter eagles, as well as 1807 dimes, more than 175,000 strikes for all varieties. The reverse die remained in excellent condition for all of the quarter eagles, only deteriorating toward the end of its use to produce the 1807 dimes.

This piece has splendid yellow luster with splashes of wispy orange toning especially evident on the reverse. The central obverse is a trifle weak, the result of reverse adjustment marks across the shield. A tiny rim disturbance is seen at 9:30 on the obverse. Population: 6 in 61, 21 finer (11/09).(#7656)

Low Mintage 1824/1 Quarter Eagle, BD-1, AU58

2094 1824/1 AU58 NGC. Breen-6127, BD-1, R.5. From a limited production of only 2,600 pieces, the 1824/1 Capped Head Left quarter eagle is a rare date in all grades. The great majority of the tiny mintage was destroyed by contemporary melters, and even circulated examples are seldom encountered today. John Dannreuther estimates a surviving population of 50-60 specimens in all grades, with the finest known specimens grading only MS64. Currently, NGC has graded eight examples in AU58, with nine finer; while PCGS has certified only three specimens in AU58, with nine finer (11/09).

All examples of this date are true overdates, with BD-1 the only variety known. The date was prized by early collectors, and the survival of the small population known today is entirely due to their efforts. An early auction appearance occurred in the Sixth Semi-Annual Sale (Woodward, 3/1865), lot 2799, "1824 Very fine, almost proof, very scarce." The lot realized a respectable $4, to J.O. Emery, a prominent early gold collector.

The present coin is an attractive specimen, with semiprooflike fields and bright yellow-gold color, overlaid with tones of orange. Traces of mint luster cling to the protected areas, near the devices. The coin is well struck, with some characteristic softness on the central design elements. The serif of the 1 is easily seen to the left of the top of the 4 in the date. A number of small abrasions in the fields surrounding the eagle are consistent with the grade. (#7663)

Classic 1826/5 Quarter Eagle AU58 Prooflike, BD-1

2095 1826/5 AU58 Prooflike NGC. Breen-6130, BD-1, High R.5. A classic rarity in a star-studded series, the 1826 is one of the top three quarter eagles struck from 1796 to 1834. According to Mint records, just 760 pieces were minted in 1826, although the actual mintage of quarter eagles bearing that date may have been a little higher.

The number of survivors is difficult to estimate, although it is probably in the range of 30 to 35 coins, the figure given by John Dannreuther in *Early U.S. Gold Coin Varieties, A Study of Die States, 1795-1834*. Other estimates range from a handful of pieces to 50 or more. The Heritage Permanent Auction Archives show just 10 previous offerings of the 1826 quarter eagle since 1993. The Smithsonian Institution has two business strikes, MS60 from the Mint Cabinet and AU58 from the Lilly Collection, ex Anderson-Dupont. Two or three pieces have been called proof in the past, although proofs of this date are probably unknown. Highly prooflike pieces such as the present coin exist.

All of those known today are from a single die pair. The obverse has sometimes been described as an 1826/5 overdate, although that is debatable. Careful examination of the date suggests that it is actually a repunched date, 1826/6. In his monograph on the quarter eagles, Walter Breen wrote that "this does not look at all like an overdate." John Dannreuther recently commented that "many, if not most, researchers now doubt the overdate status of this variety." One premise denying the overdate status is that all known 1825 quarter eagles have small stars on the obverse, while 1826 quarter eagles all have much larger stars. However, there is no denying the rarity of this issue.

Survivors are rare in all grades, with a combined NGC and PCGS population of just 22 coins, including resubmissions. Only the 1804 13 Stars rarity (13) and the 1834 Capped Bust (18) have lower NGC and PCGS combined populations. The combined average grade of those 22 submissions is 52.7, with 20 of the 22 grading events falling in the AU50 to MS61 grade range. These coins typically circulated for a short period of time before being hoarded because their gold content was worth more than face value.

Obverse die description: The date is well-spaced with the center of the curl over the left edge of the 6. The date is slightly closer to the bust than to the border, and the final digit leans slightly left. All stars are larger than in previous years. Star 1 is close to the bust and star 6 points to the center of the headband. The border has 96 dentils.

State a: perfect dies. State b: clashed dies.

Reverse die description: The reverse is the same die previously used in 1825 for BD-3 and it was used again for 1827 BD-1. The stem of the olive branch is over the right side of the D with its tip over the period following the D. The U and N are slightly low, the A in STATES leans slightly to the right, and the M in AMERICA is larger than the other letters. No letters in the legend touch. The numerator is shorter than the denominator and is titled left. The lowest arrow is connected to the bottom of the C. The border has 96 dentils.

State a: perfect dies. State b: clashed dies.

This early die state specimen exhibits fully mirrored fields on both sides, with no clash marks and no evidence of die lapping. The fields have a few insignificant blemishes, useful for pedigree purposes, and in some cases as struck. A trace of rub on the high points and a few minor slide marks on Liberty's cheek are all that separate it from a full Mint State grade. Both sides are brilliant yellow with a hint of green-gold color. A significant early quarter eagle, this 1826 is expected to generate considerable bidding interest before and during the sale.

Ex: Stack's (2/1968), lot 116.(#7665)

Bright MS63 1830 Quarter Eagle, BD-1

2096 1830 MS63 PCGS. Breen-6133, BD-1, R.4. The BD-1 of 1830 is one of "several single-variety years" known among the early quarter eagles, an unsurprising result given the annually small mintages for this red-headed stepchild of American coinage: There was simply no need for multiple die pairings. The recorded mintage for the 1830 was only 4,540 pieces, and the reverse die was reused again in 1831, 1832, 1833, and 1834. Bass-Dannreuther estimate that from 80 to 100 pieces survive today of the 1830 in all grades, of which this piece is in the upper echelon. The strike is sharp throughout, and the fields are semiprooflike with occasional patches of porosity, likely due to the quality of the original planchet. No mentionable marks appear on either side of this lustrous, bright yellow-gold piece.(#7670)

Prooflike Near-Gem 1831 Quarter Eagle, BD-1

2097 1831 MS64 NGC. Breen-6134, BD-1, R.4. The reverse of this die pairing is a carryover from 1830, an indication of the small mintages of this denomination that were the rule. Another indication of the small mintages is the number of coins auctioned as proofs, or exhibiting prooflike characteristics, as is the case here. The fields are fully prooflike on both sides, although a random scuff in the luster appears here and there. The strike is slightly soft in the centers, but it is full elsewhere. Liberty's lower hair curls, in particular, are marvelously well-detailed. The surfaces are bright yellow-gold, with minor planchet adjustment marks on a couple of the vertical shield stripes on the reverse. Bass-Dannreuther comment that "there are so many coins of this date that nearly qualify as Proofs that even recent auction appearances must be taken with a grain of salt." Census: 11 in 64, 8 finer (11/09).(#7671)

CLASSIC QUARTER EAGLE

Appealing 1834 Classic Quarter Eagle, MS64 ★

2098 1834 Classic MS64 ★ NGC. CAC. Breen-6138, Small Head, R.1. The most plentiful of four known 1834 Classic Head quarter eagle varieties. Judging from NGC/PCGS population figures, collectors can choose from a complete range of grades through near-Gem. Finer pieces are elusive. That said, a mere six coins have been designated with the NGC Star, this MS64 offering being one of them.

Rich peach-gold surfaces display occasional wisps of reddish-orange and a well executed strike leaves sharp definition on the design elements. A few scattered handling marks preclude Gem status but do not negate the coin's magnificent eye appeal that is aptly recognized by NGC and CAC. Census: 3 in 64 ★, 2 finer (11/09). (#7692)

LIBERTY QUARTER EAGLES

Elusive 1840-D Quarter Eagle, AU55

2099 1840-D AU55 NGC. Variety 1-A This issue is rare and underrated in all grades, and AU or finer pieces such as this Choice AU example are extremely rare. NGC and PCGS have combined to grade just nine finer examples of the date, including three Mint State coins. The reverse has heavy die cracks through the second T in STATES, the N in UNITED, and the M in AMERICA. The mintage figure of 3,532 coins goes a long way in explaining the rarity and especially conditional rarity of this Dahlonega Mint quarter eagle. Census: 7 in 55, 6 finer (11/09).(#7719)

Excellent 1843-C Large Date Quarter Eagle, MS62

2100 1843-C Large Date, Plain 4 MS62 NGC. Variety 1. The only Large Date variety known. The date and mintmark are nicely repunched, and that doubling is intertwined with clash marks from ATES. The obverse has a faint crack from star 8 to the border. On the reverse, the mintmarks is boldly repunched, the vertical shield lines extend up through all horizontal crossbars and the upper shield border, into the eagle's neck, some of the same vertical lines extend below the shield border, a crack joins the wing tip to the border at 10:30, and another begins at the top right of the final S, reaching the border near the O.

Our Permanent Auction Archives show just 20 auction appearances of Mint State 1843-C quarter eagles, with eight Small Date pieces and 12 Large Date coins. Those appearances translate to six individual Small Date coins and 11 Large Date coins. The present piece is tied for fourth finest of the Large Date coins that we have handled. It is sharply struck with lovely greenish-gold surfaces and reflective fields. The surfaces are lightly abraded as expected for the grade. Census: 2 in 62, 5 finer (11/09).(#7728)

Near-Gem 1847-C Quarter Eagle A C-Mint Candidate for a High Quality Type Set

2101 1847-C MS64 NGC. Variety 1. For the collector who desires to own a single high-quality example of Charlotte Mint quarter eagle coinage, this date is an excellent choice. The mintage of 23,226 ranks as the second highest of any annual quarter eagle production at the North Carolina facility, and the number of Mint State survivors also ranks at the top of the list. Jeff Garrett and Ron Guth comment: "When assembling a type set of Southern branch-mint gold coins, the 1847-C Liberty Head quarter eagle will probably represent the Charlotte quarter eagle." This greenish-gold example is a remarkable Choice Mint State coin with satiny luster, reflective fields, and sharp design definition. The surfaces are outstanding, with only a few insignificant blemishes to prevent a higher grade. Census: 4 in 64, 0 finer (11/09).(#7745)

Uncirculated 1854-C Two and a Half
One of the Finest Known

2102 1854-C MS61 NGC. Variety 1 (formerly Variety 15-I). This date is considered scarce and the present high grade example survives from a mintage of just 7,295 pieces. Only about 105 to 145 of those pieces are known today in all grades, mostly in circulated grades from Very Fine to AU. Mint State pieces are rare, regardless of the numerical level, with only 6 to 7 separate examples believed extant. This piece has bright yellow-gold color with a touch of green, and satiny luster providing slightly prooflike fields. Typical of nearly all known examples, the centers show design weakness in the centers, especially on the lower parts of the eagle. Census: 5 in 61, 9 finer (11/09).(#7770)

Rare Select 1857-O Two and a Half

2103 1857-O MS63 PCGS. The 1857-O was the final New Orleans quarter eagle. By that year, Southern gold fields were largely played out, and California bullion was coined at San Francisco instead of shipped by steamer to the Gulf Coast. Most '57-O survivors are in XF or AU grades, and those that remain in Uncirculated condition typically grade MS61 to MS62. The present example reaches the rarefied Select level, since there are no relevant marks and all devices and legends are bathed in luster. A good strike despite minor softness on the claws and left (facing) leg. A mere 34,000 pieces were struck. Encased in a green label holder. Population: 4 in 63, 1 finer (11/09). (#7784)

Exceptional 1858-C Quarter Eagle, MS63 Believed Among the Three Finest Known

2104 1858-C MS63 PCGS. Variety 1, (formerly Variety 18-J). The 1858-C is an isolated issue that probably saw extensive circulation because no quarter eagles were produced at the Charlotte Mint in 1857 or 1859. Nevertheless, this issue is the second most readily obtainable C-mint quarter eagle from the 1850s despite a paltry original mintage of 9,056 coins. It is usually seen in XF-AU, and there are probably only 15-25 coins in mint condition, none of which are finer than the present specimen. In his latest reference on the series (Zyrus Press, 2008), Winter lists three MS63 PCGS coins at the top of the Condition Census for this issue. This coin is well defined for a product of the Charlotte Mint, although there are a few areas of bluntness over the eagle's portrait. Both sides are bright with glowing fields and a predominantly orange-gold appearance. There are a few swirls of copper patina over the lower obverse and the upper left reverse. Two pedigree identifiers stand out on the coin when it is examined with a loupe: a small planchet void in the reverse field above the tip of the olive branch, and shallow, irregularly shaped area of planchet flaking to the left of the eagle's neck.

From The Cherokee County Collection, Part One.(#7787)

Elusive MS62 1862/1 Quarter Eagle Among the Finest at PCGS

2105 1862/1 MS62 PCGS. FS-301, formerly FS-002. Although listed as an overdate, the variety could actually be an upside-down 2 or something else, as Garrett and Guth point out. It is nonetheless quite rare in all grades; the MS62 grade of the present piece ranks it among the finest at PCGS. This frosty quarter eagle offers rich, deep orange-red coloration that further increases its appeal. The strike is quite bold, with all peripheral stars and Liberty's hair and beads well brought up. A popular *Guide Book* variety, and an interesting Civil War-era gold issue. Population: 2 in 62, 0 finer (11/09). (#7797)

1875 Liberty Head Quarter Eagle, AU55
Only 400 Pieces Minted

2106 1875 AU55 PCGS. The 1875 Liberty Head quarter eagle boasts one of the lowest mintages in the U.S. gold series, at a minuscule 400 pieces. In their *Encyclopedia of U.S. Gold Coins 1795-1933,* Jeff Garrett and Ron Guth estimate less than 50 specimens are known today in circulated grades, and Mint State coins are extremely rare.

The present coin features semiprooflike fields, as usually seen on this issue, with lovely reddish patina occasionally interspersed with lilac. Numerous small abrasions are peppered over each side, as often seen on this date, but a loupe is necessary to detect most of them. Population: 11 in 55, 7 finer (12/09).(#7822)

Magnificent 1892 Quarter Eagle, MS67

2107 1892 MS67 NGC. CAC. The 1892 quarter eagle saw a mintage of only 2,440 circulation strikes, making the date extremely popular among collectors. Based on an inspection of NGC/PCGS population reports, the date was saved, probably resulting from the low mintage having been an enticement to put some of these coins away at the time of issue. Relatively few of these have survived in the better grades of Mint State, however, including this magnificent Superb Gem. Its yellow-gold surfaces offer occasional blushes of orange, more so on the obverse. The design elements are crisply impressed and both sides are awash in potent luster and are impeccably preserved. Census: 1 in 67, 1 finer (11/09).(#7844)

MS68 1904 Quarter Eagle Tied for Finest Certified

2108 1904 MS68 NGC. Astonishing quality in a Coronet quarter eagle of any date. The coin is virtually perfect, only the most insignificant evidence of contact on Liberty's nose can be discerned under light magnification. Equally impressive is the luster, which swirls around the surfaces as it is angled beneath a light and shows a lovely mixture of orange-gold and pastel violet patina. The strike is also complete on all the design elements. Those interested in a one-of-a-kind representative of this popular gold type coin really should examine this lot. Census: 4 in 68, 0 finer (11/09).

From The Five Point Collection.(#7856)

PROOF LIBERTY QUARTER EAGLES

Captivating 1894 Quarter Eagle, PR66

2109 1894 PR66 PCGS. CAC (Gold Label). It is estimated that about 50 to 70 of the 122 proof quarter eagles of 1894 are extant today, a relatively large number of which have been impaired. Jeff Garrett and Ron Guth (2006) opine: "About 25% of the coins seen at auction today have been mishandled. For some reason, many of the Proof 1894 quarter eagles entered circulation briefly."

This Premium Gem offering deviates from the above profile. Its frosty devices display strong variance with the mirrored fields. Yellow-gold surfaces exhibit sharply defined design elements and have been well cared for. This captivating piece is housed in a green label holder. Population: 2 in 66, 0 finer (11/09).(#7920)

Astounding 1898 Quarter Eagle, PR67

2110 1898 PR67 PCGS. CAC (Gold Label). A large number of the original mintage of 165 proof 1898 quarter eagles have survived to the present day. Indeed, PCGS and NGC have certified more pieces than were minted, a number of which are obviously resubmitted or crossed-over specimens.

The yellow-gold and orange surfaces of this Superb Gem yield strong gold-on-black contrast at most angles of observation, though the green-insert holder does not designate a Cameo or Deep Cameo. The frosted design motifs are boldly impressed and both sides reveal immaculate preservation. The astounding eye appeal of this piece, appropriately recognized by the affixed CAC gold label, is sure to elicit spirited bidding. Population: 4 in 67, 0 finer (11/09). (#7924)

1901 Liberty Head Quarter Eagle
PR69 Ultra Cameo, Pristine Fields
Extraordinary Contrast
Tied for Finest Certified

2111 1901 PR69 Ultra Cameo NGC. The 1901 Liberty Head quarter eagle boasts the highest mintage of the series at 223 pieces. While this total may be large in the context of quarter eagle proof mintages, it is certainly a tiny number in absolute terms for any numismatic issue. Experts estimate less than 75% of the production total survives today in all grades, and David Akers states the 1901 appears less frequently at auction than the 1900. The date was considered rare as early as the John Story Jenks Collection (Henry Chapman, 12/1921), lot 5812, "1901. Brilliant proof. Very rare, few being coined in proof." Jeff Garrett and Ron Guth indicate 18 examples of the issue were offered at auction between 2003 and 2007, with an average grade of PR65.2. Of course, this total may include duplicate offerings of the same coins. This is only the sixth time Heritage has been privileged to handle an Ultra Cameo proof 1901 quarter eagle.

The year 1901 saw a shift in the Mint's production methods for proof coins. This year was the last for the distinctive cameo proofs, as the dies were polished to produce completely brilliant coins beginning in 1902. Collectors have always prized the high-contrast proofs of the earlier era, but proof sets remained popular until the matte proofs made their appearance in 1908.

The present coin is a magnificent specimen, with exceptionally strong contrast on both sides. It must be one of the first coins struck from the dies. The surfaces appear technically perfect, with attractive medium orange-gold color. The often seen orange-peel effect is evident on the reverse, but curiously is not present on the obverse. Overall visual appeal is overwhelming. The coin offered here is a realistic candidate for Finest Known, as only one other specimen has been certified in PR69 Ultra Cameo by NGC, and PCGS has not seen a coin at this level (11/09).(#97927)

Gem Proof 1902 Liberty Head Quarter Eagle Bright Reflective Surfaces

2112 1902 PR65 NGC. The Philadelphia Mint changed production methods for proof coins in 1902, polishing the dies so the devices were as reflective as the fields on most specimens seen. Collectors missed the cameo devices of earlier years, but proof sets remained popular until the matte proof designs were introduced later in the decade. A fairly large mintage of 193 Liberty Head quarter eagles was achieved in 1902, but most specimens seen today are in lower proof grades. At the Gem level, the issue is decidedly rare. To date, NGC has certified only 10 coins in PR65, with 11 finer; while PCGS has graded nine examples in PR65, with five finer (11/09).

The present coin features extraordinarily bright surfaces, with just the faintest hint of contrast when angled in the light. The surfaces are virtually perfect, with no apparent contact marks on either side. Overall eye appeal is tremendous.(#7928)

INDIAN QUARTER EAGLES

High-End MS62 1911-D Quarter Eagle The Sought-After Key to the Series

2113 1911-D MS62 NGC. CAC. The Indian quarter eagle series is the most affordable of the four 20th century gold series, with only one key date issue, the 1911-D. Want lists for Indian quarter eagles usually include the 1911-D, as it is often the last coin obtained for a complete set. Most professional numismatists recommend that collectors acquire the 1911-D first. Once the single key date in the series is purchased, the rest of the set is relatively easy, as there are only two other issues that carry a premium. The same advice is given for any series: Pursue the key date issues first. At the Uncirculated level, this MS62 is one of the better values in this key issue. The surfaces are bright with a slight reddish tinge, and there are just a couple of marks on each side that account for the grade.(#7943)

Outstanding MS64 1911-D Quarter Eagle

2114 1911-D MS64 NGC. "The 1911-D is the rarest date of the series in all grades from circulated to Gem Uncirculated. Most known examples are in the lower Mint State grades, and obtaining one in MS-60 to 62 condition can usually be accomplished with only a little searching. However, in MS-63 condition this issue is seldom available, and anything better than MS-63 is extremely difficult to locate." Those are the words of David Akers in *A Handbook of 20th-Century United States Gold Coins.* The date is at once an important key issue and a major condition rarity in the series. Auction and population data tend to obscure the true rarity of this issue in the highest grades. The substantial price jump between grades at the higher Mint State levels results in a higher number of resubmissions to the grading services. Similarly, higher price levels mean that examples will often appear in multiple auction sales until the owner gets a desired price. For those reasons, the true rarity of 1911-D quarter eagles in the highest grades will sometimes go unrecognized.

This is an attractive, high-grade example of this famous 20th century rarity. The matte-like surfaces make it possible for small abrasions to blend in virtually unnoticed. Faint golden-rose and lilac patina is intermingled over both obverse and reverse. The mintmark is remarkably strong, especially so for an issue that is often found with a very weak D. The striking details are strong in other areas as well. The mint luster is lovely and frosted an the only surface disturbance is a milling mark on the high point of the Indian's cheek.
From The Atherton Family Collection.(#7943)

1913 Indian Head Quarter Eagle, MS66 Tied for Finest Certified

2115 1913 MS66 PCGS. From a mintage of 722,000 pieces, the largest in the series, the 1913 Indian Head quarter eagle is an available date in grades up to the near-Gem level. At the MS65 level, the issue is rare, and Premium Gem examples are very rare. At the present time, NGC has certified only one coin in MS66, with none finer; while PCGS has graded five specimens at the Premium Gem level, with none finer (11/09). The present coin is a spectacular example, fully struck, with pronounced matte-like fields. The obverse surfaces are a delightful reddish color, with hints of lilac. The reverse shows decidedly more lilac coloration, with accents of red. No blemishes are detected with the unaided eye.(#7945)

PROOF INDIAN QUARTER EAGLES

Superb Matte Proof 1908 Quarter Eagle
Popular Type Coin, First Year of Issue

2116 1908 PR67 NGC. The innovative incuse Indian Head design for the quarter and half eagles made its debut in 1908, to mixed reviews. The Mint also introduced the matte proof format that year, with dark granular surfaces, much different from the reflective brilliant proofs collectors were used to. The proof mintage was large for the quarter eagle, at 236 pieces, but collectors did not like the matte format and it is likely that many sets went unsold and were melted at year's end. The issue is still the most available proof of the series, with a surviving population of 125-165 examples in all grades. The date is particularly popular as a type coin. Jeff Garrett and Ron Guth opine,"For the type collector, the 1908 Proof makes a perfect choice in terms of availability, quality, and being the first year of issue."

The present coin displays the usual dark surfaces, with a noticeable overlay of reddish patina. A full wire rim surrounds both sides. The surfaces appear technically perfect, with none of the shiny contact spots often seen on this issue. The leading grading services have not graded any coin in a higher technical grade. Census: 26 in 67, 0 finer (11/09).(#7957)

1909 Indian Head Quarter Eagle, PR63
Rare Roman Finish

2117 1909 PR63 PCGS. CAC. The matte proof coinage of 1908 proved so unpopular that the Mint switched to a new finish in 1909. Called the Roman Finish, the coins were actually struck on unfinished planchets, resulting in brighter, more reflective surfaces than the 1908 issue. The Roman proofs possessed a kind of hybrid appearance, midway between the dark, granular matte surfaces and the brightly mirrored proofs of earlier years. Unfortunately, the innovation was not viewed as an improvement by collectors, and only 139 proof quarter eagles were minted in 1909. David Akers believes many of these were melted as unsold at the year's end, and only 74 specimens were actually released. In their *Encyclopedia of U.S. Gold Coins 1795-1933,* Jeff Garrett and Ron Guth state:

> "This is far and away the most difficult issue to find in PF-64 or higher grades. For the collector, this is one of the three most difficult Proof issues to obtain in any grade, and perhaps it is the rarest overall."

The present coin is a pleasing example, with bright surfaces and a wire rim complete around both sides. A curious die break is noted from stars 3 through 6. Population: 19 in 63, 11 finer (11/09). (#7958)

Prized PR66 1910 Two and a Half

2118 1910 PR66 NGC. The briefest glance at the *Guide Book* shows the mintage of the proof 1910 quarter eagle as 682 pieces, but this purported production bears little resemblance to the reality shown but its survival today; Garrett and Guth (2006) suggest that the certified population data point to a *released* population of only 200 or so specimens, more in line with the levels found on other higher-mintage proof Indian quarter eagles. Regardless of the actual mintage, this Premium Gem proof is a definite treasure for the series collector. Yellow-gold surfaces have the semi-bright "Roman gold" texture peculiar to 1909 and 1910, and the central definition is bold. A carefully preserved and attractive specimen. Census: 30 in 66, 13 finer (11/09).

From The Atherton Family Collection.(#7959)

Appealing 1911 PR64 Quarter Eagle

2119 1911 PR64 PCGS. The 1911 Indian Head quarter eagle proofs are similar to those of 1908 which consisted of a heavy matte texture. The 1911's texture shows less granularity, however, along with a slightly darker color (Jeff Garrett and Ron Guth, 2006). Uniform khaki-gold patination on the present near-Gem displays occasional splashes of medium brown in the lower right obverse quadrant, and a well executed strike imparts crisp definition to the design elements. A few minor reverse grazes only become apparent when the coin is rotated beneath a light source. This highly appealing example is housed in a green insert holder.(#7960)

THREE DOLLAR GOLD PIECES

Outstanding 1854 Gem Three Dollar

2120 1854 MS65 NGC. The first three dollar gold pieces were struck in 1854 with a generous mintage of 138,618 pieces. This issue can be acquired without too much difficulty though the near-Gem level of preservation, though Gems are extremely challenging and anything finer is elusive.

This MS65 specimen radiates dazzling that seems to reach out to the observer. Coupled with this are exceptionally well impressed design elements. Both sides display beautiful brass-gold coloration and the smooth surfaces of each reveal no marks of note. In sum, this piece exudes outstanding eye appeal. Census: 11 in 65, 8 finer (11/09).

From The Atherton Family Collection.(#7969)

Choice XF 1854-D Three Dollar Odd-Denomination Dahlonega Gold

2121 1854-D XF45 ANACS. Odd denominations and Dahlonega gold intersect at this famous three dollar issue, struck in the initial year for the denomination and the first and last of its kind. With just 1,120 pieces struck, it stands to reason that demand far exceeds the available supply, though the size of that supply is open to debate; Q. David Bowers, in *The United States $3 Gold Pieces,* compared the question of how many 1854-D three dollar coins exist with the classic, "How many angels can dance on the head of a pin?"

What is known is that the 1854-D issue is decidedly scarce, with high demand regardless of condition. This Choice XF coin is pleasing for the grade with glimpses of original luster remaining in the protected areas. Yellow-orange surfaces are minimally abraded with a few small instances of encrustation and alloy.(#7970)

Reflective 1860 Three Dollar, MS64 ★

2122 1860 MS64 ★ NGC. CAC. The *only* Star-designated example of this issue certified by NGC as of (11/09), with only two pieces numerically finer (a 65 and a 67) in the *Census Report.* The Star attests to the quality, while the CAC sticker attests to the grade, and the virtues of both are readily evident at first glance. Flashy, mildly reflective yellow-gold fields give way to sharply struck, slightly frosted devices, creating appreciable contrast appropriate for the earliest strikes of this low-mintage issue. Only a handful of small marks in the fields combine to preclude Gem status.(#7980)

Rare 1860-S Three Dollar Gold Piece, AU58
Second Rarest S-Mint Three

2123 1860-S AU58 PCGS. Only 7,000 three dollar gold pieces were coined at the San Francisco Mint in 1860. Walter Breen reports 2,592 pieces were found to be underweight and melted at a later date, leaving a net mintage of 4,408 pieces. The date is the rarest of the early San Francisco issues and is second only to the unique 1870-S in terms of rarity in the entire S-Mint series. Few coins were saved by early collectors, and the date is particularly rare in Mint State grades. Experts believe 100-135 examples are known today, with most examples seen in the VF range. AU examples are rare and Mint State coins are virtually unobtainable.

While conservatively graded AU58, the present coin is extremely close to Mint State. Mint luster is nearly complete, and the slight softness observed on the high points is from striking weakness rather than wear. The original yellow-gold surfaces have taken on a deep reddish patina. The fields exhibit a scattering of small abrasions, consistent with the grade. A backward J-shaped planchet indent is evident near the border, below the lowest curl. Population: 4 in 58, 3 finer (11/09).(#7981)

Low Mintage 1861 Near-Gem Three Dollar

2124 1861 MS64 NGC. The 1861 three dollar saw a low mintage of fewer than 6,000 circulation strikes, and surviving examples fall mostly in the Extremely Fine to About Uncirculated range. Mint State examples are scarce through about MS63 and elusive any finer.

The yellow-gold surfaces of this near-Gem representative display partially prooflike fields highlighting somewhat the motifs, more so on the reverse. Die striations are visible over both sides, found on all high-grade examples of this issue. Aside from the typical minor softness in some of the hair curls, the design elements exhibit strong detail. A few trivial handling marks barely preclude Gem status. Census: 4 in 64, 3 finer (11/09).

From The Atherton Family Collection.(#7982)

Difficult 1863 MS64 Three Dollar

2125 1863 MS64 PCGS. The relatively low circulation-strike mintage of 5,000 1863 three dollar gold pieces combined with few being deliberately saved resulted in their rarity across the board (David Bowers, *$3 Gold Pieces*). Extremely Fine and About Uncirculated coins can be located with patience, but Mint State specimens become difficult.

The peach-gold surfaces of this near-Gem are imbued with traces of mint-green and lilac and display ebullient luster. A well executed strike leaves strong definition on the design elements except for the usual softness in the feather plumes and bow knot and adjacent wreath leaves to the right. Strong clash marks on each side do not disturb, nor do the few inoffensive handling marks. Population: 7 in 64, 10 finer (11/09).

From The Atherton Family Collection.(#7984)

Underappreciated 1864 Three Dollar, MS63

2126 1864 MS63 NGC. Ex: South Texas Collection. Estimates of the number of 1864 threes range as high as 200 pieces in all grades. That seems a generous number given a mintage of only 2,630 coins, but the key is "in all grades." We have offered very few better-grade Uncirculated 1863 threes over the past 15 years. In fact, our Auction Archives only show five appearances at various auctions in MS63 and MS64, all between 1998 and 2008. This coin is well-preserved enough at the MS63 level that fields show the die striations that are often seen that run from upper left to lower right. These striations, of course, give the coin a noticeable semiprooflike appearance. Numerous light abrasions are scattered over each side of the deep orange-gold surfaces. An overlooked and highly underappreciated rarity in the series.(#7985)

Rare Mint State 1865 Three Dollar

2127 1865 MS61 NGC. In 1865 the Civil War still raged and the payment of specie was suspended in the North, obviating the need for gold coinage. The mintage of the three dollar gold business strikes in that year was a token 1,140 coins, a quantity likely made only to prevent the proof coins (which the Mint was obligated to produce for collectors) from becoming great rarities. Mint State examples of the 1865 are extremely rare. This piece shows considerable prooflikeness, with orange-gold glints in the protected areas and hazel-blue in the fields. Census: 9 in 61, 12 finer (11/09).(#7986)

Bright 1866 Gem Three Dollar

2128 1866 MS65 NGC. Collectors apparently saved a fair number of the 4,000-piece business strike mintage of this post Civil War issue. While still scarce, Extremely Fine, About Uncirculated, and lower level Mint State specimens can be obtained with a bit of searching. Gems are extremely rare and finer examples are virtually nonexistent.

The brightly lustrous surfaces of this MS65 offering exhibit uniform brassy-gold coloration, and a decisive strike imparts excellent definition to the design elements. A handful of grade-consistent marks are undisturbing. Census: 2 in 65, 0 finer (11/09).

From The Atherton Family Collection.(#7987)

Rare MS63 1867 Three Dollar

2129 1867 MS63 PCGS. CAC. The 1867 three dollar gold piece comes from a low mintage of 2,600 circulation strikes. PCGS/NGC population reports show most certified coins to be in the About Uncirculated grade range, indicating that the issue likely did not circulate actively. Mint State pieces are extremely rare.

This Select coin's yellow-gold surfaces exhibit somewhat prooflike fields that yield noticeable contrast with the well struck design elements at various angles. Magnification brings out some wispy handling marks that limit the grade. Above average overall eye appeal. Population: 3 in 63, 6 finer (11/09).(#7988)

Rarely Seen, High Grade 1870 Three Dollar, MS64

2130 1870 MS64 NGC. For a number of years after the Civil War, gold and silver coins were rarely seen in commerce. Instead, they were hoarded by those people who could afford to do so. As a result, the Philadelphia Mint produced small amounts of coins at the time, seeing little reason to produce coinage that would also be hoarded. As a symptom of this ongoing situation, the mintage of the 1870 three dollar gold issue was a mere 3,500 pieces.

This amazing example is tied for the finest that NGC or PCGS has ever certified. It is fully lustrous and satiny with brilliant orange-gold surfaces and faint pink highlights. Few grade-limiting surface marks are evident on each side. Census: 3 in 64, 0 finer at either service (11/09).(#7991)

1873 Three Dollar Gold Piece, AU53 Key Date, Closed 3 Variety

2131 1873 Closed 3 AU53 PCGS. The 1873 three dollar gold piece is a key date in the series, with two varieties known for the date. The present coin is an example of the Closed 3 variety, with the knobs of the 3 spaced close together. Experts estimate a surviving population of only 80-120 pieces of the Closed 3 variety in all grades.

The present coin displays bright semiprooflike fields with vibrant yellow-gold color and just a hint of red. A touch of softness is evident on the high points of the design and some unusual light scratches in the right obverse field account for the grade. Population: 5 in 53, 47 finer (12/09).(#7995)

1873 Closed 3 Three Dollar, AU55
A Rare and Widely Misunderstood Issue

2132 1873 Closed 3 AU55 PCGS. Ex: South Texas Collection. The 1873 threes of both Open and Closed varieties are among the most enigmatic issues in this unusual and popular series. A good summation of the history of the possible striking sequence and speculation about numbers struck of both business strikes and proofs is presented in Q. David Bowers and Doug Winter's book on the series (2005), a worthwhile addition to anyone's library who deals with threes. The Close (or Closed) 3 business strike is the most frequently encountered of the two date variants. The mintage, however, was not recorded, leading to great speculation over the years. We believe that well under 1,000 pieces were struck. As with all known examples, the fields show bright reflectivity on each side. Undoubtedly, the initial polish on the dies never had a chance to diminish. Numerous small handling marks are seen on each side, and there is a significant accent of reddish patina.(#7995)

Brilliant Gem 1874 Three Dollar Gold

2133 1874 MS65 NGC. A seldom-seen grade for this popular type coin, one of the three usually selected for that purpose along with the 1854 (technically a distinct subtype due to the smaller denomination) and the 1878. It is worth noting, however, that of the three issues, the mintage of the 1874 is only about half that of the 1878 and about one-third that of the 1854.

In Gem condition, the comparisons are even more stark: This 1874 is one of only 13 so certified at NGC, with a single piece finer. The 1854 in Gem condition has 11 at NGC, with two finer—while the 1878 has well over a hundred Gems at NGC, with several dozen in MS66 and MS67 combined. So calling this issue a "type coin" at the Gem level underestimates its rarity and importance.

Aesthetically it is equally desirable, with brilliant, satiny yellow-gold luster. A single tick on the Indian's cheek is perhaps all that precludes an even finer grade, as the surfaces elsewhere are essentially pristine, and the strike is bold throughout. Census: 13 in 65, 1 finer (11/09).

Ex: Exclusively Internet Auction (Heritage, 9/2003), lot 14272, which brought $8,912.50.(#7998)

Brightly Reflective 1877 Three Dollar, MS61

2134 1877 MS61 PCGS. The paltry production of business strikes in this year amounted to only 1,468 pieces for a denomination that had long since become a quaint anachronism. The surfaces are prooflike as expected, and although some abrasions, field chatter, and a mediocre planchet and strike account for the grade, without a loupe the piece appears rather undergraded and quite attractive. Bowers' 2005 reference on the denomination estimates that only seven to 11 Mint State coins exist. The piece is lustrous throughout, with highly contrasted orange-gold surfaces that show strike weakness at the bottom and sides of the wreath and on the headdress feathers. The population data are almost certainly inflated by resubmissions. Population: 5 in 61, 4 finer (11/09).(#7999)

Gem 1878 Three Dollar Gold Fantastic Luster

2135 1878 MS65 NGC. CAC. The generous mintage of 83,304 business strikes ensures that even today numerous high-grade examples exist, but most of them are in the range from MS61 to MS64. Gems are quite elusive compared to the certified population overall, and they are in much demand for type purposes on the rare occasions when they appear. That popularity is here evident for another reason, the terrific luster for which the issue is noted. The devices are heavily frosted, with reddish-golden color that shows an accent of deeper red on the obverse rim between 6 and 8 o'clock. The strike is quite sharp, if a tad short of full. There are 70 pieces certified finer at NGC (11/09).(#8000)

Shining 1878 Three Dollar, MS66

2136 1878 MS66 PCGS. The 1878, with a mintage of 82,304 circulation strikes is the most common date of the three dollar gold series. This is reflected in the thousands of pieces that have been certified by PCGS and NGC. The population begins to decline in MS65, and Premium Gems are scarce.

Billowing luster exudes from each side of this MS66 coin and a decisive strike imparts sharp definition to the design features, including virtual fullness on the lower wreath, an area that sometimes shows weakness. Variegated yellow-gold and orange colors are dominant and well preserved surfaces reveal just a few minute marks. Housed in a green insert holder. Population: 63 in 66, 6 finer (11/09).(#8000)

Charming 1878 Premium Gem Three Dollar

2137 1878 MS66 NGC. Premium Gem condition is the finest most collectors can expect to locate when searching for an 1878 three dollar gold piece, and even this level of preservation will present a challenge. NGC and PCGS have graded only about 115 MS66 specimens, a number of which are likely resubmissions or crossovers. Higher-grade examples are extremely elusive.

Dazzling luster radiates from both sides of this lovely MS66 coin, each of which displays a delicate medley of yellow-gold, mint-green, peach, and light tan, accented with a streak of bluish-purple on the lower reverse. The design motifs are well impressed, save for just a touch of the usual softness on the lower wreath. A few minor ticks take nothing from the coin's charming eye appeal. Census: 53 in 66, 17 finer (11/09).

From The Atherton Family Collection.(#8000)

Deeply Patinated 1878 Three Dollar, MS67
A Spectacular Type Coin

2138 1878 MS67 NGC. The mintage of the 1878 three dollar gold piece is, at least in part, related to the Specie Resumption Act of January 1875. This Congressional act provided, among other things:

> "That the U.S. Treasury be prepared to resume the redemption of legal tender notes in specie (gold) as of January 1, 1879; and
>
> "That gradual steps be taken to reduce the number of greenbacks in circulation (millions of greenbacks were issued during the Civil War, and maintained their value only through trust in the government)".

David Bowers and Douglas Winter, in their book *The United States $3 Gold Pieces, 1854-1889*, write:

> "To provide for this, in 1878, as the time approached, it was only logical to build up a stock of such pieces, including smaller denominations for public convenience. Following this logic, the mintage of $3 coins reached 82,304 pieces (circulation strikes), the highest total since the denomination was instituted in 1854."

Today, the 1878 is the post plentiful of all dates in Mint State. Indeed, NGC and PCGS have certified approximately 6,000 examples in Uncirculated grades! The population begins to fall off in MS65 and MS66, and only 23 coins reach the lofty grade level of MS67.

This Superb Gem displays a delicate blend of yellow-gold, mint-green, apricot, and lilac patina covering surfaces that are awash in dazzling luster. While the typical 1878 is lightly struck (Bowers and Winter, p. 142), an exacting strike leaves crisp definition on the design features, including the hair, bonnet, and lower wreath, areas that are usually weak. Impeccable preservation complements these attributes, engendering captivating eye appeal. Census: 17 in 67, 0 finer (11/09).(#8000)

Captivating 1878 Three Dollar, MS67

2139 1878 MS67 NGC. The 1878 three dollar piece, with a mintage exceeding 82,000 circulation strikes, is plentiful through the near-Gem level of preservation. Gems can be located with patience and searching, and Premium Gems are very challenging. MS67 pieces are highly elusive, NGC and PCGS having certified only around 20 coins at this level, and none finer.

Strong luster emanates from from the frosty surfaces of this MS67 example and a well executed strike imparts strong detail to the design features, including Liberty's hair and plumes and the lower wreath, areas that often exhibit weakness. Peach-gold and mint-green surfaces are imbued with tints of lilac on the reverse and are devoid of blemishes. These attributes combine to yield captivating eye appeal. Census: 17 in 67, 0 finer (11/09).

From The Atherton Family Collection.(#8000)

Incredible 1879 Gem Three Dollar

2140 1879 MS65 NGC. Despite its low mintage of 3,000 circulation strikes, the 1879 three dollar population consists of numerous Mint State examples. This apparently results from coins having been shipped to banks shortly after they were minted. As there was little demand for them in the channels of commerce, however, they did not circulate. NGC/PCGS data show that most surviving 1879 threes are in the higher About Uncirculated to near-Gem range. Gems become very scarce and anything finer is elusive.

The present MS65 example exudes incredible eye appeal. Semiprooflike fields establish noticeable contrast with frosty design motifs that were in receipt of a powerful strike. Additionally, wonderful brass-gold coloration envelops both sides, each of which reveals a few trivial marks that might just barely prevent an even finer grade. Census: 18 in 65, 3 finer (11/09).

From The Atherton Family Collection.(#8001)

Rare 1881 Three Dollar Gold, MS62
Mintage of Only 500 Pieces

2141 1881 MS62 NGC. Ex: South Texas Collection. The mintage of 500 business strikes is singular in a series that is known for low mintages. Curiously, the Mint actually placed most of these 500 pieces into circulation, and as a result Uncirculated examples are rarely seen today. The two major certification services show similar numbers of MS62 and finer coins: at NGC, 8 in MS62, 11 finer; at PCGS, 8 in MS62, 13 finer (11/09). With such a low mintage the initial die polish never diminished on these coins and the fields are always bright and semireflective. The orange-gold surfaces are outlined with deeper reddish patina around the devices, and for a pedigree identifier there is a swath of longer reddish color at 6 o'clock on the obverse. Well, but not fully stuck, as usual on three dollar gold pieces.(#8003)

Low-Mintage 1883 Three Dollar, MS64 ★
An Impressive, Reflective Coin

2142 1883 MS64 ★ NGC. At first glance this important business strike actually looks like a proof due to its fully mirrored fields and satiny devices. The light yellow surfaces have hints of the watery or wavy surface that is typical of proof gold coins. The borders on both sides have pale lemon-yellow color.

The 1883 three dollar gold piece is extremely popular due to its low mintage of just 900 business strikes. Another 89 proofs were also coined. The current NGC Census Report shows that just two 1883 three dollar pieces have been certified in MS64 ★ , the only Star designated examples of the date (11/09), with seven pieces numerically finer (all MS65).

From The Cherokee County Collection, Part One.(#8005)

1888 Three Dollar Gold Piece, MS66
Coruscating Mint Luster and Rich Color

2143 1888 MS66 PCGS. A small business-strike mintage of just 5,000 pieces was produced by the Philadelphia Mint in 1888. Surprisingly the issue is readily available today. Q. David Bowers estimates a surviving population of 550-750 examples in all grades, which correlates well with current population data. The high survival rate may be due to 19th century dealer J.W. Scott, who purchased a large group of coins from the Mint and distributed them to collectors in the normal course of business. Scott's hoard may have amounted to several hundred pieces, as he had them readily available for years after 1888.

The present coin is an attractive specimen, with a sharp, but not quite full strike. The surfaces have coruscating, thick mint frost, and the pristine fields, particularly on the reverse, have a semiprooflike quality. A lovely intermixture of rose and lilac shades on the reverse is matched by the even, reddish tones on the obverse. There are no observable abrasions to limit the grade. Population: 30 in 66, 2 finer (11/09).(#8010)

PROOF THREE DOLLAR GOLD PIECES

Elusive 1854 Three Dollar Gold PR63 Cameo

2144 1854 PR63 Cameo PCGS. The recorded proof mintage of only 15 pieces appears to be on the low side, and it does not square with the fact that two different pairs of proof dies were employed. On one of these dies the ES in STATES is in a straight line, and the lettering is bolder and more deeply impressed into the die. On the other die the S is slightly lower than the E, and the lettering is not so deep. While it is possible that some catastrophic die failure occurred after one or a handful of pieces were struck, more likely is that the recorded mintage is erroneous ... or could restrikes have been made later?

Bowers' series reference offers these comments:

> "On April 28, 1854, the Mint struck 15 Proof examples that were sent by Mint Director James Ross Snowden to the Secretary of the Treasury James Guthrie in Washington. Others were retained at the Mint, including two by Chief Engraver Longacre. Interested numismatists could obtains specimens there. This was initiated what became an uninterrupted string of Proof issues, although production was exceedingly low for the next several years."

While there is no record of restrikes, this would certainly not be the only U.S. coin for which restrikes are suspected but unproven. As a one-year subtype (with small DOLLARS, 1854 only) and a first-year issue, perhaps the subsequent demand for proof examples required the striking of extra pieces beyond the original 15 coins. Various Mint personnel working there in the 1850s were far from averse to making "on-demand" issues when the correct bell was rung. But this is mere speculation. What is not speculation is that the current NGC/PCGS population data show 13 examples of the 1854 in all grades, including one circulated proof. This coin is one of two PR63 Cameo proofs at PCGS, with two finer, both PR64 Cameo. A single coin at NGC has also attained the PR64 Cameo rank, with none finer (11/09).

The present example offers luscious orange-gold fields with considerable contrast present. The S in STATES is lower than the E, without the deeply impressed lettering characteristic of the other proof die. A couple of light scrapes are noted on Liberty's cheek, and a couple of dark toning spots on the obverse: one in back of the eye, and one behind the headdress. On the reverse a similar dark spot occurs at the bottom of the 1, and a patch of light yellow-gold patina is noted through DO in DOLLARS. A delectable early proof example of this historic and unusual denomination.

Ex: Dr. Robert J. Loewinger Collection; FUN Signature Auction (1/2007), lot 3121, which realized $74,750.(#88017)

1858 Three Dollar Gold Piece, PR64 Cameo
Very Rare, Only 10-14 Minted
First Date Proofs Were Widely Offered

2145 1858 PR64 Cameo NGC. The year 1858 marked the first time proof sets were offered by the Mint on a widespread commercial basis. Collectors responded enthusiastically, and the yearly proof offerings became a profitable enterprise, but interest in proof gold coins was limited. While no records were kept of the 1858 production, experts believe only 10-14 proof three dollar gold pieces were coined. Proofs are very rare today, with Q. David Bowers estimating only 7-8 pieces known, while Jeff Garrett and Ron Guth suspect 10-12 examples may survive in all grades. For collectors, the small supply of proof 1858s is further reduced by the presence of several specimens in institutional collections. The collections of the Harry Bass Research Foundation, the ANS, and the Smithsonian all contain an example of the issue. Currently, NGC has certified only three coins in PR64 Cameo, with two finer; while PCGS has graded no examples in PR64 (11/09). This is only the second time Heritage has been privileged to offer a proof example of this date.

Perhaps the first offering of an 1858 three dollar gold piece at public auction was as part of a complete gold proof set in Sale Number Two (W. Elliot Woodward, 10/1860), lot 712, "1858 A most magnificent set of proofs, comprising $20, $10, $5, $3, $2, and $1." Notice Woodward incorrectly listed the quarter eagle value. Other early sales include the Murdoch Collection (Sotheby, Wilkinson & Hodge, 7/1903), lot 766; David S. Wilson Collection (S.H. Chapman, 3/1907), lot 245; and the William H. Woodin Collection (Thomas Elder, 3/1911), lot 1146.

The present coin is a remarkable example of this rare date. The fields are deeply mirrored, but the obverse shows occasional porosity, possibly from an improperly prepared planchet. Q. David Bowers observes "the mirror surface is usually incomplete on the obverse" of this issue, so the problem may be widespread with this date. The strike is sharp, but not quite full. Elements of contrast are definitely present on both sides, but not strong enough to merit an Ultra Cameo designation. A few hairlines in the fields limit the grade. (#88021)

1884 Three Dollar, PR66 Cameo
Strong Contrast, Attractive Color
Only Three Examples Certified Finer

2146 1884 PR66 Cameo NGC. CAC. Only 1,000 business-strike three dollar gold pieces were minted in 1884, along with 106 proofs. Harry Bass considered the 1884 to be the rarest circulation strike issue of the 1880s, and the small supply of Mint State examples puts great pressure on the tiny proof mintage. Regarding the rarity and delivery dates of the 1884, Walter Breen reports:

> "Much rarer than this mintage would suggest, and subject to much date collector pressure as only a small percentage of the 1,000 business strikes remain.—Mintage: 30 for sets Jan. 9, delivered Jan. 19; 42 on Feb. 29, 13 on June 28, 21 before Dec. 31 but delivered Jan. 10, 1885, total 106."

The coins struck in December, but not delivered until January 10 pose a problem. Mint regulations specifically prohibit selling proofs after the year in which they were dated. Both A.M. Smith and John Colvin Randall are thought to have made special arrangements to buy unsold proof coins from the mint during the 1880s. Perhaps the 21 coins delivered in January ended up with them. In any case, experts estimate only 50-65 examples survive today in all proof grades. Certainly at the PR66 Cameo level the date is extremely rare. NGC has certified only three coins in PR66 Cameo, with three finer; while PCGS has yet to see a specimen in this exalted grade (11/09).

The present coin is a magnificent specimen, with well balanced yellow-gold color, accented with a hint of red on each side. Strong contrast is evident on both sides, with notable orange-peel effect in the fields. The only flaw detectable without magnification is a tiny planchet flake in the middle of the right obverse field. (#88048)

PROOF FOUR DOLLAR GOLD PIECES
6 G ★ 3 ★ S ★ 7 ★ C ★ 7 ★ G ★ R ★ A ★ M ★ S
LIBERTY
1879
UNITED STATES OF AMERICA
E PLURIBUS UNUM
ONE STELLA
400 CENTS
DEO EST GLORIA
FOUR DOL.

Slightly Contrasted 1879 Flowing Hair Stella, PR63
Judd-1635, A Splendid Coin for the Grade

2147 1879 Flowing Hair, Judd-1635, PR63 PCGS. An item in the *Mason's Coin Collectors' Herald* from September 1880, page 15, reads as follows:

> **"STELLA AND GOLOID-METRIC PIECES.**
>
> Notwithstanding extensive advertising and offering to pay $30.00 per set for these peculiar 'Patterns,' we have to date secured but five sets. On account of the various rumors about the number of sets struck, some placing the number at 200, others at 300, we have reduced our offers to $15.00, and our sale price to $20.00."

What is not mentioned is exactly what is included in the set. While it would be nice to think that for $20 one could also obtain an 1880 Coiled Hair stella, those pieces were apparently unknown at the time. According to USPatterns.com, the 1879 Flowing Hair stellas were offered in sets that also contained the Judd-1617 and Judd-1626 patterns, both known as "goloid metric dollars" with obverse design by William Barber. (George T. Morgan also designed 1879 goloid metric dollars, which are much rarer.) The sets were offered first to Congressmen for $6.10, then to the public for $15 per set, according to that site, which adds that "the earliest resale at auction for one of these sets that I am aware of was lots 1258-1260 of Scott Stamp and Coin's July 1880 sale." We lack that catalog, but we came across another early appearance, in the Thomas Cleneay Collection (S.H. and H. Chapman, 12/1890), lot 2059: "1879 Stella ($4 gold). Metric and Goloid metric dollars. Proofs. 3 pieces." The lot brought $8.50, a price that likely indicated considerable contemporary doubt over the number of sets actually produced.

Sets containing the 1879 Flowing Hair stella and the two Barber 1879 goloid metric dollars were also produced in copper, aluminum, and white metal. There is so little documentation concerning the 1879 stellas that, as is usual in such cases, the numismatic community has substituted misinformation, disinformation, and "truthiness" instead. For example, the Judd pattern reference, 10th edition, says that the three-piece sets were sold for $6.50 each, not $6.10 as on USPatterns.com. A greater concern is this:

> "It was announced by someone, perhaps a Mint official, that 15 of the 1879 Flowing Hair $4 Stellas were struck, these as patterns, but there was a sufficient demand for them that a few hundred more were struck for congressmen, who are allowed to acquire them for $6.50 each."

It is seldom that an "announcement by someone" would still be quoted in a reputable numismatic reference as hard evidence 130 years later; but such is the absence of real documentation. The original "announcement" could just as credibly (or more so) be attributed to a well-connected 19th century coin dealer as its source, one who was trying to reduce his stock of a pricey set that he knew was produced to a larger extent than publicly known.

This is a splendid Flowing Hair example, especially for the grade. The fields show exceptionally deep reflectivity, and the devices are notably frosted, although a Cameo designation is conspicuously absent from the PCGS insert. The usual light striations are seen in the centers of each side. Close examination also reveals a few tiny planchet voids in the fields. The surfaces are bright yellow-gold with the barest overlay of reddish patina. An exceptional stella.(#8057)

6 G .3 S .7 C 7 G R A M S
LIBERTY
1879
UNITED STATES OF AMERICA
E PLURIBUS UNUM
DEO EST GLORIA
ONE STELLA
400 CENTS
FOUR DOL.

Barber-Designed 1879 Flowing Hair Stella
Judd-1635, PR67 ★ Cameo
Tied for Finest Certified

2148 1879 Flowing Hair, Judd-1635, PR67 ★ Cameo NGC. Many numismatists have commented over the years on how outlandish a conception were the 1879 stellas, metric dollars, and metric goloid dollars. Some have attributed it to naïveté on the part of Iowa Rep. John A. Kasson and/or lack of a working knowledge of international commerce among members of the Congressional Committee on Coinage, Weights, and Measures, a committee that Kasson chaired. Walter Breen in his *Complete Encyclopedia* cast Kasson as one of an "unholy trinity" of Congressional villains that included Richard A. "Silver Dick" Bland and William Darrah Kelley, cronies of Western silver-mining interests who were ever in search of new foreign and domestic uses for silver, including the twenty cent piece, the Trade and Morgan dollars, and the various international coinage concepts.

But in a perusal of the literature on the subject, what emerges as even more curious than the preposterous intended use of the stellas is the story of the so-called "originals" versus "restrike" stellas—a story that more than a few numismatists have used as the occasion to give their brains a vacation. Typical comments are these, from the 10th edition of the Judd pattern reference:

> "It was announced by someone, perhaps a Mint official, that 15 of the 1879 Flowing Hair $4 Stellas were struck, these as patterns, but there was a sufficient demand for them that a few hundred more were struck for congressmen, who are allowed to acquire them for $6.50 each. This was an era of great secrecy at the Mint, and virtually the entire pattern coinage of 1879, including the 'Washlady' and Schoolgirl silver coins, were produced for the private profit of Mint officials. ... The total number made is not known, but has been estimated to be 600 to 700, all but 15 of which are believed to have been struck in calendar year 1880 from the 1879-dated dies."

If this were indeed an "era of great secrecy at the Mint," why believe that only 15 originals were struck? It is perhaps more plausible to believe that all of the 1879 Flowing Hair coins were struck at one time and the mintage was incorrectly given as 15, with mentions of later restrikes intended to divert the curious from the intended motive, profit on the part of Mint officials and the well-connected.

Here is the story from Walter Breen:

> "Only a few original proof sets (Stella, goloid, and 'goloid metric' dollars) were made in Dec. 1879 from the Barber [Flowing Hair] designs; those with the Morgan [Coiled Hair] obvs. were clandestine issues. At least 425 additional sets followed in 1880 from the 1879 Barber dies, by order of Congress ...
>
> "As the same dies were used for original Stellas and official restrikes, distinguishing between them has been a difficult problem. Coiled hair or Morgan Stellas of 1879 are not known to have been restruck; they normally lack the central striations (on the strip from which these planchets were cut) found on most 1879 Flowing Hair Stellas and all the 1880 issues. Presumably the very rare 1879 Flowing Hair coins without central striations are the originals. None has been auctioned in many years, though many restrikes have been marketed as originals owing to their having correct weights. ..."

Again, this is remarkably fuzzy thinking for a numismatic scholar who was often piercingly astute. One first of all wonders how many 1879 Coiled Hair stellas Breen had seen, considering that only 12 to 15 are known today. All of the 1879 Coiled Hair stellas that Heritage has handled, at least three different, indeed do show striations in the center, although some catalogers have called them "roller marks." And Breen makes the assumption that the 1879 Flowing Hair "originals" are different from restrikes and were produced in a minuscule amount, despite his own evidence to the contrary. We believe that no 1879 Flowing Hair originals lacking planchet striations exist, rendering the question of whether there were two different striking periods moot.

Concerning the planchet striations, as we wrote in the Lemus Collection catalog:

> "As time goes by and no pieces appear to lack the striations, many numismatists have concluded that neither were the pattern gold pieces produced in that odd metric alloy, but rather they were struck on regular 900 fine planchets rolled out to 80% of the thickness of a half eagle, accounting for the roller marks or die striations seen on all known gold pieces."

This particular coin will require powerful magnification and a good light to discern the roller marks. And the interesting part, in addition to their extreme lightness, is that they are absolutely vertical, rather than the usual near-horizontal orientation. This is an extraordinarily attractive stella. The surfaces are bright and uniformly yellow-gold, with none of the reddish patina normally seen. Another extraordinary quality is the unfathomable depth of reflectivity seen in the fields, certainly not a given on a stella. The thick mint frost over the devices sets up a strong cameo effect against the "black" mirrored fields. There are no obvious contact marks on either side, and as for pedigree markers they appear to be limited to two small planchet flakes. Both are on the reverse, one is to the right of the inverted V at the bottom of the star, and the other is to the right of the star.

Neither of the major services has certified a Flowing Hair stella in finer condition. When one sees this coin, it is clear why. This piece is as close to technical perfection as one can ever expect. A true opportunity for the collector who has been holding out for that special coin. (#88057)

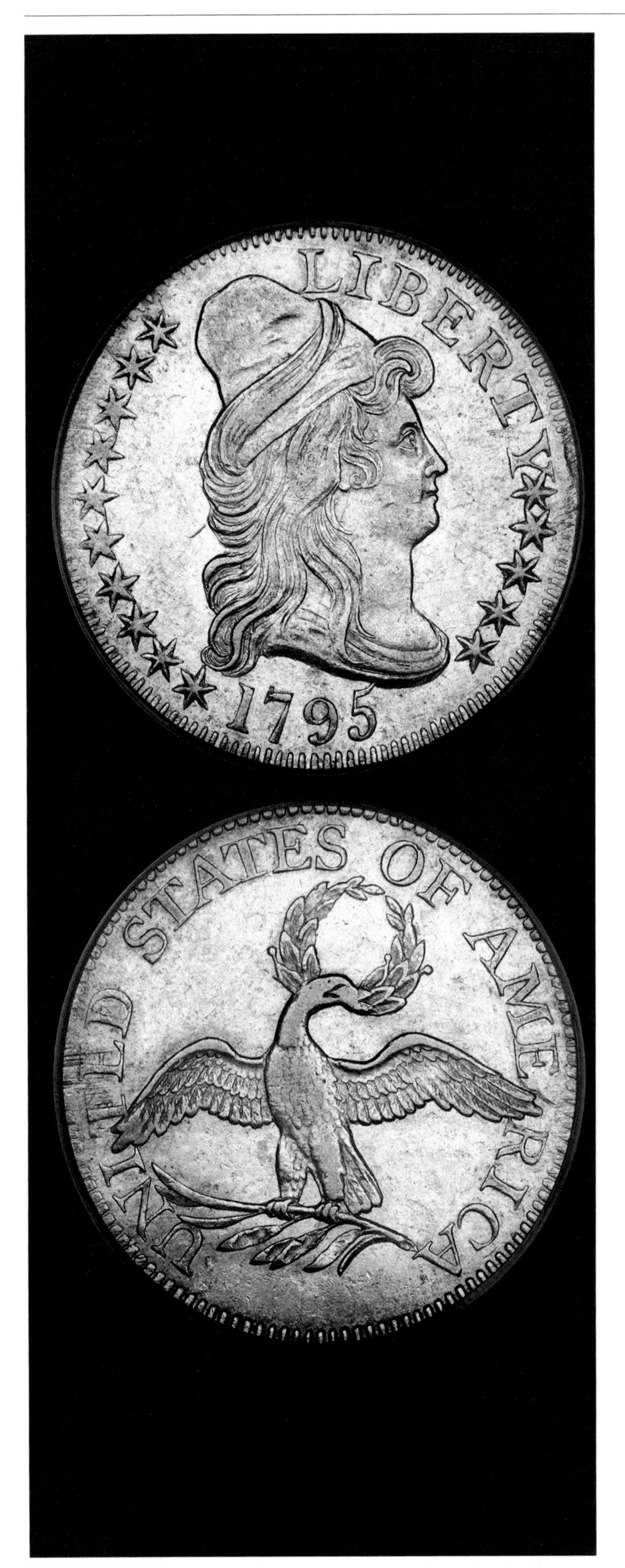

AU53 1795 Small Eagle Five Dollar, BD-4 First U.S. Gold Coin Denomination

2149 1795 Small Eagle AU53 PCGS. Breen-6412, BD-4, R.5. The Small Eagle design is appropriate, as the 1795 Small Eagle five dollar gold pieces were the first gold coins struck by the fledgling United States, only two years after its Mint in Philadelphia was founded. In the early years of coinage the Mint reported numbers of pieces coined, regardless of the date they bore; there was no requirement to strike coins only bearing the current year's date. Because of this and the large numbers of dies used—eight obverses and eight reverses—Bass and Dannreuther concluded that the mintage of 1795-dated coins might include more than the 8,707 pieces reported for the calendar year, perhaps as many as 12,000+ including those struck later.

The BD-2, BD-3, and BD-4 all share a common obverse, with each having a different reverse. On the obverse of this variety, the 5 in the date barely touches the lower drapery, and star 1 barely touches the lowest curl. Star 11 lies over the Y and touches star 12.

Breen and others believed this to be the first 1795 Small Eagle variety struck, based on the shared obverse evidence with BD-2 and BD-3. Bass and Dannreuther state that is not the case, however, due to the die crack from the edge through star 12 and into the field usually seen, along with die lapping that has removed the portion of star 1 touching the hair curl.

This AU53 piece only slight evidence of friction on the obverse, although less detail remains on the reverse due to a weaker strike than that on the obverse. Weakness is visible on the eagle's head, with some on the breast and right leg. The surfaces are still semiprooflike, with a slight reddish cast. Bass-Dannreuther estimate that from 60 to 75 examples survive.(#8066)

Choice AU 1795 BD-6 S Over D Half Eagle

2150 1795 Small Eagle AU55 NGC. Breen-6414, BD-6, R.5. The popular S over D variety with the final S in STATES punched over an errant D. There are 12 different 1795 Small Eagle varieties identified today, and they are the first Federal gold coins minted after a coinage impediment was alleviated. The Mint Act of April 2, 1792 required an excessive surety bond for mint officers, and those best suited to the job of assayer and coiner were unable to post the bond. The Mint Act asked for $10,000 bond to be posted by officers whose annual salary was only $1,500. On February 8, 1794, David Rittenhouse wrote to Congress that "a man's ability to give security depends much on accidental circumstances, little connected with either his qualifications or his moral character."

The first deposits of silver were converted to silver dollars in October 1794, and the first gold deposits were coined in July 1795. Moses Brown of Massachusetts made the first deposit of gold on February 12, 1795, providing 128 ounces. The first delivery of half eagles consisted of 744 coins that the chief coiner delivered to the Mint treasurer for distribution. Today, we are unable to identify the exact varieties that were included in that first delivery. The two S over D varieties are entirely unconnected with the other 10 die marriages in the 1795 sequence, and it is possible that these coins were the first 1795 half eagles coined that July.

This pleasing piece has faint green color in its brilliant yellow-gold surfaces with hints of reflectivity in the fields, especially near the borders. Both sides are lightly marked as expected, but there are no significant abrasions. A splendid piece, this important half eagle will make a nice addition to a specialized variety collection, or a date or type set.(#8066)

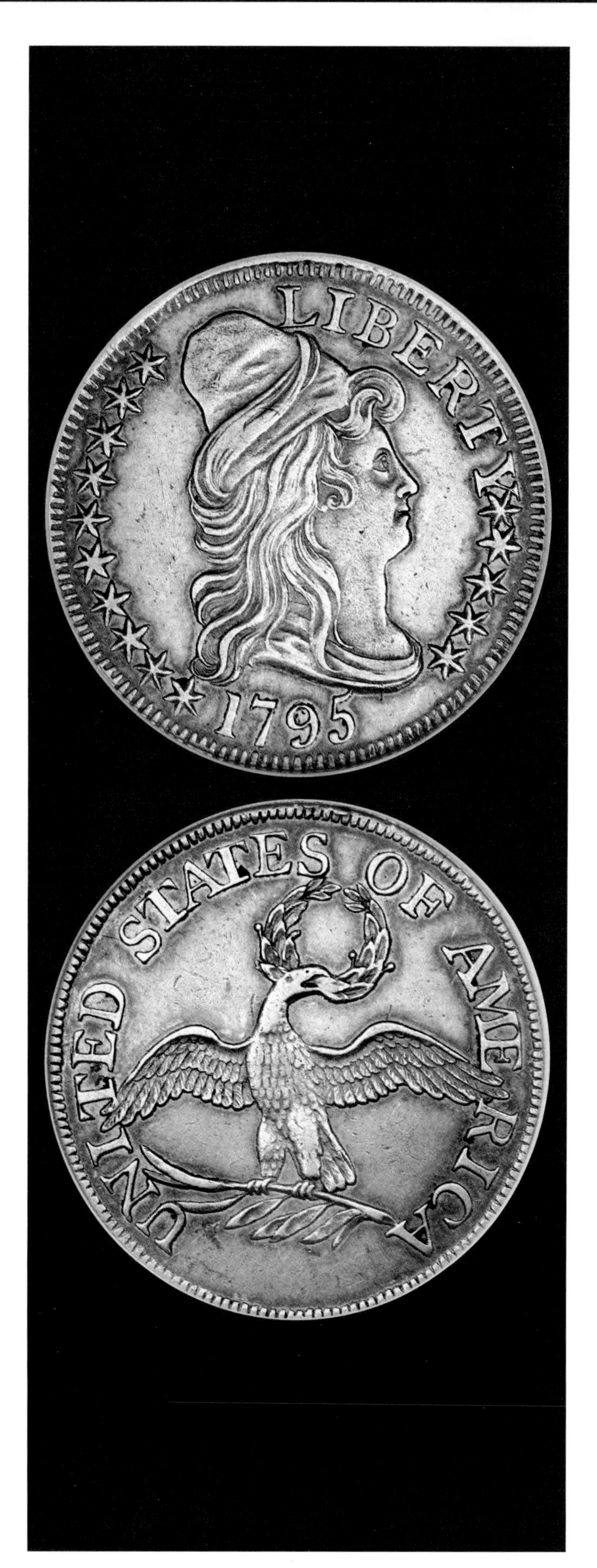

1795 Small Eagle Five Dollar BD-3, Choice AU

2151 1795 Small Eagle AU55 NGC. Breen-6412, BD-3, High R.3. Bass-Dannreuther Obverse State b/Reverse State b. The date is widely spaced and star 11 joins the Y of LIBERTY. On the reverse the tiny wreath bears four berries—two on each side—and a leaf extends to the lower foot of the I in UNITED.

There are 15 varieties of 1795 half eagle known, including 12 Small Eagle pairings and three Large Eagles. Among the Small Eagle reverses, the BD-3 at High R.3 (175-225 known, according to Bass-Dannreuther) is the only die pairing that can be considered generally available for a price. All of the other 1795 Small Eagle and Large Eagle variants range from R.5 all the way up to unique or High R.8, in the case of the 1795 Large Eagle, BD-13.

Most of the 1795 Small Eagle die pairings are in the R.5 to High R.5 range. The 1795 Small Eagles were the first gold coins struck by the U.S. Mint, in its third year of operation (gold eagles followed later in the year). As such, they are coins of immense importance to type enthusiasts, early gold specialists, and variety collectors. The very fact that the other 11 1795 Small Eagle die marriages are so much rarer places an increased burden on the BD-3; when high-grade examples do appear in the marketplace, they are eagerly bid up to high levels by members of the aforementioned factions.

This piece has antique-gold coloration with a halo of lilac and hazel around the devices on both sides, an unusual but appealing palette. There are few mentionable signs of contact, and no adjustment marks appear on either side. Tiny die cracks diagnose the die state, on the obverse from star 12 to the rim and on the reverse from the rim to the E in UNITED. This Choice AU coin should form an important addition to any collection.(#8066)

Exceptional 1795 Small Eagle Five AU58 ★, BD-3, Die State c/b

2152 1795 Small Eagle AU58 ★ NGC. Breen-6412, BD-3, High R.3. Die State c/b. Bass-Dannreuther dies 2-B. The Y in LIBERTY and star 13 touch star 12. Since this obverse is used on three varieties for the year, attribution is narrowed to BD-3 by noting the location of the eagle's left wing in relationship to the E in AMERICA—they touch only on this variety.

The Bass-Dannreuther reference suggests that Reverse Die B must be known in a terminal state, since Obverse 2 was later paired with Reverse C; the logic being that Reverse B "must have incurred some injury to force its retirement." Dannreuther continues: "Bass had two examples of this variety and knew this obverse was used again, so he anticipated finding a coin with a fatal reverse crack." This reasoning assumes that dies were only retired when severely damaged. While that was often the case with our nation's early coinage, there were exceptions. Remarriages of dies are well known in most of the early series, proving that dies were removed from the press for various reasons and then mated with another die, or even the same die, at a later date. Eventually some dies would simply vanish—for lack of a better term—from usage. They may have suffered irreparable damage, or they may have been retired for other reasons. For example, an excess supply of dies may have simply kept a few tools out of the rotation. Or, maybe the damage was to the shank and not the die face, so evidence of a terminal die state would not be visible on the last few coins struck. There are many possibilities, although we may never know the exact scenario that occurred in the early days of the first Mint.

This example is, however, from the last known state of the reverse die. The Bass-Dannreuther book states that Reverse State b shows a crack from the edge to the E of UNITED, and is referred to in that reference as a "graver's spike or die crack." The flaw noted is clearly a die gouge and not a break. In fact, on this piece we note two other engraver marks above the E and an additional spike emanating from the right side of the adjacent T—neither of which are noted in any previous writings, to our knowledge. Perhaps, then, the current offering represents the latest die state known for the BD-3 marriage.

This early five dollar was awarded the coveted ★ designation by NGC to denote exceptional eye appeal. It is likely that the lovely semiprooflike surfaces of this piece influenced the grader's decision. Since we know that Obverse 2 was lapped toward the end of the BD-3 die marriage, this example was probably struck shortly after the performance of that maintenance task. This well struck, green-gold survivor is one of only four 1795 half eagles to receive a ★ and the other three pieces are all Mint State, including an MS66 piece.

From The Cherokee County Collection, Part One.(#8066)

Elusive 1796/5 BD-1 Half Eagle, XF45

2153 1796/5 Small Eagle XF45 PCGS. Breen-6418, BD-1, High R.4. In *Early U.S. Gold Coin Varieties, A Study of Die States, 1795-1834,* John Dannreuther rates the 1796/5 half eagle as High R.4, with an estimate of 80 to 100 known examples surviving today. Our experience is different, and we feel that Dannreuther was liberal in his estimate of survivors. Prior to the present offering, we have only handled 12 examples in the last 16 years since the beginning of our Permanent Auction Archives, and only half of those pieces were unimpaired like the present specimen. Our opinion is that fewer than 50 half eagles bearing the 1796/5 overdate are still in existence today.

A comparison of mintage figures suggests that 1796 half eagles, with 6,196 coins struck, should be only slightly less rare than 1795 half eagles with 8,707 coins struck. However, mintage figures do little to explain the inner workings of the Philadelphia Mint in the 1790s. For the production of 1795-dated half eagles, the Mint made use of eight obverse dies and nine reverse dies in 12 combinations. Following that coinage, they used an extra 1795 obverse die that was overdated, along with a reverse die that had already been used, to produce the entire 1796-dated coinage from a single die combination. Novice collectors might assume that the 12 1795-dated varieties had an average mintage of 725 coins per die marriage, while more than 6,000 coins were struck from a single die the very next year.

A better interpretation of the 1795 and 1796 half eagle coinage is explained through the use of 13 die combinations to produce 14,903 coins, for an average of almost 1,150 coins per die marriage. Therefore, 1,150 pieces is the estimated mintage for 1796-dated half eagles. A second interpretation is the survival rate method. Our estimated current survival quantity reveals that about 3.6% of the original 1795-96 mintage still exists, yielding an estimated 1796 half eagle mintage of 1,377 coins. Either interpretation of the mintage figures will show that the 1796 half eagle is much rarer than 1795, and substantially undervalued today.

This lovely green-gold example has smooth surfaces with exceptional eye appeal. Only a few faint abrasions and tiny blemishes are evident, and they are consistent with the PCGS assigned XF45 grade. In fact, this is an exceptional piece for the XF45 grade, and appears to be a borderline AU example with considerable luster remaining on each side.(#8067)

Early State 1798 BD-6 Half Eagle, AU55
Perfect Obverse Die

2154 1798 Large Eagle, Small 8 AU55 PCGS. Breen-6430, BD-6, R.6. In past literature, the 8 has been called a "Small 8" compared to the "Normal 8" on BD-2 through BD-5; however, John Dannreuther corrects the notation, calling the earlier varieties "Large 8" dates and the present variety a "Normal 8."

Nearly all known examples of this die marriage, and there are only about 30 surviving, have a heavy die crack in the right obverse, from the B of LIBERTY across the hair curl, nose, chin, and down to the last star. The present piece is one of just two known to us without that obverse die crack. All examples have a reverse die crack down the right side. These cracks account for an early discard of both dies.

Housed in a green-label PCGS holder, this piece has considerable luster with bright yellow surfaces. The obverse has prominent, nearly vertical adjustment marks across the bust, and they have resulted in obvious central weakness on the reverse. Population: 16 in 55, 32 finer (11/09).(#8079)

Intriguing 1799 BD-1 Half Eagle, AU58
Obvious 1798 Clash Marks

2155 1799 Small Stars Reverse AU58 PCGS. Breen-6433, BD-1, R.5. There are nine different die marriages known for 1799, and each one is from a different reverse die. The BD-1 marriage has a reverse that was earlier used for 1798 BD-8, where it picked up bold clash marks from the 1798-dated obverse, including the complete date behind TES of STATES. Now used with a 1799 obverse, the old clash marks from the 1798 marriage are still visible, including the date! While many reverse dies in all denominations remained in use for two or more years, seldom can the actual clash marks be dated.

This pleasing piece has mild reflectivity in the fields with pale orange toning over lemon-yellow surfaces. The reverse has a small splash of powder-blue in the shield. An exciting piece from an underrated date. Population: 5 in 58, 20 finer (11/09).(#8081)

1802/1 Half Eagle, BD-8, MS61
Popular Early Gold Type Coin

2156 1802/1 MS61 NGC. CAC. Breen 6440, BD-8, R.4. A large mintage of 53,176 Capped Bust Right half eagles was achieved at the Philadelphia Mint in 1802, using overdated dies from 1801. The issue is reasonably available today, and often trades as a type coin. Eight die varieties are known for the 1802/1 half eagles, from two distinctly different obverse dies, both overdated with a 2 punched over a previous 1. The present coin is a representative of the BD-8 variety, characterized by the position of the 2 in the date touching the bust, and the S in STATES above the right side of a cloud. John Dannreuther estimates the original mintage of BD-8 as 10,000-15,000 pieces, with a surviving population of perhaps 150-200 examples.

The present coin is sharply struck, with especially pronounced definition on Liberty's hair curls and the eagle's breast feathers. The lustrous surfaces are a delightful orange-gold color. The reverse is especially clean for the grade, and if graded by that side alone would surely grade higher. On the obverse there are a couple of shallow marks and a small planchet void on Liberty's cheek that limit the grade. Census: 50 in 61, 50 finer (11/09).(#8083)

Near-Mint 1803/2 Half Eagle, BD-1

2157 1803/2 AU58 NGC. BD-1, R.4. Bass-Dannreuther Obverse State c / Reverse State c. This is an easily attributed variety due to the obvious overdate and the blundered TY on the obverse. The T is missing its right foot, and the Y is missing part of its left foot. There is another obverse that shows the 1803/2 overdate that was only used on the BD-4 die pairing. Nineteenth-century numismatist W. Elliot Woodward called them the First Overdate and Second Overdate, but on the latter the T is perfect. This piece, despite the presence of a couple of die cracks on the reverse, is still from a fairly early state of that die, which was employed until the cracks became breaks and a terminal rim cud formed. This piece shows just light wear over lustrous reddish-gold surfaces. Abrasions are scattered and minor. The lower shield, arrow shafts, and left (facing) claw on the reverse show noticeable adjustment marks.(#8084)

Gem 1806 Capped Bust Right Heraldic Eagle Five Round Top 6, 7x6 Stars, BD-6

2158 1806 Round Top 6, 7x6 Stars MS65 PCGS. CAC. Breen-6448, BD-6, R.2. A total of 64,093 Capped Bust Right, Heraldic Eagle half eagles were minted in 1806. Six die varieties are known for the date, including five varieties with a pointed 6 in the date, and the Round Top 6, BD-6 variety represented by the present coin. The BD-6 die marriage is the most available variety of the design type, and is a logical choice for type collectors. John Dannreuther estimates an original mintage of 35,000-50,000 pieces for the BD-6 variety, and believes 600-900 examples survive today in all grades. At the Gem level the issue is extremely rare. To date, NGC has certified two coins in MS65, with none finer; while PCGS has graded only this single specimen at the Gem level, with none finer (11/09).

One of the key features of the BD-6 variety, and of interest to advanced type collectors, is the placement of the obverse stars in a 7x6 pattern around the bust (previously the stars were arranged 8x5). Catalogers began to notice this distinctive arrangement as early as the Civil War era. For example, Lot 2760 of the Sixth Semi-Annual Sale (Woodward, 3/1865), reads, "1806 Six stars facing; fine and exceedingly rare." The lot sold to J.O. Emery for $8, a reasonable price in the 1860s.

The present coin is a pleasing Gem specimen, with terrific, sparkling mint luster. The bright yellow-gold surfaces show only a few, insignificant handling marks. The strike is sharpest in the center of the obverse, as usually seen on this issue. John Dannreuther believes the obverse die was placed in the anvil position when the Round Top 6 variety was struck, creating stronger obverse striking detail. Some softness is noted in the center of the reverse, where the wings and shield meet. Overall eye appeal is outstanding and the coin offered here is one of the finest survivors of this early half eagle issue. (#8089)

Late State 1808 BD-3 Half Eagle, MS62

2159 1808 MS62 NGC. Breen-6456, BD-3, R.4. This late die state piece has heavy clash marks on the obverse, as well as prominent clash marks on the reverse, including a complete 1808 date behind ES O. An obvious clash mark from the top of the cap can be seen from the arrows to the final A, the 5D, and all of the olive leaves. This may be what John Dannreuther saw when he wrote "now with crack from last A of AMERICA through denomination."

While the surfaces are lightly marked, this pleasing half eagle has excellent luster and bold design definition. Census: 38 in 62, 47 finer (11/09).(#8102)

1808/7 Capped Bust Left Half Eagle, AU58 Scarce BD-2 Variety

2160 1808/7 AU58 PCGS. Close Date, Breen-6455, BD-2, High R.4. A large total of 55,578 half eagles were coined in 1808, with four die varieties known for the date. The present coin is an example of the BD-2 variety, with the second 8 in the date punched over a 7, and a tall 1 centered over the right edge of a dentil. The BD-2 is a scarce variety with an estimated original mintage of 7,500-12,500 pieces, and a surviving population of 80-100 examples.

The present coin is an attractive specimen with strong, even reddish color over both sides. Mint luster is evident in protected areas near the devices. Evidence of porosity is noted at the centers, possibly from an improperly prepared planchet. Sharply struck in most areas, with some slight softness on the central hair curls and eagle's neck. The only noticeable surface marks are a short area of pinscratching to the left of star 12. Population: 5 in 58, 15 finer (11/09).(#8103)

Lustrous 1809/8 BD-1 Half Eagle, AU58

2161 1809/8 AU58 PCGS. CAC. Breen-6458, BD-1, High R.3. This is the only half eagle variety of the date. Coinage in 1809 was limited to half cents, large cents, dimes, half dollars, and half eagles. All 1809 half eagles are historically labeled "1809 over 8" although the undertype appears more like a misplaced 9 than an 8. John Dannreuther comments: "He [Harry W. Bass, Jr.] seems to have doubted the overdate status of this variety. The author also doubts the overdate status of this example and believes that it may only be a misplaced 9."

Regardless, it is extremely important as the only gold coin struck in 1809. This near-Mint example has a trace of pleasing violet toning in the obverse fields over green-gold surfaces with nearly full frosty mint luster.(#8104)

BD-1 1809/8 Five Dollar, MS62

2162 1809/8 MS62 NGC. Breen-6458, BD-1, High R.3. Sole variety for the year. Bass-Dannreuther Die State c/b, a combination not specifically listed in the reference but a logical extension of those present; while the obverse die crack between stars 1 through 7 also extends to the bust, as on the obverse state c, the reverse does not have the die crack between STATES and OF that defines the reverse state c. This is a well-defined yellow-orange example with few post-striking abrasions for the grade. The obverse shows striking weakness at the upper right rim, which corresponds to adjustment marks on the reverse.(#8104)

Sharp 1810 Small Date, Tall 5 Half Eagle, BD-1, MS63

2163 1810 Small Date, Tall 5 MS63 NGC. Breen-6462, BD-1, High R.3. There is not a great deal of size difference between the so-called Large Date and Small Date varieties of 1810. An easy way to tell the difference is to examine the top flags on the 1s in the date, which are nearly horizontal on the Large Date and noticeably diagonal on the Small Date. This piece displays generous mint luster radiating from frosty surfaces. The overall reddish-orange coloration mellows around the margins. The strike is sharp, with a few widely spaced adjustment marks occurring on the obverse rim between 7 and 10 o'clock. Census: 7 in 63, 4 finer (11/09).(#8106)

1810 Capped Bust Left Half Eagle, MS64
Small Date, Tall 5 Variety, BD-1
Only One Example Certified Finer

2164 1810 Small Date, Tall 5 MS64 NGC. Breen-6462, BD-1, High R.3. A substantial total of 100,287 Capped Bust Left half eagles was minted in 1810, with four major die varieties known for the date. The coin offered here is an example of the BD-1 variety, identified by the small 1 in the date nearly centered over a denticle, and the tall 5 in the denomination, with the flag to the left of the lowest feather tip. The BD-1 variety is the second most available of the four die marriages, but it is much more difficult to locate than the BD-4. Experts estimate an initial mintage of 20,000 to 30,000 pieces for the BD-1, with a surviving population of 150-225 examples in all grades. The issue is very rare at the near-Gem level, as NGC has certified only four specimens in MS64, with none finer; while PCGS has graded five examples at the Choice level, with one finer (11/09).

The half eagles of 1810 were avidly collected by early numismatists, who began to differentiate between the Large Date and Small Date varieties of the issue at a relatively early date. However, it was not until the twentieth century that all four subtypes became known. In the famous ANS Exhibition of 1914 William Woodin displayed and identified both Small Date varieties (BD-1 and BD-2), as well as the Large Date, Large 5 variety (BD-4). The Large Date, Small 5 variety (BD-3) is extremely rare, and was not known to early specialists, such as Edgar Adams and John H. Clapp. The discovery coin may have been the example in the Frederic W. Geiss Collection (B. Max Mehl, 2/1947), lot 1676. Mehl identified the coin as, "1810 Large date with small 5D." However, Mehl did not seem to realize he had identified a previously unknown variety. Knowledge of all four varieties did not become widespread until Walter Breen published his monographs in the 1960s.

The present coin is a virtually unimprovable specimen, with sharp striking details and nice, frosted luster. The natural green-gold surfaces have taken on an attractive overlay of yellow. A few light field marks limit the grade.(#8106)

1811 Small 5 Half Eagle, BD-2, MS62

2165 1811 Small 5 MS62 NGC. Breen-6464, BD-2, R.3. Bass-Dannreuther Die State e/b with prominently clashed dies. Only two die varieties are known for the 1811 half eagle. The obverse die is the same, but the reverses are readily distinguished by the size of the 5. The Large 5 variety is believed moderately scarcer. Both marriages are much more elusive than the 1807 BD-8 or the 1810 Large Date, Large 5, BD-4.

This lemon-gold early half eagle has a lustrous reverse and full luster across the obverse periphery. Both sides are refreshingly devoid of singular abrasions, and the advanced obverse die state adds to the singular appeal this coin presents.(#8109)

1811 Capped Bust Left Half Eagle, MS63
Popular Small 5, BD-2 Variety

2166 1811 Small 5 MS63 PCGS. Breen-6464, BD-2, R.3. A popular and relatively available issue, the 1811 Small 5 Capped Bust Left half eagles are prized by type collectors and series enthusiasts alike. Mint State coins are reasonably available in grades up to MS63. NGC has certified 32 examples in MS63, with 19 finer; while PCGS has graded 37 specimens at the Select level, with 13 finer (11/09).

The present coin is sharply struck throughout, with subdued satiny surfaces. The surfaces are remarkably free of contact marks for an MS63, with only a small cluster of insignificant marks above the eagle's head worthy of mention.(#8109)

1811 Capped Bust Left Half Eagle, MS64
Small 5 Variety, BD-2
Remarkable Mint Luster

2167 1811 Small 5 MS64 PCGS. CAC. Breen-6464, BD-2, R.3. The 1811 Capped Bust Left half eagle is an available, popular issue, in the context of early half eagles. In their *Encyclopedia of U.S. Gold Coins 1795-1933,* Jeff Garrett and Ron Guth indicate a surprising number of Mint State 1811 half eagles have appeared in auction catalogs over the years, but most examples seen were MS63 or lower. In MS64 the issue is decidedly rare. Including unreported resubmissions and crossovers, NGC has certified 13 coins in MS64, with six finer; while PCGS has graded 13 coins at the Choice level, with none finer (11/09).

As a date, 1811 half eagles have always been popular with numismatists, appearing at public auction as early as the A.C. Kline Sale (Moses Thomas & Sons, 6/1855), lot 185. Of course, little notice was taken of die varieties in 1855, but sophisticated numismatists began to notice the different size of the numeral in the denomination at a fairly early date. By the early 20th century, catalogers were making a clear distinction between the Small 5 and Tall 5 varieties. In the George Earle Collection (Henry Chapman, 6/1912), lot 2377 reads, "1811 Small 5. Extremely fine. Mint lustre. *Plate.*"

The present coin radiates bright mint luster, remarkable on an early five. The mint frost on the devices is thick and intense. The bright yellow-gold surfaces show occasional hints of pale rose and lilac, mostly over the devices. Recessed areas in front and behind Liberty's head show bright, semi-reflective surfaces. A few scattered marks are noted, but these are largely masked by the thick luster and have the appearance of luster grazes. There is a short grease stain (as struck) below RI. Overall visual appeal is outstanding.(#8109)

1811 Capped Bust Left Half Eagle, MS64
Small 5 Variety, BD-2
Bass-Dannreuther State d/a

2168 1811 Small 5 MS64 NGC. Breen-6464, BD-2, R.3. A large mintage of 99,581 half eagles was accomplished in 1811, with two major die varieties known for the date. The present coin is an example of the slightly more available BD-2 variety, distinguished by the smaller numeral 5 in the denomination. Perhaps 225-300 examples are known today in all grades. At the near-Gem level the issue is quite rare, as NGC has certified only 13 coins in MS64, with six finer; while PCGS has graded 13 specimens in near-Gem condition, with none finer (11/09).

The same obverse die was used on both varieties of the date, making it one of the hardiest dies of the early gold series. The reverse die employed the same Small 5 punch in the denomination used on two varieties of 1810 half eagles, but this reverse is different in other respects. The emission sequence is difficult to determine, as evidence of clashing occurs on both varieties, with the dies being lapped to remove evidence of the clashing between the different pairings. The most likely sequence seems to be BD-1, BD-2, BD-1 again, BD-2 second use. Clashing is not evident on the present coin, Bass-Dannreuther state d/a, the dies having been lapped to remove the clash marks.

The present coin is a pleasing near-Gem example, with deep reddish-tinted surfaces and frosty devices. The striking details are sharp in general, but some softness on the hair and stars is inevitable, because of the lapping of the dies. A scattering of insignificant handling marks is consistent with the grade. Overall visual appeal is excellent.(#8109)

Mint State 1811 Tall 5 Half Eagle, BD-1

2169 1811 Tall 5 MS61 NGC. Tall 5, Breen-6463, BD-1, High R.3. The scarcer of the two die marriages of 1811 half eagles, each of which receives separate listing in the *Guide Book* due to different size punches used to form the denomination. This yellow-gold Uncirculated example has attractive surfaces, and the strike is bold aside from slight softness on a small portion of the eagle's left (facing) wing. A pair of faint thin marks above the eagle's head require a loupe to locate. The open fields are moderately reflective, while cartwheel luster fills design elements. Two sets of prominent clashmarks (as produced) are visible on the fields.(#8110)

Splendid Gem 1812 BD-1 Wide 5D Half Eagle

2170 1812 MS65 NGC. Wide 5D, Breen-6466, BD-1, R.3. Two 1812 half eagle varieties are known from a single obverse die. The spacing of the denomination on the reverse provides immediate visual identification. The D is mostly under the branch stem on the Wide 5D variety, and it is mostly under the arrow feather on the Close 5D variety. This Gem is an early die state of the first struck 1812 variety, with no evidence of clash marks or other die deterioration.

We have only handled six MS65 examples of the date in all of our past sales back to 1993, with none finer. Those six pieces are equally divided between the two varieties, although the Close 5D variety is considered scarcer overall, according to John Dannreuther in *Early U.S. Gold Coin Varieties, A Study of Die State, 1795-1834*. He estimates that 300 to 450 examples of the BD-1 variety are known, with about 80 to 100 of the BD-2 variety surviving today.

The 1812 represents the final year of issue of the Capped Bust Left half eagles that were first struck in 1807 after John Reich prepared the designs. It is one of the more plentiful dates of the series, along with 1807 and 1810. These coins make excellent choices for type collectors who seek a single high quality example of the design.

This gorgeous Gem has exceptional aesthetic appeal. It is a coin that the connoisseur will appreciate for its bold strike, rich greenish-gold luster, and frosty mint surfaces. A hint of pale orange toning adds to its eye appeal. There are few marks on the exceptional surfaces with a single nick below the left (facing) wing near the E in UNITED serving as a pedigree marker. Census: 9 in 65, 0 finer (11/09).(#8112)

1813 Capped Head Left Half Eagle, BD-1, MS63 First Year of the Design Type

2171 1813 MS63 PCGS. Breen-6467, BD-1, R.2. A large mintage of 95,428 Capped Head Left half eagles was accomplished in 1813, the first year of the new design featuring the smaller bust. Two varieties are known for the date, with the present BD-1 variety most often seen. In fact, the 1813, BD-1 is the only readily available date and variety of the entire design type. The first S in STATES is located over the right side of the E in E PLURIBUS on BD-1, which employs the same obverse die as BD-2. An estimated original mintage of 60,000-75,000 pieces of the BD-1 variety was coined, with perhaps 450-650 examples surviving today in all grades.

The present coin radiates excellent mint luster, with no breaks over the high points. The attractive green-gold surfaces show underlying shades of yellow, with just a hint of reddish patina. Well, but not fully struck. A number of insignificant field marks limit the grade. Population: 63 in 63, 55 finer (11/09).(#8116)

Appealing MS61 1814/3 Half Eagle, BD-1

2172 1814/3 MS61 PCGS. BD-1, R.4. This overdate variety is the sole die pairing for the year, with the reverse a carryover from the previous year's BD-2 marriage. The remains of a 3 are obvious at the top of the 4 and at the right side, although on later-die-state examples the underdigit fades. A die center dot appears between the curl and the ear, although this piece shows none of the shield bar clashing frequently seen. The reverse shows broad double-punching on the D in the denomination, with the period adjacent high. The greenish-gold surfaces show considerable luster, and the distributed, scattered marks are relatively minor. The strike is bold, and the piece shows much eye appeal.(#8117)

1818 Capped Head Left Half Eagle, MS64
Rare 5D Over 50 Variety, BD-3
Only Two Examples Certified Finer

2173 1818 MS64 NGC. 5D Over 50, Breen 6472, BD-3, R.5. A total of 48,588 Capped Head Left half eagles were minted in 1818, with three die varieties known for the date. The present coin is a representative of the BD-3 variety, easily distinguished by the D in the denomination punched over a numeral 0. The BD-3 die marriage is the rarest variety of the date, with an estimated initial mintage of 7,500-10,000 pieces. John Dannreuther suggests perhaps 35-45 examples survive in all grades today. The issue is extremely rare at the near-Gem level, as NGC has certified only the present coin in MS64, with none finer; while PCGS has graded no examples at the near-Gem level, with two finer (11/09).

As a date, 1818 half eagles have always been prized by collectors. The BD-3 variety was first noticed by Henry Chapman in the Harlan P. Smith Collection (Chapman, 6/1906), lot 205:

> "1818 Erratic stars, one being placed beneath the lower curl of hair near the date. Rev. The D in the denomination has been cut over the letter 0 showing that the die sinker originally made it 50 instead of 5D. Uncir. Mint lustre."

The curious overstruck letter was soon forgotten by the numismatic community, except for specialists like Edgar Adams and John H. Clapp. Chapman himself did not notice it when he sold another example of the rare variety as lot 2383 of the George Earle Collection in June of 1912. On that occasion, Chapman simply noted the denomination was a "Close 5D" as opposed to the "Wide 5D" of the other two varieties. The overstrike was popularized as a distinct variety in the 1950s, when New Netherlands sold an example in one of their sales.

The present coin is a memorable specimen, with softly frosted mint luster and rich reddish color on each side. The striking details are extremely sharp, with only slight weakness on the lower hair curl and the eagle's talons. The surfaces are minimally abraded, the only mentionable flaw being a short area of shallow pinscratching to the right of the second S in STATES. The coin offered here is one of the finest survivors of this rare early half eagle variety.(#8120)

Rarity-5 1834 Capped Head, Crosslet 4 Five Dollar, BD-2, MS62

2174 1834 Capped Head, Crosslet 4 MS62 NGC. Breen-6500, BD-2, R.5. BD Obverse State a/b, Reverse State b. The 1 in the date is tall, the 4 is of the Crosslet style, and the lowest curl of Liberty's hair ends in a distinct point. These coins are quite elusive and must not be confused with the Classic Head fives, which are also found in the Plain and Crosslet 4 varieties. While the Crosslet 4 Classic Heads are also rare, the Capped Head fives of both varieties are notable rarities just as a design type.

Like their sister coinage of earlier years, the 1834 Capped Heads were the victims of mass meltings that nearly obliterated the original mintages. However, it appears that a few more may have been saved as the last of their type when the new Classic Head coins were introduced. Garrett and Guth sum up the situation regarding the pieces nicely:

> "In a series of rarities, the 1834, Crosslet 4 is among the rarest. PCGS and NGC have graded only 10 examples, among which there are, no doubt, some resubmissions that have not been removed from the charts."

Since those words were written the combined certified total now stands at 18 submissions, but the principle is the same: a high likelihood of crossovers and duplications. Interestingly, Bass-Dannreuther rate the 1834 Capped Head, Plain 4 BD-1 as rarer (30-40 known, R.5+), providing an estimate of 45-55 coins for the Crosslet 4 which, while making it still R.5, seems overly generous, given the smallish certified populations. We would be unsurprised one day soon to see the Crosslet 4 ranked Low R.6, or 25-35 examples known.

Insignificant contact in the field apparently keeps this wonderful piece from an even finer grade, but the only notable marks are in the lower left obverse field above star 1. Generous luster is present throughout the yellow-gold surfaces. On the obverse the often-seen die crack extends from the rim through stars 9 to 13, but the crack at star 6 is unseen. The reverse shows an arcing crack through all letters of AMERICA that continues into the denomination.

Bass-Dannreuther neatly capture the appeal of these early type coins:

> "The Motto issues of 1834 are very popular with collectors and they represent the last of the old tenor gold coins. The romance associated with these coins, combined with their rarity and the uniqueness of each obverse and reverse die, make them irresistible."

Census: 2 in 62, 3 finer (11/09).(#8161)

CLASSIC HALF EAGLES

Wonderful 1834 Plain 4 Five, MS64 First Classic Head Issue

2175 1834 Plain 4 MS64 NGC. First Head, Breen-6501, McCloskey 1-A, R.3. There are four types of half eagles produced in 1834: the Capped Head to Left coins with Plain 4 or Crosslet 4, and the Classic Head coins, also with Plain or Crosslet 4. The Capped Head 1834 half eagles are, of course, the last of their type, and among the Classic Heads the Crosslet 4 is much more elusive than the Plain 4 variety. The Plain 4 is appealing in high grade, however, precisely because it is the most obtainable. In MS64, 1834 Plain 4s are far from common, but when found they make wonderful type coins. NGC has certified 52 pieces in this near-Gem grade, with only eight coins finer (11/09). The surfaces of this piece are a lustrous, bright yellow-gold, with lots of eye appeal and minimal marks for the grade. A small arcing die crack connects stars 4 and 5 to the obverse rim in two places. Another plus is the bold strike, and there are no distractions save for a couple of tiny dark toning areas of little import.(#8171)

Memorable McCloskey 1-A Classic Head 1834 Plain 4 Half Eagle, MS64

2176 1834 Plain 4 MS64 PCGS. First Head, Breen-6501, McCloskey 1-A, R.3. This Script 8 variety, though scarce in an absolute sense, is one of the more available first-year Classic Head half eagle die pairs. This holds true across most grades, as the existence of this remarkable near-Gem survivor attests. From the first glance, this is an instantly captivating coin. Is it the shining lemon-gold luster? The razor-sharp striking definition? The surfaces, which are smooth even by MS64 standards? All three must play a part, but this piece also has something more—in a word, it is *special,* and a coin worth taking the time to see in person, regardless of one's interest in the series. Across all 1834 Plain 4 varieties, PCGS has graded only three coins finer (11/09). Housed in a green label holder. (#8171)

LIBERTY HALF EAGLES

1834 Classic Head, Crosslet 4
Half Eagle, MS62
Rare *Guide Book* Variety

2177 1834 Crosslet 4 MS62 PCGS. Second Head, Crosslet 4, Breen-6503, McCloskey 5-D, R.4. One of the unsung rarities among gold coins from the 1830s, the Crosslet 4 is easily the most elusive of all major variety Classic half eagles. Its rarity is, in fact, more similar to the previous two designs from 1813-29 and 1829-34 than the Classic series. The surfaces on this exceptional Crosslet 4 are boldly detailed in virtually all areas, just falling short of completeness on some of Liberty's hair curls. Both sides exhibit splendid red-orange and green-gold color, and satiny luster that is affected only by trivial scuffiness in the fields. A coin of obvious importance to the early gold specialist. Population: 5 in 62, 2 finer (11/09).

Ex: Central States Signature Auction (Heritage, 5/2005), lot 8596. (#8172)

High Grade 1840-D Tall D Five Dollar, MS62
Ex: *S.S. New York*

2178 1840-D Tall D MS62 NGC. Ex: *S.S. New York.* Variety 3-B. The opening of the 0 in the date is centered over a denticle, and the upright of the D mintmark is positioned above the left serif of the right diagonal of the V in FIVE while the right edge extends to the upright of the E in FIVE.

The 1840-D half eagle is most frequently seen in Very Fine to Extremely Fine grades. It is scarce to rare in the About Uncirculated levels of preservation, and extremely rare in Mint State (Douglas Winter, *Gold Coins of the Dahlonega Mint*).

Bright yellow-gold color covers the lustrous surfaces of this MS62 specimen. The strike is impressive, resulting in strong delineation on the design features. Only the horizontal shield lines reveal minor softness. While a handful of minute contacts define the grade, its surfaces are cleaner than many examples of this issue that tend to show conspicuous abrasions. Housed in an NGC "Shipwreck Certification" holder. Census: 3 in 62, 1 finer (9/08).(#8198)

Exceptional 1842-D Large Date Five Dollar MS61, One of the Finest Examples Known Ex: *S.S. New York*

2179 1842-D Large Date MS61 NGC. Ex: *S.S. New York.* Large Date and Letters. Reverse of 1842. Variety 9-G, the only die variety known for this issue. In *Gold Coins of the Dahlonega Mint 1838-1861,* Doug Winter states that this variety was created when the Philadelphia Mint sent a new pair of dies to Dahlonega in late 1842. The original mintage is reported as 21,691 pieces, but even this small figure seems too large in view of the coin's rarity in today's market. Recent data suggests that 85-95 examples of this variety are extant, with about 80% of this population grading in the VF-XF range. AU coins are very rare, and the issue is High R.7 in Mint State. In the context of Dahlonega half eagles, the 1842-D Large Date is second only to the famous 1861-D in absolute rarity, and is first in high-grade rarity.

The recent recovery of treasure from the wreck of the *S.S. New York* has challenged traditional wisdom about the distribution of early Southern gold. The *S.S. New York* was a light cargo and passenger ship operating between New Orleans and Galveston in the 1840s. She sank in a hurricane on September 17, 1846, with a reported loss of 17 crew members and more than $30,000 in gold. Nearly all of the U.S. coins recovered were from the New Orleans or Dahlonega mints, with only two coins from their sister mint at Charlotte. The treasure contained several outstanding numismatic rarities, including the present coin. According to a report by Doug Winter on the NGC website, the coins were conserved by Numismatic Conservation Service and certified by NGC.

The discovery of this NGC-graded MS61 coin has drastically alter the Condition Census for this issue. Previously, only three coins had been certified at the Mint State level. Experts have long agreed that the Eliasberg/Duke's Creek specimen was the finest known. The MS61 North Georgia/Green Pond example was generally listed as number two in the Condition Census, and the Byron Reed coin was number three. The present coin is a challenge to the Duke's Creek and Green Pond coins for the top spot in the Condition Census.

The yellow-gold surfaces of this stunning coin are somewhat prooflike in appearance, an effect more pronounced on the reverse than the obverse but clearly an early strike from both dies. The strike is nearly full and extremely sharp for a D-mint half eagle, with only a touch of softness visible on the high point hair. Light chatter appears in the fields, but the only singular contact marks are a scrape in the obverse left (facing) field near star 2 and two ticks on the reverse near the eagle's beak.

This piece is certified in a custom NGC encapsulation identifying its *S.S. New York* origin and bearing the notation "NGC Shipwreck Certification."(#8211)

1843-D Liberty Head Half Eagle, MS63 Medium D

2180 1843-D Medium D MS63 PCGS. Variety 10-H. The 1843-D Liberty Head half eagle is one of the most available D-Mint dates of the series and enjoys great demand as a type coin. From an original mintage of 98,452 pieces, Doug Winter estimates a surviving population of 225-250 examples in all grades. The issue is rare in any Mint State grade and prohibitively rare above MS63. To date, NGC has certified five coins at the Select level, with one finer; while PCGS has graded only four coins in MS63, with one finer (11/09).

The present coin is a solid candidate for Condition Census, as only two coins have been certified in higher technical grades. This example is fully struck, with bright mint luster and pleasing yellow-gold color. The only noticeable mark is a small diagonal abrasion above the eagle's head. Overall eye appeal is outstanding. (#8215)

Sharply Impressed 1844-D Half Eagle, MS62

2181 1844-D MS62 NGC. Variety 11-H. The 1844-D half eagle, while available with minimal difficulty in Extremely Fine and lower level About Uncirculated, is scarce in high-end AU and rare in Mint State. This MS62 specimen displays bright yellow-gold surfaces with traces of luster around and in the interstices of the design motifs. The devices are sharply impressed, a characteristic aspect of the '44-D. Planchet quality is much better than usually seen, as it is devoid of grease stains and major planchet chips. Distributed minute contact marks are for the most part inconsequential. Census: 3 in 62, 3 finer (11/09).(#8221)

Conditionally Rare 1844-O Five Dollar, MS63

2182 1844-O MS63 NGC. CAC. Many of the antebellum O-mint coins of every issue appear not to have been saved in any significant quantity. Despite its high mintage of 364,000 coins, the 1844-O half eagle is no exception. Although circulated examples are quite common, it is quite rare in Mint State, and it is an issue that legendary collector Harry W. Bass, Jr. favored. The present coin offers lots of eye appeal on the lustrous greenish-gold surfaces, with considerable prooflikeness present under light field chatter. A couple of scrapes on the neck are minor but help account for the grade. The strike is bold, save at the immediate centers. Census: 10 in 63, 6 finer (11/09). (#8222)

Small Date 1846 Five Dollar, MS63

2183 1846 Small Date MS63 NGC. The 1846 Small Date is attributable by the relatively wide spacing between the final two digits in the date. Like most early Liberty half eagles, the 1846 is an elusive coin in Mint State, and the Small Date from this year is thought to be the scarcer of the two logotypes. This lustrous yellow-gold example is boldly detailed in all areas and the bright semiprooflike surfaces have only a few wispy abrasions that account for the grade. This issue's impressively low population is perhaps modestly skewed since Small and Large Date varieties were not distinguished in the early years of certification.(#88226)

Extraordinary MS64 1848-C Five Dollar Ex: Bass, Ranked as Second Finest Known

2184 1848-C MS64 PCGS. CAC. Variety 1. A fairly substantial number (by Charlotte Mint standards) of 1848-C fives were minted, but the vast majority of the original production of 64,472 pieces has been either lost or reduced in eye appeal as a result of circulation. It is estimated that there are a total of 250-350 pieces extant today in all grades. However, well over half of the known examples are in the VF-XF grade range. Only three to five pieces are believed to grade Uncirculated. This coin is listed as second finest on Doug Winter's most recent Condition Census, and it is numerically tied with the Eliasberg coin, which is also graded MS64.

Some softness of strike is noted on the curls around Liberty's face and on the eagle's neck and right (facing) leg feathers. These features are, however, normal for the issue and do not detract from the overall pleasing eye appeal. Both sides show semiprooflike fields that glow with bright yellow-gold coloration. This piece lacks the normally encountered extensive abrasions. However, it is important to note a couple that will aid in identifying this important coin in the future: A shallow, near-vertical mark is at the end of Liberty's chin, a series of small contact marks appears between star 5 and Liberty's forehead, and a short, shallow grease stain is noted on the reverse just below the upright of the second T in STATES.

Ex: Mike Brownlee to Harry Bass, March 1972; Harry Bass Collection (Bowers and Merena, 10/1999), lot 990, where it realized $50,600; Long Beach Auction (Heritage, 2/2000), lot 6689; private collection. (#8237)

Lustrous Mint State 1849-C Half Eagle

2185 1849-C MS61 PCGS. CAC. Variety 1. The digit 1 in the date is slightly below the bust truncation, while on the reverse, in its usually seen die state, a die crack runs from the leaves directly to the rim, grazing the upper left serif of the U in UNITED. The original mintage was 64,800 pieces, although today Mint State pieces are scarce. The five finest at PCGS range from MS62-MS64, putting this piece just outside of the Condition Census. This lustrous piece has semiprooflike fields beneath the light field chatter, with attractive greenish-gold coloration. The peripheral strike is sharp, although some weakness shows on the hair beneath LIBE and on the eagle's legs, fletchings, and claws at the lower reverse. Population: 6 in 61, 5 finer (12/09). (#8241)

One of the Finest Known 1852-C Fives, MS63

2186 1852-C MS63 PCGS. CAC. Variety 1. The fields are bright and semiprooflike on this delightful Select Mint State coin, which boasts lovely orange-gold surfaces. The strike is strong in the center but somewhat weak at the peripheries. There are a few light field marks, none singularly important, that explain the grade. The mintage of this coin was a rather large (for the time and place) production of 72,574 coins. However, most of those coins circulated at the time of issue, and today several hundred survive in all grades, most of them averaging VF to XF. This MS63 PCGS example is the sole so certified, although there are three finer, all MS64. NGC has certified eight MS63s, with nine finer (11/09). Note, however, Doug Winter's comment that, unsurprisingly, the "figures are very significantly inflated by resubmissions, especially at the MS61 and MS64 level."(#8251)

1857-C Liberty Head Half Eagle, MS62 Only Three Coins Certified Finer

2187 1857-C MS62 PCGS. Variety 1. A total of 31,360 Liberty Head half eagles was produced at the Charlotte Mint in 1857, not a large mintage in the context of the series, but substantial. The issue is among the more available dates today, causing Doug Winter to theorize that a small hoard may have existed at one time. Experts estimate a surviving population of 225-275 pieces in all grades. The 1857-C is scarce at AU levels, and Mint State coins are rare. Winter believes 10-12 coins survive in Uncirculated grades. Currently, NGC has certified seven examples in MS62, with two finer; while PCGS has graded only five specimens in MS62, with a single coin finer (11/09).

The present coin is a delightful specimen, with semiprooflike fields and bright yellow-gold color. Fully struck in most areas, with some slight weakness on the eagle's neck. Identifiable by a tiny, copper-colored void above the notch in the eagle's right (facing) wing. (#8272)

Rare MS61 1859-C Five Dollar

2188 1859-C MS61 PCGS. Variety 1, the only known die pair for the 1859-C half eagle. While this issue is fairly easy to obtain in lower grades, it is extremely scarce in About Uncirculated condition and a major rarity in Mint State. PCGS and NGC have certified fewer than 20 Uncirculated coins, most all of them in MS60 and MS61. It is quite likely that a number of these are resubmissions or crossovers.

A delicate blend of yellow-gold and light green resides on the bright surfaces of this MS61 example. The obverse exhibits relatively strong definition, but the reverse reveals the usual weakness on the eagle's neck and shield. Scattered marks are relatively light, unlike the heavy, deep abrasions that so often plague surviving specimens. Population: 2 in 61, 3 finer (12/09).(#8281)

Pleasing 1859-D Medium D Select Half Eagle

2189 1859-D Medium D MS63 PCGS. Variety 36-CC, identified by upright of the Medium D mintmark partly over the upright of the E in FIVE. Easily one of the finest survivors known for this elusive late-date Dahlonega half eagle issue, listed in Doug Winter's Condition Census for the issue and previously part of the Chestatee Collection offered by Heritage in August 1999, which consisted of duplicates (!) from the incomparable Duke's Creek Collection. Considered the second finest known at that time. The two small abrasions below the truncation of the bust are unmistakable pedigree markers.

Rich orange-tinged yellow-gold luster shows slight granularity but is fine and pleasing nonetheless. Slight striking softness as usual on the central devices, though each side shows few marks for the grade. A great opportunity for the dedicated Dahlonega gold lover. Population: 3 in 63, 1 finer (11/09).

Ex: Arthur Montgomery Collection; Auction '84 (Stack's session, 8/1984), lot 1351; Ed Milas; Ed Milas Collection (Stack's, 5/1995), lot 516; Numisma '95 (Stack's/RARCOA/Akers, 11/1995), lot 1469; Chestatee Collection (Heritage, 8/1999), lot 7700.(#8282)

Memorable 1876-CC Five Dollar, MS61

2190 1876-CC MS61 NGC. Rusty Goe's April 2003 census of the finest known 1876-CC half eagles includes just two Mint State pieces, a PCGS MS66 and an NGC MS61; the former coin, the Eliasberg specimen, comes with a footnote stating that the MS64 and MS65 grading events in the NGC *Census Report* belong to the Eliasberg coin. Six years later, this MS61 survivor remains the second-finest representative of the lowest-mintage Carson City half eagle issue, a status that seems unlikely to change. This bright lemon-gold piece has a sharply struck portrait with the characteristic die lump on the neck, left of the low-hanging curl. Though a number of faint marks and wispy abrasions are present in the fields, their collective impact on the eye appeal is minimal. A memorable coin for the Carson City enthusiast.(#8340)

The Eliasberg 1899-S Half Eagle, MS69

2191 1899-S MS69 NGC. Ex: Eliasberg. Like many of the late 19th and early 20th century coins from the famed Louis E. Eliasberg, Sr. Collection, this piece was obtained at face value by John M. Clapp directly from the San Francisco Mint. It is the most pristine example of the type this cataloger has ever seen, and is certainly the finest example of the date that we have ever seen or handled. It is the finest certified by either service (the only close competition is a single PCGS MS68, with no other examples graded by either service above MS66), and is among the finest known specimens for the type.

The surfaces display intense luster with a reflective quality that is highly unusual for the issue, indicating that this piece was indeed a "special" coin set aside for an important collector. The strike is impeccable, sharp enough that it compares to many proofs of the era in this respect. A long, hard look at the surfaces under magnification does reveal a couple (literally, only a couple) of tiny, nearly insignificant abrasions. One tiny toning spot just in front of Liberty's upper lip is mentioned for accuracy and provides an easy pedigree marker for this important numismatic treasure. A stunning coin that is equal in importance alongside the Eliasberg 1899-S eagle MS69 NGC also offered in this sale, and is certainly the most important 1899-S half eagle that we have ever had the pleasure to offer. This piece is one of three certified MS69 for the entire type at NGC. We should also mention this is the **plate coin in *United States Coinage: A Study by Type*** by Jeff Garrett and Ron Guth. Population: 1 in 69, 0 finer (11/09).

Ex: San Francisco Mint, December 1899, at face value; John M. Clapp; John H. Clapp; Clapp Estate (1942); Louis E. Eliasberg, Sr.; United States Gold Coin Collection (Eliasberg Collection, Bowers and Ruddy, 10/1982), lot 599.

From The Atherton Family Collection.(#8399)

PROOF LIBERTY HALF EAGLES

Extraordinary 1839 Half Eagle, PR61
Just Two Proofs Known
The Long Hidden King Farouk Coin

2192 1839 PR61 NGC. "Semi-Unique" is an oxymoron that B. Max Mehl and other 19th and 20th century coin dealers enjoyed using, and the 1839 proof half eagle fits the definition perfectly, with only two pieces known to exist. NGC has certified a single piece that was formerly PCGS graded PR61. The other PR61 PCGS coin is the second known example, as shown in the following roster:

1. **PR61 NGC.** William H. Woodin; Waldo Newcomer; Col. E.H.R. Green; Burdette G. Johnson; King Farouk (Sotheby's, 2/1954), lot 249; Thomas Melish Sale (A. Kosoff, 4/1956), lot 1983; Paul and Art Kagin; Hollinbeck Coin Company (11/1959). **The present specimen.** This coin has been off the market for 50 years. In his *Encyclopedia of United States and Colonial Proof Coins,* Walter Breen speculated that the Farouk coin and the Melish coin, that he assigned separate entries. Today, we can confirm that they are the same coin.

2. **PR61 PCGS.** Purchased in Europe in January 1982 by Marc Emory for New England Rare Coin Galleries, as part of a three-piece 1839 gold proof set. The set was apparently the property of a European museum that was divesting its holdings of foreign (to them) coins. Later, offered provisionally in Bowers and Merena (5/1993), lots 2537-2539, but sold as a set in lot 2540.

Few 1839 proof gold coins are known to exist today, and each of the three denominations represents a distinctly different design. We are aware of three 1839 proof quarter eagles representing the Classic Head design, two 1839 proof half eagles representing the modified Liberty design, and three 1839 proof eagles representing the first Liberty design introduced in 1838.

Breen reported in his proof reference that Mint Director Robert Maskell Patterson sent two 1839 proof half eagles to Levi Woodbury, the Secretary of the Treasury, on March 22, 1839, illustrated the improved Liberty design, although he provides no documentation for his statement. If true, and with just two known today, it is likely that they are the same two coins. The modified or second Liberty Head is distinctly different from the original 1838 design that appeared on the eagles.

This piece and the 1839 proof half eagle from the European museum are from the same dies. The obverse has several areas of minor die rust, including one on the bust above the 8, and another on the neck behind the hair curl. Several other areas of die rust appear on Liberty's head and in the field around the date and most of the stars. Some past collectors and dealers have called this variety an 1839/8 overdate. High magnification observation reveals a short diagonal line that connects the ball of the 9 to its upper loop, and that feature appears to be characteristic of the original die, rather than a result of die rust. The reverse also has noticeable die rust, but no other indications of die deterioration. The overdate status is unlikely, in our opinion, as it seems that any 1838 die would feature the original head of Liberty as those on the eagles.

This proof half eagle, like the other known 1839 proof half eagle, is lower in the numerical scale due to cleaning. Hairlines are clearly visible on both sides, mostly in the fields. The obverse and reverse have fully mirrored fields that mark this coin as an unquestioned proof. The devices are fully lustrous with satiny mint frost. Both sides exhibit attractive greenish-gold color, and the devices are boldly detailed. All aspects of this coin other than the minor hairlines suggest that it is a first-rate specimen.(#8428)

1863 Half Eagle, PR66 ★ Ultra Cameo
Likely Less Than a Dozen Known

2193 1863 PR66 ★ Ultra Cameo NGC. Few business strikes survive of this low-mintage half eagle issue, produced at the height of the Civil War to the extent of a mere 2,442 pieces. The 1863 quarter eagle, a legendary rarity, was not made at all as a business strike, but the proof half eagle is almost certainly rarer. Only 30 examples each of the quarter eagle and half eagle are recorded in proof format, but today 15-20 pieces of the quarter eagle are known, compared to about a dozen or less of the half eagle. The 30 gold proof sets of the year were delivered on March 23, with a few extra pieces of the one dollar and three dollar pieces, according to Breen. (Some of those proof gold pieces may have been later melted, according to an exchange Breen reports between coin dealer Samuel H. Chapman and early proof gold collector John F. McCoy, whose collection was auctioned in 1864 over a period of nearly a week.) Both the business strike and proof half eagles are of the Type Two reverse, introduced on the P-mint coins in 1860.

The 1989 Breen *Proof Encyclopedia* states "not more than a dozen around"; more-recent references, such as Garrett and Guth, estimate 10 to 12 examples, consistent with the combined NGC/PCGS population data. NGC has certified only four coins, including one impaired PR50, two PR65 Cameos, and this PR66 ★ Ultra Cameo as the finest. PCGS has graded six coins, the finest a single PR65 Deep Cameo (11/09).

This appears to be only the second time we have offered a proof 1863 half eagle in any grade since we began maintaining our Permanent Auction Archives, the first a PR64 Deep Cameo PCGS coin that brought $69,000 in our Dallas Signature Auction (11/2005, lot 2421).

The present coin is well-balanced, with even, moderate yellow-gold patina on each side and little evidence of contact. It is perhaps only a few light, undistracting field hairlines that preclude an even finer grade. Liberty's cheek in particularly is clean, as are the devices throughout. For pedigree purposes we note a tiny planchet indent, as made, in the field over Liberty's head, between stars 7 and 8. The strike is fully brought up, as expected. This coin poses an important opportunity to obtain the finest certified example of this momentous rarity.(#98453)

Brilliant PR64 Cameo 1889 Half Eagle

2194 1889 PR64 Cameo NGC. CAC. The business strike production of this issue was a skimpy 7,520 pieces, and only 45 proofs were produced, also on the low side. Today only 15 to 20 proof specimens are known including examples in museum collections, most of them in the PR64 grade of the present piece. This near-Gem proof displays intense field-device contrast on both sides, with brilliant luster and attractive yellow-gold coloration throughout. A couple of tiny grayish contact marks are noted on Liberty's neck. NGC has certified nine examples in PR64 Cameo, with only three finer (11/09). (#88484)

Admirable 1891 Half Eagle, PR64 Deep Cameo

2195 1891 PR64 Deep Cameo PCGS. CAC. The recorded mintage is only 53 examples for the 1891 half eagle, and perhaps 20 different pieces exist today; the population data are skewed due to duplications. Most of the survivors average the near-Gem level of the present coin, which boasts the splendid, deep field reflectivity and thick frost expected for a Deep Cameo coin. The surfaces are a pretty, pleasing canary-yellow. Abrasions are remarkably few, although we do see a couple of wispy contact marks in the fields. Nonetheless, we believe the coin is high-end for the assigned grade. Population: 7 in 64 Deep Cameo, 0 finer (12/09).(#98486)

1896 Half Eagle, PR64 ★ Ultra Cameo
One of the Finest Examples
Known of This Popular Date

2196 1896 PR64 ★ Ultra Cameo NGC. A total of 103 proof Liberty Head half eagles were coined in 1896, certainly a modest figure in absolute terms, but still the largest proof half eagle mintage of the 19th century. However, the coins are much rarer than the production total suggests. Jeff Garrett and Ron Guth believe only 25-30 examples survive today in all grades. In PR64 Ultra Cameo the 1896 is a R.7 issue. NGC has graded one coin PR64 Ultra Cameo, with seven finer; while PCGS has certified one example at this exalted level, with three finer (11/09).

The present coin exhibits profound contrast between the reflective fields and the frosty devices, earning the coveted ★ designation. The characteristic orange-peel effect is most noticeable on the obverse. A few tiny marks are present on both sides, two below the eagle's beak, and one in the lower right obverse field, out from star 12, and undoubtedly account for the grade. Overall eye appeal is outstanding. NGC has graded only one coin in PR64 ★ Ultra Cameo, with three finer (11/09).(#98491)

1900 Liberty Head Half Eagle, PR66 Cameo
Reported Proof Mintage of 230 Pieces
Low Survival Rate, Strong Cameo Contrast

2197 1900 PR66 Cameo NGC. CAC. The Mint anticipated a large demand for proof sets in 1900, perhaps because of optimism over the new century. In his Golden Jubilee Sale (B. Max Mehl, 5/1950), lot 409, Mehl noted, "Apparently collectors began to realize the charm of collecting these beautiful gold proofs, as we note by the mint report that 230 proofs were struck." In spite of the large mintage, the largest of any Liberty Head half eagle, the date is not noticeably more common than other proofs of the era. Perhaps much of the original mintage went unsold, and was melted at the end of the year, or the issue may have had an unusually low survival rate, with a disproportionate number of examples being destroyed in the Gold Recall of the 1930s. In any case, Jeff Garrett and Ron Guth estimate only 75-100 specimens are known today in all proof grades. In PR66 Cameo the date is very rare, as NGC has certified only five coins in this grade, with four finer; while PCGS has not seen any example in this category (11/09). Garrett and Guth report an unusually fine specimen, possibly Ex:Pittman, sold for $218,000 in early 2008.

The coin offered here is an amazing specimen, with pristine fields and an even orange-gold color. The brightly reflective fields contrast boldly with the frosty devices to produce the desirable cameo effect. The Mint changed production methods in 1901, and coins minted after that date generally lack the popular cameo contrast. The only possible identifier is a tiny mark on the lower, front part of the bust truncation, and that may be too small to be useful. Overall visual appeal is exceptional.(#88495)

Scarce 1908-S Premium Gem Five Dollar

2198 1908-S MS66 PCGS. The 1908-S half eagle is one of the most common dates in all grades despite the low mintage of 82,000 pieces. The certified population begins to decline between the near-Gem and Gem levels. Premium Gems are scarce and finer pieces are rare.

The lustrous peach-gold surfaces of this MS66 offering are splashed with mint-green, orange, and lilac and exhibit well struck design features, including the headdress feathers. Some trivial grazes in the raised, exposed upper reverse fields do not detract. Housed in a green label holder. Population: 13 in 66, 8 finer (11/09).(#8512)

Popular Gem 1909 Half Eagle

2199 1909 MS65 NGC. For the dedicated type collector, the 1909 Indian half eagle issue, though not so heavily produced as its D-mint counterpart, is still one of the most accessible dates in Gem condition, being merely scarce rather than rare at that level. Still, "scarce" in the context of the series is challenging enough to drive prices into the five figures. This charming MS65 example has bold orange-gold luster and crisp central design definition. Remarkably smooth surfaces show no more than a handful of tiny marks, mostly in unobtrusive parts of the reverse fields. Census: 49 in 65, 6 finer (11/09).

From The Atherton Family Collection.(#8513)

Lovely Gem 1913-S Half Eagle
Only MS65 at PCGS

2200 1913-S MS65 PCGS. Although the 1909-O and 1911-D half eagles are well-known keys to the series, there are numerous conditional rarities than stand out from the pack in the Indian half eagle series as the upper Mint State levels are scaled. Those conditional rarities include all of the S-mint issues from 1912 through 1915.

Concerning the 1913-S, Akers' *Handbook of United States Gold Coins 1907-1933* notes that:

> "The 1913-S ranks ahead of the 1911-S and 1916-S in terms of both overall and high-grade rarity. MS-63s are very scarce and coins that grade MS-64 are nothing short of rare. Gems are virtually unobtainable."

This is a hands-down Gem under any accepted grading interpretation. As such, it is another entry in our Platinum Night offerings that is certain to pique the interest of Registry Set collectors, as well as gold specialists, series aficionados, or any other collector who appreciates coins that are both truly rare and aesthetically beautiful.

Both the production values and subsequent surface preservation are remarkable on both sides. There is little of the peripheral strike weakness so often seen on examples of the issue, and the mintmark is well-struck. Only a couple of the lower headdress feathers are a bit indistinct. The coloration is appealing, with lilac and jade accents complementing the predominantly peach-gold patina. The Indian's cheek is completely free of pesky abrasions, large or small. This is the only Gem certified of the issue at PCGS, although one piece has been graded even finer (11/09).

PCGS Registry Set Note

This coin would upgrade four of the current Top 5 Indian Head $5 Gold, Circulation Strikes (1908-1929) Registry Sets—most of them by several points.(#8526)

1914 Indian Head Quarter Eagle PR66 Challenging Matte Proof Date

2201 1914 PR66 NGC. The Mint revised its proof production methods for the final time in 1914, retaining the sandblast finish, but with coarser surface granules. The public failed to appreciate the new format, and few of the 125 proof half eagles minted in 1914 were actually sold. The issue is the second most difficult date of the series to locate in today's market. We estimate that only 35-50 examples are extant in all grades. Including both leading grading services, only 12 coins have been certified in PR66, with 11 finer (11/09).

The present coin exhibits finely grained surfaces, with atypical pronounced yellow color. The surfaces appear technically perfect, with no discernable marks or shiny spots. Overall visual appeal is all one could ask for.(#8545)

EARLY EAGLES

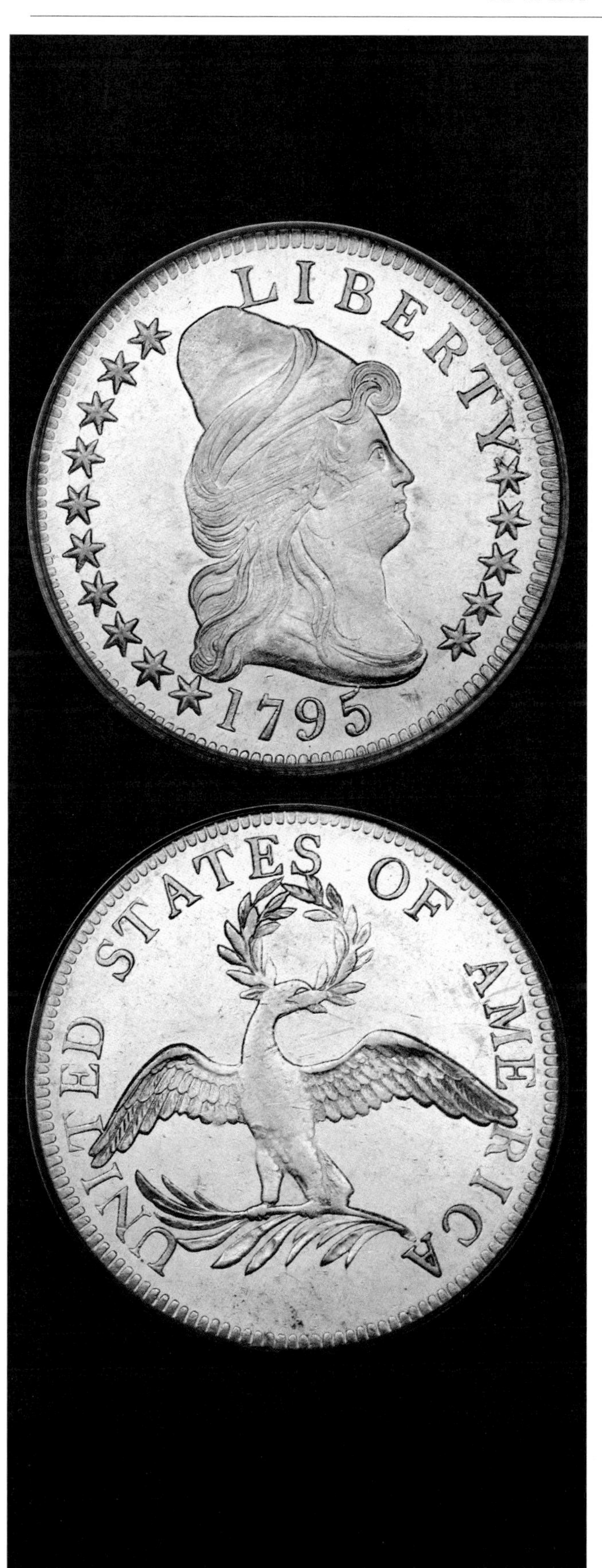

Semiprooflike 1795 13 Leaves Eagle
BD-1, MS62
Advanced Obverse Die State

2202 1795 13 Leaves MS62 PCGS. Breen-6830, Taraszka-1, BD-1, R.3. Bass-Dannreuther Obverse Die State c (late) / Reverse Die State a. Star 11 is extremely close to the Y in LIBERTY, and star 1 virtually touches the lowest hair curl. The flag of the 5 in the date overlaps the bust drapery. On the reverse a leaf tip brushes the lower left corner of the U in UNITED.

The Draped Bust, Small Eagle type ten dollar pieces were made only from 1795 to 1797, when the reverse design was superseded by the Large Eagle or Heraldic Eagle reverse. Of the estimated 13,000-15,000 tens produced of the Small Eagle type, the 1795 Small Eagle is the most widely seen date.

There are five known die marriages of 1795 eagles, created from three obverse and three reverse dies—two of them 13 Leaves, one 9 Leaves. The obverse of the BD-1 saw its single use in that pairing, while the reverse is shared with BD-2. The BD-2 obverse was paired with the 9 Leaves Reverse for BD-3, and with a different 13 Leaves Reverse for BD-5. Finally, the latter 13 Leaves Reverse was paired with a different obverse to create the BD-4.

Of the four 13 Leaves marriages, the BD-1 is the most available. Bass-Dannreuther estimate that from one-half to two-thirds of all surviving 1795 eagles are of the BD-1 pairing. Remembering that the BD-1 obverse is unique to this variety while the reverse was also used on the BD-2, it is not as surprising as it might be at first blush to note that the obverse die state of the present example seems considerably more advanced than that of the reverse. The obverse die appears not far from failure, and as such represents the terminal die state, or nearly so, quite a bit more advanced than the Bass specimen that was described as Obverse State c but appears more like State b. The obverse crack from star 9 runs all the way through star 1 and down into the field below the digits. Another crack connects the 9 and 5; yet another connects the forward bust tip with the right-side stars, and there appears to be advanced crumbling of the die at the rim above TY.

On the reverse, however, none of the die cracks mentioned in Bass-Dannreuther appear, and it looks as if the die was fairly fresh when this coin was struck. This is a simply marvelous example of this important first-year gold coin issue, with lots of semiprooflike flash radiating from the fields. The even green-gold coloration is consistent on both sides. The obverse shows crosshatched major adjustment marks in the center. A tiny planchet void appears under a loupe to the right of the 5, but this is quibbling. Any contact marks or other impairments are trivial compared to the broad appeal this piece presents to all viewers. Population: 16 in 62, 18 finer (11/09). (#8551)

1797 Capped Bust Right Ten, MS61
Heraldic Eagle, BD-4
First Year of Type

2203 1797 Large Eagle MS61 PCGS. Breen-6834, Taraszka-12, BD-4, High R.4. The Heraldic Eagle reverse was used for the first time in 1797, after the Small Eagle design was retired part way through the year. Mint records indicate a production total of 10,940 pieces for the design, with three different die marriages known. The same obverse die was used in all three marriages, so keys to the varieties are found on the reverse. The present coin is a representative of the BD-4 variety, characterized by the long, thin neck of the eagle, and the position of the arrows on the reverse, with one arrow tip nearly to the end of N in UNITED. The most available variety of the date, BD-4 had an estimated initial mintage of 3,500-5,000 pieces. John Dannreuther estimates 90-110 examples are known today.

Eagles of 1797 have been popular numismatic items since the early days of the hobby, but knowledge of specific die varieties only developed in the 20th century. In the George Earle Collection (Henry Chapman, 6/1912), lots 2289, 2290, and 2291 were all examples of different varieties of 1797 eagles. Chapman correctly identified lot 2289 as the obvious Small Eagle variety, but he believed the other two lots were of an identical Heraldic Eagle design. In fact, plates of the two lots reveal that lot 2290 was a BD-2 specimen, while lot 2291 was the subtly different BD-4. Extensive, systematic knowledge of die varieties of early gold denominations has only become available in recent times, thanks to research by specialists such as Harry Bass and John Dannreuther.

The present coin features bright, semiprooflike fields, with yellow-gold color overlaid with a slight reddish patina. The striking details are a little soft on the hair curls, but the eagle's plumage is complete. The usual die crack through the second 7 is visible, as well as a crack between E and R in AMERICA. Numerous small abrasions are scattered about the surfaces, but none are worthy of individual mention. Population: 16 in 61, 15 finer (11/09).(#8559)

A 15% BUYER'S PREMIUM ($14 MIN.) APPLIES TO ALL LOTS.

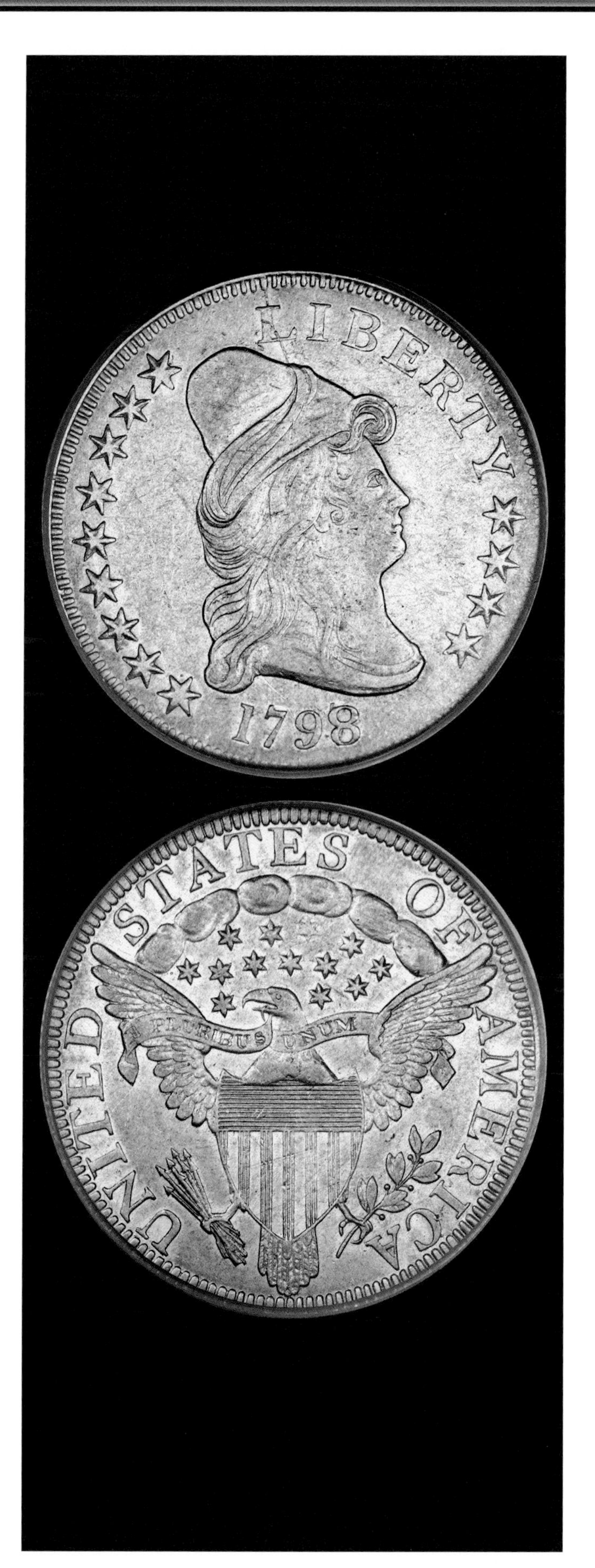

Elusive 1798/7 9x4 Stars Eagle, BD-1, XF45

2204 1798/7 9x4 Stars XF45 PCGS. Breen-6836, Taraszka-9, BD-1, High R.4. The obverse has an unbalanced appearance as the engraver placed nine stars along the left border, leaving a need for just four stars on the right. LIBERTY is especially widely spaced. The reverse is a multi-year die that was also used for 1797 BD-3. In fact, the reverse die was used for both 1798/7 overdates before the 1797 BD-3 and BD-4 eagles were minted. A die crack develops on the reverse of 1797 BD-3 after that die was used with the two 1798/7 varieties. This example has three obverse die cracks, including a prominent crack through the L, cap, and hair, exiting the hair into the left field toward star 3, a second crack from the border to the R crosses the field to the fore curl and continues faintly to join the first crack in the hair, and a third crack branches from the junction of the other two cracks to the hair just above the ear.

Once called a major rarity, the 1798/7 9x4 Stars eagle is scarce, with between 80 and 100 examples known today, according to John Dannreuther in Early U.S. Gold Coin Varieties, A Study of Die States, 1795-1834. While we have been unable to construct a complete pedigree lineup of this variety, we have a database that includes 191 auction listings in grades from Fine to MS63. The XF45 grade falls almost exactly in the middle of that database, with 87 finer auction appearances and 93 lesser appearances.

A pleasing Choice XF, this specimen has light greenish-gold surfaces and retains generous portions of luster, including field reflectivity around the devices. The surfaces have myriad tiny marks that are consistent with the grade. None of those marks are significant. A pleasing and desirable early eagle.(#8560)

Satiny 1799 BD-7 Eagle, MS62

2205 1799 Small Stars Obverse MS62 PCGS. Irregular Date, Small Stars, Breen-6840, Taraszka-19, BD-7, R.3. The Irregular Date obverse is recognized by the unusual spacing of the date, with the 1 extremely low and far from the hair curl, and the second 9 high, nearly touching the drapery. This variety is the second most plentiful 1799 eagle, and it is the most widely available of the Small Stars obverse type. This example has satiny luster with lovely yellow-gold brilliance and pleasing surfaces. Only a few scattered marks are evident on each side. Population: 20 in 62, 17 finer (11/09). (#98562)

Lustrous 1801 BD-2 Eagle, Unc Details

2206 1801 PCGS Genuine. Breen-6843, Taraszka-25, BD-2, R.2. The BD-2 die combination is recognized by the position of star 1 (far from the curl) and star 8 (close to the cap). On the elusive BD-1 die combination, they have exactly the opposite relationship. The PCGS number ending in .92 suggests Cleaning as the reason, or perhaps one of the reasons, that PCGS deemed this coin not gradable. The 1801 BD-2 eagle is one of the most widely available early eagle varieties, a wonderful choice for the date or type collector. This piece has light green-gold luster with reflective fields and bold design motifs.(#8564)

Pleasing 1801 BD-2 Eagle, AU50

2207 1801 AU50 PCGS. Breen-6843, Taraszka-25, BD-2, R.2. The plentiful 1801 BD-2 variety is usually recognize by the relationship of the bottom and top stars on the left to the central design motif. However, there are other differences between this variety and 1801 BD-1. Star 13 is distant from the drapery on BD-1 and appears to touch on BD-2. The L nearly touches the cap on BD-1, and is clearly separated on BD-2. All of these relationships suggest that the bust of Liberty is leaning back a little on BD-2.

This pleasing example has faint green-gold luster with traces of pale rose toning and slightly reflective fields. It is an attractive coin that is destined for a quality type collection.(#8564)

Lovely 1801 BD-2 Eagle, AU53

2208 1801 AU53 PCGS. Breen-6843, Taraszka-25, BD-2, R.2. A great coin for the design collector, the 1801 BD-2 eagle is handily the most plentiful variety of all early eagles struck from 1795 to 1804, with 600 to 800 examples known, including many in AU and Mint State grades. This pleasing piece is housed in a green-label holder and exhibits lovely green-gold surfaces with considerable lemon-yellow toning splashed over both sides. It is an early die state with no evidence of clash marks, lapping, or die cracks on either side. Here is an excellent opportunity to acquire a lovely early ten.(#8564)

Early-State 1801 Eagle, BD-2, MS60

2209 1801 MS60 NGC. Breen-6843, Taraszka-25, BD-2, R.2. Bass-Dannreuther Obverse State a / Reverse State a. Star 8 nearly touches the Liberty cap and has two points facing toward the cap. Star 13 also nearly touches the forward tip of the bust. Star 9 has an extra tine of metal pointed towards the Y. The reverse has lumps at the bottom left of the first T and A in STATES.

What is most interesting about this piece, however, is not a feature that it has, but *one that it lacks,* namely the usually seen "vertical spines in cap," as Bass called them. These spines have many times been called the result of die clashing with the vertical stripes in the shield on the reverse, but we remain unconvinced of that fact. Neither their width nor overall appearance seems to match the reverse shield lines or any other reverse feature. In many ways, the "spines" resemble some sort of addition made by hand after the dies were produced. If this is true, their discovery at the Mint would explain why a obverse die that showed no die cracks on the 600-800 examples known today was suddenly retired. Bass-Dannreuther write, "The obverse here is not known with any serious damage, so its cause of retirement is not known."

Whether the "spines" are the result of die clashing or other cause, the present coin is clearly from a die state previous to their creation. This piece has somewhat prooflike surfaces on both sides, with generous luster and scattered small ticks, scrapes, and abrasions that explain the grade. We can see no evidence of tiny die cracks on the obverse. We have gone back though our Permanent Auction Archives and discovered only a tiny minority of examples we have sold in the past that lack this feature. An interesting coin that could be the subject of fruitful research for the specialist.(#8564)

Attractive MS61 1801 Eagle, BD-2

2210 1801 MS61 PCGS. Breen-6843, Taraszka-25, BD-2, R.2. Star 8 is near the cap—nearer than on the much-rarer BD-1—while star 1 is further away from the curl and star 13 is closer to the bust than on BD-1. Numerous nearly vertical spines on the cap appear to be an added decoration to the die of some sort. On the reverse the eagle's upper beak nearly touches a star just below. Only two die marriages are known for the 1801 eagles, although the recorded mintage was large, at 44,344 coins. Not all of them were necessarily dated 1801, however, as the small number of dies and other evidence suggests that some of that number may have been dated 1800 or even 1799. The reverse die was used for both the BD-1 and BD-2 of 1801, then reused for the BD-3 of 1803.

This example offers attractive greenish-gold coloration with a small patch of hazel at the bust tip. Minor horizontal planchet adjustment marks appear on the lower shield. This would make a wonderful addition to a high grade type set.(#8564)

Lot 2211

LIBERTY
1801
UNITED STATES OF AMERICA
E PLURIBUS UNUM

Gem 1801 Capped Bust Right Eagle, BD-2
Popular Condition Rarity
Tied for Finest Certified

2211 1801 MS65 NGC. Breen-6843, Taraszka-25, BD-2, R.2. Mint records show 44,344 ten dollar gold pieces were coined in 1801, with two die varieties known for the date. However, researchers believe some of the large production was actually dated 1800, and a few examples maybe even 1799. The present coin is an example of the BD-2 variety, the most available for the date, easily recognized by the location of the obverse stars. Star 8 is close to the cap, with two points pointing to the cap, while star 13 nearly touches the bust. The stars have longer, more spindly points than the BD-1 variety. The original mintage of the BD-2 variety is estimated as 30,000-40,000 pieces, with perhaps 600-800 examples known today in all grades. The issue is not difficult to locate in lower Mint State grades, and it is a popular choice for a type collection, but it is very rare at the Gem level. Currently, NGC has certified only two coins in MS65, with none finer; while PCGS has graded three examples at the Gem level, with none finer (11/09).

Because of their beauty and impressive size, the eagles of 1801 have been popular with collectors since the earliest days of the hobby. The date appears in auction catalogs as early as the A.C. Kline Collection (Moses Thomas & Sons, 6/1855), lot 175, and remained a frequent offering in catalogs throughout the 1860s. A particularly nice specimen, reminiscent of the coin offered here, appeared in the Sixth Semi-Annual Sale (W. Elliot Woodward, 3/1865), lot 2740, "1801 Splendid, perfectly uncirculated, almost proof; very scarce." The lot realized $17, a respectable sum at the time, to John F. McCoy. McCoy was one of the most prominent collectors of the Civil War era, but he had sold his main collection through Woodward the year before. The McCoy sale was a blockbuster auction that set the all-time record for total prices realized up to that time. Perhaps McCoy was acting as an agent for another collector when he purchased the spectacular 1801 eagle at the later sale, or he may have been starting a second collection of his own. In any case, the coin he purchased sounds like a memorable specimen, and one can only wonder if it might be an early appearance of the coin offered here.

Of course, little notice was taken of subtle differences in die characteristics during the 1860s. Only rudimentary studies of early gold die varieties were attempted by numismatists before the 20th century. In the early days of the last century, specialists such as John H. Clapp and Edgar Adams laid the groundwork for serious study of early gold die varieties, and their findings began to appear in auction catalogs of the time. In the William H. Woodin Collection (Thomas Elder, 3/1911), lots 1195 and 1196 offered both varieties of 1801 eagle, and the cataloger was careful to differentiate between them. The coin in lot 1196 represented the BD-2 variety, and Elder described it as a magnificent specimen:

> "1801. Stars on obv. slightly smaller. On reverse, star does not quite touch top of eagle's beak. Gem proof piece with mint luster. Finest 1801 I have ever offered. Plate."

The lot realized $39, a good price in the early 20th century. One cannot help but notice the similarities between Elder's description and Woodward's characterization of the coin in his earlier sale. No proofs are known for this date, so the coin must have been a particularly fine Uncirculated specimen. Again, one can only wonder if the citations both refer to the same coin, and if the coin offered here is a later appearance of the same extraordinary example.

The present coin is certainly well preserved, with medium orange-gold color, and lovely, satiny mint luster. The centers are fully struck, but slight softness is noted around the margins. A short die crack is evident, moving downward from Liberty's earlobe. Some light adjustment marks are detected through the letters LIBERT. The only flaw worthy of mention is a mark in the left obverse field, to the right of star 3. The coin offered here is one of the finest surviving early eagles, and is worthy of a place in the finest early gold collection.(#8564)

1803 Small Stars Reverse Ten, BD-3, MS63 A High Grade, Sharply Struck Example Of This Popular Early Type

2212 1803 Small Stars Reverse MS63 NGC. Breen-6844, Taraszka-28, BD-3, R.4. The 1803 Capped Bust Right, Heraldic Eagle ten dollar gold piece boasts a small mintage of 15,017 pieces. Six different die varieties are known for this issue, with one obverse die used in all six marriages. The reverse die used for BD-3 is characterized by the position of the eagle's beak nearly touching the star below its point, and the right foot of E in STATES positioned over a cloud space. BD-3 is the most available variety of the date, but it is still scarce in absolute terms. In *Early U.S. Gold Coin Varieties,* John Dannreuther estimates 150-200 examples of this issue are still extant in all grades. Mint State 1803 eagles are rarities, even the "common" varieties. NGC has certified 18 examples of this issue at the MS63 level, with nine finer; while PCGS has graded nine Choice specimens, with only 11 finer (11/09).

Die marriages were of little interest to collectors of the 19th century, and catalogers seldom differentiated between varieties in their lot descriptions. Numismatists became more conscious of these important differences in the early part of the 20th century, and auction catalogs began to describe the small stars reverse in basic detail. In the Stickney Collection (Henry Chapman, 6/1907), lot 623, an 1803 eagle is described: "1803 R. Small stars. Extremely fine. Mint lustre. See plate." The coin sold for $25, a good price at the time.

The present coin is sharply struck, with complete detail on the feathers on the eagle's breast. The surfaces display bright, satiny luster, with attractive reddish patina on each side. A few light obverse abrasions can be detected with a loupe. Rarity, historic interest, and strong visual appeal combine to make this offering an important opportunity for the early gold specialist.(#8565)

AU Details 1803 'Extra Star' Eagle, BD-5

2213 1803 Large Reverse Stars, Extra Star—Altered Surface—NGC. AU Details. Breen-6845, Taraszka-30, BD-5, High R.4. This is the famous "Star on Cloud" variety, of which Bass-Dannreuther wrote:

> "Bass owned two examples of this scarce and popular variety. The curious 14th star seems to have been discovered by Harry Bass. Although the die combination was previously known, no one had noticed the tiny star atop the cloud below (O)F. Bass saw this on an example he purchased in 1966."

Bass-Dannreuther estimate that from 90 to 110 examples exist today of this variety in all grades. The present piece still appears to bear much original luster, although the fields on both sides, the obverse more prominently, have been expertly smoothed. A deep gash runs through ED, the wing, and ST on the reverse. Despite the caveats, much appeal is present on this large and important early type coin.(#88565)

Late Die State 1804 BD-1 Eagle, AU55

2214 1804 Crosslet 4 AU55 NGC. Breen-6847, Taraszka-31, BD-1, High R.4. This piece has all the cracks described by Taraszka, and also has an obverse crack from the border through star 11 to Liberty's lower lip. There is also an extremely faint crack between the tops of L and I.

The early eagles began with coins dated 1795, and ended with coins dated 1804, although the last eagles struck at the Mint during that time frame were actually dated 1803. The 1803 BD-6 eagles and the 1804 BD-1 eagles share a common reverse die, and that die is in a later die state on the few surviving examples of the 1803 BD-6.

At one time the 1804 eagles were thought to be extremely rare. In his 1960s era monograph, Walter Breen suggested that about 25 to 30 examples survived in all grades, calling it Low R.6. At that time, Breen had yet to understand the emission sequence, writing that "the single 1804 obverse die was not put into use until the latter part of December." In his 1980 auction analysis, David Akers noted the rarity of the issue that he said was "about the same rarity as the 1796." More recently, Jeff Garrett and Ron Guth state that "it is easier to find any other date among early eagles." Today an estimated 80 to 100 examples survive, still placing this issue solidly in the scarce category. Writing about the 1804 BD-1 eagle variety, John Dannreuther notes that "the 1804's rarity has been exaggerated by some numismatists and researchers, as today it is believed between 80 and 100 examples still survive. This still is a scarce issue and the 1804 date makes it extremely popular. It is the only 1804-dated eagle that is available to collect."

This attractive piece has light green-gold surfaces with reflective fields on both sides. Some minor scuffing in the left and right obverse fields is inconsequential. Most design details are sharply defined, although Liberty's profile is typically weak.(#8566)

Near Terminal 1804 BD-1 Crosslet 4 Eagle, MS62

2215 1804 Crosslet 4 MS62 NGC. Breen-6847, Taraszka-31, BD-1, High R.4. This piece is slightly later than the other 1804 in this sale, with all the other cracks plus a short crack from the nose tip.

Mint records show six deliveries of 1804 eagles totaling 9,795 coins from June 1 to the end of the year. It is believed that most of those coins were dated 1803, although exactly how many were 1803 eagles and how many others were 1804 is unknown. The generally reported mintage of 1804 is 3,757 coins, the total of the final two delivery warrants during the year. On December 28, 1804, the coiner delivered 2,515 pieces, and on December 31, another 1,242 pieces. However, there is a problem with that figure that apparently came from Breen in his monograph. Since the final eagles coined at the Philadelphia Mint were dated 1803, those 1803s had to be included in the latest delivery. Any attempt to determine exact mintages of each and every variety would require an extensive study of dates, varieties, die states, survival rates, and emission sequences. A quick study suggests that the actual mintage was about 3,500 coins, followed by the final 257 coins from the last two deliveries, the latter being the 1803 BD-6 eagles.

Satiny bright yellow-gold luster is accented by splashes of lilac and orange toning. This piece should be rather easy to identify, as it has a large planchet lamination defect crossing the upper left (facing) wing from the D to the first S.(#8566)

LIBERTY EAGLES

1883-O Liberty Head Eagle, XF45
Low Mintage Rarity

2216 1883-O XF45 PCGS. The 1883-O boasts the lowest mintage of any branch mint Liberty Head eagle, at a mere 800 pieces. It is the rarest O-Mint eagle and one of the rarest coins of any denomination from the New Orleans Mint. Doug Winter estimates a surviving population of 35-45 examples in all grades, of which perhaps 14-18 specimens are in the XF range.

Collecting large denomination gold coins did not become popular in this country until the late 1930s, so early auction appearances of the 1883-O eagle are few and far between. The catalogers of Sale Number 399 (Morgenthau, 5/1939), appreciated the rarity of the 1883-O when they described lot 384 of that sale, "1883 O Extremely fine and excessively rare." Auction appearances are still uncommon today, with an example typically showing up maybe twice a year. Garrett and Guth remark, "Ownership of an 1883-O eagle is the mark of an advanced collector." The present offering represents an important opportunity for gold specialists to obtain an example of this rare date.

The present coin exhibits original surfaces, with gray-lilac patina over attractive shades of red. Semiprooflike luster remains evident in the protected areas. A speckling of blue dots appears on the top third of the obverse surface. Wear and handling marks are consistent with the grade. Population: 7 in 45, 12 finer (11/09).(#8701)

Bold Near-Gem 1897-S Ten Dollar

2217 1897-S MS64 PCGS. CAC. Although the original production was a substantial one approaching a quarter-million pieces, most of the 1897-S eagles circulated, and today the average grade, even of certified coins, is a bit less than Choice AU. Mint State examples are on the rare side, and most of them tend to be lower-Mint State examples. This near-Gem is exceptional for its surfaces and relative lack of singular abrasions. Glorious cartwheel luster radiates from both sides, with attractive orange-yellow patina. The strike is impeccable. Population: 2 in 64, 4 finer (11/09).(#8739)

The Eliasberg 1899-S Eagle, MS69
One of Only Three Liberty Eagles
So Graded for the Entire Type

2218 1899-S MS69 NGC. Ex: Eliasberg. Stunning. Awe-Inspiring. Breathtaking. Those are a few of the words one could use to describe the beauty of this spectacular piece, perhaps the finest Liberty eagle that we have ever had the pleasure to behold. Like most of the other S-mint coins obtained by Louis E. Eliasberg, Sr. from the John H. Clapp Collection in 1942, this piece was purchased directly from San Francisco Mint for face value at the time of issue. While not a proof, it is described by Bowers and Ruddy in their 1982 sale of the gold portion of the Eliasberg Collection as a "specimen."

While the term was obviously there used in the loose sense of the word, this coin is certainly a special piece that was set aside at the time of striking because of its near-pristine surfaces. It falls just short of perfection, as close inspection indicates a couple of tiny abrasions that are insignificant overall. It is sharply struck, beautifully lustrous, and is as close to perfect as one could ever expect to find. The single finest 1899-S at PCGS is an MS67, while at NGC this piece is the single finest by four grade points. A few wispy die cracks appear on each side near the peripheries. This stunning beauty could be the ultimate type example for the Liberty eagle series, and in fact it is one of only three for the entire type certified in this highest grade at NGC. This piece is the ***plate coin in* United States Coinage: A Study by Type** *by Jeff Garrett and Ron Guth.* Population: 1 in 69, 0 finer (11/09).

Ex: Obtained by John M. Clapp directly from the San Francisco Mint, December 1899, at face value; John H. Clapp; Clapp Estate (1942); Louis E. Eliasberg, Sr.; United States Gold Coin Collection (Eliasberg Collection, Bowers and Ruddy, 10/1982), lot 820.

From The Atherton Family Collection.(#8744)

Marvelous MS66 1900 Eagle

2219 1900 MS66 NGC. The 1900 has a well-deserved reputation as a type issue, with Garrett and Guth noting its easy availability through Select Mint State and even a step above. Gem and better coins are rarities, however, and this MS66 example is one of just five in the combined certified population, with none finer (11/09). Both sides offer wonderful, satiny luster with hints of orange against otherwise yellow-gold surfaces. Sharply struck central devices share the texture of the fields. Carefully preserved with only slight striking softness visible at the obverse stars.(#8745)

Memorable Gem 1903 Eagle One of Two Finest at PCGS

2220 1903 MS65 PCGS. This example of the 1903 eagle in Gem condition is not only a memorable presentation, it represents excellent collector value, as a low-mintage, well-produced issue that is priced at a modest premium as higher-mintage issues in the same series. The mintage was only 125,800 pieces. The strike is full, and the frosty surfaces offer rich, mellow orange-gold coloration with tinges of jade-green near the obverse rims. The reverse sports a similar palette. No significant contact is present, and this MS65 piece is one of only two so certified at PCGS, with none finer (12/09).(#8752)

PROOF LIBERTY EAGLES

1864 Liberty Head Eagle, PR65 Cameo
Dramatic Cameo Contrast
Only 50 Examples Minted

2221 1864 PR65 Cameo NGC. CAC. Records indicate 50 proof Liberty Head eagles were struck in 1864, a large total for the era. Ordering gold proofs from the Mint was a complicated, expensive process during the Civil War years, because the Mint would not accept federal greenback notes at par for gold transactions. Collectors had to pay steep premiums for any gold coins purchased with paper currency. Alternatively, collectors could choose to pay for their purchases with other gold coins, which had to be purchased from bullion dealers at exorbitant prices. Faced with these difficulties, and the understandable preoccupation with the war effort, few collectors were willing to go to the trouble and expense of ordering proofs. It is doubtful if more than 20 gold proof sets were actually sold in 1864, the rest being melted at the end of the year. Proof 1864 eagles are decidedly rare today in all grades. Both Walter Breen and David Akers estimate a surviving population of 12-15 examples. Population data from the leading grading services has been inflated by resubmissions and crossovers. Even so, NGC has certified only two examples in PR65 Cameo, with none finer; while PCGS has yet to see a coin in this category (11/09).

The present coin displays profound cameo contrast, suggestive of an Ultra Cameo designation. An illimitable depth of reflectivity in the fields contrasts starkly with the frosty devices, producing the classic white-on-black flash of cameo contrast. The surfaces are a rich, reddish -gold color. The only pedigree markers are some insignificant contact marks below ES in STATES and F in OF on the reverse. (#88800)

Elusive 1867 Eagle, PR64 ★ Ultra Cameo
Possibly the Rarest 1860s Ten Dollar

2222 1867 PR64 ★ Ultra Cameo NGC. CAC. Even business strike gold coins from the year 1867 are rare: The gold dollar, quarter eagle, three dollar, the P-mint five dollar, and the eagle all saw productions well under 10,000 pieces, and the only gold coins that saw six-digit productions were the 1867 P- and S-mint double eagle issues.

Although for some unknown reason the production of gold proof sets in this year was 50 coins as opposed to the 25 or 30 typical of other years in the 1860s, it is likely that some—perhaps half—of those extra proofs were melted, as the proof gold issues of 1867 are uniformly rarer than a production of 50 pieces each would indicate. Breen's classic reference on proof coins estimates less than 18 survivors for the gold dollar, 15-20 of the three dollar, fewer than 10 for the half eagle and double eagle, and 12 to 15 of the eagle.

Dave Bowers, in cataloging the Louis E. Eliasberg, Sr., proof 1867 eagle ("United States Gold Coin Collection," Bowers and Ruddy, 10/1982, lot 727), wrote that only seven or eight proofs "can be verified today." The coin, a Gem proof, brought an impressive $17,600 nearly three decades ago.

More recently Garrett and Guth have provided this concerning the 1867 ten dollar:

> "Despite a higher mintage for this year, the 1867 is an exceedingly rare date in Proof condition. It is at least as rare as any other date from this decade and may, in fact, be the rarest. Auction appearances are very infrequent ... ."

Like most known examples, the present piece offers pronounced orange-peel effect on each side, with bright yellow-gold color and marvelously intense contrast between the thickly frosted devices and brilliantly mirrored fields. For pedigree purposes, we note a few light hairlines in the reverse right field, and a tiny dotlike planchet flaw, as made, in the field near the top of the last A in AMERICA. In PR64 ★ Ultra Cameo this piece is the only one certified, although that service has also certified one PR64 Cameo coin and one each in PR65 Cameo and PR66 Cameo. Interestingly, PCGS has certified but a single impaired proof, PR55 (11/09).(#98807)

Very Rare 1882 Eagle, PR66 Cameo

2223 1882 PR66 Cameo NGC. CAC. Slowly but surely, the annual mintages of proof gold eagles crept upward during the 1860s and 1870s, to a point in the 1880s where a uniform 40 gold proof sets were being produced annually. But 19th century Mint reports on proof coinage are notoriously unreliable, not so much for the original figures as when remeltings of unknown quantities and date of coins are involved. If buyers were unavailable for all of a year's coinage (or that of prior years, in some cases), the proofs could be simply melted or otherwise disposed of, with no record ever produced of the reduction in net distribution.

Despite the recorded mintage of 40 coins for the 1882 proof eagle, Garrett and Guth posit that "previous estimates of 12 to 15 examples are probably accurate, if not a trifle overstated." The authors here likely refer to David Akers' previous estimate using the same range, dating from his 1980 eagles reference where he says that "proofs of 1882 are very rare." NGC has certified 10 pieces of the 1882 proof eagle in all grades, ranging from an impaired PR58 Cameo to this single PR66 Cameo, numerically tied with a single PR66 Ultra Cameo. PCGS has graded only five examples, with two PR64 the finest (11/09). This gives a total of 15 coins, less a near-certain number of duplicates and three examples at the Smithsonian and ANS, so the number of pieces available in the marketplace could be only eight or 10 different coins.

This largely pristine specimen has medium golden-orange color and abundant eye appeal, including the expected bold strike and considerable field-device contrast. For pedigree purposes we mention a tiny planchet flaw on Liberty's chin and another between stars 5 and 6. Census: 1 in 66 Cameo, 0 finer (11/09).(#88822)

Amazing 1890 Eagle, PR66 ★ Ultra Cameo

2224 1890 PR66 ★ Ultra Cameo NGC. For a Philadelphia Mint issue the number of business strike eagles produced in 1890 was on the small side, at 57,980 coins. Typical mintages of the era were in the six- and even seven-digit range as, for example, 1893's 1.84 million eagles. The small business strike production appears as a smaller number of Mint State coins certified, with the finest business strikes at NGC a couple of MS65s.

It is unclear how much upward pressure such a paucity of high-grade business strikes might or might not exert on the proofs of the year, produced to the extent of only 63 coins. It is safe to say, however, that this piece is numerically finer than any certified business strike of the issue at both NGC and PCGS (which has certified a single Gem and none finer).

Although the certified populations of proofs show their normal inflation due to resubmissions, it is likely that perhaps half of the original mintage survives today—perhaps 25 to 30 different pieces. This coin is also, without a doubt, aesthetically at the head of the pack of proof survivors as well. It is numerically tied with six other "submission events" at NGC in PR66 Ultra Cameo, and with a single PR66 Deep Cameo at PCGS (11/09). It is one of only two in PR66 ★ Ultra Cameo. It is highly likely that those figures are also inflated by resubmissions.

This is the only PR66 Deep/Ultra Cameo piece we have ever offered. The only other PR66 we offered, from the Ed Trompeter Collection, was a Cameo NGC example that brought $54,050 back in our 1999 FUN Signature Auction (Heritage, 1/1999, lot 8252). This coin is the first offering of a PR66 Ultra Cameo that we have discovered since an offering six years ago (Goldbergs, 2/2003, lot 1846). That coin appears to be a different example from the present piece, as it bears a tiny luster break on Liberty's neck that this coin does not possess.

The present coin offers intense reflectivity, with typical orange-peel surfaces and pristine orange-yellow surfaces. The curls behind the neck are incomplete due to die polishing, as Breen's *Proof Encyclopedia* notes, along with thinning on some of the shield stripes. A tiny line connecting the bun bottom with the rear curls is a pedigree marker, but it appears to be of Mint origin rather than post-strike contact. A simply amazing specimen for the finest cabinet. Census: 2 in 66 ★ Ultra Cameo, 0 finer (11/09).(#98830)

1895 Liberty Head Eagle, PR65, Tied for Finest Certified Within the Designation Bright Color, Good Contrast

2225 1895 PR65 PCGS. CAC (Gold Sticker). Only 56 Liberty Head eagles were struck in proof format in 1895, a small mintage even by 19th century proof standards. Walter Breen estimated "Under 30 survive, possibly under 25," while David Akers stated "Of the 56 specimens minted, perhaps 20-25 still exist." A search of auction records reveals this is only the fifth time Heritage has been privileged to handle a proof 1895 eagle in any grade, the third appearance at the Gem level. Certainly, coins in PR65 are very rare. Only seven specimens have been certified in PR65 by PCGS, with none finer; while NGC has not seen an example with this designation (11/09).

Proof coins were very popular with numismatists during the 19th century and the Mint's production standards were especially high in the 1890s. Collectors such as Virgil Brand made a standard practice of ordering multiple examples of favorite denominations every year. On February 16, 1895, Brand received a proof double eagle and eagle, two proof half eagles, 10 proof quarter eagles, 10 proof sets containing the cent through dollar, and 20 minor proof sets as part of his customary yearly order from the Mint. Brand placed an identical order in 1896. The popularity of proof sets continued until the advent of the matte proof era in 1908.

The gold CAC sticker confirms the exceptional quality of this specimen, backed by John Albanese's guarantee to purchase this coin at this grade level. The fields are mirrored and the devices are covered with rich mint frost, creating a strong, but unacknowledged, element of contrast on both sides. The reverse shows the orange-peel effect characteristic of many proofs of the era, but the effect is not evident on the obverse. The surfaces are bright yellow-gold, with the merest hint of red. The fields are free of significant distractions, although some flaws on the holder may be mistaken for handling marks. Overall eye appeal is outstanding.(#8835)

Grand PR64 Ultra Cameo 1897 Ten

2226 1897 PR64 Ultra Cameo NGC. CAC. As noted by Garrett and Guth in their *Encyclopedia of U.S. Gold Coins,* "The 1897 eagle always comes with cameo contrast, often with heavy frosting on the central devices." This Ultra Cameo specimen takes the statement to its logical extreme, with thick golden-frost blanketing the broad, smooth areas of the portrait as well as the intricate details of the eagle's feathers. The yellow-gold mirrors show minor cloudiness, but this scarcely detracts from the outstanding contrast. Only a few minor hairlines scattered in the fields preclude an even finer designation. Census: 1 in 64 Ultra Cameo, 4 finer (11/09).(#98837)

Appealing Gem Cameo Proof 1901 Eagle

2227 1901 PR65 Cameo NGC. CAC. The recorded proof production was 85 pieces, although most survivors today fail to achieve the Gem level. In PR65 Cameo this coin is one of only two so certified at NGC, and there are two examples finer (12/09). PCGS has certified one example each in PR65 Cameo, PR65 Deep Cameo, and PR66 Cameo and PR66 Deep Cameo.

The present NGC PR65 Cameo offers instant eye appeal. The surfaces are well-contrasted, seemingly on the cusp of an Ultra Cameo designation. Orange-gold predominates, with tinges of hazel near the obverse rim. The strike is impeccable, as expected, and mentionable contact is absent.(#88841)

Flashy 1906 Eagle, PR64 Cameo

2228 1906 PR64 Cameo NGC. The 1906 proof ten dollar gold piece saw a mintage of only 77 pieces and surviving coins are very scarce. As might be expected, Cameos are even more difficult to locate. The brass-gold surfaces of this near-Gem Cameo display a nearly gold-and-black contrast at certain angles, and an exacting strike brings out complete delineation on the design elements. Faint hairlines in the obverse field preclude attainment of Gem classification. A couple of alloy spots in Liberty's hair, one on the upper right neck, and one under the curl might help pedigree the coin. Census: 5 in 64 Cameo, 13 finer (11/09).(#88846)

Near-Gem 1907 Indian Head Eagle, MS64 Wire Rim, Judd-1901 Saint-Gaudens' Original Design

2229 1907 Wire Rim MS64 NGC. CAC. David Akers reports a net mintage of just 472 Wire Rim ten dollar gold pieces in 1907, with 542 pieces initially struck, and 70 unsold specimens melted between 1915 and 1918. The coins were never released into circulation. Instead, the issue was distributed to Congressmen and Treasury Department officials, and sold to private citizens who ordered them from the Mint. The issue has a high survival rate, and experts estimate a surviving population of 325-400 examples in Mint State grades today.

Wire Rim tens are technically a pattern issue (Judd-1901) but like 1856 Flying Eagle cents, they were struck in sufficient numbers that regular issue collectors have long considered them part of the collectible series. The Wire Rim design has always been prized by collectors, as it is the only available issue that shows Saint-Gaudens' original design for the coins. An early auction appearance was in the William H. Woodin Collection (Thomas Elder, 3/1911), lot 1259. The lot was preceded by an example of the Rolled Edge design in lot 1258 to which Elder refers in his description, "1907. Similar type, with sharp 'wire edge'. Only 550 struck. Rare. Unc. Plate." Elder seems to have been well informed about the issue at this early date.

The present coin is a pleasing near-Gem specimen, with compelling eye appeal. The obverse surfaces have a curious fine granular texture, similar to a matte proof, but the reverse shows the usual swirling die polish marks. Most of the surfaces exhibit the bright yellow-gold color usually seen on this issue, but there is also a slight overlay of reddish patina. A couple of faint handling marks are clustered to the left of the E in E PLURIBUS, the only flaws worthy of mention. Census: 80 in 64, 62 finer (11/09).(#8850)

Important Gem 1907 Wire Rim Ten

2230 1907 Wire Rim MS65 NGC. The 1907 Wire Rim eagle is an experimental issue—but it is one that would have reached circulation had Teddy Roosevelt and Augustus Saint-Gaudens had their way, and had its design been more practical for coinage and commerce. Although it is listed in the Judd pattern reference (Judd-1901; Judd-1774 before the eighth edition), even the Judd editors waffle on the status of the piece: "Regular or pattern? This point can be debated."

The 1907 Wire Rim eagle, for all intents, can be included in the same class as another august group, the 1879 Flowing Hair stellas. Both were experimental designs, both are listed as patterns, and both were made as delicacies for the well-connected.

Notwithstanding its technical status, the 1907 Wire Rim is widely pursued and collected alongside the regular-issue coins beginning with the 1907 No Periods. Similarly, the 1879 Flowing Hair stellas are often collected as part of a complete U.S. gold type set. Garrett and Guth, in *100 Greatest U.S. Coins,* discuss this in conjunction with the 1907 Rolled Rim issue that followed: "Reportedly, 500 were struck and this design type is considered experimental per conventional wisdom, although research has revealed that, in fact, these were made as delicacies to be distributed by Mint officials, Treasury Department officials, and others. To acquire one of these, you needed a 'connection'! "

Akers' *Handbook* of 20th century gold notes an original mintage of 542 coins, of which "70 pieces were melted between 1915 and 1918," leaving a net distribution of 472 coins.

This MS65 NGC-certified piece, of distinctly finer surface quality than the average, is a stunning work of numismatic art. Deep, consistent apricot-orange coloration lends splendid eye appeal. The obverse presents a wonderful cameo appearance—more through the design than through any obvious field-device contrast—and is virtually pristine save for a trivial mark or two. Two minuscule dark flecks on Liberty's jawline are mentioned for pedigree purposes only. The reverse is equally appealing. Census: 32 in 65, 30 finer (11/09). (#8850)

Gem 1907 Indian Head Ten, Wire Rim
Only 472 Examples Released
Represents Original Design, Judd-1901

2231 1907 Wire Rim MS65 PCGS. CAC. The 1907 Wire Rim Indian Head eagle represents Augustus Saint-Gaudens' original design for the ten dollar gold piece. The eponymous rim is a delicate, knife-like feature around both sides of the coin, resulting from metal being squeezed between the collar and the dies during the striking process. Prized by collectors today, the Wire Rim caused difficulties in the ejection process and made stacking the coins problematic. Accordingly, the design was modified at least twice by Chief Engraver Charles Barber; Saint-Gaudens' assistant, Henry Hering; and his son, Homer; to produce the No Periods design eventually used for mass production in 1907.

The Wire Rim coins were never released into circulation. They were presented to Congressmen and other VIPs to demonstrate the new design and sold at face value to museums and private collectors. The issue was available for order for several years after 1907, and Henry Chapman is known to have purchased a group of them in 1912. The unsold remainder of the mintage was melted after 1915. Roger Burdette has determined that only 472 Wire Rim eagles were actually released. The issue is listed as a pattern in the standard literature, but most collectors consider it an integral part of the collectible series.

The present coin is a blazing Gem specimen, with bright mint luster. Both sides exude bright yellow-gold color, beneath rich reddish patina. The striking details are noticeably sharper at the centers, with the softness seen on the peripheries of all examples of this issue. The only noticeable "flaws" are a tiny planchet void at the forefront of the eagle's wing, and a couple of other small, insignificant field marks. Overall eye appeal is outstanding. Population: 49 in 65, 20 finer (11/09).(#8850)

1907 Indian Head Eagle, Unc Details Rolled Edge, Net Mintage of 50 Pieces

2232 1907 Rolled Edge—Cleaned—ANACS. Unc Details, Net AU50. The Rolled Edge design was the first modification made to Saint-Gaudens' original design for the ten dollar gold piece, after the Wire Rim design proved impractical. Chief Engraver Charles Barber added a border to the original design and 31,500 examples were initially struck. More problems arose before the issue was released into circulation, and a total of 31,450 of the coins were melted. Only 50 specimens were saved through private orders placed at the Mint and through the Assay Commission.

The present coin features bright surfaces, probably the result of a cleaning long ago. The pronounced matte-like surfaces are a pleasing yellow-gold color. The only marks of note are an irregular planchet void at the back of the eagle's tail feathers and an almost imperceptible, shallow scratch from stars 1-4.(#8851)

Premium Gem 1907 Indian Head Eagle No Periods

2233 1907 No Periods MS66 PCGS. CAC. According to Mint Superintendent Landis 238,864 Indian Head, No Periods eagles were minted at the Philadelphia facility in 1907, along with 542 Wire Rim examples. Apparently, many examples were saved of this first-date-of-issue design, as it is readily available in Mint State grades today. The issue is easily located in grades through MS64, making this date a popular choice with type collectors. The date is scarce at the Gem level, and coins finer than MS66 are rare.

The present coin is a splendid specimen, with thick mint frost and delightful color. The original surfaces are accented with intermingled shades of rose and lilac on both sides. No noticeable marks are present to the naked eye, but magnification reveals a few minor marks on Liberty's cheek. This example combines high technical grade with stunning visual appeal. Population: 70 in 66, 6 finer (11/09).(#8852)

1908 Indian Head, No Motto Eagle, MS65
Popular Low Mintage Date

2234 1908 No Motto MS65 PCGS. The 1908 No Motto Indian Head eagle is an underrated date, with a small mintage of 33,500 pieces. The tiny production figure is only one-tenth of its With Motto counterpart. The fleeting opportunity that this Gem No Motto eagle represents should be obvious to knowledgeable gold specialists. Intermingled swirls of steel-blue, champagne-orange, and yellow-gold color compete for dominance on the obverse, but the reverse shows continuous orange-gold color. There is no criticism that we can offer to either the smooth surfaces or powerfully struck devices. A low mintage, conditionally scarce issue whose desirability among type collectors is unflagging. Population: 23 in 65, 11 finer (12/09). (#8853)

1908 Indian Head Eagle, MS68
Fully Struck, With Amazing Mint Frost
Tied for Finest Certified

2235 1908 Motto MS68 NGC. The motto IN GOD WE TRUST was not present on Saint-Gaudens' original 1907 designs for the eagle and double eagle denominations because President Theodore Roosevelt objected to the use of the deity's name on coinage. Congress felt differently, and mandated the return of the motto in 1908. Accordingly, Chief Engraver Charles Barber placed the motto on the reverse, before the eagle's breast early in the year.

From a large mintage of 341,300 pieces, the 1908 Indian Head With Motto eagle is readily available in most grades today. David Akers reports:

> "By Indian Eagle standards, the 1908 Motto is a plentiful issue. Examples that grade MS-60 to MS-64 are offered on a regular basis, while MS-65s, even though scarce, are still obtainable with a bit of searching. There are even a fair number of MS-66s in the market, but Superb Gems are very rare and seldom encountered."

The present coin is a Superb Gem of unbelievable quality. This piece is finer than the MS67 coin in the famous Phillip H. Morse Collection, and tops the specimen in Jim O'Neal's fabulous collection of ten dollar gold coins. The fine-grain, matte-like surfaces are virtually perfect. Close inspection reveals only two small marks, one across the front of the eagle's tail feathers, and another at the forefront of the eagle's wing. Amazing mint frost covers the matte-like surfaces, and the vibrant color is primarily reddish-gold with occasional hints of lilac. The striking details are full throughout. Certainly, this specimen is one of the finest ten dollar gold coins of any date surviving today. NGC has certified only three coins in MS68 with none finer; while PCGS has graded four examples in this exalted grade, with none finer (11/09).(#8859)

Scarce, High Grade 1909-D Ten Dollar MS66, Ex: Morse, O'Neal

2236 1909-D MS66 PCGS. Ex: O'Neal. Breen-7109. The 1909-D is one of the scarcer issues among early ten dollar Indians, and is much more challenging than its mintage of 121,540 pieces would seem to indicate. David Akers contends in *A Handbook of 20th-Century United States Gold Coins* that it is one of the most underrated issues in the series, and is actually one of the rarest in an absolute sense. "Even in MS60 this issue is very rare and in MS63 or MS64 condition, it can be located only with great difficulty," says Akers.

In Gem and better condition the 1909-D is extremely rare. PCGS and NGC combined have certified only eight examples in MS65. Another eight coins have earned the Premium Gem level of preservation, and a mere three pieces are classified as MS67. Neither service has certified any specimen finer. Moreover, our records indicate that the '09-D in these higher Mint State grades has appeared in major auction sales fewer than 20 times within the past 15 to 20 years.

In his May 1998 catalog of the Thaine Price Collection, Akers writes that a number of 1909-D ten dollar coins that were not previously known to the numismatic community have come onto the market in recent years. He goes on to say that most of these are of minimal Uncirculated quality, with only a few even reaching the Choice level.

Walter Breen, in his 1988 *Encyclopedia of U.S. and Colonial Coins,* identifies two variants of the D mintmark on the 1909. The first variety has a broad D opposite the arrow points, and parallel with the upright of the T in TEN. The second variety has the mintmark below the arrow points. Breen says this was an intentional change in position to give a less cramped effect. According to Breen, the first variety is scarcer in Uncirculated grades than is the second variety.

The current MS66 coin has a satiny appearance, and yields pleasing glowing luster and evenly distributed honey-gold color. The design elements are sharply impressed, with resultant excellent definition in the feathers on the headdress and on the eagle. The mintmark is located opposite the arrow points and is broad, confirming the Breen-7109 variety. The surfaces on both sides are well preserved, and display just a couple of minute marks on the Indian's cheek, and another in the right (facing) reverse field. A small planchet void is located below and to the right of IN GOD WE TRUST, and will serve, along with the previously mentioned unobtrusive contact marks, as a pedigree identifier. Population: 5 in 66, 2 finer (11/09).

Ex: Phillip H. Morse Collection of Saint-Gaudens Coinage (Heritage Auction Galleries, 11/2005), lot 6506; The Jim O'Neal Collection of Saint-Gaudens Eagles (Heritage, 1/2009), lot 3509.(#8863)

Scarce 1911 MS66 Ten Dollar

2237 1911 MS66 NGC. The 1911 is one of the commonest issues in the Indian Head ten dollar series and one of the easiest eagles to obtain in Mint State. This can be partially attributed to the discovery of 30 to 40 Mint State coins in the early 1990s (*The Coinage of Augustus Saint-Gaudens,* 2006). Gems and Premium Gems are scarce, however, and higher-grade coins are quite rare.

The wheat-gold surfaces of this MS66 example are tinted with light green and a well executed strike imparts sharp detail to the design motifs. The satiny fields yield pleasing luster on both sides. Census: 51 in 66, 11 finer (11/09).(#8868)

Gorgeous Premium Gem 1911 Eagle

2238 1911 MS66 NGC. CAC. While not accessible to quite the same extent as the late 1926 and 1932 issues, the 1911 has established itself as a date of choice among type collectors seeking an earlier With Motto year. This reputation has developed thanks to the eye appeal of extraordinary specimens such as the present Premium Gem. Lemon-gold surfaces are fantastically lustrous, with the cartwheel effect on the obverse especially bold. The finer details of the feathers on each side are unusually crisp, and only a handful of tiny marks to the left of the portrait preclude an even higher grade. NGC has certified just 11 numerically finer examples (11/09). (#8868)

1911 Indian Head Eagle, MS66
A Colorful Example

2239 1911 MS66 PCGS. CAC. The large mintage of 505,500 pieces makes the 1911 Indian Head eagle an available date, popular with both type and series specialists. Of course, at the Premium Gem level examples are scarce, and anything finer is quite rare. The present coin is a spectacular example, with equal amounts of attractive reddish-gold and lilac color on each side. Soft mint frost overlays the pristine, matte-like surfaces. As expected with an MS66 example, no mentionable marks are evident, except for a tiny planchet void (as struck) to the right of M in UNUM. Population: 19 in 66, 8 finer (11/09).(#8868)

Lustrous 1912 Eagle, MS66

2240 1912 MS66 NGC. The 1912 is one of the more available issues of the type, and examples are readily obtainable through the near-Gem level of preservation. Gems are scarce, however, and Premium Gems fall into the rare category. Anything finer is virtually unobtainable.

The slightly granular surfaces of this MS66 example yield ebullient luster and yellow-gold patina imbued with tints of light green. A solid strike manifests itself in strong definition on the design elements and close examination reveals just a few minute marks that are well within the parameters of the grade designation. Census: 17 in 66, 1 finer (11/09).(#8871)

The O'Neal 1914 Eagle, MS65

2241 1914 MS65 PCGS. CAC. Ex: O'Neal. While the San Francisco and the occasional Denver issue are most prominent in collectors' minds, the generally higher-mintage Philadelphia coins have a couple of champions, even among With Motto pieces. While the 1909 is rated slightly higher in terms of high-grade collecting difficulty, the 1914 sports the lowest mintage of any Philadelphia With Motto Saint-Gaudens eagle issue. With much of Philadelphia's gold coinage dedicated to overseas trade, particularly European transactions, it is hardly coincidental that Philadelphia's smallest With Motto eagle output should come in the same year that the simmering hostilities in Europe broke out into full-fledged warfare.

Rich yellow-gold surfaces show occasional peach accents and a touch of green-gold at the upper reverse, and while the fields show a touch of the usual granularity, the luster is above-average even by the standards of the issue. Surfaces are carefully preserved and highly suggestive of an even finer grade, though a handful of modest faults are present on each side. PCGS has graded just nine numerically finer pieces (11/09).(#8875)

Important 1915 Indian Ten, MS66

2242 1915 MS66 NGC. In terms of both relative and absolute scarcity, the 1915 eagle is a fairly common date. That usually translates into a coin which is popular for type purposes. At the MS66 level, however, this issue is a rarity. Only a total of 27 pieces have received such a grade from NGC and PCGS combined, with a mere five examples seen even finer at MS67 (11/09). The present Premium Gem is well struck and displays vibrant mint luster. The original green-gold surfaces are devoid of reeding marks and exhibit only faint and inconsequential grazes. An opportunity to acquire one of the highest graded representatives of this World War issue. No more examples would be struck at Philadelphia until 1926, since gold coins little circulated and exporters preferred the more convenient double eagle.(#8878)

PROOF INDIAN EAGLE

Lovely 1909 Ten Dollar, PR64

2243 1909 PR64 NGC. CAC. The 1909 Indian Head proof ten dollar had a mintage of 74 specimens. While it has been variously reported that 20 or fewer examples still exist, we believe the number to be higher, in the order of perhaps 30 to 45 pieces. NGC and PCGS combined have seen about 80 '09 proof tens, many of which are obviously resubmitted or cross-over pieces.

This near-Gem offering possesses pretty lemon-gold color and sharply struck design features. Its surfaces have the "Roman" finish typical of '09 proofs, displaying a brighter appearance than the unpopular dark matte or "sandblast" finish used to strike most proof 1908 Indian eagles. A highly attractive coin despite a few minute marks that deny Gem classification. Census: 21 in 64, 25 finer (11/09).(#8891)

LIBERTY DOUBLE EAGLES

1852-O Liberty Head Double Eagle Scarce in AU58

2244 1852-O AU58 NGC. From a substantial mintage of 190,000 pieces, the 1852-O Liberty Head double eagle is an available date, and always in great demand with type collectors. Doug Winter estimates a surviving population of 900-1100 examples in all grades, with perhaps 200-250 specimens extant in AU. The issue does become scarce in higher AU grades, and Mint State coins are rare.

The present coin is especially attractive, with bright semiproof-like fields, and a remarkably sharp, uniform strike over all the design elements. There are two small marks in the lower obverse field, and one on the reverse just under the eagle's left (facing) wing. Census: 79 in 58, 14 finer (11/09).(#8907)

Stunning MS63 1856-S Twenty
Ex: *S.S. Central America*

2245 1856-S No Serif, Left S MS63 PCGS. Ex: *S.S. Central America*. Variety 17O, *SSCA* 5611. As the name implies, the U in UNITED is almost entirely lacking its left serif. The left half of the crossbar of the A in STATES is also missing. While most of the double eagles recovered from the *S.S. Central America* were 1857-S coins, a much, much smaller number were 1856-S double eagles. While this coin, like other *SSCA* coins is certified with a special gold-label PCGS insert, the online PCGS *Population Report* does not distinguish between the *SSCA* and normal coins. It is nonetheless instructive to note that, while the number of 1857-S double eagles graded MS63 at PCGS is 832, the number of 1856-S pieces in that grade is 70. This is a simply stunning coin, with a full strike, brilliant, radiant cartwheel luster, and rich orange-gold coloration tinged with greenish-gold near the obverse rim. The lot includes a faux-book presentation case. Population: 16 in 63, 23 finer (11/09).(#70024)

Scarce AU58 1866-S Twenty Dollar Motto

2246 1866-S Motto AU58 NGC. During the first part of the year, 1866-S double eagles were struck with the old No Motto (i.e., Type One) reverse. Beginning in March, more than 842,000 double eagles were struck using the new With Motto (i.e., Type Two) reverse. Examples of this issue are most frequently encountered in the Extremely Fine to low-end About Uncirculated. High-end AUs are scarce and Uncirculated coins are rare. The latter are not found above MS62, at least with certification.

The yellow-gold surfaces of this near-Mint State example display luster around and within the interstices of the design motifs. An above average strike leaves relatively strong detail on the design features, including the shield and wing feathers, elements that are usually weak. Distributed light marks are visible, but these are of less severity than ordinarily seen.

From The Atherton Family Collection.(#8950)

Popular 1866-S Motto Twenty, Mint State

2247 1866-S Motto MS60 PCGS. Garrett and Guth nicely sum up the situation for this popular issue, writing, "Very few coins of the date have turned up in Mint State in the last 140 years." The popularity is a combination of the Motto type with the popular Old West mintmark of San Francisco. This piece offers radiant luster emanating from orange-gold surfaces; the numerous abrasions on both sides, some large, preclude a finer grade, but there is strictly no sign of wear or friction on the high points. A bold die crack on the obverse runs from the rear curls where they meet the neck, diagonally down through the 8 in the date, through the base of the 1, and thence to the rim. Population: 5 in 60, 18 finer (12/09).(#8950)

Appealing 1869-S Double Eagle, MS62

2248 1869-S MS62 NGC. The 1869-S twenty dollar is plentiful in Extremely Fine and About Uncirculated grades. Mint State examples are rare, most being in the MS60 to MS61 range, the finest condition most collectors are likely to encounter of this issue.

Rich peach-gold patination on this MS62 specimen displays subtle traces of mint-green. Its design features exhibit better definition than typically seen, though the first three stars reveal the usual softness in the centers. Most of Liberty's hair, the shield, and the eagle's plumage are strong. The luster also appears above average, though its flow is occasionally broken by light to moderate marks. All in all, an appealing piece for the designated grade.

From The Atherton Family Collection.(#8956)

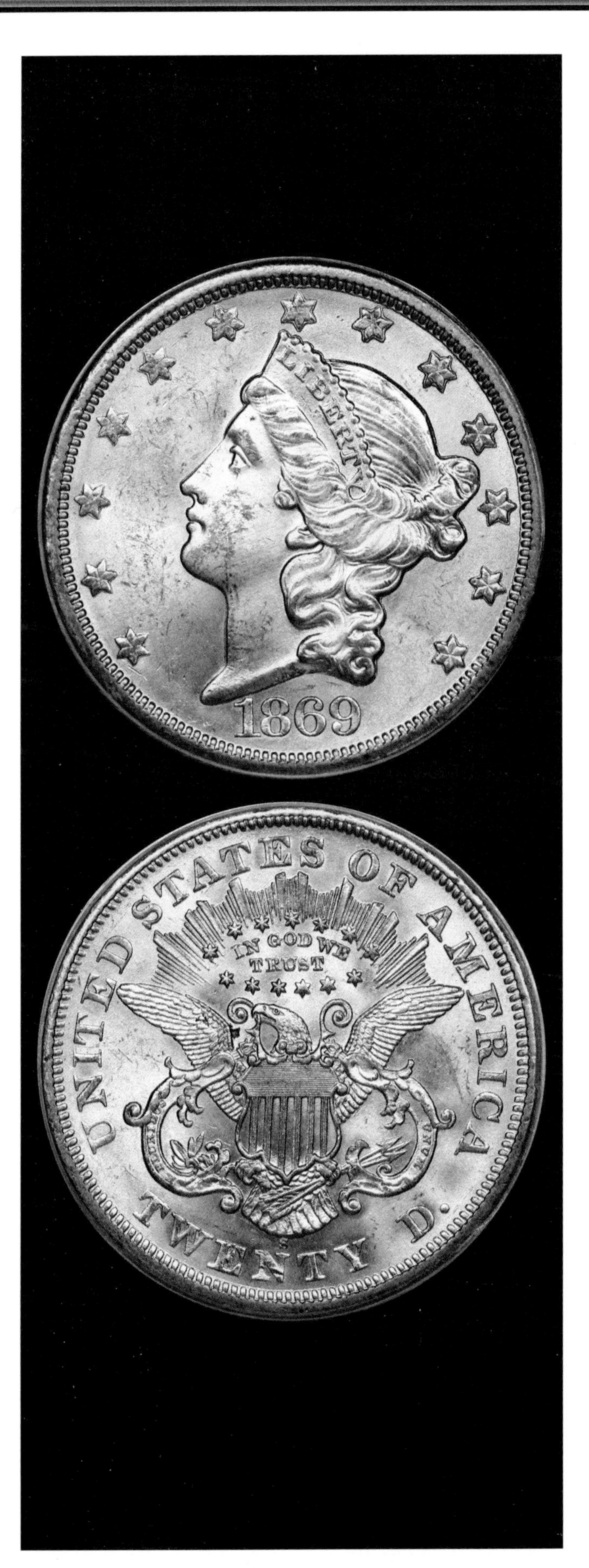

Fantastic MS64 1869-S Twenty

2249 1869-S MS64 PCGS. CAC. While Type Two Liberty double eagles are desired as a category, within the group, the 1869-S does little to distinguish itself in the midrange circulated grades, as Garrett and Guth note in their *Encyclopedia of U.S. Gold Coins*. Beyond XF45, however, a new pattern emerges: "The majority of coins offered at auction in the last two decades have been About Uncirculated. Mint State examples are very rare, most being only at the MS-60 or MS-61 level. Many great collections of the past have lacked the date in Mint State."

The level of challenge progresses as the grade increases. In the words of Garrett and Guth, "Although the date is very rare in Mint State, a few choice examples are known." Among Choice coins, "a few" is appropriate indeed; there is a combined population of 14 MS64-graded pieces, nine graded by NGC and five by PCGS, with none finer (11/09). As with most certified populations, there is a distinct possibility that the figures include at least one resubmission.

As one of five PCGS-graded pieces, the present near-Gem is of particular importance to Registry enthusiasts. Pale straw-gold and deeper canary-yellow shadings mingle in the immensely lustrous, faintly frosty fields. While the portrait and the obverse stars show a degree of striking softness, the surface quality is remarkable; Liberty's cheek shows no marks of any significance, only a small luster scrape. While the few abrasions on the reverse render the grade technically accurate, its eye appeal far surpasses the traditional understanding of an MS64 coin.(#8956)

LIBERTY
1870
UNITED STATES OF AMERICA
IN GOD WE TRUST
CC
TWENTY D.

Legendary 1870-CC Double Eagle, XF40

2250 1870-CC XF40 NGC. The highly influential numismatic writing pair of Garrett and Guth have covered the broad expanse of classic U.S. gold, but few of the issues they surveyed received as much praise as the 1870-CC double eagle. In each of the three editions of their coffee-table delight, *100 Greatest U.S. Coins,* the 1870-CC twenty has held a place in the the book, progressing from a rank of 74th in the first edition printed in 2003 to 64th in the most recent version, copyright 2009.

As Garrett and Guth explain in *100 Greatest U.S. Coins,* the 1870-CC double eagles are inextricably linked to the mining history and development of the Old West:

> "In 1870, a new U.S. branch mint opened at Carson City, Nevada. Because of the Comstock Lode and other mineral discoveries, the West was producing an abundance of precious metals. It was felt that a coining facility in Carson City, only about 15 miles from the Comstock Lode, would be useful to the inhabitants ..."

Garrett and Guth also list a variety of reasons why the 1870-CC twenty has become so famous, highlighting the influence of collectors of Carson City coinage, those interested in the mystique of the Old West (such as the Japanese purchasers of the 1980s, as noted by Doug Winter in his *Gold Coins of the Carson City Mint* from 2001), and those with a penchant for the hefty gold double eagle denomination in general.

With these groups all pursuing the relative handful of 1870-CC twenties still extant, it is little wonder that demand should far outstrip the current supply. In their rarity note for *100 Greatest U.S. Coins,* Garrett and Guth state: "Most experts agree that between 35 and 45 examples are known to exist in all grades." Further, earlier: "Nearly all examples of this great rarity are owned by serious collectors and are seldom offered for sale." With this in mind, the opportunity—the remarkable *luxury*—offered to collectors by this auction is staggering: the ability to choose between *two* 1870-CC twenties to be sold on the same night!

It is worth noting that while the present example took the "serious collector" path (one need only look at the other Atherton Family Collection pieces to know that the presence of this 1870-CC double eagle is no fluke), the other 1870-CC twenty, to be offered immediately after this piece, comes from a German source and was previously unknown to American collectors. Their appearance together in this auction is the happiest of numismatic coincidences.

Like all its fellows, this XF representative shows the effects of what must have been years of hardscrabble wear in Nevada or perhaps elsewhere in the West. The softly struck portrait and stars appear more worn than they actually are, though the yellow-gold fields still show appreciable luster, which corrects this faulty impression. Both sides exhibit light to moderate abrasions, though in the context of the 1870-CC double eagle issue, this is an appealing survivor. In their 2006 *Encyclopedia of U.S. Gold Coins,* Garrett and Guth offered the 1870-CC double eagle this simple tribute: "The 1870-CC double eagle is one of the true classics of the series." This Platinum Night is one of the best opportunities in years to own the legend. Census: 6 in 40, 13 finer (11/09).
From The Atherton Family Collection.(#8958)

1870
UNITED STATES OF AMERICA
IN GOD WE TRUST
TWENTY D.

Rare 1870-CC Liberty Double Eagle, XF45

2251 1870-CC XF45 PCGS. There are only 40 to 50 known 1870-CC double eagles that survive from an original mintage of just 3,789 coins. It ranks high among the list of known double eagle rarities, a list that includes business strikes of the 1854-O, 1856-O, 1881, 1882, and others. Market appearances of the 1870-CC twenty are also rare, and any appearance must be considered a major opportunity for the advanced collector of Liberty double eagles or Carson City gold coins. We have only offered 15 examples at auction since the beginning of our Permanent Auction Archives in 1993. Only three of those appearances are graded higher than the present piece. It is the first double eagle struck at Carson City in the opening year of that branch mint. However, contemporary coin collectors were rare in that region, so few were saved from circulation.

The present specimen that PCGS grades XF45 is actually a new piece to the numismatic community, coming from the Rheinland-Pfalz area of Western Germany. The grandfather of the gentleman that brought the coin to Heritage was in the U.S. in the early 20th century, and he wanted to bring a few double eagles back to his family in Germany. Most of the coins he acquired were Saint-Gaudens pieces, but he also wanted one coin from the "old west," and acquired this 1870-CC twenty. The coin remained hidden in an old piece of furniture for nearly 100 years until his grandson retrieved the coin just a few years ago. The younger man had little knowledge of coins, and failed to understand the significance of this piece until he contacted the Heritage European representatives.

The mystique of the 1870-CC twenty is a combination of both historic and numismatic influences. This piece represents the early history of the Carson City area, from its first settlers in 1851 until the Mint was opened in 1870. The new facility was a direct result of the Comstock Lode and the silver interests in Nevada, although many gold coins were also produced over the next quarter century. This piece also represents the charm of the old West, today as it did a century ago for a visitor from Germany.

The numismatic importance is a combination of its overall rarity, and its condition rarity. With only 40 to 50 coins known, the date is easily one of the rarest double eagles with only a few contenders. The low mintage and immediate circulation of all those coins explains its condition rarity. Nearly all examples are in the VF to XF grade range, typically with heavily abraded surfaces. The finest certified examples include an NGC AU55, a single AU53 PCGS coin, two AU53 NGC coins, four AU50 PCGS examples, and three AU50 NGC pieces. The present XF45 specimen is tied for the 12th best certified at NGC and PCGS, combined.

This specimen exhibits the usual light abrasions always associated with the 1870-CC double eagle, although they are less severe than those on many of the known examples. Typical of 1870-CC twenties is the peripheral weakness seen among the stars on the obverse, and the legend on the reverse. The surfaces are light yellow with traces of luster still visible in the protected areas. Traces of green and orange accents add to its overall appeal. This is a remarkable and extremely important specimen.(#8958)

Prized AU53 1871-CC Twenty

2252 1871-CC AU53 NGC. Doug Winter notes in his *Gold Coins of the Carson City Mint* (2001), "The 1871-CC is the second rarest Carson City double eagle. When available, the typical piece grades Very Fine to Extremely Fine. This is a very scarce date in About Uncirculated and most of the pieces known in this grade range are no better than About Uncirculated-50."

Winter continues by noting the issue's increasing rarity through the various tiers of the AU grade band. For most collectors of Carson City double eagles, this AU53 representative is well-placed at the confluence of ambition and availability. Attractive green-gold coloration and a solid strike for the issue are the chief highlights. The mildly abraded surfaces offer slight reflectivity.(#8961)

Appealing, Scarce Choice AU 1871-CC Twenty

2253 1871-CC AU55 PCGS. The 1871-CC double eagle circulated widely in Nevada, and quantities also found their way overseas. Moreover, most survivors show heavy bagmarks. Extremely Fine and About Uncirculated coins are the most often encountered specimens, while Mint State examples are rare, with a mere six having been certified, primarily in MS60 and MS61.

This Choice AU is therefore a very special offering. First of all, while it does reveal a few light marks, they are not severe and do not detract from the coin's overall appeal. Second, its design features are well defined, including sharpness in the star centers. Finally, its yellow-gold surfaces are splashed with lilac and grayish-blue, especially on the obverse, and retain a good amount of luster in the areas around and the interstices of the design motifs. Population: 9 in 55, 0 finer (11/09).

From The Atherton Family Collection.(#8961)

Attractive 1872 Double Eagle, MS62

2254 1872 MS62 NGC. Within the series of Type Two double eagles there are several conditionally scarce P-mints, with issues such as the 1868 or 1870 being two of the more high profile dates. The unheralded 1872 is an issue with a larger mintage that often goes unnoticed. Granted, an AU55 or AU58 example can be obtained without too much difficulty, but finding something better than a heavily abraded Unc. can require a great deal of patience. Offered here is a well struck coin with attractive yellow-gold coloration blushed with apricot. Only a reeding mark trio to the left of Liberty's ear precludes what might well be an important advance in grade. Census: 12 in 62, 2 finer (11/09).

From The Atherton Family Collection.(#8963)

Well Struck 1874 Twenty Dollar, MS62

2255 1874 MS62 NGC. An examination of certified population data indicate that the majority of extant 1874 double eagles fall into the Extremely Fine to About Uncirculated range. A number of Mint State coins have also been graded, nearly all in MS60 to MS61. The issue is extremely scarce in MS62 and is rarely encountered any finer.

The lustrous apricot-gold surfaces of the current MS62 offering are uniformly well struck, including full radials in the obverse stars and sharpness on the eagle's plumage. Some scattered marks prevent the attainment of the next highest grade. We hasten to add, however, that these are fewer and of less severity that typically found on the vast majority of Mint State survivors. Census: 18 in 62, 3 finer (11/09).

From The Atherton Family Collection.(#8970)

Pleasing 1875-S Select Double Eagle
An Important Condition Rarity

2256 1875-S MS63 NGC. While many of the 1.230 million 1875-S double eagles were shipped overseas for trade, large numbers have returned to America over the past few decades, resulting in a large supply to satisfy collector demand. Most extant specimens are in the About Uncirculated grades. The issue is available in Mint State, but is primarily limited to MS60 and MS61. MS62s are scarce and finer examples are rare.

Pleasing luster endows this Select offering and an impressive strike delivers strong definition to the design elements, including most of Liberty's hair that frequently shows flatness on many examples. Yellow-gold surfaces are tinged with hints of light green and are minimally abraded. A few grease streaks in the lower left reverse quadrant are noted. Census: 11 in 63, 5 finer (11/09).

From The Atherton Family Collection.(#8975)

Lot 2257

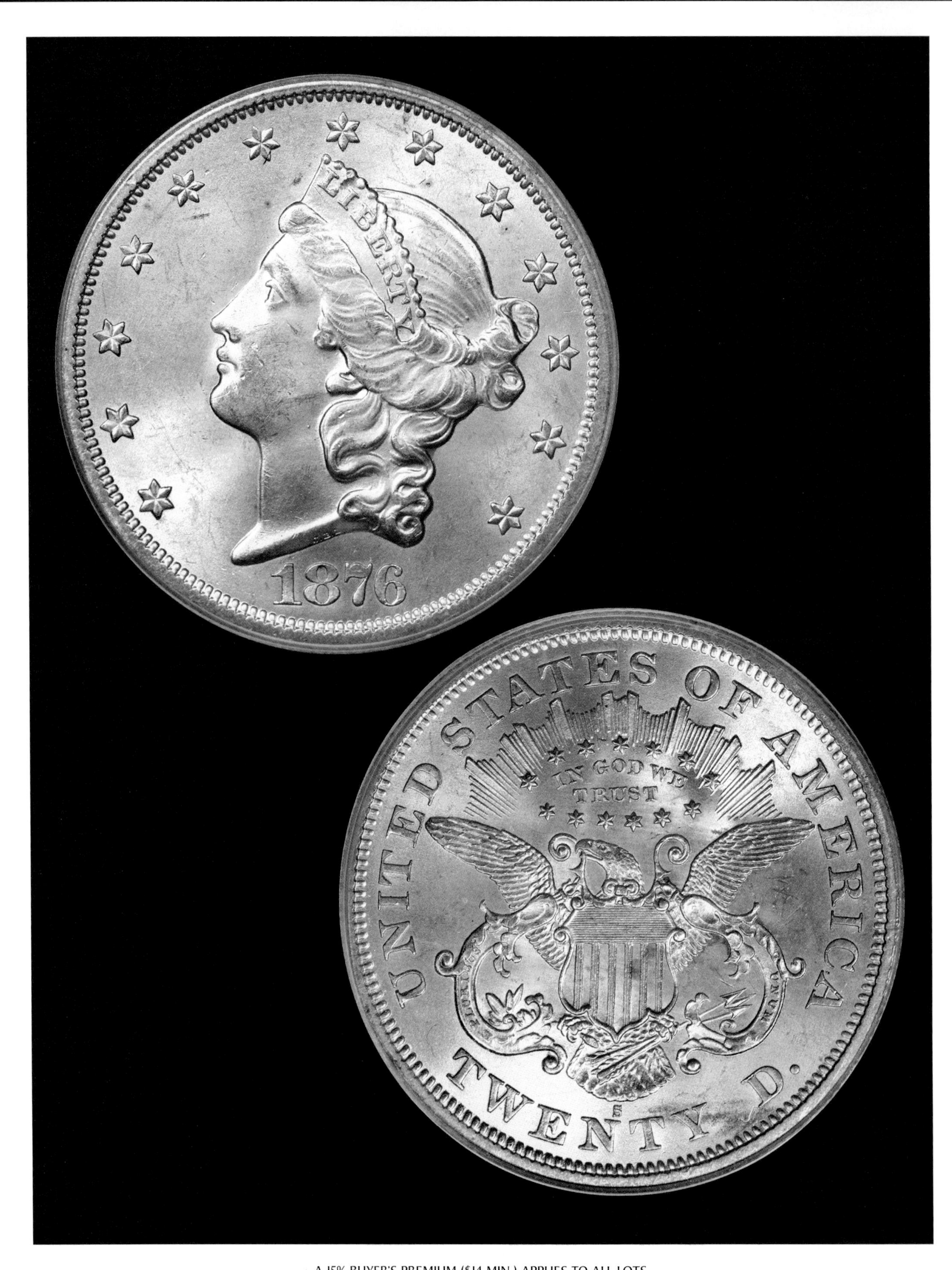
LIBERTY
1876
UNITED STATES OF AMERICA
IN GOD WE TRUST
S
TWENTY D.

Astounding Gem 1876-S Twenty
Sole Finest Certified by PCGS

2257 1876-S MS65 PCGS. CAC. A Gem 1876-S double eagle is a rare treat, indeed; in fact, this is the first time Heritage has had the privilege of offering one at public auction! Garrett and Guth, in their *Encyclopedia of U.S. Gold Coins,* note that while the issue was heavily repatriated from both Europe and South America, "Choice and gem examples are very rare. Three [pieces] have been certified at the MS-65 level, but none have traded at auction in recent years."

The statement was true at the time of publication, but in its March 2009 Baltimore auction, Bowers and Merena offered one of the two NGC-certified MS65 pieces as part of the Southerly Collection. The description of the Southerly Collection piece begins with the following intriguing assessment:

> "... the Type II Double Eagle series is one of the most conditionally challenging in all of U.S. numismatics. There is perhaps no better indication of the veracity of this statement than the combined PCGS and NGC population *for the entire type* [italics theirs] in grades at and above MS-65. Just eight (!) examples of all issues have been so graded by the major certification services, and most of those coins are off the market in tightly held collections."

The statement remains accurate as of (11/09). To elaborate, there are four certification events each for NGC and PCGS. The NGC pieces are spread across three dates and three grade levels: an 1875 is graded MS66, an 1875-S is certified as MS67, and two 1876-S examples rate an MS65. The PCGS coins include an 1869 graded MS65, an 1873 Open 3 also assessed as an MS65, an 1875-S in MS67, and a single 1876-S graded as MS65 (the present specimen). The exceedingly slow pace of public transactions involving Gem and better Type Two double eagles has frustrated attempts to build a full roster.

That said, it seems a virtual certainty that while there are eight certification events listed, these eight events likely translate to only six or seven actual coins. The 1875-S issue is represented in both the NGC *Census Report* and PCGS *Population Report* as MS67, with the next highest grade MS64, which hardly seems coincidental. The population of three total 1876-S twenties in MS65 also presents the possibility of a resubmission. There are at least two distinct 1876-S Gems, however; the NGC-certified coin offered in March 2009 could not possibly be the same as this PCGS-graded piece, which is housed in an old green label holder.

As one of just a handful of Gems among all Type Two double eagle issues, this coin is of high importance to the top-shelf type collector, and as the sole finest PCGS-certified example of its issue, it is also a singular trump for the Registry enthusiast. Beyond those appeals, it is a simply beautiful example, offering both strong cartwheel luster in the yellow-gold fields on each side and subtle frostiness on the portrait. The obverse definition, while not absolute, is more than adequate, and the reverse offers greater sharpness. Small color nuances appear as a line along Liberty's jaw and a small spot within the shield. Most notably, the surfaces are remarkably well-preserved, with only a few small ticks present on the peripheral parts of the portrait and a handful of marks scattered in the fields. A coin of immense quality that has been recognized by both PCGS and CAC.(#8978)

Exceptional 1877-S Double Eagle, MS63
A Notable Condition Rarity

2258 1877-S MS63 PCGS. The 1877-S double eagle was shipped to European and South American countries in large quantities shortly after it was produced. Most of the returning examples are in the Extremely Fine to lower Mint State levels and are heavily abraded. The issue becomes rare in MS63, the condition of the coin in this lot, and is virtually unobtainable any finer.

Lustrous yellow-gold surfaces are imbued with mint-green, orange, and lilac and exhibit sharply struck design features, including the obverse stars that are often weak on surviving examples. Scattered minute marks and grazes are much less extensive and severe than ordinarily encountered. Population: 21 in 63, 3 finer (11/09).
From The Atherton Family Collection.(#8984)

Low-Mintage 1881 Double Eagle, AU53

2259 1881 AU53 PCGS. Garrett and Guth (2006) note: "The 1881 Philadelphia double eagle is the start of a series of very low-mintage issues. ... Predictably, the 1881 issue is a major rarity in all grades. It is estimated that fewer than 40 coins are known." That figure would make up only about 2% of the 2,199 business strikes produced. This well-defined straw-yellow example, lightly marked overall but with few significant abrasions, is modestly worn with significant reflective luster remaining in the fields. A narrow horizontal alloy streak passes through the shield. Attractive and important, a noteworthy survivor. Population: 3 in 53, 7 finer (11/09).(#8994)

1882-CC Liberty Head Twenty, MS62 Only One Coin Certified Finer

2260 1882-CC MS62 NGC. Variety 1-A. The 1882-CC is one of the more available Liberty Head double eagles from the Carson City Mint. In spite of the relatively small mintage of 39,140 pieces, the issue has appeared regularly in auction catalogs and dealer offerings in recent decades. Jeff Garrett and Ron Guth believe the date may have been represented in European hoards and repatriated in fairly large numbers. Doug Winter estimates a surviving population of 800-900 pieces in all grades. The issue becomes scarce in higher AU grades, and experts believe only 30-35 examples are extant in Mint State.

The present coin is at the pinnacle of obtainable pieces, as only one coin has been certified finer at either of the leading grading services (11/09). This impressive example is fully struck, with bright yellow-gold surfaces and semiprooflike fields. Lightly abraded and nice for the grade, the only mentionable mark is between F and A on the reverse. Census: 11 in 62, 0 finer (11/09).(#8997)

Attractive 1883-S Double Eagle, MS64 One of Finest Known

2261 1883-S MS64 NGC. Large quantities of 1883-S double eagles were struck for international trade (1.189 million pieces). The coins were apparently carelessly handled, resulting in the vast majority of surviving examples falling into the About Uncirculated to MS62 grade range. The issue becomes scarce in MS63 and rare in near-Gem. Neither NGC nor PCGS has certified any pieces finer.

Not only is this MS64 offering one of the finest known of the date, but its design features are sharply delineated, including the centers that are sometimes incomplete. Attractive rose-gold coloration adorns highly lustrous surfaces that reveal the expected number of bagmarks, but are completely devoid of copper stains, a rather common affliction of this issue. Census: 5 in 64, 0 finer (11/09).

From The Atherton Family Collection.(#9000)

Frosty 1884-S Twenty, MS64

2262 1884-S MS64 PCGS. Among Type Three twenties, the 1884-S is fairly ubiquitous in the lower Mint State grades, up through MS63. Nearly a thousand pieces in MS63 have been certified by NGC and PCGS together, less duplicates. In MS64, however, the certified population plunges precipitously. NGC and PCGS together have graded only 25 coins in MS64, with five finer (11/09). This PCGS-certified near-Gem boasts over-the-top eye appeal, a combination of the rich reddish-orange coloration, cartwheel luster, and frosty, near-abrasion-free surfaces. Population: 17 in 64, 1 finer (11/09).

From The Atherton Family Collection.(#9002)

1885 Liberty Head Twenty, AU55
Low Mintage Date
Prooflike Surfaces

2263 1885 AU55 PCGS. The 1885 Liberty Head double eagle boasts the second lowest business-strike mintage of any double eagle, at 751 pieces. Few examples were saved at the time of issue because most advanced collectors of the era preferred to order proofs from the Mint, rather than save a business strike from circulation. The issue is rare in all grades today, with fewer than 100 examples known. Most examples seen are in AU grades, and Mint State pieces are quite rare.

Because the mintage was so small, the dies did not experience much wear, and business-strike coins have reflective, prooflike surfaces. Virtually all early auction appearances of the 1885 double eagle describe the coin offered as a proof, but we suspect many coins were actually prooflike business strikes. For example, the coin offered in the Murdoch Collection (Sotheby, Wilkinson & Hodge, 7/1903), lot 692 is located in the section of the catalog reserved for proof double eagles, but the cataloger describes the coin as "slightly scratched" and "very fine." As no other 1885 gold proof coins from any denomination are offered in the catalog, it seems unlikely that Murdoch purchased his 1885 double eagle from the Mint as part of a proof set. A more likely scenario is that the coin was a business strike that made its way to Europe in normal channels of foreign trade, and Murdoch acquired it from a bullion broker or pawn shop. When his collection was sold, the British cataloger was fooled by the reflective surface and categorized the coin as a proof. Even in this country, numismatists often confused the proof and business-strike issues of 1885 until recent times.

The present coin is an appealing specimen, with the prooflike surfaces always seen on this date. The surfaces are tinted a rich, even reddish color and are lightly abraded for the grade. Two tiny milling marks in the right obverse field serve as pedigree markers. Population: 10 in 55, 17 finer (11/09).(#9003)

Famous, Low-Mintage 1885 Twenty, AU58
Generally the Finest Grade Obtainable

2264 1885 AU58 PCGS. The decade of the 1880s is notorious for deeply mirrored business strikes and softly defined proofs, a situation that years ago caused a blurring between the two (usually depending upon which was more valuable). In recent decades, scholarship in most series has risen to such a level that diagnostics are now known that clearly differentiates between coins struck for circulation and proofs. With an issue such as the 1885 twenty, with a mintage of only 750 pieces, this can be important to know. In his double eagle *Guide Book,* Q. David Bowers lists the characteristics:

> "The date on the circulation strikes is placed slightly differently form that on the Proofs, farther to the left, with 8 centered under the B (J.B.L.), while on the Proofs the center of the 8 is ever so slightly to the right. The date is lower than on the Proofs. On the circulation strike the 5 is much closer to the dentils than to the curl above, while on the Proofs it is just slightly closer to the dentils than the curl above."

This is an unquestioned business strike. The fields are reflective, but lack the depth seen on first-strike coins and proofs. The surfaces are peppered with numerous tiny abrasions, but the only ones worthy of individual mention are on Liberty's neck, one at the top and the other at the bottom. The strike is sharp throughout and the surfaces display even reddish patina. In general, the 1885 is unavailable in mint condition. Both services combined have only graded 20 coins finer than AU58 (several of which were undoubtedly resubmissions). Population: 10 in 58, 7 finer (11/09).

From The Atherton Family Collection.(#9003)

Lovely Near-Gem 1885-S Twenty Dollar

2265 1885-S MS64 PCGS. Like so many of its Type Three brethren, the 1885-S is a rarity in grades above MS63. This has been a favorite series of astute collectors for many years, as there were numerous underrated S-mint issues that could be bought for little premium. With the recent advances in gold prices and the accompanying fervor for gold coins, the series has been "waking up" to fresh price increases. This is a lovely near-Gem example, with coruscating luster over mellow orange-red surfaces. Only a couple of minor abrasions appear to keep this piece from an even finer Gem grade. Population: 30 in 64, 1 finer (11/09).

From The Atherton Family Collection.(#9005)

Bold MS64 1890-S Double Eagle

2266 1890-S MS64 NGC. Despite a plentiful mintage exceeding 800,000 pieces, the 1890-S is another Type Three twenty whose certified populations plummet at the near-Gem level. Even Select examples are scarce. The present near-Gem is a tale of two colors, with orange-gold in the centers bounded by greenish-gold at the margins on both sides. Bountiful luster appears, and there are relatively few abrasions. The strike is well-executed, as is the case with most Type Three twenties. Among the handful of finest certified at either service. Census: 7 in 64, 1 finer (11/09).

From The Atherton Family Collection.(#9015)

LIBERTY
1891
UNITED STATES OF AMERICA
IN GOD WE TRUST
E PLURIBUS UNUM
TWENTY DOLLARS

Low Mintage 1891 Liberty Head Double Eagle, MS63
Second Finest Certified

2267 1891 MS63 PCGS. CAC. Only 1,390 business strike Liberty Head double eagles were minted in 1891, supplemented by 52 proof examples. Despite the minuscule production figure, the 1891 has been overshadowed by the rare dates of the 1880s, and the true rarity of the issue has never been appreciated. Few numismatists were interested in collecting double eagles in 1891 and the tiny supply of proof issues was undoubtedly adequate to satisfy contemporary demand. In their *Encyclopedia of U.S. Gold Coins 1795-1933,* Jeff Garrett and Ron Guth comment:

> "Most of the important collections of previous generations did not have a circulation-strike example of the 1891 double eagle. Collectors considered a Proof example to be preferable and not a distinctly different issue. Modern numismatists now realize the importance and rarity of many previously overlooked Philadelphia issues. The 1891 double eagle is a prime example."

Nearly all early auction appearances of the 1891 double eagle feature proof examples, confirming the preference for this format noted by Garrett and Guth. An early appearance was in the William H. Woodin Collection (Thomas Elder, 3/1911), lot 1380, "1891. Brilliant proof. V. Rare. Only 1,442 of all kinds struck." The lot realized only $26, indicative of the low esteem in which proof coins in general were held by 1911 (while proof sets were popular in the 1890s, their popularity declined dramatically during the matte proof era, beginning in 1907). The fabulous Garrett Collection contained a complete gold proof set of 1891, probably purchased by Robert Garrett through Henry Chapman. The James Ten Eyck Collection (B. Max Mehl, 5/1922) also included a complete gold proof set of 1891 in lot 332, which realized $44.25.

Even when an early appearance was described as a business strike, it often turned out to be an impaired proof. The coin in lot 816 of the Smith, Dickie and Other Collections (Elder, 11/1935) was described as, "1891. $20. P. Mint. Only 1,442 struck. Fine and very rare. Worth $75." When the coin surfaced many years later as lot 4044 of the Norweb Collection (Bowers and Merena, 11/1988), the cataloger described it as, "**1891 Proof-50.** A Proof which spent a few months of its life in circulation, and which has various marks and evidences of handling over the Proof surface, although abundant Proof areas can still be seen."

It has only been in recent times that uncirculated examples of the 1891 double eagle began to appear on an equal footing with their proof cousins at public auction. A search of auction records over the last 15 years reveals only six offerings of an 1891 double eagle in Mint State grades through the major auction firms. The finest known example is the piece in The Dallas Bank Collection (Sotheby's/Stack's, 10/2001), lot 111, which realized $80,500. The coin appeared again in the FUN Signature Auction (Heritage, 1/2005), lot 30540, where it realized $155,250.

The number of surviving 1891 double eagles is the subject of some debate among the experts. In 1988, Walter Breen estimated a dozen business strikes were still extant, accompanied by perhaps 15-18 proofs. In the same year, the catalogers of the Norweb Collection speculated that as many as two dozen regular-issue examples might have survived, along with an equal number of proofs. By 1999, Doug Winter and Michael Fuljenz had revised the total upward to 35-45 business strikes and 20 proofs. Today, using population data from third-party grading services, experts still estimate a population of fewer than 100 examples in all grades. At the MS63 level, the issue is extremely rare. The present coin is the only specimen certified at the Select level by either of the major grading services, and only the Dallas Bank example has been graded finer (11/09).

The coin offered here is a magnificent example, with bright mint luster and semiprooflike fields on both sides. The strike is full over all design elements. A pair of faint alloy streaks are present on the obverse, one running diagonally down behind Liberty's head, and the other starting at a small copper colored void in the upper left obverse field. The reverse is virtually blemish free, while a few small abrasions in the obverse fields define the grade.(#9016)

Appealing 1891-CC Double Eagle, AU58

2268 1891-CC AU58 NGC. The 1891-CC twenty is an important rarity, and has the second lowest mintage of any double eagle from this mint (5,000 pieces), behind the 1870-CC (3,789 coins). It is extremely difficult to locate in Mint State, and when seen in that condition is likely to be between MS60 and MS62. A mere two MS63 have been certified, and none finer.

Just a trace of wear on the very highest design points keep this specimen from the Mint State grades. The fields are very slightly reflective and each side has nearly complete luster and is sharply struck. Hints of rose, sky-blue, and lavender toning confined to the peripheries, mostly on the reverse, add to the overall aesthetic appeal. A few minute bag marks and luster grazes are noted on the obverse, but do not distract. Census: 69 in 58, 36 finer (11/09). (#9017)

Extraordinary 1892 Double Eagle MS66 ★ Deep Prooflike

2269 1892 MS66 ★ Deep Prooflike NGC. The 1892 is a well-known and highly respected issue in the Type Three series. Only 4,523 business strikes were produced, with another 93 proofs struck. The rarity and value of this issue are such that the mintmark has been removed from 1892-S coins in the past. It is reliably estimated that some 130-140 coins survive today in all grades. Most survivors are in XF-AU and Mint State coins are quite rare, especially above MS62.

The 1892 is generally seen with numerous and heavy abrasions, which makes this coin all the more special. This piece is similar in overall texture and appearance to the 1976 ANA example, but the pedigree identifiers on that coin do not exactly match this one. The strike is full, as usually seen, with complete radial lines on the stars and fully defined hair detail on Liberty. The fields are fully and deeply prooflike on each side, this coin apparently being one of the first struck from the new (polished) dies from this year. Additionally, the devices are heavily frosted, with the result that both obverse and reverse have a pronounced cameo effect. Abrasions are minimal, aside from several tiny marks in the left obverse field. Please note, quite a few scuffs appear on the holder; they are *not* on the coin. A speck of copper color appears in the field in front of the juncture of Liberty's throat and neck. Needless to say, this is a very rare offering with this degree of technical merit, one equally rare with this amount of aesthetic appeal. The finest certified at PCGS are three examples in MS64; at NGC this is the only MS66 Deep Prooflike, although a couple of non-Prooflike coins are numerically finer (11/09).

Ex: 2004 FUN Signature (Heritage, 1/2004), lot 3188, which brought $36,800.

From The Atherton Family Collection.(#9019)

Lustrous Gem 1900-S Twenty Dollar

2270 1900-S MS65 NGC. The 1900-S double eagle was struck to the extent of more than 2.4 million coins, and Mint State examples are quite attractive and well-made, when they are found. Gem examples are nonetheless scarce, although lower Mint State grades are available for a price. Less than a dozen Gems of this issue are certified at NGC and PCGS combined, less an unknown number of duplications, as always.

The present Gem is lustrous, with yellow-gold surfaces and some light smoke-gray accents. A couple of tiny marks on Liberty's cheek are the only mentionable abrasions. Census: 7 in 65, 2 finer (11/09).

From The Atherton Family Collection.(#9038)

Low-Mintage 1902 Twenty, MS63

2271 1902 MS63 PCGS. CAC. Neophyte collectors are always surprised to hear that the mintage of this overlooked P-mint issue is an astoundingly low 31,140 coins. This piece, certified in a green-label holder, offers attractive luster emanating from the greenish-gold surfaces on each side. The strike is well-detailed throughout, stopping just short of full. A few trivial contact marks on each side appear to preclude an even finer grade, but the issue is an elusive one, even at this Mint State level; finer examples are few and far between. Population: 64 in 63, 9 finer (12/09). (#9041)

1904 Liberty Head Double Eagle, MS66
A Wonderful Type Coin With a Hint of Semireflectivity in the Fields

2272 1904 MS66 PCGS. From a huge mintage of more than 6.2 million pieces, the 1904 Liberty Head double eagle is the most available date of the series. Accordingly, the issue enjoys great popularity with investors and type collectors, as well as series enthusiasts. Large numbers were used in foreign trade and preserved in European banks, to be repatriated in recent times. The issue is easily located in grades up to the Gem level, and even MS66 coins can only be called scarce. However, improving on a Premium Gem example, such as the present coin, is almost impossible. Currently, NGC has certified only a single coin finer than MS66, while PCGS has graded two specimens above the Premium Gem level (11/09).

The present coin is fully struck, with hints of a semiprooflike finish in the fields of both sides. The surfaces are a pleasing, even reddish-gold color. As expected with an MS66 coin, the surfaces exhibit no mentionable blemishes.(#9045)

Marvelous 1904 Double Eagle, MS66

2273 1904 MS66 NGC. As a review of NGC and PCGS population figures readily shows, the 1904 twenty dollar is easily obtainable through the Gem level of preservation. The number of certified coins drops significantly from just under 10,000 MS65 pieces to about 350 in Premium Gem. Finer examples are rarely encountered.

Scintillating luster endows both sides of this marvelous MS66 specimen and a powerful strike imparts bold definition to the design elements. Attractive yellow-gold surfaces are devoid of significant marks. The technical quality and aesthetic appeal of this piece make it an excellent choice for a high-grade type collection.

From The Atherton Family Collection.(#9045)

Intensely Contrasted 1873 Closed 3 Double Eagle, PR64 Ultra Cameo

2274 1873 Closed 3 PR64 Ultra Cameo NGC. CAC. Although these are still often called Closed 3, the loops of the numeral are not entirely closed, bur rather *closer together* than on the Open 3 style that preceded it. Many numismatists have turned to the "Close 3" terminology, which more accurately describes the variety. The year also marked another transition, although not among the gold issues—that of the No Arrows/With Arrows varieties in the minor silver coinage, signaling a slight alteration to even metric weights. As a result, the complete proof set of the year contains more coins (20) than any other, a fact that exerted a peculiar fascination for noted collector Harry X Boosel, long known as "Mr. 1873."

All of the 25 recorded double eagle proofs are of the Closed 3 (or Close 3) type, although business strikes of the Open 3 variety were produced later in the year in Philadelphia and San Francisco, but none in Carson City. Garrett and Guth comment concerning the issue:

> "The 1873 issue is among the most difficult of the Proof Type 2 double eagles to locate. Very few have been offered for sale in recent decades. There are only 10 to 12 coins known in all grades, including at least two in museum collections. Of the few that have survived, several are slightly impaired. The Proof gold coinage of 1873 has one of the lowest mintage figures for the era and is very popular as such."

A perusal of our Permanent Auction Archives indicates that this is the first time we have ever offered a proof example of this elusive date, since we began recordkeeping in 1993. In fact, we can locate only five trades of this coin in the past 30 years. The most recent that we know of was the ex: Trompeter Collection specimen, a Gem Cameo NGC coin that American Numismatic Rarities offered (1/2005, lot 1023) which garnered $155,250.

This piece displays marvelous, intense contrast on both sides between the deeply reflective, mirrored fields and thickly frosted devices. A slight pinkish-gold cast appears on each side. For pedigree purposes we mention a few tiny lint marks visible under magnification, most notably by stars 11 and 13. The combined population data appear to contain numerous duplicates. Census: 1 in 65 Ultra Cameo, 1 finer (11/09).(#99088)

Rare 1896 Liberty Head Double Eagle, PR65 Deeply Reflective Fields, Frosty Devices

2275 1896 PR65 PCGS. CAC (Gold Sticker). At 128 pieces, the 1896 Liberty Head twenty enjoys the largest proof mintage of any 19th century double eagle. Of course, in absolute terms, the production figure is still extremely small, and the issue is rarer than one would expect in today's market. In their *Encyclopedia of U.S. Gold Coins 1795-1933,* Jeff Garrett and Ron Guth estimate only 45-50 specimens are known today in all proof grades. At the Gem Proof level coins are very rare. Currently, NGC has certified only a single coin in PR65, with none finer; while PCGS has graded five specimens in PR65, with three finer (11/09).

Few collectors were interested in collecting double eagles in 1896, but a small number of specialists and advanced collectors did order gold proofs from the Mint every year. For example, Virgil Brand recorded his receipt of his usual order of proofs, including a double eagle, on August 24, 1896. John H. Clapp received his proof 1896 double eagle in November of that year. New York collector James Ten Eyck apparently purchased a gold proof set from the Mint every year. In the sale of his collection by B. Max Mehl on May 2,1922, lot 337 reads, "1896 $20., $10., $5., $2.50. Very Scarce." Modern collectors have this small group of numismatists to thank for the minuscule supply of 1896 proof double eagles that we know today.

The outstanding quality of the present specimen is attested to by the gold CAC sticker. The insert does not indicate a Cameo designation, but significant elements of contrast are present on both sides. The fields display an unfathomable depth of reflectivity, while thick mint frost covers the fully impressed devices. The surfaces appear pristine at first glance, and only the slightest signs of contact are revealed by close examination. Tremendous visual appeal, coupled with high technical grade make this offering an important opportunity for the discerning collector.(#9112)

Magnificent 1900 Double Eagle PR65 Deep Cameo

2276 1900 PR65 Deep Cameo PCGS. The turn of the new century brought a new reverse hub to the double eagle, though few collectors probably noticed. The back of the eagle's neck is smooth, a minor design change that lasted through the end of the series in 1907. Proofs dated 1900 are similar to the business strikes, only on a much smaller scale. Both proofs and coins struck for circulation are among the more obtainable dates among later Type Three twenties. However, there were 1.8 million business strikes produced, but only 124 proofs were minted. It is estimated today that roughly three dozen proofs are believed to exist in all grades.

This is one of the finest 1900 proof twenties we have seen. Comparing this coin to the photo of the PR66 Cameo we offered in March 2008, at first glance this piece actually appears to be technically finer, lacking the tiny planchet flaws that were scattered across the face of that coin. However, the grade of this piece vs. the PR66 is most likely explained by the presence of a shallow planchet flake next to star 12—a"defect" that was on the coin when it left the Mint 110 years ago. Otherwise the surfaces are bright orange-gold with just the faintest trace of orange-peel in the fields. The depth of mirrored reflectivity is unfathomable, and set against the "black" proof fields is thick mint frost on the devices. We see no obvious or mentionable post-striking defects on either side of this magnificent proof twenty. Population: 5 in 65 Deep Cameo, 0 finer (11/09).

From The Atherton Family Collection.(#99116)

Select Proof 1905 Double Eagle

2277 1905 PR63 NGC. The proof 1905 double eagles are associated with a lower-mintage business strike issue, though gold proofs, unlike their copper or silver counterparts, are usually rarities in their own right and rarely contemplated as substitutes for circulating issues. This sharply defined Select specimen has gleaming yellow-gold surfaces with hints of lemon color and impressive mirrors. While the obverse shows a number of hairlines in the portrait area and a few contact marks on Liberty's forehead, the piece remains strongly appealing to the unaided eye. One of just 92 proofs for the year. Census: 3 in 63, 8 finer (11/09).(#9121)

Remarkable 1906 Double Eagle, PR66

2278 1906 PR66 NGC. The 1906 proof double eagles were produced to the extent of 94 coins. By 1906 there were many more collectors of means than even a decade earlier, and sales of the proof double eagles would have been much higher. It is possible that most of the 94 coins produced actually found buyers by 1906 (the Mint regularly melted unsold proof coins without reducing reported production figures), although time and attrition took their toll later on. The population data at NGC and PCGS are wildly skewed by duplications, crackouts, and resubmissions.

Garrett and Guth in their *Gold Encyclopedia* offer this concerning the issue:

> "The 1906 double eagle is a very rare issue in Proof. Of the 94 coins struck, there are probably just 45 to 50 coins known in all grades. Most of the coins seen of the date are of PF-64 quality. For some reason, many pieces are softly struck on the reverse. Gem examples are also seen less often than many of the dates from 1898 to 1905. There is also added desirability due to the rarity of circulation-strike examples."

In PR66 this is the sole finest certified at NGC, although two PR66 Cameos are its numeric equal. The finest at PCGS are a couple of PR65 coins. This is a fully brilliant Premium Gem with just a hint of cameo contrast. Every detail on each side is boldly defined. The surfaces are virtually pristine with only a couple of faint hairlines. (There are quite a few scuffs on the slab that are *not* on the coin.) A tiny disturbance on Liberty's cheek appears to be a planchet lamination rather than post-strike contact. The best pedigree identifier we can cite is a faint diagonal line from the underside of the eagle's left (facing) wing below the T in UNITED. A coin of remarkable quality. Census: 1 in 66, 0 finer (11/09).

Ex: Pittsburgh Signature (Heritage, 8/2004), lot 7710, which brought $74,750.

From The Atherton Family Collection.(#9122)

Final-Year 1907 Liberty Twenty, PR63 Cameo

2279 1907 Liberty PR63 Cameo NGC. A small proof mintage of 78 Liberty Head double eagles was accomplished in 1907, the smallest proof mintage of the 20th century. Anticipation of the new Saint-Gaudens design, which began production in November, probably limited the mintage of the older design gold proof sets. However, the survival rate is high, with perhaps 40-50 examples still extant. An early auction appearance of a 1907 proof set was in the James Ten Eyck Collection (B. Max Mehl, 5/1922), lot 347. Mehl noted, "1907 Old type. $20., $10., $5., $2.50. Perfect brilliant proofs. Rare. The $20. in brilliant proof is far more rare than the rare variety St. Gaudens type."

The present coin is a splendid specimen of this historic issue. Attractive yellow-gold surfaces are enhanced by deeply reflective fields and a full strike. In the *Encyclopedia of U.S. Gold Coins 1795-1933,* Jeff Garrett and Ron Guth note most examples of this date lack Cameo devices, but NGC has awarded this piece the coveted Cameo designation. A few small handling marks limit the grade.

From The Cherokee County Collection, Part One.(#89123)

HIGH RELIEF DOUBLE EAGLES

Bright Yellow-Gold 1907 High Relief Twenty MS62, Wire Rim

2280 1907 High Relief, Wire Rim MS62 PCGS. The Saint-Gaudens double eagles are widely acclaimed for their aesthetic appeal, and the 1907 High Relief issue is particularly stunning. The design, however, went through several significant revisions before the first coins were struck. President Roosevelt's original plan was to have Saint-Gaudens redesign all of the gold coins and the cent, and the artist experimented with several different sketches depending on the denomination. Of course, in the end Saint-Gaudens would only create new eagles and double eagles.

For the obverse of the double eagle, Saint-Gaudens wanted a forward-striding figure of Liberty, much like what was ultimately used, but with wings and a small feather headdress. He had planned to have a standing eagle on the reverse, but for unknown reasons moved that to the ten dollar. Roger Burdette (2006) speculates that Saint-Gaudens "realized his compositions were too complicated. By simplifying Liberty - removing superfluous wings and headdress, converting her into a dynamic obverse figure full of motion and life - he now needed to pair it with a reverse of similar character."

The iconic flying eagle design was originally intended to be the obverse of the cent, but Saint-Gaudens moved it to the double eagle. At this point plans for the cent, quarter eagle, and half eagle were postponed indefinitely, and were eventually taken up by different artists. Numismatists can debate the artistic merits of some of the preliminary sketches and patterns for the double eagle, but essentially all can agree that the end result was outstanding. These High Relief twenties have been highly desirable among collectors for over a century.

This example has bright yellow-gold surfaces, lacking the usually seen reddish tint. The presence of yellow seems to make the swirling die polish marks in the field more apparent. Magnification shows a few small contact marks, which undoubtedly account for the grade, but none are immediately apparent to the unaided eye.(#9135)

Outstanding Wire Rim MCMVII Double Eagle, MS65

2281 1907 High Relief, Wire Rim MS65 PCGS. It is well known that Theodore Roosevelt was the catalyst for the redesign of American coinage in the early 20th century, and he played an active role throughout their production. His vision for American coinage provided much of Saint-Gaudens' inspiration for the 1907 High Relief double eagles that are so popular among collectors today. On November 6, 1905, after a visit to the Smithsonian Institution, the President wrote to Saint-Gaudens with "a suggestion." He continued,

> "It seems to me worth while to try for a really good coinage, though I suppose there will be a great revolt about it! I was looking at some gold coins of Alexander the Great today, and I was struck by their high relief. Would not it be well to have our coins on high relief, and also to have the rims raised? The point of having the rim raised would be, of course, to protect the figure on the coin; and if we have the figures in high relief, like the figures on the old Greek coins, they will surely last longer ..."

Saint-Gaudens heartily embraced Roosevelt's idea and, after several setbacks, he created the remarkable high relief design for the double eagle. According to Philadelphia Mint Superintendent John Landis, the relief had to be reduced by about 20% so that the coins could be struck with only three blows to the die, as opposed to the seven originally required. Nonetheless, the result was a masterpiece of numismatic art. These pieces may not have been the most practical for commerce, but they are considered by many to be the most beautiful American coins ever issued.

This Gem has remarkably clean surfaces, pronounced satiny mint luster, and the usual reddish patina seen on almost all original High Reliefs. Evidence of the numerous blows from the hydraulic press are evident as all the folds in the gown are complete and the lettering on the upper reverse is obviously separated from the rim. There are no obvious or mentionable contact marks on either side of this impressive piece. The wire rim appears to be complete around both sides, but it is difficult to say for certain as the holder partially obscures the rim on the obverse.

From The Ralph P. Muller Collection.(#9135)

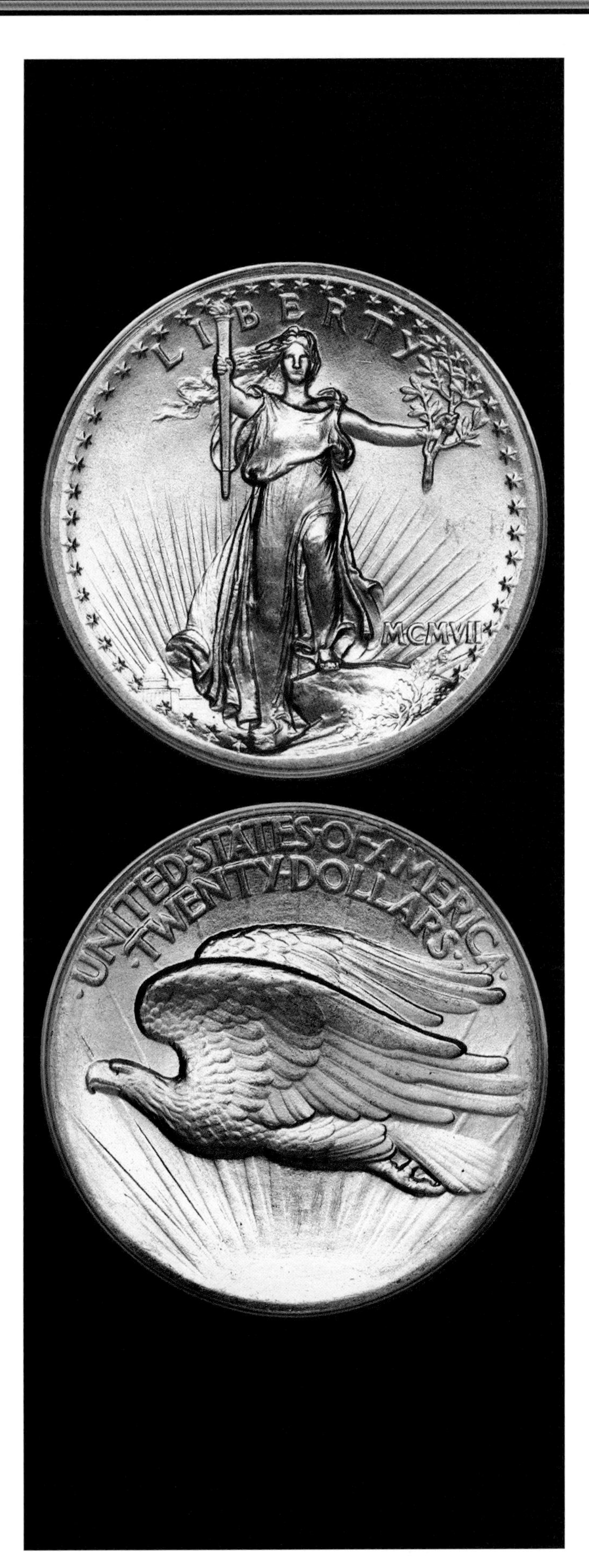

Exceptionally Well-Preserved 1907 High Relief Twenty Wire Rim, MS66

2282 1907 High Relief, Wire Rim MS66 PCGS. We do not know for certain when Roosevelt decided to redesign the nation's coinage, but he had made up his mind by early 1905. Saint-Gaudens and the President likely discussed the idea at the American Institute of Architect's dinner on January 12, 1905 at the White House, and five days later Roosevelt sent the artist a letter asking if he could make designs for the "gold coins and the one cent pieces."

By selecting an outside artist to redesign the coins, the president offended the Mint's Chief Engraver Charles Barber, whose large ego was no secret. Barber also had clashed with Saint-Gaudens on several occasions in the past. Their rivalry during the redesign has been mentioned on countless occasions, and even before Saint-Gaudens got to work on sketches he knew that Barber would be an obstacle.

In 2003 Susan Grewe Tripp discovered an interesting letter dated January 14, 1905 from Saint-Gaudens to his brother Louis, who was also an artist. He wrote, "Barber is a S.O.A.B. but I had a talk with the President who ordered [Treasury] Secretary Shaw in my presence to cut Barber's head off if he didn't do our bidding." This comical anecdote tells a lot about Roosevelt's colorful personality, but it also shows that Saint-Gaudens must have been hesitant about accepting the President's commission and made his opinion of Barber very clear. Roosevelt's support gave Saint-Gaudens a level of protection from Barber, and it was through his persistence that the 1907 High Relief double eagles were struck.

This is an exquisitely preserved example of the High Relief, a coin that more closely approaches art than anything else produced in the U.S. Mint. The surfaces are astonishingly free from the usual contact marks. In fact, we only see one, and it is located on the obverse below the T in LIBERTY. The rich, satiny mint luster has the usual overlay of light reddish patina. An outstanding, high-grade High Relief that will be sure to raise eyebrows at lot viewing and also at the price it realizes.(#9135)

LIBERTY
MCMVII
UNITED STATES OF AMERICA
TWENTY DOLLARS

Essentially Perfect MS67 1907 High Relief Twenty
Ex: Phillip H. Morse

2283 1907 High Relief, Wire Rim MS67 NGC. Augustus Saint-Gaudens was the undisputed master of American sculpture at the time he was commissioned to redesign the eagle and double eagle. When Saint-Gaudens became a cameo cutter in New York City at age 13, American art was dominated by portrait painting. Paris was the center of the art world, and Saint-Gaudens studied there from 1867 to 1875. On his return to the United States, he found the country in the midst of what Mark Twain called the "Gilded Age"-and art was an essential part of the culture.

Saint-Gaudens did not just participate in this artistic movement, but he became a guiding force for American artists. He introduced the country to the French ideals and, according to art historian Henry J. Duffy, "his works engaged the audience in a more immediate way than any other American sculpture at the time." Many of Saint-Gaudens' sculptures and friezes were placed in public areas, such as parks and museums, where thousands of people could interact with them. However, perhaps none of his other works affected as many people on a daily basis as his ten and twenty dollar coins.

Saint-Gaudens was a revolutionary not only in sculpture, but in coinage. Most Americans were concerned about the value of their coins, not the appearance. Theodore Roosevelt and Augustus Saint-Gaudens thought that while a coin was an instrument of commerce, it could also be a work of art. This notion resulted in the redesign of American coins by some of the country's leading artists. Saint-Gaudens' extraordinary 1907 High Relief double eagle represents the pinnacle of this coinage renaissance.

This extraordinary High Relief previously appeared in our auction of the Phillip H. Morse Collection. The following is an updated version of the description as it appeared in that landmark offering from 2005:

> "The 1907 High Relief Wire Rim twenty dollar, according to the Census reports, is readily available in Mint State grades through MS64. It becomes considerably scarcer in Gem and Premium Gem, and very challenging in MS67 and higher grades. Indeed, a total of just 23 MS67 specimens, the grade of the piece in the current lot, have been seen by both NGC and PCGS, along with 5 coins grading higher (11/09). Moreover, according to our auction records, only eight Superb Gems have made appearances over the past 29 years. We present a review of four of these sales below.
>
> "In its August 1978 sale of the Kaufman Sale, RARCOA offered a piece described as having "magnificent deep golden toning" (lot 1907). The specimen appearing in Superior's October 1989 of the Heifetz Collection (lot 5200) is described as follows: "the strike is spectacular, crisp and bold, with no signs of weakness." The 1907 High Relief in Superior's May 1990 sale is called "Perfect-sleek, elegant, pleasing to the eye and impeccable" (lot 5790). Finally, a Superb Gem we sold in our August 1997 ANA Sale is described thus: 'the radiant, satiny luster has a gleam that is unique to High Reliefs'" (lot 7873).

The descriptors applied to the foregoing MS67 High Reliefs can be applied to the present coin from the Phillip Morse Collection. It has deep yellow-gold toning over a satiny finish with radiant luster. The strike is exquisite, with all of the design elements displaying excellent definition, and the surfaces are impeccably preserved, exhibiting not even a few minor abrasions that might serve as pedigree markers. Indeed, the only identifiers on this coin are a couple of light alloy spots, one in the middle of the eagle's lowest tail feather, and another on a feathertip over the eagle's leg. A faint wire rim is noted along the right (facing) obverse.

Ex: Phillip H. Morse Collection of Saint-Gaudens Coinage (Heritage, 11/2005), lot 6524.

From The Five Point Collection.(#9135)

Satiny MS65 1907 Flat Rim High Relief Twenty

2284 1907 High Relief, Flat Rim MS65 PCGS. CAC. Augustus Saint-Gaudens has received many accolades from numismatists for his outstanding design for the double eagles, and deservedly so. However, his assistant, Henry Hering, who played a significant role in the creation of these coins, is often overlooked.

In early June 1900 Saint-Gaudens was diagnosed with cancer and, although the tumor was removed, he was plagued by intense pains for the rest of his life. The ailing artist made sketches and provided guidance for the new coins, but it was Henry Hering who did all of the relief modeling, in addition to serving in Saint-Gaudens' absence at meetings with Mint officials. His efforts were instrumental in the ultimate production of the 1907 High Relief double eagles.

The Mint was not satisfied with the high relief models that Hering submitted; nevertheless 12,367 pieces were struck due to President Roosevelt' insistence. These coins are considered by collectors as the ideal form of Saint-Gaudens' masterful design. Although still beautiful in their own right, the later Saint-Gaudens twenties lack the same charm of the High Reliefs.

Hering was working on a reduced relief model that could have satisfied both the Mint and Saint-Gaudens' wishes, but he could not finish in time. Roger Burdette (2006) writes,

> "Had these low relief models been delivered in a timely manner in June, it is possible the entire 1907 issue of double eagles from the new designs would have had higher relief than typical coins and would have been made from Saint-Gaudens' original work not Charles Barber's re-engrave".

Even during production, adjustments were made to Saint-Gaudens' twenties. A thin 'fin' or bit of extruded metal squeezed between the dies and collar, resulting in what we know today as the Wire Rim. Mint personnel saw this as a striking defect, and late in the production run corrective measures were taken. This is one such example, and it shows almost no trace of the wire rim. Additionally, the surfaces display thick, satiny mint luster with a pronounced accent of reddish patina on each side. The Flat Rim coins are several times scarcer than their Wire Rim counterparts. This would make a lovely addition to an advanced type set or collection of Saint-Gaudens twenties.

From The Ralph P. Muller Collection.(#9136)

PROOF HIGH RELIEF DOUBLE EAGLE

1907 Saint-Gaudens Double Eagle, PR64 High Relief, Wire Rim

2285 1907 High Relief PR64 NGC. The proof issues of 1907 are controversial, with some numismatists believing all High Reliefs should be considered proofs and others vehemently opposed to classifying any examples as proofs. Even the grading services are split on this issue, with PCGS refusing to certify High Relief coins as proofs, while NGC recognizes certain specimens as legitimate proof examples. Characteristics such as an extremely sharp strike and swirling die polish lines in the fields are among the diagnostic features used by NGC to certify proofs. No records were kept of the number of proof examples struck in 1907, but the number must have been quite small.

The present coin shows the full strike and fine swirling die polish lines diagnostic of proofs of this date. The surfaces are silky smooth, with satiny luster, and attractive reddish color. A couple of tiny rim bumps on the reverse account for the grade, as the surfaces show minimal signs of contact, suggestive of a Gem designation. Census: 89 in 64, 71 finer (11/09).(#9132)

SAINT-GAUDENS DOUBLE EAGLES

Gem 1908 Motto Double Eagle

2286 1908 Motto MS65 PCGS. While the No Motto double eagles of 1908 are readily available in high grades today, thanks to the Wells Fargo hoard, the much lower-mintage Motto twenties of the same year are far more elusive. Gems are borderline condition rarities and anything finer easily qualifies; PCGS has certified just 10 such pieces (11/09). This marvelous MS65 survivor offers strong wheat-gold luster and pleasing overall definition, though the torch and the hand holding it show slight striking softness. The central devices are clean for the grade, though a number of small ticks appear on the surrounding rays.

From The Ralph P. Muller Collection.(#9147)

Gem 1908 Motto Twenty With Great Luster and Color

2287 1908 Motto MS65 PCGS. Ex: Brahin. Against the objections of President Theodore Roosevelt, Congress voted to restore the motto IN GOD WE TRUST to national gold coinage beginning in 1908. This is the first year of the new design with 46 tiny stars around the obverse border. Although most type collectors are content with a single coin to illustrate the With Motto design, detail-oriented collectors realize that two coins are necessary. In 1912, two additional stars were added to the obverse to represent the last of the continental United States, New Mexico and Arizona. This is a sharply struck Gem with brilliant honey-gold and lilac colored luster and pristine surfaces. It is elusive in Gem quality, and only a few finer examples have been certified by PCGS. Population: 41 in 65, 10 finer (11/09).(#9147)

Beautiful 1908-D Motto Double Eagle, MS65

2288 1908-D Motto MS65 PCGS. The highly lustrous surfaces of this Gem are patinated in shades of beautiful apricot-gold, mint-green, and lilac. Exquisite definition characterizes the design elements and the few grade-consistent marks are unbothersome. Scarce in Gem and rare any finer.
From The Ralph P. Muller Collection.(#9148)

Low Mintage MS61 1908-S Double Eagle

2289 1908-S MS61 PCGS. With only 22,000 pieces struck, a figure just over twice the production of the legendary High Relief twenties, it is little wonder that examples would be elusive regardless of grade, and the date's famously low mintage has attracted many collectors otherwise not interested in the series. This MS61 survivor has moderately abraded, softly lustrous surfaces, gold-orange with areas of deeper alloy at the high points. Overall eye appeal is strong despite these scattered faults. A coin of definite interest.(#9149)

Frosty Gem 1908-S Double Eagle

2290 1908-S MS65 PCGS. Akers' useful *Handbook of 20th Century United States Gold Coins (1907-1933)* offers these comments concerning the 1908-S double eagle:

> "The 1908-S is rare in lower Mint State grades and extremely so at or above the MS-65 level. This is one of the few Saint-Gaudens Double Eagles that is seen much more often in circulated grades than in Mint State. There are no more than 40 coins extant that grade MS-65 or finer, and the 1908-S is equally as rare as the 1932 in high grades."

There appear to be numerous reasons why most 1908-S double eagles are found in circulated grades. A chief one undoubtedly was the longstanding "hard money" tradition of the Old West, where gold dust, then private gold, then federal coinage were the favored forms of exchange and anything else traded at substantial discounts. Even when parity between paper money, gold, and silver was achieved after the Civil War for the first time in decades in 1878, the Western states continued to show a preference for gold coins in particular, while much of the rest of the country was comfortable with paper currency backed by gold or silver.

Even though Augustus Heaton had published his seminal *Mint Marks* pamphlet in 1893, listing "causes of attractiveness" of U.S. coins, it would be decades before collecting by mintmark would truly catch on, spurred by the introduction of coin boards. And certainly few collectors paid much attention to mintmarks on the largest gold denomination—as they could not afford to collect them regardless. Finally, their status as second-year issues ensured that fewer were saved than had they been first-year. It appears that most of the 22,000 pieces produced quietly entered circulation, where they stayed at least a short time.

The present Gem has yellow-gold coloration rather than the usually encountered reddish-orange patina, but the surfaces are highly lustrous and well-frosted. The strike is full, also typical for this well-made issue, and there are no mentionable marks. This prized Gem should form a bedrock addition to a fine collection of Saint-Gaudens double eagles. Population: 14 in 65, 14 finer (11/09).

PCGS Set Registry Note

Of the top five current PCGS Saint-Gaudens $20 Gold, Circulation Strikes (1907-1932) collections, this piece would upgrade four of the five, the sole exception being the Dr. and Mrs. Stephen L. Duckor Set #2.(#9149)

Remarkable 1908-S Twenty Dollar, MS66

2291 1908-S MS66 NGC. CAC. The year 1908 was one of transitions at our nation's mints. Ending a 115-year-old monopoly on copper coinage, Philadelphia would no longer be the only mint producing cents once San Francisco got into the act, making Indian cents in 1908 and 1909 before switching to the new Lincoln design. (Although it opened in 1906, the Denver Mint would not join the cent fray until 1911.) Denver and San Francisco had already moved to the new Indian Head and Saint-Gaudens designs for the half eagle, eagle, and double eagle among the gold coin denominations, but Philadelphia struck both types of the half eagle, including the old Liberty Head type.

Another transition was going on, contemporaneous with those already mentioned: Even though the new designs were fostered by President Roosevelt and originally embodied by Augustus Saint-Gaudens and Bela Pratt, it was over the president's strenuous objection (that a reference to God on something so mercantile as money amounted to sacrilege) that Congress insisted upon the motto IN GOD WE TRUST on coinage. But the quarter eagles and half eagles, struck later in the year, all bore the motto, while eagles and double eagles of the new designs were struck both with and without the motto (although not all coins were struck at all mints).

So it was that Philadelphia and Denver struck both No Motto and With Motto twenties and tens, while San Francisco struck only With Motto coins of both denominations. In the case of the double eagle, only 22,000 pieces were struck. As the second year of the new Saint-Gaudens design rather than the first and with the plethora of frankly more-flashy coins appearing the preceding year, it appears that most examples circulated, as the general public had lesser incentive to save the second-year coins. Most certified examples, while elusive in any grade, average about Choice AU or so.

The present Premium Gem coin is a remarkable exception to the rule, as one of only six so certified at NGC, with none finer. PCGS has certified nine MS66 examples, with five finer (11/09). It exhibits the usual lavish mint frost for which the issue is well-known in high grade, and the reddish-gold color is also typical, with a slight tinge of lilac intermingled over each side. The strike is full and, as expected of the grade, there are no mentionable distractions.

From The Ralph P. Muller Collection.(#9149)

1909 Saint-Gaudens Double Eagle, MS65
Underrated Condition Rarity

2292 1909 MS65 NGC. At the Gem level, the 1909 Saint-Gaudens double eagle is a "sleeper" in the series, with its true rarity overlooked by most collectors. Experts estimate only 20-25 examples survive in MS65, and population data correlates well with this estimate.

The present coin is an impressive, fully struck Gem, with every detail of the intricate design brought up in clear definition. The surfaces are a satiny yellow-gold color, with a tinge of orange. A shallow, horizontal mark in the center of the obverse is the only mentionable flaw on this memorable specimen. Census: 8 in 65, 4 finer (11/09). (#9150)

Gem 1909 Saint-Gaudens Twenty
Vibrant Mint Luster

2293 1909 MS65 PCGS. CAC. Seldom encountered at the Gem level, the 1909 "perfect date" Saint-Gaudens double eagle is an underrated issue in the series. Few examples were saved by collectors at the time of issue, and early auction appearances were infrequent.

The outstanding feature of the coin offered here is its extraordinary, vibrant luster. The devices are richly frosted, and the surfaces are a subtle orange-gold and pale green color. Striking details are sharp throughout. The only detectable flaws are a tiny planchet flake out of the upper obverse, and a shallow luster graze across the sun. Overall eye appeal is outstanding. Population: 21 in 65, 7 finer (12/09).(#9150)

Magnificent 1909 Double Eagle, MS66

2294 1909 MS66 PCGS. The 1909 is one of the most underrated issues in the Saint-Gaudens double eagle series. This is probably due, at least in part, to its relative availability in the lower levels of Mint State. Indeed, PCGS and NGC have certified more than 2,000 Mint State pieces through MS63. The population declines to about 300 or so in near-Gem and fewer than 30 coins in MS65. The two services have seen just 11 Premium Gem examples and none finer.

The current MS66 offering is one of the lofty 1909 twenty dollar gold pieces. Its satiny surfaces yield captivating luster and are patinated in a delicate blend of peach-gold and mint-green. The strike is virtually unimprovable, manifesting itself in razor-sharp delineation on Liberty's facial features, gown lines, fingers, and toes and on the eagle's plumage. The intricacies of the panes in the Capitol building also stand out. For some reason most 1909 double eagles suffer from scattered bagmarks, accounting for most surviving examples being confined to the MS60 to MS63 grade range. This specimen reveals just a few unobtrusive marks that are completely within the parameters of the grade designation. We mention one at the top of the tenth obverse ray, one in the center of the branch arm, and another in the upper left reverse sun only because they might help to identify the coin for pedigree purposes. This magnificent piece is sure to elicit spirited bidding among aficionados of Saint-Gaudens gold coinage. Population: 7 in 66, 0 finer (11/09).

From The Ralph P. Muller Collection.(#9150)

Marvelous 1909/8 Twenty Dollar, MS66
Among the Finest Certified

2295 1909/8 MS66 PCGS. FS-301. This is an issue that holds a particular fascination for the present cataloger (GH) as well as many other numismatists. As the sole overdate in the Saint-Gaudens series, its appeal is undeniable. Yet it is certainly not alone in its status as a popular 20th century overdate coin, keeping company as it does with the 1918/7-D Buffalo nickel, the 1918/7-S Standing Liberty quarter, the 1942/1-P and -D Mercury dimes, and the 1943/2-P Jefferson nickel. Some collectors—not all—would add the 1914/3-PDS Buffalos to that list, although they are much more controversial.

However, a considerable difference exists between the 1909/8 and most of the other overdates above: While the "wartime overdates" made during World War I and World War II are usually laid at the feet of the mints' having some of their most-skilled personnel serving in the armed forces—hence the mistakes in die hubbing—the 1909/8 is not a wartime production. It is a dual-hub error like the other overdates—although some numismatists who should have known better believed otherwise at its discovery in 1910. Edgar H. Adams wrote these in the June 1910 issue of *The Numismatist*:

> "Overstruck dates are those where the die of one year has been altered to do service for the succeeding one. The last figure in the date is usually gouged out and replaced by the new one, but seldom is this operation conducted so skillfully that traces of it are not left. Of course the reason for this is to save money in the making of the dies, and the practice has by no means been abandoned altogether, for careful scrutiny of the Saint-Gaudens $20 piece of 1909 will reveal traces of what seems to have been the alteration of the figure 8 to 9."

Another interesting anomaly that can serve for authentication purposes on some, not all, specimens is the diagonal die crack that often appears inside the O in IN GOD WE TRUST (not seen here). This would seem to point to a limited number of reverse dies, despite perhaps half of the 1909 Philadelphia double eagles being overdates. The present Premium Gem is among the four finest certified at PCGS, and there are none graded finer at either service (11/09). Marvelous, abundant frosty luster is the hallmark of this piece. The coin is yellow-gold overall, with considerable areas of reddish-gold and lilac intermixed on each side. The strike is uniformly sharp, further increasing the enormous appeal.
From The Ralph P. Muller Collection.(#9151)

Conditionally Rare MS66 1909-S Twenty

2296 1909-S MS66 NGC. CAC. In his *Guide Book of Double Eagle Gold Coins,* Q. David Bowers comments on this issue: "The 1909-S double eagle is readily available in Mint State grades through MS-64, with MS-65 being scarce to rare." The unspoken implication is that even finer pieces, such as this Premium Gem, are distinctly rare, and that implication is correct: NGC has graded just nine coins at the MS66 level and none finer (11/09).

Bowers continues in his commentary, stating that "[m]ost are highly lustrous and very attractive." This coin exemplifies those attributes, with orange-accented yellow-gold luster a highlight of its eye appeal. Well-defined for the issue with only a single flaw worth mentioning, a curving depression below Liberty's branch arm.

From The Ralph P. Muller Collection.(#9153)

Frosted MS66 1910-S Double Eagle Scarce in Such Superior Condition

2297 1910-S MS66 PCGS. Extremely scarce in MS66 condition with only 13 other pieces so graded by both major services, and another nine finer (11/09). Of the two finishes known for the 1910-S this is a frosted coin, and as such it is scarcer than the usual satin-like finish. The rich reddish-gold color of the coin is accented by a faint trace of lilac around the devices and peripheries. The devices are fully struck throughout, and there are no mentionable abrasions on either side of this magnificent coin.

Ex: Phillip H. Morse Collection of Saint-Gaudens Coinage (Heritage, 11/2005), lot 6586.(#9156)

Frosty Gem 1911 Double Eagle

2298 1911 MS65 PCGS. The 1911 is a scarcer P-mint issue among the Saint-Gaudens double eagles; Gems are much more elusive than neophytes might believe. PCGS has certified only 33 pieces in MS65, with nine finer (12/09). It is also an issue where "cherrypicking is advised," as Bowers notes, and if so many cherrypickers can stop their hunt at this coin. Rolling cartwheel luster emanates from the frosty, mattelike surfaces, greenish-gold at the rims and orange-gold in the centers. The strike is bold, and there are no singular abrasions. A faint bit of die grease appears near the date, but it is totally undistracting.(#9157)

Premium Gem 1911 Double Eagle

2299 1911 MS66 NGC. As Q. David Bowers writes of the 1911 in his *Guide Book of Double Eagle Gold Coins,* "The 1911 is one of the scarcer double eagles of the era, but, fortunately, enough nice MS-63 and MS-64 coins are in the market that you will have no trouble finding one." An MS66 coin, on the other hand, usually entails a good deal more searching. This Premium Gem offers deep yellow-gold luster with finely granular texture. The obverse shows a partial wire rim, while the reverse shows a small rim abrasion near 12 o'clock. The centers are well-preserved save for a few marks on Liberty's leg. Census: 12 in 66, 3 finer (11/09).

From The Ralph P. Muller Collection.(#9157)

MS66 1911 Double Eagle
Tied for Finest Certified by PCGS

2300 **1911 MS66 PCGS.** Garrett and Guth note: "Like other Philadelphia Mint issues from this period, the 1911 double eagle is very scarce in gem MS-65 grades or finer." In the "or finer" category, the issue is decidedly *rare:* PCGS has graded just nine pieces as MS66 and none finer (11/09). This shining Premium Gem has generally sharp design definition, like most of its fellows, but it also boasts decidedly above-average luster. Smooth yellow-gold surfaces complete the eye appeal. A memorable high-end representative that offers plenty of allure for the dedicated Registry collector.(#9157)

1911-S Saint-Gaudens Double Eagle, MS66
Fully Struck With Soft Mint Frost

2301 **1911-S MS66 PCGS.** The 1911-S Saint-Gaudens double eagle is scarce at the Premium Gem level, and prohibitively rare in any higher technical grade. Only one coin has been certified finer ay NGC and PCGS combined (12/09).

The present coin is fully struck throughout, with exquisite detail on all design elements. The surfaces are predominantly reddish in color, with subtle accents of lilac interspersed on the obverse. Soft mint frost is evident on the devices and no mentionable marks are detected. Overall visual appeal is undeniable. Population: 23 in 66, 1 finer (12/09).(#9159)

Premium Gem 1911-S Saint-Gaudens Twenty
Challenging High Grade Issue

2302 1911-S MS66 PCGS. From a mintage of 775,750 pieces, the 1911-S Saint-Gaudens double eagle is an available date in grades up to MS64. A hoard of mostly lower Mint State coins surfaced in El Salvador, including a few pieces at the Gem level. Only a handful of specimens exist at the Premium Gem level, however, and Superb Gems are virtually unobtainable.

The present coin exhibits the fine, matte-like granularity in the fields that characterizes this issue. The surfaces display softly frosted mint luster and an even reddish-gold color. The pristine fields display no mentionable flaws. Population: 23 in 66, 1 finer (12/09). (#9159)

Gem 1912 Saint-Gaudens Double Eagle
Exceptional Frosted Mint Luster

2303 1912 MS65 PCGS. The 1912 Saint-Gaudens double eagle boasts a small mintage of 149,700 pieces. If not for the emergence of several European hoards in the 1960s and 1970s, the issue would be quite rare today. As it is, the date is scarce-to-rare in all grades, and Gem examples are decidedly elusive.

The coin offered here exhibits unusually frosty luster, which tends to overpower the usually seen fine granularity in the fields. Well struck, with a few tiny marks evident in the fields, but none of individual significance. Population: 28 in 65, 5 finer (12/09). (#9160)

Appealing MS65 1912 Double Eagle

2304 1912 MS65 NGC. In the 21st century update to the influential David Akers *Handbook of 20th Century United States Gold Coins 1907-1933,* the author offers this early "general comment" on the issue, "The Philadelphia Mint was the only coinage facility to strike Double Eagles in 1912, and it produced fewer than 150,000 coins for commercial use." This Gem never saw circulation, but it is possible—should that be probable?—that it was put to "commercial use" as part of an overseas payment but never actually spent. Regardless, this is a beautiful orange-gold Gem with stunning luster and a crisp strike. Aside from an abrasion in the lower left obverse field, the surfaces are well-preserved. NGC has graded just three numerically finer examples (11/09).

From The Ralph P. Muller Collection.(#9160)

High-End Gem 1913 Twenty Rarely Found in This Grade

2305 1913 MS65 PCGS. CAC. Though the 1913 double eagle's mintage of nearly 170,000 pieces is higher than for many of the surrounding Philadelphia issues, it is one of the more elusive condition rarities known to the series. International tension had risen dramatically in the early years of the 20th century, particularly with the formation of the Triple Alliance and Triple Entente in Europe, and after the outbreak of World War I in 1914, the double eagles that would have been used for international commerce had nowhere to go.

When he described the Dr. Thaine B. Price example in 1998, David Akers commented: "As a date, the 1913 is much more rare than the 1912; in fact, it is the rarest of the With Motto issues from 1908-1915, especially in Choice Uncirculated or better condition. Gems are prohibitively rare, and for all practical purposes, unobtainable ..." The present piece is tied with eight others for the finest example certified by PCGS (11/09).

The strike is unusually bold for this normally weak issue; while most examples have a flat appearance that is similar to the 1907 and 1908 No Motto coins, this coin offers delightful detail, particularly on the peripheral elements. In his *Guide Book* to the series, Dave Bowers did a little fishing on the subject of strike: "Somewhat similar to the 1912, the 1913 requires cherrypicking in order to reel in a sharp one."

While most examples of the 1913 double eagle exhibit dull green-gold fields, this aesthetically superior Gem's pristine surfaces exhibit creamy yellow-gold luster with traces of honey-gold near the borders and delicate rose accents. Only a few tiny marks in unimportant areas establish this desirable survivor as a "mere" Gem. This worthy Gem is sure to delight the successful bidder.(#9161)

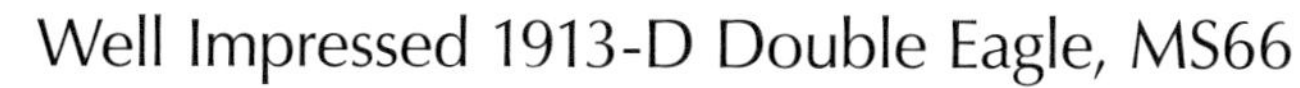

Well Impressed 1913-D Double Eagle, MS66

2306 1913-D MS66 NGC. Many 1913-D double eagles survived in European or South American bank vaults before returning to the States over the past several decades. This renders a sufficient population of near-Gems. Full Gems can be located with patience and searching, but finer examples are very elusive.

The highly lustrous surfaces of this Premium Gem display peach coloration imbued with hints of mint-green. The design elements are well impressed, including most of the panes on the Capitol building, Liberty's facial features and branch-hand fingers, and the eagle's plumage. A mark on the mid torch and another on the adjacent arm are undisturbing, but mentioned solely for pedigree purposes. Census: 8 in 66, 0 finer (11/09).(#9162)

Low-Mintage 1913-S Twenty, MS65

2307 1913-S MS65 PCGS. The 1913-S, while not the rarest Saint-Gaudens double eagle issue today, still holds considerable importance by virtue of its low mintage, just 34,000 pieces. Gem and better examples of the date are particularly elusive; PCGS has graded just 21 coins at the MS65 level and only one finer (11/09). This attractive example has a strong strike overall, with only slight softness visible at the top of the torch. The strong yellow-gold luster shows a hint of satin, and while there is a rim bruise near 6 o'clock on the reverse, abrasions are few otherwise.

From The Ralph P. Muller Collection.(#9163)

Low Mintage 1914 Saint-Gaudens Twenty, MS65

2308 1914 MS65 PCGS. CAC. The 1914 Saint-Gaudens double eagle boasts a low mintage of 95,250 pieces, and is considered a "better date" in all grades. The issue is a rarity in higher grades. David Akers reports, "Most Mint State examples grade no finer than MS-64, through which grade the 1914 is a very scarce coin. Gems are nothing short of rare." The present coin possesses extraordinary thick, frosty mint luster, unusual on a 1914. The surfaces are slightly granular, with a matte-like finish. Attractive orange-gold color predominates, except over the eagle, where there is the occasional dab of lilac. Population: 37 in 65, 3 finer (11/09).

From The Ralph P. Muller Collection.(#9164)

Appealing 1914-D Double Eagle, MS66

2309 1914-D MS66 PCGS. Mint State 1914-D twenties are common through MS64. Gems can be located with patience, but Premium Gems such as the current offering present a challenge. Higher-grade coins are virtually unobtainable. Frosty luster endows both sides, each of which displays rich orange patina splashed with lilac on the reverse. Sharply struck and revealing just a few unimportant marks. Overall, this piece possesses breathtaking eye appeal. Population: 55 in 66, 1 finer (11/09).

From The Ralph P. Muller Collection.(#9165)

Bold Gem 1915 Double Eagle Tied for Finest at PCGS

2310 1915 MS65 PCGS. The 1915 double eagle is an issue that is quite well-produced, but it is nearly always found in Mint State grades from MS60 through MS64. Gems are rare, and it is an issue unknown any finer, save for a single MS66 piece certified at NGC. PCGS has certified 35 examples in MS65, with none finer (11/09). This Gem offers generous luster with mellow orange-gold predominating, contrasting against the tinges of greenish-gold that gravitate towards the peripheries on each side. The strike is uniformly bold. A tiny copper alloy spot appears just at the eagle's beak.(#9167)

Fantastic Gem 1915 Double Eagle

2311 1915 MS65 PCGS. CAC. The outbreak of World War I and the resulting disruption of overseas trade removed much of the Mint's reason for striking double eagles, yet production actually *increased* from 1914 to 1915, going back above six figures. This increase is deceptive, however, because Philadelphia would not strike double eagles from 1916 through 1919. This Gem, tied with 33 others for finest known to PCGS (11/09), has strong design definition and bold luster. The obverse has elements of reddish-orange color, while the reverse is brighter yellow-gold. Minimally abraded and gorgeous.
From The Ralph P. Muller Collection.(#9167)

Fully Struck Gem 1915 Twenty Dollar

2312 1915 MS65 NGC. Turning the usual equation topsy-turvy, this Philadelphia Mint issue is scarcer than its mintmarked sibling of the same year, the 1915-S. Most of the 1915 Philadelphia twenties found in the marketplace are Mint State, but most are in the lower Mint State grades from MS60 to MS63. The certified populations thin considerably in MS64 and dramatically in MS65, where PCGS has certified 34 coins and this NGC-certified piece is one of only 40 so graded, with one finer (11/09). The coin is fully struck, with yellow-gold color and a light, even overlay of reddish patina. A minor scuff on the left side of the sun is the only noticeable mark.
From The Five Point Collection.(#9167)

Lot 2313

LIBERTY
1920
UNITED·STATES·OF·AMERICA
TWENTY·DOLLARS
IN·GOD·WE·TRUST

Seldom-Seen 1920-S Twenty, MS64
First Absolute and Condition Rarity in the Saint-Gaudens Series

2313 1920-S MS64 PCGS. The 1920-S is the first regular issue in the Saint-Gaudens series that is a major rarity. As with many issues in this challenging series mintage has little to do with availability, or in this case non-availability, of the 1920-S. The mintage was 558,000 pieces, but after the Gold Recall Act of 1933 almost the entire production was melted during the 1930s. Unlike most other mintmarked dates from the 1920s, the 1920-S has never returned to this country from the usual sources in Europe or Central America. Only a few circulated pieces have returned over the past 50 years, most likely coins that were released into circulation at the time of issue. From the scant documentary evidence uncovered, almost the entire mintage was bagged and held in government vaults immediately after striking. Roger Burdette recently uncovered letters between T. Louis Comparette, curator of the Philadelphia Mint's coin collection from 1905 to 1922, and George Godard, Connecticut State Librarian. Comparette made "special arrangements" to acquire two examples of each coin issued by the mints (for obverse and reverse display purposes). He acknowledged in a letter dated May 5, 1920 to Godard that his actions were "irregular." Burdette continues the story, quoting Comparette:

> " 'Herewith I am sending you a [1920] Twenty Dollar gold piece, just struck. It is for the Reserve Funds and not to be issued for general circulation, and the securing of the specimens for others than the government collection is probably irregular, so please do not let the fact become public knowledge. For others will demand specimens as soon as they learn that a few have them are out.' "

Six months later Comparette reminded Godard that the Mitchelson Collection had gotten a good 'deal' on the double eagle transaction:

> "'By the way, you and the Senator [Connecticut Senator Hall] were lucky in re the 1920 Double-eagles. But very few of them got out. All the rest are under seal along with the reserve funds, and the repeated efforts of scores to secure specimens have so far proved unavailing. I have been trying to get a specimen for the American Society in New York, but in vain. ... Sometime, undoubtedly, they will be obtainable, but nobody now can surmise when. Perhaps the next Secretary of the Treasury will find a way to be accommodating and release a bag of them for the hungry collectors.' "

Apparently that day never came for the "hungry collectors." From the estimated number of survivors, it appears that the 1920-S twenties that exist today are limited to those acquired by the few collectors who had connections with Mint personnel.

Estimates of the number known have varied widely over the years. Twenty years ago Walter Breen estimated that only eight to 12 pieces survived, a number that is clearly on the low side. We estimate that 80-100 coins exist today in all grades. NGC and PCGS have seen a total of 169 submissions, with a large number clustering in the AU58-MS63 range. An MS64 coin is usually the highest grade obtainable, and there is a precipitous drop off above that level. Probably only 15-20 coins survive in MS64, with five or six pieces in MS65 or MS66. These numbers underscore the condition rarity of the 1920-S, as well as its absolute rarity. In fact, it is ranked third in the 53-coin series in high grade rarity, trailing only the 1921 and the uncollectible 1933. In high grade rarity it outranks the legendary 1927-D, almost all of the dozen or so known examples are in mint condition.

This piece shows the typical strike softness on the Capitol building on the lower left obverse. Liberty's nose is only slightly soft, and the toes are fully brought up. The reverse design is fully struck. Few abrasions appear on this lustrous near-Gem, the most prominent a horizontal nick above Liberty's left (facing) leg and a couple of marks above and below the eagle's beak. The surfaces are nicely frosted, as often seen on 1920-S twenties, with a complement of rich reddish patina is seen over each side.

From The Ralph P. Muller Collection.(#9171)

1920-S Saint-Gaudens Double Eagle, MS64

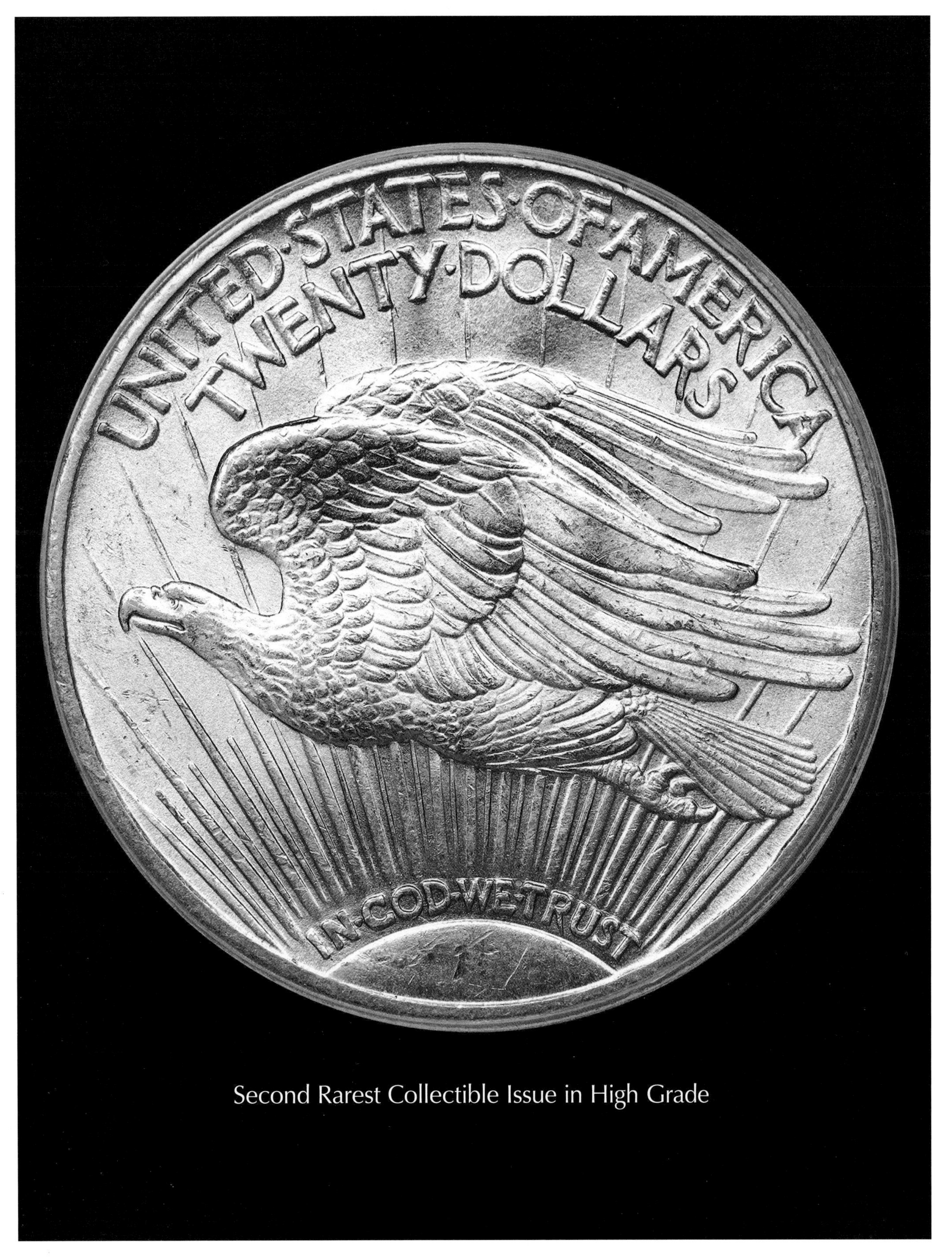

Second Rarest Collectible Issue in High Grade

1920-S Saint-Gaudens Double Eagle, MS64
Second Rarest Collectible Issue in High Grade

2314 1920-S MS64 PCGS. CAC. Ex: Brahin. The 1920-S Saint-Gaudens double eagle, with an original mintage of 558,000 pieces, is one of the outstanding rarities of the series. Most examples were apparently kept in government vaults until the 1930s, when nearly the entire mintage was melted. Noted gold specialist David Akers nicely summarized the rarity of the 1920-S in his recently published *A Handbook of 20th Century United States Gold Coins 1907-1933:*

> "The 1920-S is one of the prime rarities in the Saint-Gaudens Double Eagle series, if not in the entire 20th century U.S. gold series. In fact, it is the rarest collectible Saint-Gaudens Double Eagle after only the 1927-D, 1930-S and 1921. The 1920-S is actually rarer than the 1927-D and 1930-S in high grades. Virtually the entire mintage was destroyed during the gold recall of the 1930s—the first of several Saint-Gaudens Double Eagles from the 1920s and 1930s to suffer this fate. The majority of survivors fall somewhere in the Choice AU to MS-64 grade range. High-grade examples, of which there are very few, were almost certainly obtained at the time of issue by collectors who had close ties to Mint or other government officials."

Historically, numismatists estimated the rarity of an issue by keeping track of specimens seen at shows, auction appearances, and in dealer's advertisements. Experts were able to form an accurate impression of a coin's availability on the market at any particular time. Of course, the perceptions changed if a coin became more available through hoard or shipwreck finds. The 1920-S has never been included in such a find, and the supply of high grade coins has remained constant for decades.

In recent times, the importance of data from third party grading services has become a dominant factor in determining the overall rarity of certain issues. Unfortunately, in the case of the 1920-S, the data has been distorted by resubmissions and crossovers, and no longer reflects the true rarity of the issue in higher Mint State grades. To date, NGC has certified 13 examples in MS64, with two finer, at MS65; PCGS has graded 11 specimens in MS64, with four examples in MS65, and two coins in MS66 (10/09). To test this data, we have conducted a search of auction records to see how many coins have appeared at auction and private sale in grades MS64 and above since 1990. The resulting roster reveals that only six coins account for all appearances of the date in MS64, while two separate examples have been cataloged at the Gem level, and two specimens are known in MS66. There are also two coins reported in institutional collections, one MS64 and one MS67. The roster shows a total of seven coins in MS64, versus 24 coins certified by the grading services; two examples in MS65, versus six seen by NGC and PCGS; and the two coins in Premium Gem condition coincide exactly with the population data. It is easy to understand how the population data came to be inflated when the roster is studied for duplicate appearances of the same coin. The Reed Hawn specimen has appeared in six different auctions since 1990, and the Thaine Price coin has appeared in five. It has become common practice to resubmit such a coin to the grading services before any auction appearance, in the hopes of receiving an upgrade. In recent times, some attempt has been made to adjust the population totals when this occurs, but there was no such accounting effort in earlier days. Of course, some auction appearances may have been overlooked, as this is the first attempt to compile such a listing, and it is conceivable that a few high grade specimens have not been offered at auction in the last 20 years. Still, the disparity between the 24 coins certified in MS64 and the seven near-Gem examples that can be documented from the census is dramatic. The roster provides a compelling argument that the 1920-S is much rarer at the near-Gem level than the population data indicate.

The extraordinary near-Gem specimen presented in this lot displays bright peach-gold surfaces that are imbued with just the slightest hint of mint-green undertones. Strike can be a problem on most 1920-S double eagles, and some minor softness is noted on the Capitol building of this example. All in all, though, the design features are strongly impressed, particularly on the fingers of both hands, on the olive branch, and on the eagle's breast feathers. Both sides are well preserved, and reveal fewer handling marks than expected, suggestive of an even higher grade. Outstanding visual appeal and the high technical grade make this specimen an appropriate choice for a fine Registry Set of double eagles.

The following roster of MS64 and finer specimens has been compiled from a study of auction records and private transactions over the past two decades.

1. **MS66 PCGS.** Louis Eliasberg; The United States Gold Coin Collection (Bowers and Ruddy, 10/1982), lot 1051, not certified at the time, graded Select Brilliant Uncirculated by the cataloger; Dr. Steven Duckor; Phillip H. Morse; The Phillip H. Morse Collection (Heritage, 11/2005), lot 6641 (realized $ 517,500).
2. **MS66 PCGS.** A coin with an unknown pedigree sold by Todd Imhof of Heritage Auction Galleries to Dr. Steven Duckor in early 2006.
3. **MS65 PCGS.** Jeff Browning; The "Dallas Bank" Collection (Sotheby's/Stack's, 10/2001), lot 185, not certified at the time, graded Gem Brilliant Uncirculated by the cataloger; Pittsburgh ANA (Heritage, 8/2004), lot 7782; "Dr. EJC" PCGS Registry Set Collection; (the Akers and Bowers plate coin).
4. **MS65 PCGS.** Milwaukee ANA (Heritage, 8/2007), lot 2074, (realized $264,500).
5. **MS64 PCGS.** Reed Hawn Collection (Stack's, 10/1993), lot 1118, not certified at the time, graded Choice Brilliant Uncirculated by the cataloger; Long Beach Signature Sale (Heritage, 6/2000), lot 7702; Philadelphia ANA (Heritage, 8/2000), lot 7599; Benson Part II (Goldberg, 2/2002), lot 2271; Dallas Signature Sale (Heritage, 10/2008), lot 2486; Los Angeles ANA (Heritage, 7/2009), lot 1128.
6. **MS64 PCGS.** Dr. Thaine B. Price Collection (Akers, 5/1998), lot 100, not certified at the time, graded Very Choice Uncirculated by the cataloger; Dr. Richard Ariagno Collection (Goldberg, 5/1999), lot 895; FUN Signature Auction (Heritage,1/2003), lot 9326; San Francisco ANA (Heritage, 7/2005), lot 10428; Long Beach Signature Sale (Heritage, 9/2009), lot 1129.
7. **MS64 PCGS.** Phillip H. Morse Collection (Heritage, 11/2005), lot 6642; Pre-Long Beach Auction (Goldberg, 9/2007), lot 3523.
8. **MS64 PCGS.** FUN Signature Auction (Heritage, 1/2007), lot 3287.
9. **MS64 PCGS.** The Rarities Sale (Bowers and Merena, 10/2004), lot 940.
10. **Very Choice Uncirculated 64.** Auction '90 (Akers, 8/1990), lot 1988.

Other Known Specimens:

A. A coin in the collection of the American Numismatic Society, reported as a Superb Gem by Jeff Garrett and Ron Guth.
B. A coin in the National Numismatic Collection, Smithsonian Institution, reported to grade at least MS64 by Garrett and Guth.

From The Jay Brahin Collection.(#9171)

Lot 2315

LIBERTY
1921
UNITED STATES OF AMERICA
TWENTY DOLLARS
IN GOD WE TRUST

Near-Gem 1921 Saint-Gaudens Twenty
Second Only to the 1933 in High Grade Rarity

2315 1921 MS64 PCGS. The 1921 double eagle is one of the legendary rarities in the Saint-Gaudens series. It is often compared to the 1920-S. However, it is only comparable in the total number of pieces known of each. The 1921 differs significantly from the 1920-S because of the lack of Uncirculated survivors. The majority of 1921 twenties are in circulated grades. It is significant that the Thaine Price Collection lacked a 1921, and the Browning, Eliasberg, Amon Carter, and Floyd Starr collections all had AU coins. Clearly the challenge for the advanced collector of Saint-Gaudens twenties is not to hold out for a Gem or better example, but just to have the opportunity to acquire a coin in any grade. That said, there are a couple of extraordinary pieces known, both of which trace their origin to George Godard, who provided the Museum of Connecticut History with coins through Louis Comparette after the death of Joseph Mitchelson in 1911. Both of Godard's coins (an MS66 and MS65) were sold in 1982, and the coins were reunited in the Phillip H. Morse Collection. The MS66 brought $1,092,500 and the MS65 realized $805,000 when we sold both in November 2005. There is also an intriguing coin that is called a Roman Finish proof striking. This unusual coin traces its pedigree to Raymond T. Baker, Mint director in 1921, and was struck on the occasion of his nephew's birth.

As a high grade rarity, the 1921 is second only to the 1933. Both major services have graded a total of 154 pieces in grades that range from VF35 to MS66. We estimate that no more than 45 to 60 circulated pieces exist, plus another 55 to 70 examples in Uncirculated grades. Most of the Mint State coins cluster around MS62, but that total is a mere 34 pieces (minus obvious resubmissions). In MS63 and finer, the survivors known probably number no more than 20 pieces.

Obviously almost the entire mintage of 528,500 pieces was melted in the 1930s, a situation that does compare to the 1920-S. In both cases, the number known today has remained stable over the past 50 years with only a few (Walter Breen says five) examples recovered from European sources. The rarity of the 1921 was recognized early on. Breen writes that forgeries of the 1921 were made in Europe before 1953. Such pieces show the numerals leaning to the right and lettering that differs from genuine pieces.

In an interesting and remarkable letter first published in the June 2006 American Numismatic Rarities auction catalog, Dr. Charles W. Green writes to Louis Eliasberg in February 1947. Dr. Green had inquired of Mint officials about the availability of Saint-Gaudens twenties, realizing at an early date how rare certain issues were relative to their mintage. Mint officials told Dr. Green "the true record would be, not the number struck, but the number 'put out'; that is actually issued from the producing mints, all the rest having gone to the melt and of course very possibly some of those put out went to the melt also." He listed several rarities, among which was the 1921: "Of the 1921 Philadelphia double eagle, only 25 coins were put out. So there we have a perfect record of rarity. The rest went to the melt." It is natural to assume that with certain rarities more pieces were rescued prior to melting by Treasury Department or Mint employees. Such would seem to be the case with the 1921, with the number known at least six times larger than the number "put out."

The 1921 has brought strong prices at auction since double eagles were first collected as a series beginning in the late 1930s. Henry Morgenthau's Sale Number 399 (5/1939) had a 1921 that he termed "excessively rare" and the coin brought $260. Five years later, the 1921 in the Belden Roach Collection (Mehl, 2/1944) realized $945. At that time, Mehl stated "After making some inquiry, I found that not more than four or five specimens were known to exist." The Bell coin (Stack's, 12/1944) crossed the four-figure mark at public auction when it brought $1,125.

The 1921 is such a rare coin in Uncirculated grades that not much is known about its luster characteristics. It is generally regarded as having a satiny finish rather than a frosted surface, but this is one of the few coins that display soft mint frost. Additionally, the color is a lovely reddish-gold with a pale accent of lime-green around the margins. Striking details are usually incomplete on the high grade pieces known, and this piece follows suit, with soft definition on Liberty's nose, toes, and the center of the eagle's breast. This piece is easily identifiable by a star-shaped mark or possible die flaw in the center of Liberty's forehead. Apparently all 1921 twenties show peripheral die cracks on the reverse. With a mintage of more than half a million pieces, it is obvious that numerous die pairings were used; no single set of die cracks should fit all known pieces. This coin shows the usually seen cracks from below the eagle's beak, through the beak, and into UN. The tops of TWENTY are all connected by another crack, and an even more prominent one begins at the R in AMERICA and terminates in the eagle's tailfeathers. Perhaps most noticeable is an arc-shaped crack through the sun on the lower reverse that parallels the rim.

The opportunity to acquire a 1921 in any grade is rare. This splendid MS64 affords the advanced collector a seldom-seen chance to add this rarity to a first-rate set of Saint-Gaudens twenties.

From The Ralph P. Muller Collection.(#9172)

Shining MS65 1922-S Double Eagle

2316 1922-S MS65 NGC. As a whole, the 1922-S double eagle issue rates as "formerly rare," once nearly inaccessible but now much more readily collectible thanks to repatriation. Mostly Choice or lesser-grade pieces have returned to U.S. ownership, however, leaving Gem and better coins conditionally rare. This MS65 coin is brightly lustrous with yellow and orange hues that alternate at various angles. Light toning over each side clearly suggests long-term storage. Minimally abraded save for shallow flaws at the left obverse field and a curving abrasion on the eagle's wing. Census: 12 in 65, 3 finer (11/09).

From The Ralph P. Muller Collection.(#9174)

Frosty MS67 1923-D Double Eagle

2317 1923-D MS67 PCGS. The 1923-D Saint-Gaudens issue is widely renowned for its remarkably high quality. The usual production criteria for high-grade 1923-Ds include surfaces showing bountiful luster and attractive color, a strike that is uniformly bold, a paucity of marks and that most essential ingredient, eye appeal. The present Superb Gem typifies why 1923-Ds are the ultimate type coin. Thick, frosted mint luster abounds throughout. The surfaces offer great reddish color with a tinge of lilac around the margin on the obverse. The strike is sharp, and there are no mentionable distractions; quite the contrary, the eye appeal is as about as fine as can be imagined. Population: 59 in 67, 0 finer (11/09).

From The Five Point Collection.(#9176)

Shining Superb Gem 1924 Double Eagle

2318 1924 MS67 PCGS. CAC. As a PCGS-graded coin, this Superb Gem 1924 double eagle is of definite interest to Registry enthusiasts as well as high-end type collectors, and the old green label holder gives it added cachet among certain circles. No simple numeric grade, however, can communicate this coin's beauty. Powerfully lustrous fields are primarily sun-yellow with pale blue-silver peripheral overtones in arcs and dots along the obverse rim and also at the bottom of the reverse. Strong striking quality overall, with only slight weakness on the torch and hand, and fantastic surface preservation. PCGS has certified just one coin as numerically finer (11/09). (#9177)

LIBERTY
1924
D
UNITED·STATES·OF·AMERICA
TWENTY·DOLLARS
IN·GOD·WE·TRUST

1924-D Saint-Gaudens Double Eagle Rarity, MS65
Blazing Mint Luster

2319 1924-D MS65 PCGS. CAC. Ex: Brahin. One keen market participant calls this amazing Gem "a real monster" and stated that "it is better than 90% of the common dates I see in MS66." Our Permanent Auction Archives record three MS66 PCGS coins, seven MS65 PCGS examples, and six MS65 NGC pieces. Those 16 auction appearances include just 10 different coins. All three MS66 appearances are for a single coin, the exceptional piece from the Amon Carter Collection. The Brahin specimen that is offered here is nearly the equal of that MS66 coin, and it is clearly finer than the nine different MS65 pieces that have made 13 appearances in our past auctions. The typical 1924-D twenty has heavily abraded surfaces, and the appearance of an MS64 with smooth surfaces would be enough to coin the collector's attention. But what if the coin was a Gem MS65? Such a coin would go far beyond the typical collector's experience, and it would become a landmark event when it crosses the auction block. That is what we expect for the present piece.

Like most branch mint issues from the 1920s, the 1924-D Saint-Gaudens double eagle was a rare coin in the 1940s, when collecting double eagles first became popular in this country. Most of the copious mintage of over 3 million pieces was held in Treasury vaults and subsequently melted in the late 1930s. Shortly thereafter, the date began to turn up in auction catalogs, such as the piece in J.C. Morgenthau's May 1939 sale, lot 552, "1924 D Uncirculated and very scarce." The coin realized $73, a strong price in the 1930s for a coin that could have been purchased from the Treasury Department at face value until 1933. Fortunately, a few bags escaped the Gold Recall and later surfaced in foreign banks. In the second edition of *A Handbook of 20th Century United States Gold Coins 1907-1933,* David Akers explains further developments in the 1924-D story:

> "Prior to the mid-1950s, the 1924-D was considered to be an extremely rare issue. The subsequent discovery of several small hoards, however, permanently altered the overall rarity ranking of this issue. Today, the 1924-D is only a median rarity in the Saint-Gaudens Double Eagle series. Since most of the hoard coins are of low quality, however, the 1924-D remains scarce in MS64 and very rare at or above the MS65 grade level."

Akers estimates a surviving population of 12-15 examples at the Gem level, with two or three specimens in higher grades. Population data from third party grading services corresponds closely with this estimate. To date, NGC has certified nine examples in MS65, with a single finer coin; while PCGS has graded nine specimens at the Gem level, with two finer (10/09). Of course, that population data undoubtedly includes resubmissions.

In the mid-twenties, the Denver and San Francisco Mints followed a policy of poor production resulting from extended die life, coupled with low quality control. The majority of survivors show extreme die wear near the borders. Jeff Garrett and Ron Guth write in their *Encyclopedia of U.S. Gold Coins 1795-1833* that "a coin grading MS-64 is about as nice as a collector can hope to secure."

The outstanding characteristic of the present coin is its blazing mint luster. The vibrant surfaces are a bright yellow-gold at the centers, with a subtle reddish patina at the margins. Coupled with a sharp strike, the overwhelming luster gives this coin the visual appeal of a Premium Gem. A small mark on Liberty's face is all that prevents a higher grade. Unlike most examples, this piece has crisp peripheral definition. This piece is a bold exception to that rule. We believe that this stunning Gem is the fourth or fifth finest 1924-D Saint-Gaudens double eagle in the Census listing of the best coins of the issue that survive today.
From The Jay Brahin Collection.(#9178)

Conditionally Challenging 1924-D Twenty, MS65

2320 1924-D MS65 NGC. The 1924-D double eagle is among many Saint-Gaudens double eagle issues whose perception of rarity has gradually shifted over the decades. In this regard it has much in common with other former rarities, including 1924-S, 1926-D, 1926-S, and 1927-S.

The 1924-D double eagle at one time was considered a premier rarity. As often seen, the determining factor was not so much mintage as meltage, the latter determined by how many were actually shipped overseas and available for later repatriation. David Akers, in his useful 20th century gold coin *Handbook,* writes concerning the 1924-D:

> "From an overall rarity standpoint, the 1924-D is nearly identical in all respects to the 1924-S and 1926-S, although it is much rarer than the 1926-S in high grades. Prior to the mid-1950s, the 1924-D was considered to be an extremely rare issue. The subsequent discovery of several small hoards, however, permanently altered the overall rarity ranking of this issue. Today, the 1924-D is only a median rarity in the Saint-Gaudens Double Eagle series. Since most of the hoard coins are of low quality, however, the 1924-D remains scarce in MS-64 and very rare at or above the MS-65 grade level."

The present Gem 1924-D, while thus a respectable but unremarkable rarity overall in the Saint-Gaudens series compared to several other issues, is conditionally much more elusive at the MS65 level than some of the aforementioned dates. We made a comparison of the combined population data from NGC and PCGS (10/09) for the 1924-D and 1926-S that bears out Akers' hypothesis:

1924-D Combined Totals. MS63-246, MS64-258, *MS65-18, MS66-3.*
1926-S Combined Totals. MS63-330, MS64-582, *MS65-48, MS66-5.*

We have italicized the relative totals in Gem or finer grades for easier reference, but it is clear that the 1924-D is more elusive than the 1926-S in Gem or higher by a factor of nearly 3 to 1, irrespective of duplicates.

More than a century after the introduction of the Saint-Gaudens series and with the current high prices for gold bullion and rare gold coins, it seems almost certain that the relative rarity rankings for the series, which were largely established (except for the 1933) by the 1950s-1960s, are likely to remain little changed as the series moves into a new century.

The striking details on 1924-D twenties is often weak. This piece shows some irregularity in that regard, with the Capitol building weak, as is the nose of Liberty. However, Liberty's toes and all the eagle's plumage is fully brought up. The surfaces display the usual frosted mint luster one expects for this issue, and each side has an even layer of reddish patina. Abrasions are slight, and none are worthy of individual mention.

From The Ralph P. Muller Collection.(#9178)

1924-S Saint-Gaudens Double Eagle, MS64
Only 259,000 Examples Released

2321 1924-S MS64 PCGS. CAC. A large mintage of 2.9 million Saint-Gaudens double eagles was achieved by the San Francisco Mint in 1924, but only 259,000 examples were officially released. Most of the coins released were used in foreign trade. The balance of the mintage was melted and stored as ingots in Fort Knox after the Gold Recall of 1933.

The issue was extremely rare in the 1940s, and the 1924-S was regarded as the rarest date of the series. In the Dr. Charles W. Green Collection (B. Max Mehl, 4/1949), lot 879, the cataloger reported, "To the best of my knowledge, only three specimens are known to exist." In the 1950s and 1960s, numerous examples used in foreign trade were discovered in European banks, and the 1924-S was demoted from the "rarest of the rare" to the scarce category. Most examples recovered in recent decades were in MS63 and lower grades. Near-Gem and finer examples are still challenging today.

The present coin exhibits extraordinary mint luster, with intermingled rose and lilac color on each side. The surfaces are lightly abraded for the grade. Overall visual appeal is strong, as attested by the CAC sticker. Population: 95 in 64, 3 finer (11/09).
From The Ralph P. Muller Collection.(#9179)

Elusive Gem 1925-D Saint-Gaudens Twenty
Popular Condition Rarity

2322 1925-D MS65 PCGS. The 1925-D Saint-Gaudens double eagle is an elusive issue in all grades today, in spite of its large original mintage of 2.9 million pieces. In *A Guide Book of Double Eagle Gold Coins,* Q. David Bowers estimates a surviving population of 500 to 800 examples in Mint State, with a group of 50 to 80 specimens in circulated grades. The contradiction between the sizeable production figure and the meager supply available today is a familiar story with later dates in the Saint-Gaudens series. During the 1930s and 1940s the contrast was even more dramatic. David Akers explains the situation in the Thaine B. Price Collection (Akers, 5/1998), lot 109:

> "The 1925-D is another issue that, at one time, was widely regarded to be a major rarity in any condition. It was considered to be more rare than the 1922-S, 1924-D and 1925-S, not to mention such now famous rarities as 1920-S, 1929, 1931 and 1932. The 1950's, however, brought significant changes to the relative rarity rankings of Saint-Gaudens Double Eagles since many formerly rare issues were discovered in European banks. The 1925-D was one of those issues, and although large hoards of the 1925-D were never discovered, several small groups were uncovered over the years amounting to perhaps several hundred pieces total."

Bowers believes the bulk of the 1925-D mintage was stored in Treasury vaults as backing for paper money, or in U.S. banks as reserves, with only a few thousand specimens exported to foreign banks. The coins stored in domestic banks and Treasury depositories were eventually melted, after the Gold Recall of 1933. Most examples known today were exported, and returned to this country after a lengthy hiatus. Today, Jeff Garrett and Ron Guth consider the 1925-D the 12th rarest date in the 54-coin series.

While its relative rarity versus other issues in the Saint-Gaudens series has varied over the years, the status of the 1925-D as a prime condition rarity has never been in doubt. NGC has certified only seven examples at the Gem level, with a single coin finer, at MS66; PCGS has graded four specimens at the MS65 level, with two finer, at MS66 (10/09).

Collecting large denomination gold coins did not become popular in the United States until the late 1930s. The major motivation for collecting double eagles was the realization by collectors, such as Louis Eliasberg and Charles Green, that a collection of gold coins was a legal opportunity for American citizens to own gold. Unfortunately, few collectors were astute enough to take advantage of the loophole before the window of opportunity closed. In the Norweb Collection (Stack's, 11/2006), lot 1475, Bowers relates:

> "In 1932 the Treasury Department put out a list of coins available for face value, including many older dates. There were 10 double eagles on the list. The lineup is significant as it likely indicates that they were being held as reserves in the Treasury Building, Washington, as backing for Gold Certificates. The 10 double eagles on the list: 25-D $20, 1925-S $20, 1926-D $20, 1926-S $20, 1927-D $20, 1927-S $20, 1930-S $20, 1931 $20, 1931-D $20, 1932 $20. Anyone caring to send $200 to the Treasury in 1932 for one of each would have received coins that today would be worth over $3,000,000, not bad as an investment!"

It is worth noting, all the dates on the Treasury list are seldom encountered today.

The present coin is a magnificent specimen, with richly frosted surfaces and a deep, even, reddish patina on both sides. The reverse surfaces are highlighted by pronounced shades of lilac on the eagle's wings. The strike is sharp, but not quite full, as slight softness is noted on Liberty's nose and toes. Handling marks are minimal, with only a short, horizontal mark on the bent (right facing) leg discernable to the naked eye. Overall eye appeal is outstanding. The combination of exquisite visual appeal and high technical grade make this coin a candidate for the finest Registry Set.
From The Ralph P. Muller Collection.(#9181)

1925-S Saint-Gaudens Double Eagle, MS63

2323 1925-S MS63 PCGS. For many later issues in the Saint-Gaudens double eagle series, there is simply no relationship between the size of the original mintage and the availability of the coins today. The 1925-S is a case in point. In the Thaine B. Price Collection (Akers, 5/1998), lot 110, David Akers expounds:

> "Despite its extremely high mintage of 3,776,500 pieces (third highest mintage of the series after only the ultra-common 1924 and 1928) the 1925-S is one of the major rarities in the series and has long been regarded as such.—Also, unlike most of the other rare mintmarked issues of the 1920's, the 1925-S is actually seen more often in high grade circulated condition than it is in mint state condition, meaning that the 1925-S Double Eagles were put into circulation and not just stored as gold reserves the way most other $20 issues were."

Akers' statement about the unusual availability of circulated examples is explained by the research of Dr. Charles Green, which shows that 454,700 1925-S double eagles were actually released into circulation, while the balance of the large mintage was melted after the Gold Recall of 1933. In *A Guide Book of Double Eagle Gold Coins,* Q. David Bowers estimates a surviving population of 600 to 1,000 examples of the date in all grades today.

The present coin is an attractive specimen, with thick, frosted mint luster and even orange-gold color throughout. A few small abrasions in the fields and on Liberty's face are consistent with the grade. Population: 77 in 63, 25 finer (11/09).
From The Ralph P. Muller Collection.(#9182)

Select Mint State 1925-S Double Eagle

2324 1925-S MS63 PCGS. The 1925-S double eagle demonstrates amply why the original mintages in this widely collected series have nothing to do with their ultimate rarity. Despite an original mintage approaching 4 million pieces, the issue is elusive in MS63 or finer grades. In his *Guide Book of Double Eagle Gold Coins,* Q. David Bowers comments, "The 1925-S is a sleeper. The large mintage belies the rarity of this coin. The population of 1925-S double eagles is about evenly divided between high grade worn pieces and lower level Mint State examples, although some notable gems exist, some of which appeared on the market in the late 1980s."

One of the many wonderful attributes of the Garrett-Guth *Gold Encyclopedia* (this is not a commercial, but every serious gold collector/investor owes it to him/herself to acquire a copy) is the auction analysis from 1991 through 2005 for every gold issue. During that time, according to the authors, 126 pieces of the 1925-S changed hands, with an average grade of 57.8. The population summary shows 513 pieces graded (between NGC, PCGS, and ANACS), with an average grade of 59.8.

The current example, graded MS63 by PCGS, shows a population of 77 pieces, with 25 finer, while NGC shows 34 MS63 examples, with 17 coins graded finer (11/09). This specimen offers fine-grained, mattelike surfaces that are delectably colored in intense hues of orange-gold. Excellent luster radiates from each side, and this coin shows little of the strike weakness that sometime afflicts this issue near the lower obverse border. The strike is a bit blunt on Liberty's head, however, and a few light abrasions on her right (facing) leg and well hidden in other places confirm the grade. Two fine, light die cracks are seen on the reverse, both running through the eagle's head. This is an extremely appealing coin, one that would cost a great deal more at the next Uncirculated level.(#9182)

LIBERTY
1925
UNITED·STATES·OF·AMERICA
TWENTY·DOLLARS
IN·GOD·WE·TRUST

1925-S Saint-Gaudens Double Eagle, MS65
Akers 'Significant Example'
Very Rare in Gem

2325 1925-S MS65 PCGS. CAC. Ex: Brahin. Called a "sleeper" by Q. David Bowers, the 1925-S Saint-Gaudens double eagle is definitely an underrated coin today. The large mintage of nearly 3.8 million pieces influences the thinking of potential buyers, but in reality, the production total is meaningless when evaluating the coin's availability. Experts estimate a surviving Mint State population of 275-330 pieces, with a like number extant in circulated grades. Most examples seen are in the AU55 to AU58 range, and the issue is extremely rare at the Gem level. In *A Handbook of 20th Century United States Gold Coins 1907-1933,* David Akers comments:

> "Scarce-to-rare in all grades, the 1925-S is one of the leading condition rarities in the Saint-Gaudens Double Eagle series. Even MS-64s are elusive, and the combined population of Gems and Superb Gems is fewer than 10 coins. The 1925-S is the only mintmarked Double Eagle from the 1920s that is easier to locate in circulated condition than Mint State."

Population data from the leading grading services supports Akers' evaluation of the 1925-S as a prime condition rarity. Currently, NGC has certified only two examples in MS65, with two higher; while PCGS has graded two specimens at the Gem level, with three higher (10/09).

As Akers mentioned, the 1925-S is the only branch-mint issue of the era that is frequently encountered in circulated grades. A significant effort must have been made to circulate the coins at their time of issue, in contrast to the other dates of the period, which were stored in Treasury vaults as backing for U.S. currency. In 1947, Dr. Charles Green conducted research in mint records which revealed that 454,700 double eagles were officially released by the San Francisco Mint in 1925. The unusually high number of circulated 1925-S double eagles are evidence of this release. A small number of coins was used in international trade, and preserved in European banks. These European holdings surfaced in later years to provide the bulk of the 1925-S population in lower Uncirculated grades we know today. The few Gem or finer specimens were doubtlessly purchased by collectors directly from the San Francisco Mint and carefully preserved over the following decades. The great majority of the Mintage, the third largest of the series, was destroyed after the Gold Recall of 1933.

A diligent search of auction records over the last 15 years reveals only eight occasions when a 1925-S was offered in MS65 or better condition by the major auction firms. Outstanding examples include the incredible PCGS graded MS68 Norweb/Price coin, which sold for $209,000 back in 1998, and the PCGS MS67 Morse example (Heritage, 11/2005), lot 6681, which realized $287,500. The finest known Norweb/Price example probably traces its origins back to King Farouk's collection. Included in lot 185 of The Palace Collections of Egypt (Sotheby's, 2/1954) were 17 Saint-Gaudens double eagles, probably the most valuable group of twenties ever offered in a single lot. The dates included the 1930-S, 1931, 1931-D, 1932, and 1933, as well as the 1925-S, and other dates from the 1920s. Of course, the 1933 was withdrawn before the sale, surfacing again in 2003 when it sold for the all-time record price of $7.5 million. The lot in the Farouk sale was knocked down to David Spink, who was acting as an agent of Mrs. Norweb at the sale.

This highly lustrous representative is a magnificent example of the issue. The present coin stands out among the extremely small number of Gem Mint State survivors, being especially well struck and without the often-seen peripheral die cracks. One curving die break is noted from the eagle's wing down through its head, and into the field below. Lovely, subtle colors accent the smooth surfaces. Pale reddish-gold centers are highlighted with a touch of lilac at the margins. Surface marks are minimal, and the overall eye appeal is simply outstanding. The coin offered here is listed as the number five specimen in David Akers' census of Significant Examples.

Ex: The Phillip H. Morse Collection of Saint-Gaudens Coinage (Heritage, 11/2005), lot 6682.

From The Jay Brahin Collection.(#9182)

Satiny MS63 1926-D Twenty

2326 1926-D MS63 PCGS. The 1926-D is a very elusive issue in the Saint-Gaudens series, and the appearance of three high grade examples in this auction is certainly atypical. Even though 481,000 pieces were minted, most were apparently melted in the 1930s with a few dozen ending up in European banks. The coins from European sources typically are lower grade Uncs, the average coin being no better than MS61-62. PCGS has certified 48 pieces in MS63 with only 24 finer (11/09). This is pleasing example that is well defined throughout with only a few small marks scattered about. Light reddish color is noted and the surfaces display attractive satiny mint luster.(#9184)

1926-D Saint Gaudens Double Eagle, MS64 Important Condition Rarity

2327 1926-D MS64 PCGS. CAC. The 1926-D Saint-Gaudens double eagle has a storied past. In the mid-1940s the issue was considered one of the least available dates in the series, ahead of such 20th century rarities as the 1927-D and the Ultra High Relief. Its status as the "rarest of the rare" was shared by only the 1924-S and the 1926-S. The discovery of small numbers of key-date double eagles in European banks in the 1950s changed the relative rarity rankings of all the key issues. Today the 1926-D is regarded as a rare date, but it no longer challenges the 1927-D or 1933 for top honors in absolute rarity. However, as a condition rarity, it remains a top contender. In the Thaine B. Price Collection (Akers, 5/1998), lot 112, David Akers called the 1926-D "one of the premier condition rarities of the Saint-Gaudens Double Eagle series." Akers went on to report:

> "The 'World's Greatest Collection' sale in 1946 represented the very first offering of this rare issue at public auction and the Dr. Charles W. Green sale conducted by B. Max Mehl in 1949 was the second. The Menjou sale in 1950 was only the third time that the 1926-D had ever been sold publicly. At the time of those three sales, the 1926-D was generally regarded as the ultimate rarity in the Saint-Gaudens series along with the 1924-S and 1926-S. The discovery in the intervening years of some rather low quality Uncirculated specimens has dimmed the fame of the 1926-D to a degree, but its status as a great condition rarity remains unchallenged and unsurpassed among the issues of this popular series."

Population data from the leading grading services supports Akers' assessment of the 1926-D as a prime condition rarity. At the near-Gem level, the issue is quite rare. NGC has certified only nine coins in MS64, with none finer; while PCGS has graded 19 examples at the near-Gem level, with five finer (11/09).

The present coin is a delightful specimen, with pleasing orange-gold surfaces highlighted by hints of lilac on the reverse center. The 1926-D is often seen with extensive weakness on the peripheral design elements, but the coin offered here exhibits only slight softness on the Capitol and some of the stars. The surfaces radiate rich satiny luster. A few marks above the eagle's head and to the left of the tail feathers, and a short horizontal mark across Liberty's head limit the grade.

From The Ralph P. Muller Collection.(#9184)

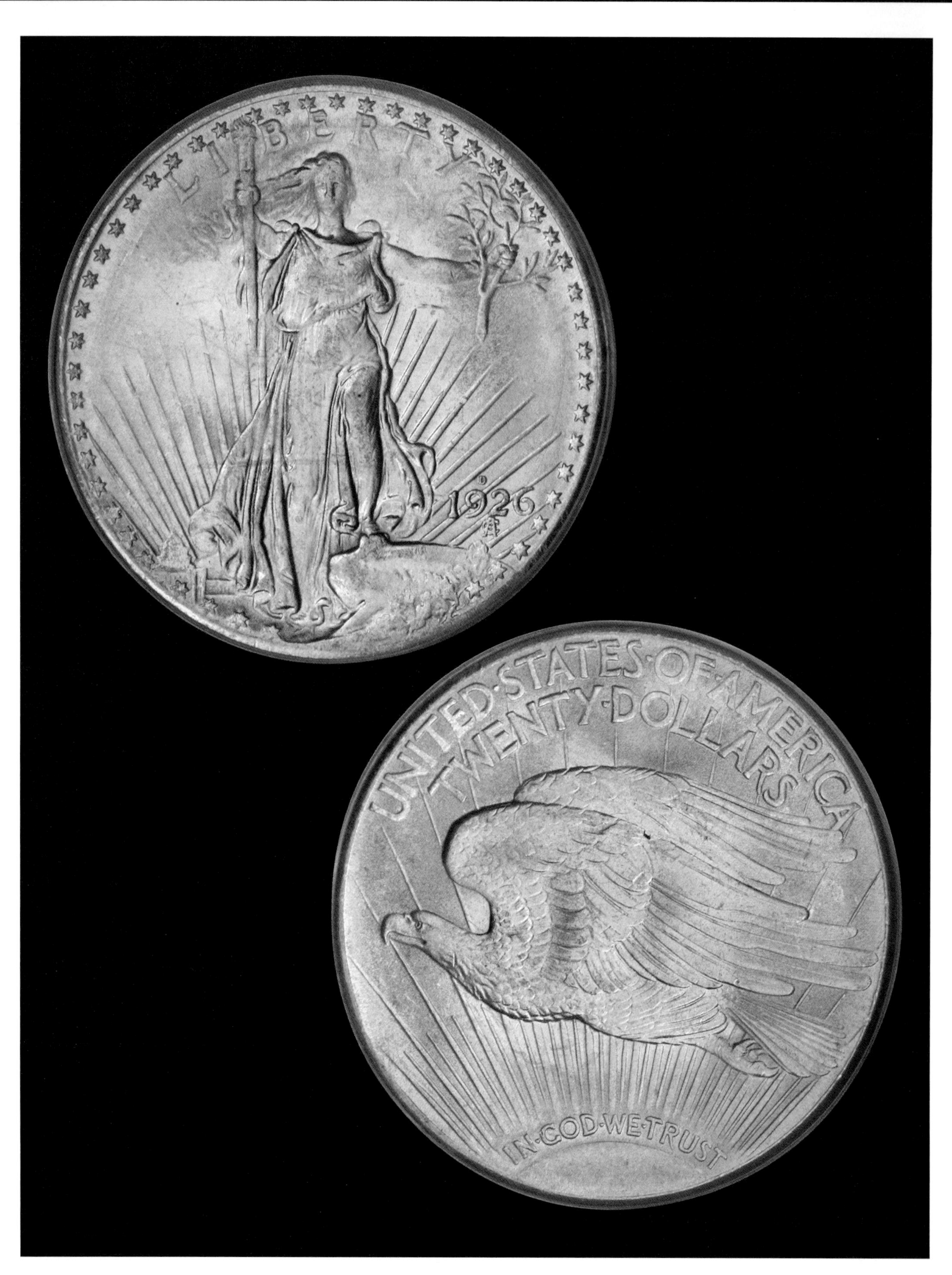
LIBERTY
1926
D
UNITED·STATES·OF·AMERICA
TWENTY·DOLLARS
IN·GOD·WE·TRUST

1926-D Saint-Gaudens Double Eagle, MS65
Premier Condition Rarity

2328 1926-D MS65 PCGS. CAC. Ex: Brahin. "The 1926-D is one of the rarest and most underrated issues in the series," writes David Akers in *A Handbook of 20th Century United States Gold Coins 1907-1933.* The date is a premier condition rarity in the Saint-Gaudens series, and the present coin is a magnificent representative. In terms of overall rarity, Akers rates the 1926-D favorably with the 1925-S. He continues:

> " Until the 1950s, in fact, the 1926-D was thought to be rarer than the legendary 1927-D. While a few pieces have turned up in foreign banks since then, there has never been a find that even approaches the status of a hoard in terms of size or significance. When offered in today's market, which is not often, the 1926-D almost always grades somewhere in the MS-60 to MS-63 range. A full MS-64 is a very rare coin, while Gems are encountered only once in a very long while. In fact, there are only five-to-seven examples surviving that grade MS-65 or finer, and none of these pieces are Superb Gems."

Data from third party grading services supports Akers assessment of the rarity of the 1926-D in high grades. Currently, PCGS has certified three MS65 examples and two MS66 coins; NGC has yet to see any Gem or finer specimens (10/09). It is also noteworthy in this regard that the 1926-D has, to the best of our knowledge, made only eight appearances in MS65 or better grades through the major auction firms in the last 15 or so years. The most prominent of these is the PCGS graded MS66 Morse specimen, which realized $345,000 when we offered it in November 2005. The finest known example may be a specimen in the Smithsonian, which Jeff Garrett and Ron Guth report is a Superb Gem.

The Denver Mint coined 481,000 double eagles in 1926, a smallish mintage for the series, but certainly not indicative of the coin's rarity today. Like many other mintmarked issues of the 1920s, the 1926-D was primarily used to back U.S. currency, and most of the mintage was held in reserve in Treasury vaults or domestic banks. After the Gold Recall of 1933, the great majority of the mintage was melted and stored as ingots at Fort Knox. Only a handful of specimens were released into circulation domestically, and only 30-45 coins are known today in circulated grades. A few bags were probably used in foreign trade, and these examples found refuge in foreign banks during the great Recall. Almost all specimens known today in lower Uncirculated grades, perhaps 175-200 examples, are from these European holdings. Fortunately, a few Gem specimens were purchased directly from the Mint and preserved by dedicated collectors to provide the available population of a half dozen or so high grade coins known today.

The 1926-D did not appear at auction until the mid-1940s. Probably the first appearance was in the World's Greatest Collection (Numismatic Gallery, 1/1946), lot 1044, where it realized $1,300. The coin went on to even greater heights in its next appearance, as lot 916 of the Dr. Charles W. Green Collection (B. Max Mehl, 4/1949), where it realized $2,500. The Green auction was a breakthrough in double eagle collecting, and the number of collectors pursuing the big gold coins probably at least doubled after this sale. The 1926-D was definitely in the front rank of American rarities at the time, and was considered by most to be the rarest Saint-Gaudens double eagle. Fortunately for present day collectors, small numbers of 1926-D double eagles began to turn up in the early 1950s from the European sources alluded to before. By the time of the Adolphe Menjou Collection (Numismatic Gallery, 6/1950), the effect of the European finds began to be felt. The catalogers still touted the issue as a great rarity, but the price realized declined to $2,000. This trend has continued in recent times, with the result that the 1926-D has become an underrated coin in the current market. Garrett and Guth rate the 1926-D as the 10th rarest date in the 54 coin series today.

The Gem example presented here displays dazzling luster that radiates from satiny peach and yellow-gold surfaces, tinged with traces of emerald and reddish-gold at the margins. A sharp strike occurs on the design elements, save for the usual softness in the Capitol dome. A die ejection mark in the upper left obverse border is seen to some degree on several higher grade 1926-D twenties. In addition to the Morse MS66 coin, we have only handled three MS65 coins in our past sales, including this piece from the Kutasi Collection. This is a highly attractive and appealing Gem that easily ranks in the Condition Census of all 1926-D twenties.

Ex: Charlotte Collection (Stack's, 3/1991), lot 1215; later, Kutasi Collection (Heritage, 1/2007), lot 3300; Heritage (5/2007), lot 2803.

From The Jay Brahin Collection.(#9184)

Elusive Gem 1926-S Double Eagle

2329 1926-S MS65 PCGS. The 1926-S is among several mint-marked Saint-Gaudens issues—1924-S, 1925-D, 1926-D, 1927-S—that were once considered among the rarest in the series. Today those issues are still scarce, but more available than formerly due to hoard discoveries and repatriations of overseas caches.

In the case of the 1926-S, however, Gems are still quite rare. PCGS has certified 28 in MS65 (less duplicates, as always), with only three pieces finer (11/09). The present Gem offers rolling, thick mint luster. Most of the patina is an even orange-gold, with deeper reddish patina on the obverse surrounding a center of lilac. The strike is uniformly sharp, save for some bluntness on Liberty's toes. Both sides are clean and lack obvious marks.

From The Five Point Collection.(#9185)

One of the Finest Known 1926-S Twenties, MS66

2330 1926-S MS66 PCGS. The 1926-S was considered at one time to be one of the Big Three in the Saint-Gaudens series of double eagles, along with 1924-S and 1926-D. It outranked such luminaries as the 1920-S, 1930-S, and even the 1927-D. To underscore the rarity of this issue, Max Mehl stated in his mail bid sale of the Dr. Green Collection in 1949 that he believed only three pieces were known. Bidders in that sale drove the price of Green's 1926-S to $1,525—more than three times what the 1930-S brought ($450) and more than twice what his 1927-D realized ($630). Akers notes that in the Menjou Sale (1950), the 1926-S "was conspicuous by its absence; it was the only late date Saint-Gaudens Double Eagle other than the 1927-D that was missing from that famous sale."

Then in the 1950s, small quantities of 1926-S twenties began to turn up in Europe. Over the next 20 years the status of the '26-S plummeted from "unobtainable" to "very scarce." Today it is considered a medium rarity among the other mintmarked Saints from the mid-1920s. Almost all known 1926-S double eagles are in mint condition, but they are heavily concentrated in the MS62-64 grade range. At the Gem level, the '26-S retains much of its former glory with fewer than two dozen pieces known today and Gems regularly bring $20,000-25,000 when offered at public auction. The highest price paid (to date) for this date is the PCGS MS66 coin in the Thaine Price Collection (1998), a fabulous coin that brought an astonishing $77,000.

Again, as with the 1924-S and 1925-S, the 1926-S is often seen with die cracks, an indication that the dies were used long after they should have been retired. Die bulging is also sometimes seen around the rim, giving the peripheral stars a raised and connected appearance. The striking definition is usually quite strong, and a minority of survivors show the "beveled" rims from previous years. Mint luster varies from strongly frosted to satiny, and coloration is usually medium yellow-gold to green-gold. This particular coin shows many of those traits, including the beveled rim and occasional peripheral die cracks. However, die bulging is not noted. The mint luster is especially pronounced and frosted, with an intermingling of reddish-gold and lilac on each side. The striking details are strong throughout. This is one of the finest 1926-S twenties offered at auction in recent years. Population: 3 in 66, 0 finer (11/09).

From The Ralph P. Muller Collection.(#9185)

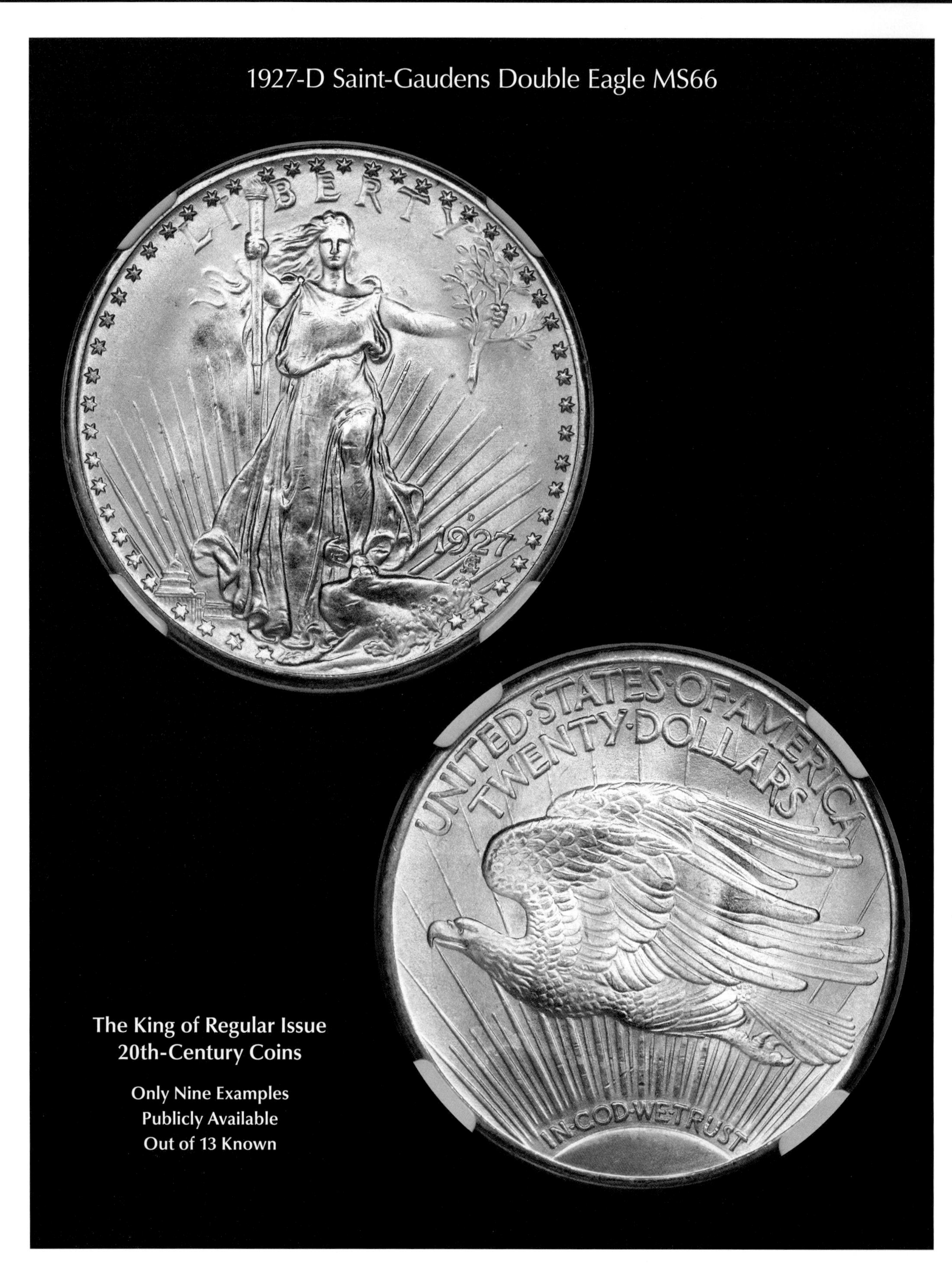
1927-D Saint-Gaudens Double Eagle MS66
LIBERTY
1927
UNITED·STATES·OF·AMERICA
TWENTY·DOLLARS
IN·GOD·WE·TRUST
The King of Regular Issue
20th-Century Coins
Only Nine Examples
Publicly Available
Out of 13 Known

2331 1927-D MS66 PCGS. Heritage is excited and privileged to offer an example of the 1927-D Saint-Gaudens double eagle, the most elusive regular-issue U.S. coin of the 20th century. This specimen is certified MS66 by PCGS, one of five so graded. PCGS has graded eight pieces from MS63 to a single MS67, placing this coin in a tie for second-finest and comfortably at the high end of the Condition Census (11/09). Of the 13 total coins certified at both services, four or five likely represent duplications or crossovers from one service to the other. Based on the detailed pedigree research and previously unpublished photos that we present below, we can document a maximum of 13 specimens today, of which only nine coins (and possibly as few as seven) are publicly held and available–at least theoretically–in the numismatic marketplace. The Smithsonian Institution possesses three examples that are presumed off the market forever; another has reposed in the Connecticut State Library's Museum of Connecticut History since its acquisition directly from the Denver Mint in 1927.

The King of 20th-Century Regular Issues

The Morse specimen illustrates the 1927-D double eagle entry in *The Coinage of Augustus Saint-Gaudens*.

The 1927-D double eagle has earned a longstanding and well-deserved reputation as the rarest regular-issue U.S. coin–gold or otherwise–of the 20th century, although it was the late 1940s-early 1950s before that perception was generally acknowledged. Examples of the 1927-D double eagles have been responsible for many record-shattering performances in the decades after they first appeared in the numismatic spotlight during the 1940s, in the process gaining recognition as legendary rarities and dethroning numerous other issues.

Heritage has been privileged to offer three different examples at auction over the past 15 years. The MS67 PCGS specimen from the Phillip H. Morse Collection of Saint-Gaudens Coinage brought $1,897,500 when we offered it in our Dallas Signature Auction (11/2005, lot 6697). A couple of years ago, that price was the fourth all-time highest paid for a U.S. coin at public auction, behind the famous 1933 Saint-Gaudens twenty, the Childs 1804 Original silver dollar, and a 1907 Ultra High Relief, Lettered Edge double eagle, PR69 PCGS, also from the Morse Collection.

The price paid for the Morse 1927-D still holds the number 7 spot of the Top 250 Coin Prices as recorded in the current (2010) *Guide Book;* the crucial distinction between the two rankings is "U.S. coins," since the two 1787 Brasher doubloons in the *Guide Book*, numbers 4 and 6, are technically not U.S. coins but pre-Federal issues. (Omitting those coins, the Morse 1927-D would rank number 5 in the *Guide Book*.) The appearances of the Queller Collection 1804 Original silver dollar which we handled in our Central States Signature Auction (4/2008, lot 2089), also bumped the Morse Collection 1927-D down a notch. The price paid for the Morse Collection 1927-D remains the sixth-highest price ever attained in a Heritage auction.

A Gem 1927-D certified by NGC, from The Delbert McDougal Set of $20 Saint-Gaudens Coins, brought another record price of $1,322,500 in our FUN Signature Auction (1/2006, lot 3624). That coin holds the current number 22 all-time price record in the 2010 *Guide Book* (tied with numbers 21 and 23).

George Godard and The Connecticut State Library

Connecticut State Library

George Seymour Godard (1865-1936) was a Connecticut blueblood whose family had lived in Granby, Connecticut, for nine generations at the time of his birth. He attended Wesleyan University and obtained a Bachelor of Divinity degree from Yale in 1895. By 1900 he held the post of Connecticut State Librarian, which he would occupy until his death. He was responsible among other duties for curating the magnificent currency, coin, and medals collection of Joseph C. Mitchelson, whose bequest to the Connecticut State Library in 1911–valued then at $70,000–made it the second most important collection in the United States, behind only the National Numismatic Collection. The collection, now housed in the Museum of Connecticut History, has continued to grow over the years and includes many remarkable, rare, and unique specimens. The collection spans the era from the 17th century to the present and includes such items as the 1737-39 Higley coppers, more than 200 varieties of Connecticut coppers, and an MCMVII proof Ultra High Relief double eagle.

Godard was so diligent at preserving state records that he earned the nickname "Preservation Godard" for his efforts. Godard took up the task of keeping the Connecticut State Library's numismatic collections up-to-date after the Mitchelson bequest, endeavoring to obtain specimens of each current year's coins. In so doing he occasionally relied on T. Louis Comparette, curator of the Philadelphia Mint's numismatic collection from 1905 until his death in 1922. Both Comparette and Godard had the custom of acquiring two specimens of desired issues for their museum collections, so that both sides could be displayed simultaneously. Comparette had "inside connections" at the Mint and was not averse to using them, as well as outside contacts, to obtain pieces for the Mint Museum.

But after Comparette's passing, Godard obtained the two examples of the 1927-D double eagle directly from the Denver Mint. The present piece–an MS66 PCGS specimen making its second appearance with us–is one of those two coins, with a pedigree tying it back directly to Godard and the Denver Mint in 1927. Both pieces reposed in the Connecticut State Library Museum of Connecticut History until 1995, when the museum consigned one of its two coins to Heritage. It garnered $390,500 in our Long Beach Signature Auction (6/1995, lot 6026, as MS66 NGC). That price, still today, is number 201 in the Top 250 prices in the *Guide Book*. (It is fascinating to note that only four years ago, the 2006 *Guide Book* listed that same price record as number 88 all-time highest.)

The current Museum of Connecticut History collections curator, Dave Corrigan (whose kind assistance we gratefully acknowledge), says that the proceeds from that coin and others consigned to the 1995 Heritage sale continue to this day funding museum acquisitions. Please note in the roster that follows, to our knowledge the photo of the second piece still in the museum has never been published.

We are also indebted to Dr. Richard Doty, curator of the Smithsonian Institution's National Numismatic Collection, and Karen Lee for furnishing Heritage with never-before-published images of two 1927-D double eagles in the national collection. We thank both institutions and their curators for their helpfulness and cooperation.

Augustus Saint-Gaudens (courtesy of the Saint Gaudens National Historic Site)

Modern Comparisons to Other Rarities

The significance of the present offering, as the rarest 20th century regular issue coin and the key to Saint-Gaudens regular issue double eagles, can scarcely be overstated. While at various times other 20th century gold issues have been thought rarer than the 1927-D, modern-day thinking puts this coin at the head of the pack among regular issue coins dated in the 1900s–a position it has securely occupied since the 1950s, when its incredible rarity was finally appreciated. The closest comparisons that can be made are with other members of the Saint-Gaudens series, and among those the only two that are of comparable rarity are the 1933 double eagle and the 1907 Ultra High Relief:

1907 Ultra High Relief. Even if one considers this the key to a complete set of Saint-Gaudens double eagles as some collectors do, the fact remains that it is not a regular issue. It is nonetheless much desired for its fidelity to "The Saint's" original, unalloyed artistic vision–but it is a pattern coin under any reasonable definition, issued only in proof format. Even though it is a proof pattern issue, the 1907 or MCMVII Ultra High Relief had an estimated original mintage of 16-22 coins. Modern survival estimates range from about 12 to 15 coins all told--not far different from the survival estimates for the 1927-D.

1933 Double Eagle. Numismatists know this issue well from the single example now legal to own, a Gem specimen formerly in the King Farouk Collection that set the all-time world-record price for a coin–$7,590,020–at auction in July 2002. But 10 other examples of the 1933 double eagle, formerly in the estate of Philadelphia jeweler Israel "Izzy" Switt and "discovered" in a safe deposit box in 2005, are currently the subject of hot dispute in our judicial system concerning whether they were properly released from the Mint–as Switt's heirs maintain through their attorney–or stolen from the Mint by Switt, as the government alleges.

If they are eventually adjudicated legal to own and join the Farouk coin, the possibility exists of a total of 11 examples being numismatically available. (Or more; other surviving pieces are rumored, and among the government's latest moves in September is to try to expand the litigation's scope to cover any future 1933s that might be uncovered.) If that occurs, the 1927-D will still slightly edge out the 1933s for the title of most elusive 20th century among "regular issues," at least in terms of those potentially available to collectors. But for now, the 1933 cannot be considered a "regular issue" and is essentially noncollectible.

The 1927-D Double Eagle in Numismatic History

The Saint-Gaudens double eagles, perhaps more than any other U.S. coin series of the 20th century, have been the subject of prodigious mintages, exportations, repatriations, large discovery hoards, and mass extinction events that make the original production figures meaningless. While some issues with high mintages are still common today, others are extremely rare. A key factor has been not only how many were melted over the decades, but more especially which issues were exported (thus avoiding near-total annihilation in some cases) or otherwise cached away so as to be rediscovered later (the vast Wells Fargo Hoard of 1908 No Motto twenties comes to mind).

Subsequent discoveries and reimportations over several decades of numismatic history have shifted the numismatic landscape, continually altering the perception of which series issues are viewed rarest and their interrelationships. In some cases, as with the 1927-D, the fortunate survival of a few specimens almost appears to be the luck of the draw. In that respect, without undue hyperbole we believe close cousins to the 1927-D double eagles may be the fabulously rare 1822 half eagles, of which but three are known. They, too, were the subject of mass meltings of nearly their entire design type, the survivors more a matter of serendipity than foresight.

What precedes the physical description of the present offering is an examination of those shifting perceptions and interrelationships over the decades.

The Early Years: 1927-1933

The Denver Mint reportedly made 180,000 examples of the 1927-D double eagle, using four different die pairs, although most examples known today are from a single pair. The original mintage of the issue, while on the low side, certainly suggests neither its later rarity nor its eventual reputation as the rarest collectible regular-issue coin of the 20th century. The reasons for the nominal mintage are uncertain today. There were healthy emissions of 1927-D cents, nickels, and dimes. But the 1927-D quarter and dollar mintages were smallish; no half dollars were made at all. In the gold series, Denver had made no quarter eagles since the 1925-D, and no half eagles or eagles since the 1914-D.

The current Denver Mint began striking coinage in 1906, but the 1927-D double eagles are its rarest business-strike coins to date, discounting the fabled 1964-D Peace dollars.

The situation for double eagles was of a pattern all its own, however. Before the 1927-D the Denver Mint had produced double eagles yearly since 1923, in plentiful numbers exceeding 8 million total coins for the 1923-D through 1926-D double eagle issues. There simply may have been little need for double eagles, given the productions of the preceding years. The 180,000 1927-Ds made certainly would not have signaled *major rarity* to the few collectors of the era who could afford to collect Uncirculated double eagles. In fact, the 1927-D's mintage was many times higher than several earlier Saint-Gaudens twenties, including the 1908-S (22,000), 1909-D (52,500), 1913-S (34,000), or 1914 (95,250).

As with so many series issues, the clue to the 1927-D's rarity today is more survival than production. Although today we believe that only 13 or 14 examples are known (see the roster below), Bowers notes in his double eagle *Guide Book* that "interestingly, double eagles of this date and mint were available for face value from the Treasury Department from 1927 to the early 1930s." While many Saint-Gaudens issues can today be considered "less rare than formerly thought" due to the extensive repatriations of overseas gold coin hoards after World War II, the 1927-D is most particularly and noticeably *not* among them.

A good example of the "formerly rare" issues in the Saint-Gaudens series is the 1924-S, of which Bowers writes in his *Guide Book of Double Eagle Gold Coins*:

> "The 1924-S is a wonderful double eagle. At one time it was considered to be one of the greatest rarities in the series, handily outclassing the famous MCMVII Ultra High Relief and the incredible Proofs of 1883 and 1884. The appearance of a specimen at auction was a momentous event. Today, following the tapping of overseas hoards, the 1924-S remains elusive, but enough exist that they come onto the market with regularity, usually in lower Mint State grades."

As decade after decade passes by, however, the 1927-D–unlike the 1924-S and many others–appears to have been an issue that was almost entirely melted shortly after the great Gold Recall of 1933, implemented by President Franklin D. Roosevelt in the darkest days of the Great Depression.

The 1927-D Double Eagle During the 1940s

The Great Depression lingered for years, an unwelcome guest that destroyed lives, dissolved fortunes, dampened commerce, and forced record numbers of Americans to seek public or private assistance. Not long after, the Second World War embroiled much of the world from 1939 to 1945. From the time of their production through the Bank Holiday and Gold Recall of 1933, the numismatic world heard little of the 1927-D double eagles until 1944. In that year Stack's offered the first specimen known to appear at public auction, the J.F. Bell specimen. The Stack's catalog description is laconic in the extreme:

F.C.C. Boyd, early owner of a 1927-D double eagle whose 'World's Greatest Collection' was auctioned in 1946

"**1927 "D" Brilliant Uncirculated.** We doubt that more than a dozen are known. Very rare and choice."

The Bell coin realized $500–a considerable sum at that time, but certainly not a record-breaking performance. (For greater context, the record price of the 1940s was $11,575 for the Dunham 1822 half eagle in 1941, a record for any coin that would be broken only in the 1960s.) Another 1927-D in the World's Greatest Collection of F.C.C. Boyd, auctioned in 1946, realized $650.

A somewhat later appearance was in B. Max Mehl's 1949 auction of the Dr. Charles Green specimen, a coin that we believe to be the same coin as the Bell specimen. Here is how Mehl described it:

> "1927 D. Uncirculated with full mint lustre. Another great rarity. With an auction record of over $900. Catalogs $600. I think this coin is almost as rare as the 1926 D. This specimen is from the Bell Sale, in 1944, at $500."

This appearance realized $630. After considerable effort we have failed to locate the specific auction record over $900 that Mehl mentions; we believe it may actually have been a private sale, a competitive bid Mehl knew about that was later reduced, or possibly just an outright error. The prices realized during this era, while substantial, tell us there was as yet little comprehension of how truly rare the 1927-D was–or, more properly, *would become in relation to other series issues.*

The 1927-D Double Eagle During the 1950s

The 1950s were an era when the top 10 auction records included $10,500 for an AU 1799 large cent (Abe Kosoff's Sloss sale in 1959) and $8,000 for an 1804 Restrike silver dollar in XF (Stack's Davis-Graves sale of 1956). For our purposes, we make special note of the 1957 Schmandt Collection sale by Stack's, which also included a consignment from an "Eastern University." Lot 1072 was described as follows:

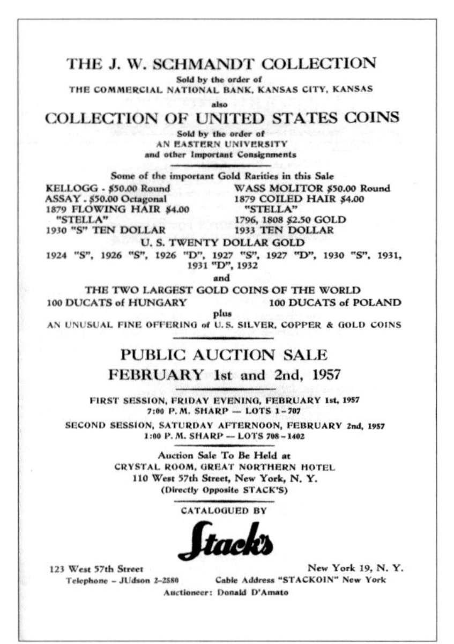

THE J. W. SCHMANDT COLLECTION
Sold by the order of
THE COMMERCIAL NATIONAL BANK, KANSAS CITY, KANSAS
also
COLLECTION OF UNITED STATES COINS
Sold by the order of
AN EASTERN UNIVERSITY
and other Important Consignments

Some of the important Gold Rarities in this Sale

KELLOGG - $50.00 Round	WASS MOLITOR $50.00 Round
ASSAY - $50.00 Octagonal	1879 COILED HAIR $4.00 "STELLA"
1879 FLOWING HAIR $4.00 "STELLA"	1796, 1808 $2.50 GOLD
1930 "S" TEN DOLLAR	1933 TEN DOLLAR

U. S. TWENTY DOLLAR GOLD
1924 "S", 1926 "S", 1926 "D", 1927 "S", 1927 "D", 1930 "S", 1931, 1931 "D", 1932
and
THE TWO LARGEST GOLD COINS OF THE WORLD
100 DUCATS of HUNGARY   100 DUCATS of POLAND
plus
AN UNUSUAL FINE OFFERING of U.S. SILVER, COPPER & GOLD COINS

PUBLIC AUCTION SALE
FEBRUARY 1st and 2nd, 1957

FIRST SESSION, FRIDAY EVENING, FEBRUARY 1st, 1957
7:00 P. M. SHARP — LOTS 1-707
SECOND SESSION, SATURDAY AFTERNOON, FEBRUARY 2nd, 1957
1:00 P. M. SHARP — LOTS 708-1402

Auction Sale To Be Held at
CRYSTAL ROOM, GREAT NORTHERN HOTEL
110 West 57th Street, New York, N. Y.
(Directly Opposite STACK'S)

CATALOGUED BY
Stack's
123 West 57th Street   New York 19, N. Y.
Telephone - JUdson 2-2580   Cable Address "STACKOIN" New York
Auctioneer: Donald D'Amato

The 1957 Stack's Schmandt Eastern University auction in 1957 was where the 1927-D's true rarity began to be recognized.

> **"THE VERY RARE 1927 'D' $20.00**
> 1072 **1927 'D'** It is quite difficult to find words to describe another rare $20.00 after writing about the earlier lots, but this is rarer than the 1927 'S'. Should easily bring in excess of catalog. Lacking in the Davis Graves, Baldenhofer, Melish and many other collections. A beautiful yellow gold, Brilliant Uncirculated. **PLATE**."

What had apparently brought about writer's exhaustion on the part of the cataloger was the presence on the previous page of a 1926-D double eagle, and further on the same page of a 1931-D. For the latter the cataloger says:

> "1075 **1931 'D'** One has to search high and low to find the last auction or private sale record on this coin. While not attributed as rare as the 1926 'D' it runs it a very close second. If we were to run a table on rarity of Denver Mint $20.00, we would place it in this order: 1926 D first, 1931 D second, 1927 D third, which gives one an idea of its rarity. This should bring about $1250.00. Brilliant Uncirculated with full lustre and a beautiful strike. **PLATE**"

Despite all the foregoing, the Stack's description of the 1926-D is fairly terse:

> "1070 **1926 'D'** The rarest coin from the Denver Mint, and also in our opinion the rarest double eagle. Should bring far in excess of catalog as there is a $2500 record. Brilliant Uncirculated. **PLATE**"

Paying little heed to all the trumpeting, the marketplace was ahead of the cataloger in this auction. The 1926-D only brought a meager $500, while the 1927-D cleared $1,230 and the 1931-D garnered $1,625. Even then the 1927-D was beginning to gain greater visibility, although it still played second fiddle to the 1931-D in this instance. As a further reference, we note that the 1957 edition of the *Guide Book* listed the 1926-D and 1926-S each at $1,000 in Uncirculated, compared to the 1927-D and 1927-S at $750, and $700 each for the 1924-S and 1931-D.

The 1927-D During the 1960s and 1970s

Although they took some time to filter into the numismatic market, during the 1950s and into the 1960s additional specimens of rare-date double eagles would occasionally turn up in small caches. A period of intense searching of the various hoards known–most in Europe but also including some in Latin America–would occasionally uncover a shiny 1926-D, or a nice 1931-D or 1924-S, and the sporadic appearance of a 1930-S or one of the other later-date issues from the 1924-1932 era was always a possibility.

But no 1927-D double eagles turned up, then or later. The 1926-D and 1924-S had fallen from their high thrones of previous years. A March 1969 Stack's auction of the James Dines Collection included several rare (and formerly rare) Saint-Gaudens issues, each merely described as "BU." While a 1931-D and 1932 each realized $3,200 and a 1930-S realized $2,600, a 1926-D sold for only $725. There was no 1927-D in the Dines Collection.

Clarke E. Gilhousen

The consignor of the 1927-D double eagle in the Gilhousen Collection of 1973 had been seeking an example for 35 years and considered it his "greatest acquisition."

It is also in the 1960s that a 1927-D double eagle first set one of the top 10 auction records for the decade. An Uncirculated example in the Lester Merkin sale of October 1969 brought $32,000. That amount is surpassed at public auctions during the 1960s only by two appearances of the 1913 Liberty Head nickel and one of an 1804 Restrike silver dollar.

An anonymous collector (we believe it was Edwards Metcalf) bought the same Merkin coin shortly after the sale for an amount in excess of the $32,000 it had brought. That trade also would have been a record for the 1960s, had it been a public auction.

That same coin from the Merkin sale was reconsigned to the Gilhousen sale in 1973. The cataloger wrote that the consignor had been seeking a 1927-D double eagle for 35 years and considered it his "greatest acquisition." (It is nonetheless surprising that he held it less than four years.) The coin brought $60,000. In contrast, "BU" examples of the 1930-S and 1932 in the Gilhousen sale brought $7,000 and $5,500, respectively. And how had the mighty fallen: A 1926-D in AU brought only $1,300 in Gilhousen. In the following year, Texas oilman H. Jeff Browning paid $175,000 for his 1927-D, a coin whose previous origins we have been unable to trace.

Clearly, the 1927-D was an issue that had come into its own as a legendary rarity of the first rank, while erstwhile contenders had been cast down from on high.

The 1927-D in the 1980s to the Present

The 1980s saw further price advances. By 1981 an AU58 example--the only circulated specimen on the roster that follows--sold for $220,000 in a Stack's auction, increasing to $242,000 in a Bowers and Merena appearance in 1987 before falling back the next year to $187,000. Meanwhile the Eliasberg (U.S. Gold Coin Collection) specimen, an MS66 that originated in the World's Greatest Collection of F.C.C. Boyd, brought $176,000 in 1982. That piece has since seen a number of private trades. Another MS66 in the Stack's 1985 sale of the Primary Bartle Collection brought $275,000, an amount just short of the Top 10 auction records for the decade. This was an era when an 1804 Restrike silver dollar brought $308,000 and the Eliasberg 1822 half eagle garnered $687,500; the top price for the entire 1980s was the $990,000 realized for the Dexter 1804 Original silver dollar.

Louis E. Eliasberg, Sr., whose 1927-D double eagle sold for $176,000 in 1982

By the 1990s, the finest example known, an MS67 PCGS example in the Stack's 1991 Charlotte Collection auction, would bring in $522,500. The present example, an MS66 PCGS piece with a provenance tying it directly back to the Connecticut State Library and the Denver Mint in 1927, would trade in its first Heritage appearance in 1995 (as MS66 NGC) for $390,500. The Dallas Bank Collection example, an MS66 PCGS coin offered by Sotheby's-Stack's in 2001, was the one that Jeff Browning acquired for $175,000 in 1974. The 2001 appearance brought $402,500, and it would trade in 2005 privately for $1,650,000.

We handled the 1927-D from the 1985 Primary Bartle Collection sale in 2006 as part of the Delbert McDougal Set of $20 Saint-Gaudens Coins, by which time it managed to bring in an amazing sum of $1,322,500 for the happy consignor. This was again just short of the Top 10 auction records for the 2000s. Finally, what brought just over a half-million dollars in the 1991 Charlotte Collection sale, an MS67 PCGS specimen, would end up in the Heritage 2005 auction of the illustrious Phillip H. Morse Collection, where it would bring an unprecedented total of $1,897,500. In a 2008 compilation by P. Scott Rubin of auction records published in *Coin Values* magazine, that sale was worth the number 3 top auction record of the 2000s. And although a number of other higher prices have intervened, in the 2010 *Guide Book* that sale is still the number 7 spot in the Top 250 Coin Prices Realized at Auction.

Physical Description

MS66 PCGS. The surfaces display thick mint frost throughout. The centers are bright yellow-gold while the margins are more deeply colored, with a noticeable accent of lilac. The striking details are fully brought up in all areas. This example is most immediately identifiable on the obverse by an alloy spot in the left field and a couple of short contact marks across both of Liberty's legs. A short mark below the EN of TWENTY appears in the upper reverse field, and a couple of small ticks on OD W in the motto.

David Akers' 20th century gold coin *Handbook* notes that most, but not all, known specimens of the 1927-D were struck from a single pair of dies, although four die pairs are recorded. Akers describes the obverse die cracks to include one "thin, spindly die crack [that] joins star to star through the top of the letter L in LIBERTY," and another that "begins at the base of the letter L in LIBERTY and runs through the adjacent letter I before terminating at the torch in Liberty's left (facing) hand." On the reverse "a thin, nearly vertical die crack bisects the eagle's beak."

On the present coin, a short star-to-star die crack passes through the top of the L in LIBERTY; another longer crack passes from the bottom of the L through the top of the torch and to the B. On the reverse a long, near-vertical crack passes through the eagle's beak, and a very short die crack runs from above the eagle's eye across the adjoining ray.

An Unprecedented Opportunity

The present 1927-D double eagle marks an unprecedented opportunity to acquire the rarest regular-issue coin made in at least the past 100 years. It is also an opportunity that is fleeting, as during the past 30 years or so an example of the 1927-D appears at auction on average about once every two years. The high grade of the current Premium Gem example makes this opportunity even more important, as it is tied for second finest with numerous other examples (including what are clearly duplications) and surpassed in grade only by the ex: Morse specimen.

Registry Set Collectors Note

The ownership of any 1927-D double eagle is one of those marks of rare accomplishment that turns a memorable collection into a world-class one. As of this writing there are eight current NGC and 12 PCGS Saint-Gaudens Registry Sets with a completion of 80%, for a total of 20 Registry Sets at both services combined. *As amazing as it may seem, every one of those current sets is lacking an example of the 1927-D.*

NGC Census: 1 in AU58, 1 in MS65, 3 in MS66.
PCGS Population: 1 in MS63, 1 in MS65, 5 in MS66, 1 in MS67 (11/09).

1927-D Saint-Gaudens Double Eagle

Heritage Revised Roster (November 2009)

The following roster considers all available sources and relies heavily on photographs in past auction catalogs. We attempt to rank each coin from highest to lowest grade, in some cases estimating how the coin would probably grade if submitted to a third-party grading service today. Despite our best efforts, it is possible that the list below still contains some duplications, as one coin has not been seen since 1957, another since 1973. There are at most 13 pieces known, of which only nine are publicly held and theoretically available in the numismatic marketplace. It is possible that as few as seven specimens are publicly available. *Four of the following are permanently impounded in museum collections; those pieces are listed separately.*

Publicly Held Specimens

1. MS67 PCGS. Charlotte Collection (Stack's, 3/1991), lot 1217, $522,500; Jay Parrino; Phillip H. Morse Collection of Saint-Gaudens Coinage (Heritage, 11/2005), lot 6697, $1,897,500; Todd Imhof (then at Pinnacle) on behalf of a private client. A small diagonal mark appears at the center of Liberty's waist.

2. MS66 PCGS. Primary Bartle Collection (Stack's, 10/1985), lot 868, $275,000; Superior (8/1992), lot 686, unsold; Delbert McDougal Set of $20 Saint-Gaudens Coins (Heritage, 1/2006), lot 3624, $1,322,500; Heritage (1/2007), lot 3303, unsold. A mark at the midpoint of the fourth ray right of Liberty identifies this example.

3. MS66 PCGS. H. Jeff Browning, acquired 9/24/1974 from an unknown source for $175,000; Dallas Bank Collection (Sotheby's-Stack's, 10/2001), lot 206, $402,500; ANA Sale (Bowers and Merena, 8/2003), lot 4417, unsold; later, Rare Coin Wholesalers (6/2005, $1,650,000); Legend Numismatics; BRS Legacy Collection (6/2005). Small marks appear on the rays above the 19 in the date.

4. MS66. F.C.C. Boyd; World's Greatest Collection (Numismatic Gallery, 1/1946), lot 1045, $650; Stack's (privately); Louis E. Eliasberg, Sr.; U.S. Gold Coin Collection (Bowers and Ruddy, 10/1982), lot 1067, $176,000; later, Dr. William Crawford. This coin was later the subject of a July 2005 NGC press release where it was stated that the coin was submitted by an anonymous Western dealer at the 2005 New York Invitational Coin Show, and that it was previously from an old private collection; later, North American Certified Trading (1/2006); East Coast dealer. The coin is graded MS65 in the Eliasberg catalog, but the illustration suggests MS66 or MS67. The obverse has a tiny spot in the field just above the right (facing) shoulder. There appears to be an alloy spot on the fourth feather down from the top of the eagle's wing, below the S in DOLLARS.

5. MS66 PCGS. The present specimen. Denver Mint (1927); Museum of Connecticut History-Connecticut State Library (Heritage, 6/1995), lot 6026, $390,500 (as MS66 NGC); Jay Parrino; numerous intermediaries. See Physical Description**.**

6. MS66 NGC. James Kelly (late 1940s); private Lima, Ohio collector, $2,000; Auction '84 (Paramount, 7/1984), lot 999, $198,000; Dr. Steven Duckor; Dr. Thaine B. Price (David Akers, 5/1998), lot 115, $577,500; Superior (3/2001), lot 989. Several tiny marks or spots are visible on or between the rays left of Liberty.

7. MS64. Lester Merkin (10/1969), lot 526, $32,000; anonymous collector (perhaps Edwards Metcalf), after 10/1969, $32,000+; Gilhousen Collection (Superior, 2/1973), lot 1041, $60,000. A small spot is evident below the second L in DOLLARS. A small field mark is visible below the forearm.

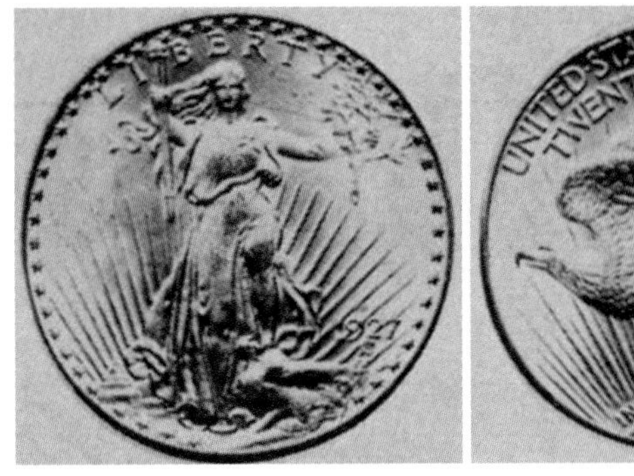

8. MS64. An Eastern university; Stack's (2/1957), lot 1072; present location unknown. A small spot is visible in the field below the tip of the fourth feather down from the top of the eagle.

9. AU58 NGC. Stack's (12/1981), lot 1252, $220,000; Bowers and Merena (10/1987), lot 2201, $242,000; Charles Kramer Collection (Stack's and Superior, 11/1988), lot 913, $187,000; Superior (2/1992), lot 3339, unsold; Superior (1/1993), lot 1595, $137,500. Slight rub is noted on Liberty's right (facing) knee. A diagonal field mark is visible between the end of Liberty's flowing hair and the rays below. Small marks are evident on the top part of the eagle's left (forward) wing. This appears to be the only piece that has signs of wear.

Museum Specimens

10. MS66. Smithsonian Institution 1984.1046.0812. Likely obtained directly from the Denver Mint in the late 1920s-early 1930s. The Smithsonian Institution holds three different examples of the 1927-D double eagle. Two are believed obtained directly from the Denver Mint; the third came from the famous Josiah K. Lilly Collection, which the Smithsonian took possession of in 1968. This coin is depicted in Jeff Garrett and Ron Guth's *Encyclopedia of U.S. Gold Coins 1795-1933* and is illustrated on the Smithsonian website. A tiny tick appears on Liberty's exposed right (facing) knee, and a small mark shows on the ray just left of the D mintmark and one slightly further down the ray above the 9. The strike is incredibly sharp. On the reverse, a wispy die crack runs through the crossbar of (AMERIC)A, through two adjacent feathers and into the field below, a diagnostic shared with the Smithsonian coin 11, just below. The reverse shows a small scrape through three rays above (TRU)ST on the right side. On the lower left rays, there are tiny ticks on rays 5, 7, and 9 counting from the left inward. *Images courtesy of the National Numismatic Collection, Smithsonian Institution.*

11. MS65. Smithsonian Institution NU283645. J.F. Bell Collection (Stack's, 12/1944), lot 1004, $500. The Dr. Charles Green coin (B. Max Mehl, 4/1949, lot 917, $630) is unplated in the catalog, but Mehl specifically attributes the coin as the J.F. Bell specimen in his lot description. Robert Schermerhorn; Stack's (privately, 1953); Josiah K. Lilly; Smithsonian Institution (1968). The Bell sale was the first public offering of a 1927-D double eagle. ***This previously unpublished image of the specimen in the National Numismatic Collection has been plate-matched to the photo in the Bell catalog.*** (The Bell image is in black and white and not high-quality, although good for the era, and we have identified numerous identical marks on both coins. Nonetheless, some of the die cracks and contact marks described cannot be seen on the Bell image.) On the obverse, a near-vertical nick appears near the bottom end of the olive stem, clearly visible on both the Bell and SI images. There is a tiny dark spot below the L of LIBERTY, and a spot on Liberty's right (facing) knee. Luster grazes in the left field have a triangular-shaped top, with the bottom ending precisely at the tip of the third long ray from the left (visible on both). A small smudge appears at the top of the sixth long ray from the left. A scrape appears on Liberty's belly, running slightly upward from left to right, below the waist (visible on both the SI and Bell images). The Smithsonian image shows a thin die break running from the tip of L through I and across the torch. It also shows a small, wispy die crack traversing the crossbar of the last A in AMERICA, through the eagle's adjacent two rear feathers and out into the field. There is a near-vertical die crack through the forward portion of the eagle's beak. *Images courtesy of the National Numismatic Collection, Smithsonian Institution.*

12. MS66. Smithsonian Institution 1985.0441.1523. Likely obtained directly from the Denver Mint in the late 1920s-early 1930s. ***Previously unpublished images.*** This coin has a couple of amazing similarities and several distinct differences from the Bell-Lilly-Smithsonian coin 11, just above. A nick appears at the bottom of the olive branch, but on this coin the nick is more diagonal than near-vertical, about paralleling the bottom stem edge. A tiny dark spot appears just to the right of the nick, in the field. There is also a near-identical (to the Bell coin) mark on Liberty's belly, but here it is just about horizontal. The luster grazes in the left obverse field are more minor on this piece, without a triangular top and not quite meeting the tip of the third long ray counting from the left. A tiny dark spot appears between the fifth and sixth long rays counting from the left, two-thirds of the way down toward Liberty's gown fold. On the reverse there is no visible crack through the eagle's beak. A minute die crack is scarcely visible *below the crossbar of the last A*, near the bottom right of that letter. What appears to be a small raised die line connects the top of the eagle's upper breast with the lower part of the forewing just above. Vertically below the R in DOLLARS on the top feather of the eagle's outside (left) wing, a diagonal mark clearly shows. *Images courtesy of the National Numismatic Collection, Smithsonian Institution.*

13. MS66. Denver Mint (1927); **Museum of Connecticut History--Connecticut State Library C08433.** ***Previously unpublished images.*** This well-struck coin is one of two 1927-Ds obtained directly from the Denver Mint in the year of issue by then-Connecticut State Librarian George S. Godard, with its sibling, No. 5, being the coin currently offered. This specimen has two near-parallel reverse toning streaks that provide a clear identification, running through the eagle's rear tail feathers to the rim beneath CA. A small die crack runs through the crossbar of the last A in AMERICA, through the eagle's longest tail feather and out in the field. A smaller crack connects the tops of CA, and there appear to be traces of the usually seen straight-line vertical crack through the eagle's beak. On the obverse a tiny tick appears near the top of the fourth ray counting from the right, along with the usually seen straight die crack through LI and the torch. Some light field marks appear between the olive branch, Liberty's right (facing) arm, and TY.

From The Ralph P. Muller Collection.(#9187)

Elusive MS62 1927-S Double Eagle

2332 1927-S MS62 PCGS. Although Mint records show over 3.1 million double eagles produced at San Francisco in 1927, that figure is utterly disconnected from the numismatic reality of today. While the 1927-S is not of the supreme rarity that characterizes its Denver counterpart, it is nonetheless highly prized and elusive. As Garrett and Guth recount: "This tremendous mintage did little to provide coins for future collectors. Virtually the entire mintage was destroyed in the 1930s, leaving just a few hundred around today for collectors to fight over."

Interestingly for an issue that saw little circulation, the 1927-S appears frequently in worn grades, as shown by the NGC *Census Report* and the PCGS *Population Report*. In fact, the mean grade for the combined certified population is a mere 59.9, which puts virtually any Mint State coin, including the present MS62 piece, ahead of the curve.

Deep sun-gold shadings prevail on this desirable and satiny 1927-S twenty, though a hint of orange is present on the reverse. It is well struck overall, though the edges show a degree of the usual beveling and the peripheral stars are a trifle soft. A number of wispy abrasions are present in the fields and a handful of small digs appear on the central devices, yet the overall eye appeal is far better than the MS62 grade might suggest. An excellent candidate for most double eagle cabinets, even one that has mainly Select or better pieces. Population: 49 in 62, 34 finer (11/09).(#9188)

LIBERTY
1927
UNITED STATES OF AMERICA
TWENTY DOLLARS
IN GOD WE TRUST

Exceptional MS65 1927-S Twenty
One of the Keys to the Saint-Gaudens Series

2333 1927-S MS65 PCGS. CAC. The 1927-S is not only a celebrated issue in the Saint-Gaudens series in its own right, but its closest cousin, the fabulously rare 1927-D double eagle, further augments its considerable fame. That the 1927-S has maintained such an elite status is made all the more impressive when one considers the number of issues in the series today considered "less rare than previously thought"—almost invariably due to discoveries of small caches of coins in Europe or Latin America, which mostly occurred in the 1940s through the early 1960s. While the 1927-S has not been entirely immune to that phenomenon, far fewer examples have been found than many other issues that constitute the last decade or so in the manufacture of the denomination.

The only Saint-Gaudens double eagles that we can say with certainty to have entirely escaped the "former rarity syndrome" are the 1927-D and the 1933. Of course the status of 10 1933s confiscated by the federal government from the Langbord family is still the subject of current litigation. And so far as is known, there have been no new 1927-Ds uncovered overseas, if at all, in many decades, as its first known auction appearance in the 1944 J.F. Bell Collection was accompanied by a description speculating that no more than a dozen were known, and today we can account for only 13 examples.

On the other hand, the 1926-D in the 1940s was thought rarer than the 1927-D, and yet today, due to those selfsame repatriations, several hundred examples are known, most of them Mint State.

The 1927-S, however, bears more similarities to the 1927-D than to the 1926-D. In the companion volume to the Phillip H. Morse Collection which we handled in 2005, we wrote this concerning the 1927-S issue:

> "The 1927-S is one of the rarest and best-known issues in the Saint-Gaudens series of double eagles. In 1988, David Akers ranked the 1927-S as tenth in overall rarity out of the 54-coin series. Fifty years ago it was considered as the fourth rarest, trailing only the 1924-S, 1926-D, and 1926-S. Since that time, a few 1927-S twenties have turned up, one or two at a time but nothing approaching the quantities of, say, the 1926-S. This is in spite of the fact that 3.1 million pieces were produced. The key status of the 1927-S is based on absolute rarity rather than conditional rarity. In all grades, there are probably only 160-170 pieces extant today, but curiously, two-thirds of the pieces known are Uncirculated—and there are several that are known at the Superb level."

As further testament to the modern day rarity of the 1927-S, we note that when the final prices were tallied in the Morse Collection, the finest known 1927-D, an MS67 PCGS example, was in first place. The second, third, and fifth-highest price records went to the incredibly rare 1921s, in MS66, MS65, and MS64, respectively (the 1921 is extremely rare above MS63). Fourth place went to an incredibly rare 1920-S in MS66—and the sixth-highest price went to a 1927-S double eagle in MS67, the single finest known.

This piece in MS66 is one of only a half-dozen so certified at NGC and PCGS combined (two at PCGS and four at NGC), and there are only three examples certified finer, two MS67 at NGC and one at PCGS (10/09).

Like other 1927-S twenties we have handled, this example has dynamic luster characteristics. The intensity of the mint luster and intermingled reddish-gold and lilac colors give it a resemblance to a high grade 1923-D. The surfaces are remarkably free from abrasions, with the only one of note for pedigree purposes located in the left obverse field. An outstanding example of this key Saint-Gaudens twenty.
From The Ralph P. Muller Collection.(#9188)

LIBERTY
1927
UNITED·STATES·OF·AMERICA
TWENTY·DOLLARS
IN·GOD·WE·TRUST

Key 1927-S Saint-Gaudens Twenty, MS66
Only 3,750 Examples Released

2334 1927-S MS66 PCGS. CAC. Ex: Brahin. Like all of the mintmarked issues from the late 1920s, the 1927-S Saint-Gaudens double eagle is a key date in the series. The large mintage of 3.1 million pieces was almost totally destroyed after the Gold Recall of 1933, and only a small number of examples surfaced in European holdings in the 1950s. In *A Handbook of 20th Century United States Gold Coins 1907-1933,* David Akers reports:

> "Five decades ago, the 1927-S was considered to be the fourth-rarest issue in the Saint-Gaudens Double Eagle series after the 1924-S, 1926-D and 1926-S. Even the 1920-S, 1921 and, yes, the 1927-D were thought to be more plentiful than the 1927-S. This all changed in the late 1950s when individual examples began to show up in shipments of U.S. gold coins from Europe. By the end of the 20th century between 100 and 200 pieces had arrived, although at no time was there ever a hoard of this issue. Typically grading MS-60 to MS-64, the 1927-S is particularly rare as a Gem and all but unknown any finer than MS-66."

Akers was particularly well qualified to comment on the small presence of the 1927-S in European hoards. As a principal of the Paramount International Coin Company, he was privy to many records of transactions between Jim Kelly and Paul Wittlin, who was the main conduit for bringing European holdings to the U.S. coin market. In Price List 8 (Paramount,1974), Akers made the following observations about the 1927-S:

> "This is the first example of this rare date that we have owned in several years and even when we were regularly receiving shipments of rare double eagles from our European buyer Paul Wittlin, the 1927-S was conspicuous by its absence although in such shipments we received as many as six 1921's at one time or two 1870-CC's, or half a dozen 1891's! Of course, the days of such shipments are far behind us and will never be repeated again, but the fact remains that even in those bountiful days the 1927-S was seldom sent to us and this is a strong indicator of the coin's rarity."

Akers currently ranks the 1927-S as the 9th rarest issue of the 53 coin collectible series, with a surviving population of 120-140 examples in Mint State grades. NGC has certified four coins in MS66, with two finer; while PCGS has graded only two examples at the Premium Gem level, with one finer (10/09).

In the waning days of the Great Depression, with most forms of gold bullion deemed illegal for U.S. citizens to own, a few astute numismatists realized collecting large denomination gold coins was a viable opportunity to invest in the precious metal. Saint-Gaudens double eagles began to appear in numismatic auctions in the late 1930s, even though many of the coins were less than 10 years old. One early appearance of the 1927-S was in Sale Number 399 (Morgenthau, 5/1939), lot 554, "1927 S Extremely fine and scarce." The lot realized $67, a strong price for that era.

In the 1940s, collecting twenty dollar gold coins became widespread for the first time. Collectors such as Louis Eliasberg and Dr. Charles W. Green formed important collections of double eagles during the decade, and much attention was focused on the denomination. Regarding the 1927-S, Green's research in Mint Records revealed the startling fact that only 3,750 specimens of the date were actually released by the San Francisco Mint before the Recall. Apparently, more than 3 million examples of the issue were melted and stored as ingots in Fort Knox. The effective mintage of the 1927-S is the minuscule total of coins actually released, and this explains its rarity today.

The presently-offered Premium Gem displays peach-gold patina that is accompanied on the obverse by tinges of light tan, and on the reverse by subtle yellow-green undertones and occasional splashes of reddish color. Attractive luster radiates from both faces, and the motifs are well impressed. The Capitol building, which is typically weak on this issue, exhibits nice detail in most of the panes. Liberty's facial features, the fingers on both hands, the toes, and the eagle's plumage are all sharp. A solitary light copper spot in the lower left obverse field and a small mark in the middle of Liberty's outstretched left arm may help pedigree this rarity. The present coin is listed as the number three specimen in David Akers' census of Significant Examples.

Ex: Rarities Sale (Bowers and Merena, 7/2002), lot 931.

From The Jay Brahin Collection.(#9188)

LIBERTY
1929
UNITED·STATES·OF·AMERICA
TWENTY·DOLLARS
IN·GOD·WE·TRUST

1929 Saint-Gaudens Double Eagle, MS65
Late-Date Rarity
Only 25,170 Coins Released

2335 1929 MS65 PCGS. CAC. Ex: Brahin/Browning. "Easily comparable to the lovely Price example. This specimen can take its place in the ranks of the best." Those were the comments about this piece in the catalog of the Dallas Bank Collection. Our consigner is also enamored of this coin, writing that "it is a complex mirrored/satiny colorful coin that could easily be in a MS66 holder and no one would consider it overgraded."

The 1929 is the first issue in the group of late-date Saint-Gaudens double eagles that collectors have always regarded as major rarities. While its appearance in European hoards in recent years has made the issue more available than the other late dates, the 1929 is still a challenging issue in Mint State grades, especially at the Gem level. Indeed, David Akers believes the 1929 is rarer in high grades than the 1931 and 1932. In terms of absolute rarity, Akers rates the 1929 as the 11th rarest date in the 53 coin series, with a surviving population of 175-230 examples in Mint State grades. Other estimates of the total surviving population have ranged from a low of 60 coins to a high of 1,750 coins, but both of those extremes are entirely unrealistic. Nearly all known 1929 double eagles, like survivors of the other late dates through 1933, are found in lower Mint State grades. Circulated pieces are virtually non-existent. According to Akers, "most examples are noticeably abraded, although the occasional MS-64 with relatively smooth-looking surfaces is available. Exceptionally well-preserved 1929 Double Eagles are few and very far between."

Saint-Gaudens double eagles first attracted attention as a popular collecting discipline in the late 1930s. Early research by Dr. Charles E. Green revealed that only 25,170 double eagles had been released by the Philadelphia Mint in 1929. The rest of the large mintage of nearly 1.8 million pieces was destroyed after the Gold recall of 1933, explaining the rarity of the date today. When Green sold his holdings as the Dr. Charles W. Green Collection (B. Max Mehl, 4/1949), Mehl described the 1929 in lot 799 as:

> "I unhesitatingly class the coin as extremely rare, far more so than is generally recognized. This is the first specimen that I have offered in my Sales. Such great collections as the Roach, Atwater and others did not have it. There have only been three or four offered at auction at all. The coin has an auction record of $290.00. I believe it to be as rare as the 1921."

A group of about 80 coins surfaced in the 1980s, and another mini-hoard of 10 pieces was handled by Jeff Garrett in the early 1990s, increasing the availability of the 1929 to its present levels. NGC has certified four coins in MS65, with one finer; while PCGS has graded 22 specimens at the Gem level, with five finer (10/09). While it is not unusual to find a Choice MS64 example in a collection, Gems are seldom seen, even in the best collections. Here is an opportunity to acquire a remarkable Gem 1929 double eagle.

The present coin is sharply struck, with attractive and uniform brilliant yellow-gold surfaces and bright mint frost that forms shimmering satin luster. The reverse is accented by richly variegated shades of lilac, intermingled with subtle yellow and rose color. Its overall eye appeal is absolutely amazing.

Ex: Dallas Bank Collection (Sotheby's/Stack's, 10/2001), lot 209.

From The Jay Brahin Collection.(#9190)

Frosty Gem 1929 Double Eagle, Rare So Fine

2336 1929 MS65 PCGS. The 1929 Philadelphia twenty dollar begins a string of renowned low-survival issues that culminate in the magical 1933 coins, one of them legal to own, the other contested pieces currently the subject of hot litigation, cancelled press releases, moves and countermoves.

All of the 1929-1932 issues, which include the 1929, 1930-S, 1931, 1931-D, and 1932, are famous among numismatists and collectors of this celebrated series of large gold coins. The 1929 double eagle has a significance that is sometimes overlooked or forgotten, in that it bears the date of the year that began the Great Depression, beginning with the stock market crash of October 29, 1929.

All of the 1929-32 dates are rare, although the 1929 has seen a few more hoard discoveries and repatriations of overseas holdings than the other issues in the series. Nonetheless, the 1929 should almost be viewed as two separate issues, since in Gem grade or finer it is prohibitively rare. Akers in his updated *Handbook* writes the following concerning the 1929:

> "The 1929 is the least rare of the group in an absolute sense, but it is still a challenging issue to locate in all Mint State grades. When offered in today's market, the 1929 is apt to grade MS-60 to MS-64. The population falls off markedly in MS-65, and the issue is currently unknown any finer than MS-66. In fact, the 1929 is rarer in high grades than the 1931 and 1932."

The certified data from NGC and PCGS verify Akers' assertion, as barring duplications there are less than two dozen Gems certified, with only a half-dozen or fewer at the MS66 level. This splendid Gem offers swirling luster over frosted surfaces. The obverse is an even orange-gold, while the reverse shows shades of lilac interspersed on the eagle. The strike is sharp if a trifle short of full, but the eye appeal is over the top.

From The Ralph P. Muller Collection.(#9190)

Lot 2337

LIBERTY
1930
UNITED·STATES·OF·AMERICA
TWENTY·DOLLARS
IN·GOD·WE·TRUST

Elusive 1930-S Saint-Gaudens Twenty, MS65
Underrated, Low Mintage Issue
Key to the Late Date Series

2337 1930-S MS65 PCGS. CAC. The 1930-S Saint-Gaudens double eagle is, historically, the most underappreciated coin in this popular series. Previously, the true rarity of the later dates in the series was overshadowed by the more celebrated Ultra High Reliefs, the ultra-rare 1927-D issue, and the controversial 1933 date. While collectors have long recognized that all the dates from 1929-1932 are elusive, the coins have never received the attention garnered by the "Big Three." Today, recently published research from numismatists such as Q. David Bowers, David Akers, Jeff Garrett, and Ron Guth, and data from the major grading services, have established the importance of this group of dates. The coins are now coming into their own, perceived by collectors as desirable, historic rarities. The 1930-S is emerging as the undisputed star of this elite group of double eagles.

Even among specialists, the relative rarity of the later dates in the Saint-Gaudens double eagle series has only recently become clear. When David Akers published his study of double eagles in 1982, he believed coins such as the 1931-D were scarcer than the 1930-S. After reviewing more recent data, Akers reevaluated this position. In his recently published *Handbook of 20th Century United States Gold Coins,* Akers states: "The 1930-S is by far the rarest of the 1929-1932 issues in this series and, discounting the essentially uncollectable 1933, only the 1927-D is rarer when we consider the entire Saint-Gaudens series."

Q. David Bowers concurs with Akers' assessment, asserting "The 1930-S stands as a highly important rarity, second (and at a distance) only to the 1927-D among rarities in the Type 6 double eagle series, up to 1932." Heritage was privileged to offer another specimen of the 1930-S double eagle in the recent Long Beach Signature Auction (Heritage, 9/2009), lot 1984. In the lot description for that coin, we published the following study:

> "Essentially 'rarer than all but the 1927-D' is quite a breathtaking statement for connoisseurs of the series. We could not resist making a comparison:
> "—For the 1920-S, 1927-D, 1927-S, 1929, 1930-S, 1931, 1931-D, and 1932, PCGS has certified, in all grades, respectively: 86, 7, 135, 164, 40, 79, 97, and 69 pieces (less duplicates). (9/09).
> "—For the 1920-S, 1927-D, 1927-S, 1929, 1930-S, 1931, 1931-D, and 1932, NGC has certified, in all grades, respectively: 82, 5, 124, 129, 19, 40, 48, and 69 pieces (less duplicates). (9/09).
> "If we assume that the certified population reflects the total population, and that all of the issues above have the same percentages of duplicates (both reasonable but not necessarily true assumptions, nor yet provably false), then the data certainly appear to support Akers' astonishing assertion. Even if some issues have a higher percentage of duplicates, the differences are compelling."

The 1930-S boasts an original mintage of just 74,000 pieces, the third lowest of the series. The coins were not widely circulated at their date of issue, and all but a tiny portion of the mintage was melted in the Gold Recall of the mid-1930s. In the catalog of the Norweb Collection (Stack's, 11/2006), a remarkable piece of correspondence between Dr. Charles Green and Louis Eliasberg is reproduced. In this document, Green tells of a consultation he had with the assistant director of the Mint in which many Mint records were made available for him to study. Green was able to determine the exact number of double eagles released by the various Mint facilities for many important dates in the 1920s and 1930s. Regarding the 1930-S double eagle, Green states only 3,250 examples of this issue were officially released from the San Francisco Mint before the Gold Recall. Experts estimate a surviving population of just 40-60 specimens today.

The first appearance of a 1930-S double eagle at public auction was in the J.F. Bell Collection (Stack's, 12/1944), lot 991. The coin was described as "Brilliant Uncirculated" and realized $475, a strong price at the time (the 1927-D in that sale only realized $25 more). The same coin was offered in the Dr. Charles Green Collection (Mehl, 4/1949), lot 883. Green was an important numismatic scholar of this period, and he was an early student of the Saint-Gaudens series, as shown by the research alluded to above. The Green catalog is one of the few important sales of U.S. gold coins from this era that was not included in Akers' survey when he published his seminal work. The catalog provides much interesting information for the modern researcher.

In his *Complete Encyclopedia of U.S. and Colonial Coins,* Walter Breen reported most surviving 1930-S double eagles had been repatriated "from European banks about 1960." Numismatic evidence, particularly the condition of the coins themselves, has cast some doubt on this statement in recent years. Nearly all examples seen are Uncirculated, with most coins grading MS64 and above. A typical example is lustrous, with strong eye appeal and a sharp strike. The coins just seem too nice to be hoard specimens. Garrett and Guth opine, "Those that did survive were likely held by American coin collectors or dealers, and it is almost certain that none were shipped overseas from this Western mint." However, there is strong anecdotal evidence that Breen was correct about at least some of the coins emerging from European holdings. In the catalog of the Lake Michigan and Springdale Collections (American Numismatic Rarities, 6/2006), lot 2787, the following conversation between John Ford (speaking) and Q. David Bowers is recalled:

> "I remember that Paul Wittlin, who used to buy gold coins for Jim Kelly in Paris and other places in Europe, got into a major argument with Kelly in 1960, and for a time they stopped doing business together (they later reconciled). Wittlin approached me with four gem 1930-S twenties he had just purchased, and I bought the lot for about $750 apiece. I took them with me to the ANA Convention in Atlanta in 1961, and put one of them in a case. Harvey Stack spotted it, and we made a deal for $1,000, and then I told him I had three more—and he bought them all. Later I met the man in Paris from whom Wittlin had bought them—he was a coin dealer in that city—and I learned that he had charged Wittlin $400 each. So, that is how four of these found their way to America."

It is clear from Ford's reminiscence that at least a few of the 1930-S double eagles were saved from the melting pot by foreign bankers.

The present coin is a magnificent specimen of this sought-after date. The surfaces are radiantly lustrous, with an attractive layer of crimson patina. Handling marks are consistent with the grade. We note a light mark in the left (facing) obverse field at about 9 o'clock, extending from a star to the rays. The strike is impressive, as usually seen on this issue. Exquisite detail shows on all design elements, especially on the eagle's feathers and the pillars of the Capitol. Fabulous eye appeal complements the high technical grade to make this offering a coin to remember.
From The Ralph P. Muller Collection.(#9191)

Marvelous 1931 Saint-Gaudens Double Eagle, MS65

Bowers: 'One of the Key Issues in the Series'

2338 1931 MS65 PCGS. The Philadelphia Mint achieved a large mintage of more than 2.9 million double eagles in 1931. If original mintage were the only factor in a coins rarity, the 1931 Saint-Gaudens double eagle would be a common coin indeed. However, as numismatists have long known, mintage statistics are meaningless when discussing the rarity of the later issues of this series. Distribution is the true key to their rarity; the great majority of the 1931 production was melted and transformed into ingots in 1937, after the Gold Recall of 1933. Historically, not everyone in the numismatic community understood the relative rarity of the 1931. In the catalog of the Thaine B. Price Collection (Akers, 5/1998), lot 120, David Akers mused:

> "For many years, the 1931 was considered to be the second most common of the rare late date issues of the Saint-Gaudens series, i.e. those issues from 1929-1932. It was considered to be more rare than the 1929, but less rare than the other three, in particular, the 1932.— That misconception has been corrected now, and today the 1931 is appropriately regarded as the second rarest of the late date issues with respect to population rarity after only the 1930-S."

The actual number of 1931 Philadelphia Mint double eagles available today is a source of some disagreement. Q. David Bowers calls the 1931 "one of the key issues in the series" and estimates a surviving population of 80-120 Mint State specimens, with half a dozen or so examples in circulated grades still extant. Those figures coincide well with current population data from the leading grading services, where NGC and PCGS combined have certified a total of 119 specimens in all grades (10/09). Elsewhere in the present catalog we have mentioned Dr. Charles Green's research on the Saint-Gaudens double eagle series. This research has come to light through the efforts of Q. David Bowers, Dr. George Fuld, and Richard Eliasberg. According to Green's study, a shockingly low 45 coins of this denomination were distributed through official channels in 1931. On the other end of the spectrum, Jeff Garrett and Ron Guth estimate a surviving population of 1931s from 200 to 300 pieces, an estimate that seems overlarge.

The first auction appearance of a 1931 double eagle probably occurred in the Needham, Herrick and Other Collections (Thomas Elder, 9/1937), lot 1393. Elder's description stated, "1931. $20. Of the U.S. St. Gaudens type. A very rare year. First ever offered at auction sale! Value $350. Brilliant Uncirculated. Of greatest rarity." We have been unable to discover the price realized, but Elder's estimate is an indication of how great the demand was for this date in 1937. While Elder's estimate certainly seems high, it is small compared to the $1,250 Col. James Flanagan paid for the 1933 double eagle he purchased from B. Max Mehl just two months later. Clearly, the late date double eagles were exciting coins in the late 1930s.

The rare Gem offered here displays richly frosted surfaces and exhibits a delightful cartwheel effect when rotated slowly under a light. The strike is sharp, with crisp detail present on all design elements. The surfaces are an attractive, bright greenish-yellow, with a faint undertone of red. Both sides show a scattering of insignificant handling marks and luster grazes, entirely consistent with the grade. Overpowering luster is the standout feature of this specimen. The combination of high technical grade and intense visual appeal makes this offering a rare opportunity for the discerning collector.

From The Ralph P. Muller Collection.(#9192)

1931-D Saint-Gaudens Double Eagle, MS65 Condition Rarity, Radiant Surfaces

2339 1931-D MS65 PCGS. CAC. Ex: Brahin/Connecticut State Library. Any collector with a strong budget and a desire can assemble a nearly complete set of Saint-Gaudens double eagles. However, it is the patient collector that will assemble a World-Class set. Just finding every date and mintmark issue is a challenge, but patience is required to find just the right coin for each issue. Quality is the key word for the best collections, combining grade with eye appeal. The present coin is an example of the best quality. It is more than just a Gem, possessing the aesthetic characteristics of the finest coins known today.

During the throws of the depression, there was little need for coinage. For example, the Denver Mint only made cents, dimes, and double eagles in 1931. Only 106,500 of those double eagles were coined in Denver, and nearly all of the mintage remained inside Mint and treasury vaults until the time came to melt the coins a few years later. Only those few coins that were saved by collectors at the time of issue are preserved today.

The 1931-D is the second rarest D-Mint Saint-Gaudens double eagle, behind the legendary 1927-D. From a small mintage of 106,500 pieces, the 1931-D is considered the eighth rarest date in the 53 coin series. David Akers recalls that 30 years ago the 1931-D was a serious challenger to the 1930-S for the title of rarest late date Saint-Gaudens twenty. A small hoard of 15-20 pieces surfaced in the early 1980s, however, raising the availability of the 1931-D to about the same level as the 1931 and 1932 issues. Today, experts believe perhaps 95-110 examples survive in Mint State, with only a handful of coins known in circulated grades. In higher grades the 1931-D is quite rare. NGC has certified only six coins at the Gem level, with a single specimen finer; while PCGS has graded fourteen examples in MS65, with four finer.

The present coin can trace its provenance back to its date of issue, as it was part of the deaccessioned holdings of the Connecticut State Library. Elsewhere in this catalog we have told the story of Librarian George Godard and his special relationship with T. Louis Comparette, curator of the Mint Collection in the early 20th century. Godard updated the collection of the Library every year by purchasing coins directly from the mints, or from the coins provided for assay purposes if none were available through regular channels, using funds allocated for the purpose. This practice was continued, even after Comparette's death in 1922.

The coin offered here displays the bold impression that typifies the issue, but its radiant surfaces are anything but common. The typical 1931-D twenty is among the least attractive of the late-date issues, but this piece displays swirling, frosty luster and bright, reddish-gold surfaces that yield to copper and lilac on the eagle's wing. The surfaces are essentially devoid of post-production impairments although, for pedigree purposes alone, we note a small lateral abrasion on Liberty's lower right leg. This piece truly possesses the quality of the best available 1931-D double eagles and it will make a nice addition to a World-Class collection.

Ex: Museum of Connecticut History Collection (Heritage, 6/1995), lot 6033; Phillip H. Morse Collection, Part II (Heritage, 12/2005), lot 2081.

From The Jay Brahin Collection.(#9193)

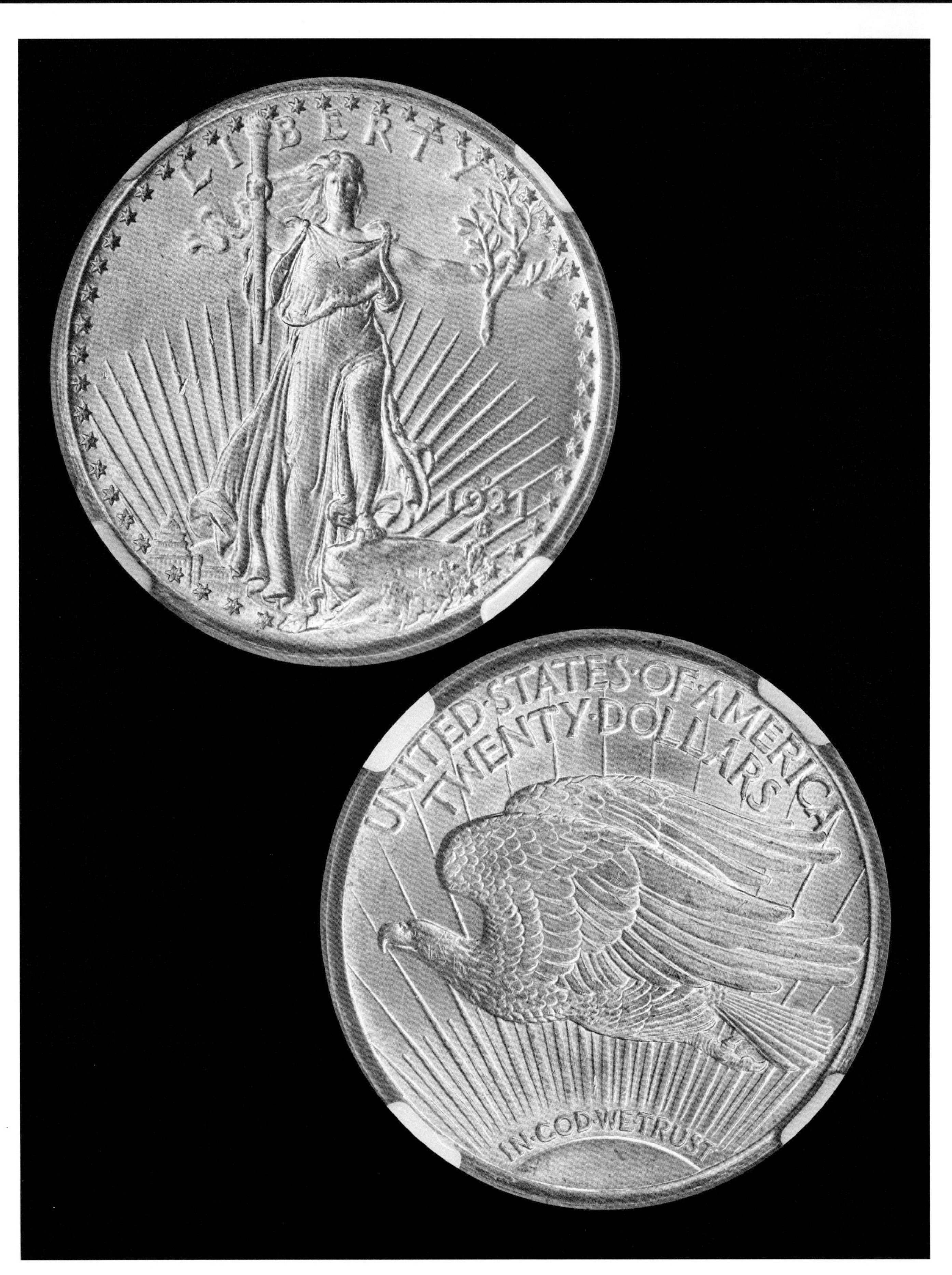

A 15% BUYER'S PREMIUM ($14 MIN.) APPLIES TO ALL LOTS.

Impressive 1931-D Saint-Gaudens Double Eagle, MS66
Second Rarest Issue from the Denver Mint
Scarce Late Date Key

2340 1931-D MS66 PCGS. The 1931-D Saint-Gaudens double eagle claims the sixth lowest mintage of the series, a paltry 106,500 pieces. The issue was probably intended for use in foreign trade, as there was little call for large denomination coins in the domestic economy during the Great Depression. Whatever their intended purpose, it seems certain that only a few specimens were ever released into circulation, and the great majority of the coins were melted after the Gold Recall of 1933. Today, experts estimate a surviving population of 100-150 specimens, with nearly all examples seen in Uncirculated grades.

Collectors have always prized Denver Mint Saint-Gaudens double eagles, but accurate information about the relative rarity of issues in the series has been particularly hard to come by. Today the 1931-D is recognized as one of the rarer issues and a great prize, but its place in the series was not always understood. When David Akers cataloged the 1931-D in the Thaine B. Price Collection (Akers, 5/1998), lot 121, he had this to say about the issue:

> "In the distant past, the 1931-D was widely regarded as the fourth or fifth rarest issue of the Saint-Gaudens Double Eagle series, surpassed in rarity only by the 1924-S, 1926-D and 1926-S, as well as possibly the 1927-S, although the latter was usually considered about the equal of the 1931-D. The 1927-D, now the premier issue of the series, was actually thought to be less rare than this issue until the early-1950s when small quantities of the 1931-D first began showing up in European banks. Over the next two decades, several mini-hoards of the 1931-D were discovered, but relatively few of these pieces graded better than Choice Uncirculated and the majority were heavily marked and lackluster."

Today numismatists consider the 1931-D to be the second rarest issue from the Denver facility behind the 1927-D, and its status as a condition rarity is undiminished. Coins at the Gem level are decidedly rare, and extremely rare any finer. This is the only coin NGC has certified at the MS66 level (PCGS has graded four) and none are finer (11/09).

Dr. Charles Green was a keen student of the Saint-Gaudens double eagle series, as well as an important collector and correspondent of Louis Eliasberg during the 1930s and 1940s. He was given access to many Mint records from the 1920s and 1930s, enabling him to determine the exact number of coins the Mint released into circulation during key dates of this period. Unfortunately, the Denver Mint records were in such disarray that he was unable to review them when he made his study in 1947. In his letter to Louis Eliasberg, reproduced in the Lake Michigan and Springdale collections (American Numismatic Rarities, 6/2006), Green reported:

> "As to the Denver mint, the records apparently were in bad shape as far as answering my query was concerned. It was stated that it would take a year to provide the information whereupon Mrs. Ross, the Director, because of the rush of work there, told the Denver Mint to forego the matter."

If the Mint was totally confused about the number of coins released during the years in question, it is no wonder the numismatic community had a false picture of the relative rarity of the Denver issues.

The early auction history of the 1931-D reflects the initial confusion about its rarity, and the gradual understanding of its true place in the series that numismatists have attained over the years. Possibly the first auction appearance of the issue was in Sale Number 399 (Morgenthau, 5/1939), lot 557. Wayte Raymond and J.G. MacAllister were the proprietors of the Morgenthau firm, and they were famous for their terse commentary. The lot description read simply, "1931 D Uncirculated and extremely rare." If this was indeed the first offering of this date, it proved an auspicious beginning. The lot realized $130, a significant sum for a coin that could be purchased for face value from the Mint only six years previously.

The issue appeared in several sales in the mid-1940s, and prices continued to be uniformly high, but the gap between the 1931-D and the 1927-D began to close, as the extreme rarity of the latter coin became more apparent. Of course, the 1926-D was still perceived as the rarest coin in the series throughout the decade. Charles Green decided to sell his collection in a landmark auction through dealer B. Max Mehl on April 26, 1949. Lot 918 was impressively presented as:

> **"The Excessively Rare 1931 Denver Mint $20.00 Gold Piece**
> **"1931 $20.00 Gold, Denver Mint.** Uncirculated. Perfect in every respect, full frosty mint luster. Extremely rare and valuable. Record in the Bell Sale, in 1944, $1,100.00. Dr. Green purchased this specimen in a Philadelphia Sale, December, 1944, for $920.00. The coin catalogs now at $750.00. It is a great rarity and it is worth well into the four-figure mark."

The lot realized $760, slightly more than its catalog value, but still the lowest price of the 1940s. The 1927-D was close behind, at $630, while the 1926-D continued to lead the pack at $2,500.

The impact of repatriation of European holdings began to be apparent in the 1950s, but catalogers were slow to revise their rarity rankings. An example of the 1931-D double eagle was featured in the J.W. Schmandt Collection (Stack's, 2/1957), lot 1075. In the lot description, the Stack's cataloger reiterated the old beliefs about the relative rarity of the Denver issues, which were clearly out of date by that time.

The cataloger correctly positioned the 1931-D as the second rarest issue in the series, but he continued to record the more numerous 1926-D in the number one spot, with the true champion 1927-D in third place. Collectors were clearly ahead of the catalogers at this juncture, in terms of understanding the true rarity of these issues. The 1926-D in the sale declined sharply, realizing only $500, because knowledge of the finds in Europe had spread. The 1927-D gained more ground, realizing $1,230, while the 1931-D posted an impressive gain at $1,625. Apparently, the public had not become aware of the smaller number of 1931-D coins that had emerged from overseas havens, but the adjustment would soon be made.

By the time of the Wolfson Collection (Stack's, 10/1962), the true order of rarity among the Denver Mint issues had finally been established. Lot 1043 of that sale expounds:

> **"1931 'D'** Uncirculated, with full mint bloom. This coin is the second rarest Denver Mint Double Eagle of the St. Gaudens design, exceeded in rarity only by the elusive and extremely rare 1927 'D'. It is interesting to record here that 15 years ago it was not too difficult to locate a 1927 'D' and yet almost impossible to find a 1931 'D'. Since the recent demand for rare dates and mintmarks has far exceeded the supply, we have been better able to determine which coins are rarer than others. The 1927 'D' is definitely rarer than the 1931 'D'."

The 1931-D was the last double eagle produced at the Denver Mint. A period of 31 years after its date of issue, the true place of the 1931-D double eagle was finally established throughout the numismatic community. The lot realized $1,750, while the once-mighty 1926-D garnered only $500. Despite the emergence of a hoard of 15-20 pieces in 1984, the 1931-D continues to hold its place as the second rarest Saint-Gaudens double eagle from the Denver Mint today.

The mint luster on this piece is nothing short of spectacular. It is frosted and both sides exhibit richly intermingled reddish-gold and lilac patina. As usually seen, the striking details are complete throughout. Only two small marks can be used as pedigree identifiers: One is located on the obverse across ray 7 in the left field; the other is a short, diagonal mark on the top of the sun. This is an opportunity for the Saint-Gaudens specialist to acquire one of the finest examples known of this late-date rarity.
From The Ralph P. Muller Collection.(#9193)

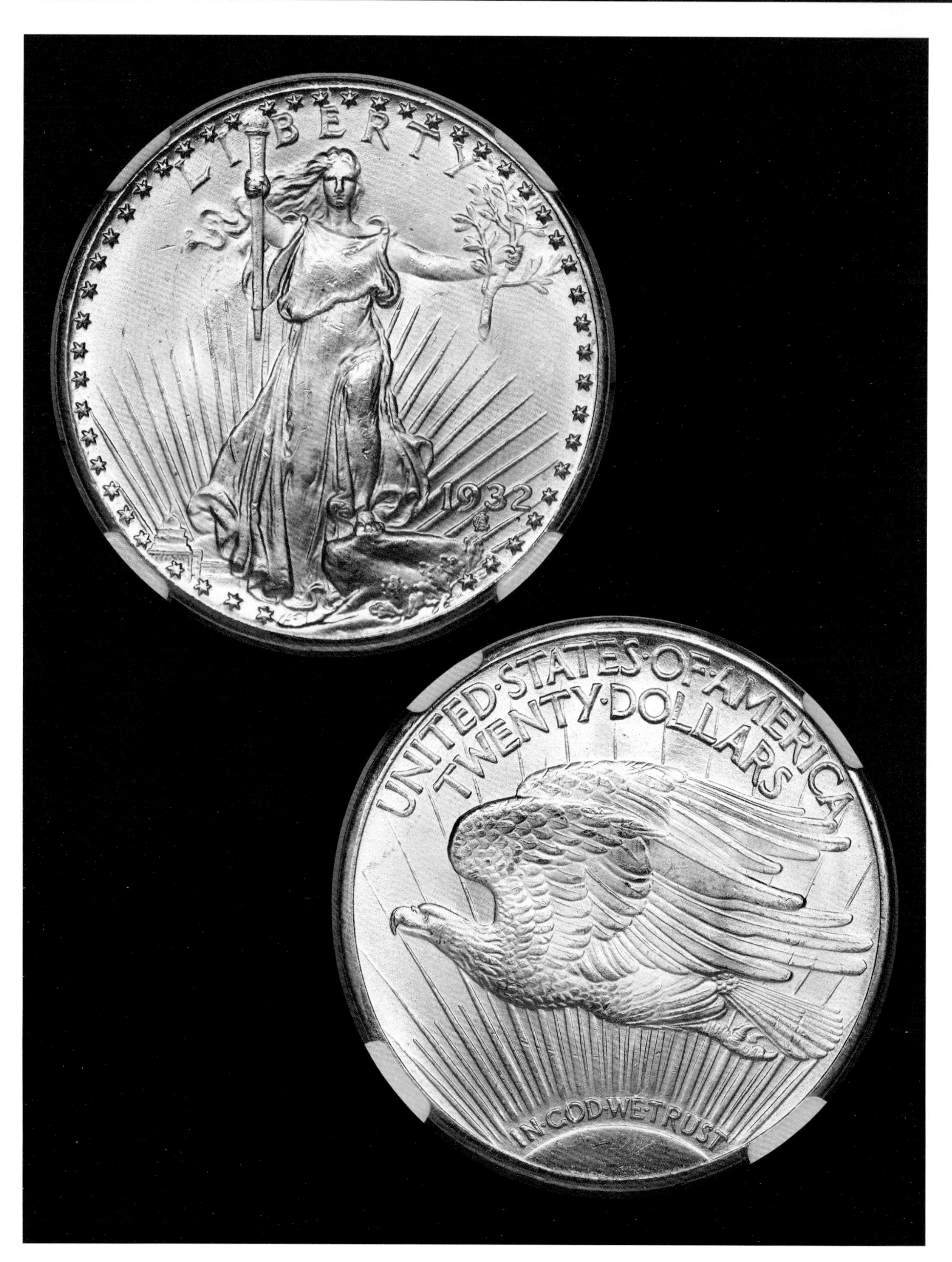
LIBERTY
1932
UNITED·STATES·OF·AMERICA
TWENTY·DOLLARS
IN·GOD·WE·TRUST

Spectacular 1932 Saint-Gaudens Twenty, MS66
Last Collectible Date of the Series
Among the Finest Certified

2341 1932 MS66 PCGS. For the present time, the 1932 Saint-Gaudens double eagle is the last collectible date in this popular series. If the current struggle over the legal status of the 1933 issue is resolved in favor of the Langbords, 1932 will become the penultimate date for the series, and numismatists will have at least 11 legal-to-own 1933 double eagles to pursue for their collections. Statistically, the task of securing one of those examples will not be that much more difficult than finding a specimen of the 1932 date in Premium Gem condition now. In *A Guide Book of Double Eagle Gold Coins,* Q. David Bowers estimates a total of 11 surviving specimens of the issue at the MS66 level today, exactly the same as the available number of 1933 double eagles if the Langbords win their case. Population data from the leading grading services indicates a slightly higher total of MS66 specimens, but those figures are probably inflated by resubmissions and crossovers. Neither NGC nor PCGS has certified a specimen at the Superb Gem level, but in the *Encyclopedia of U.S. Gold Coins 1795-1933,* Jeff Garrett and Ron Guth report the specimen in the Smithsonian would probably grade MS67.

A large mintage of more than 1.1 million double eagles was accomplished at the Philadelphia Mint in 1932, but only a small portion of that mintage escaped the melting pot after the Gold Recall of 1933. In the catalog of the Norweb Collection (Stack's, 11/2006), lot 1487, the cataloger explained:

> "It is likely that no double eagles of this date were ever released either into circulation or for export. So far as we have been able to determine, all known today trace their pedigree to examples provided to collectors for face value in 1932, a courtesy that had been extended for several years (and which also included other denominations), or pieces that Treasury employees saved from the unfortunate melt of 1937 by selling them to Philadelphia and New York City dealers for modest premiums."

Examples seen today are almost always in Uncirculated grades, sharply struck, with lustrous surfaces. Research that Dr. Charles Green conducted in the 1940s indicates only 110 double eagles were officially released by the Philadelphia Mint in 1932. Bowers estimates a total surviving population of 60-80 specimens in Mint State grades, with only one or two circulated examples surviving. David Akers ranks the 1932 as the eighth rarest date in the 54-coin series.

Numismatists appreciated the rarity of the 1932 from the start, and its status as the last date readily available to the public added special interest to any appearance. The first public auction offering was probably in the Needham, Herrick and Others Collections (Thomas Elder, 9/1937), lot 1394. The lot directly followed a 1931 double eagle, and Elder commented, "1932 $20. Same type. Brilliant Uncirculated. Of greatest rarity. None struck for circulation. Value $350." Elder's estimate is quite impressive for a coin that could be purchased at the Mint for face value only five years before. Perhaps he was aware of the market for 1933 double eagles, which were selling for much higher premiums in that era.

The 1932 double eagle was featured in lot 1680 of the Flanagan Collection (Stack's, 3/1944). The lot directly preceded the first offering of a 1933 double eagle at public auction, but that coin was seized by the Secret Service and later destroyed. The 1932 double eagle realized $240, on a $200 estimate, to J.F. Bell. Bell (whose real name was Jacob Shapiro), resold the coin in December of the same year in lot 892 of Stack's famous sale of his collection. The 1932 double eagle realized $300, a substantial $60 profit in those days on a coin he held less than seven months.

In recent times the 1932 appears at auction perhaps three or four times per year, on average. At the Premium Gem level, offerings are much less frequent. A search of auction records reveals 16 appearances of the date in MS66 grade since 1990. Some notable specimens include the Norweb coin in 1988, the Thaine Price specimen in 1998, the example in the Browning Collection in 2001, and the Phillip H. Morse coin in 2005.

Regarding the high quality of the 1932 double eagle, the authors of *The Coinage of Augustus Saint-Gaudens as Illustrated by the Phillip H. Morse Collection* concur that:

> "As a rule, a high-grade 1932 is a great-looking coin with outstanding luster and color. According to Akers, it is superior in this regard to the other late-date issues, except possibly the 1930-S. The color is typically medium to rich yellow or greenish yellow-gold, but some examples exhibit light to medium orange and greenish-gold patina. Most 1932s are very frosty, but some have a satiny texture. Most specimens are sharply struck, though some of the satiny coins reveal softness on Liberty's figure. All in all, the eye appeal for this issue is well above average for the series."

That could well describe this example. The surfaces have a decided frosted texture and the striking definition is strong throughout. The reddish-gold patina shows just the slightest hint of lilac around the margin on the obverse. There are no mentionable abrasions on either side. This is a spectacular example of this famous rarity.
From The Ralph P. Muller Collection.(#9194)

1908 With Motto Twenty, PR67
First-Year Matte Proof

2342 1908 Motto PR67 NGC. Adoption of Augustus Saint-Gaudens' new designs for the ten and twenty dollar gold pieces required the rethinking of proof gold production as it had been practiced prior to 1908. Because of the radically different design compared to the previous Coronet Head coinage, it was impossible to produce proofs in the pre-1908 style, with polished fields. The reason was die curvature and texture of the field, known in Mint parlance as "ground." While it has been asserted in the past that the Mint adopted the sandblast or "matte" technique of proofing coins for collectors because it was popular in Europe, the fact is the design of the coins themselves required a different technique. In fact, sandblast proofing was not new to the United States, but its use had previously been restricted to medals. And it was medals that all four gold denominations in 1908 were modeled after.

Sandblast proofs give the finished coin a dull, non-reflective surface. Proofs were struck on a hydraulic press from new, carefully impressed dies (as with the previous brilliant method). While the dies and planchets were not polished, as they were on brilliant finish proofs, the planchets were carefully selected for smooth surfaces. An interesting passage in Roger Burdette's 1905-1908 volume of the *Renaissance* trilogy states:

> "Correctly called sandblast proof since this describes how the pieces were made. Surface very delicate and easily marred. Sandblasting tends to exaggerate the color of the gold, particularly the greenish specimens (caused by excess silver in the alloy)."

History repeated itself in 1908 with the Mint overestimating the popularity of the new sandblast proofs, just as James Ross Snowden had overestimated the reception by the collecting public to the widespread availability of proof coinage in 1858. Five hundred gold proof sets were struck in 1908, but only 101 twenties were reportedly sold (the remainder melted at year's end). Of that number somewhere between 45 and 60 examples are believed known today as recognizable proof strikings.

The color and texture of the surfaces of 1908 sandblast proofs are noticeably different from later years. Proofs from this year have distinctly deeper color, usually khaki-green, but some are olive-gold or even mustard-gold. The individual grains are much coarser than seen on later sandblast proofs. These two attributes—color and texture—are usually enough to identify a 1908 sandblast proof with the date covered. This particular coin has a subtle green-gold cast, but it is not nearly as deep as many proofs from this year. The surfaces are nearly perfect, with only the most minute contact evident with a strong magnifier.

From The Ralph P. Muller Collection.(#9205)

Impressive PR66 1911 Double Eagle First Year of Issue After Resumption of the Matte Proof Process

2343 1911 PR66 NGC. A hundred years ago the Mint was considerably more responsive to collectors and sensitive to public criticism than today. It is difficult to imagine how a small group of present-day collectors could significantly influence how proof coins are manufactured. But in 1910 highly influential collector, William H. Woodin, wrote Assistant Secretary of the Treasury Abram Piatt Andrew his opinion of the "Roman" Finish gold coins made in 1909 and 1910:

> "If any collectors objected to this finish [the sandblast finish from 1908] it was because they did not understand that the St. Gaudens designs are not adapted to the production of polished proofs. The present proofs of the St. Gaudens designs and of the Pratt designs are simply rotten. I know of no other way to express it ... "

Woodin was one of the foremost collectors in the early 20th century: he co-authored the first reference on patterns, and 23 years later was appointed Secretary of the Treasury by Franklin Roosevelt. His influence was extensive in both Mint affairs and numismatic circles. Once he expressed his dissatisfaction with the "Roman" finish of 1909-1910, Andrew asked Woodin to become the point man to see if the ANA would pass a resolution in favor of reverting to the sandblast finish of 1908. Woodin took on the task, but first warned the newly appointed Mint director that "I can get quite a number of letters favoring dull proof coins from collectors, but I could not get all collectors to agree on anything. They are a very peculiar class of people as a rule, and you would be amused if you could hear some of their ideas."

The resolution recommending a switch back to sandblast proofs passed at the ANA convention on September 7, 1910. Andrew wrote to Woodin later that month: "I have referred your correspondence with regard to the matter to the Director, and I have little doubt that he will agree with the desires of the American Numismatic Association."

When one looks at the mintages of proof twenties, it is difficult to reach the same conclusion that Woodin and the ANA came to in 1910. By all accounts, the 1908 sandblast proofs were unpopular. Undoubtedly, collectors did not suspect such a finish when they ordered their gold proof sets and 101 proofs were sold that year. In 1909, the first of only two years for the Roman finish only 67 proof twenties were sold. Collectors likely thought they would receive a sandblast finish coin again in 1909, thus the low number. In 1910 collectors bought 167 proofs, the highest number in the series. One might reasonably conclude that collectors did indeed like the untreated finish. In 1911 the production dropped to 100 proofs, and for the rest of the series numbers were far below 100.

Over the years experts have estimated that survivors number from 20 to 25 examples. Based on those we have seen coupled with data from the major grading services, we believe that somewhere between 40 and 50 proof 1911s survive. As a rule, the texture of 1911 proof twenties is similar to that from 1908, with coarser granules over the matte surface. Generally, however, the color is not as dark as seen on the first year of issue. On this piece, the granularity is virtually identical to the 1908, and the color is more reddish-tinted than the typical olive or khaki on the 1908. A few shiny spots are seen over the high points on each side, but the only notable contact mark is on the long ray below the eagle's beak.

From The Ralph P. Muller Collection.(#9208)

Nearly Perfect 1912 PR67 Saint-Gaudens Twenty

2344 1912 PR67 NGC. The 1912 proof double eagle saw a dramatic drop in the mintage from 100 pieces the year before to only 74-an augur of even lower productions to come in the future. A curious anomaly is seen in the number of survivors for 1911 and 1912; the estimated number of pieces extant today is virtually identical. In each case probably 40-50 pieces are believed known, which indicates that either a significantly higher number of 1911 proof twenties were spent or melted, or a higher percentage of 1912 twenties were saved by collectors.

The surfaces of 1912 matte proof or sandblast finish twenties differ noticeably from 1908 and 1911. The finish on 1912 pieces has a much finer granularity and is several shades lighter than either of the two previous years. Roger Burdette explains in his *1905-1908 Renaissance* reference that results could vary from one year to the next, depending on which Mint personnel performed the work and how carefully they followed directions.

Proofs from 1912 exemplify the difference between the previous brilliant proof method (pre-1908) and those from the matte proof era (1908-1915). Brilliant proofs exhibit a solid sheet of mirrored reflectivity, the only interruption being the so-called orange-peel effect that was often inadvertently created by overheating planchets in the annealing furnace at a temperature intended for a harder base metal. Sandblast or matte proofs show thousands of tiny granules that disperse light individually. This effect is best seen when examined with a magnifier. Each granule will reflect light in a different direction, giving the coin an overall "dull" appearance when seen at arm's length, but when viewed up close the randomly directed tiny granules display a collective sparkling effect. The 1912 proof twenties often show color similar to that on 1911 twenties, usually dark yellow-gold or "mustard" color. This particular coin is yellow-gold, with microscopic grains from the sandblast finish distinctly different from the 1908 and 1911 issues. There is a tiny speck of russet color (an alloy spot?) on the reverse, directly below the A in DOLLARS that can be used as a pedigree identifier. Census: 12 in 67, 1 finer (11/09).

From The Ralph P. Muller Collection.(#9209)

Superb Matte Proof 1913 Twenty
A Magnificent Example

2345 1913 PR67 NGC. The production of matte proof gold continued to decline in 1913. The mintages from 1911 through 1915 indicate that the core number of collectors for these coins varied between 50 and 100. In 1913 only 58 proof twenties were produced. The overall level of preservation is quite high for the 1913, rivaled only by the 1908 and 1911. Because of the high level of preservation and lack of attrition compared to other years, the 1913 proof twenty ranks sixth of the 10 sandblast and "Roman" finish proofs in both overall and high-grade rarity. Both major services combined have graded 72 coins, a number obviously representing numerous resubmissions. Our best estimate is that no more than 35-40 different coins survive today.

The sandblast surface of this coin has even finer granules than the 1912 in the Ferrari Collection. While the finish on the 1913 proof twenty is sometimes compared to that on the 1908 in the standard literature for the series, that is not our experience from this group of coins. The 1908's texture is significantly coarser than the 1912 or the present 1913. This piece also displays atypical color; the references lead one to expect a brownish-gold or khaki-gold coin, but this example is much closer to a reddish-tinted yellow-gold. When closely examining the coin with a magnifier one has to wonder why, despite its already lofty grade level, it is not graded even higher. We note two "imperfections," one on each side. On the seventh ray on the right of the obverse, above the 9 in the date, a tiny cluster of what appear to be specks of grease was struck into the coin during manufacture. On the reverse, another fleck of grease was struck into the end of the eagle's tailfeathers. Most 1913 proof twenties show a partial wire rim around both sides, especially the reverse. This piece shows a complete wire rim around the reverse, with none on the obverse. One curious feature we have never noticed in the past (and the literature does not mention) is the reverse has a slight clockwise rotation relative to the obverse. This may be a unique occurrence among 1913 proof twenties, perhaps in the entire series.

For sheer visual impact, this magnificent coin is one of the finest (maybe *the* finest) example in this extraordinary set of proof twenties.

From The Ralph P. Muller Collection.(#9210)

Interesting PR67 1914 Twenty Dollar

2346 1914 PR67 NGC. The production of proof twenties remained low in 1914—but was higher than the previous year by 12 pieces. Various numismatic authors have commented on the production schedule for proof twenties for 1914. The main point of curiosity is the striking of the coins late in the year, with a secondary interest in the significant number rejected and melted. The first batch, 35 pieces, was not struck until September 28, a point of interest as proofs are normally struck at the first of the year. Of those 35 proofs struck in late September, 10 were melted. On November 4 another 35 proofs were produced, and again 10 were melted. The final batch was struck on December 19—30 pieces—and again 10 coins were rejected and melted. Thus, the net mintage of 70 proof twenties.

The consistent number of 10 coins rejected and melted is interesting. One can speculate variously what this means. One theory can be linked to a sentence from Roger Burdette's *1905-1908 Renaissance* reference: "Results of sandblasting and other techniques often varied from coin to coin and year to year, depending on which assistant did the work and whether procedures were followed carefully." What we know for certain from direct examination of 1914 proof twenties is that the surface texture is noticeably different from previous years. The coins generally have a coarser finish. This may suggest that a different assistant worked on the 1914 coins, thereby explaining the different appearance. It might also explain what appears to be a mandatory rejection of 10 proofs from each striking period. When examined in the Mint, only the finest were accepted and sent out to collectors who ordered them.

The certification of 45 pieces by both major services speaks volumes about the rarity of this year. This total number has only increased by one since we cataloged the Phillip H. Morse Collection that appeared in our November 2005 auction. When resubmissions are subtracted, it is difficult to arrive at more than 25 to 30 individual coins that survive today in all grades (one as low as PR50).

The surfaces of this magnificent piece do indeed show more granularity than the previous three years. There is evidence of slight imperfections in the sandblasting technique in the right obverse field, seen as a few nearly horizontal, raised flecks in that area. These "flecks" are covered by the sandblasting, so they either predate the application or were a part of it. We also note a darker, reddish-tinted streak in the right obverse field. None of these have any effect on the technical grade of this coin, and close examination of each side fails to reveal any post-striking defects. The coin has a pronounced green-gold hue, nearly khaki-gold as often seen on 1908 proofs. At the PR67 level, this piece represents an opportunity to acquire one of the finest examples known of the 1914. Only five other pieces have been so graded, with only one example (also an NGC coin) graded finer.
From The Ralph P. Muller Collection.(#9211)

Low Mintage, Final Year 1915 Gem Matte Proof Twenty

2347 1915 PR65 NGC. The 1915 proof twenty was a milestone in the series of sandblast (matte) proof twenties for two reasons. The mintage was a mere 50 pieces, lowest in the series, and it was the final year of issue for this special finish on U.S. gold coinage. The minuscule mintage probably represented the core number of collectors in the country who would purchase a proof twenty for their collection each year, regardless of the method of manufacture. The last time only 50 proof double eagles were produced was in 1894. The years between then and the end of the Coronet series in 1907 ranged from 50 pieces up to a high of 158 proofs in 1903. The new dime, quarter, and half dollar that went into production in 1916 had different field curvature and unevenness, similar to the twenty dollar coins, and accordingly were unsuited for traditional brilliant proofing methods. Philadelphia Mint Superintendent Adam Joyce pointed this out in a letter to Mint Director F.J.H. von Engelken on October 17, 1916:

> " ... the only difference between the proofs and the regular [nickel and silver] coins being the sharper edge and design. ... In order to distinguish gold proofs from the regular issue, it has been necessary to give them a sandblast finish, which changes the appearance of the coins to such an extent that it is almost impossible to put them in circulation. This is something I am not sure we have a right to do."

When those reasons were coupled with the additional paperwork and lost revenue producing each proof coin, von Engelken discontinued the manufacture of proof coinage the following day.

NGC and PCGS combined have certified only 51 proof 1915 twenties. Most known examples cluster tightly in the PR64-PR65 range, with few higher or lower. We estimate that probably no more than 30 individual pieces exist today in all grades. This year has the same coarse finish as seen on the 1914 twenties. The surfaces are usually darker than on 1911-1913 coins. Nevertheless, magnification shows bright, sparkling individual facets on each side. This PR65 example displays the expected coarser texture, as seen on the 1914 in the Ferrari Collection. The color is just slightly more yellow than the 1914, however. A couple of shiny spots are seen over the high points of the design, and the only contact marks (tiny ones at that) are widely scattered over the reverse.

From The Ralph P. Muller Collection.(#9212)

Very Rare 128 Grains, 22 Carats C. Bechtler Five Dollar, K-23, AU58

2348 (1837-42) C. Bechtler Five Dollar, 128G. 22C. AU58 NGC. K-23, R.6. The very rare C. Bechtler five dollar struck to a stated 128 grains - 22 carats standard. This near-Mint example, if it ever circulated, did so only briefly. The sun-yellow surfaces remain immensely lustrous, and the protected areas around the devices exhibit considerable reflectivity. Only minor evidence of friction precludes a finer designation, and neither side shows any individually significant abrasions. Softly struck with ill-defined obverse rims, though the reverse rims are uneven but complete. Listed on page 361 of the 2010 *Guide Book*.(#10103)

Rare K-10 C. Bechtler 67 G, 21 C. Quarter Eagle, MS60 With Lamination

2349 (1837-42) C. Bechtler Quarter Eagle, 67G. 21C.—Obverse Lamination—MS60 NGC. K-10, R.5. A significant, largely retained planchet lamination affects the G in 67 G and the spaces above and below. That side also shows a significant planchet void at the C in CAROLINA, which corresponds to the prominent reverse die break above the second E in BECHTLER. Both sides offer strong yellow-gold luster with no trace of actual wear, and the coin has considerable eye appeal despite its production flaws. A valuable survivor of this rare C. Bechtler quarter eagle variant, the only one made at the 67 grains standard. Listed on page 360 of the 2010 *Guide Book*.(#10067)

Lustrous 1861 Clark, Gruber Quarter Eagle, K-5a, MS62

2350 1861 Clark, Gruber & Co. Quarter Eagle MS62 NGC. K-5a, R.4. Two points of the star above the P in PIKE are recut, and recutting also shows on the P in PIKE in the coronet. The 1861 Clark, Gruber designs imitated federal-style coinage, replacing the embarrassingly naïve depictions of a perfectly triangular Pike's Peak on the 1860 coinage.

This piece shows greenish-gold surfaces with a few stray contact marks but full luster, along with some moderate strike weakness in the center that is typical of the issue. This piece is tied with a handful of others in this grade, but there are few finer. Listed on page 378 of the 2010 *Guide Book*. Census: 10 in 62, 3 finer (11/09). (#10139)

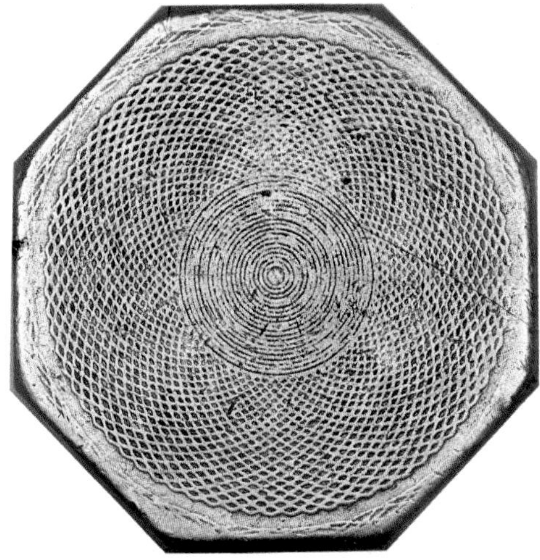

XF Sharpness 1851 Humbert Fifty 880 Thous, Reeded Edge, K-5

2351 1851 Humbert Fifty Dollar, Reeded Edge, 880 Thous.—Reverse Scratched—NCS. XF Details. K-5, Low R.5. A faint straight pinscratch crosses the reverse between 10:30 and 3:30, but hardly seems worthy of a 'Scratched' designation. The eagle's shield and rock show wear consistent with the XF Sharpness grade. The wings display luster and impressive plumage detail. A few small bagmarks are scattered above the eagle and throughout AMERICA. Moderate rim dings are present at 4 o'clock on the obverse, and at 4 and 11 o'clock on the reverse. Circulated slugs often have small bruises on the rim corners, due to the softness of the alloy, the indifference of frontier commerce, and the sheer weight of the piece. Listed on page 363 of the 2010 *Guide Book*.(#10211)

Outstanding 1851 Humbert K-6 Slug, AU53

2352 1851 Humbert Fifty Dollar, Reeded Edge, 887 Thous. AU53 PCGS. K-6, R.4. The massive 50 dollar gold slugs, or ingots as they were called at the time, are among the most popular gold coins issued in California. They are often classified in the same series as private and territorial gold coins; however, the issuing authority for these pieces was the United States of America, with Augustus Humbert as U.S. assayer, so calling them private gold pieces is incorrect. Since California officially became a state in September 1850, the term territorial gold coinage is also incorrect. In fact, the various U.S. Assay Office gold coins issued in California should be considered a regular issue gold coins just like any gold coin issued struck in Philadelphia or any branch mint. As such, they can be considered the only regular issue U.S. 50 dollar gold coins.

This lovely piece has an excellent blend of green, lilac, and orange over bright yellow-gold surfaces with considerable remaining luster. A short time in commerce resulted in a number of minor surface ticks and nicks, but they have obviously been present for a long time as the orange toning is visible inside most of those marks. The edges and rims are quite well preserved, and the corners of this octagonal piece are little marred. This outstanding slug is an excellent representative of the "Days of '49." Listed on page 364 of the 2010 *Guide Book*.(#10214)

Near-Mint (1849) Miners Bank Ten Dollar, K-1

2353 (1849) Miners Bank Ten Dollar AU58 NGC. K-1, R.6. The Miners Bank was among the first issuers of California gold coins. The earliest evidence of the Wright & Co. firm's existence comes not from coins but currency, one dollar bills dated March 1, 1849, despite a provision in the California Constitution prohibiting the utterance of paper currency.

We consider the coin's obverse to be the side with the MINERS BANK legend and the denomination, although NGC has inserted the coin with the opposite side facing forward. At any rate, the obverse reads MINERS BANK with two stars, one on each side, and SAN FRANCISCO around the rim. TEN. D. is in the center. The reverse bears an eagle similar to the federal-style coins, shield on its breast and clutching arrows and laurel leaves, with 13 stars below and CALIFORNIA above.

Kagin's reference on Territorial gold notes that the copper-alloyed pieces, K-1, were struck in the East with a collar producing normal rims, then the dies were brought West where silver-alloyed coins were struck with beveled rims and no collar, causing an anomaly at the top of the I in CALIFORNIA.

This piece is of the first type, with normal rims and orange-gold coloration caused by the copper alloy (coins with a greater percentage of silver in the alloy will produce a more greenish-gold color). This is a well-centered coin with only light field chatter on each side that separates it from Mint State. Much luster remains, and the eye appeal is outstanding. Listed on page 368 of the 2010 *Guide Book*. Census: 4 in 58, 7 finer (11/09).(#10236)

Noteworthy 1849 Moffat & Co. Five, K-4a, MS62

2354 1849 Moffat & Co. Five Dollar MS62 PCGS. K-4a, R.4. Die crumbling is prevalent, but no cud is yet present above the D in GOLD. The straw-gold surfaces are luminous and display no obvious marks. A loupe reveals a solitary hair-thin line on Liberty's neck, and the highpoints of the hair show slight blending of detail. Luster is particularly evident on the reverse. An important example from the first year of private gold coinage in California. Moffat & Co. was the second facility to coin gold, after Norris, Gregg, & Norris. Moffat continued minting through 1853, albeit in the name of the U.S. Assay Office. Listed on page 363 of the 2010 *Guide Book*. Population: 9 in 62, 5 finer (11/09).(#10240)

Rare 1849 Mormon Quarter Eagle, K-1, AU50

2355 1849 Mormon Quarter Eagle AU50 PCGS. K-1, High R.5. Struck from gold dust collected along the American River in California, soon after the Gold Rush began in 1848-49. Although coined from the native California gold, additional alloys were added which brought the fineness below the stated value on the coins. Repudiation by bankers followed, and few merchants accepted these pieces outside the Mormon Church. The vast majority of the issue was eventually melted. A full set of 1849 Mormon Gold was offered in The Dr. George Alfred Lawrence Collection (Thomas Elder, 6/1929), with the quarter eagle as lot 1374, "1849. $2 1/2. Same type as preceding only value. TWO. AND. HALF. DO. Near fine. (Ellsworth Coll'n) VR. **Plate.**"

The present coin features bright, even yellow-gold color, and the minutely grainy surfaces exhibit only small, individually indistinguishable marks. The obverse die is buckled through the lower portion of the all seeing eye, which weakens that area, and is diagnostic for this issue. Population: 5 in 50, 11 finer (11/09).(#10259)

Lustrous 1849 Norris, Gregg, & Norris Five Dollar, K-2, AU50

2356 1849 Norris, Gregg, & Norris Five Dollar, Plain Edge AU50 PCGS. K-2, R.5. Period after ALLOY. Dan Brown's *The Lost Symbol* is a fitting read for these coins, as it was more than a half-century between their production and when the source of their enigmatic "N.G. & N." stamp finally was revealed. Among U.S. Assayer of Gold Augustus Humbert's coins sold in 1902 was a perfect example of the issue, wrapped in a piece of paper reading, "From my friends, Norris, Grigg & Norris." (Today's commonly accepted "Gregg" was also spelled "Grigg" and "Grieg" in contemporary sources.) Today they are considered the very first of the California gold issuers, having produced coins as early as May 1849. As such, their historic coinage is highly prized by collectors.

The coins appear to have circulated well, proof that they were accepted in commerce. Early assays by Eckfeldt and Dubois substantiated the firm's claim that they weighed 1 percent more than federal half eagles and sold in major cities in the East at the same premium. The present AU example is attractive and problem-free, showing a complete 5 on the high point of the shield—the first detail that wear will efface. The surfaces are antique-gold, with considerable luster remaining. A few small hits dot the surfaces, mostly on the reverse, which account for the grade. Listed on page 360 of the 2010 *Guide Book*. Population: 5 in 50, 19 finer (11/09).(#10279)

Famous 1849 Norris, Gregg, & Norris Five Dollar, Reeded Edge, K-4, XF40

2357 1849 Norris, Gregg, & Norris Five Dollar R.E. XF40 PCGS. Period, K-4, R.4. One of the most famous "solved enigmas" of American numismatics is the meaning of the initials "N. G & N." on the territorial half eagles now known as Norris, Gregg & Norris. The key was a note found among the possessions of Augustus Humbert, the famous California coiner and assayer, who should have known the truth as well as anyone! This dusky orange-gold example saw appreciable use in California commerce, as suggested by its wear and scattered abrasions, yet it remains highly pleasing. Listed on page 362 of the 2010 *Guide Book*. For all Reeded Edge varieties, Population: 11 in 40, 30 finer (11/09).(#10282)

Splendid 1852 Wass Molitor Ten Dollar Large Head, Wide Date, K-4, MS62 Tied for Finest at PCGS

2358 1852 Wass Molitor Ten Dollar, Large Head, Wide Date MS62 PCGS. K-4, R.5. The firm of Wass, Molitor & Co. produced only five dollar and ten dollar pieces in 1852, while in 1855 they made ten dollars, twenty dollars, and fifty dollars. The ten dollar denomination was the only one that repeated in 1855. The 1852 fives and tens are both known with so-called Small Head and Large Head styles (although Kagin calls the ten dollar pieces "Long Neck" and "Short Neck," respectively, for the Small Head and Large Head.) The 1852 ten dollars are known with three date styles: High Narrow Date, Low Narrow Date, and Wide Date, as here. All of the 1852 Wide Date tens are of the Large Head (or Short Neck) type. The Large Head, Wide Date shows the 2 in the date slanted to the left at its top and partially protruding from under the bust truncation. All known examples of the 1852 K-4 ten show numerous obverse die cracks—Kagin enumerates 10; see that reference for the detailed list—as well as three others on the reverse. Clearly this was a die that was stressed and ready to crack, or cracked already, before any coins were struck—or, at least, any that survive today.

The present piece shows wonderfully deep, rich orange-gold color with lots of luster remaining. Scattered minor abrasions, mostly seen under a loupe, account for the grade. The softness on the reverse is a function of the obverse die being cut too deeply rather than wear. In MS62 the present piece appears to be the finest that we have ever offered of this variety, by two grade points. Any serious collector knows that the gap between MS60 and MS62 can be a huge void, and this coin makes a splendid representative of the immense difference in the two grades. Listed on page 372 of the 2010 *Guide Book*. Population: 2 in 62, 0 finer (11/09).(#10348)

S.S. CENTRAL AMERICA GOLD BARS

Important Harris, Marchand & Co. Gold Ingot From the *S.S. Central America*, 18.41 Ounces

2359 Small- to Medium-Sized Harris, Marchand & Co. Gold Ingot. CAGB-127. Serial number 6510, 18.41 oz, 712 fine, stamped value $270.96. An infrequently encountered assayer compared to Justh & Hunter or Kellogg & Humbert, though at just over three dozen ingots recovered, the Harris, Marchand & Co. imprint is more accessible than a number of others. In his *A California Gold Rush History,* Q. David Bowers lists a number of attributes for the Harris, Marchand & Co. ingots as a class: "Nearly all of the ingots display irregular alignment of numerals and many have irregular letter alignment as well. Most bars have rather rough surfaces ... Save for the finely crafted hallmark and the curved logotype with the company name, most imprinting is rustic."

The hallmark bears further attention; as Bowers notes, Harris, Marchand & Co. "... *[original italicized]* is the only firm that used a coin-die style hallmark on its ingots." This hallmark takes the form of an all-seeing eye surrounded by rays and flanked left and right by five-pointed stars, which separate the words MARCHAND / ESSAYEUR. The broad circular field is the only significant area on which this ingot shows truly smooth surfaces.

The ingot's main face, read as oriented with the corner cut at upper left, states NO *[line below O]* 6510 / *[curving]* HARRIS MARCHAND & CO / [hallmark]. From there, the north face lists the value of $270.96, the south face has *[upside down]* 712 FINE, and the east face has 18.41 OZ, with dots below both letters. Overall color is light yellow-gold with deep red encrustation at parts of the hallmark, the beginning and end of the curved imprint, a line at the lower right part of the main face, and at the bottom halves of the digits in 712. A memorable shipwreck ingot that offers a different perspective on the California Gold Rush.

Ex: FUN 2002 (Heritage, 1/2002), lot 7904.

NO.4146.
185.21 OZS.
876 FINE
$3353.87

Justh & Hunter Gold Ingot, 185.21 Ounces
Attractive Smooth Surfaces
Ex: *S.S. Central America*

2360 Justh & Hunter 185-Ounce Gold Ingot. Emil (or Emanuel) Justh was a follower of Lajos Kossuth, the famous Hungarian freedom fighter. Kossuth took advantage of the general wave of unrest that swept across all of Europe in 1848 to further the cause of Hungarian freedom from Austria. Unfortunately, his movement was crushed by Russian intervention in 1849, and Kossuth fled into exile in the United States and Great Britain. With his political future looking bleak at home, Justh opportunely heeded the siren song of the Gold Rush. He left his home in Verboca, Hungary and made his way to the German port of Hamburg. From there, he boarded ship on the *Gellert* and sailed directly for San Francisco on May 18, 1850. After 159 days at sea, he arrived on November 15 of that same year. Justh was a lithographer by profession in Hungary, and he began his career in San Francisco as a lithographer. In 1852, he and another immigrant named F.I. Goerlitz formed a short-lived general Ship and Customs House Broker business. This partnership lasted less than a month, and apparently Justh then found employment at the new Assay Office as an assayer.

Justh's future business partner, Solomon Hillen Hunter, arrived in San Francisco aboard the steamship *Sonora* on March 3, 1855. Ironically, prior to boarding this ship on the Pacific side of Panama, Hunter was a passenger on the *S.S. George Law.* Shortly thereafter, the *George Law* was renamed the *S.S. Central America.* So, Solomon Hunter was actually on board the famous treasure ship two years before it sank in the Atlantic with more than 80 gold ingots stamped with his name.

In 1855, Justh and Hunter formed a partnership in San Francisco to assay gold. The firm prospered and in the following year they opened a branch office in Marysville. In spite of its good reputation, the partnership only lasted a couple of years and was dissolved on July 10, 1858. Of course, by then millions of dollars in Justh and Hunter ingots, including the present specimen, as well as bars of numerous other California gold refiners lay at the bottom of the ocean, enough bullion to be a factor in the Panic of 1857.

Solomon Hunter returned to New York in 1858 and was last listed in the *Baltimore City Directory* in 1860. Emil Justh continued to lead a colorful life. In 1861, Justh sold his refinery to Kellogg, Hewston & Co. as he intended to go east. True to his word, Justh sailed to New York City and began a career as a stockbroker.

In 1871, Justh had a "complicated" divorce case. The 45-year old stockbroker had the following sordid account of his life included in the *New York Times* from October 21:

> "On Wednesday last John T. Burleigh of No. 23 Dey Street, appeared before Judge Shandley, at Jefferson Market Police Court, and stated that several important letters, and a check for $30, were stolen from his safe by a private detective named A.A. Ackerman, at the instance of Emil Justh, a banker residing at No. 63 Exchange Place. Yesterday Sergt. McComb proceeded to the residence of Mr. Justh, to arrest him on the charge, but the latter refused to accompany him to the Station, and when force was used, presented a revolver at the officer's head. Patrolman Tully witnessed the occurrence, and before the weapon could be discharged wrenched it from his hand. He was then conveyed to the Station, where the letters were found in his possession. These letters, Justh alleges, afford proof of the seduction of his wife by Burleigh, and he desired to use them in proceedings for divorce now pending. Justh was discharged from custody, and Judge Shandley retained the letters in his possession for the present."

Apparently, Justh had retained the spirit of the Wild West in his Eastern life. His temerity in threatening the police with a gun could have ended badly, but the luck of the Gold Rush was still with him. Justh later moved to Paris, where he died in December 1883.

The present offering is a clean, problem-free ingot, with remarkably smooth surfaces. It measures 149 x 71 x 29 mm. The top is impressed: NO. 4146/Justh & Hunter (curved company imprint)/185.21 OZS 876 FINE/$3353.87. The inscriptions are attractively laid out in a horizontal pattern, with ample space between the lines. The weight in ounces and the fineness are logically recorded on the same line. The bottom side was unevenly inscribed with the individual ingot number, but only the 46 is visible. The back side of the ingot features a long depressed area often seen on these ingots, the result of the casting process. The depression is filled with a reddish-russet patina, most likely caused by contact with the rusting iron ribs of the ship (see *A California Gold Rush History* for details). The item offered here is an important memento from this historic California assayer and refiner.

No 615
KELLOGG
&
HUMB
ASSAY
102.17 OZ
903
FINE
$1907.17

Kellogg & Humbert Gold Ingot, 102.17 Ounces
Ideal Representative California Ingot
Ex: *S.S. Central America*

2361 Kellogg & Humbert Assayers 102-Ounce Gold Ingot. Kellogg and Humbert were a highly respected private partnership that was formed in April 1855 and remained in business until 1860. The firm's name is closely associated with the treasure of the *S.S. Central America*, as they manufactured far and away the greatest number of gold bars recovered from that famous shipwreck. The partnership is also well known for its twenty and fifty dollar gold pieces that were created in an era in which the recently opened San Francisco Mint could not keep up with demand for coinage.

John Glover Kellogg was born on December 3, 1823, in Marvellus, Onondaga County, New York. He studied law and passed the bar, but succumbed to the call of the goldfields before he could set up in practice. He sailed aboard the bark *Belvedere* on February 13, 1849, taking the long route around Cape Horn, and arrived in San Francisco on October 12 of the same year.

Upon arrival, Kellogg sought employment with the highly esteemed Moffat & Co., a private coining firm that later became the United States Assay Office of Gold, and eventually turned over operations to the firm of Curtis, Perry and Ward. Kellogg later formed a partnership with assayer G.F. Richter and operated with great success, minting approximately $6 million in twenty dollar gold pieces used in the regional economy.

Augustus Humbert was born on July 2, 1815, in Switzerland. After immigrating to the United States, Humbert was appointed United States Assayer of Gold in San Francisco. He joined Kellogg in the firm of Kellogg & Humbert in April 1855. The new firm operated as an assaying and coining firm, with offices at No. 104 Montgomery Street in San Francisco.

When the San Francisco Mint was first established in April of 1854 its operations were hampered by shortages of many critical supplies, such as alloy and parting acids. The facility was not able to satisfy the need for coinage in the booming Western economy. Kellogg & Humbert helped supply the shortfall, primarily by issuing twenty dollar gold coins until the end of 1855, when the Mint was fully operational. A newspaper article in May 1855 revealed that Kellogg & Co. delivered 50% more coinage than the San Francisco Mint during this period, with an output of $60,000 to $80,000 per day.

Kellogg and Humbert dissolved their partnership in 1860. Kellogg organized other business ventures, returned to New York for a time, and finally returned to California to manage the Pacific Refinery and Bullion Exchange. He died on April 21, 1886. Humbert retired from the firm in 1860 and returned to New York. He arrived onboard the *Northern Light* on June 27,1860. He died suddenly in Paris, France on June 6, 1873. Humbert's coin collection was auctioned by the Chapman brothers, on behalf of his heirs, in May of 1902. Lot 716 was a Kellogg & Co. proof fifty dollar gold piece from 1855.

For those who desire a single representative ingot of California native gold, the present ingot is ideal. Few such ingots have survived outside of shipwreck finds over the years, due to the high intrinsic gold value. This particular ingot, along with many other Kellogg and Humbert bars, was recovered from the *S.S. Central America*. Indeed, more Kellogg & Humbert ingots were represented in the treasure than those of any other assay firm. Many recovered ingots in the treasure were sold at auction by Christie's New York office on December 14, 2000. The ingots varied in size and fineness with the smallest ingots realizing higher premiums over current gold value. Although not as many buyer's were in the market for the larger size ingots, today these represent an ideal combination for desirability and value.

This medium-sized ingot measures 55 x 112 x 29 mm, and has bright yellow-gold color throughout. The top side was intended to read: No. 615 / KELLOGG & HUMBERT ASSAYERS / 102.17 Oz / 903 FINE / $1907.17. Three large gas bubbles from the casting process have slightly distorted the inscription. One bubble makes the company imprint read HUMB ASSAY, rather than HUMBERT ASSAYERS. Another bubble is located just to the left of F in FINE. The third bubble is just barely touches the top of the 0 in the value. On the back side the individual bar number 615 is repeated. Opposing corners have the assay chip that is so-well known on these ingots. It is instructive to note the .903 fineness is actually higher than the standard for gold coins.

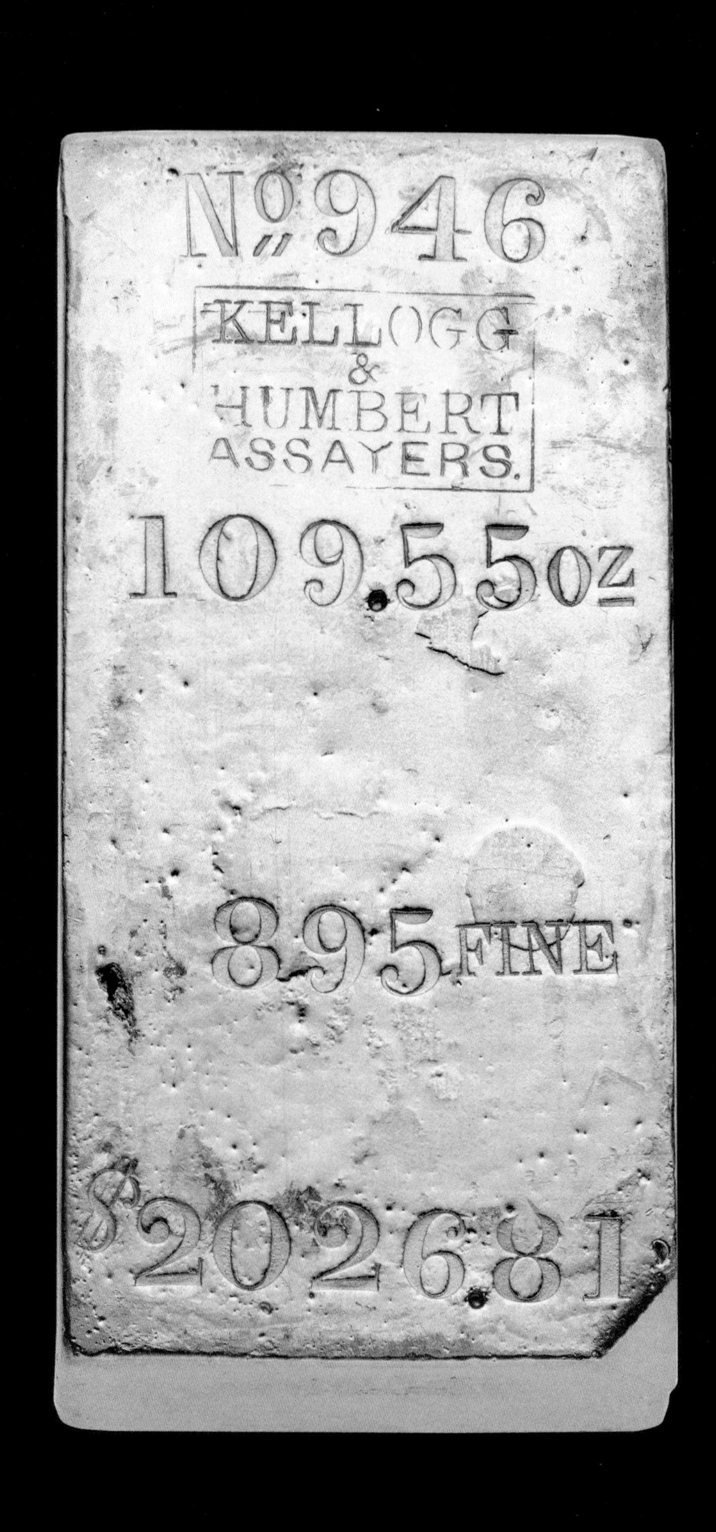
No 946
KELLOGG
&
HUMBERT
ASSAYERS.
109.55 oz
895 FINE
$2026.81

Impressive 109.55 Oz. Gold Ingot Kellogg & Humbert, Recovered From the *S.S. Central America*

2362 "Very Large Size" 109.55 Oz. Kellogg & Humbert Gold Ingot. CAGB-701. Kellogg & Humbert No. 946. The most famous sunken ships make history twice: first when they are lost and then when they are found. In the aftermath of September 12, 1857, when the *S.S. Central America* sank in the aftermath of a hurricane, her vast golden cargo—valued at $2 million at a time when the price of gold was fixed at $20.67 an ounce—was also lost, along with over 400 passengers. In the 1980s and 1990s, when other news and disasters had eclipsed her loss, she made history again: the search for the *S.S. Central America* led to her discovery, recovery, and years of litigious buffoonery.

When the *S.S. Central America* went down in 1857, her loss shook the financial world and contributed to the Panic of 1857. When her treasure was brought back to the light, the world of numismatics faced its own upheaval: the 1857-S double eagle suddenly became the most available Type One double eagle in Mint State, and the ingots of the *S.S. Central America* were unlike anything collectors and scholars had ever seen. For the past decade, collectors have grappled with a transformed and tantalizing world, where territorial gold ingots can be found outside the great museum collections, and with the price of gold recently reaching record highs, interest in these hefty and historic items has intensified.

At just shy of 110 ounces, this lot is a "very large size" ingot by the standards of Q. David Bowers, as found in his great work on the shipwreck and the events leading to it, *A California Gold Rush History.* An excellent starter summary of the characteristics of this ingot comes from the same source:

> "*Serial number:* 946. Kellogg & Humbert. *Ounces:* 109.55. Mold K&H-04. *Fineness*: 895. *Value (1857):* $2,026.81. Very large size ingot. Inscriptions on face, $ sign high and leans right. Vertically oriented. Reverse stamped with repetition of serial number, but in different font."

Several points warrant additional commentary. The broad "face" and its opposite, which shows a sizable hollow from the casting process, are the only two sides to show any stamps. The main face reads, from top to bottom, NO *[line below O to indicate abbreviation]* 946 / *[imprint of KELLOGG & HUMBERT ASSAYERS on four lines within rectangular punch, incomplete at lower left]* / 109.55 OZ *[line below Z, reason as before]* / 895 FINE / $2026.81. On the opposing face are the simple numerals 946, in a different font as noted by Bowers, right-side-up in the space above the casting hollow.

The qualities of the surfaces themselves also deserve certain notes. All sides are primarily bright, light yellow-gold with only one small area of encrustation noted to the left of 895 FINE on the main face. On all sides but the bottom face are a number of small pits left by air bubbles trapped during casting, as well as the scattered marks that must be expected from the ingot's tumble to the bottom of the ocean, not to mention the effort of returning it to the open air.

The bar has two corner cuts, one at the lower right of the main face and the other diagonally opposite along the back face. The back face shows considerably more texture than the rest of the ingot, not only at the casting hollow but beyond it as well. This lot comes with a decorative wood carrying case with rope handles, metal hasp, and a metal padlock with two keys. A decoration on the lid reads KELLOGG & HUMBERT / ASSAYERS / No. 108 MONTGOMERY STREET / SAN FRANCISCO.

A California Gold Rush History
Number 29 of 400

2363 ***A California Gold Rush History.*** Arguably the most legendary book by author Q. David Bowers, *A California Gold Rush History* covers the California Gold Rush and the *S.S. Central America* treasure. This volume, number 29 in its edition of 400, comes with a number of gold flakes recovered from the *S.S. Central America;* these are mounted inside the front cover, behind a clear plastic window. The greater treasure, of course, is the knowledge found within the more than 1000 large-format gilt-edged pages. Upper front corner bumped, otherwise well-preserved. Comes with sturdy outer storage case of issue. This important addition to a high-caliber numismatic library is also a perfect complement to another piece of the *S.S. Central America* treasure, such as a coin or ingot.

NUGGETS

Five Water-Tumbled Gold Nuggets

2364 **Five Water-Tumbled Gold Nuggets from Alaska**. These five specimens all exhibit a great degree of water tumbling, their surfaces rubbed almost entirely smooth, bringing the bright yellow color to a gleaming finish. Highly attractive, they have the appearance of shining golden putty, folded and molded by hand. Some retain narrow, deeper crevices where the crystalline texture is still visible to provide a pleasing contrast, and two of the pieces are enlivened by the inclusion of small sections of the opaque white quartz around which the gold originally developed. The largest nugget measures approximately 2-3/8 x 1¼ x ½ inches; the smallest approximately 1¼ x ¾ x ½ inches; and the total weight of all five is 15.9 troy oz (494.5 grams).

Impressive Gold Nugget

2365 Victoria, Australia Gold Nugget. 275.5 Grams. Gold has been a popular currency for over 4,000 years, due in part to its aesthetic appeal, a characteristic perfectly demonstrated in this wonderful nugget. The folded, twisted form of this nugget gives the impression of a large mass of crushed gold leaf, fantastically folded in on itself with the raised rounded areas rubbed smooth by water tumbling and the crevices and depressions retaining a more textured, brittle appearance. Deep in the center of the nugget are visible fragments of the host rock about which the nugget developed. This fine specimen measures approximately 2.37 x 1.62 x 1.62 inches and weighs 8.86 troy ounces (275.5 grams).

Voluminous Australian Gold Nugget

2366 Western Australia Gold Nugget. 598.8 Grams. Gold nuggets weighing more than five ounces are extremely rare. This remarkably fine and large specimen measures approximately 2.5 x 2.5 x 1.62 inches, and weighs an impressive 19.25 troy ounces (598.8 grams).

The smooth-rubbed undulating form of this nugget is testament to extensive alluvial action, the natural growths gently smoothed by constant, repeated water-tumbling. Interspersed throughout are characterful crevices and caverns that retain a textured appearance, as though deliberately molded.

Rare 1851 Seated Dollar Pattern in Copper Judd-132 Restrike, PR63 Brown

2367 1851 Dollar, Judd-132 Restrike, Pollock-159, Low R.7, PR63 Brown PCGS. CAC. Both obverse and reverse dies feature the designs used to coin the 1851 silver dollar restrikes. The obverse can be distinguished from the original 1851 dies because the date is centered on the restrikes. On the original dies the date is slanted upward. Struck in copper with a reeded edge. The 10th edition of the Judd book states "Restrikes, possibly from a newly created obverse die, after the spring of 1859." This, of course, makes these pieces one more of Mint Director James Ross Snowden's "delicacies" struck as trade bait for collectors of that era. The surfaces are lightly hairlined, and have since retoned a lovely olive-brown color. When closely examined, the surfaces show a few light contact marks that account for the grade. Still, a rare example of one of the most famous dates in the Seated dollar series.(#11563)

Annular 1852 Judd-140 Pattern Gold Dollar, PR65

2368 1852 Gold Dollar, Judd-140, Pollock-167, Low R.7, PR65 PCGS. CAC. One of the proposed solutions to the problem of the undersized and easily lost gold dollar was an annular pattern. The large center perforation (as struck) and narrow margin forces a simple design. The obverse has only USA above the hole with 1852 below, while the reverse has a series of laurel sprigs amidst heavy concentric die lines. Curiously, no denomination is stated. Struck in copper-nickel with a plain edge. Light golden-brown toning enriches unperturbed, well struck surfaces.(#11589)

Gem Proof 1865 With Motto Seated Dollar Pattern Struck in Silver, Judd-434

2369 1865 Dollar, Judd-434, Pollock-507, Low R.7, PR65 NGC. CAC. The obverse die features the standard Seated Liberty motif used in regular-issue coinage in 1865. The reverse die consists of the familiar perched eagle design also used on circulation strikes and proofs of 1865, with the addition of a scroll above the eagle's head with the motto IN GOD WE TRUST. Struck in silver with a reeded edge.

The With Motto reverse die is the same physical die that appears on regular issue Seated dollars struck from 1866 to 1870. A prominent die line begins beneath the right serif of the N of IN and passes through the G and O of GOD to the lower ribbon border beneath the D. Another die line runs through IN G, and yet another runs through WE from the scroll fold to the left.

With the first regular use of the reverse die in 1866, a careful comparison of such regular issue proof dollars to the reverse of this piece may finally determine the answer to the question about the status of these patterns as originals struck in 1865, or restrikes struck at a later date. The question has been debated frequently in numismatic circles, with no conclusive answer. If it could be determined that the reverse of this pattern is an earlier die state than the 1866 proof dollars, then it would be proven that these patterns were struck before the proofs in 1866.

This gorgeous proof has faint lilac and gold toning over the deeply mirrored fields and frosty devices. It is not designated as a Cameo proof, although another examination by the grading service might change their opinion. Both sides have excellent design details and pristine surfaces. Census: 1 in 65, 0 finer (11/09).(#60619)

1871 Standard Silver Quarter Pattern Judd-1096, PR66 Ex: Bass

2370 1871 Standard Silver Quarter Dollar, Judd-1096, Pollock-1097, Low R.7, PR66 PCGS. CAC. Ex: Bass. The Longacre Seated design that features an Indian princess representing Liberty. Her hand steadies a globe, while the other hand holds a Liberty pole with cap on top. There are flags behind her. The reverse expresses the denomination and depicts a wreath of cotton and corn. Struck in silver with a reeded edge. Deeply reflective on each side with lovely rose colored toning around the obverse margin and multicolored iridescence around the reverse. A high grade example with an outstanding pedigree.

Purchased by Harry Bass from Stanley Kesselman, 11/1971; Bass I (Bowers and Merena, 5/1999), lot 1139; Baltimore Signature (Heritage, 7/2003), lot 10024, which realized $9,775.(#61355)

1871 Gold Dollar in Copper, Judd-1161 R.8, PR64 Brown

2371 1871 Gold Dollar, Judd-1161, Pollock-1303, R.8, PR64 Brown NGC. Ex: Simpson. This extremely rare pattern is struck in copper from regular dies for the 1871 gold dollar. The Judd pattern reference lists it as R.8, calling it a die trial. USPatterns.com notes there are less than four specimens known, saying that the pieces were likely deliberately struck for sale to collectors rather than being a die trial of any sort. This piece has prooflike pinkish surfaces with a couple of dots of blue near the rims on each side. A small planchet indentation, as made, appears just below the Indian princess's chin. A few tiny abrasions dot the surfaces, none of them bothersome. Extremely rare. Census: 2 in 64 Brown, 1 finer (11/09). (#61423)

Extremely Rare 1873 Trade Dollar in Copper
Judd-1327, PR64 Brown
One of Four Pieces Known

2372 1873 Trade Dollar, Judd-1327, Pollock-1472, High R.7, PR64 Brown PCGS. Regular die trials piece for the adopted Trade dollar. Struck in copper with a reeded edge. According to our records, this is the first Judd-1327 we have handled. The reason is clear after a little investigation. Of the four pieces known, two are in the "Wyoming Collection," one was sold in ANR's 2006 FUN Sale, and this is the fourth.

The surfaces are deep chocolate-brown over each side. The striking details are complete throughout. The only marks that could be used as pedigree identifiers (and they are faint) are a tight cluster of tiny marks in the reverse field just below the final A in AMERICA. (#61615)

UNITED STATES OF AMERICA
LIBERTY
1874
DOLLARS
10
STERLING
£2·1·1
MARKEN
41·99
KRONEN
37·31
GULDEN
20·73
FRANCS
51·81
16·72
GRAMS
900 FINE
UBIQUE

1874 Dana Bickford Ten Dollar in Gold, PR65 Deep Cameo, Judd-1373
One of Only Two Pieces Known

2373 1874 Bickford Ten Dollar, Judd-1373, Pollock-1518, R.8, PR65 Deep Cameo PCGS. The Bickford pattern ten dollar gold piece, known to pattern collectors as Judd-1373, is one of the most celebrated issues in the U.S. pattern series. Only two examples are known, placing the issue at the pinnacle of rarity. Both known examples have been meticulously preserved, and their size, attractive design, and majestic gold composition combine to make them breathtakingly beautiful numismatic patterns. The rich and mysterious history shared by these pieces adds to their irresistible appeal.

The Design

On the obverse, a fresh-faced, youthful Liberty faces left, with her hair tied back and wearing a diadem, ornamented with six stars, reading LIBERTY. UNITED STATES OF AMERICA rings the rim; the date 1874 is below. Liberty has an olive wreath tied around her neck. On the reverse a rope design forms six separate cartouches around the rim. In the center is the Latin word UBIQUE "everywhere," with 16.72 GRAMS 900 FINE in three lines. In the cartouches are the coin's exchange values in various international currencies: DOLLARS 10; STERLING 2.1.1; MARKEN 41.99; KRONEN 37.31; GULDEN 20.73; FRANCS 51.81. Struck in gold, with a reeded edge. The diameter is the same as a twenty dollar, but the planchet is thinner.

Bickford's Proposal

Dana Bickford's proposal for an international coinage captured the public's attention in the mid-1870s. The following article explaining the situation was originally published in *The Coin and Stamp Journal* in Kansas City, Missouri (February 1876 issue). It has been reprinted in several sources since that time:

> "The leading journals throughout this country and Europe are discussing the necessity for an 'international coin,' having been aroused to its importance by a resolution offered in the Senate by Senator Sherman. But Mr. Sherman's plan will meet with the same difficulty that our government has contended with for years, viz., to obtain a coin having a relation of value to the present coins of other nations, without having their denominational value and design changed. This difficulty has been overcome, and to Mr. Dana Bickford, of New York City, the original inventor of the automatic knitting machines, belongs the honor.
>
> "Mr. Bickford, while traveling in Europe, experienced the difficulties and inconveniences that European travelers are subjected to, of having to provide money current in each country he visited, and at times ignorant of its value in our money. Having upon one occasion been particularly annoyed, he determined, if possible, to overcome the difficulty, and being a man of great inventive capacity, was not long in arriving at his present plan, and designed a coin that shows on its face its value in our money and that of the principal commercial nations of the world.
>
> "The United States and foreign governments have endeavored for years, and spent thousands of dollars, to perfect a system of 'international coinage,' but have been unable to get a coin that would prove acceptable to the principal nations, as each one has a peculiar design for its coin, which it is unwilling to change entirely. With Mr. Bickford's coin this difficulty is removed, as each government can fully display its design and value on one side, and on the other show the value of the coin in the currencies of the different nations, also the fineness of the metal and number of grammes without altering their values, and but slightly changing designs.
>
> "Shortly after Mr. Bickford returned from Europe he called on Dr. Henry R. Linderman, the director of the Mint, and submitted to him his design for an international coin. After carefully examining it the director was so impressed with its importance, and the great saving the adoption of such a coin would be to our government, that with his usual foresight and penetration he at once ordered sample coins struck off at the Philadelphia Mint, which proved entirely satisfactory and practical. It is not generally known that the annual expense to our government for recoinage and waste on coin entering this country from abroad is half a million dollars, and the same waste and expense is incurred by foreign governments."

Unfortunately, Bickford's idea was ahead of its time, and more than a century would pass before his dream was at least partially realized by the euro.

An Unknown Rarity

The Bickford pattern ten dollar gold pieces, Judd-1373, were not known to numismatists of the 19th century. The design was struck in copper, aluminum, and nickel compositions, as well as gold, with both plain and reeded edges. Examples of the design in copper appeared in various auction catalogs of the period, but even the greatest pattern collections of the era did not include an example of Judd-1373. Robert Coulton Davis published the first important work on U.S. pattern coins in the *Coin Collector's Journal* in 1885, where he described both plain and reeded edge varieties of the design in copper, but he was unaware of the strikings in other metals.

The issue remained closeted in the early 20th century. A five-page article was published in the *Numismatist* in July 1906 that described the Bickford patterns in copper, but made no mention of the gold striking. Numismatists remained unaware of the existence of these patterns until the publication of *United States Pattern, Trial, and Experimental Pieces,* by Edgar Adams and William Woodin in 1913. Listed as number 1366 in that reference, the authors revealed the following information about the gold Bickford pattern eagles for the first time:

> "Gold. Reeded Edge. (Only two specimens known in this metal, one of which is in the collection of W.W.C. Wilson of Montreal, Canada, and the other is owned by William H. Woodin of New York City.)"

Pattern collectors were amazed to learn of the existence of the familiar Bickford patterns in a precious metal variant, as the copper pieces had been well known since their date of striking. The dramatic tale of their discovery is still being pieced together today. In his *United States Gold Patterns* (1975) David Akers offers two possible sources for the new patterns. The first scenario involves the activities of William Idler, an old-time coin dealer with particularly good connections at the Mint. Idler's collection was being marketed by his son-in-law, John W. Haseltine, at the time. Alternatively, Akers suggests the coins may have been part of the hoard of patterns William Woodin received in the famous exchange for the gold half union patterns.

Haseltine and Idler

William Idler was a Philadelphia coin dealer of the 1860s who enjoyed a special relationship with the staff and officials of the Mint. He used his contacts to secure examples of many pattern delicacies and restrikes that were not available to other numismatists. His prize possession was a Class Three 1804 dollar that he used to make electrotypes for favored clients. When he died in 1901, his holdings and numismatic contacts passed to his son-in-law and fellow coin dealer, Captain John W. Haseltine.

Haseltine developed his Mint connections to an even greater degree than Idler. He became the Mint's marketing pipeline for all the 1801, 1802, and 1803 proof restrike dollars, as well as most of the Class Three 1804 dollars made in the 1870s. He continued to market patterns and restrikes throughout his career, obtaining examples directly from the Mint, or selling specimens from Idler's collection. In the early 20th century, he was responsible for the first appearances of the 1884 and 1885 Trade dollars.

In time it became popular to assume that any newly discovered numismatic phenomenon probably originated with the activities of Haseltine or Idler in conjunction with greedy Mint officials. While these suspicions were often well grounded, modern numismatists have learned that clandestine deals were not the exclusive property of these two gentlemen. Writing mainly about the contemporary scandal of the half union patterns in the *Numismatist* in July 1910, Edgar Adams hints that the nefarious parties were not Haseltine and Idler, but someone much closer to the Mint:

> "It has been generally stated, usually as a supposition, that the unknown coins that have recently come to light were from the Idler collection. The senior Mr. Idler, who died some years ago, was a dealer who was supposed to have a very considerable stock and, also, favorable opportunities at the mint. The Idler stock passed to other hands and has been quietly marketed. When the great *unknowns* were heralded, the conclusion was jumped at that they were 'from the Idler collection,' some explanation was necessary, and as this served quite well, it was left to pass uncorrected. The Idler collection had some good things, but not the *good things* that most interest Uncle Sam. No, they did not come from the Idler collection, they never were that far away from home."

Clearly, Adams knew the source of the half union patterns, and many other hitherto unknown pieces, such as the Bickford gold eagles, was not the infamous Idler- Haseltine dynasty, but someone even more intimately associated with the Mint.

Woodin's Trade

One of the greatest stories in American numismatics involves the sale and recovery of the 1877 fifty dollar half union patterns by the Mint in the early 20th century. The fabulous trade William Woodin supposedly transacted with Mint officials to secure their return is almost certainly the conduit by which the gold Bickford pattern eagles entered the numismatic marketplace. However, like most good stories in numismatics, the details of Woodin's trade have been deliberately obscured to protect the guilty. Only in recent times have the full details of the transaction emerged from the shadows.

The traditional story, as outlined in an article by Edgar Adams in the July 1909 *Numismatist,* tells of Woodin purchasing the two half unions from Haseltine for $10,000 each, a record price for any coin at the time. The publication of this story resulted in much public dissatisfaction, as it was generally felt the coins were national treasures that should never have been sold to a private individual. The government threatened legal action to recover the coins and, after much maneuvering, a settlement was agreed to in which Woodin returned the half unions to the Mint in exchange for "three crates" of pattern coins, with Haseltine acting as the middleman. William Woodin became the premier collector of patterns in the country at one stroke. His giant pattern windfall included specimens of many issues that were extremely rare, or even unknown before that time.

Even though Adams named Haseltine as the seller of the half union patterns in his 1909 article, his own words in 1910 show that he knew the real source was someone much closer to the Mint. Noted pattern researcher Saul Teichman has recently uncovered the true source of the half union patterns, and the identity of the individual who reimbursed Woodin when the deal was reversed. Haseltine was merely the front man acting as agent for former Chief Coiner A. Louden Snowden. Noting a gap in the Mint's pattern collection corresponding to Snowden's tenure there, Teichman believes Snowden acquired many patterns during his time at the Mint, essentially paying bullion prices for the rare pieces. As Teichman says:

> "If one looks at the Mint collection, there is a gap with regard to coins from 1874-1877. This is probably not an accident. I believe all of the gold patterns from the 1872 Amazonian set, the two Bickfords, the two 1875 Sailors Head sets, the two 1876 double eagles in addition to the two 1877 half unions come from Snowden as well as most of the 1877 half dollars and the silver 1876 dollar patterns."}

Teichman also refers to a June 7, 1910 letter from Woodin's attorney to U.S. Attorney Henry W. Wise that establishes Snowden as the owner of the half unions at the time of the transaction, and explains how he came to possess them in the first place. The letter was sold in George Kolbe's sale of the Ford Library, and has been reprinted on the USPatterns.com website. We excerpt from the letter:

> "Col. Snowden, who had originally purchased these coins from the Director of the Mint in Philadelphia by depositing the bullion value and the charge for pattern pieces to save them from being melted down, in the course of negotiations between himself and Dr. Andrew, Director of the Mints, came to an agreement with the latter over all matters in dispute between them, and proposed to Mr. Woodin to repay him the $20,000 he had paid for these pieces, in order that he might carry out his arrangement with Dr. Andrew. Mr. Woodin after numerous visits to Philadelphia and Washington and conference with Dr. Andrew, both there and in this city, decided to accept this offer, returned the 50's to Col. Snowden, and I thereupon notified Mr. Pratt, as did Mr. Woodin, that the incident was closed."

So, as Teichman's research confirms, Snowden was the source for the coins. Having obtained the half unions in a questionable deal during his years of service at the Mint, he was the individual who had to restore them to the Mint and repay Woodin for his loss. The only means for him to do this was to hand over to Woodin all the patterns he had acquired over the years, including the Bickford eagle patterns in gold. Interestingly, there was even a cover story in place to explain the absence of the half unions after Snowden acquired them. Robert Coulton Davis was aware the gold coins existed when he published his seminal work on patterns, but he was told they had been melted:

> "One specimen of each of these patterns was struck in gold and placed in the coin cabinet at the Philadelphia Mint. But afterward, as no appropriation had been made for them, they were melted up, much to the regret of those interested in coins, for they were the only coins of this denomination in gold that have ever come from the United States Mint."

Of course, Snowden later claimed he purchased the patterns to prevent them from being melted. Once the mystery of their first appearance is solved, the further history of these remarkable patterns is well documented (see roster below). It is interesting to note Woodin did not display an example of Judd-1373 in the 1914 ANS Exhibition, even though their existence had first been published in his book the previous year. Perhaps he was gun-shy after his experience with the half unions, and did not want to further advertise his ownership of the rare gold patterns. Another striking circumstance is the lack of early auction appearances. Neither specimen was offered at public auction until 1979, a full 66 years after their discovery.

Roster of Bickford Pattern Eagles in Gold, Judd-1373

1. Ex: Philadelphia Mint in 1874; A. Louden Snowden; William H. Woodin; F.C.C. Boyd; Dr. J.H. Judd; Abe Kosoff; *Illustrated History of United States Coinage* (Kosoff, 1962), lot 467; acquired in a trade by Dr. John Wilkison in 1962; sold to Paramount, 9/1973; A-Mark in 1976; repurchased by Paramount in 11/1978; Auction '85 (Paramount, 7/1985), lot 1306, realized $82,500; Randolph S. Rothschild; 68th Anniversary Sale (Stack's, 10/2003), lot 1118, realized $276,000; Judd and Akers plate coin. **The present coin.**

2. Ex: Philadelphia Mint in 1874; A. Louden Snowden; possibly William H. Woodin; W.W.C. Wilson; sold through F.C.C. Boyd to Virgil Brand in 1919 for $2,000 (Brand Journal number 90921); Brand Estate; sold by Abe Kosoff to Dr. John Wilkison for $8,000 in the 1940s; sold to Paramount, 9/1973; A-Mark in 1976; repurchased by Paramount in 11/1978; Auction '79 (Paramount, 7/1979), lot 184, did not sell; later sold to Julian Leidman; ANA Convention Sale(Bowers and Ruddy, 7/1981), lot 2433, realized $90,000; Ed Trompeter; Trompeter Collection (Superior, 2/1992), lot 137, realized $198,000; Baltimore Auction (Superior, 7/1993), lot 695, realized $154,000; Bob Cohen; sold to Harlan White in 1994; the Holecek Family Trust; 65th Anniversary Sale (Stack's, 10/2000), lot 1621; a Southern collection; Simpson Collection.

The surfaces of this piece are extraordinary. The fields are deeply mirrored, and as the insert states the devices are heavily frosted, giving the coin a profound cameo contrast. The color is bright yellow-gold throughout. Discerning which of the two examples this piece is turned out to be an extraordinarily difficult task. It came down to this: There is a tiny planchet flake just above the end of the top ribbon on the obverse, a minute planchet mark in the field just above the curve of that same ribbon, and on the reverse there is a squiggly lint mark below the 2 in the value beneath GULDEN. These are consistent with the black and white photos from the Stack's (10/2003) Sale.

Few coins or patterns can rival the absolute rarity and desirability of a Bickford ten dollar in gold. We are proud to be able to offer this example for sale at public auction, and we know the next owner will be just as proud to be the steward of this premier rarity. (#61677)

1875 Twenty Cent Pattern in Copper Judd-1400, PR66 Red and Brown

2374 1875 Twenty Cents, Judd-1400, Pollock-1543, Low R.7, PR66 Red and Brown PCGS. The obverse represents Liberty seated at the seashore, with an "illogical steamship" (Judd)—sails billowing before, steam blowing behind. The reverse is similar to the adopted twenty cent design of 1875, with minor differences in the olive leaves. Struck in copper with a plain edge. USPatterns.com suggests that a dozen or so are known. This piece displays a reverse that is nearly half mint red, with complementary glints of blue and violet. The red on the obverse is confined to the protected areas around the devices. A glossy, smooth, pristine piece with no visible impairments. This is the finest certified at PCGS regardless of color. Population: 1 in 66 Red and Brown, 0 finer (12/09).(#71707)

Beautiful PR64 Brown 1876 Gold Dollar Pattern Struck in Copper, Judd-1478

2375 1876 Gold Dollar, Judd-1478, Pollock-1631, R.8, PR64 Brown PCGS. CAC. Like the 1871 gold dollar pattern struck in copper (Judd-1161), this 1876 gold dollar is also struck in copper from regular dies for the gold dollar of the year. Judd lists it as a die trial, but a more-logical explanation of their existence comes from USPatterns.com, which says the pieces were likely struck as part of complete off-metal sets for sale to collectors. The explanation is even more compelling, due to the popularity of the nation's Centennial observances and related coinage.

Some of the more rampant excesses of the Mint striking and restriking coins for sale to collectors seem to have come during the tenures of Mint Director Henry Richard Linderman, who served a first term from 1867-69 and a second term from 1873-78. It was during the latter period that the first Class III 1804 silver dollars appeared, around 1875. Many of the so-called off-metal or fantasy restrike Gobrecht silver dollars are believed to hail from the same period.

This piece has pinkish-gold and aqua-blue coloration on the obverse, while the reverse is more uniformly and beautifully blue-green. A tiny planchet indent, as made, appears in the obverse field behind Liberty's head, but there is no visible post-strike contact. Population: 1 in 64 Brown, 0 finer (11/09).(#61800)

Sparkling 1876 Five Dollar Struck in Copper
Judd-1484, PR65 Red and Brown
R.8, Possibly Only Two Known

2376 1876 Five Dollar, Judd-1484, Pollock-1637, R.8, PR65 Red and Brown NGC. This copper five dollar pattern is struck from the regular dies for the 1876 half eagle. Judd lists as a die trial; USPatterns.com calls it a pattern likely deliberately struck for sale to collectors. This piece is one of two certified at NGC, both PR65 Red and Brown (or one coin was submitted twice), and there are no other Judd-1484s certified in any grade at NGC. PCGS has certified a single PR65 Red and Brown, although we believe that to be the Harry W. Bass, Jr. specimen, and a different example as far as we can ascertain. This may nonetheless be one of only two examples in existence, a conclusion that USPatterns.com supports as well. This is a attractive, sparkling Gem with lots of field-device contrast and plenty of mint orange-red remaining in the fields on both sides, punctuated by dollops of cobalt-blue. The Centennial dating only increases the appeal, now as well as it did when made.(#71806)

Previously Unknown 1877
Judd-1515 Half Dollar
PR64 Red and Brown

2377 1877 Morgan Half Dollar, Judd-1515, Pollock-1679, R.7, PR64 Red and Brown PCGS. The obverse is similar to the Morgan dollar, but the head of Liberty is surrounded by a beaded circle, with 13 stars and E PLURIBUS UNUM around the edge. The date 1877 is below. On the reverse a so-called "defiant eagle" is perched on a scroll inscribed IN GOD WE TRUST. An olive branch points left, and three arrowheads point right. Struck in copper with a reeded edge. In our public auctions, We have handled three examples of this design combination in silver, but never before in copper.

The provenance of all five known examples of this pattern issue are recorded at USPatterns.com. However, the present piece is different than any of those five, so it is a sixth known example. Illustrations of the other five may be found as follows:

1. PR67 Brown NGC. American Numismatic Rarities (6/2005), lot 417.
2. PR66 Red and Brown PCGS. American Numismatic Rarities (3/2005), lot 1070.
3. PR65 Red and Brown PCGS. Superior (10/1989), lot 3274.
4. Gem Proof. 1981 ANA (Bowers and Ruddy, 7/1981), lot 234.
5. PR64 Red and Brown PCGS. The present specimen with no previous record.
6. Choice Proof. Bowers and Ruddy (11/1976), lot 981.

This near-Gem is an exceptional example of the extremely rare 1877 Judd-1515 half Dollar. Although they are a little subdued, the surfaces on both sides are much closer to Red than they are to Brown. The devices have delicate medium brown toning with accents of pale blue and lilac. A remarkable and extremely important half dollar.(#71853)

Extremely Rare Judd-1539A 1877 Pattern Half Dollar, Ex: Lemus, PR65

2378 1877 Half Dollar, Judd-1539A, Pollock-1707, R.8, PR65 NGC. The obverse centers around a bust of Liberty facing left. Liberty wears a Phrygian cap and laurel wreath, with the word LIBERTY inscribed on the cap band. The bust is surrounded by 13 stars arranged seven to the left and six to the right. IN GOD WE TRUST is inscribed above with the date below. The reverse features an eagle standing on a tablet inscribed E PLURIBUS UNUM, and clutching an olive branch and three arrows. The eagle's left talon supports a shield. The legend UNITED STATES OF AMERICA is at the border above, with the denomination HALF DOLLAR below. Struck in silver with a reeded edge. USPatterns.com can trace only three examples of Judd-1539A today. The present coin is the finest of the three, and has been offered at auction only a handful of times since 1886. The importance of this offering cannot be overstated.

The present coin possesses the intangible quality known as eye appeal in abundance. The deeply reflective fields are covered with vivid shades of olive, lilac, and gold. The strike is marvelous, with crisp detail in the hair and star centrils. The intricate beauty of Barber's design is fully realized on this extremely rare pattern. As previously indicated, this piece is the finest of the three known examples, and its importance cannot be overstated.

Ex: Maris Collection (New York Coin and Stamp, 6/1886), lot 206; T. Harrison Garrett; Garrett Collection (Bowers and Ruddy, 11/1979), lot 392; Randolph S. Rothschild Collection (Stack's, 10/2003), lot 1091; The Lemus Collection (Heritage, 1/2009), lot 1884.(#61881)

1879 'Morgan Dime,' Judd-1588, PR67

2379 1879 Morgan Ten Cents, Judd-1588, Pollock-1781, High R.6, PR67 NGC. CAC. An example of the popular "Morgan dime" pattern. The obverse features the portrait of Liberty as used on the Morgan dollar, here adapted to the format of a dime. The 13 stars on the Morgan dollar are here replaced by UNITED STATES OF AMERICA, with the date below the bust. Otherwise, the obverse is nearly indistinguishable from the dollar design. The reverse has ONE DIME in the center, encircled by a wreath composed of six bunches of four laurel leaves each. The second U in PLURIBUS is repunched. Struck in silver with a reeded edge. The Judd reference notes the "unusual style" of the doubled parallel branches or vines that extend all the way around the reverse.

The "Morgan dimes" are popular not only with pattern and Morgan dollar aficionados, but also with specialists in the various dime series, especially the contemporaneous Seated Liberty design. Fortunately, the Judd-1588, while still quite rare, has a surviving population of perhaps a dozen examples. This is a splendid silver-gold and blue-green toned piece with lots of contrast that appears at a minimum deserving of a Cameo designation, although the moderate-intensity color may have precluded it. Census: 2 in 67 (including one Ultra Cameo), 2 finer (11/09).(#61965)

PR65 Brown 1879 Metric Dollar, Judd-1623

2380 1879 Metric Dollar, Judd-1623, Pollock-1819, Low R.7, PR65 Brown PCGS. CAC. The obverse features the metric dollar design of George T. Morgan, featuring a bland, rarely seen head of Liberty, her hair brushed back and fastened in a bun, with a wide ribbon atop her head reading LIBERTY in incused lettering. The reverse is the standard metric dollar design, with DEO EST GLORIA prominent in a cartouche above the central composition. Struck in copper with a reeded edge.

The various metric coinage proposals occupied the Mint and the Congressional Subcommittee on Coinage, Weights, and Measures for far too long a time, as in the end they all came to nought. This is a marvelous Gem that it is a shame to label Brown. The obverse has a melange of violet, blue, and reddish-orange, while the reverse has much red remaining, and both sides have generous field-device contrast. This piece is the finest PCGS-certified Brown coin, although one PR67 Red and Brown is numerically finer (11/09). (#62001)

1882 Liberty Head Nickel Pattern
Judd-1690, PR66

2381 1882 Liberty Head Five Cents, Judd-1690, Pollock-1892, R.5, PR66 PCGS. Extremely popular as a transitional pattern, Judd-1690 employs an obverse similar to the adopted 1883 Liberty Head nickel, with a slightly different arrangement of the stars. On Judd-1690, the stars behind Liberty's head seem slightly wider spaced than on the adopted design. The reverse is the same as the regular-issue of 1883, the infamous NO CENTS variety. Struck in nickel with a plain edge.

Judd-1690 enjoyed great popularity with pattern collectors as early as the 1880s. An example was offered at public auction in the Woodside Collection (New York Coin & Stamp, 4/1892), lot 385, "1882 Five Cents: same as adopted type of 1883: nickel: proof; rare." Note the cataloger failed to notice the subtle difference in star placement.

The present coin is a magnificent example, with deeply reflective fields and light golden-steel toning on both sides. Population: 8 in 66, 2 finer (11/09).(#62095)

1943 Experimental Pieces Including A Previously Unreported and Unique Experimental Piece Struck in 1942 With 1943 Lincoln Cent Dies

2382 Five-Piece 1943 Experimental Cent Collection NGC. The five individual pieces represent only part of the experimentation that took place during World War II to assist the war effort. Copper and other elements including tin and nickel were desperately needed for ammunition, so a substitute was sought for the cent and five cent pieces.

The five pieces in this lot are housed in an NGC holder. Each piece came in a brown envelope with notes and include:

1. **A blank planchet for a zinc coated steel cent, Type One,** before passing through the upsetting machine to form a raised lip for the border. This piece retains its bright bluish-tinted gray surface with little evidence of corrosion. 2.7 grams. This piece is reportedly from the "First test run of zinc plated steel [in] 1943."
2. **1942 Judd-2054 AU55 NGC.** This piece combines the LIBERTY and JUSTICE obverse with the UNITED STATES MINT reverse. It is struck on a zinc-coated steel planchet that shows pale blue-gray color and minor corrosion. Only about half a dozen of these experimental pieces are believed known today. 2.56 grams. The accompanying envelope is annotated: "No denomination 'coin' used for testing metals at Philadelphia Mint."
3. **A copper-coated steel blank, Type One,** showing slight corrosion and other minor imperfections. 2.9 grams. The accompanying envelope identifies this as a "test blank of copper-plated steel for one cent piece—January 1943."
4. **1943 Judd-2085 Lincoln cent. AU58 NGC.** Reportedly on a blank plated with 4% antimony and 6% iron, per NGC. We are unable to state if they had actual metallurgical analysis performed on this piece. Lightly worn with dark gray-brown surfaces. 2.7 grams. The accompanying envelope is annotated: "Experimental Zinc & Antimony on steel. Dec. 1942." According to David Camire, an NGC consultant, this is a previously unreported pattern for the 1943 cents that was "subjected to nondestructive, X-ray fluorescence." Camire continued that "the testing determined the composition to be '90 percent zinc, 4 percent antimony, 6 percent iron plating" according to the *Coin World* article mentioned below.

   The USPatterns.com website reports that "It differs from the regular zinc coated steel cent of this year in that the plating includes antimony and iron. According to researcher Roger Burdette, it is probable that the antimony was added to make the coin darker in color in order to make it less likely to be confused with a dime which, apparently happened often."
5. **A blank planchet for a zinc-coated steel cent, Type One,** with bright blue-gray surfaces and minor corrosion. Also from the first test run at the Philadelphia Mint in 1943.

Accompanying this lot is a *Coin World* article about the five pieces from the September 21, 2009 issue of that weekly newspaper. The article, written by *Coin World* reporter Paul Gilkes, identified the owners as "the children of a former Philadelphia Mint metallurgist [now deceased] who worked on finding an alternative to the pre-1943 bronze cent."(Total: 5 pieces)

ERRORS

Remarkable Double Denomination Mule
1993-D Cent With Dime Reverse
MS65 Red

2383 1993-D Lincoln Cent—Struck with Dime Reverse Die—MS65 Red PCGS. U.S. coins struck with dies of different denominations are extremely rare. Until recent years, none were known. The most famous among those are the Sacagawea dollar reverse, paired with a statehood quarter obverse, of which ten examples are known, per Fred Weinberg. In our April 2006 Central States Signature, a 1999 cent with a dime reverse hammered down for $138,000, the largest prices realized for an error coin in a Heritage auction, excluding the 1944-S steel cent that sold for $373,750 in our 2008 ANA Signature.

Aside from malfeasance of a mint worker, the muled denomination error is only possible when the denominations involved are similar in diameter. A cent is 19 mm, and a dime is 17.9 mm, a difference of 1.1 mm or approximately 5%. Given the billions of cents struck annually at the Federal mints, it was inevitable that an absent-minded worker would pair cent and dime dies. Presumably, the mistake was discovered and the struck pieces were destroyed before dispersal, with the single exception of the present survivor.

This lustrous Gem shows the characteristics expected of a cent and dime mule. The dime side has a broad, tall rim, since metal was forced into the collar of the dime die by the wider diameter cent die opposite. As a result, the cent side has a soft strike near the rim, since metal in the vicinity flowed into the dime collar. The strike on the devices is normal. The lustrous surfaces are pristine aside from a solitary faint graze above the date. The color is predominantly orange, with shades of fire-red and olive-green occasionally present.

This auction provides an unusual opportunity to acquire two different cent/dime mules, one on a cent planchet and the other on a dime planchet. It is unlikely that such a fortuitous combination will again appear in consecutive auction lots.

From The Alfred V. Melson Collection, Part One.

Amazing Double Denomination Cent and Dime Mule
Roosevelt Dime With 1995 Cent Obverse

2384 1995 Roosevelt Dime—Struck With Cent Obverse Die—MS64 NGC. An astounding mint error that prior to the 1990s was believed impossible to occur. Only the narrow difference in die diameter between the cent and dime makes it plausible that a busy mint worker could erroneously pair dies of different denominations. Most likely, a press run was made from this die pairing and detected by an inspector, possibly the operator of the mint press. Perhaps the entire batch was melted, aside from the present coin.

This satiny near-Gem displays the characteristics expected of a dime struck with a cent obverse die. The obverse has only a partial rim. IN GOD WE TRUST and the L in LIBERTY are tight against the border. This is because the dime planchet was less in diameter than the cent die. On the dime side, the border displays minor softness of strike, principally on ES OF AM. This was partly due to the die alignment, but also because of metal flow of the planchet toward the collar to fill the unexpectedly wide cent obverse die. The strike on the cent is sharp except for minor incompleteness on the truncation of Lincoln's bust near the VDB initials.

As is the case with the prior lot, also an important cent and dime mule, the dies are rotated approximately 15% from usual coin turn. One hopes that the buyer of the previous lot also purchases the present piece, since these two extremely rare cent and dime mules belong together.

From The Alfred V. Melson Collection, Part One.

Please also refer to lot 2433 in the Indian cent section of this catalog for a 1905 Indian cent struck in gold on a quarter eagle planchet.

COLONIALS

Rarely Seen MS62 1662 Oak Tree Twopence Small Date, Noe-29

2385 1662 Oak Tree Twopence MS62 NGC. Small Date. Noe-29, Crosby 1-A2. R.6. 13.0 gn. Struck from poorly aligned dies, the obverse is about 20% off-center at 6 o'clock, while the reverse is normally centered. Lustrous obverse and reverse surfaces are toned deep silver-gray, with traces of bluish patina. A minor planchet void is evident at 3 o'clock, relative to the obverse. This piece is finer than either Hain Collection coin, and finer than the second Ford Collection example. Listed on page 36 of the 2010 *Guide Book*. Census: 4 in 62, 3 finer (11/09).(#17)

Popular 1652 Noe-5 Oak Tree Shilling, MS61

2386 1652 Oak Tree Shilling MS61 NGC. IN at bottom. Crosby 2-D, Noe-5, W-470, R.2. 66.4 grains. The obverse of Noe-5 is typically found off-center and off the planchet at 6 o'clock, with a wide margin at 12 o'clock. The reverse is common to Noe-4, 5, 6, and 7, and usually has a vertical die crack from 2 o'clock to 4 o'clock, as on this example. Both sides have pleasing, lustrous silver-gray surfaces with splashes of darker toning. Close inspection reveals a few minor imperfections that have accumulated over the last 357 years. Listed on page 37 of the 2010 *Guide Book*.(#20)

Historic St. Patrick Halfpenny, XF40

2387 (1670-75) St. Patrick Halfpenny XF40 PCGS. Breen-204, Vlack 1-A, W-11540. After he arrived in New Jersey in 1681, Mark Newby (1638-1683) became a member of the legislature, and had passed a law that made his St. Patrick's pieces current money. Newby settled in the vicinity of present day Camden, New Jersey, along with other Irish settlers.

A medium brown example that has impressive detail and no apparent abrasions. The brass splasher on the crown is centered slightly left. Much nicer than usually seen for this Irish import. Listed on page 39 of the 2010 *Guide Book*. Population: 6 in 40, 0 finer (11/09).(#46)

Rare 1723 Hibernia Farthing in Silver W-12500, MS64

2388 1723 Hibernia Pattern Farthing, Silver MS64 PCGS. One dot after 1723, Martin 3.3-Bc.3, W-12500, R.5. The Hibernia farthing in silver, once considered virtually unobtainable, is now "merely" rare thanks to the later 20th century discovery of a hoard of the W-12500 pieces. This seems to have fueled collector desire for the variant all the more, especially for high-grade examples such as this near-Gem. The devices are well-defined, and the fields remain strongly lustrous through ample toning. Deep blue and lighter olive-gold shadings show occasional glints of bright silver-white. Listed on page 42 of the 2010 *Guide Book*. Population: 5 in 64, 3 finer (11/09).(#179)

Extremely Rare Broad Axe Higley Copper
VALUE ME AS YOU PLEASE
Freidus 3.3-C, Choice Fine

2389 (1737) Higley Copper, Broad Axe Fine 15 PCGS. Crosby 25, Breen-242, Freidus 3.3-C, W-8280, URS-3. 137.5 gn, 27.9 mm, 1.3-1.5 mm thick, per its 2004 Ford Collection auction appearance, where the piece was graded "Overall Very Fine." Further cataloged by Michael Hodder as:

> "Both sides are toned in a deep, rich and even olive brown shade. The surfaces in most places are smooth and hard, granularity being confined principally to the centers. Partial central detail showing, the top of the deer's figure soft, legend at lower left and pointing hand indistinct but sharp elsewhere.
>
> "On the reverse, the broadaxe is about as bold as ever seen given the die failure on this side and the legend around is complete save for the last three letters, which are faint to indistinct. Struck on a flawed planchet, with linear defects showing at the lower left on the obverse. Reverse cut from edge into center, quite possibly to test the metal ...
>
> Another addition to the 1994 [Dan Freidus Higley] census and a nicer coin than Eliasberg:44 which was porous and dark."

We are aware of only six examples of Freidus 3.3-C, including the present piece, Ford II:272, and the four coins listed in Freidus' census. Eliasberg:44, referred to above, is Fr. 3.3-D. Garrett:1305, Roper:152, and Hain:204 are the more available Fr. 3.2-C. Listed on page 47 of the 2010 *Guide Book* PCGS Population for all Deer/Broad Axe die varieties: 2 in 15, 0 finer (11/09).

Ex: Hillyer Ryder; Dr. Thomas Hall; F.C.C. Boyd Estate; John J. Ford, Jr. Collection, Part II (Stack's, 5/2004), lot 273.(#213)

Rare New Yorke in America Token
Undated, Brass, Fine 15

2390 Undated New Yorke Token, Brass Fine 15 PCGS. Rulau NY 621, R.6. This rare token was issued by Francis Lovelace, the British governor of New York from 1668-1673. The obverse design features Cupid and Psyche (Crosby says Venus) under five palm trees. The mythological figures are believed to be a play on the issuer's name, and the eagle on the reverse is identical to the crest on the Lovelace coat of arms. Other facts that help establish an approximate date for the token include the spelling of the city's name. The name New Yorke was adopted in 1664, when the British occupied the city, and the final E was dropped from the spelling around 1710.

The token is farthing size, and the weight, composition, and die axis are similar to the 1670 farthing tokens of Bristol, England. The tokens may have been manufactured in Bristol, as there is no evidence that they ever circulated in this country. The discovery specimen was a pewter example located in the Hague about 1850. Today, approximately 10 pieces are known in brass, with four examples in pewter. The token is listed on page 45 of the 2010 *Guide Book*.

The present example shows even, well-balanced wear over each side. The high points are tan-yellow, and contrast sharply against the russet patina that surrounds and is seen within the recesses of the devices. The surfaces are clean and problem free, except for a few spots of corrosion on the reverse. Population: 3 in 15, 0 finer (11/09). (#226)

Desirable 1776 Continental Dollar, XF45
Newman 1-C, CURENCY Variety

2391 1776 Continental Dollar, CURENCY, Pewter XF45 NGC. Newman 1-C, Hodder 1-A.3, W-8445, R.3. Late die state. The obverse has a solid break over GI of FUGIO and another joining the last N and last T in CONTINENTAL. Light wear and minor surface marks are consistent with the grade of this wonderful piece. The surfaces are pleasing with only slight verdigris. This plentiful variety is usually available in a rather wide range of grades. The present piece will provide collectors with an excellent compromise between grade and price. Listed on page 81 of the 2010 *Guide Book*. (#791)

Select 1776 Continental Dollar, MS63
Newman 1-C, CURENCY

2392 1776 Continental Dollar, CURENCY, Pewter MS63 PCGS. CAC. Newman 1-C, Hodder 1-A.3, W-8445, R.3. Intermediate die state. Newman 1-C is easily the most plentiful single variety among all surviving Continental dollars, and the intermediate die state is seen more often than the early or late die states. The Continental dollars were issued in conjunction with coinage proposals and requests at the time of our nation's independence. Today they are tangible reminders of the struggle that ensued against the British leading up to the Declaration of Independence and, eventually, the Constitution.

The denomination of the Continental coinage has been debated over recent years, with cent and dollar the two likely choices. Some have suggested that the pewter pieces were intended to be cents, and the silver pieces dollars. We tend to stay with numismatic tradition in this regard and call all of these pieces dollars unless someone provides convincing evidence to the contrary.

This Select Mint State piece is exceptional, with brilliant gray luster and considerable light ivory reflectivity in the protected areas of the design on both sides. The strike of this Select Mint State coin is excellent, and its overall aesthetic appeal is remarkable. For the history connoisseur who appreciates outstanding quality, this MS63 example with its reflective surfaces is a coin that will be a welcome collection addition. Listed on page 81 of the 2010 *Guide Book.* (#791)

Famous Bar Copper, AU55

2393 (1785) Bar Copper AU55 PCGS. Breen-1145, W-8520, R.4. The *Whitman Encyclopedia of Colonial and Early American Coins* comments on the supposed origin of the Bar coppers: "It is believed that these were produced in Birmingham, England, by a Thomas Wyon, according to researcher Russell Rulau (though facts are scarce)." The Bar coppers have long attracted more theories than facts, such as the idea that soldiers' buttons inspired the design, but such speculation has only fueled the Bar coppers' mystique. This modestly worn example was struck slightly off-center like many of its fellows, this one oriented toward 4 o'clock on the obverse. Luminous mushroom-brown surfaces show only a few flecks of deeper color. Listed on page 69 of the 2009 *Guide Book*.(#599)

Near-Gem 1787 Immunis Columbia Eagle Reverse Tied for Finest Certified

2394 1787 Immunis Columbia Piece, Eagle Reverse MS64 Brown PCGS. Ex: Troy Wiseman Collection. Crosby Pl. VIII, 8, Breen-1137, W-5680, High R.4. Breen believed this scarce issue was originally intended as a pattern for Continental Congress coinage. Later, it was struck for circulation, possibly at the Rahway Mills private mint in New Jersey. The only collectible Immune/Immunis Columbia variety; the *Guide Book* also lists several extremely rare issues, dated 1785 or 1786, paired with various dies such as a Nova Constellatio obverse, a Vermont obverse, and a New Jersey reverse. Rarest of all is the unique gold example of the 1785 Immune Columbia Blunt Rays NOVA CONSTELATIO, obtained by the Mint collection in 1843 from Matthew Stickney in exchange for an 1804 Class I Original silver dollar.

The present medium brown Immunis Columbia Eagle Reverse example is sharply struck and uncommonly smooth. Luster glimmers throughout the major devices. A light die crack descends from the eagle's beak, and dentils are clashed onto the reverse border near 9 o'clock. Mint-made die lines pierce the eagle's head and reach the U in UNITED. Minor die rust, also as made, is seen beneath the O in COLUMBIA. Most survivors are in well worn or corroded condition; this remarkable example ranks among the finest known. As of (11/09), NGC and PCGS have certified a combined total of three pieces as MS64 Brown, with none finer. Listed on page 53 of the 2010 *Guide Book*.

Ex: Troy Wiseman Collection (Heritage, 1/2007), lot 752, which realized $46,000.(#841)

Near-Gem Silver 1796 Castorland Medal Original Dies, Reeded Edge

2395 1796 Castorland Medal, Silver MS64 PCGS. Ex: Troy Wiseman Collection. Breen-1058, W-9100, R.4. Reeded Edge. The line between original and restrike Castorland medals has always been confusing. Even experts disagree, notably Walter Breen and John Ford. Ford stated in a conversation in 1997 that originals do not have die rust on the reverse, are slightly convex, and the finest he knew of was a VF35. Breen, on the other hand, on page 106 of his *Complete Encyclopedia* states that originals have old style lettering; on the obverse the A is below the M, 1 is embedded on a border bead. On the reverse, S is far below AL, M below AG, UG touch. Further, "all originals seen to date have traces of rust near vessel handle but no bulge at PARENS and no break at final S; restrikes from these dies show both failures in various states."

This original dies example does indeed show die rust around the vessel handle; however, there is no perceptible bulging of the die in the center or around PARENS. The fields are notably reflective on each side with a few stray marks. The surfaces are toned medium gray with considerable underlying rose and lilac coloration. This is a high grade and very attractive example of a failed social experiment that resulted in the foundation of modern day Carthage, New York. Listed on page 73 of the 2010 *Guide Book.*

Ex: Troy Wiseman Collection (Heritage, 1/2007), lot 749, which realized $16,100.(#653)

Impressive MS62 Brown Washington Cent Born Virginia, Inscribed Reverse, Baker-60

2396 1792 Washington Born Virginia Cent, Inscribed Reverse MS62 Brown NGC. W-10730, Baker-60, R.6. Although John Gregory Hancock's 1791 Small Eagle and Large Eagle cents are relatively common, his Born Virginia Washington pieces were apparently coined in much smaller quantities. When encountered, survivors tend to be circulated and exhibit weakness on the central reverse legends. This MS62 example is far superior to the other two examples listed in the NGC *Census Report,* both of which are VF (11/09). It boasts a sharp, even strike and consistent dark walnut-brown toning. A tiny obverse rim nick at 3 o'clock and a faded mark in front of the nose are consistent with the grade. Listed on page 78 of the 2010 *Guide Book.* (#723)

Important XF 1792 Getz Cent Copper, Baker-25, Small Eagle

2397 1792 Washington Getz Pattern Cent, Small Eagle, Copper XF40 PCGS. Baker-25, W-10775, R.6. 32 mm, plain edge. The dies for this well executed pattern cent were engraved by Peter Getz of Lancaster, Pennsylvania. Getz based his designs on those of young Birmingham, England engraver John Gregory Hancock, specifically his 1791 Small Eagle cent (Baker-16). The reverse legend was changed from ONE CENT to UNITED STATES OF AMERICA, since silver strikings were intended, perhaps to serve as a half dollar, as suggested by Walter Breen. The reverse for this design replicates the Great Seal. It is believed that the coins were actually struck in Harper's coachhouse on 6th Street in Philadelphia. This historic structure housed the U.S. Mint's machinery in 1792 before the first Mint building was occupied. This building was also the location for the striking of the 1792 half dismes.

This piece shows lovely chocolate-brown patina. The only planchet flaw of any note is an angling depression from the first T in STATES down through star 1 and beyond. Post-strike flaws that are worthy of note are a diagonal mark across Washington's temple and three tiny rim nicks, two at the 6 o'clock position and one at 7 o'clock, all convenient markers for pedigree tracing. According to the 1999 Rulau-Fuld revision of the classic Baker reference, circa 30 pieces are known for Baker-25.

Silver pieces were also struck from the dies with various edge designs, as were large flan (36 mm) copper pieces. Breen speculated that this coinage was completed prior to December 21, 1791, despite the date, in order to have examples available for Robert Morris to pass out as samples to congressmen when his coinage bill was introduced. However, Washington disapproved of presidential portraits on U.S. coins, which he considered monarchical, and congressional legislation to establish the United States Mint was modified to instead use "a device emblematic of liberty." This bill was passed and signed into law by President Washington on April 2, 1792. Population: 1 in 40, 3 finer (12/09).

Ex: Denver Signature (Heritage, 8/2006), lot 5015, which realized $43,125.(#921)

HALF CENTS

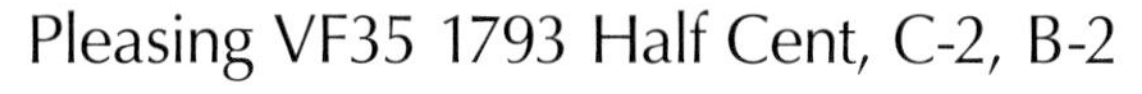

Pleasing VF35 1793 Half Cent, C-2, B-2

2398 1793 VF35 PCGS. C-2, B-2, R.3. The second of four 1793 half cent varieties in both the Cohen and Breen references, the C-2 half cent is considered the second issue in the emission sequence for the date. Minor abrasions and rim bumps are present on this otherwise pleasing medium brown example. Some of the surface marks appear to be lamination defects present when it was struck. A few splashes of lighter orange-tan and darker steel are evident on each side. The commercial sharpness of this piece is finer than the PCGS grade suggests. MRB Fine 12.(#1000)

Attractive XF40 1793 Half Cent, C-4, B-4

2399 1793 XF40 PCGS. C-4, B-4, Low R.3. This is the first year of issue for the half cent denomination, and it is a one-year design type with the profile of Liberty facing to the left. Beginning the next year, the profile is facing to the right. Although it is not known with certainty, it is believed that the designer of this type was Joseph Wright who is best known for his 1793 Liberty Cap large cent design. These half cents were coined from mid-July through mid-September, at about the same time as the Liberty Cap cents were produced. This wonderful example has glossy, smooth surfaces with splendid reddish-brown color and only light wear on the highest points. A few tiny field marks are noted, but the overall quality is choice with excellent eye appeal. MRB VF30.(#1000)

Curious 1796 C-2 With Pole Half Cent, AU55

2400 1796 With Pole AU55 PCGS. C-2, B-2, High R.4. Breen State I. Manley State 1.0. EAC 45. An early die state with repunching of the 9 clear. The existing population of 1796 half cents is too small to clearly establish distinct die states or a suitable emission sequence.

The 1796 half cent is the classic rarity of the denomination from a mintage of just 1,390 coins. Perhaps 10% of those coins still exist today, nearly all in very low grades. We estimate the existence of about 25 No Pole coins and perhaps 120 With Pole coins. Certain issues, such as the 1796 half cent and the 1901-S quarter, are known in high grade and low grade, but virtually unknown between these extremes. Nearly all known 1796 half cents, of both varieties, exist in Mint State and also below Fine. Those that grade VF, XF, and AU, such as this piece, are extremely rare.

Walter Breen described two subvarieties for the With Pole pieces, struck on rolled copper planchets or on spoiled cents. His spoiled cent subvariety, like the thick planchet 1795 coins, should weigh at least 100 grains, compared to the 84 grain standard for the issue. To date, we are only aware of a single thick planchet piece, discussed in Breen's *Half Cent Encyclopedia*. This example has many curious marks on the reverse that give the appearance of undertype, but from what? Look in the dentils over TED and TATE, on and between the upper leaves of both branches, at OF AM, and elsewhere. In addition to its excellent preservation, this piece may provide an important discovery for the advanced numismatist.

This lovely example has reflective fields on both sides, with excellent luster. Aside from the usual minor abrasions resulting from brief circulation, the surfaces are exceptional. Slight weakness is evident at the center of the reverse, but all other design elements are bold. MRB AU50.

Ex: Julian Leidman; Jim McGuigan; Benson Collection Sale (Goldberg Coins, 2/2002), lot 32; Stuart Levine (2/2002).(#1027)

Condition Census 1805 C-2 Half Cent, VF30

2401 1805 Small 5, Stems VF30 NGC. C-2, B-2, R.5. This is the rarest 1805 variety, and one of the most important half cent varieties of any year. Although it has a few microscopic scratches on each side, the surfaces and color are as fine as any 1805 C-2 we have handled. Both sides are dark chocolate with some lighter tan and maroon. A small patch of corrosion on the reverse is barely noticeable. According to *Copper Quotes by Robinson,* there are only two VF coins and three Fine examples known. This piece is clearly in the Condition Census for the variety. MRB Fine 15.(#1087)

Double Struck C-3 1808 Half Cent Second Strike 90% Off Center, VF30

2402 1808—Double Struck, Second Strike 90% Off Center—VF30 NGC. C-3, B-3, R.1. Manley Die State 1.0 without any indication of the vertical die streaks that appear on the right obverse field of most better grade examples. This is a well-known variety whose second 8 in the date was formed by stacking two small 0 punches normally used to form the fraction denominator. Struck from medal turn dies.

This coin is prominently **double struck.** The first strike was normal, but the piece failed to fully eject from the screw press and was struck a second time, 90% off center at 1 o'clock relative to the first strike. The second strike is off center toward 11 o'clock and shows the 08 in the date and the lower portion of the bust tip. The second strike is uniface obverse; the reverse die was blocked by a newly fed planchet, which is not included. A medium brown midgrade example with smooth surfaces save for faint thin marks above the H in HALF and on the lower right obverse field. MRB Fine 15.(#1107)

LARGE CENTS

Pleasing 1793 Chain Cent, Fine 12
Popular High R Variety, S-3

2403 1793 Chain AMERICA Fine 12 PCGS. S-3, B-4, Low R.3. The anomalous high R in LIBERTY is distinctive. The obverse displays rich chocolate-brown shadings with occasional slate-gray elements, while the reverse shows a more even balance between the two colors. The level of remaining detail is pleasing for the grade; aside from the 3 in the date, all peripheral elements are plain. The chain is similarly strong, with only one weak link at the upper left.

This attractive S-3 example, from the most available of the Chain cent varieties, should be of particular interest to type collectors. As an essentially problem-free representative of the place where "United States coin history starts," to quote Paul M. Green in his March 25, 2003 Item of the Week column for *Numismatic News*, it offers an attractive blend of eye appeal and history. MRB 10.(#1341)

Sharp 1793 S-3 Chain Cent, XF Details

2404 1793 Chain AMERICA—Burnished—NGC. XF Details. S-3, B-4, Low R.3. The S-3 die marriage is far the most plentiful of the 1793 Chain cents, and for that reason it is a popular choice of date and type collectors who have varying reasons for acquiring specific coins. For some, perfect surfaces and color are the primary requirement with less emphasis on the amount of detail that remains. For others, the opposite is true, with surfaces and color being secondary to detail. The present specimen is ideal for the second group as it shows exceptional detail, but has been burnished to lessen the effects of old corrosion or other impediments. The end result is a surprisingly attractive, well detailed Chain cent that should prove to be affordable for many collectors. MRB VG8.(#1341)

Pleasing 1793 S-4 Chain Periods Cent, VF20

2405 1793 Chain Periods VF20 PCGS. S-4, B-5, R.3. The Chain Periods variety is a popular subtype of the Chain cent design, and it was the last variety coined before the change to the Wreath design. Housed in a green-label PCGS holder, this Chain cent has pleasing olive-brown surfaces with splashes of lighter tan. There are a few grade-consistent handling marks, but none of any severity. This piece is far finer than most Chain cents that we encounter, regardless of grade. It is almost certainly within the top two dozen surviving Chain Period cents. MRB Fine 12.

From The Chandler Collection, Part Two.(#91341)

Mid-Grade 1793 Chain Cent, VF20 S-4, 'Periods' Variety

2406 1793 Chain Periods VF20 PCGS. CAC. S-4, B-5, High R.3. The periods on the obverse, following both the date and LIBERTY, are the hallmark of this die and they are both clearly visible. Possibly engraved by Joseph Wright, as the design has a slightly different treatment and the periods are reminiscent of his 1792 pattern quarter where this device was also employed. The deep brown surfaces reflect an unusually sharp strike for this often-weak issue. Several moderate-sized marks are seen on the obverse, the most prominent of which are at the center of that side. A couple of small rim bumps are also noted at the 5 to 6 o'clock positions on the obverse. Still, a pleasing, mid-grade example of America's first one cent issue. MRB 8. Population: 4 in 20, 16 finer (9/06).(#91341)

Condition Census 1793
S-11a Vine and Bars Cent, AU58
The Dr. French Specimen; Plated in Breen

2407 1793 Wreath Cent, Vine and Bars AU58 PCGS. S-11a, B-16a, High R.4. **The Breen Plate Coin.** Breen Die State I with perfect dies aside from a faint reverse bulge between ONE and CENT. The S-11 die combination is known with three edge types, creating three different sub-varieties cataloged as S-11a (Vine and Bars edge), S-11b (Lettered edge with two leaves), and S-11c (Lettered edge with one leaf). Of the three, S-11a is clearly scarcer than the others.

Del Bland wrote in his Condition Census that this piece has "a long line-like planchet defect in the left obverse field." It is that planchet defect that positively identifies this as the Dr. French specimen, and the ANS replacement coin. The American Numismatic Society large cent episode involving Dr. Sheldon has been discussed many times, and needs little further discussion here. The ANS released this coin in exchange for the original Clapp Collection specimen that was removed from the museum several decades ago. The Clapp specimen carries an MS60 grade, while this piece carries an XF45 grade in the Bland Condition Census, and a conservative XF40 grade in the latest Noyes Condition Census. Our own opinion is in line with Del Bland, leaning toward the AU50 level.

The planchet defect that Bland discusses in no way detracts from the splendid appearance of this glossy cent. The olive-brown surfaces show faint iridescence, with reflective fields, traces of cartwheel luster, and bold devices. Traces of light orange appear on the obverse border outside the beads from 9 o'clock to 11 o'clock. Splashes of light orange patina appear behind TATES of AMER on the reverse. The surfaces are remarkable and far finer than most known examples of any 1793 Wreath cent. Based on the strict grading of early copper specialists, less than 20 Mint State Wreath cents exist of all die varieties, followed by about two dozen AU pieces. Most of the top grade pieces will be found in specialized collections, leaving few others for date and type collectors. We place this piece among the finest Wreath cents that are currently available in the market. MRB XF45.

Ex: Dr. George French (B. Max Mehl, 1929 Fixed Price List), lot 12; Henry Sternberg Collection (J.C. Morgenthau, 4/1933), lot 8; Dr. William H. Sheldon; Charles R. Mathewson; Copley Coin Company; Dr. William H. Sheldon; ANS; American Numismatic Rarities (7/2003), lot 107.(#1347)

Lovely 1795 S-75 Lettered Edge Cent MS65 Red and Brown

2408 1795 Lettered Edge MS65 Red and Brown NGC. S-75, B-3, R.3. Die State V, with minor buckling of the obverse date near the border from 6 o'clock to 8 o'clock. The combination of a lettered edge with a double leaf at the top of the right branch on the reverse identifies this plentiful variety. It is the only readily available 1795 Lettered Edge cent in Mint State grades, with more than a dozen known. Bland records 18 Mint State examples and Noyes records 14 Mint state pieces. There are just four Mint State S-74 cents and one S-76a.

Breen stated that this variety is often found on defective planchets, writing that "even Mint State survivors show granularity or minute pit marks." This piece shows some minor pitting on the reverse in the area of STATES, and just opposite the obverse die buckling. What we see here, and what Breen was describing, are original planchet marks that remained due to weak striking pressure at that area. The balance of the coin is smooth and satiny, with excellent luster, faded from original red to light tan with a few splashes of darker brown and traces of iridescence.

We are unable to match this piece to any of those currently recorded in the various Condition Census lists compiled by Bill Noyes or Del Bland. It is possibly one of those that has not been seen in recent times, with no available photograph, or perhaps a new specimen previously unknown to the copper community. MRB MS60.(#1378)

The Naftzger Duplicate
1796 S-84 Cent, AU58
Fifth Finest Known

2409 1796 Liberty Cap AU58 PCGS. S-84, B-5, R.3. Bill Noyes tells us in his photo book of 1795 to 1797 cents that there are four Mint State S-84 cents in the Condition Census. He places the present piece, which he grades AU55, in fifth place. Del Bland also grades the coin AU55 and places it in eighth position. Although each side has a few marks, the overall appearance of this light olive cent is outstanding, with glossy surfaces are excellent design definition.

When R.E. Naftzger, Jr., purchased the Sheldon Collection in 1972, he already owned the Gem Beckwith specimen and the current example. Sheldon had the other Gem specimen that is now listed in the Noyes Census, so the present piece became the third line coin that was sold when New Netherlands auctioned the Naftzger duplicates in November 1973. MRB AU55.

Ex: Robert Coulton Davis (New York Coin & Stamp Co., 1/1890), lot 2530; Harlan P. Smith; Virgil M. Brand; Hillyer Ryder (5/1945); Wayte Raymond; New Netherlands Coin Co. (9/1953), lot 247; C. Douglas Smith; A. Kosoff; R.E. Naftzger, Jr.; Abner Kreisberg (9/1967), lot 381; Quality Sales Corp. (6/1968), lot 65; R.E. Naftzger, Jr. (New Netherlands Coin Co., 11/1973), lot 403; Charles E. Harrison; to the present consigner.(#1392)

Attractive 1797 S-135 Cent, MS65 Brown

2410 1797 Reverse of 1797, Stems MS65 Brown PCGS. S-135, B-5, R.3. Breen Die State V with die chips over the C of AMERICA, a faint die bulge at D ST, and clash marks on both sides. A die scratch through the leaves below RI of AMERICA distinguishes this variety from S-123, the other Nichols' Find 1797 cent. Like the other two Nichols' Find varieties (including 1796 S-119), the S-135 is more often seen in Mint State grades than in lower circulated grades. Like most examples of the variety, the central obverse is a little indistinct. The surfaces are pleasing medium brown with traces of luster remaining in the protected areas. An attractive and desirable cent. MRB MS60. Population: 8 in 65 Brown, 2 finer (11/09).(#1422)

Desirable 1799 S-189 Cent, VF25

2411 1799 VF25 PCGS. S-189, B-3, R.2. Only a faint trace of the reverse die chip, sometimes called the "mintmark" of 1799 Normal Date cents, is visible on this example. Although slightly dark as usual for the date, this piece has pleasing surfaces with nothing more than grade-consistent abrasions on each side. The date and LIBERTY are both bold, an important characteristic that is seldom encountered. One or the other is usually weak. This is an attractive 1799 large cent that should generate considerable bidding activity before falling to the auctioneer's hammer. MRB Fine 12.(#1443)

2412 No Lot.

Desirable 1804 S-266 Cent, AU55
Tied for Tenth Finest
The Dr. French Specimen

2413 1804 AU55 PCGS. S-266c, B-1, R.2. Medium brown surfaces host splashes of deeper steel toning, and additional traces of tan that is faded from mint color. The surfaces have minor abrasions, including a small scratch on Liberty's face, keeping the strict EAC grade below the sharpness grade. Del Bland and Bill Noyes each grade this piece VF35. MRB XF40.

Ex: Major William Boerum Wetmore (S.H. and H. Chapman, 6/1906), lot 578; Dr. Lewis H. Adler (3/1917); B. Max Mehl; Dr. George P. French (B. Max Mehl, 1929 FPL), lot 338; H.A. Stoddard (1934); B. Max Mehl; T. James Clarke (1954); R.E. Naftzger, Jr. (2/1992); Eric Streiner; Jay Parrino; Gene Sherman; Superior (9/1997), lot 68; Superior (5/1999), lot 1484.(#1504)

The Sheldon Plate 1807 S-271 Comet Cent
MS64 Brown
The Rasmussen Specimen

2414 1807 Comet MS64 Brown PCGS. CAC. S-271, B-1, R.1. **The obverse of this example is plated in both editions of Sheldon's work.** Breen Die State IV or later, with numerous raised die flaws and clash marks on the obverse. This plentiful die marriage is usually seen with the massive "Comet" die defects in the upper left obverse field. These defects are present on the vast majority of known examples. In fact, some early die state examples are marketed as the "Eclipsed Comet" variety, and they are scarcer but clearly less popular. It is one of only a few instances where a die state (as opposed to a die variety) has its own listing in the *Guide Book.* The obverse die defects are called "linear die flaws" by Breen, indicating that they are different than die breaks that create similar raised areas on coins of other varieties. The dies, especially the obverse, have also received several sets of clash marks.

This is a splendid Comet with fully lustrous golden-brown color, accented by lighter tan faded from red luster, and also by pale sea-green toning. Most details remain crisp, and both the obverse and the reverse impressions are well-centered. Later die states often have some axial misalignment with the obverse centered and the reverse slightly off-center. Bill Noyes grades this coin MS62 and Del Bland calls it MS61, but both agree that it is the third finest known Comet cent. Only the Newcomb specimen and the Parmelee-Helfenstein coin are finer. MRB MS63.

Ex: Homer K. Downing; A. Kosoff (Numismatic Gallery, privately 5/1947); R.E. Naftzger, Jr.; A. Kosoff (10/1959), lot 100; Stack's; Dorothy Nelson (Stack's, 2/1976), lot 76; William R.T. Smith (4/1977); C. Douglas Smith (12/1979); Myles Z. Gerson; Del Bland (3/1982); C. Douglas Smith; Herman Halpern (12/1986); R.E. Naftzger, Jr. (2/1992); Eric Streiner (4/1992); John B. MacDonald (8/1999); Wes Rasmussen (Heritage, 1/2005), lot 3329.(#1531)

Scarce S-278 1808 Cent, MS63 Brown
Ex: Dan Holmes

2415 1808 MS63 Brown PCGS. S-278, B-2, R.3. The scarcest die pair for the year, distinguished by the second S in STATES having its right edge aligned with the leaftip below. Though both sides of this Classic large cent show considerable die erosion (from the later die state) as well as striking softness, grading by surface indicates no actual wear. Deep brown color is the norm, though occasional silvery highlights are also present. Tiny dark areas at star 6 and to the right of the date correspond with small depressions, thought to be planchet flaws by the cataloger of the coin's Dan Holmes Collection auction appearance. MRB AU55.

Ex: Bowers and Merena (11/2002), lot 400; Denis Loring; Dan Holmes; The Dan Holmes Collection (Goldberg, 9/2009), lot 550. (#1543)

PROOF LARGE CENT

Proof-Only 1849 N-18 Cent, PR64 Red

2416 1849 PR64 Red PCGS. N-18, R.6. This proof-only variety has bright golden-red surfaces on the obverse with subdued red on the reverse. Both sides are peppered with tiny spots, limiting the grade of this otherwise beautiful piece. This example is finer than most 1849 N-18 cents. Bob Grellman writes that "this variety's status as a proof-only strike is not in question, but it does not represent the mint's finest effort." Housed in a green-label PCGS holder, this is the finest PCGS certified 1849 proof cent with full red color. Population: 2 in 64 Red, 0 finer (11/09). MRB PR63.(#1978)

FLYING EAGLE CENTS

Lustrous MS63 1856 Flying Eagle Cent, Snow-3

2417 1856 MS63 PCGS. Snow-3. The Snow-3 1856 Flying Eagles are mostly business strikes, and they constitute the examples actually struck in 1856 and distributed to Congressmen and Washington VIPS in support of the effort to launch the new-style small cents. Most of the Snow-9s are proofs, restrikes from a few years later struck for collectors. The repunched flag on the top of the 5 in the date makes attribution of the Snow-3 relatively easy, although the present specimen also shows strike doubling on most of the peripheral legends. Generous luster proceeds from both sides of this Select Mint State coin, which has predominantly honey-gold surfaces with considerable field-device contrast. The strike is fairly weak on the peripheries, with softness on the eagle's head and tail and the wreath on the reverse. Population: 40 in 63, 49 finer (11/09).(#2013)

Prized Select 1856 Flying Eagle Cent

2418 1856 MS63 PCGS. CAC. Snow-9. PCGS does not recognize proofs of the 1856 Flying Eagle cent, though NGC and others have been convinced by various arguments. Early small cent guru Rick Snow has presented evidence both for and against, such as an exacting strike counterbalanced by poor mirrors or planchet flaws. This Select specimen exemplifies many of the contradictions of the issue. While the bold definition is consistent with a proof striking, reflectivity on the streaky autumn-brown surfaces is almost non-existent and several planchet cracks are noted on each side. Population: 40 in 63, 49 finer (11/09).

From The Five Point Collection.(#2013)

Prooflike MS65 1856 Flying Eagle Cent
Ex: Walsh, Snow-3, Die Stage A

2419 1856 MS65 PCGS. Ex: Joshua and Ally Walsh. Snow-3. Die Stage A. The obverse die of this variety is easily identifiable by repunching on the 5 in the date, although one will need a loupe to discern this feature on the present example. This die was also used to strike coins of the Snow-1 and Snow-10 varieties. The most evident reverse diagnostics are the high leaves at the C and T in CENT. This reverse die was also used to strike Snow-8.

According to Snow (2001), examples of Snow-3 are the second most frequently encountered 1856 Flying Eagle cents in today's market. This die pair was used from 1856 through early 1857. The first coins produced were copper die trial pieces (Judd-281, Pollock-213), of which only two examples are accounted for today. The Mint then struck 634-800 business strike 1856 Flying Eagle cents of the Snow-3 die marriage using copper-nickel planchets. Snow asserts that these coins were prepared for two purposes: to test the press and dies in a simulated business strike run, and to provide examples of the proposed copper-nickel cent to members of Congress.

The first copper-nickel examples of Snow-3 that emerged from the dies are prooflike in finish with moderately reflective mirrors in the fields. These coins are known as Die Stage A, and they can be easily mistaken for proofs by collectors who are not aware of the other diagnostics for Snow-3. All examples of this variety lack the completeness of strike that proof 1856 Flying Eagle cents display. The present coin, while certainly sharp in overall detail, exhibits a little softness of strike over the eagle's breast feathers. In addition, the reverse devices, particularly the cotton leaves in the wreath, have rounded edges. As befits the die stage, this coin displays moderately reflective fields. The color is a warm, original, honey-gold shade with swirls of medium tan and lilac patina here and there. Both sides are free of bothersome handling marks, although a tiny carbon fleck in the obverse field above the date is noted.

From 1856-1860, the Philadelphia Mint produced 659-850 business strike 1856 Flying Eagle cents during two distinct striking periods. During the same time, the Mint delivered 1,025-1,550 proofs. With a lower original mintage, the business strikes, which are of the Snow-3, Snow-6, Snow-7, Snow-8, and Snow-10 varieties, are more highly prized by Flying Eagle cent specialists. This Gem is certified in a green label holder.(#2013)

Early Die State 1858/7 Flying Eagle Cent, MS64

2420 1858/7 MS64 PCGS. FS-301, formerly FS-006. Snow-1. Die Stage A. This is one of the finest examples of this very popular 19th century overdate. One must look carefully to find any imperfections on the evenly toned, light brown surfaces. Even the strike is impressive with the overall definition as full as typically seen for the variety. There is, nonetheless, slight weakness over the upper right quadrant of the reverse, but Snow states that this is characteristic of the variety. Only very rarely is an 1858/7 cent seen with any more detail in this area than that seen on this particular coin. The striking softness associated with the 1858/7 has resulted in considerable resistance on the part of the grading services to certify any examples higher than MS64. Since NGC and PCGS have recently come to understand the peculiar striking characteristics of this variety, a few examples have received an MS65 designation. Indeed, the present representative has the look of a higher grade.

A very early die state, remnants of the 7 underdigit show clearly above and to the right of the final 8 in the date. The diagnostic die dot above the date, which is actually the left base of a misplaced 1, is bold and triangular in shape. In addition, the broken wing tip is just about connected to the wing. There are also light die striations (as produced) visible diagonally from the lower left to the upper right of the coin, and additional die file marks are visible under the date. These features are only visible on the earliest die states.

The die state of a particular 1858/7 Flying Eagle cent is very important because nearly 75% of all examples produced are late die states with no evidence of the 7 showing. Richard Snow states that collectors who desire top quality examples of this date demand to see the 7! Clearly, the present lot represents an important opportunity for the advanced collector to acquire one of the finest examples of this popular and rare overdate. This issue is normally collected as part of the regular issue Flying Eagle series, adding further to its desirability.

Ex: "Heathgate" Collection (Goldberg Coins, 2/2001), lot 1082; Joseph P. Gorrell Collection (Heritage, 1/2003), lot 4406. Accompanied by an Eagle Eye Photo Seal and certificate.(#2022)

Impressive 1856 Snow-9 Flying Eagle Cent, PR64

2421 1856 PR64 PCGS. CAC. Snow-9, a proof-only variety. The green label PCGS holder that houses this coin identifies it as a Choice proof, and it exhibits exceptional workmanship. The surfaces are nicely mirrored, finer than usual for the 1856 Flying Eagle cents, and the strike is bold with every detail sharp and crisp. Both sides have delightful light tan surfaces with wonderful iridescent toning. Only a few minuscule spots or flecks are evident on each side, and abrasions are entirely absent. PCGS has only certified 46 finer proofs of this important issue (11/09).(#2037)

Delightful Gem Proof 1857 Flying Eagle Cent

2422 1857 PR65 NGC. Snow-PR2. Although not generally manufactured to the same degree of quality as coins from the PR1 dies, those of the PR2 variety are certainly among the 50 proof Flying Eagle cents delivered in 1857. The present example is strongly reflective in the fields with full striking definition throughout. The medium-tan surfaces reveal blushes of champagne iridescence at direct angles, and the surfaces are free of singularly mentionable blemishes. The proof Flying Eagle cents of 1857 and 1858 are not as widely publicized as those of the first-year 1856, but they are of greater rarity, which makes the presence of multiple die pairs for the 1857 proofs all the more intriguing.(#2040)

Cameo PR65 1857 Flying Eagle Cent
A Deeply Reflective, Starkly Contrasted Example

2423 1857 Flying Eagle PR65 Cameo NGC. Snow-PR1. As a rule, proof Flying Eagle cents dated 1857 and 1858 are actually rarer than those of 1856, and pieces exhibiting any degree of contrast are almost non-existent. Current population data supports the rarity of such pieces. This Gem example has lovely light tan color with traces of pale gold toning. A few inactive spots are evident on each side, mostly hidden within the devices and not obviously apparent. The fields are deeply mirrored around sharply defined and highly lustrous devices, and these physical characteristics are compiled into an aesthetically pleasing piece that will surely please the collector of 19th century proof type coins.

This issue predates by a year the systematic production of proof coins for sale by the Mint to active collectors of the time. The current edition of the *Guide Book* inexplicably reports a proof mintage of 485 coins, an extraordinary high figure that is not supported by population information. In *A Guide Book of Flying Eagle and Indian Head Cents,* Richard Snow estimates an actual mintage of just 50 proofs and Dave Bowers published an estimated mintage of 50 to 100 proofs in his *Buyer's Guide* to the series. Auction records also support the lower mintage and a similarly low population. In the current market place, with multiple examples of many different rarities offered in single sales, it is instructive to learn that we have only offered proof 1857 Flying Eagle cents on 55 previous occasions (as both Cameo and non-Cameo) over 17 years.

In Volume One of *The Flying Eagle and Indian Cent Attribution Guide,* Snow has identified three different varieties for the 1857 proof Flying Eagle cents. This example is from the PR1 dies identified by Snow with the comment: "PR1 is typically found with deep mirrors and a unquestionable proof look." This Gem Cameo proof clearly matches his comments. Census: 2 in 65 Cameo, 1 finer (11/09). (#82040)

Notable PR66 Cameo 1858 Cent Small Letters Obverse

2424 1858 Small Letters PR66 Cameo NGC. Snow-PR2. A Small Letters obverse paired with a Low Leaves reverse; Snow describes the main reverse diagnostic as a "[d]iagonal die line in denticles below the right ribbon end." This is plain on the present piece once one knows where to look. This is a remarkable Premium Gem specimen that makes a wonderful first impression. Bright lemon-gold and orange fields show subtle blue-green accents, and the mildly frosted devices stand out from the mirrors. On closer inspection, a few tiny flyspecks (such as the one below the claw) and contact marks are visible, but their influence on the eye appeal is minimal. NGC has graded just two PR66 Cameo examples of the Small Letters variety with none finer in the contrast category (11/09).

Rarely Seen 1873 Open 3 Cent, MS66 Red

2425 1873 Open 3 MS66 Red NGC. Struck in the latter part of the year, the Open 3 is the more available of the two date variants. Snow estimates that of the 11.6 million 1873 cents minted, 9.0 million were of the Open 3 variety. This is a remarkable Condition Census 1873 Open 3 cent, with excellent sharpness throughout and splendid orange-gold surfaces that display blushes of rose patina across the center of the obverse. We have only offered four examples (including this piece in 2003) in the past 16 years at auction.
From The Five Point Collection.(#2108)

MS66 Red 1873 Open 3 Cent Ex: Joshua and Ally Walsh

2426 1873 Open 3 MS66 Red PCGS. Ex: Joshua and Ally Walsh Collection. The relatively low mintage for the 1873 issue is divided into Closed 3, Open 3, and Doubled LIBERTY varieties. While the Open 3 is not rare in lower grades, only a tiny fraction of the survivors can match the original copper-gold color of this immaculately preserved Premium Gem. The delightfully lustrous surfaces also offer subtle rose accents. Well struck with all four diamonds visible and immense visual appeal. For pedigree purposes, an opaque toning spot is seen within the O of ONE. Population: 4 in 66 Red, 0 finer (12/09).(#2108)

Highly Unusual 1877 Cent Struck on a Venezuelan One Centavo Planchet, MS61

2427 1877 Cent—Struck on a Venezuela One Centavo Planchet—MS61 NGC. 2.3 gm. Judd-1496, Pollock-1649, R.8. Although it is listed in the standard pattern references, this piece is not a true pattern but a Mint error. This fascinating piece made its way into the two major pattern references due to its appearance, which is suggestive of a deliberately struck off-metal pattern. Later research revealed the truth, and the most recent edition of Judd, while it maintains the listing for this singular item, indicates its true status as a mint error.

While the Philadelphia Mint struck no contract coinage for Venezuela in 1877, a leftover copper-nickel planchet from the previous year's production of one centavo coins somehow mixed in with the bronze blanks for cents and was struck. The result was this fascinating and distinctive specimen.

The feathers of the headdress are weak at the tips, owing to the underweight nature of the planchet, and the lower part of the wreath is similarly ill-defined. By contrast, the soft lower right corner of the N in ONE is a diagnostic for this important issue. Occasional sage accents grace the otherwise nickel-gray surfaces, which are smooth and attractive.

Any Uncirculated 1877 cent is highly desirable due to its status as a low mintage key date. Finding such an example struck on a foreign planchet is an opportunity unlikely to surface again.

Ex: Bowers and Merena 2003 Baltimore ANA Auction, lot 3158.

1877 Indian Cent, MS65 Red and Brown

2428 1877 MS65 Red and Brown PCGS. Die Pair 2, per Snow. The date is spaced apart, with the 18 in the date not touching (they touch or nearly so on Die Pair 1). A raised die dot appears at the juncture of the hair and neck, just above the ribbon. The bottom of the N in ONE is weaker than the surrounding letters. This piece shows generous luster proceeding from both sides, with a pleasing mix of honey-gold, almond, and mahogany coloration prevailing. Even under a high-powered loupe, there are remarkably few distractions seen. All four diamonds and the L on the ribbon are visible, if not bold, and there is no carbon. Series aficionados will no doubt give this piece the important notice it deserves. Population: 48 in 65 Red and Brown, 3 finer (12/09).(#2128)

1877 Indian Head Cent
MS66 Red and Brown
Tied for Finest Certified

2429 1877 MS66 Red and Brown NGC. Only 852,500 cents were minted in 1877, the smallest mintage for the denomination since 1823. The Mint redeemed and reissued nearly 10 million cents in 1877 which, when coupled with the low demand for small change in the depressed economy, made a large production of cents unnecessary. The survival rate for the date is also surprisingly low, making the 1877 the rarest Indian Head cent. The present coin is a delightful specimen, with predominately red surfaces, evenly and lightly mellowed, with just a touch of brown. The strike is sharp, but not quite full. Full detail is present on the feathers, but there is some localized weakness on the second diamond from the top and the lower reverse wreath. Currently, consulting both leading grading services, the coin offered here is tied for finest certified in the Red and Brown category. Census: 8 in 66 Red and Brown, 0 finer (11/09).(#2128)

1877 Gem Indian Cent With Glowing Mint Red Luster

2430 1877 MS65 Red NGC. A shortage of copper resulted in the mint's limited production of Indian cents in 1877. A paltry total of 852,500 pieces were struck, and, while the final-year 1909-S has a lower mintage (309,000 pieces), the '77 is the undisputed key to this widely collected series. It seems likely that while the 1909-S survived in sufficient numbers (thanks to heightened public awareness of numismatics in the early 20th century), most examples of the 1877 production entered economic channels. Not so with the present Gem, whose surfaces are smooth with virtually no blemishes to report. Both sides are aglow with rich orange-red luster, and the strike is bold in most areas. A little softness of detail is noted on the obverse at the tips of the feathers in Liberty's headdress. For future identification, a small mark resembling a lintmark is visible in the left obverse field under the A of STATES.

From The Five Point Collection.(#2129)

Exceptional MS66 Full Red 1888 Cent

2431 1888 MS66 Red PCGS. The mintage for the 1888 dropped significantly from the previous year. While 37.9 million pieces were still struck, full red (and high grade) examples are difficult to locate. An immensely attractive Indian cent, the surfaces are bright with even orange-red color over both sides with no signs of mellowing or browning anywhere. As Snow indicates, the color is a bit paler than seen in previous years, most likely because of the source of the planchets. The mint luster is thickly layered on both obverse and reverse, giving this coin an undeniable attractiveness. Population: 12 in 66 Red, 1 finer (11/09).

From The Five Point Collection.(#2168)

2432 No lot.

UNITED STATES OF AMERICA
LIBERTY
1905
ONE
CENT

Breathtaking 1905 Gold Indian Cent, MS64

2433 1905 Indian Cent—Struck on a Quarter Eagle Planchet—MS64 PCGS. Weight: 64.5 grains, the standard weight of a quarter eagle. Exactly five Indian cents are known on gold planchets, according to information available to us. Among them are three dated 1900, this piece dated 1905, and an example dated 1906. The Judd pattern reference lists 1900 and 1907 gold cents in the section on mint errors. However, Andrew W. Pollock, III, listed the 1900 gold Indian cents as P-1990 in the regular pattern section of his reference. Pollock writes: "Listed in Judd as a mint error, but it is difficult to imagine that a Mint employee would be so careless as to feed gold planchets into a coinage press fitted with one-cent piece dies." Pollock suggests that these pieces may have been deliberately struck for one or more collectors.

The following Census of gold Indian cents and additional information about them is compiled from a variety of sources, including www.uspatterns.com , www.minterrornews.com , Donald Taxay's 1976 *Catalogue and Encyclopedia,* Andrew Pollock's 1994 *United States Patterns and Related Issues,* the Judd reference, and selected auction catalogs. Conversations with Fred Weinberg and Richard Snow provided additional background.

1900 MS65 PCGS. Col. E.H.R. Green; B.G. Johnson; John Beck (Abner Kreisberg Corporation, 1/1975), lot 609; Mike Byers; Auction '89 (Superior, 7/1989), lot 856; Bowers and Merena (8/1991), lot 4103; recently PCGS authenticated as a 1900 Indian cent struck on a gold $2.50 planchet, and graded MS65. The 1991 ANA catalog gives a weight of 65.8 grains, 1.3 grains too much for a quarter eagle planchet.

1900 AU55. Heritage (8/1993), lot 8000. The 1993 ANA catalog gives a weight of 4.35 grams (67.12 grains), 2.62 grains too much for a quarter eagle planchet.

1900. Michael Hodder reported in a May 14, 1996 letter to Q. David Bowers that he had personally seen three different pieces, all with weights in the range of 65.8 to 67.1 grains. See Bowers' *A Buyer's and Enthusiast's Guide to Flying Eagle and Indian Cents,* p. 427.

1905 MS64 PCGS. Apparently unknown to the numismatic community prior to the current offering. Weight: 64.5 grains, the standard weight for a quarter eagle planchet.

1906 AU58 NGC. Stack's (6/2004), lot 4097; Stack's (9/2009), lot 4299. Weight: 64.4 grains, within the 0.25 grain tolerance for a quarter eagle planchet.

1907. Listed in the Judd pattern book, and in Donald Taxay's Catalogue and Encyclopedia [of] U.S. Coins. *The 1907 gold Indian cent is currently unlocated.*

One example dated 1900 is also known in silver, from the identical dies as the 1900 gold Indian cents, suggesting they were all made at or near the same time. Rick Snow writes in *A Guide Book of Flying Eagle and Indian Head Cents* that "both the silver and gold examples are struck from the same dies, with light roughness on the reverse die, probably from die rust." That all three 1900 pieces have higher weights suggests that they were specially made, perhaps without the knowledge of Mint officials. Fred Weinberg explained to this cataloger that "the weights vary because in all probability, they were on planchets that might not have been filed down to the proper weight spread." Hand adjusting of individual gold planchets continued in the Mint until circa 1910. Those three pieces are almost certainly fancy pieces made for collectors, while the 1905 and 1906 examples, on correct weight planchets, are more likely pieces truly made in error, and substantially more important as such.

This example is slightly off-center toward 9 o'clock, the tops of UNITED STATES off the planchet. The strike is weak at the date, feather tips, RICA, the outer parts of the wreath, and the ribbon bow. The weakness seems counter to expectations of the soft gold, but the diameter is at least a full millimeter less than an Indian cent, meaning that the metal flowed out and was insufficient to accept the design from the deepest recesses of the dies. Both sides have fully brilliant yellow surfaces with frosty mint luster. A few faint hairlines on the cheek prevent a Gem grade assignment. This stunning gold Indian cent is one of the truly amazing error coins we have ever handled.

Splendid 1909 VDB Cent
Doubled Die Obverse
FS-1101, MS66 Red

2434 1909 VDB Doubled Die Obverse FS-1101 MS66 Red PCGS. According to the *Cherrypickers' Guide,* the FS-1102 is marginally rarer than the the FS-1101. Both, however, are growing quite elusive in the finest grades—a circumstance due not only to the *Cherrypickers'* reference, but also to the increasing spread of variety collecting, the various major/complete variety sets in the PCGS Set Registry, and their certification of varieties, as here. The die-doubling on the FS-1101 is readily evident on both the date digits and the RTY of LIBERTY. This piece boasts splendid fiery-red surfaces with no mentionable carbon, save for a single fleck under the T of CENT on the reverse, and great eye appeal. This coin, among the finest certified, would upgrade most of the major and complete variety sets in the PCGS Set Registry, as it is a component of both collections. Population for the variety: 3 in 66 Red, 0 finer (12/09).(#37633)

Remarkable Full Red MS66 1909-S VDB Cent

2435 1909-S VDB MS66 Red PCGS. This is a remarkable Premium Gem example with bright red luster on both sides. All of the design elements are sharply detailed, and the surfaces are pristine without any spots or other blemishes. The only reason we can find for a grade below the Superb Gem level is a slight mellowing of the original color. The "SVDB" is a favorite with collectors, and is well-known to specialists and novice collectors alike. It is possibly the single most widely known coin in all of American numismatics. PCGS has only certified nine full Red examples of this date in higher grades (11/09). (#2428)

Impressive 1912-D Cent, MS66 Red

2436 1912-D MS66 Red PCGS. This piece in MS66 Red is one of only a dozen so certified at PCGS, and we would be surprised if a good number of those were not resubmissions. As recently as four years ago, PCGS had certified only four coins in this grade. This is a marvelous piece, boldly struck and with absolutely no visible carbon. The only mentionable strike softness is on the first A of AMERICA. The date, mintmark, and all other devices on both sides are sharp and well-detailed. An impressive semikey Lincoln for a fine Registry Set. Population: 12 in 66 Red, 0 finer (12/09).(#2455)

Low Mintage 1914-D Lincoln Cent, MS65 Red

2437 1914-D MS65 Red PCGS. The 1914-D Lincoln cent is a low mintage issue that did not attract much attention until the 1930s, when coin boards and folders became popular. Few examples were saved from the original mintage of 1.2 million pieces and Mint State examples were extremely difficult to locate when collectors belatedly recognized the importance of the issue. Specimens with fully Red surfaces, such as the present coin, are especially elusive. The surfaces of this coin radiate blazing mint red color, much lighter and more evenly tinted than usually seen. The strike is full, with slight evidence of metal flow in the fields. Both obverse and reverse are almost carbon-free, extremely unusual on Mint State specimens of this date. Overall eye appeal is stunning. Population: 55 in 65 Red, 3 finer (11/09).

From The Five Point Collection.(#2473)

Key 1914-D Lincoln Cent, MS65 Red

2438 1914-D MS65 Red PCGS. The 1914-D is an elusive key date in the Lincoln cent series, with an original mintage of less than 1.2 million pieces. The issue is especially difficult to locate with full Red surfaces. The coin offered here features unusually bright, but undoubtedly original surfaces. The attractively variegated color ranges from light orange-red to full cherry-red (the color usually seen on this issue). The design elements show fully struck, exquisitely detailing on each side. Some light carbon flecks—present on nearly all Mint State survivors unless they were dipped or cyanided (David Bowers, 2008, p. 146)—are noted here. Extremely difficult to locate any finer, as both grading services have certified a total of only eight examples in finer grades (11/09).(#2473)

Wonderful 1917 Doubled Die Cent MS65 Red and Brown

2439 1917 Doubled Die Obverse MS65 Red and Brown PCGS. Breen-2081, FS-101, formerly FS-013. Slightly faded mint Red and attractive for this exceedingly rare issue. To date, this coin is tied for the finest with one other example graded by PCGS in the Red and Brown category. A few more are graded that retain the full Red color, some of which technically exceed the present coin. Boldly struck with clear doubling on the 9, 7 and TRUST. For the Lincoln cent collector, this is one of the premier rarities in the entire series, and a coin which is difficult to find in any grade. This desirable *Guide Book* variety is described in *Cherrypickers'* as "certainly one of the top five Lincoln Cent varieties. Extremely rare in mint state." An exceptional opportunity for the specialist to obtain a wonderful example of this issue.

In 1917 the U.S. mints were focused on producing the new quarters and half dollars, both of which were introduced in 1916, but production really got humming in 1917. Apparently the doubled die obverse was caused when the master hub shifted slightly while this die was being manufactured. Population: 2 in 65 Red and Brown, 0 finer (12/09).(#92496)

Splendid 1918 Cent, MS67 Red

2440 1918 MS67 Red PCGS. CAC. The designer's V.D.B. initials were restored to the cent in 1918, placed on Lincoln's shoulder next to the rim. Fully Red 1918 cents can be located through the Gem level of preservation. Premium Gems are considerable more challenging and higher-grade pieces are rare.

Strong luster emanates from the orange-gold surfaces of this Red Superb Gem and a powerful strike delivers bold delineation to the design elements. Close examination reveals no mentionable contact marks, toning spots, or carbon flecks. Splendid eye appeal is evident on both sides. Population: 9 in 67 Red, 1 finer (11/09). (#2506)

Red-Tinged 1922 No D, Weak Reverse Cent Die Pair 3, MS64 Red and Brown

2441 1922 No D Weak Reverse MS64 Red and Brown PCGS. CAC. Die Pair 3, identifiable by the weak second 2 in the date and the distended O in ONE. Generous amounts of mint red cling to the surfaces—most of the obverse, and the periphery on the reverse—unusual for any 1922 No D cent. The central obverse is chiefly ice-blue, and the reverse has more variegated central color. As always seen (and diagnostic), the reverse is soft due to both the strike and prolonged die use, particularly on the wheat stalks, where about half the detail is absent. As is sometimes the case with this die pair, the ghost of a mintmark can be seen under magnification. This coin is tied with a small handful of Weak Reverse coins at PCGS for the finest numerically certified, regardless of color designation. A real prize for the Lincoln cent specialist. Population: 9 in 64 Red and Brown, 0 finer (11/09).(#2541)

Type One 1936 Doubled Die Obverse Lincoln Cent MS66 Red, FS-101

2442 1936 Doubled Die Obverse Type One MS66 Red PCGS. CAC. FS-101, formerly FS-014. This bold doubled die is in hot demand from variety collectors. The comments from *Cherrypickers'* are instructive, rating the variant with a liquidity factor of L-5, "will sell easily, and often above listed value" and interest factor of I-4, "high interest (most variety collectors interested)." Bold north-south doubling on TRUST is the key for the variety, as this piece shows, but all peripheral letters, the date, and the forward edge of Lincoln's coat all exhibit prominent doubling. This piece offers unturned orange-red surfaces with lots of eye appeal and only a few minor flecks on the lower reverse. A well-struck and thoroughly lustrous example. Population: 6 in 66 Red, 1 finer (11/09). (#82650)

Bright 1943 Cent Struck on a Curacao 25 Cent Planchet XF40 One of Only Three Pieces Known

2443 1943 Cent—Struck on Curacao 25 Cent Planchet—XF40 NGC. 3.5 grams. This is the third example we have handled of this World War Two-created rarity. The other two were in our 2001 Central States Sale, lot 5942; 2001 ANA Sale, lot 5466; 2005 Central States Sale, lot 8214 (which was a reappearance of the 2001 Central States coin). Similar to the famous copper cents of 1943, these two coins have a different origin but were produced in the same manner as the copper cents by "old" planchets remaining in the hopper and then struck with the next year's cent production. Rather than recreate the wheel, here is the background to how this coin was struck in 1943, taken from our 2001 catalog:

> "This coin was born out of the turmoil of the Second World War. In the spring of 1940, Nazi Germany overran the Netherlands in a campaign that also saw the conquest of France and Belgium. The Dutch colonies of Surinam (in northern South America), Curacao (an island in the Caribbean Sea north of Surinam, and part of the Netherlands Antilles), and the Netherlands West Indies came under the protection of the Allied powers. Curacao was particularly important to the war effort, as its refineries delivered more than 60% of the oil used by the Allies. In addition to providing troops to protect Curacao's shores, the United States also produced coinage for the Dutch colony. In 1943, the Philadelphia Mint delivered 2.5 million 25 cent coins (KM-38) for shipment to Curacao."

Apparently after the production run of Curacao 25 cent pieces, the Mint resumed striking U.S. cents, and this piece was mistakenly struck on one of the few (perhaps as few as two?) remaining Curacao planchets. The surfaces are bright and silvery in appearance on each side. Numerous tiny abrasions are peppered over each side, but the only marks we see that could be used for pedigree purposes are located on the reverse between the N and E of ONE. An exceptionally rare opportunity for the error specialist.

Famous 1943 Cent in Bronze, AU58
Legendary Off-Metal Error Rarity

2444 1943 Cent—Struck on a Bronze Planchet—AU58 PCGS. Few coins are so misunderstood, so mysterious, so *legendary* as the 1943 cents struck in bronze, known informally as the 1943 "copper" cents. When the Mint switched from bronze to zinc-plated steel for cent coinage, a handful of leftover bronze planchets nevertheless found their way into the coining press and were stamped with the date 1943. This occurred at all three Mint facilities to strike cents that year, though a majority of the known 1943 bronze or "copper" cents were struck in Philadelphia, not Denver or San Francisco. Fewer than 20 are known.

The difference between the normal steel cents of 1943 and the anomalous bronze cents of the same year has captured the imagination of generations of collectors; David Lange, in his *The Complete Guide to Lincoln Cents,* titled the section on the 1943 bronze cents "Error Coin Royalty." There are many more impostors than kings when it comes to the 1943 bronze cent; many genuine 1943 *steel* cents have been copper-plated, and even after testing with a magnet weeds out the plated pretenders, a few more deceptive fakes exist. The authenticity of this near-Mint 1943 bronze cent, however, is unimpeachable.

Almost from the outset, the 1943 bronze cents were the subject of misinformation. Henry Ford, the automobile titan, supposedly offered a new car in exchange for a 1943 "copper" cent, for example; this was not the first coin hoax centered around Ford. Erroneous prices also figure prominently into 1943 bronze cent tall tales; Lange cites a 1959 report that an example sold for $40,000, and as he notes, "Given that coins such as the 1804 silver dollar were then valued in the $10,000-$15,000 range, this figure seems fanciful."

Similarly, news dispatches in 1999 about a 1943 bronze cent supposedly spent as an ordinary coin overestimated its value; the original wire report claimed it was worth a quarter of a million dollars, a number that increased to a cool half-million as the story was retold! Still, there is a positive side to the coin's history of rumor, which was further fueled by dealers advertising to buy examples for wild sums. As authors Jeff Garrett and Ron Guth note in *100 Greatest U.S. Coins,* "many of today's collectors got their start by searching for a 1943 bronze cent in pocket change."

As an AU58 example, the present 1943 bronze cent ranks highly among the known survivors; it must have circulated only briefly before it was recognized as unusual and pulled from circulation. The violet-brown and mahogany surfaces have picked up a few light abrasions, and the obverse shows a faint fingerprint pattern to the toning. A long, thin abrasion in the upper right obverse field, which passes between TRUST and Lincoln's head, is the most readily identifiable pedigree marker.

From The Kiev Collection.

Famous 1944 Steel Cent, AU55
Prized Off-Metal Rarity

2445 1944 Cent—Struck on a Zinc-Plated Steel Planchet—AU55 PCGS. The 1943 bronze cent and the 1944 steel cent are two sides of the same error: planchets left over from one year's cent coinage—bronze planchets from 1942, or steel planchets from 1943—carried over to the next year's production. Thus, a handful of 1943-dated cents were struck in bronze when they should have been made out of steel, and similarly, a handful of 1944-dated cents were struck in steel when they should have been made out of shellcase alloy.

This modestly worn 1944 steel cent has pale gray surfaces with minor spotting through the obverse fields and a reddish area at the loop of the R in AMERICA. While the portrait of Lincoln shows slight softness, owing to the harder-than-expected planchet, the lines of the wheat ears remain bold.

From The Alfred V. Melson Collection, Part One.

1944-D Cent Struck on Steel Planchet
A Branch Mint Rarity, AU53

2446 1944-D Cent—Struck on a Zinc-Coated Steel Planchet—AU53 PCGS. Branch mint 1944 steel cents are far more elusive than their Philadelphia counterparts. While the main Mint put leftover steel cent blanks to use striking emergency coinage for Belgium, which greatly lengthened the time in which a steel cent planchet could have come between 1944-dated cent dies, neither Denver nor San Francisco used steel cent blanks after 1943, creating a much narrower window in which 1944-dated steel cents might have been struck.

This delightful 1944-D steel cent circulated briefly before being saved, as shown by the minor wear over the devices. Pale blue tints from the zinc plating mingle with the pale steel-gray of the planchet underneath. Spots are visible along the obverse rim and also on the reverse, most noticeably to the right of the E in ONE and around the word STATES. An important and unusual selection for the collector of numismatic exotica.

From The Alfred V. Melson Collection, Part One.

Unusually Bright MS65 Red 1955 Doubled Die Cent

2447 1955 Doubled Die Obverse MS65 Red PCGS. Due to the manner in which 1955 Doubled Die cents were released to the public, i.e., through vending machines in the Boston area in the summer of 1955, most survivors today show subdued mint red color at best, and most are brown or have just a bit of red remaining. This coin has unusually bright, shimmering orange-red luster with faint traces of cherry-red around the obverse devices. A few flyspecks of carbon are seen over each side, but there are no large spots or obvious abrasions on either the obverse or reverse of this lovely and highly lustrous Gem example. Population: 18 in 65 Red, 0 finer (11/09).
From The Five Point Collection.(#2827)

PROOF LINCOLN CENTS

Impressive 1909 VDB Cent, PR65 Red

2448 1909 VDB PR65 Red PCGS. Although business strike 1909 VDB cents are plentiful, proofs are infrequently encountered. Only 1,194 proofs were minted, and only a fraction of those survive today. Example such as this brilliant proof are seldom seen. The surfaces are satiny with brilliant original Red color and wisps of iridescence on each side. The strike is excellent with pinpoint details. The reverse has a raised die line from the rim to the period after the D and a tiny crescent-shaped die chip right of the M in UNUM, both die markers for the matte proofs. Population: 7 in 65 Red, 9 finer (11/09). (#3302)

Full Red PR66 1912 Matte Proof Cent

2449 1912 PR66 Red NGC. We cannot overstate the importance of this Gem full red proof Lincoln cent for specialists in this long-lived and popular series. Only two 1912 examples have received a PR66 Red grade from the major grading services: the present example and a specimen at PCGS. None are finer (11/09). As befits the issue, both sides display a matte finish that is coarser than that seen on the typical survivor from the two preceding proof deliveries. The texture is undisturbed by even a single noteworthy handling mark, and each side has only two nearly microscopic carbon flecks. Needle-sharp striking definition characterizes all of the fully lustrous, straw-gold features. This coin is from a middle to later state of the dies as outlined in Lange's Lincoln cent reference, showing numerous die polish lines through 91 in the date, through ERTY, and above the T in TRUST.

In terms of total number of coins known, the 1912 is not as rare as either the 1909 VDB or the 1916. However, David Lange notes that the 1912, as a full red Gem, is the rarest of the three issues. The author also speculates that many of the 2,145 proof Lincoln cents prepared in 1912 may have been melted as unsold. Census: 1 in 66 Red, 0 finer (11/09).

From The Five Point Collection.(#3314)

Rare 1916 Gem Red Proof Cent

2450 1916 PR65 Red PCGS. Most of the surviving 1916 proof cents out of the original mintage of 600 pieces (2010 *Guide Book*) are Brown or Red and Brown. Fully red, unspotted, and fully struck pieces are rare. The present Gem offering displays copper-orange luster on matte surfaces. A well executed strike leaves crisp definition on the design features, including Lincoln's hair and bow tie and the grains and lines of the wheat stalks. A few minuscule toning spots are visible on each side but the coin is carbon free, and a small mark concealed in Lincoln's beard is within the parameters of the numerical grade. Population: 10 in 65 Red, 3 finer (11/09).(#3326)

PROOF TWO CENT PIECE

1873 Open 3 Two Cent Piece, PR66 Red
Tied for Finest Certified

2451 1873 Open 3 PR66 Red PCGS. The five cent nickel denomination proved much more popular than the two cent piece in the late 1860s. Mintages of the latter denomination declined steadily until 1873, the final year of the denomination, when only proof examples were produced. Two major varieties are known for the year, from the self-explanatory Open 3 and Closed 3 dies. The present coin is a representative of the less available Open 3 variety, with the knobs of the 3 distinctly separate. Walter Breen believed the Open 3 coins were restrikes, and they are listed as such in the *Guide Book,* with an estimated mintage of 500 pieces. Alternatively, some experts believe the Open 3 coins were included in the 500 silver proof sets delivered after July 21, 1873 containing the Trade dollar and With Arrows coins. The issue is scarce in all grades today, and very rare at the PR66 Red level.

The present coin features pristine surfaces, with light, fragile red color. Currently, NGC has certified only three coins in PR66 Red, with none finer; while PCGS has graded five coins in PR66 Red, with none finer (11/09).(#3656)

THREE CENT NICKEL

Difficult 1885 Three Cent Nickel, MS66

2452 1885 MS66 PCGS. CAC. The year 1885 saw a scant mintage of 1,000 three cent nickel business strikes, the lowest circulation-strike production in the series. As expected, this date is difficult to locate in any grade level. PCGS and NGC have certified only about 100 specimens in all levels of preservation.

The light gray surfaces of this Premium Gem display blushes of subtle gold and ice-blue when viewed under magnification, and an exacting strike leaves virtually complete definition on the design elements, including the lines of the III denomination. A few minuscule flecks are undisturbing. Housed in a green label holder. Population: 10 in 66, 2 finer (11/09).(#3753)

2453 No Lot.

Richly Toned 1908 Liberty Nickel, MS67 Sole Finest Certified

2454 1908 MS67 NGC. The 1908 Liberty nickel is among the most difficult series issues of the 1900s to find in high Mint State grades. This is a marvelous Superb Gem with strong mint luster shining through the multicolored toning. The obverse displays ice-blue patina in the center, with rich olive and amber tones around the periphery. On the reverse glints of jade complement the predominating rose-gray coloration. The strike is nearly full, save for the often-weak lower left ear of corn on the reverse and stars 1 and 2 on the obverse. An essential for the NGC Registry Set collector, as the sole example of this issue at either service to date meriting this highest MS67 grade.(#3869)

PROOF LIBERTY NICKELS

Legendary 1913 Liberty Nickel
King of 20th Century Coins

Olsen Specimen

Olsen-Farouk-Hydeman-Buss-Hawn

Hawaii Five-O Star

Most Famous of Five Known

2455 1913 Liberty PR64 NGC.

THE OLSEN SPECIMEN

Recently dubbed "The Mona Lisa of Rare Coins," the Olsen specimen is the second finest of just five known examples and is currently graded PR64 NGC. It was the first 1913 Liberty Head nickel offered for sale in a public auction, and the only specimen that professional numismatist B. Max Mehl ever handled, despite his extensive advertising campaign that promoted the famously rare coin. It also holds the record as the first coin to break the $100,000 price barrier in 1972, while another 1913 nickel, the Eliasberg specimen, became the first coin to break the $1,000,000 price barrier some 24 years later. It is certainly possible that a 1913 Liberty nickel, perhaps the Olsen specimen, will someday become the first coin to break the $10,000,000 price barrier.

Jeff Garrett and Ron Guth, authors of *The 100 Greatest U.S. Coins,* noted in the 2009 third edition that the Olsen specimen "has been viewed ... by more people than any other." In *A Guide Book of Shield and Liberty Head Nickels,* Q. David Bowers describes the Olsen specimen as the most famous of all 1913 Liberty Head nickels. "This particular coin is probably the most highly publicized of the five specimens," writes Bowers.

John Dannreuther considers it to be the second of five 1913 Liberty nickels struck. His detailed analysis, discussed later, indicates that the Smithsonian specimen was the first coin struck, followed by the Olsen specimen, and then the other three. Of those three coins (another specimen is in the ANA) in private hands today, the Olsen specimen was struck before the other two. A professional numismatist from Memphis, Tennessee, Dannreuther is well respected among his peers for his critical eye and careful reasoning. He was one of six numismatists chosen for the authentication team when the Walton specimen of the 1913 nickel reappeared in 2003, after a 40-year absence.

Describing it in his 1961 catalog of the Edwin Hydeman Collection, Abe Kosoff stated that it "is a superb coin, sharply struck, as choice a specimen as could possibly be attained. It has been handled with utmost care, a statement which, unfortunately, cannot be made of two of the pieces." In 1985 the Superior cataloger wrote that the coin has "a needle-sharp strike with partial wire rims and slightly prooflike surfaces; all overlaid with a uniform matte-like gray finish and completely free from nicks and scratches." Eight years later, Stack's offered the Olsen specimen as part of the Reed Hawn Collection, paraphrasing the earlier Superior description: "Pleasing and uniform matte gray surfaces free from disfiguring marks. Partially reflective prooflike surfaces and a needle-sharp strike with raised wire rims in places."

Bowers, himself once an owner of the Olsen specimen, calls it "a very nice coin in a lower Mint State classification." However, NGC and PCGS have both graded the coin PR64. While there is a difference of opinion among some about terminology, the difference between a Mint State designation and a proof designation for an issue with just five pieces known is moot.

Past owners of the Olsen specimen, beginning with Fred Olsen, include Egyptian King Farouk, department store owner Edwin Hydeman, Los Angeles Lakers owner Dr. Jerry Buss, Texas oilman and numismatist Reed Hawn, and Dwight Manley, distributor of the *S.S. Central America* treasure. The current owner desires anonymity, but would certainly hold his own with those before him. The provenance is impressive, and the next collector who owns this coin will be in good company. In *Million Dollar Nickels,* Ray Knight observes: "Owning one of these treasures automatically elevates the holder upon a pedestal of honor in the numismatic community."

The Olsen specimen is sharp and complete in its design definition. Every star on the obverse is fully defined, Liberty's hair detail is crisp, and the individual agricultural elements are sharp. Similarly, every element of the wreath on the reverse is bold, down to the individual kernels in each ear of corn. The surfaces are fully pleasing and attractive, with uniform surfaces that show exceptional mirrored reflectivity. The surfaces are pristine, without any marks. Only a slight matte appearance separates this piece from a full PR65 grade.

The current offering is only the 12th time that any 1913 Liberty Head nickel has been offered at public auction since their first auction appearance in November 1944.

A STARRING ROLE

After the Olsen nickel broke the $100,000 price barrier, it became the "central character" of a *Hawaii Five-O* episode appropriately titled "The $100,000 Nickel." The genuine Olsen specimen was only used for the close-up shots during filming. For all other scenes the nickel had its own "stunt double."

Hawaii Five-O was a popular television police series starring Jack Lord as Steve McGarrett, the head of the elite state police unit in Hawaii. His partner and second in command was Danny "Danno" Williams, played by James MacArthur. Nearly every episode ended with McGarrett saying to Williams, "Book 'em, Danno." The series was broadcast on CBS from September 1968 to April 1980 and was filmed almost exclusively in Hawaii, one of the big draws for its fans.

The plot of "The $100,000 Nickel," originally aired on December 11, 1973, involved a coin convention and auction held at the Ilikai Hotel in Honolulu. A 1903 Liberty nickel was carefully altered to 1913 and used in a sleight-of-hand trick to steal the real 1913 nickel. Victor Buono played Eric Damien, a thief who orchestrates the robbery. With the switch detected before Damien can leave the hotel, he drops the coin into a vending machine, expecting to recover it later. Meanwhile, money from the vending machine was already collected, and a struggle ensued for the coin. That struggle resulted in coins being scattered over the ground, whereupon a young boy picked up the nickel and later spent it. Finally, after passing through many hands, the nickel was returned to its owner, apparently unharmed during its ordeal.

The publicity shot that is reprinted here shows Victor Buono inspecting the 1913 Liberty nickel. However, Buono is holding the magnifying glass between the nickel and the camera while he is inspecting the reverse of the coin.

Victor Charles Buono was born in San Diego, California, on February 3, 1938, and died in San Bernardino, California, on January 1, 1982. He was raised in San Diego and graduated from St. Augustine High School. His introduction to the performing arts came at the hand of his maternal grandmother, Myrtle Glied, a vaudeville performer. He first appeared on network TV in 1959. He also appeared in a number of movies, including *Who's Minding the Mint?*.

THE KING OF 20TH CENTURY COINS

While the 1804 silver dollar rightfully holds the title The King of Coins, there is no doubt that the 1913 Liberty Head nickel is the King of 20th Century Coins. The 1913 nickel holds the number one position in the third edition of *100 Greatest U.S. Coins.* Garrett and Guth comment: "Twenty years ago, if you asked any collector or dealer to name the three most valuable American coins, the response would most likely have been the following: 1804 Silver Dollar, 1894-S Dime, and 1913 Liberty Head Nickel. Today the 1913 Liberty Head nickel has taken the lead, gaining the top position in the 100 greatest U.S. coins." The dynamics of the rare coin market have changed in recent years. According to Garrett and Guth, the 1913 Liberty head nickel's "recent surge in popularity may be due in part to the publicity that has attended its last few appearances."

Each time a 1913 Liberty Head nickel breaks a previous price barrier, and it has happened twice with prices entering six figures and later seven figures, the fame of this rarity becomes even greater. A starring role in television increases its fame, as does each story, article, auction appearance, or book about the coin. It has even appeared in comic books and children's publications, such as *Weekly Reader.* Sprinkle in a little mystery, and the 1913 Liberty Head nickel makes its case as the most famous rarity in numismatics.

SAM BROWN AND HIS NICKELS

Samuel W. Brown is considered the mastermind behind the 1913 Liberty Head nickels. Brown was employed at the Philadelphia Mint from December 1903 through November 1913, putting him at the right place and time. He was also the first person to make any reference to the possible existence of such coins, in the form of a small advertisement in the December 1919 issue of *The Numismatist* to purchase examples. Further, Brown was the first person to publicly share any of the coins in the form of a coin convention exhibit, just a few months later. Although circumstantial, the evidence points a finger directly at Sam Brown, likely with the assistance of one or more accomplices.

Brown worked as a clerk or storekeeper, according to his employment transcript, resigning to enter business for his own account. He was born in Brownstown, Pennsylvania, circa 1879, and died in North Tonawanda, New York, in June 1944. It seems that Brown was always well liked and respected. After resigning from the Mint, he relocated to North Tonawanda late in 1913, where he was associated with Wayne Fahnestock in the Frontier Chocolate Company. He was later associated with the Pierce-Brown Company and retired in 1924 at the age of 45. He was a Mason and a past master of Sutherland Lodge No. 826. Brown also served as district deputy grandmaster of the Niagara Orleans district and as a member of the Shrine club and the Ismailia temple. Serving several terms on the Board of Education, he was mayor of North Tonawanda in 1932 and 1933.

Ray Knight comments: "The mysterious Mr. Brown confounds understanding. Just when you think you have him pegged as a crafty, scheming thief, he conducts the rest of his life in what appears to be a completely exemplary manner."

THE HOBBS EPISODE

The authors of *Million Dollar Nickels* observe: "The whole affair of the 1913 Liberty nickels would possibly never have come up—and the coins may never have been created—had it not been for The Hobbs Episode."

Treasury Secretary Franklin MacVeagh had an opportunity to make a permanent mark on the U.S. coinage before his term expired in 1913. The nickel was the only coin whose design could be changed under the 25-year law that states coin designs must remain in production for 25 years before they can be changed. MacVeagh served as Secretary of the Treasury from March 8, 1909, to March 5, 1913. After seeing James Earle Fraser's designs for the Buffalo nickel, he awarded Fraser the commission. In his annual report, Mint Director George Roberts stated about the Buffalo design: "The coin is distinctively characteristic of America, and in its execution promises to take high artistic rank among the coinages of the world." Everything was coming along smoothly, and the Buffalo nickel was about to become a reality—until the Hobbs episode began.

Hobbs Manufacturing Company began business as a manufacturer of paper box machinery, originally in Lynn and Boston, relocating to Worcester, Massachusetts, in 1891. In 1910 the firm began production of vending machines for postage stamps, railroad ticket sales, and change-making.

Officials from Hobbs Manufacturing found the new Indian/Buffalo nickel entirely unsatisfactory, demanding change after change to the Fraser design. Fraser sent a set of Hobbs-approved models to Charles Barber, who received them on December 26, 1912. He went to work reducing them and preparing dies, with test strikes minted on January 7, 1913. Hobbs was still unsatisfied and demanded more changes. Another six weeks of meetings and changes took place until MacVeagh had had enough. He certainly wanted the Buffalo nickel released before his term expired, and a meeting with Hobbs representatives on February 15, 1913, put an end to the episode. MacVeagh advised Roberts to proceed with production of the new nickels, and production finally commenced on February 21. All of the delays provided an opportunity for a special coinage.

PRODUCTION FACT AND FICTION

Much of what we know or think we know about the 1913 Liberty Head nickel remains undocumented. It seems that factual accuracy has never been a concern of numismatists in the past. John Dannreuther sums up the problem: "Once a rumor is repeated and put into print, it becomes fact. When one person repeats it and the next guy repeats it and the next guy repeats it, it becomes absolute fact. Then it becomes part of numismatic lore." Fortunately, the approach of 21st century numismatic research is a fresh look at past lore and legends. Instead of assuming that a story is correct, current research is verifying the source material and eliminating the speculation.

There has been considerable discussion about how and when the 1913 Liberty nickels were made. The coins made their first public appearance in 1920, in the possession of Samuel W. Brown. Circumstantial evidence points to Brown, although it is unlikely that he actually struck the five coins himself. He was a clerk or storekeeper at the Mint, rather than a coiner or someone with knowledge of coin production. Brown almost certainly had one or more accomplices, but who were they?

In *Million Dollar Nickels,* the authors devote an entire chapter, "Covert Origins," to the mystery of their production. The truth may never be known, as the facts are most likely buried with those responsible. Some have speculated that the coins were made late in 1912, while others suggest early 1913, and some have even said that they could have been made as late as 1919, although the latter is highly improbable.

Lee Hewitt made several suggestions in the March 1958 issue of *Numismatic Scrapbook Magazine:*

1. They were struck to exchange for coins needed for the Mint cabinet.
2. The coiner and engraver were merely amusing themselves when they struck the coins.
3. They were struck exclusively for a wealthy collector.

Five years later in September 1963, Hewitt suggested they were die trials. Don Taxay responded that they were made expressly for Brown, and that they are fantasy pieces. In 1968, Clyde Mervis reported that the coins were die trials, and that a worker carelessly tossed the coins in a desk drawer where they remained for an unspecified period of time. David Bowers and Walter Breen have both mentioned possible accomplices. In the Eliasberg catalog, Bowers went so far as to suggest it may have been George Morgan.

There have been a number of individuals identified as possible accomplices, from engraver Charles Barber to assistant engraver George T. Morgan, numismatist Stephen Nagy who supposedly had ties to the Mint, to an unidentified security guard who was reportedly fired in 1918. In *Million Dollar Nickels,* the authors suggest that Brown may have been an accomplice for someone else. "A different angle must consider that Brown was not the mastermind of the deed that someone else put in motion and he was only a cog in the plan. He may only have assisted in the plot. He may not have even been present when the coins were struck but received them at a later time, perhaps much later."

DEPARTMENT OF COMMERCE AND LABOR—BUREAU OF THE CENSUS
THIRTEENTH CENSUS OF THE UNITED STATES: 1910—POPULATION

State Pennsylvania
County Philadelphia
Name of incorporated place Philadelphia City
Enumerated by me on the 18th day of April, 1910. L. E. Neagley, Enumerator.

The 1910 Federal Census provides us with names of two others who might have been accomplices, although we are now introducing further speculation. In 1910 Brown was a workman at the U.S. Mint, residing at the boarding house of Carrie Corn, at 1611 South Oxford St. Two other boarders at the same residence, Henry B. Shuman and a Mr. Wenger, were both machinists at the Mint. In 1920 Shuman was listed as a "counter of money" at the Mint, while Wenger is not further identified.

The most likely time of production was the last two weeks of 1912 or the first week of 1913. Before the December 13 order to do nothing about the 1913 nickels came from Mint Director Roberts, Mint employees would have no reason to think that 1913 Liberty Head nickels would be out of the ordinary. Within a week after the first of January, the dies would most likely have been destroyed. The actual dies were probably a pair intended for proof coin production, already given the special polishing necessary for proofs. The striking was rushed, as indicated by the reverse die that was loose in the press. Each of the five coins has a slightly different amount of detail on the reverse, and the difference is attributed to a reverse die that was not firmly seated in the coning press.

For nearly 90 years, everything that has been discussed about the origins of the 1913 Liberty Head nickels is pure speculation, or educated guess at the best. There are only a few facts to aid in a solution to the mystery:

1. Dies for 1913 Liberty nickels were made in the last two months of 1912. We know this as records show 10 sets of 1913 Liberty nickel dies were shipped to San Francisco on November 25, 1912. Philadelphia Mint proof dies would have been made about the same time.
2. Mint Director George Roberts told his staff on December 13, 1912, to do nothing about the five cent coinage until new designs are ready.
3. The first Buffalo nickels were coined on February 21, 1913.
4. Five different 1913 Liberty Head nickels exist, and each shows some degree of reflectivity or mirrored surface.
5. Samuel W. Brown first exhibited the coins in 1920, after advertising to purchase them in December 1919.
6. Brown worked at the Mint from 1903 until 1913, when he resigned in November.

EMISSION SEQUENCE

Smithsonian Specimen

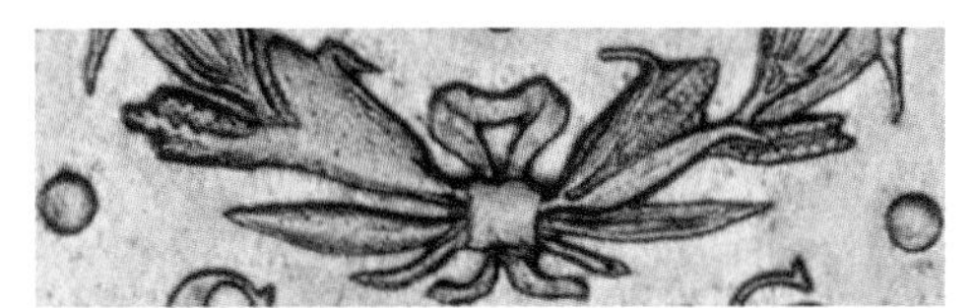

Walton Specimen

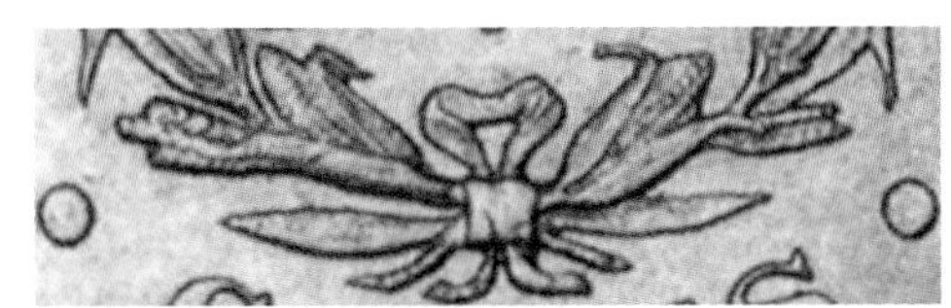

Olsen Specimen

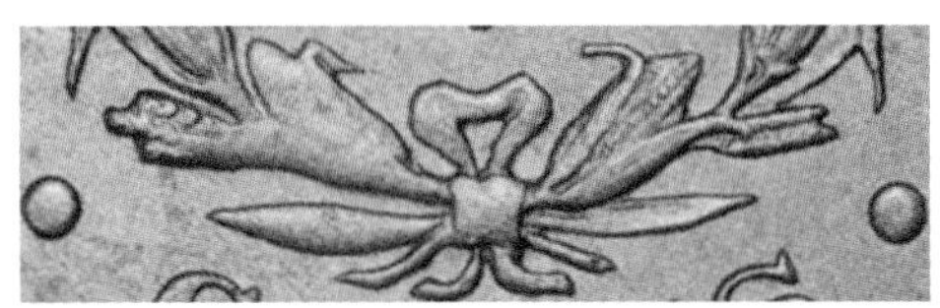

McDermott Specimen

Eliasberg Specimen

Because the reverse die was not fully seated in the coin press and each coin has slightly diminished reverse detail, it is actually possible to determine with a high degree of accuracy the order that each coin was struck. That is exactly what John Dannreuther did on the night of July 30, 2003.

As part of the six-person authentication team studying all five 1913 Liberty nickels, Dannreuther compared the existing reverse detail on each coin. The key location is the bottom of the wreath, including the ribbon bow and the two ears of corn. The photographic evidence is more difficult to place in order than the actual coins, but clearly the Smithsonian, Olsen, and Eliasberg coins were struck before the Walton and McDermott coins. Dannreuther concluded that the Smithsonian coin was first, followed in order by the Olsen, Eliasberg, Walton, and McDermott specimens.

EARLY PROVENANCE PERIOD

Samuel Brown; August Wagner; Stephen K. Nagy (circa 1924); Wayte Raymond (circa 1924); Col. E.H.R. Green; Col. Green Estate (12/1941); Eric P. Newman and Burdette G. Johnson.

All five 1913 Liberty Head nickels remained together from the day they were made until 1943 when Eric Newman became the last collector to own the five coins. Different numismatic observers have varied opinions regarding the early provenance of the five coins. According to Knight: "It hasn't always been easy to figure who the owners really are. Constructing a reliable pedigree for the 1913 Liberty Head nickels becomes an article of faith for certain periods in the provenance records."

The name **Samuel W. Brown** appears at the beginning of every provenance record constructed for each of the five known 1913 nickels. Circumstantial evidence clearly points to Brown as the first owner of these nickels, although others were likely involved in their production. We do know that all five coins remained together for many years, from the day they were struck until Eric Newman dispersed them individually in the 1940s.

In his *Guide Book* to the series, Dave Bowers suggests that **Stephen K. Nagy** may have been involved as a Brown accomplice, and that Nagy retained ownership of the coins until 1924. Aside from mentioning personal conversations with Nagy, Bowers provides no other documentation.

August Wagner advertised the five coins for sale late in 1923 and early in 1924. It is unclear whether Wagner actually owned the coins at that time, or if he had them on consignment from the true owner.

FOR SALE.

Five (5) Five-Cent Liberty Head 1913 Coins. Proof.

The only Five-Cent Liberty Head Coins of this design and year in existence.

AUGUST WAGNER,
31st and York Sts.,
Philadelphia, Pa.

Wayte Raymond handled the coins circa 1924, placing them with his most important client, **Col. E.H.R. Green.** Raymond was most likely a dealer intermediary in the transaction rather than an actual owner of the coins. Various sources give different dates for the transaction, normally between 1924 and 1926.

Colonel Edward Howland Robinson Green was the son of Hetty Green, the famous "Witch of Wall Street" who at one time was considered the richest woman in the world. Col. Green was an avid collector of many things. At one time, for example, he owned the entire sheet of "Inverted Jenny" airmail stamps, a philatelic rarity of noted fame. The coins passed into his estate in 1936 and remained there for several years.

Working with his mentor, **Burdette G. Johnson,** St. Louis collector **Eric P. Newman** acquired the five coins in December 1941 for $2,000. The total purchase price was less than Samuel Brown offered to pay for the coins in 1919.

Newman made the initial contact with executors of the Col. Green estate through his desire to acquire a rare U.S. demand note from St. Louis. The response was that he would have to buy all of the Missouri currency, which he did. He and B.G. Johnson formed a partnership to acquire additional portions of the Green Collection, eventually including all five 1913 Liberty Head nickels. Two of the coins were purchased on December 16, 1941, for $500 each, and the other three were purchased on December 29, 1941, for $333 each. The dates represent receipt of payment by the Green estate executors.

Newman retained the finest piece (the Eliasberg specimen) for his own collection and sold the other four through Johnson. Two pieces were sold to James Kelly on March 11, 1943, for $750 each, another was sold to Kelly on March 17, 1943, for $750, and one piece was sold to F.C.C. Boyd on April 22, 1943, for $1,000. Transaction dates are from copies of Johnson's original invoices in Newman's possession.

MODERN PROVENANCE PERIOD

From 1943 to the present day, each of the five nickels has traveled a different road. Here is a record of the provenance for each nickel, along with a photo of each coin. They are presented in the assumed order that each coin was actually struck.

The Norweb-Smithsonian Specimen PR60.

Eric P. Newman; B.G. Johnson (4/22/1943); F.C.C. Boyd (1944); Numismatic Gallery (1944); King Farouk (1952); Government of Egypt (Sotheby's, 2/1954), lot 1695; Abe Kosoff and Sol Kaplan (1954); Emery May Holden Norweb (1978); Smithsonian Institution.

The authors of *Million Dollar Nickels* comment: "Owned by a Middle Eastern potentate, a rebellious North African government, an American Ambassador's wife, and the prestigious Smithsonian Institution, this specimen can easily lay claim to having the most stately masters."

The Olsen-Hawn Specimen PR64 NGC. The Present Specimen.

Eric P. Newman; B.G. Johnson (3/1943); James F. Kelly (1943); Fred E. Olsen; B. Max Mehl (11/1944), lot 1551; King Farouk; Numismatic Fine Arts (5/1946), lot 1058, unsold; King Farouk; B. Max Mehl (6/1947), lot 2798; Edwin Hydeman (Abe Kosoff, 3/1961), lot 280, unsold; Edwin Hydeman (1972); World Wide Coin Investments; World Wide Coin Investments and Bowers and Ruddy Galleries; World Wide Coin Investments; Robert L. Hughes Enterprises (1977); Superior Galleries (1977); Dr. Jerry Buss (Superior Galleries, 1/1985), lot 366; Reed Hawn (Stack's, 10/1993), lot 245; Spectrum Numismatics; Nevada Investor (7/2002); Bruce Morelan and Legend Numismatics (2004); John Albanese and Blanchard & Co., Inc.; private collection.

Circa 1975, Bowers and Ruddy Galleries purchased a half interest in the Olsen specimen, but then had second thoughts and sold their share back to World Wide. Continental Coin Corporation is sometimes mentioned in the provenance of this coin following World Wide Coin Investments. However, Warren Tucker states that his firm sold the coin directly to Robert Hughes.

The Eliasberg Specimen PR66 PCGS

Eric P. Newman (11/2/1948); Numismatic Gallery (12/16/1948); Louis E. Eliasberg, Sr. (1976); Eliasberg Estate (Bowers and Merena, 5/1996), lot 807; Jay Parrino; Superior (3/2001), lot 728; Dwight Manley (2003); Edward C. Lee (2005); Legend Numismatics (2005); Legend Collection (Bruce Morelan); Stack's (1/2007), lot 1599; anonymous California collector.

This is the finest of five 1913 Liberty Head nickels, which Eric Newman originally chose for his own collection. Abe Kosoff convinced Newman to sell the coin so that he could place it with Louis Eliasberg.

The Walton Specimen PR62

Eric P. Newman; B.G. Johnson (3/1943); James F. Kelly (1943); Dr. Conway Anderson Bolt (1945); George O. Walton (1962); Melva W. Givens (1992); Givens Estate.

From March 9, 1962 until July 30, 2003, the Walton specimen was believed lost to numismatics. The complete and remarkable story is told in *Million Dollar Nickels.*

The McDermott-ANA Specimen PR55 NGC

Eric P. Newman; B.G. Johnson (3/1943); James F. Kelly (1943); J.V. McDermott (1966); Elizabeth McDermott; Paramount (8/1967), lot 2241; Aubrey and Adeline Bebee (1989); American Numismatic Association.

McDermott was fond of carrying this piece in his pocket, so that he could show it to anyone on request, thus explaining its lower state of preservation today.

OWNERSHIP REGISTRY

Many important individuals have owned a 1913 Liberty Head nickel, from King Farouk to Emery May Holden Norweb. A brief biographical sketch of each individual is presented

THE EARLY PERIOD

Samuel Brown is discussed above.

Colonel Edward Howland Robinson Green was born in London, England, on August 22, 1868, and died at Lake Placid, New York, on June 8, 1936. He was the son of Hetty Green, the "Witch of Wall Street," and her husband, Edward Henry Green. He was educated at Fordham College, studied law in Chicago, and married Mabel E. Harlow on July 10, 1917. Green was a director of the Baltimore and Ohio Railroad, and president of the Texas Midland Railroad. His home of record was Terrell, Texas, where he moved in 1892 to represent his mother in pending railroad transactions. Green was active in politics as a Republican, attended several Republican National Conventions, and served as a director of the 1904 St. Louis World's Fair (or International Exposition). In 1910 Green was appointed an honorary colonel by Texas Democratic Governor Oscar Colquitt. He was an avid coin and stamp collector whose total estate was estimated in excess of $40 million.

Burdette G. Johnson was born in DeSoto, Missouri, on January 2, 1885, and died in St. Louis on February 24, 1947. He was the son of William A. Johnson and Luella (Conway) Johnson. In 1910 he resided at 2844 LaFayette Avenue in St. Louis, living there with his parents, grandmother, two uncles, and a cousin. Eight years later, he resided with his father at 2108 South Spring Street, and operated his business at 1155 North 11th Street. He was the proprietor of St. Louis Stamp and Coin Company, operating the business from 1907 until his death 40 years later. Johnson was a mentor of Eric Newman beginning in the 1920s, and the two eventually handled considerable portions of the Colonel Green coin collection, including all five 1913 Liberty Head nickels. Johnson also handled material from the Virgil Brand estate through his brother Armin Brand. He died on a St. Louis streetcar while commuting to work.

Stephen Kenneth Nagy, Jr. was born in Newark, New Jersey, on January 15, 1884, and died in Philadelphia on August 29, 1958. Nagy owned an antique business in Philadelphia, handling a variety of objects including rare coins. In 1942 he resided at 1536 N. Willington Street in Philadelphia, and operated his business at 8 South 18th Street. He was married to Gertrude Devers, the daughter of Minnie Devers who resided with them for many years. They were married between 1910 and 1920. It is often stated that Nagy was the son-in-law of famous 19th century coin dealer and Civil War hero Captain John W. Haseltine. No such connection has been located in any historical records.

Eric Pfeiffer Newman was born in St. Louis, Missouri, on May 25, 1911. He graduated from MIT in 1932, and from the Washington University (Missouri) School of Law in 1935. While a student at MIT, he met Col. Green, clearly unaware that he would eventually handle material from Green's estate. He began his law practice in 1935 and married Evelyn Edison in 1939. His grandfather gave him an 1859 Indian cent in 1920, starting his interest in numismatics. He soon became acquainted with B.G. Johnson, who encouraged him to learn about the coins he wanted to buy. He has written many books and articles about numismatics and remains an active numismatist today at age 98.

Wayte Raymond was born in South Norwalk, Connecticut, on November 9, 1886, and died in New York City on September 23, 1956. He joined the ANA in 1902 and issued fixed price lists from 1908 to 1911. Raymond then entered in partnership with Elmer Sears to form the United States Coin Company, conducting 43 auction sales from 1912 to 1918. He later operated the numismatic division of J.C. Morgenthau with James G. Macallister, conducting over 50 auctions. He also conducted 69 sales under his own name. Raymond was publisher of the *Coin Collector's Journal* from 1934 until 1954, the *Standard Catalog of United States Coins,* and others. Among his many clients was Colonel Green. Raymond's paternal ancestry dates to the 1630s in Massachusetts.

August Wagner advertised the five 1913 Liberty Head nickels for sale in late 1923 and early 1924 from his business in Philadelphia. His advertisement appeared in *The Numismatist,* suggesting that he was an ANA member, although former ANA historian Jack Ogilvie stated in a letter to Eric Newman that Wagner was not an ANA member.

Wagner was a real estate broker in Philadelphia, according to the 1910, 1920, and 1930 Federal Census records. His World War I draft registration card gives his residence as "NE cor. 65th and Camac" in the community of Oak Lane, and his business address as "NW cor 31st and York." He was born in Pennsylvania on April 26, 1881, and was the father of five children with his wife, Alice. He was living in 1942, having registered for the World War II draft, and was apparently deceased before 1950, as his wife is listed alone in a 1950 Philadelphia city directory. Past articles have described Wagner variously as a coin dealer or a stamp dealer, and it is certainly possible that he did both, but real estate seems to have been his primary profession.

THE MODERN PERIOD—INDIVIDUALS

Aubrey and Adeline Bebee [ANA] were collectors and dealers in Omaha, Nebraska. Aubrey was born in Arkansas on July 9, 1906, and died in Omaha, Nebraska, on May 5, 1992. He married Adeline Dorsey in 1930. He was employed as a real estate salesman, bookkeeper, and hotel manager. The couple opened a coin shop in Chicago in 1941 and relocated to Omaha in 1952. They conducted the 1955 ANA auction. Aubrey Bebee was charter member number one of the Professional Numismatists Guild. They paid $46,000 for the McDermott 1913 Liberty Head nickel in 1967, representing a new price record for any coin at that time. In 1985 they purchased the Jerry Buss specimen of the 1804 silver dollar and eventually donated both coins to the ANA.

Dr. Conway Anderson Bolt [Walton] was born in South Carolina on September 14, 1900, and died in Monroe, North Carolina, on November 23, 1973. He was the son of William Franklin Bolt and Mary Eulalia Pitts. He married Martha Eloise Seabrook in 1928, and they had at least one son, Conway Anderson Bolt, Jr. Most of his collection was sold by Stack's in April 1966, with remainders sold by Pine Tree Auctions in 1975. A family history notation found on the internet states that Dr. Bolt was the presiding physician at the birth of country singer Randy Travis in 1959.

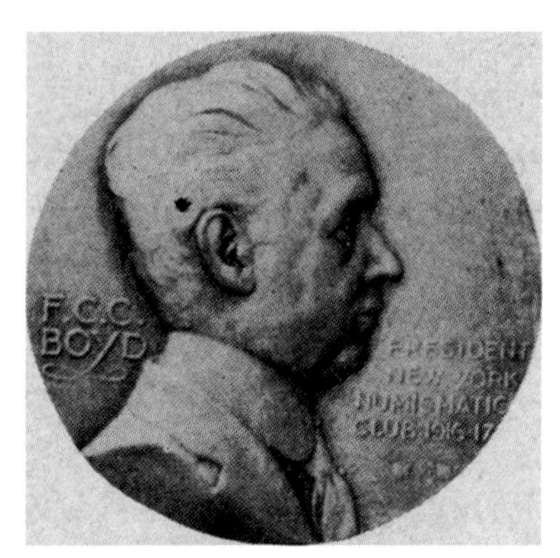

Frederick C.C. Boyd [Norweb] was a collector and dealer who was born in New York City on April 10, 1886, and died in East Orange, New Jersey, on September 7, 1958. He was the son of James Boyd and Arabella Sherwood. Boyd was apprenticed to a printer at age 13 and employed as a traveling salesman at 17. He was eventually associated with the Union News Company and retired as the company's vice president in 1946. Boyd served on the board of the National Recovery Administration in the 1930s, and on the board of the Office of Price Administration during World War II. He held life member number 5 in the ANA and conducted the 1922 ANA auction. He was also a Life Fellow of the American Numismatic Society, a member of the Bronx Coin Club, Chicago Coin Club, and New York Numismatic Club, holding every office in the latter except Vice President. He was the owner of the "World's Greatest Collection," sold in a series of six auctions held by Numismatic Gallery in 1945 and 1946.

Dr. Jerry Buss [Olsen] was born in Salt Lake City, Utah, on January 27, 1933, and graduated from the University of Wyoming. He received his Ph.D. in chemistry from the University of Southern California in 1957 and was employed in the aerospace industry. He began a real estate business in 1959, eventually growing to a multimillion-dollar business. Buss is well known as the owner of the Los Angeles Lakers basketball franchise. He is also well known as a poker player, finishing third in a seven-card stud event at the 1991 World Series of Poker and recently appeared on the *High Stakes Poker* television show.

Louis Edward Eliasberg, Sr. [Eliasberg] was born in Selma, Alabama on February 12, 1896, and died in Baltimore, Maryland, on February 20, 1976. He was the son of Adolph and Hortense (Schwartz) Eliasberg. In 1927 he married Hortense Miller Kahn, and they had two sons, Louis, Jr., and Richard. Eliasberg was a Baltimore financier and the president of Finance Company of America. Eliasberg formed the only complete collection of U.S. regular issue coins, following *Green's Mint Record and Type Table*. He often publicly displayed the coins, and in April 1953 *Life* magazine did a feature story about the Eliasberg Collection.

King Farouk I [Norweb, Olsen] of Egypt was the son of King Fuad I, born on February 11, 1920. Farouk assumed the throne at age 16. He married Queen Farida in 1938, and they had two daughters. He then divorced her and married Narrima Sadak in 1951. The couple had a son, Ahmed Fuad II. However, his reign was considered one of incompetence, and he was deposed by the Egyptian army in 1952. He lived in exile in Monaco and later Rome and died on March 18, 1965. Farouk was a renowned gourmand and an avid collector in many different fields.

Melva Walton Givens [Walton] was George Walton's sister. She was born in Virginia on August 19, 1913, and died in Salem, Virginia, on March 25, 1992. At the time of her death, she had owned the Walton specimen for 30 years, although she never knew it. In 1962 the nickel was called an altered date, although the observation was incorrect. She has the special distinction as the only 1913 Liberty nickel owner who was born in 1913.

Reed Hawn [Olsen] was born in Corpus Christi, Texas, on August 20, 1949, and currently lives in Austin, Texas. He attended the University of Texas in Austin and holds a Bachelor of Arts degree in English. He is married with three children. His business ventures include oil and gas, as well as Arabian horses. Hawn's collection was built primarily through Stack's, with additional assistance of the late Jerry Cohen.

Edwin McMasters Hydeman [Olsen] was born in Morristown, Pennsylvania, on March 2, 1904, and died in Miami, Florida, on December 3, 1989. He was the son of Leon Hydeman and Helen Lederman. He was a resident of York, Pennsylvania, and the owner of a department store in that city.

John Vere McDermott [ANA] was born in Wisconsin on November 10, 1897, and died in South Milwaukee, Wisconsin, on September 29, 1966. He was employed as a steeplejack and later operated a vending machine business and a coin business. Mac, as he was known to all, was described as a person as memorable as his nickel, which he often carried loose in his pocket. His wife, Elizabeth ("Betts") consigned the coin to James Kelly and Paramount after his death, and she died in Lubbock, Texas, later that same year on December 18, 1967.

Bruce Morelan is a Pacific Northwest businessman and a partner in Legend Numismatics. He began collecting coins at the age of six when his grandmother gave him three coins that she saved in her teapot for many decades--a Trade dollar, a half dime and a three cent nickel. Morelan began his collection by forming the finest set of Trade dollars in memory of this event. After buying and selling ultra rarities such as the Eliasberg 1884 and 1885 Trade dollars, the Olsen and Eliasberg 1913 Liberty nickels, Morelan went on to form the finest set of Seated dollars ever completed and remains active in numismatics today.

Will W. Neil [Olsen] never actually owned a 1913 Liberty nickel, but the Olsen specimen was included in the June 1947 catalog of his collection.

Emery May (Holden) Norweb [Norweb] was born on November 30, 1895 in Salt Lake City, Utah, and died on March 27, 1984, in Cleveland, Ohio. She was the granddaughter of Liberty Emery Holden, who was the founder of the *Cleveland Plain Dealer* newspaper, still published today. She was the daughter of Albert Fairchild Holden, who gave her an interest in numismatics. She married Raymond Henry Norweb, Sr., in Paris in 1917, where she drove an ambulance and worked in French hospitals. The couple's first child, R. Henry Norweb, Jr., was born in August 1918 in a cellar during an air raid. Mrs. Norweb was president of the Cleveland Museum of Art from 1962 to 1971. She was a member of the American Numismatic Association for almost 70 years, joining in 1914. Much of the Norweb Collection was sold in the late 1980s by Bowers and Merena, but Ambassador and Mrs. Norweb made several donations, including their 1913 Liberty nickel that was presented to the Smithsonian in 1978. Although billed as the Norweb Collection and usually considered the coin collection of Ambassador Norweb, the true collector was Mrs. Norweb, whose interest was encouraged by her father. She holds an ANA membership record of 70 years.

Fred E. Olsen [Olsen] was born in England in 1891 and finished his technical training at the University of Toronto. He later lived in Alton, Illinois, where he was employed as technical director at the Western Cartridge Company. Known as an explosives authority, Olsen developed a new method of making smokeless gunpowder, gaining him national fame. Olsen died in 1986 at his home in Guilford, Connecticut.

George Owen Walton [Walton] was born on May 15, 1907, in Rocky Mount, Virginia, and died on March 9, 1962, in an auto accident outside of Wilson, North Carolina. He was described as a quiet and secretive man. He divided his time between Charlotte, North Carolina, and Roanoke, Virginia. Those who knew Walton understood that he was an estate appraiser for banks. It had also been reported that he worked as a government intelligence agent during World War II. Walton was known as a coin collector who also collected guns and ammunition, rare books and documents, stamps, watches, and ivory.

THE MODERN PERIOD—COMPANIES AND ORGANIZATIONS

American Numismatic Association [ANA] is the national coin collector's organization in Colorado Springs, Colorado. The ANA was founded by Dr. George Heath of Monroe, Michigan, in October 1891. Heath was the publisher of a magazine called *The Numismatist* that has since become the association's journal. It has been published continuously since 1888. The ANA currently has more than 30,000 members.

The ANA Mission Statement from their website, www.money.org, states that "The American Numismatic Association is a nonprofit educational organization dedicated to educating and encouraging people to study and collect money and related items. With nearly 33,000 members, the Association serves the academic community, collectors and the general public with an interest in numismatics." The ANA helps all people discover and explore the world of money through its vast array of programs including its education and outreach, museum, library, publications, conventions and seminars.

John Albanese has nearly 30 years of numismatic experience, and was one of the original founders of PCGS before he left that firm and began his own grading service, NGC. He is a leading professional numismatist who is a noted authority on coin grading. He serves as a consulting associate to Blanchard & Co., Inc., a numismatic investment firm founded by Donald Doyle in New Orleans. The firm describes its operation as "the largest and most respected retail dealer in rare coins and precious metals in the United States," according to their website.

Blanchard & Co., Inc. [Olsen] is a numismatic investment firm founded by Donald Doyle in New Orleans, Louisiana. The firm describes its operation as "the largest and most respected retail dealer in rare coins and precious metals in the United States," according to the company website.

Bowers and Ruddy Galleries [Olsen] was a partnership of Q. David Bowers and James Ruddy, operating in Los Angeles, California, from 1972 to 1983. For much of that time they were a subsidiary of General Mills. The firm conducted more than 60 auctions, including the famous Garrett Collection and the gold portion of the Louis Eliasberg Collection. They also had a sales department, and published the *Rare Coin Review.* Earlier, Dave Bowers and James Ruddy operated Empire Coin Company in the late 1950s and early 1960s.

Bowers and Merena Galleries [Eliasberg] was a partnership of Q. David Bowers and Raymond N. Merena, operating in Wolfeboro, New Hampshire, from 1983 to 2003. In 2000, the firm was sold to Collector's Universe, a public company from California. Bowers remained as president until January 2003. Paul Montgomery became president, and six months later moved the company to Mandeville, Louisiana. About a year after that, Spectrum Numismatics purchased Bowers and Merena Galleries, and moved the company to Irvine, California.

Q. David Bowers [Eliasberg, Olsen] was born in Honesdale, Pennsylvania, on October 21, 1938. Bowers began his coin business in 1953 in Wilkes-Barre, Pennsylvania, and soon entered into partnership with James Ruddy, operating Empire Coins in Johnson City, New York. Empire Coins sold to Paramount International Coin Corporation in 1966. Later, Bowers operated Hathaway and Bowers Galleries with Terry Hathaway, and again with Ruddy in Bowers and Ruddy Galleries. Both firms were in the Los Angeles area. In 1983 Bowers entered a partnership with Raymond N. Merena in Bowers and Merena Galleries. They sold the business to Collectors Universe in 2000, and Merena retired. Bowers left the firm in January 2003 and was soon associated with American Numismatic Rarities. He is currently chairman of Stack's.

Robert L. Hughes [Olsen] is a California professional numismatist who has been active for several decades and is one of the nation's leading experts in pattern coins.

Bruce Smith is the founder of Integrity Asset Management, LLC, based in Covington,Louisiana, a firm that handles "top tier assets from many platforms." The company is "based on the belief that our customers' needs are of the utmost importance," according to their website. Smith serves as the agent for the current consigner of the Olsen 1913 Liberty Head nickel.

Sol Kaplan [Norweb] was born in Odessa, Russia, on December 24, 1899, and died in Cincinnati, Ohio, on January 31, 1974. He was the son of Morris Kaplan and emigrated with his family about 1910. He was the proprietor of Cincinnati Stamp and Coin Co. His obituary in *The Numismatist* described him as "a colorful, dedicated, and legendary professional numismatist." He was an active member of the Professional Numismatists Guild, serving several offices including president. Today, the PNG presents the Sol Kaplan award to those who work toward combating fraud and theft in the numismatic marketplace.

James F. Kelly [Walton, Olsen, ANA] bought three of the five nickels from Eric Newman and Burdette G. Johnson, the only individual to handle more than two different 1913 nickels after they were split up. Kelly was born on April 20, 1907, and died on December 27, 1968. He was a coin dealer in Dayton, Ohio, and eventually became a founder of Paramount International Coin Company. He worked closely with Johnson in the 1940s.

Edward C. Lee [Eliasberg] of Merrimack, New Hampshire, has been a professional numismatist since 1958. He purchased the Eliasberg specimen in 2003 with the comment that he "planned to retire on a nickel."

Legend Numismatics {Eliasberg, Olsen] is a New Jersey rare coin firm operated by partners Bruce Morelan, Laura Sperber, and George Huang. They have handled both the Eliasberg specimen, and the Olsen specimen, along with many other important rarities in all series.

Dwight Manley [Eliasberg] was born in Whittier, California, in 1966 and raised in Brea, California. He formerly served as president of United Sports Agency, and as a managing partner of the California Gold Marketing Group. His sports clients have included Karl Malone and Dennis Rodman. His California Gold Marketing Group purchased the $100 million treasure of the *S.S. Central America,* the single largest numismatic purchase ever recorded. His accomplishments also include 18 months as the national manager for the Jockeys' Guild, a position he held without compensation while keeping the organization out of bankruptcy. Manley, who began collecting coins at age 6, is a major supporter of the American Numismatic Association. He is a managing partner in a real estate holding company, Manley Fanticola.

The photo shows Edward C. Lee (left), with Dwight Manley.

B. Max Mehl [Olsen] was born in Russia in 1884. He was a shoe salesman who became a coin dealer at the age of 16 and conducted his first auction in December 1903. That auction was a 33-lot mail bid sale that appeared in *The Numismatist.* John Adams writes in *United States Numismatic Literature, Volume Two,* that Mehl's career should never have happened. According to Adams, Mehl was "an immigrant Jew in a then-gentile hobby ... he was located in Fort Worth, Texas, at a time when 95 percent of the business was done on the East Coast; and ... Lilliputian in stature and colorless in terms of personality, he adopted a business plan that relied on creativity and promotion."

Mehl did more to promote coin collecting than any other individual in the 20th century, or perhaps ever. He spent millions of dollars advertising to buy and sell rare coins. The 1913 Liberty nickel was a favorite subject of his advertising. The advertisement reproduced here appeared in the January 6, 1935 issue of the *San Antonio* (Texas) *Light* and is typical of his advertising style. Throughout his campaign, Mehl knew the whereabouts of all five 1913 nickels.

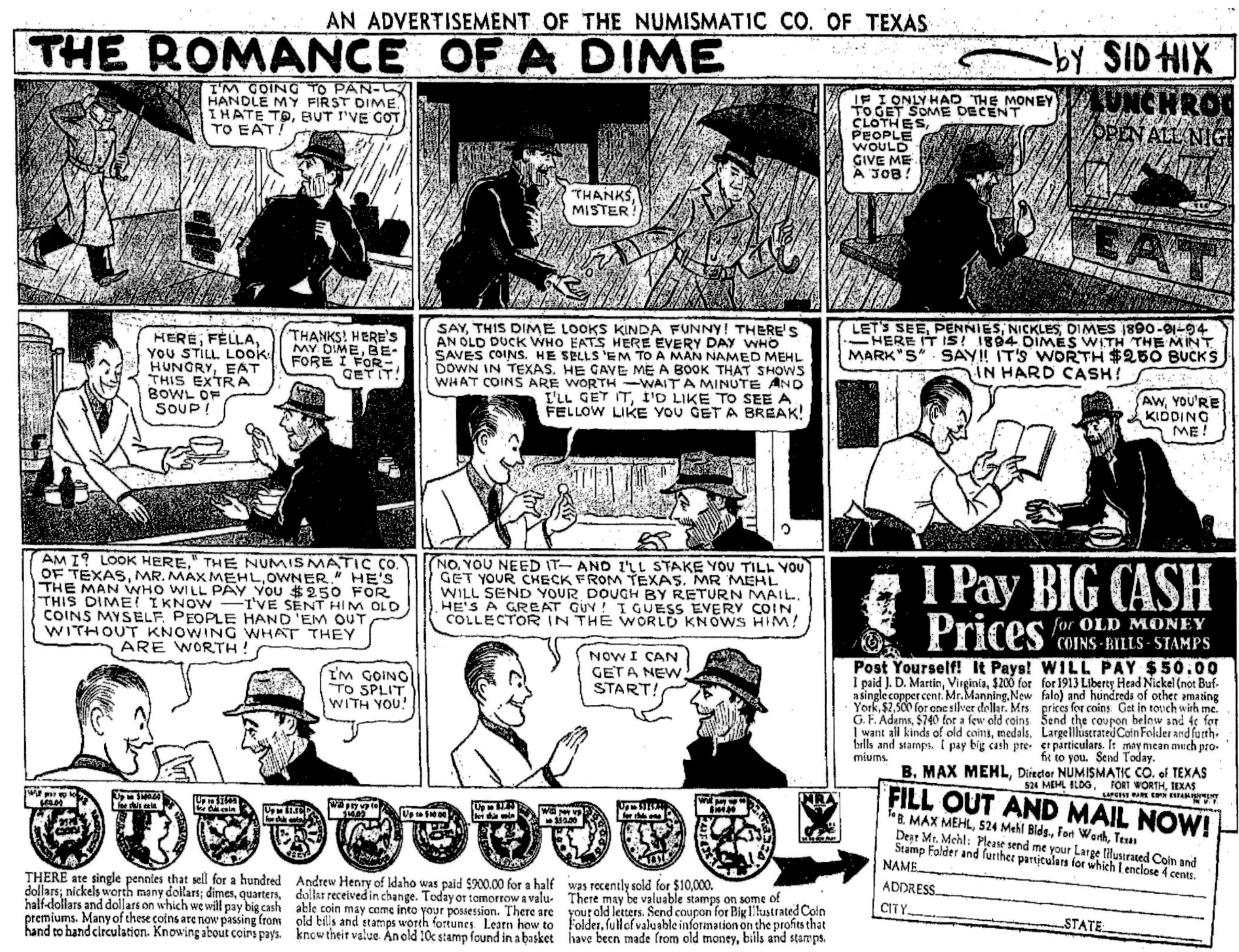

Numismatic Fine Arts [Olsen] was operated by Edward Gans and Henry Grunthal, who also operated as independent coin dealers in New York. Their second mail bid sale, offering the Olsen specimen of the 1913 Liberty nickel was held on May 21, 1946. The partnership conducted 13 sales from November 1945 to March 1953. Afterward, Edward Gans conducted three additional sales in 1954, 1955, and 1960. The firm is unrelated to a later firm of the same name operated in California.

Edward Gans [Olsen] was born in Hamburg, Germany, on August 27, 1887, and died in Berkeley, California, on February 13, 1991, age 103. He was a banker in Germany, relocating to Berlin in 1909, to New York City in 1938, and to Berkeley in 1953. He conducted an independent coin business, and also conducted auctions with Henry Grunthal under the name Numismatic Fine Arts.

Henry Grunthal [Olsen] was born in Germany on August 11, 1905, and died in Bronx, New York, on September 8, 2001. He was the son of German numismatist Hugo Grunthal. An ANA member since 1929, Grunthal emigrated to the United States in 1938. He was educated at the University of Berlin and at the Sorbonne in Paris, studying archaeology and art history. He conducted an independent coin business in New York City and also conducted auctions with Edward Gans as Numismatic Fine Arts. In 1953, Grunthal joined the curatorial staff at the American Numismatic Society.

Numismatic Galleries [Eliasberg] was a partnership of Abe Kosoff and Abner Kreisberg. Although they handled many rarities privately, such as the 1913 Liberty Head nickel, they are primarily known for their many important auction events. Best known is the F.C.C. Boyd Collection that they handled in a series of six auctions in 1945 and 1946, billed as the "World's Greatest Collection."

Abe Kosoff [Norweb, Eliasberg] was born in New York on December 31, 1912, and died in Palm Springs, California, on March 19, 1983. He has been called The Dean of American Numismatics and was a founder of the Professional Numismatists Guild.

Abner Kreisberg [Eliasberg] was born on May 28, 1904, and lived in Beverly Hills, California. He died on July 10, 1997. He was a partner with Abe Kosoff in Numismatic Galleries until July 1954 and later conducted auction sales with Hans Schulman. He held additional auctions with Jerry Cohen, who became his partner after he and Kosoff parted.

Paramount International Coin Corporation [ANA] was founded in 1964 by Q. David Bowers, Michael DiSalle, Max Humbert, James Kelly, and James Ruddy. The firm conducted more than 75 auctions from 1965 to 1986 and was a participant in the annual "Apostrophe Auctions."

Jay Parrino [Eliasberg] is the proprietor of The Mint in Kansas City, Missouri. He was the successful buyer of the 1913 Liberty Head nickel at the Eliasberg sale in May 1996, becoming the first person in history to pay more than $1 million for a single coin.

Smithsonian Institution [Norweb] was established in 1846 for the purpose of the "increase and diffusion of knowledge among men" through the bequest of James Smithson, a British scientist who himself had never visited the United States. It soon became a depository for government collections. Today the organization operates 19 museums, nine research centers, and the National Zoo. In 2008 the museums had more than 25 million visitors, with another 3 million visitors to the zoo.

Spectrum Numismatics [Olsen] is a rare coin firm in Irvine, California, and the parent company of Bowers and Merena Galleries.

Stack's [Olsen, Eliasberg] of New York City began as a business of the Stack family, conducting several hundred coin auctions beginning with their first sale in October 1935. They are the parent company of Coin Galleries, holding additional regular auction sales. Today there is no member of the Stack family associated with the firm.

Superior Galleries [Olsen] of Los Angeles, California, began as a business of the Goldberg family. Their first auction sale was held in September 1970. They held a number of important sales, especially in the field of early copper coins. Today there is no member of the Goldberg family associated with the firm.

World Wide Coin Investments [Olsen] was a partnership in Atlanta, Georgia, operated by John Hamrick and Warren Tucker. The firm handled three major rarities: the 1913 nickel, an 1804 silver dollar, and an 1894-S Barber dime. They frequently displayed all three coins at conventions in the early to mid-1970s.

John Hamrick [Olsen] was a partner with Warren Tucker in World Wide Coin during the 1970s, at the time they handled the Olsen specimen of the 1913 nickel, along with an 1894-S dime and an 1804 silver dollar. Hamrick began collecting coins in 1953 and opened his first coin shop 10 years later, while he was a student at George Institute of Technology.

Warren Tucker [Olsen] was a partner with John Hamrick in World Wide Coin during the 1970s, at the time that they handled the Olsen specimen of the 1913 nickel, along with an 1894-S dime and an 1804 silver dollar. They often displayed the trio at coin shows and conventions, where the present cataloger (Mark Borckardt) first saw the three coins. Today, Tucker is director of world coin auctions for Heritage.

AUCTION APPEARANCES

B. Max Mehl, November 1944, lot 1551, $3,750 [Olsen]

The Olsen sale included several important rarities in addition to the 1913 nickel. Among the offerings were an excellent selection of pattern coins that included a quintuple stella in gold, a complete set of four dollar gold pieces, 1884 and 1885 Trade dollars, a Mint State 1797 half dollar, and a Massachusetts NE sixpence.

Numismatic Fine Arts, May 1946, lot 1058, $2,450 (unsold) [Olsen]

The second mail bid sale of Edward Gans and Henry Grunthal was originally scheduled to close on May 7, 1946, but the date was changed to May 21. The sale included 1,140 lots of American and world coins.

Lot No. 1551

The RENOWNED U. S. 1913 LIBERTY HEAD NICKEL

1913 U. S. Five-Cent Nickel with **LIBERTY HEAD.** Uncirculated, sharp, with bold impression. Only five specimens struck and this is claimed to be the sharpest and best of the lot. Of excessive rarity.

I plead guilty to being responsible for making this coin so famous, having used it in all of my national advertising for a period of about a quarter of a century, during which time it appeared in advertising totalling an expenditure of well over a Million Dollars!

As is well known, the regular issue of the Liberty head nickels was discontinued in 1912, and the Buffalo nickels appeared in 1913, but apparently a few specimens, only five of the Liberty head type were struck in 1913. The entire lot was purchased about fifteen years after their issue by the late Col. E. H. R. Green. All five specimens were immediately absorbed by private collectors. Mr. Olson paid no less than $900.00 for this coin. And since its purchase, he was offered $1,000.00 for it by the dealer of whom he purchased it. I mention this so as to give you an idea of the value of the coin, as I am sure of receiving numerous inquiries as to its probable worth. To the collector of today, this coin is better known and of greater fame than our 1804 Silver Dollar. It is, of course, considered as one of our greatest rarities from every point of view, and rightly so. One owner of a specimen of this great coin recently wrote me that he considered his coin worth $5,000.00. It is difficult to place a value on a coin of this kind, but in my opinion, the price offered for this coin recently by a dealer, that of $1,000.00, I consider very nominal. Certainly, this great coin will prove a most gratifying source of possession to the fortunate owner and also a profitable investment as well.

B. Max Mehl, June 1947, lot 2798, $3,750 [Olsen]

Although the 1913 nickel was consigned by Mehl and never owned by Will W. Neil, the Neil sale had an impressive offering of numismatic delicacies, including a Mint State 1794 dollar, 1804 silver dollar, 1870-S silver dollar, 1838-O half dollar, 1894-S dime, 1843 proof set, a set of stellas, and numerous other properties.

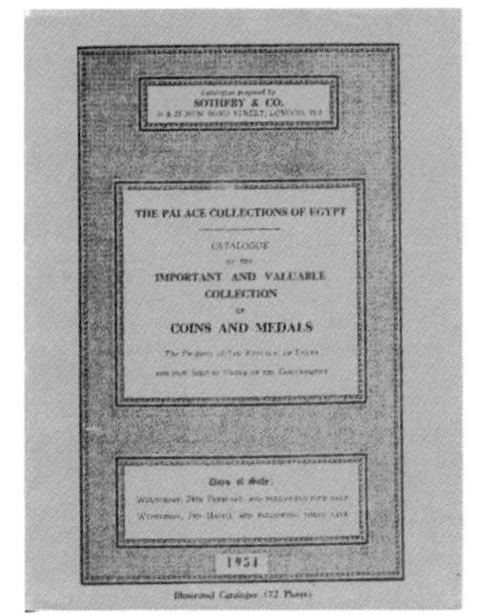

Sotheby's, February 1954, lot 1695, $3,747 [Norweb]

Sotheby's was selected to handle the King Farouk Collection on behalf of the Government of Egypt. The collection was billed as "The Palace Collections of Egypt," since Farouk had been deposed. The catalog was poorly prepared, grouping together extremely important coins into large lots by denomination. The 1913 Liberty Head nickel, for example, was part of a collection of 149 nickels from 1866 to 1948 that was offered in a single lot. Abe Kosoff and Sol Kaplan successfully requested that the 1913 nickel be taken out of the lot and sold separately, and they purchased it for 1,300 pounds (about $3,747).

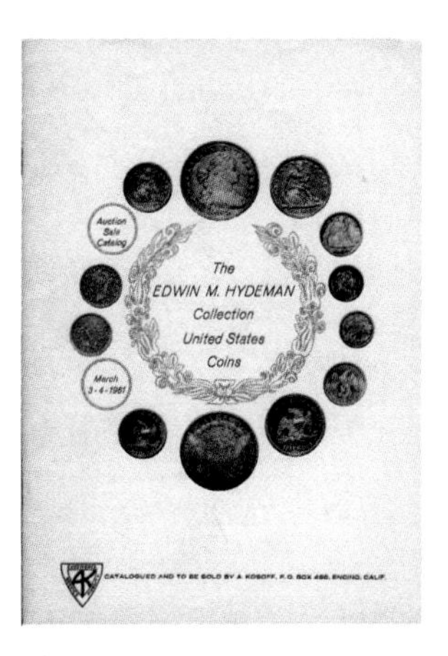

Abe Kosoff, March 1961, lot 280, $50,000 (unsold) [Olsen]

Two full pages in the catalog were devoted to the 1913 nickel. The sale was remarkable for its offering of the 1913 nickel, an 1804 silver dollar, an 1894-S dime, an 1876-CC twenty-cent piece, and the 1866 No Motto half dollar and dollar. Following Abe Kosoff's tradition, the first lot was an 1856 Flying Eagle cent.

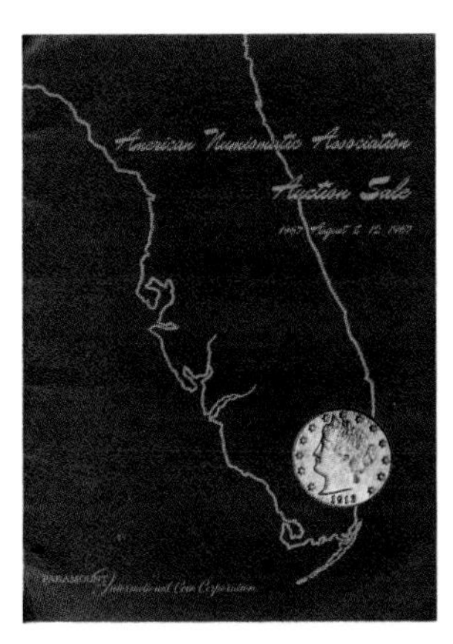

Paramount, August 1967, lot 2241, $46,000 [McDermott]

Paramount International Coin Corporation was selected to handle the American Numismatic Association auction in 1967.

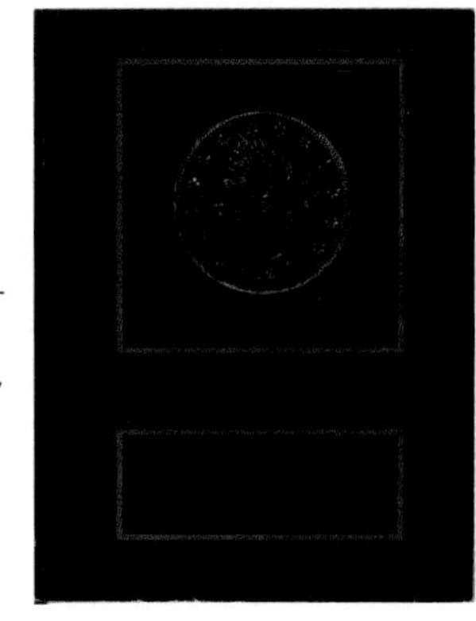

Superior, January 1985, lot 366, $385,000 [Olsen]

Dr. Jerry Buss sold his collection in 1985 due to changing interests and a concern that he was neglecting his coins. Buss said: "I guess I just decided that I would rather sell it than neglect it." In his biography, Superior continued: "Since he is unable to give the proper attention or time to his hobby, Dr. Buss has decided to dispose of his coin collection." Consisting of nearly 2,300 lots, the sale ranged from Colonial and U.S. coins to foreign and ancients. The big three of U.S. coin rarities, the 1913 Liberty Head nickel, the 1894-S Barber dime, and the 1804 silver dollar, were offered.

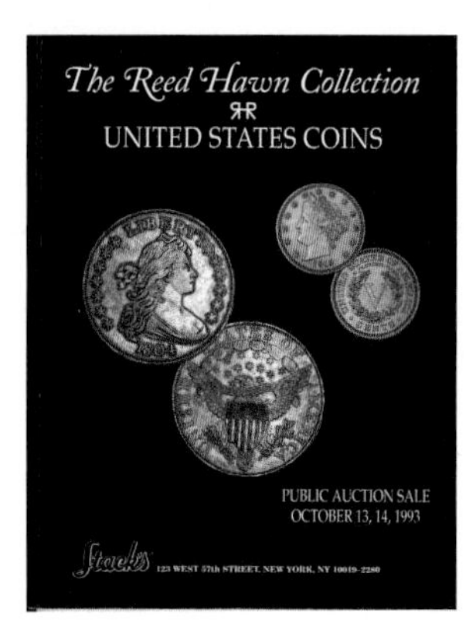

Stack's, October 1993, lot 245, $962,500 [Olsen]

The Reed Hawn Collection included the Olsen specimen of the 1913 nickel alongside the Mickley Class I 1804 silver dollar. The sale included many other important coins, such as proof examples of the 1864-L Indian cent, 1864 Small Motto two cent, 1867 Rays nickel, and seven Gobrecht dollars.

Bowers and Merena, May 1996, lot 807, $1,485,000 [Eliasberg]

The Eliasberg Collection was the only complete collection of U.S. coins ever formed, and it will likely always hold that distinction. The collection was sold in three different auction events. First were the gold coins that Bowers and Ruddy sold in October 1982. They were followed by Colonials through dimes in May 1996, and twenty cent pieces through silver dollars in April 1997.

Superior, March 2001, lot 728, $1,840,000 [Eliasberg]

The Eliasberg specimen was offered on behalf of Jay Parrino, who purchased the coin at the Eliasberg sale. Superior held the auction in conjunction with the Spring 2001 ANA Convention held in Salt Lake City, Utah.

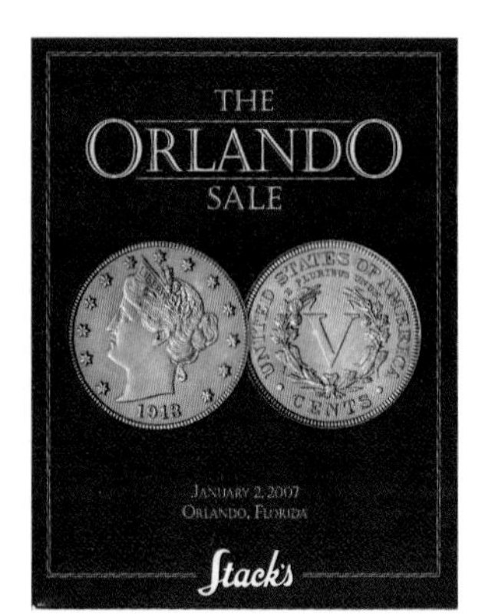

Stack's, January 2007, lot 1599, unsold [Eliasberg]

Stack's offered the Eliasberg specimen on behalf of Bruce Morelan and Laura Sperber. The coin failed to meet its reserve.

SELECTED SOURCES

Adams, John W. *United States Numismatic Literature, Volume II.* Crestline, California: George Frederick Kolbe Publications, 1990.

Bowers, Q. David. *A Guide Book of Shield and Liberty Head Nickels.* Atlanta: Whitman Publishing, LLC, 2006.

Garrett, Jeff and Ron Guth. *The 100 Greatest U.S. Coins.* Atlanta: Whitman Publishing, LLC, 2009.

Gengerke, Martin. *American Numismatic Auctions. 8th Edition.* Woodside, NY: the author, 1990.

Montgomery, Paul, Mark Borckardt, and Ray Knight. *Million Dollar Nickels: Mysteries of the Illicit 1913 Liberty Head Nickels Revealed.* Irvine, CA: Zyrus Press, 2005.

Smith, Pete. *American Numismatic Biographies.* Rocky River, OH: Gold Leaf Press, 1992.

www.ancestry.com accessed on multiple occasions for biography details of various individuals.

(#3912)

BUFFALO NICKELS

Popular 1916 Doubled Die Obverse Buffalo Nickel, FS-101, VF30

2456 1916 Doubled Die Obverse VF30 NGC. FS-101, formerly FS-016. The doubled date is most obvious on this variety, as the point where the doubling between the dies is greatest. The result is one (19)16 drastically below the other, especially visible on upper and lower loops of the 6. Curiously, the lower two-thirds of the 19(16) is virtually absent. Less-obvious die doubling is also visible at the front of the Indian's profile, the braid, the rear feathers, and the ribbons hanging down near the date. The 1916 Doubled Die is is a high-visibility and high-demand variety in the series, as well as a popular *Guide Book* listing. The present piece offers bold appeal, with medium silver-gray surfaces and no visible problems. Some interesting die striations appear on the reverse, and a full horn is visible save for the tip. Census: 3 in 30, 59 finer (11/09).(#3931)

Attractive Choice AU 1918/7-D Buffalo Nickel Reverse Terminal Die State

2457 1918/7-D AU55 PCGS. This Choice AU coin, an uncommonly high-end representative of the 1918/7-D overdate, shows deep reddish color, with considerable amounts of lilac interspersed and brightness beneath the patina. The piece is sharply struck and shows just a mere hint of high-point friction. Most intriguing about this example is the extremely late die state of the reverse: the surface exists on three distinct planes, separated by cracks through the bison's body with a prominent die break at the word FIVE. It is not hard to imagine a worn-out, cracking die suddenly shattering and injuring the other die in the pair; perhaps this specimen is a clue to what caused the retirement of the famous overdated obverse die. Population: 22 in 55, 72 finer (12/09).(#3939)

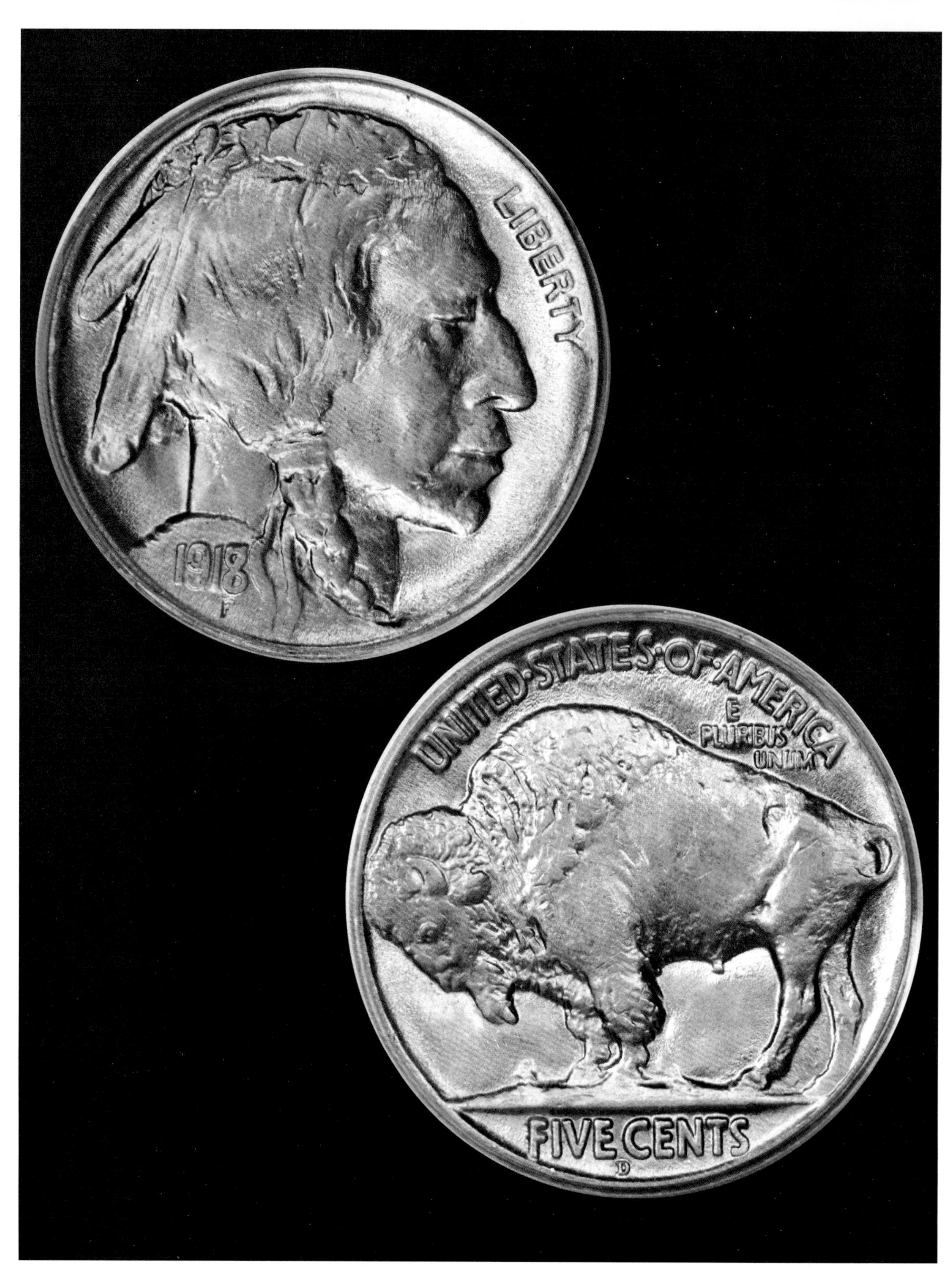
LIBERTY
1918
F
UNITED·STATES·OF·AMERICA
E
PLURIBUS
UNUM
FIVE CENTS
D

Gem 1918/7-D Buffalo Nickel
Satiny Surfaces, With an Extraordinary Strike
Tied for Finest Certified

2458 1918/7-D MS65 PCGS. FS-101, formerly FS-016.5. The years 1917 and 1918 saw an unprecedented production of small change at all of the U.S. Mints. This heightened production was in response to a serious shortage of small denomination coinage, possibly caused by hoarding and the transportation of much small change overseas. More than one million American soldiers served on European battlefields in the last two years of World War I, and every one of them carried at least a few cents and nickels with him. The coins were eagerly accepted by French merchants, who particularly liked the nickel. David Lange tells of this contemporary newspaper account, "The French like the American 5-cent piece. 'Elle est jolie,' they say, comparing it to the French coin of the same denomination with a square hole in the center." To make up for this drain on the domestic supply of coinage, all U.S. Mints were working overtime in late 1917.

One unintended consequence of this extra Mint activity was the production of several important overdates in the coinage of 1918. Both the quarters of the San Francisco Mint and the nickels of the Denver Mint are known in overdate varieties, and each variety is a prized rarity to collectors today. The overdate dies were created by a hubbing error that occurred in late 1917, when dies dated 1917 were still in use and dies for the next year were hurriedly manufactured. In *The Complete Guide to Buffalo Nickels,* David Lange describes the likely sequence of events:

> "In sinking a working die, two or more impressions had to be taken from a working hub. Between each impression, the developing die was taken to the furnace to be annealed, or softened, since the first impression caused the metal to become workhardened. It was then ready for another impression. Amid the haste to produce new dies, a working die that had already been impressed with a hub dated 1917 was then either inadvertently or intentionally given another impression from a hub dated 1918. The result was an overdate."

The overdate feature went unnoticed by numismatists of the early 20th century and the coins circulated extensively for a long period before it was discovered. Exactly when the error was first noticed is unclear. David Lange references an appearance on March 15, 1930, in an auction held by dealer Paul Lange of The Hobby Shop. Q. David Bowers notes an appearance in a Barney Bluestone catalog in 1931. Neither of these events was widely noticed by the numismatic fraternity, and the issue languished in obscurity until the late 1930s when collecting Buffalo nickels became widespread. By the time of the Adolphe Menjou Sale (Numismatic Gallery, 6/1950), catalogers had become familiar with the variety. Lot 597 of that sale reads, "1918 over 17 D. Only fine but rare, lists in very fine condition at $50.00."

An important step in the developing popularity of the coin was its listing in the first edition of the *Guide Book of United States Coins 1947.* The *Guide Book* was actually published in 1946, but had the following year's date on the cover. The variety was listed on page 88 as "1918D over 7." The price was listed as $40.00 in fine and $150.00 in Uncirculated. The popularity of the *Guide Book* ensured that knowledge of the variety would spread and its value would increase accordingly.

The exact mintage of 1918/7-D Buffalo nickels is unknown, but Bowers estimates an original production figure of about 100,000 pieces. Because the coins circulated for so long before the variety was noticed, the great majority of the surviving population is in lower circulated grades. The typical example seen today is in the VG-VF range. Many example doubtless exist in grades below VG, and more than 100 specimens have been graded, but the overdate is difficult to detect because of wear on the date. Coins grading AU are seldom encountered, and Mint State specimens are rare. The number of surviving specimens in Mint State grades is another mystery. Population data in the lower Uncirculated grades has been distorted by resubmissions. Walter Breen guessed possibly six specimens survive in Uncirculated grades, but that estimate is certainly too low. Lange estimates approximately two dozen example are extant in Mint State grades, a more reasonable figure. We would not be surprised if the real total was larger still, say around 35-40 pieces. The two major grading services have certified a total of seven specimens at the Gem level, with four at NGC and three at PCGS. Neither service has graded an example in any higher grade (11/09).

All 1918/7-D nickels are from the same die pair. The present coin shows fine traces of a die crack extending from the braid across the Indian's face. A few specimens from an early die state are reported without the die break, but the feature is generally considered diagnostic. The coin offered here is truly a magnificent specimen. The warm, thick, satiny surfaces are lightly toned, with a pale overlay of gold and occasional hints of lilac. The considerable visual appeal is augmented by the amazingly sharp strike, which imparts nearly full detail to all design elements. The only mark of distinction is a glancing, diagonal mark on the bison's body, between the withers and the hump. The high technical grade, intense aesthetic appeal, and fascinating history of this coin combine to make this offering one of the most desirable examples of 20th century coinage.(#3939)

Memorable 1920-S Buffalo Nickel, MS65

2459 1920-S MS65 NGC. One could easily cite the lovely original toning, but in this case the bold impression, particularly on the reverse of this normally strike-challenged issue, must take center stage. The strike on the reverse is far and away finer than usual, with a bold full horn and fur on the bison, and nearly a split tail. The braid and central details on the obverse are also sharp, although the bottom halves of the 19 are a bit hazy and some of LIBERTY blends into the rim due to die wear. Both sides, the obverse more so, show orange-peel effect. The patina is a delicate and delightful blend of rose, gold, and olive. A memorable example of this elusive issue. Census: 15 in 65, 1 finer (11/09).(#3946)

Superb Gem 1925 Buffalo Nickel Tied for Finest Certified

2460 1925 MS67 PCGS. This piece should perk up the interest of Registry Set collectors, as it is one of the seven examples of the issue so certified at PCGS, and there are none finer (11/09). NGC has certified only four in this ultimate grade. This Superb Gem would upgrade at least one, and likely more, of the current Top 5 Buffalo Nickels Basic Set, Circulation Strikes (1913-1938) Registry Sets at PCGS. The obverse is golden-gray and well struck, although some light die rust appears in the fields. The reverse has shades of pinkish-gold and ice-blue, and both sides are remarkably pristine. The strike is somewhat soft on the Indian's braid, but bold elsewhere, especially on the reverse.(#3954)

Splendid 1927-D Buffalo, MS66

2461 1927-D MS66 NGC. NGC has certified four 1927-D Buffalo nickels in MS66 with none finer, and PCGS has certified three in MS66, also with none finer (11/09). That is an extremely small total population when one considers the number of people who are enamored of this series. Although shy of a full strike, this Premium Gem shows considerably more detail than most examples of the issue. It is highly lustrous with vibrant mint frost and incredible iridescent toning on the obverse. The reverse is brighter with gold violet and blue toning. The Buffalo nickel enthusiast will want to bid boldly for this piece.(#3961)

PROOF JEFFERSON NICKEL

Flawless 1952 Jefferson Nickel PR68 Deep Cameo, Sole Finest at PCGS

2462 1952 PR68 Deep Cameo PCGS. For many years the finest Jefferson nickels of this issue were a handful of PR67 Deep Cameo examples at PCGS. More recently this piece has assumed the lead, and is now the finest and only PR68 with the vaunted Deep Cameo designation added. This example offers quicksilver surfaces with no more than a hint of golden color, and deep, flawless mirrored reflectivity. As the only "Pop 1" highest-grade Jefferson with Deep Cameo surfaces currently certified at PCGS from the difficult 1938-1959 era, this piece could see runaway bidding from series enthusiasts. Population: 1 in 68 Deep Cameo, 0 finer (12/09).(#94184)

1792 Half Disme, Judd-7, XF45
Historic Early Pattern

2463 1792 Half Disme, Judd-7, Pollock-7, R.4, XF45 PCGS. The famous 1792 half disme is one of the most coveted issues in all of American numismatics, and rightly so. It was (possibly) designed by British engraver William Russell Birch, and (probably) struck in the coachhouse cellar of John Harper, a Philadelphia sawmaker. The original issue of 1,500 (or 2,000) pieces was allegedly made using silver bullion contributed by George Washington, perhaps even from his own personal silverware. This story is, alas, unconfirmed.

Such is the history of the 1792 half disme. Many of the facts about these fascinating pieces are simply unknown, but can be reasonably deduced: like the name of their designer. William Russell Birch executed other coin designs very similar to that of the half disme, making him the most likely candidate for authorship. Other facts (like the original number produced) are likely to remain uncertain; possibly forever. That will not reduce the ongoing fascination of numismatists with these coins, however. They are simply too interesting to ignore.

The issue was avidly collected by early numismatists, and auction appearances are frequently encountered as early as the 1860s. One particularly nice specimen was offered as lot 2864 of the Sixth Semi-Annual Sale (Woodward, 3/1865): "Martha Washington Half Disme, 1792; a splendid proof; a finer coin is not known; in this condition of the highest rarity." The lot realized $40, a large sum at the time, to a collector named Hoffman.

The present coin is an attractive example of this popular issue, with gray-blue toning and light tinges of golden-rose in the fields. It is largely free of the issues or distracting problems that plague these early coins, with only one shallow planchet flaw located to the left of the eagle. It also exhibits a few crisscrossing adjustment marks in the center. The wear is even and the strike is uniform, resulting in rewarding detail remaining in the hair, and a strong profile to admire. A lively example that will certainly attract well-deserved attention when it crosses the auction block. Population: 2 in 45, 34 finer (11/09). (#11020)

Amazing Prooflike MS67 1795 Half Dime V-5, LM-8

2464 1795 MS67 Prooflike NGC. V-5, LM-8, R-3. Although not fully struck, this example is much sharper than most that we have seen. Only one or two others that have been seen in recent years are similar to this example for overall strike and quality. The obverse is sharply detailed with only a slight merging of the two lowest hair strands. All other design features, and especially those at the center, are boldly detailed. The reverse is equally bold, again with only a slight merging of the detail where the wing intersects the left branch, below T of UNITED. Due to the rotated reverse die, this point on the reverse is exactly opposite the slightly weak hair detail on the obverse. All other detail on the reverse is boldly defined, including the eagle's breast feathers which are almost never found with any definition. The obverse is cracked from the border to the digit 7, on to Liberty's neck and cheek, exiting just below the eye, and continuing to the right arm of Y and the border. This bisecting crack forms a small chip covering the top of the digit 7. Another short crack connects star 13 to the border. Fine hairline cracks join the last four stars on the right, and an extremely faint branch of the first crack extends to Liberty's chin. A die crack on the reverse, through TED, and described by Russell Logan and John McCloskey, is present but extremely light. In fact, this crack is so faint that it is easy to miss, even on such a high grade coin.

The surfaces of this Superb Gem example are amazing. The fields on both sides are fully mirrored with the exception of a small area of mint frost on each side. On the obverse, this is adjacent to Liberty's neck and chin, and on the reverse, around the eagle's head and over the wing on the right. Much like the minor strike weakness on each side, these areas of mint frost are opposite each other on the two sides. Because the reverse die is rotated, there is no easy explanation as to the relative location of these frosty areas. The balance of the fields on both sides are fully prooflike, as indicated by NGC. These small areas of mint frost suggest that the flat surface of the fields on the die did not fully come in contact with the surface of the planchet, thus one or both dies must have been sunken slightly in this area. This would suggest that one of these dies was lightly polished or lapped in this area, probably to repair minor damage, such as a clash mark. These details suggest that this is *not* a specimen or special strike, as much as we would like to think otherwise. In the 1998 Bowers and Merena catalog, the status of this coin was discussed: "Probably not a specimen striking, although we realize that such terms as *specimen* and *Proof* are often assigned to silver coins of the 1790s if they exhibit prooflike characteristics. Without entering into this controversy, it certainly is correct to say that the piece is *very special in its superb quality,* quite special in overall appearance."

Today, we are certainly not suggesting that this brilliant and Superb Gem example is anything more than an incredible example of the 1795 half dime production. Perhaps it is one of the coins from the hoard mentioned by Walter Breen in his *Proof Encyclopedia.* He described a hoard of approximately 100 examples, including some of this die marriage, which was found in the late 1870s or early 1880s. The Wadsworth-Rea hoard included some examples that "have vaguely shiny or partly mirrorlike surfaces." Breen further noted that those coins are "generally weak in centers, central hair and breast feathers being flat." The exceptional strike on this example, however, might preclude its status as one of these hoard coins.

Ex: Bowers and Merena (8/1998), lot 82; Jack Lee Collection, III (Heritage, 11/2005), lot 2057.(#4251)

Near-Gem 1796 LIKERTY Half Dime, V-1, LM-1 Among the Finest Known

2465 1796 MS64 PCGS. V-1, LM-1, R.3. The more available of the two die varieties for this issue, though scarce in its own right, known in the *Guide Book* as the LIKERTY variation for the breaks near the vertical stroke at the upper and lower loops of the B. Interestingly, there are more *Guide Book* entries for this issue than there are die marriages; the 1796, 6 Over 5 corresponds to the V-2 or LM-2 and the 1796 LIKERTY is the V-1 or LM-1. These are the only two die varieties established for the year and denomination, leaving the "plain" 1796 entry sandwiched between the two an enigma.

The year 1796 marked the half dime's transition from the Flowing Hair obverse to the Draped Bust design, a shift that took place a year earlier for the half dollar and dollar, the other silver denominations then in production. With a stated mintage of just 10,230 pieces split between the two 1796 half dime varieties, it is little wonder that the date as a whole is scarce in an absolute sense, nor does it come as a surprise when Logan and McCloskey describe both variants as "usually seen well worn."

Such truths make the existence of coins such as the present near-Gem all the more remarkable. Its luster is gorgeous, and the strike is remarkably bold on the fine details of Liberty's hair. Ice-blue, violet, and russet shadings are dominant with occasional elements of light silver-gray glimmer at the margins. A remarkably appealing representative that is easy to appreciate. For all 1796 half dime varieties combined, Population: 4 in 64, 3 finer (11/09).(#4254)

Choice AU 1796/5 Half Dime, V-2, LM-2

2466 1796/5 AU55 PCGS. V-2, LM-2, R.6. The 1796/5 is a rare variety that is usually found in well-worn condition, although some of the certified examples are high-grade. Remains of a previous 5 are quite plain under the subsequent 6. The B in LIBERTY is defective, made from the same punch that was used to create the LIKERTY variety. The 1796/5 is also a well-known and popular *Guide Book* variant. The present Choice AU example is certified in an old small-size green-label holder. The surfaces still retain much luster and have alluring silver-gold coloration on each side. A wispy, arcing scrape appears below LIBERTY and a couple of stars, but otherwise there is no significant contact. Some faint adjustment marks appear on the lower reverse, and the usual die crack runs from the rim to T3 through the eagle's breast, the clouds, the right ribbon tip, and back to the rim.(#4255)

The Ed Price 1797 16 Stars Half Dime, MS62 V-4, LM-2, Logan-McCloskey Plate Coin

2467 1797 16 Stars MS62 NGC. Ex: Price. V-4, LM-2, R.4. **The Logan-McCloskey plate coin.** The first 7 in the date is small, while the second one is quite large. The stars are arranged 9 left and 7 right, and on the reverse there is no outside berry below the D of UNITED. A leaf is quite close beneath the first T of STATES.

The obverse die was first used on this die pairing, then subsequently used on the V-3, LM-3 marriage. On the first use here, extensive die clashing developed, most visible before Liberty's face and above her head. A die crack appears from the rim through star 8. The reverse also is extensively clashed—from the juncture of the top two leaves through the O(F), through and below TES, and above and left of the eagle's left (facing) wing—and cracked, most prominently from the rim down through E of UNITED. A small rim cud connects the dentils over ME.

This is a difficult variety that is seldom seen in Mint State. This piece has much delightful luster remaining on pinkish-gold surfaces. A couple of tiny dark spots and planchet voids are as made and undistracting, in any case, but helping to explain the grade. The centers are fairly weakly struck on each side, but there is little sign of post-strike contact on this fascinating and well-preserved coin. (#4259)

BUST HALF DIME

Astounding MS68 1830 Half Dime, V-1, LM-14 Sole Finest Certified by NGC

2468 1830 MS68 NGC. V-1, LM-14, R.3. The reverse, with second T in STATES over the left side of the second U in PLURIBUS, is diagnostic for the variety. The Logan-McCloskey reference notes, "A scarce die marriage, but nice high grade examples of this marriage have been discovered over the years." This MS68 example, the sole finest certified by NGC (11/09), certainly would qualify. Both sides offer wonderful detail and lustrous silver-gray fields that show glimmers of green-gold close to the rims. Exquisitely preserved, as demanded of the grade, and virtually flawless to the unaided eye. (#4277)

SEATED HALF DIMES

1838 Seated Liberty Half Dime, MS68 ★ Large Stars, No Drapery, V-8 Tied for Finest Certified

2469 1838 Large Stars, No Drapery MS68 ★ NGC. V-8. A stunning Superb Gem. As of (11/09), only three examples of this date have been certified at the seemingly unobtainable grade of MS68★ at NGC. Part of a large mintage of 2.2 million pieces, the 1838 Large Stars half dime is an available date, and the issue enjoys great popularity as a type coin.

The present coin is a magnificent specimen, with untoned centers surrounded by bands of iridescent rose and cobalt-blue. Well defined features, mark-free surfaces, and radiant luster define the technical grade, while a combination of the aforementioned qualities and the aesthetically pleasing coloration explains the ★ notation on the NGC label. The attribution of this V-8 specimen is confirmed by the position of star 1, not low, but close to the rock on the obverse and a die crack from the reverse rim through the left side of M in AMERICA. Partial dentilation from 6 o'clock to 12 o'clock on the reverse is common to the issue. Census: 3 in 68 ★, 0 finer (11/09). (#4317)

Distinctive 1853-O No Arrows Half Dime, MS63

2470 1853-O No Arrows MS63 PCGS. CAC. The port city of New Orleans had an unceasing need for coinage in the years leading up to the Civil War, and as a rule, the pieces produced there circulated rather than sitting in vaults. This makes a number of silver issues, particularly those struck before the weight adjustment of 1853, rarities in Mint State. The 1853-O No Arrows, the last of those issues, is among the most elusive, its mintage of 160,000 pieces having experienced considerable attrition. The present Select coin is a distinctly high-end survivor, boldly impressed with warm gold-orange patina and hints of blue and green over strong and appealing luster. Population: 1 in 63, 5 finer (11/09).(#4352)

PROOF SEATED HALF DIMES

Early and Rare 1842 Half Dime, PR64

2471 1842 PR64 NGC. An exceptional early Seated proof half dime. Walter Breen, in his *Encyclopedia of United States and Colonial Proof Coins,* cited only seven known examples, and the NGC and PCGS total populations are 5 and 1, respectively. Still other sources claim a mintage of 8 pieces. Whatever the true figure, it is clear that this is an extreme rarity, and the example offered here is graded a respectable PR64. Violet-gold patina covers each side, and blue-green toning also appears within the wreath on the reverse. The strike is crisp, and the devices reveal few flaws, though a handful of hairlines and tiny contact marks are scattered in the fields. In light of the history and overall eye appeal of this piece, such minor troubles are forgivable and are unlikely to lessen anyone's appreciation of this diminutive silver proof.(#4418)

Sharp 1796 Ten Cent, JR-4, AU58

2472 1796 AU58 PCGS. JR-4, R.4. The 9 and 6 in the date are close, star 15 is close to the bust, leaves number 17 left and 13 right, right upright of N in UNITED recut at top.

Both sides of this near-Mint State specimen are colorfully toned in a medley of purple, forest-green, reddish-gold, yellow-green, and violet, joined by deep aqua-blue on the reverse. The design elements are well centered on the planchet and exhibit uniformly sharp delineation. Devoid of mentionable contacts and adjustment marks. The high technical quality and aesthetic appeal of this piece will make it a favorite of either the variety or type collector.(#4461)

Stunning MS66 JR-1 1796 Dime
An Important Type Coin

2473 1796 MS66 NGC. JR-1, R.3. The most instantly recognizable of the 1796 dime varieties, thanks to the die break or "cud" at star 1 that appears on virtually all known examples, the JR-1 is also scarce in an absolute sense, though it is also the year's most readily available die variety across the grading spectrum. This piece is from a later die state, with prominent crack in the field just to the right of Liberty's face as well as prominent clash marks throughout.

Beyond the needs of die-variety enthusiasts, the JR-1 is of particular importance to type and *Guide Book* collectors. As the first year of issue for dimes, the 1796 date was saved in quantity, and it follows logically that the JR-1 has a plurality of high-grade specimens. This holds true in practice, especially for coins in Gem and better condition. Among the eight 1796 dimes graded MS66 by NGC (there are three finer), a look at Heritage's Permanent Auction Archives shows that at least three distinct coins are of the JR-1 variety (11/09).

This Premium Gem offers beautiful blue-green peripheral toning over otherwise light silver-gray surfaces. In accordance with comments in *Early United States Dimes,* this later-state coin has a "shallow central portion," though this weakness is localized and the portrait is sharp for the date. Both sides are attractively lustrous and minimally marked. A gorgeous coin capable of inspiring spirited bidding.(#4461)

BUST DIMES

MS63 1805 4 Berries Dime, JR-2

2474 1805 4 Berries MS63 NGC. JR-2, R.2. The dimes of 1805 are known only by two die marriages that share a common obverse, with a small spine protruding from the top of the 5 in the date. The reverses show four or five berries, with the present 4 Berries reverse having narrow A's and leaves that are clear of the peripheral lettering.

This coin shows appealing medium-gray and golden highlights on each side, with few relevant abrasions. Some light adjustment marks appear in the central obverse. The strike is fairly sharp in the center, although some of the dentilation is softly defined. Census: 22 in 63, 54 finer (11/09).(#4477)

Popular JR-1 1820 STATESOF Dime, MS65

2475 1820 STATESOF MS65 NGC. JR-1, R.4. The STATESOF variety is one of several famous engraving blunders in early U.S. coinage. Letters in the reverse legend were improperly spaced, crowding OF between STATES and AMERICA. The first STATESOF dimes were struck in 1814. The reverse die was then placed in storage, where it gathered dust until 1820, since no dimes were struck in intervening years. The die returned to use in 1820, paired with a fresh 1820-dated obverse, to strike the scarce JR-1 marriage.

This high grade representative has light gold and plum peripheral toning. The obverse die is sunken between stars 2 and 4, and this weakens those stars as well as the final letters in UNITED, which are opposite on the reverse. Otherwise, the strike is exceptional, and both sides are attractively preserved. For the variety, Census: 4 in 65, 1 finer (11/09).
From The Five Point Collection.(#4494)

Marvelous MS66 1831 Dime, JR-3

2476 1831 MS66 NGC. JR-3, R.1. The first 1 in the date appears high, and the upright of the second 1 is under a curl. On the reverse the scroll begins under the upright of the D in UNITED and extends nearly to the middle of the M in AMERICA. The I in the motto is centered under the right edge of the last T. The top arrow feather is detached at the eagle's claw. This is a marvelously well-preserved dime that could pass muster for a much-younger coinage, save for the design. The silver-white surfaces are free of even the smallest visible distractions, and the strike is well-executed save for minor softness on the eagle's head and claws. Census: 10 in 66, 6 finer (11/09). (#4520)

Stunning 1831 JR-4 Dime, MS66

2477 1831 MS66 PCGS. CAC. JR-4, R.2. The 1831 JR-4 dime is a plentiful variety, although examples as nice as this piece are seldom encountered. That is equally true for all other varieties of the date and the type. For all nine years from 1829 to 1837, PCGS has only certified 46 submissions in MS66 and just 19 finer pieces. This stunning Premium Gem is housed in an older green-label PCGS holder. It presents sharp design elements with brilliant satin luster and wisps of gold and iridescent toning on both sides. Population: 6 in 66, 5 finer (11/09).(#4520)

Gorgeous Near-Mint 1846 Dime, AU58

2478 1846 AU58 PCGS. CAC. In *The Complete Guide to Liberty Seated Dimes,* Brian Greer writes of the 1846: "Fairly scarce in any grade and rare in XF and above. This is the lowest mintage Stars Obverse seated dime (excluding varieties)." With just 31,300 pieces struck, the 1846 dime has less than half the mintage of the more famous 1844 issue, the "Little Orphan Annie." This gorgeous near-Mint representative offers impressive luster with just a hint of friction on the high points. Elegant lavender, gold, and sea-green shadings grace each side, and marks are minimal. Population: 2 in 58, 2 finer (11/09).(#4588)

Key Issue 1873-CC Arrows Dime, XF45

2479 1873-CC Arrows XF45 PCGS. CAC. The 1873-CC with Arrows is one of the key dates in the Seated Liberty dime series. When found, examples usually grade from Good to Very Fine; higher grade pieces are difficult to locate. Of the approximately 80 specimens certified by PCGS and NGC, about 60 or so grade from Fair 2 to VF20; a mere three Mint State coins have been seen.

The Choice XF example in this lot displays light gray fields that highlight silvery devices that are nicely defined. Both sides are remarkably smooth and clean, a refreshing change from what is typically found on surviving examples that usually have porous surfaces, or other problems. The collector putting together a set of Seated dimes should give this Choice coin serious consideration, as a comparable piece may not come along for some time. Population: 2 in 45, 2 finer (12/07).(#4666)

Sharp 1874-CC Arrows Dime, AU50 Details

2480 1874-CC Arrows—Corroded—ANACS. AU50 Details. A major rarity in the series, the 1874-CC dime has a mintage of just 10,817 coins, and of those few that survive, the typical example is very well worn, grading far below the present example. The average certified grade is only VF, and those averages tend to favor higher grade coins. This piece is very well struck with excellent detail on both sides. The surfaces are lightly granular with minor corrosion on both sides, but it is evenly distributed and non-distracting. A small splash of iridescent toning at the upper left obverse adds character. (#4669)

PROOF SEATED DIMES

Important 1837 No Stars Dime, Gem Proof

2481 1837 No Stars PR65 NGC. Greer-102. All proofs of this first-year issue are of the Large Date variety. Writing in 1977, Breen states that perhaps 20 examples of this rare first-year proof are extant, some of which are impaired. In his 1988 *Encyclopedia,* however, the author states that "30+" proof 1837 No Stars dimes are extant. Regardless of which, if either, of these estimates is accurate, there is no doubt that this proof issue is one of the premier rarities in the Seated Dime series.

An unquestionably important coin for first-year proof type purposes, this is a fully original Gem with medium cobalt-blue, reddish-purple, and gold patination. The fields shimmer as the coin rotates beneath a light and the devices are extraordinarily well struck. The quintessential representative of Christian Gobrecht's original conception of the Seated Liberty Dime. Census: 2 in 65, 3 finer (11/09). (#4718)

Gorgeous 1855 Seated Dime, PR65

2482 1855 Arrows PR65 NGC. It is thought that just 12 to 15 proof 1855 Seated dimes exist, according to Garry Fortin at www.seateddimevarieties.com, and every known example shows hub doubling at the date and arrows, a diagnostic of proofs. The same obverse is also known on business strikes, so the existence of the date doubling will not prove that a coin is a proof. However, the lack of that doubling will prove that a coin is not a proof. This Gem rich gold toning over deeply mirrored fields and frosty devices, with splashes of iridescence to heighten its aesthetic appeal. Census: 2 in 65, 0 finer (11/09).(#4744)

'The Coin Without a Country'
Judd-233 1859 Transitional Dime, PR66
Ex: Eliasberg

2483 1859 Transitional PR66 PCGS. CAC. Judd-233, Pollock-280, High R.6. Popularly known as "The Coin Without a Country," as the starred obverse used for regular issue 1838-1859 dimes is combined with the cereal wreath reverse of 1860-1891 issues, with no indication anywhere of the country of origin. Struck in silver with a reeded edge.

While the 1859 Transitional dimes often are collected by pattern enthusiasts (and as noted at the top of the description, they are assigned number 233 in Judd), other authorities have considered the coins fantasies rather than patterns. In the description of this coin for the Louis E. Eliasberg, Sr. collection, the cataloger wrote: "The distribution arrangement for the 1859 transitional dime is not known, but it certainly must have been regarded as a delicacy when it was struck, significantly during the term of Mint Director James Ross Snowden."

If Eliasberg had any such concerns, he did not let them get in the way of collecting the issue, and by now, the Transitional dimes of 1859 have tradition on their side. This Premium Gem proof, amply frosted on the devices, has strong mirrors beneath rich patina, which the Eliasberg catalog termed "Delicate lilac, gold, and iridescent toning." To this, we add that strike and surface quality are both excellent. Housed in a holder with green insert and green CAC label.

Ex: The Louis E. Eliasberg, Sr. Collection (Bowers and Merena, 5/1996), lot 1168.(#4749)

BARBER DIMES

Impeccable 1881 Seated Dime, PR68 ★ Cameo

2484 1881 PR68 ★ Cameo NGC. The business strike mintages of dimes from 1879-1881 were on the scrawny side—24,000 coins in the case of 1881—complemented by a normally small quotient of proof coins, 975 pieces. This is the only Cameo example certified PR68 by NGC and the only Star coin in that grade (two non-Cameo pieces are graded PR68 without the Star) (11/09). As expected, the surfaces are amazingly impeccable on this coin. Blinding reflectivity cascades from silver-white surfaces, ringed with a thin circle of pinkish-gold, and the strike and field-device contrast are equally bold. A finer type coin is unimaginable.(#84778)

Important 1894-O Barber Dime, MS66 Tied for Finest Graded at PCGS

2485 1894-O MS66 PCGS. Ex: Duckor. Both sides are exquisitely detailed, with bright, semiprooflike fields, strong overall luster, and faint iridescent toning. The obverse and reverse are essentially brilliant, with only the faintest traces of gold at the rims. Close examination reveals a few wispy hairlines on Liberty's cheek, but the balance of the coin is essentially perfect and problem-free, as it should be for the grade. No varieties have been reported for this low-mintage issue, although we note that this example has the mintmark tilted noticeably to the left. This lovely example is an important condition rarity at the Premium Gem level. Population: 6 in 66, 0 finer (9/09). (#4804)

Elusive 1896-O Barber Dime, MS66

2486 1896-O MS66 PCGS. The 1896-O is the third of four early O-mint issues in the series, from 1894-O to 1897-O—each with a mintage under 1 million coins—that are among the most difficult to find in Mint State grades. The 1896-O is also an underrated issue compared to the key-date 1895-O. This piece is well-struck on both sides, save for minor softness on the 6 in the date. Silver-gold patina graces the obverse and much of the reverse, where a small area of aqua and cinnamon joins the fray. At the Premium Gem level, this coin is one of only handful so graded at PCGS, and there are none finer. Population: 7 in 66, 0 finer (12/09). (#4810)

MERCURY DIMES

1916-D Dime, MS62 Full Bands A Low-Mintage Issue With Few High Grade Examples Known

2487 1916-D MS62 Full Bands NGC. The 1916-D is the "Holy Grail" of Mercury dime collectors. The constant demand for the issue is fueled not only by collectors of this series, but also by some nonspecialists who simply want an example of this legendary coin for their collection. Consequently, the popularity of the 1916-D keeps its price high in all levels of preservation.

Despite its low mintage (264,000 pieces) and first-year-of-issue status, the 1916-D was not saved in great numbers. This is reinforced by inspection of PCGS/NGC population figures. The two services have to date (11/09) certified about 550 Mint State coins, most in MS64 and below. Conversely, they have graded more than 2,000 examples in grades Poor through AG3 and over 1,500 in the two grades of Good.

Why did so many 1916-D dimes enter the channels of commerce and remain there to become heavily worn? Paul Green, in a 2005 article in Littleton Coin Company's *Collector's Corner*, suggests an answer:

> "... many collectors in the first quarter of the past century were still collecting only by date. The Augustus Heaton work on branch mint issues in the 1890s had helped to alert some to the idea of collecting by date and mint mark ... but there has long been a strong belief that many did not really start collecting in the way we do today until the albums and guides of the 1930s alerted them to the possibilities."

The surfaces of this piece show light golden-rose toning on both obverse and reverse and the underlying mint luster is remarkably bright. The central horizontal bands, as well as the diagonal bands are fully defined.(#4907)

Exceptional 1918-D Dime, MS65 Full Bands

2488 1918-D MS65 Full Bands PCGS. Ex: Scheppman Collection. This issue's ample mintage of over 22 million pieces, combined with the strains of wartime production, makes the 1918-D dime one of the most poorly produced Mercury issues. In his *The Complete Guide to Mercury Dimes,* Lange gives a grim assessment that " ... this date offers relatively few coins which will satisfy collectors."

At the MS65 Full Bands grade level, the 1918-D is the premier rarity among D-mint issues in this long-lived and widely collected series. This impressive and obviously important Gem is not only fully impressed over the all-important crossbands, but the peripheral devices are sharply detailed throughout. Both sides exhibit a warm, matte-like texture that is veiled in original pastel-gold and ice-blue patina. A smattering of olive-tan color is seen at the lower obverse border, and the surfaces are pleasingly preserved, even by the standards of the Gem designation. Population: 19 in 65 Full Bands, 3 finer (11/09).(#4919)

Sharp 1919-D Gem Full Bands Dime

2489 1919-D MS65 Full Bands NGC. Despite a mintage of almost 10 million pieces, the 1919-D dime is elusive in the better grades of Mint State, particularly so with Full Bands. Unfortunately, peripheral weakness is common on this issue, even on those with Full Bands. The present Gem offering is a refreshing exception, for not only are the middle, diagonal, and upper and lower bands full, but so are the peripheral elements. All lettering near the rim is sharp, as are the date digits and mintmark. Untoned surfaces display bright luster and reveal only a couple of inoffensive grade-consistent marks. A light crack occurs at the L of LIBERTY and another on the lower left neck. Census: 6 in 65 Full Bands, 0 finer (11/09).(#4925)

Remarkable 1925 Mercury Dime MS68 Full Bands

2490 1925 MS68 Full Bands PCGS. One of only three Full Bands examples of the 1925 certified in MS68 at PCGS, this coin would upgrade every one of the current Top 5 Mercury Dimes FB Basic Set, Circulation Strikes (1916-1945) Registry Sets at PCGS. This piece boasts razor-sharp separation on the all-important central bands and all of the bands, even the sometimes-weak diagonals. Another typical problem area for the issue is the date, where many examples show a mushy final digit. Not so the present piece, with a crisp lower loop on the 5 and a clear space between it and the rim. The surfaces are satiny and silver-gold, with bits of olive-gray confined to the lower reverse.(#4949)

Exceptional 1925-S Dime, MS67 Full Bands

2491 1925-S MS67 Full Bands NGC. The 1925-S is considered the most poorly made date in the Mercury dime series. David Lange writes in his *Mercury Dimes* reference that both obverse and reverse are plagued by heavy die polishing and erosion and a generally weak strike throughout, especially the reverse periphery

Despite this date's reputation, the present Superb Gem displays full delineation not only on the bands but on most of the peripheral letters as well. These are frequently indistinct on some '25-S specimens. Dappled medium intensity gold, red, lime-green, and sea-green patina races over the obverse, ceding to mere hints of this color palette on the reverse. Lustrous surfaces are well preserved. Census: 5 in 67 Full Bands, 0 finer (11/09).(#4953)

Solidly Struck 1927-S Ten Cent, MS66 Full Bands

2492 1927-S MS66 Full Bands PCGS. Ex: Scheppman Collection. The shining surfaces host devices that are solidly impressed at both the centers and the peripheries. The margins show elements of tan, bronze, yellow-gold, green, and violet patina, while the remainder of each side is essentially brilliant. Powerful visual appeal for this San Francisco issue.

Paradoxically, while Lange compares the 1927-S favorably to earlier S-mint dimes, he notes that the 1927-S pieces are far more elusive with Full Bands, and combined with a low general mintage and a tiny pool of Mint State pieces, the Full Bands coins for the year are particularly challenging. An attractive and carefully preserved representative such as the present exemplar should draw the attention of dedicated connoisseurs.(#4965)

Radiant Gem Full Bands 1942/1-D Dime

2493 1942/1-D MS65 Full Bands PCGS. CAC. The 1942/1-D Mercury dime overdate is both more difficult to see and more elusive—facts which may be interconnected, as its existence went undetected for much longer than for its Philadelphia cousin. Both varieties are the result of dual-hub errors, likely produced towards the end of 1941 when working dies were being made of both years. It is interesting to learn, per Lange's reference, that the variety also features a repunched mintmark that is clearly visible with a loupe. This specimen offers radiant luster over silver-white surfaces lightly tinged with pinkish-gold and ice-blue. Not merely the crucial central bands, but all bands on the fasces are fully struck. Population: 16 in 65 Full Bands, 13 finer (12/09).(#5041)

Exceptional Strike Rarity 1945 Dime MS66 Full Bands

2494 1945 MS66 Full Bands PCGS. Collectors have long tried to assemble sets of this popular series in Mint State with full central bands. By the mid-1970s, specialists were well aware that the seemingly common 1945 was in fact a major rarity with Full Bands. The Philadelphia Mint may have had a labor shortage in 1945 due to World War II, at the same time that the wartime economy was booming. The mints also had to strike substantial quantities of world coinage, further straining resources. Given these circumstances, it is understandable that the Philadelphia Mint wished to increase die life for 1945 dimes, and the nearly 160 million pieces struck were produced from dies spaced slightly too far apart. This lustrous Premium Gem has light yellow-gold toning and is minimally marked. A couple of die polish areas are visible at the obverse margins. Population: 13 in 66 Full Bands, 3 finer (11/09).(#5057)

PROOF ROOSEVELT DIMES

1968 Roosevelt Dime, PR67 Rare No S Proof Key Modern Rarity

2495 1968 No S PR67 PCGS. After the three-year proof striking hiatus from 1965 to 1967, production resumed in 1968, not at Philadelphia but at San Francisco. When the S mintmark was left off a dime obverse die, however, a new modern error rarity was created. (This error was later repeated on the dime in 1970, 1975, and 1983.) The present coin is a deeply mirrored, mostly brilliant specimen, with just a slight overlay of pale golden toning. The surfaces are technically perfect, except for a tiny planchet flaw in the field below O in OF on the reverse. Population: 5 in 67, 5 finer (12/09).(#5245)

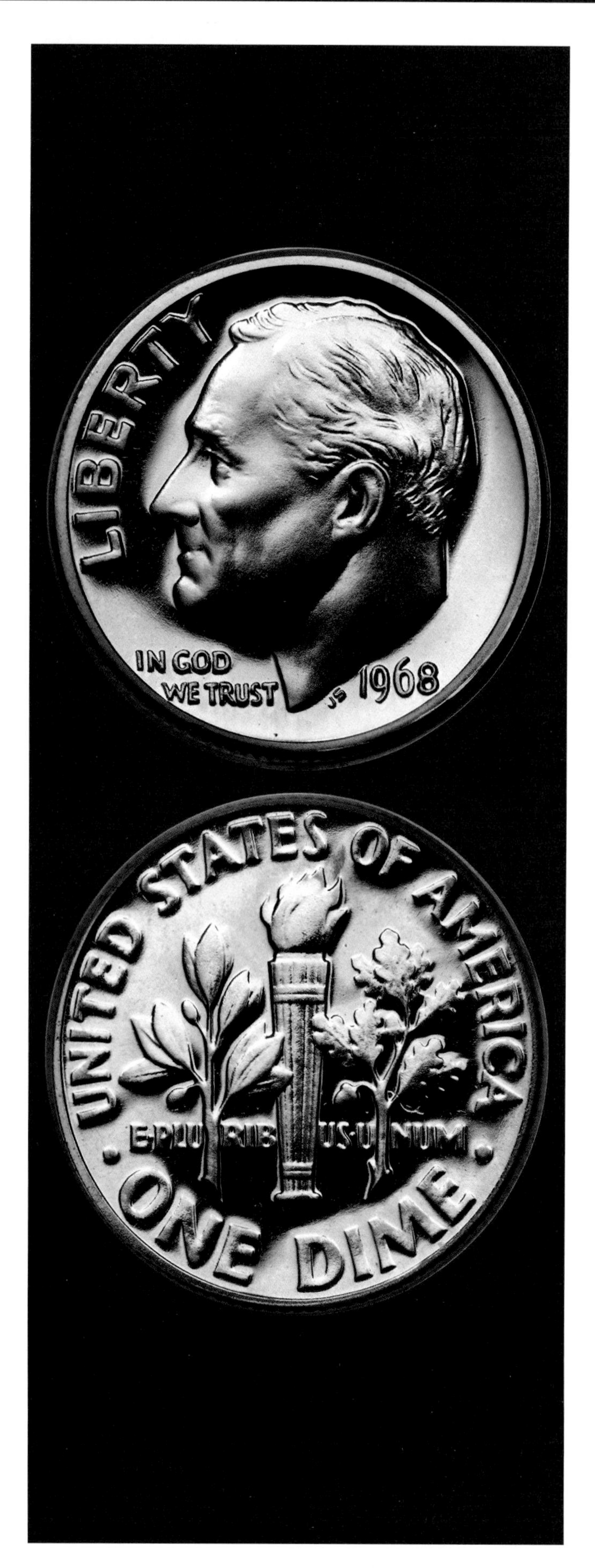

Popular PR68 1968 No S Dime
Tied for Finest at PCGS

2496 1968 No S PR68 PCGS. The first No S proof dime issue occurred in 1968, resulting from an incomplete die that had the mintmark left off. Since proofs were always produced in Philadelphia before 1964, and none were minted in 1965-1967, the 1968 issue was the first date in which this error could possibly happen. The Philadelphia Mint was historically responsible for producing all coinage dies, including adding the mintmarks, which were then shipped to the branch mints for coinage. It is easy to understand how one S-less die could slip through the net in the first year of proof production after the hiatus. The error was repeated in three later years (1970, 1975, and 1983), with the 1968 issue the second rarest of the dates. The Philadelphia Mint's 200-year monopoly on die production finally ended in 1996, when the Denver Mint opened its own die shop.

Reports of the S-less dime were first published in *Coin World* on June 28, 1968, causing much excitement in the numismatic community. The variety is mentioned, but not individually listed, in the 2010 *Guide Book*. The *Guide Book* does list the complete 1968 proof set with the No S dime. The number of No S dimes minted is unknown but presumed to be extremely small. Walter Breen estimated a population of only six examples known in 1988, but population data from the grading services indicates a larger number of survivors. Perhaps 15-25 examples in all proof grades is a more accurate estimate.

This is a PR68 specimen from the variety that started the sequence, carefully preserved and minimally toned with potent mirrors. Both sides are mildly contrasted with a touch of frost visible on the devices, though not enough for a Cameo designation. Among coins not graded as Cameo or Deep Cameo, this piece is tied with four others for finest certified by PCGS (11/09).(#5245)

TWENTY CENT PIECES

1876 Twenty Cent Piece, MS66
Lovely Toning Over Semiprooflike Fields

2497 1876 MS66 PCGS. CAC. From a minuscule business-strike mintage of 14,460 pieces, the 1876 twenty cent piece is a scarce coin in all grades, and quite rare at the Premium Gem level. The public never accepted the odd denomination, and 1876 was the final year of business-strike production. Proofs were minted for two more years, and the denomination was dropped after 1878.

The present coin is a visual delight. The reflective, semiprooflike fields glow beneath multiple layers of toning. The obverse fields are primarily a deep blue, yielding to gray on the central device. The same deep blue hue covers the reverse margins, but the center is a delightful gray-rose. The striking details are sharp, with full definition at the top of the wing. The only detectable marks are a couple of faint field marks, left and right of Liberty. Population: 11 in 66, 2 finer (11/09).(#5299)

Superb Gem 1876 Twenty Cent Piece
Tied for Finest Certified

2498 1876 MS67 PCGS. CAC. Authorized in March 1875, the unfortunate twenty cent piece soon proved unpopular and unnecessary. Business strikes were minted for only two years, including the small mintage of 14,460 pieces achieved by the Philadelphia Mint in 1876. Proof-only mintages were issued in 1877 and 1878, and the denomination was discontinued on May 2, 1878. Twenty cent pieces were heavily melted in later years, and the 1876 is a scarce date in all grades today. At the Superb Gem level, NGC has certified five examples, with none finer; while PCGS has graded only two specimens, with none finer (11/09).

The present coin is a stunning Superb Gem, with brilliant fields and virtually perfect surfaces. The striking details are sharp throughout. The intense visual appeal and high technical grade make this example a fitting choice for the finest type set or date collection. (#5299)

PROOF TWENTY CENT PIECE

1877 Twenty Cent Piece
Pristine Superb Gem Proof

2499 1877 PR67 NGC. The short career of the twenty cent piece was over nearly as soon as it began. The single year of 1875 was the only such that could be called its heyday, and by 1877 and 1878 the only mintages were small emissions of proofs. This 1877 proof is one of only 350 recorded for the year, although the combined NGC/PCGS population data total nearly 500 pieces because of the many duplications. This Superb Gem offers lovely pale blue and rose toning intermixed on each side, with strong proof mirrors flashing through. Even under a strong loupe, there are no visible impairments of any kind. Among the finest certified. Census: 3 in 67, 0 finer (11/09).(#5305)

EARLY QUARTER

Scarce B-1 1804 Quarter, VF25

2500 1804 VF25 ANACS. B-1, R.3. The die scratch at star 9 on the obverse is diagnostic. The B-1 variety of the 1804 quarter is the more available of two for the year, but still scarce in an absolute sense. This is an appealing midrange representative, silver-gray with elements of gold and violet on the obverse. The margins of that side show deeper charcoal color, as does most of the reverse. The surfaces show an assortment of the usual shallow abrasions and pinscratches, as well as a small rim bump visible above the R in LIBERTY. Housed in a small-format ANACS holder.(#5312)

Admirable 1804 Quarter, B-1, XF

2501 1804 XF40 NGC. B-1, R.3. The small die flaw between stars 8 and 9 confirms the variety, as do the usually seen "collar" clash marks before the bustline, appearing as an extra fold of cloth. For a coin with 20 points of wear this piece is remarkably clean, showing no mentionable abrasions save for a couple of faint scrapes below the U in UNITED. There are no planchet adjustment marks on either side, the strike is well-centered, and full dentilation appears around the rims. Medium dove-gray surfaces show darker charcoal tinges near the device peripheries. An original and compelling example of this popular first-year Heraldic Eagle type. Census: 3 in 40, 13 finer (11/09).(#5312)

Attractive 1806 Quarter, B-2, MS64

2502 1806 MS64 PCGS. B-2, R.2. The variety is attributed by defects in the foot of 1 in the date that touches the curl, and defects in T in LIBERTY at the left and the foot of I at right. On the reverse, the C of 25 C touches the tail, there are 11 arrowheads, all Ts have a shorter lower left serif, AME of AMERICA joined at base, and 2 inside and 3 outside berries. Incipient rim crumbling and several reverse cracks point to Tompkins Die Stages 3/4-5.

Medium intensity gray, grayish-purple, and golden-gray toning bathe both sides of this near-Gem, joined by a splash of orange-brown on Liberty's neck. The design features are generally well defined except for the often-seen softness in some of the obverse stars. A few unobtrusive handling marks are unbothersome. Housed in a green label holder. Population for the issue: 9 in 64, 2 finer (11/09).(#5314)

One of the Finest Known 1815 Quarters, B-1 MS66

2503 1815 MS66 PCGS. B-1, R.1. Late Die State. This was the only quarter dollar issued during the decade from 1808 to 1817, and the first year of issue for the Capped Bust design. The mintage of 69,232 quarters of December 16, 1815, were all delivered to the Planter's Bank of New Orleans, while the 20,003 coins delivered on January 10, 1816 were probably sent to the Bank of the United States in Philadelphia, according to Steve Tompkins in *Early United States Quarters 1796-1838*.

The December delivery was sent upon request of the Planter's Bank, who apparently needed the coins as a replacement for Mexican two reales coins of a similar value. An exchange of letters took place between Bailly Blanchard, cashier of the Planter's Bank, and Mint Director Robert L. Patterson. Blanchard insisted that the bank could only use quarter dollars, while Patterson wanted to send the entire amount in dimes. More than six months elapsed from the first letter requesting the coins and the date they were delivered.

Several die states are known for the 1815 quarter, and this piece is a later die state with light clash marks on each side, especially visible on the reverse. It is probably one of the later January 10 coins. It is also a lovely Condition Census candidate with full silver luster beneath heavy iridescent toning, deepening to steel along the borders. Population: 3 in 66, 0 finer (11/09).(#5321)

Untoned MS65 1818 Quarter, B-3
A Rare and Overlooked Type Coin

2504 1818 MS65 NGC. B-3, R.3. The repeating date is equally and widely spaced, and the last 8 is uncentered (right of) the lowest hair curl. Both 1s in the date have broken feet at their left sides. This is technically the 1818/5 overdate die from the B-1 die marriage, but reground so that the traces of the 5 no longer show.

On this piece there is visible die clashing on both sides. The coin is essentially brilliant, displaying just a bit of peripheral color. The surfaces are thickly coated in superb mint frost and show generous luster that is seldom seen on early type coins. The strike is full throughout, save for minor weakness on Liberty's highest hair curls. There are no mentionable abrasions. A wonderful type coin or representative of this available variety. For the date, Census: 26 in 65, 13 finer (11/09).(#5322)

Finest Certified B-3 1818 Quarter, MS66

2505 1818 MS66 NGC. B-3, R.3. Die State II. The obverse die is shared with the B-1 die pairing, and both are sometimes called 1818/5 overdates, although on the B-3 the 5 is no longer visible under the last 8. The date is quite wide and equally spaced, and relatively high above the border. The second 8 is to the right (uncentered) under the curl, and star 1 points between the first and second drapery folds. On the reverse, the scroll's left end is under the upright of the D, and its right end is centered under the right foot of A. All T's are defective at bottom right, and a crack extends from the edge through the lower arrowhead and the two arrow shafts above, up toward the eagle. The defective left feet in both 1s of the date confirm the die state.

The 1818 quarter, from a mintage of 361,174 pieces, is readily obtainable in circulated grades. Even Mint State coins are occasionally available through MS64 or MS65. Premium Gems, however, are very difficult to locate, as evidenced by the 22 coins certified for the 1818/5 by NGC and PCGS, and only one is found finer (11/09).

The silvery surfaces of this amazing MS66 example are awash in full luster and display whispers of cobalt-blue and light tan at the margins. The design features are sharply detailed throughout. The dentilation is full on both sides, and no mentionable contact marks are evident. Some light clash marks are visible on the reverse. This is an outstanding piece for a high grade type set. For all NGC-certified 1818s, Census: 12 in 66, 1 finer (11/09). This is the finest and only B-3 certified as such at either service.(#5322)

Multicolored 1828 Gem Quarter, B-1

2506 1828 MS65 NGC. B-1, R.1. The 1828 is the final issue in the large size Capped Bust quarter series. For this variety, star 1 is close to the bust. The denomination has a curl base 2 and a fancy top 5. The T's on the reverse are defective at the bottom right, as with all varieties of this year.

The present coin is toned in shades of deep green and gold on the lower two-thirds of the obverse, while the upper portions are light steel-gray. The patina is matched on the reverse, where the lower portion is lighter and the rest is deep blue, green, and russet. Flashy luster shines in the periphery. The strike is sharp save for Liberty's uppermost curls, and all of the stars have fully defined centrils.

Although B-1 is a common variety, the 1828 is rare in Gem condition and it is virtually impossible to locate in a higher grade. This piece is the perfect coin for the type collector who demands the utmost quality. Census for the issue: 3 in 65, 1 finer (11/09). (#5342)

Appealing 1837 Quarter, B-1, MS65

2507 1837 MS65 PCGS. CAC. B-1, R.3. The 7 in the date is centered under the left edge of the hair curl, identifying the obverse. The reverse eagle has no tongue, the 2 has a curl base, and the base of E in UNITED is below that of T. According to Steve Tompkins' reference (2008) this is die stage 2/1, identified by a die crack traversing the lower obverse border and a crack from D through STATE to dentils.

Attractive luster exudes from surfaces toned in light to medium shades of sky-blue, bluish-purple, golden-orange, gray, and lime-green. A well executed strike sharpens the design elements except for softness in the centrils of the stars at the upper border, and both sides are nicely preserved. Great overall eye appeal. Population for the issue: 10 in 65, 8 finer (11/09).(#5356)

SEATED QUARTERS

Gem 1838 No Drapery Quarter

2508 1838 No Drapery MS65 NGC. The device punches for what would become the Seated Liberty quarter were completed by Christian Gobrecht during the summer of 1838. After 20 "specimens" were sent to Treasury Secretary Levi Woodbury, regular production commenced on September 29. The Philadelphia Mint produced at least 466,000 examples this year, all of which, like their 1839 and 1840-O No Drapery counterparts, lacked obverse drapery folds at Liberty's right (facing) elbow.

All three of these issues are scarce in problem-free Uncirculated preservation, and what few coins have been certified at the upper reaches of the Mint State grading scale are usually snatched up quickly by type collectors when they appear on the market. This example sports an uncommonly bold strike, and there are remarkably few abrasions for the type. It is frosty and undeniably attractive with just a hint of golden patina over the obverse. Census: 5 in 65, 3 finer (11/09).

From The Five Point Collection.(#5391)

LIBERTY
1838
UNITED STATES OF AMERICA
QUAR. DOL.

Immaculate 1838 No Drapery Quarter, MS68

2509 1838 No Drapery MS68 PCGS. CAC. R.W. Julian's article "Gobrecht's Seated Liberty," published in the July 2003 edition of the magazine *Coins,* offers an excellent overview of how the eponymous design made its way to the quarter dollar. The Liberty Seated obverse, which Julian credits to a collaboration between engraver Christian Gobrecht and artists Titian Peale and Thomas Sully, was created for the silver dollar, but its use spread quickly to other denominations:

> "The designs were so well received that [Mint Director Robert] Patterson soon sought permission to improve the looks of the dimes and half dimes by putting the seated figure on the obverse. ... Once the dimes and half dimes had received the seated figure of Liberty, the quarter dollar came next. Gobrecht prepared the dies in the summer of 1838 and in September several trial pieces were sent to Treasury Secretary Levi Woodbury and President Martin Van Buren for their inspection. Approval was soon forthcoming and coinage quickly began. Demand was strong enough that 466,000 pieces were struck by year's end."

Julian further notes that while Gobrecht's obverse design was artistically successful, it created certain technical challenges that Mint Director Patterson decided to rectify. In a different article, "Collectors Clamor for Seated Liberty Quarters" in the February 29, 2000 edition of *Numismatic News,* Julian describes the change made and how it affects the way today's collectors approach the series:

> "The quarter coinage of 1838-1840, without drapery, is increasingly obtained by type collectors because of the distinct difference in the obverse dies. This variety was struck at Philadelphia in 1838 and 1839 but also at New Orleans in 1840; the dies for the latter were sent off before all the changes were in place. Philadelphia coined only the variety with drapery in 1840.
>
> "Sculptor Robert Ball Hughes had been hired by Director Patterson to slightly redesign the silver coinage, especially the Seated Liberty figures; the change of drapery at the elbow is a mark of Hughes' work. The point of the make-over was to reduce the height of the figure so that the coins would strike up better in the available coining presses."

While the 2010 edition of the *Guide Book* does not specify the No Drapery Seated quarters as a subtype, many collectors do consider them such, among them James W. Lull, previous owner of the present example; he assembled a high-end type collection which included both this 1838 quarter and an 1857 quarter, which would be redundant for type purposes if not for the No Drapery versus Drapery nicety.

The second Julian quote references what may be considered this Superb Gem beauty's only flaw, that its strike is soft at the peripheries; still, in light of the issue's striking weakness being ever-present, this is forgivable. Otherwise, the eye appeal has no need for redemption; the bold silver-white luster on each side shines through occasional splashes of milky patina. Essentially unmarked and frosty, with a small sliver of startling brilliance between the T and E of STATES on the reverse. In a prior appearance, the cataloger mentioned that this MS68 PCGS example had a peer at NGC, a coin graded MS68 ★; this listing no longer appears in the *Census Report,* and the logical conclusion is that the MS68 ★ coin was recertified, this time by PCGS; possibly that coin and the present lot are one and the same. Population: 1 in 68, 0 finer (11/09).

Ex: James W. Lull Collection (Bowers and Merena, 1/2005), lot 681.(#5391)

Richly Toned MS65 1853 Arrows and Rays Quarter

2510 1853 Arrows and Rays MS65 NGC. Mint Director George Eckert convinced Congress it was necessary to reduce the weight of minor silver coinage to discourage hoarding. The act of February 21, 1853 specified a new weight for the quarter of 96 grains, down from the previous weight of 103.125 grains. To mark this change, arrowheads were placed on either side of the date, and rays were placed above the eagle on the new coins. The arrows remained on the quarter design until 1856, creating a three-year type coin. A large mintage of 15.3 million pieces was achieved.

The present coin is a pleasing example of this interesting date. All design elements are sharp, and the fields are blemish-free. Abundant mint luster is evident, under accents of gold and lavender toning. A better type coin would be difficult to find. Census: 26 in 65, 9 finer (11/09).(#5426)

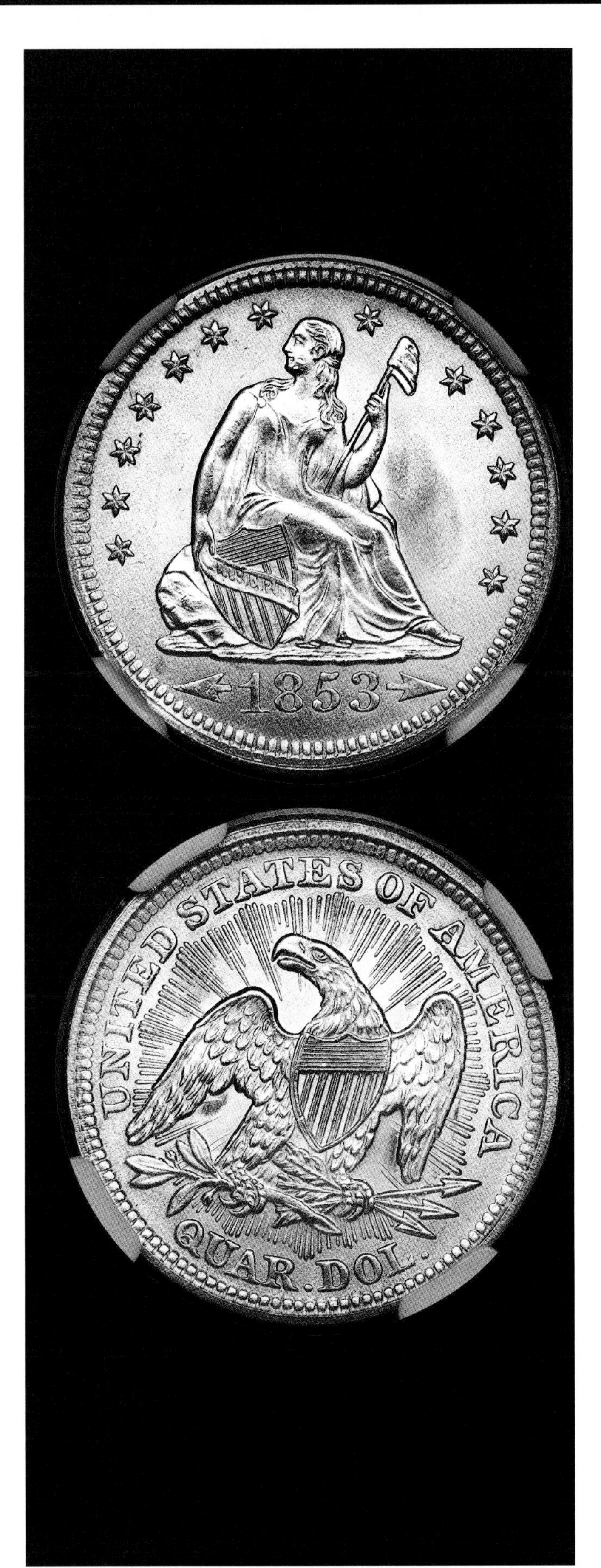

Brilliant 1853 Arrows and Rays Quarter
A Spectacular MS67 Example

2511 1853 Arrows and Rays MS67 NGC. For several years leading up to 1853 U.S. silver coins were worth more melted than in their coined form. This was good for bullion dealers at the time as it provided them with an "endless chain" of profit. However, it was distinctly bad for other commercial interests and common people who needed small denomination coinage to make change in their everyday transactions. For commercial usage in the early part of 1853, quarters were best suited by default as half dimes and dimes were too cumbersome to pay off debts and half dollars were not struck until May 21. As a result, after the Act of February 21, 1853 was passed to remedy the situation, the Mint was closed to visitors and the coinage of copper was suspended. By the middle of April the Director was able to offer coins for sale, and in the first few weeks only quarters were sold as they bridged the gap between the three cent silver and the gold dollar.

These new quarters weighed 96 grains, compared to the former 103 1/8 grain weight. To denote the reduction in weight arrowheads were placed on each side of the date and rays were placed around the reverse. This design format lasted only one year, with a reminder of the reduced weight carried on through 1855 with arrowheads only. More than 15 million quarters were struck of the Arrows and Rays design and they were a smashing success. One Philadelphia paper reported that the Mint had "fully overcome the complaint among the small dealers of a want of change." The new coins served their purpose excellently. For the first time since the establishment of the Mint in 1793 the nation had an adequate supply of fractional coins of uniform quality.

This particular piece is one of the finest examples extant of this one-year type. All too often found with heavily toned surfaces, this is a brilliant coin with silky-smooth, satin-like mint luster. Fully struck throughout, each side is nearly abrasion-free. Both obverse and reverse display a granular texture around the margins from metal flow in those areas. Population: 3 in 67, 0 finer (11/09).

From The Five Point Collection.(#5426)

Rare 1853-O Arrows and Rays Quarter, MS64

2512 1853-O Arrows and Rays MS64 PCGS. Larry Briggs recent series update in the *Coin Dealer Newsletter* called this issue "fairly easy to locate in all grades AG-XF; AU coins very scarce and Mint State coins downright rare." The one-year type with the Rays reverse shows a curiosity of the issue, as the large O mintmark lies over the rays underneath. Like many examples, the present near-Gem displays a "halo" effect around many of the devices, an attempt, per Briggs, to reengrave the dies to prolong their life. The obverse die nonetheless appears in an advanced state. Aside from the prominent halo effect on the right-side stars, an extremely bold die clash runs from Liberty's lower curls through the pole and upraised forearm. A couple of wispy die cracks appear elsewhere on that side.

Considerable luster emanates from surfaces that show little post-strike contact. The coloration is largely silver-gold, with daubs of jade, ochre, and mauve more visible on the reverse. A prize for the Seated quarter, type, or New Orleans specialists, and among the finest at PCGS. Population: 5 in 64, 0 finer (11/09).(#5428)

Prized 1857-S Seated Quarter, MS64 Tied for Finest at PCGS

2513 1857-S MS64 PCGS. CAC. After opening in 1854, the San Francisco Mint produced its first Seated quarters the following year. Mintages, while on the smallish side, continued even through the difficult Civil War era, with the sole exception of 1863. The mintage in 1857 was typical of the era, a skimpy 82,000 coins. Briggs notes in his *Coin Dealer Newsletter* update (December 2007) that Mint State examples are rare and "usually well-struck with creamy luster." This piece is certified in an older small-size green-label holder and offers such a bold strike, with memorable patina. Gold, saffron, and ice-blue hues appear on both sides, with considerable untoned silver-gray luster beneath. A couple of reeding marks left of the date and a small scrape in the left obverse field explain the grade but are unbothersome. Population: 3 in 64, 0 finer (11/09).(#5444)

1860 Seated Liberty Quarter, MS66
Only One Example Certified Finer

2514 1860 MS66 PCGS. CAC. Type Two Obverse, Type One Reverse. From a business strike mintage of 804,400 pieces, the 1860 Seated Liberty quarter is one of the more available No Motto dates. Most examples seen are in lower circulated grades, with Fine/VF coins predominating. Larry Briggs gives Mint State coins an R.4 rating, and examples at the Premium Gem level are extremely rare. Currently NGC has certified only two coins in MS66, with one finer; while PCGS has graded two examples at the Premium Gem level, with none finer (11/09).

The present coin is a lovely Premium Gem with delightful iridescent toning. The surfaces are covered with thick gray patina, yielding to cobalt-blue and russet at the margins. The striking details are stronger on the left, with the right obverse stars missing centrils. One small handling mark is noted, in the right obverse field. Overall eye appeal is outstanding.(#5451)

1868 Seated Liberty Quarter, MS66
Tied for Finest Certified

2515 1868 MS66 PCGS. CAC. Though it has a lower mintage than its S-mint counterpart (29,400 pieces versus 96,000 pieces), the 1868 quarter is more available in Mint State grades, since virtually all of the San Francisco coins experienced heavy circulation. Still, in grades above Gem, the 1868 proves itself a fantastic rarity, with only three pieces at that level in the combined certified population and none finer (11/09).

This enticing piece offers surprisingly strong luster beneath moderate aqua, azure, violet, and orange concentric toning. The strike is crisp, and the surfaces are immaculate and semiprooflike. The contrast between the reflective surfaces and frosty devices gives this specimen an unusual cameo appearance. A simply marvelous coin that is destined for an honored place in a top-drawer collection. (#5472)

Semiprooflike MS66 1869 Quarter
Tied for Finest Certified

2516 1869 MS66 PCGS. A mere 16,000 pieces were struck for circulation of the 1869 quarter, plus another 600 proofs for collectors. Scarce in all grades and especially so in mint condition. Only 22 pieces have been certified by both of the major services in MS60 and better grades. This piece is tied as finest certified with another MS66 that has been graded by NGC (11/09). This coin would truly be a centerpiece of a collection of With Motto quarters. The fields are bright and semireflective, a quality that is apparent even through the rich layers of gray-rose and cobalt-blue toning. The flashiness in the fields is due in large part to faintly visible die polishing marks on each side.

The initial appearance of this piece suggestive of a quarter struck 10 years later. The reason, of course, is because the coins struck beginning in 1879 were low mintage dates such as this one. This meant the initial die polish and reflectivity did not wear off the dies from repeated striking, as one would see on a higher mintage coin. While the means of production were similar in each case, what is singular and noteworthy about this coin is the earliness of the date. It is unusual to locate such high grade pieces from 1869. It must be remembered that the low mintages that began in the early part of the Civil War were not automatically suspended once the Union was reunited. This piece is sharply struck and, of course, devoid of any mentionable surface flaws.(#5474)

Remarkable 1882 Seated Quarter, MS68

2517 1882 MS68 NGC. CAC. All of the Seated quarters in the 1880s are important rarities in higher Mint State grades, and this piece is one of the most remarkable from that decade. As expected for the grade, neither side reveals even the smallest abrasion; the small flaw between Liberty's head and the cap is a tiny planchet void, as made. Incredible original color includes, on the obverse, a concentric ring of vivid blue-green, with violet outside and cinnamon-gold on the inside. The reverse is similarly shaded, if a bit less spectacularly. Some die clashing appears on both sides. Census: 5 in 68, 0 finer (11/09).(#5514)

LIBERTY
1853
UNITED STATES OF AMERICA
QUAR. DOL.

Rare 1853 Arrows and Rays Seated Quarter, PR65 Cameo

2518 1853 Arrows and Rays PR65 Cameo NGC. Walter Breen's *Proof Encyclopedia* records a total of five proofs and Larry Briggs' Liberty Seated quarter reference does likewise, probably following Breen's lead. Breen identifies (citing no reference) the occasion for the pieces' striking on March 3 as the introduction of the new Arrows and Rays subtype, whose business-strike coinage began on April 26. (This remark apparently dates to Harold Newlin in the 1880s, who pegged the striking of proof half dimes to that date. Breen leapt, rightly or wrongly, to the conclusion that all Arrows and Rays proofs were struck at that same time.) The right arrow point nearly touches a dentil; the shield point is over the right base of the 1 in the date. The left base of the 1 is about over the center of a dentil. Light recutting is visible south on the 53 and the right arrow. The bottom of the flag on the 1 is even with the left arrow shaft. On the reverse some faint die file marks are visible above the ER in AMERICA, and some die polish lines in the loop of the Q. Most of these die markers for the proof coinage are documented in either the Breen or Briggs references.

As any serious collector of 19th century proof coinage knows, proof coins of any denomination and year before 1858 or so are quite rare. This piece should be doubly popular, as it is not only incredibly rare in its own right, but it is also a one-year proof representative of the important Arrows and Rays subtype. (While the 1853 and 1854 are often collected and considered as a single type, the 1854 Seated quarters lack the Rays reverse, technically making the two issues distinct subtypes.) The proof 1853 Arrows and Rays quarter is considered the most important proof issue in the Seated Liberty quarter collection.

Although this coin is not attributed as such by NGC, it is clearly the specimen from the Louis E. Eliasberg, Sr. Collection, where Q. David Bowers cataloged it as "MS-64, prooflike," going into extensive detail on why the piece might be a true proof—at least, as that term might apply to coins dated 1853. Among the similarities he cites that are visible on this piece are "delicate champagne toning over mirror surfaces" and the die finishing lines just inside the denticles over stars 11 and 12. A small patch of darker toning midway down Liberty's right (facing) calf is a match, as is the tiny rim crease just above the Liberty cap, between stars 8 and 9 (this is, however, apparently in the die, as some other specimens in the roster below show the same feature). The color plate in the Eliasberg catalog is also a dead match.

The following roster, updated since our Phil Kaufman and Scott Rudolph offerings, shows the present coin to be probably the third finest known of the eight coins enumerated. A few of the pieces may be prooflike business strikes, and there may be some duplication; only five of the following pieces have been certified as proofs.

1. **PR67 NGC.** Heritage (7/2008), lot 1640. Unsold. Different from any of the pieces below.
2. **PR66 Cameo NGC.** Phil Kaufman Collection (Heritage, 8/2007), lot 1785; Scott Rudolph Collection (Heritage, 1/2009), lot 3766, which realized $230,000. This piece matches none of the following coins.
3. **PR65 Cameo NGC. The present coin.** Acquired by J.M. Clapp (as "Uncirculated") at an early date, probably before 1894; John H. Clapp; Clapp estate, 1942, to Louis E. Eliasberg, Sr.; Louis E. Eliasberg, Sr. Collection (Bowers and Merena, 4/1997), lot 1454; Heritage (1/1998), lot 6782; David Lawrence (3/2005), lot 1522; unknown intermediaries. In the Eliasberg catalog, Dave Bowers described this piece as MS64, prooflike, noting "possibly a candidate for 'proof' attribution." Since the time of that sale, it has been certified as a proof.
4. **PR64 NGC.** Jerome Kern Collection (B. Max Mehl, 5/1950), lot 1445; John Jay Pittman (David Akers, 5/1998), lot 1325; Bowers and Merena (8/1999), lot 141; Goldberg Coins (2/2002), lot 704; Superior (1/2004), lot 287.
5. **MS64, prooflike.** Thomas L. Elder; Norweb Collection (Bowers and Merena, 3/1988), lot 1594. Dave Bowers cataloged this as a prooflike business strike in the Norweb catalog, but a decade later Dave Akers included it in his census of proofs.
6. **PR63 PCGS.** Auction '80 (Stack's), lot 1184; Auction '90 (Stack's), lot 143; Stack's (5/1992), lot 2659; Superior (6/1999), lot 2099; Superior (10/2000), lot 4360; Goldberg Coins (5/2001), lot 561; Superior (1/2004), lot 2354.
7. **Proof.** Lester Merkin (6/1968), lot 291; Stack's (10/1990), lot 1638.
8. **Proof.** National Numismatic Collection; Smithsonian Institution.(#85548)

Rare 1856 Seated Liberty Quarter, PR65
Only 25-30 Pieces Minted in Proof

2519 1856 PR65 PCGS. CAC. The Philadelphia Mint began its program of commercial proof production in 1858, when Mint Director James Ross Snowden published ordering instructions and a list of prices for obtaining proof examples of various denominations from that facility. Before that date, no official records were kept of proof production, and the number of coins minted was quite limited. Regarding the 1856 proof mintage, Walter Breen comments, "In some ways this is one of the most difficult and complicated dates of the series." Breen estimates the proof quarter mintage as less than 30 pieces, while Larry Briggs estimates the total as 25+ examples. Proof quarters of 1856 are quite rare in all grades today, with Gem specimens almost unobtainable. NGC has certified four coins in PR65, with two examples finer; while PCGS has graded only one example at the Gem Proof level, with none finer (11/09).

Briggs designates the proof die marriage as combination 10-H, with a diagnostic die bulge on the reverse from the first A in AMERICA to the eagle's wing, down through the arrow shafts to the L of DOL. The present coin features reflective proof surfaces under delightful gray, blue, and violet toning. Numerous die striations are evident in the fields, as usually seen on this issue. The strike is remarkably sharp, with only slight softness on stars 12 and 13. The coin offered here is one of the most attractive survivors from the tiny proof mintage and we expect intense competition from series enthusiasts when this lot is called.(#5552)

BARBER QUARTERS

Outstanding 1893-S Quarter, MS66

2520 1893-S MS66 PCGS. CAC. Breen-4135. Mintmark Far Right. The 1893-S is difficult to locate in all grades and Premium Gems such as the present offering are extremely rare. Radiantly lustrous surfaces exhibit sharply struck design elements and are remarkably well preserved. Cobalt-blue, lavender, and gold-orange toning covers the obverse and is confined to the margins of the reverse. The CAC label affirms the outstanding eye appeal. Population: 2 in 66, 2 finer (11/09).(#5606)

Problem-Free VG8 1901-S Barber Quarter

2521 1901-S VG8 PCGS. CAC. The 1901-S is the unchallenged key to the series, and every collector who takes up the task of completing the Barber quarter set knows that sooner or later he or she will need to face the difficulties—aesthetic and financial—of acquiring one. Most of the examples seen are in the lowest or highest grades, with little material in-between. A quick survey of our own auction offerings reveals many in the Fair-Good range, along with some spectacular high-Mint State pieces. This problem-free VG8 shows a full rim on both sides, with the L, Y, and part of the T visible in LIBERTY. The medium dove-gray surfaces are largely unblemished. (#5630)

Problem-Free 1901-S Quarter, VG8

2522 1901-S VG8 PCGS. Natural bluish-gray patina with soft gold undertones shows on both sides of this key date Very Good representative. The rims are sharp for the grade designation and display a considerable amount of dentilation. Liberty's jawline is strong as is most of the eye and lower ear. L and Y of LIBERTY are clear, as are the tops of I and T. The reverse shield exhibits complete separation from the adjacent wings and tail, and most of the letters in PLURIBUS and the UN of UNUM show clearly. Close inspection with a loupe reveals remarkably clean surfaces for a coin that experienced moderate to heavy circulation. The Barber quarter specialist seeking a nice problem-free '01-S will not want to miss out on this particular offering.(#5630)

Splendid 1902-S Barber Quarter, MS67
Tied for Finest at PCGS

2523 1902-S MS67 PCGS. CAC. The 1902-S quarter is an extremely elusive issue in the Barber series. For many years PCGS had certified but a single 1902-S in MS67, a coin we have had the privilege to handle numerous times since 1994. We at first thought that the present coin was an "old friend" coming back for a return visit—something we always enjoy at Heritage—but it is, in fact, a second example in MS67 that has recently joined the ranks of finest at PCGS. The splendid surfaces on this piece show a mixture of untoned silver-gray mixed with lilac and olive-gray in varying degrees on both sides. As the grade demands, there are essentially no distractions on this piece, although a hint of the normal strike softness appears at the upper right shield corner. The strike elsewhere is quite sharp. As further testament to the elusiveness of this issue, we note that the fabulous John C. Hugon Collection (Heritage, 1/2005), which contained many landmark rarities in the Barber series, managed "only" an MS65 NGC example of the 1902-S. Population: 2 in 67, 0 finer.(#5633)

Dazzling 1909-S Quarter, MS67
Among Finest Certified

2524 1909-S MS67 PCGS. CAC. The 1909-S is infrequently encountered in the better Mint State grades and almost never in the lofty condition of MS67, that of the present specimen. Dazzling luster emanates from immaculately preserved surfaces beautifully toned in peripheral electric-blue and golden-brown. A sharp strike leaves excellent definition on the design motifs save for a touch of softness on the upper right shield corner. Population: 2 in 67, 0 finer (11/09). (#5656)

PROOF BARBER QUARTER

Appealing 1897 PR68 Cameo Quarter

2525 1897 PR68 Cameo NGC. Judging from NGC/PCGS population figures, a fair number of 1897 proof quarters have managed to survive the ravages of time, including several designated as Cameos. Specimens in the lofty grade of PR68, however, such as this Cameo, are extremely elusive.

Satiny motifs appear to be suspended over the deeply mirrored fields. The strike was powerful, leaving complete delineation on the design features, including the upper right shield corner and the arrow feathers and adjacent claw, elements that are sometimes weak. Pastel yellow, violet, orange, green, and lavender coloration resides on both sides, each of which is impeccably preserved. A small planchet chip occurs on the outer left (facing) wing. Census: 7 in 68 Cameo, 0 finer (11/09).(#85683)

STANDING LIBERTY QUARTERS

Near-Mint 1916 Standing Liberty Quarter
Original, Variegated Toning

2526 1916 AU58 PCGS. The February 2007 edition of the magazine *Coins* contains the article "Rare Beauty," by Tom LaMarre, which offers a brief but well-written introduction to the Standing Liberty quarter series:

> "The Mint struck Standing Liberty quarters from 1916-1930. Many collectors consider the design an artistic masterpiece. But it was difficult to strike and did not hold up very well in circulation. So the Mint replaced the Standing Liberty quarter with the Washington quarter in 1932. By then, collectors already prized the rare, first-year 1916 Standing Liberty quarter."

Collectors still do so today, especially high-quality pieces such as this one. This is an unquestionably original example that shows variegated medium to darker gray toning over each side and pale blue toning also across the reverse. Just the slightest touch of friction is seen over the high points. An excellent representative of this scarce and valuable first-year issue.(#5704)

Unusually Lustrous MS62 1916 Standing Liberty Quarter

2527 1916 MS62 ANACS. In his book *Standing Liberty Quarters,* specialist J.H. Cline notes of the 1916 issue: "This coin has long been the most sought-after coin in the series, even more so than the 1918/7-S. The 1916 has, of course, the lowest mintage of all dates and mintmarks, except the overdate." Later, Cline also credits the coin's status as the first of its kind as the primary reason for its popularity, curiously relegating the date's obvious rarity to second place. It has, however, remained a collector favorite since the date of issue. This example has lovely rose toning over each side with a hint of lilac. The mint luster is surprisingly strong for an MS62 and gives this coin an unexpected dimension of desirability. The grade is primarily derived from a couple of short marks in the center of the shield. (#5704)

Uncirculated 1916 Type One Standing Liberty Quarter, Full Head

2528 1916 MS60 Full Head PCGS. While the design change that added a chain mail drape to Liberty is the most famous such alteration to take place during the evolution of the Standing Liberty quarter, it is not the only one. The recessed date revision of 1925 is similarly of great importance, and even among the so-called Type One quarters, there are appreciable differences between coins dated 1916 and those of the next year, as Eric von Klinger describes in an article for the September 24, 2007 edition of *Coin World:*

> "The differences most often pointed out lie in the treatment of Liberty's big toe and the bottom of the gown, in relation to the pedestal with the date. On the 1916, the toe overlaps the pedestal. To the viewer's left of that foot, the bottom edge of the gown is nearly straight and well separated from the pedestal. On the 1917 the big toe is on top of the pedestal; the bottom of the gown is more rounded and closer to the bottom of the pedestal."

The von Klinger article also cites J.H. Cline, who notes a number of additional diagnostics that can clue in a collector that a coin dates to 1916 or 1917, even in the absence of a date. The impressive preservation of this example, however, means that no such subtle diagnostics are needed to identify it. The obverse has an impressive amount of mint luster for an MS60 coin. The reverse, however, displays less 'pop.' Both sides are covered in rose-gray toning, and the reverse is slightly deeper in hue. There are no mentionable abrasions on either side.(#5705)

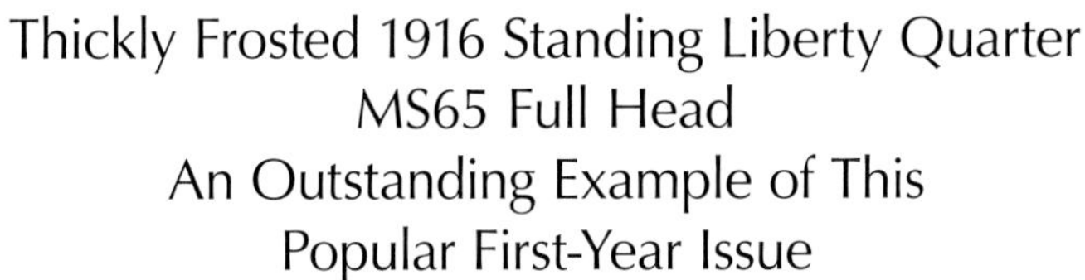

Thickly Frosted 1916 Standing Liberty Quarter MS65 Full Head
An Outstanding Example of This Popular First-Year Issue

2529 1916 MS65 Full Head PCGS. In a *Numismatic News* article dated October 31, 2006, "Philly Standing Liberty Quarters Start Rare," Paul M. Green alludes to the design issues that delayed the Standing Liberty quarter: "There were some problems making final decisions on the new quarter and by the time it was ready for production it was already well into December ... [The branch mints] would have been unable to produce the new coins before the early days of 1917. In fact, Philadelphia barely managed to get the 1916 Standing Liberty quarter out anyway, with a mintage of just 52,000 pieces."

As a result, relatively few examples were available much less set aside, and the date became an instant rarity because of its low mintage. It is avidly sought after in all grades, and is especially elusive in Gem condition. This is a lovely example that displays rich, frosted mint luster with a slight accent of rose and golden color on each side. The strike is sharply defined in all areas, and the only mentionable (but still minute) mark is in the center of the shield.(#5705)

Rare Gem Full Head 1918-S Quarter

2530 1918-S MS65 Full Head PCGS. The 1918-S at 11 million coins had, by far, the largest S-mint coinage of the entire Standing Liberty quarter series. However, an unintended consequence was a high percentage of coins lacking a Full Head. Cline's reference estimates that only about 3% of the issue has Full Head details. Some of the examples are "just made it" coins, but this piece is definitely not such a piece, and it is quite rare as such. A clear ear hole and three olive sprigs are blatantly visible, with complete separation of the brow and hairline all along the profile. A couple of shield rivets are faint, as normal. This piece has lustrous silver-gray surfaces with good eye appeal overall. Population: 32 in 65 Full Head, 6 finer (11/09).(#5725)

Choice AU 1918/7-S Quarter

2531 1918/7-S AU55 NGC. The extensive popularity of the 1918/7-S quarter reaches well beyond specialist circles, since overdates as a class have their own adherents and enthusiasts. In "The Ten Top Error Coins," an article in the June 1996 edition of *Coins* by Al Doyle, the 1918/7-S Standing Liberty quarter ranks at #6 on the list, which also includes other memorable overdates, such as the Denver and Philadelphia 1942/1 dimes and the New Orleans and Philadelphia 1887/6 Morgan dollars. Similarly, this charming piece is sure to rank highly with the successful bidder. Only slight, even wear is seen over the high points, and each side displays muted gray patina with a tinge of golden. A few shallow field marks are seen on the reverse, but none are worthy of individual mention.(#5726)

Bright AU58 1918/7-S Standing Liberty Quarter

2532 1918/7-S AU58 PCGS. FS-101, formerly FS-008.5. The overdated 1918/7-S quarter presents a significant challenge across the grading scale. The date, which was on an exposed plaque until a design change for 1925, would wear away quickly and thus take away what would otherwise make a lower-grade coin distinctive. At the high end, by contrast, few 1918-S quarters of any stripe were saved at all, making better-grade coins similarly elusive and significantly reducing the pool of upper-tier overdate survivors. This is a bright, uniformly untoned example that retains nearly complete mint luster. Just the slightest hint of high point friction can be seen when the coin is closely examined. The striking details are surprisingly strong for the issue, and Liberty's head detail is almost complete.(#5726)

Sharply Struck 1919 Quarter MS67 Full Head

2533 1919 MS67 Full Head PCGS. The 1919 quarter is relatively available through the Premium Gem level of preservation, even with a Full Head. Superb Gems with fullness in Liberty's head, such as the coin in the present lot, are extremely scarce, however, and finer examples are virtually unobtainable.

A well executed strike transcends the fullness in Liberty's head to include boldness on the chain mail, rivets, and inner shield. Even the date digits, that are often weak in the first 1 especially, are strong. Lustrous surfaces are color free except for barely discernible wisps of light tan on the lower left reverse. A couple of unobtrusive minute marks do not detract. Population: 11 in 67 Full Head, 2 finer (11/09). (#5729)

Incredible 1928-S Quarter MS68 Full Head

2534 1928-S MS68 Full Head NGC. The obverse of this incredible coin is mottled in hues of emerald, amber, and violet, with untoned silver peeking though the interstices. The reverse offers more moderate charcoal-gray and ice-blue patina with untoned areas. Both sides display generous luster. A thoroughgoing examination under a loupe fails to reveal even the slightest mark, as expected of the lofty grade. Three clear olive sprigs appear, although a couple of the shield rivets are missing. This MS68 Full Head coin is one of only two so certified at NGC, and there are, understandably, none finer (11/09).(#5771)

Rare O-106 1794 Half Dollar, Fine 15

2535 1794 Fine 15 PCGS. O-106, Low R.6. This variety is identified by the following: on the obverse, star 2 is attached to the lowest curl, and star 1 is well below the curl; on the reverse, there are 21 berries, the only reverse with such (10 left and 11 right).

A medley of sky-blue, lavender, yellow-gold, and gray patination covers both sides of this Choice Fine half dollar. The design elements exhibit relatively strong definition for the type and designated grade. The expected number of contacts for a moderately circulated coin are evident, but notable adjustment marks are lacking.(#6051)

Late State 1794 O-101a Half Dollar, XF45

2536 1794 XF45 NGC. O-101a, High R.3. Star 1 pierces the low curl. The reverse has a die crack from the wreath to the border between UNITED and STATES, and another crack through the F to the wreath, following the branch upward toward the final S. This is the usually seen 1794 variety, although none of the 11 die varieties are encountered with any frequency. Probably half of all 1794 half dollars are from the O-101 die marriage, and few of those survivors can match the grade and quality of this piece. There are only about a dozen finer examples, including all states of the O-101 die combination.

There were two deliveries of 1794 half dollars, including 5,300 pieces on December 1, 1794, and 18,164 pieces on February 4, 1795. Those two deliveries account for the entire mintage of 23,464 coins. The current population of the variety suggests that half of all 1794 half dollars struck at the Mint were from this die pair, which tells us that certainly some, and probably all 1794 O-101 half dollars were actually minted in 1795.

This piece has distinctive toning with sea-green, deep blue, and iridescence blended together, along with splashes of ivory that retain some luster. The surfaces are lightly abraded as expected, although mostly hidden beneath the toning. A few moderate adjustment marks, mostly on the reverse, are also hidden beneath the toning. Census: 16 in 45, 17 finer (11/09).(#6051)

Near-Census 1795 O-117 Half Dollar, AU50

2537 1795 2 Leaves AU50 PCGS. O-117, R.4. Housed in a green-label PCGS holder, this amazing 1795 half dollar faint bluish-gray patina over lighter silver surfaces with a trace of champagne toning on each side. The surfaces are lightly marked as expected for the grade, although none of those marks are severe, and they should not be confused with the clash marks that are also present on both sides. Overton states that the field is unfinished beneath the chin, although the marks in that region also appear to be clash marks. This is an early die state before the obverse cracked below the bust point. Only about 10 AU or better examples of this variety have been sold in auctions over the last decade, and most of those are the late die state coins.

From The Chandler Collection, Part Two.(#6052)

Medium to Deeply Patinated 1806/5 Half Dollar, O-102, MS63

2538 1806/5 MS63 PCGS. O-102, R.3. The top of the underdigit 5 is visible near the top of the 6. The stars are large, and star 12 is recut with a broken point near the highest point of star 13. This is called a six-berry reverse; however, it usually only shows five berries because of heavy die clashing (which is the case here). More easily attributable by the bold line to the right of the upper right corner of the shield. A die crack runs through the tops of UNITE and another from N to the wing.

Medium to deep bluish-purple toning covers both sides with brownish-green peripheral accents. The design elements are well struck except for the usual softness on the eagle's breast and neck. A few light ticks do not detract. Population for the issue: 1 in 63, 0 finer (11/09).(#6077)

Satiny 1806 O-109 Half Dollar
MS62 Pointed 6, No Stem

2539 1806 Pointed 6, No Stem MS62 PCGS. O-109, R.1. This lovely example has all of the characteristics of the O-109a die state, with the exception of the obverse die crack through star 12. Other cracks are present, clash marks are plain, obverse stars and reverse letters are drawn to the edge, and only a few remnants of the border denticles are visible. A sharp strike imparts excellent, nearly full design definition on both sides, with satiny silver luster beneath ivory, lavender, and peripheral steel-blue toning. Although a common variety, few finer examples are known. Population: 6 in 62, 13 finer (11/09).(#6073)

Splendid 1806 Half Dollar, O-118
MS62 Pointed 6, Stem

2540 1806 Pointed 6, Stem MS62 NGC. O-118, R.3. On this Pointed 6, Stem variety, the left side of the Y is recut, while the T is not. A leaf points below the right side of I in AMERICA. There are five berries, four with long stems. Two tiny die defect lines appear above the right shield tip—one just left of the tip, one below the second U in UNUM.

This splendid type coin offers original pinkish-gold centers with ice-blue margins. Considerable luster is evident, and although a couple of minor abrasions explain the grade, the eye appeal is strong. Numerous tiny peripheral die cracks appear on the reverse. (#6071)

Possibly Finest 1806 O-116 Half Dollar, MS65

2541 1806 Pointed 6, Stem MS65 PCGS. CAC. O-116, R.3. The boldly recut TY in LIBERTY immediately identifies this obverse, which was used with four different reverse dies to coin O-114, 115, 116, and 117. O-115 is the usual variety seen with this obverse, while O-116 is next, followed by O-114 and O-117. It is believed that the Overton sequence of O-114 through 117 is the same order that these coins were originally minted.

This Gem shows the prominent die crack through the date and all stars on the left, continuing through the centers of LIB, and in the other direction to the border below the final star. A branch crack is seen outside the first three stars at the left, and an additional crack starts at the outer point of star 7 and joins the tops of LIBER. The recutting on T remains bold, while the recutting on Y is weakened due to die erosion. The reverse has a crack from below the tail to the tops of all letters in UNITED STATES. Clash marks are evident near OF.

A few high grade examples of O-116 are known, including this piece and the MS65 NGC coin that we sold in our May 2009 CSNS sale. These two are probably tied for the finest known examples of the variety, and they are followed closely by two or three MS64 coins, and a few MS63 pieces, the latter including the lovely Eliasberg specimen.

This remarkable example has fully lustrous, frosty silver surfaces beneath rich gold, cobalt-blue, pale green, and lilac-brown toning on both sides. It is fully original and attractive with typical design definition. The hair details behind the forehead are a trifle indistinct and the base of the wing just left of the shield is similarly weak. However, the surfaces are pristine and the overall aesthetic appeal is exceptional. Population: 6 in 65, 4 finer (11/09).(#6071)

The Overton Plate 1807 O-115 Half Dollar Rarity, VF20 The Finest of Four Known

2542 1807 Draped Bust VF20 PCGS. O-115, High R.7. This is the finest of just four known examples of the recently discovered 1807 O-115 half dollar. The first example was located in June 2004, and three additional pieces have been found since. The others grade Fine 15, Fine 12, and VG8. The O-115 variety number is out of sequence, since O-111 through O-114 are all Capped Bust half dollars.

The obverse is a newly discovered die with the T in LIBERTY slightly higher than the neighboring R, higher above the R than on any other 1807 Draped Bust obverse. The reverse was also used for 1807 O-103 and O-104. There is no evidence of the reverse die crack found in late states of O-103, so the O-104 and O-115 varieties were both struck before O-103.

This wonderful piece is fully original with deep silver-gray and steel patina, showing minor splashes of lighter silver color. The surfaces are exceptional with only a few insignificant abrasions. (#6079)

Splendid 1807 Draped Bust Half O-108, MS64

2543 1807 Draped Bust MS64 PCGS. O-108, R.3. This die pairing is easily identified by star 7's position well above the base of the L in LIBERTY. On the reverse the F in OF is missing its right foot. This splendid near-Gem, certified in a green-label holder, is struck from late-state dies that show numerous cracks. Much of the obverse periphery is covered with a series of interconnected cracks, and the reverse die is in an equally advanced state close to total failure. This silver-white piece shows just a hint of golden coloration, but save for a single scrape behind Liberty's eye there are remarkably few singular abrasions. No adjustment marks are present. Population: 10 in 64, 7 finer (11/09).(#6079)

BUST HALF DOLLAR

Magnificent 1831 Half Dollar, MS66
Finest Known of the O-111 Variety

2544 1831 MS66 PCGS. CAC. O-111, R.1. A wavy die crack joins the digits of the date and extends left and right from the date. A similar crack joins all left-side stars, and another joins stars 8 through 10. On the reverse lines 2 and 3 of stripe 1 are joined, although slightly separated at their tops, and the right side of the I in PLURIBUS is centered under the second T in STATES.

This boldly lustrous Premium Gem piece is extremely well struck for the issue, although die erosion draws the peripheral elements toward the rims. Its overall eye appeal, however, is off the charts, with light silver-gray and champagne centers delicately tinged with iridescent blue and lilac. A couple of unobtrusive dotlike indentations on the lower bust are of no consequence. The finest known of this variety, listed in Herrman, August 2009. Population for the issue: 4 in 66, 0 finer (11/09).

Ex: Pittman Collection, Part III (David Akers, 5/1998), lot 1496; Franklin Collection Part 2 (Stack's, 1/2008), lot 471.(#6159)

SEATED HALF DOLLARS

1845-O No Drapery Half Dollar, MS64
Tied for Finest Certified

2545 1845-O No Drapery MS64 PCGS. CAC. From a large mintage of more than 2 million pieces, the 1845-O Seated Liberty half dollar is an available date in lower circulated grades, becomes scarce in AU, and is rare in Mint State. For all varieties, PCGS has certified nine in MS64 and only two in MS65. Even rarer is the 1845-O No Drapery that is offered here, with only two MS64 PCGS coins and none finer (12/09).

The No Drapery variety is a late die state with excessive die polishing removing the drapery at Liberty's elbow. While many partial drapery pieces exist with remnants of the drapery remaining, the true No Drapery pieces are extremely rare.

The present coin is a memorable example, with bright luster and semiprooflike fields. Both sides have a slight overlay of golden-rose patina, with a scattering of russet and blue around the borders. The luster is so strong the coin seems brilliant, despite the attractive toning. Fully struck in all areas except star 7, which is only sharp. A coin worthy of the finest collection of Seated Liberty half dollars and sure to inspire spirited bidding when this lot is called.(#6250)

Popular 1854-O Arrows Half, MS66

2546 1854-O Arrows MS66 NGC. When the weights of half dimes through half dollars were slightly reduced in 1853, newly minted examples featured arrows at the date to distinguish them from the earlier coins. Rays were also added to the reverse of quarters and halves, which created a one-year type. The rays were removed the following year, but the arrows remained until 1856, at which point the original design was resumed. The 1854-O, with its mintage of more than 5 million pieces, is popular as a representative of the two-year Arrows at Date, No Rays type. Despite its relatively high mintage, the '54-O is rare in MS66 and virtually impossible to locate any finer. PCGS and NGC combined report only four pieces finer (11/09).

A hint of rose toning accents the mostly silver-gray surfaces of the present coin. The strike is razor-sharp at the centers, while the stars around the obverse show some softness. Both sides are remarkably clean and exhibit powerful luster throughout. This exceptional piece would be a welcome addition to even the finest collections. (#6280)

Desirable 1854-O Arrows Half, MS67

2547 1854-O Arrows MS67 NGC. While the 1854-O Arrows Seated half dollar had an enormous mintage of more than 5 million pieces, its status as a mintmarked high-mintage With Arrows half puts it in the "sweet spot" for type collectors. The present piece is one of only two Superb Gems certified at NGC and PCGS combined, and there are only two finer (9/09). While the surfaces of this lovely coin are still largely brilliant silver-gray, glints of translucent pink, gold, and jade appear, enhancing the already considerable eye appeal. Both dies were well used by the time this coin was minted, showing numerous die cracks and minor rim breaks. Census: 1 in 67, 2 finer (11/09).(#6280)

CONFEDERATE STATES OF AMERICA

1861 Confederate Restrike Half Dollar, MS63

2548 1861 Scott Restrike MS63 PCGS. Breen-8002. In 1879, dealer J.W. Scott acquired the reverse die used to mint the Confederate half dollars, of which only four original specimens are known. Scott then obtained a supply of original 1861-dated half dollars and proceeded to grind off the reverse design of each coin. Using the one-sided coins as planchets, Scott restruck 500 examples of the CSA issue for sale as promotional items at $2 each. The items were reasonably popular, appearing at auction as early as the J.N.T. Levick Collection (Woodward, 5/1884), lot 2467, "The Confederate Half Dollar, 1861; rev., Struck from the original die; silver, fine, and becoming very scarce." According to David Proskey, Scott sold about 250 of his restrikes in early offerings, and maintained a supply for over 30 years, eventually raising the price to $15 per piece.

The method of manufacture caused a flattening of the obverse design in the CSA restrikes, readily apparent on this example. The reverse design is sharply defined and shows much brightness in the fields. Mostly untoned, with light gray patina in places. Population: 10 in 63, 5 finer (11/09).(#340402)

SEATED HALF DOLLARS

Rare, Pleasing 1867 MS66 Half Dollar

2549 1867 MS66 PCGS. The 1867 half dollar, with a circulation strike mintage under half a million pieces, is a better date overall and rare in Mint State. Indeed, PCGS and NGC have certified only 100 pieces in all grades. Mint State examples are rare.

Electric-blue, lavender, and golden-brown patination concentrates at the margins of this Premium Gem, more extensively so on the obverse. Lustrous surfaces exhibit crisply struck design features, none of which reveal even a hint of weakness. This is a well cared for piece showing just a couple of trivial marks. Population: 2 in 66, 1 finer (11/09).

Ex: Superior (9/1999), lot 1291.(#6321)

Important 1870-CC Half Dollar, VF35

2550 1870-CC VF35 PCGS. The Carson City Mint began production in 1870 with quarters, half dollars, silver dollars, half eagles, eagles, and double eagles. All denominations are scarce or rare, and every 1870-CC coin, regardless of its denomination is in high demand. This pleasing piece falls just short of XF, with minor blemishes on each side that are consistent with the grade. It is an excellent piece that will fit nicely in a Seated half dollar collection, an 1870-CC denomination set, or a Carson City type set. Population: 12 in 35, 22 finer (11/09).(#6328)

Handsome 1872-S Gem Half Dollar From the Eliasberg Collection

2551 1872-S MS65 PCGS. CAC. Ex: Eliasberg. WB-102. Medium-Small Mintmark. The 1872-S ranks among the most elusive San Francisco Mint Seated half dollars, as indicated by perusal of PCGS/NGC population data.

Soft violet, gray, orange, blue, and beige patina is slightly deeper on the obverse of this lovely Gem, and a well executed strike imparts sharp detail to the design elements. The planchet shows striations on both obverse and reverse, but are more obvious on the reverse, and the partially prooflike fields offset the motifs at various angles. Exquisitely preserved throughout. A handsome coin with a great pedigree! Population: 2 in 65, 0 finer (11/09).(#6335)

New Style 1873-CC Half Dollar MS64 Arrows at the Date

2552 1873-CC Arrows MS64 PCGS. CAC. Arrowheads were placed beside the date on all half dollars minted after April 1873 to indicate a small weight change in the planchet. The new coins contained slightly more silver than their earlier counterparts, and were designed to have an exact metric weight of 12.5 grams. At the Carson City Mint, 214,560 half dollars were struck using the new standard in 1873. The issue is scarce in all grades today, and Mint State examples are rare. NGC has graded four coins at the MS64 level, with two finer; while PCGS has certified seven examples in MS64, with two finer (11/09).

The coin offered here is sharply struck throughout, with attractive steel-gray toning, accented by horizontal streaks of russet and lilac. The surfaces show a minimum number of handling marks for the grade. Since this issue is virtually unobtainable at the Gem level, the present specimen represents an important opportunity for advanced type collectors and half dollar specialists.(#6344)

Shining Superb Gem 1879 Half Dollar

2553 1879 MS67 PCGS. CAC. Type Two Reverse. Like the Seated half dollar issues of the 1880s, the 1879 coins, minted in the wake of the passage of silver-purchase legislation, had only a token mintage of circulation-strike pieces while unwanted silver dollars were made by the millions. Despite the meager mintage, a number of high-grade examples have survived, including this Superb Gem, which is housed in a green label holder. Both sides are immensely lustrous with considerable reflectivity. Occasional hints of cloud-white and champagne toning visit surfaces that shine silver-white elsewhere. Population: 13 in 67, 2 finer (11/09).(#6361)

PROOF SEATED HALF DOLLARS

Ex: Kaufman 1839 No Drapery Half, PR62
One of Only Three Proofs Believed Known

2554 **1839 No Drapery PR62 NGC.** Ex: P. Kaufman. To the best of our knowledge, the Kaufman 1839 No Drapery proof half dollar is one of only three pieces known. We trace its provenance to F.C.C. Boyd and World's Greatest Collection. It appears to be the only late die state example, with a bisecting reverse crack that is unseen on the other two examples.

All three known 1839 No Drapery proof half dollars appear to have a crack extending through the outer parts of MERICA and HALF DOL, continuing to a point below the left (facing) wing (an interesting question that arises here is why the Mint would use a cracked reverse die to strike proofs), and the proofs have several other characteristics that distinguish them. The Kaufman coin is identified by the following: an additional bisecting crack from the reverse rim at 7 o'clock that travels through the leaf and eagle's left (facing) leg, the lower shield, middle of the left wing, to the right foot of the R in AMERICA; and a heavy clash mark within the lower right reverse shield.

A second example, the Hawn specimen, is easily distinguished by a spot over the right upright of the N in UNITED. It also lacks the bisecting reverse crack. That piece most recently appeared in our January 2007 FUN sale, lot 988. Additionally, its pedigree can be traced to the Stack's August 1973 sale of the Reed Hawn Collection, lot 125, and it has appeared in several sales during the last 10 years.

The third 1839 No Drapery half dollar appeared in the October 1996 Stack's sale, lot 300. A small chip out of the edge above first S of STATES identifies it.

The three known examples of this proof rarity are:

1. **PR64 PCGS.** Reed Hawn (Stack's, 8.1973), lot 125; Bowers and Merena (8/1999), lot 199; Goldberg Coins (2.2001), lot 1752; 2002 ANA Sale (Superior), lot 973; Heritage (1/2004), lot 5941; Richmond Collection (David Lawrence, 3/2005); Heritage (1/2007), lot 988.
2. **PR62 NGC.** F.C.C. Boyd (World's Greatest Collection, Numismatic Gallery, 4/1945), lot 246; 1946 ANA (Abe Kosoff), lot 812; Stack's (3/1965), lot 440; 1976 ANA (Stack's, 8/1976), lot 1172; Stack's (12/1985), lot 942; Worrell Collection (Superior, 9/1993), lot 712.
3. **Proof.** Stack's (10/1996), lot 300. Unknown previous pedigree.

Additional appearances:

A. PR63 PCGS. Heritage (9/2002), lot 13257; Heritage (12/2002), lot 19261.

B. Will W. Neil (B. Max Mehl, 6/1947), lot 474.

C. 1948 ANA, lot 1766.

The Kaufman coin, with the additional bisecting reverse crack and the reverse clash mark, was likely the last of the three 1839 No Drapery proof half dollars to be struck.

Several additional attributes stand out on the Kaufman coin that are sure to draw the attention of the Seated Liberty proof aficionado. It possesses delightful field-motif contrast, regardless of the angle from which it is viewed. While not designated a Cameo on the NGC holder, deeply mirrored fields highlight the frosty devices. The rims are bold and squared off, and exhibit fully struck dentilation. An impressive strike provides complete definition on the design features that appears to further accentuate the contrast with the fields. Brilliant fields display barely discernible wisps of sky-blue and gold-tan color under magnification, slightly more so on the obverse. A scattering of inoffensive contact marks and some faint hairlines in the fields are all that preclude the achievement of a significantly higher grade. Indeed, this imposing PR62 coin has fewer marks than seen on many finer-graded pieces.(#6381)

Extremely Rare 1849 Half, PR65
Ex: Phil Kaufman

2555 1849 PR65 NGC. Ex: P. Kaufman. This splendid Gem 1849 proof half dollar pedigrees to the Floyd Starr Collection, though this is not indicated on the NGC insert. While NGC and PCGS have certified a total of 10 specimens, at least three are probably resubmissions, as numismatic researchers are in agreement that no more than six or seven examples exist. An analysis of appearances known to us results in the following roster:

1. **PR66 NGC**. John Jay Pittman (David Akers, 5/1998), lot 1536; Rarities Sale (Bowers and Merena, 8/1999), lot 205; George "Buddy" Byers (Stack's, 10/2006), lot 1150. (We are unable to locate an appearance of a PCGS-graded PR66; perhaps it is the same as this specimen.)

2. **PR65 NGC**. The Kaufman coin. Floyd T. Starr Collection (Stack's, 10/1992), lot 549; Superior (7/1993), lot 421.

3. **PR64 NGC**. The Richmond Sale, Part III (David Lawrence, 3/2005), lot 1793.

4. **PR64 PCGS**. Long Beach Sale (Heritage, 9/2005), lot 3265. Catalogers note that a contact mark on Liberty's eye brow identifies the coin.

Additional Appearances.

A. **PR64**. Louis E. Eliasberg, Sr. Collection (Bowers and Merena, 4/1997), lot 1947.

B. **Brilliant Proof**. James A. Stack Collection (Stack's, 3/1975), lot 453.

C. **Brilliant Proof**. John Work Garrett Collection, Johns Hopkins University (Stack's, 3/1976), lot 214.

Iridescent cobalt-blue toning, imbued with splashes of orange and lavender, dominates the obverse of the Kaufman coin, while slightly deeper hues of blue uniformly spread across the reverse. A well executed strike imparts razor-sharp definition to the design elements. Close inspection reveals no mentionable contact marks or hairlines. A beautiful example of this extremely rare issue. (#6393)

BARBER HALF DOLLARS

Outstanding 1892 Barber Half Dollar, MS67

2556 1892 MS67 PCGS. CAC. The 1892 is the most readily available date in the Barber half series in high grades, because the collecting public saved considerable numbers in the first year of issue. Even this "common" issue, however, is anything but available in this lofty condition; PCGS has graded just 11 coins as MS67, with only one finer (11/09).

The appeal of this piece is instantaneous and enormous, beginning with copper-gold surfaces laced with jade-green, aqua, mauve, and amber. The strike is bold and shows little of the reverse weakness so often seen. A tiny planchet lamination in the area of the designer's initial B on the bust truncation is neither easily visible nor distracting. Finally, the luster is excellent, a final affirmation of this outstanding coin's Superb Gem status.(#6461)

All-Brilliant 1899-S Barber Half, MS67 Tied for Second Finest Certified

2557 1899-S MS67 NGC. This coin is stark white in color and highly lustrous. The surfaces are pristine and show virtually no handling ticks or milling marks, as one would expect for this exemplary grade. Even the strike is superb, with no signs of weakness seen, even on the eagle's claws and the clutch of arrows. This piece is identifiable by a minor speck located just below the upper right star on the obverse. This piece is simply amazing, as the surfaces, luster, and strike are so close to perfection. NGC and PCGS have graded a combined five pieces this high with a single coin graded higher (11/09). (#6485)

Sensational 1904-O Barber Half, MS66

2558 **1904-O MS66 PCGS.** The 1904-O Barber half dollar is one of the major condition rarities in the series, despite a mintage well in excess of 1 million coins. Most entered circulation and are now well worn, if they survive at all. This amazing piece is housed in an older generation PCGS holder and exhibits intense silver frost with iridescent splashes on both sides. The strike is remarkably well executed with only slight weakness at the lower reverse. The right edge of the shield, arrow feathers, and eagle's tail feathers are weak, but all remaining detail is strong. In the 16 years since this Superior offered this coin, PCGS has only certified three more in MS66 and just two finer coins. Population: 4 in 66, 2 finer (11/09).

Ex: Superior (5/1993), lot 584.(#6499)

Stunning Superb Gem 1907-D Half

2559 1907-D MS67 PCGS. CAC. As conditionally rare Barber halves go, the 1907-D gets little press. Neither a particularly low-mintage date (over 3.8 million pieces struck) nor a heavily saved one, the 1907-D simply slipped through the cracks at the time of issue, and to a certain extent, it continues to do so. Heritage, however, recognizes the rarity of the 1907-D half dollar in MS67; PCGS has certified just three examples at that level and none finer (11/09). With the offering of this Superb Gem, Heritage will have auctioned all three of those coins.

The memorable FUN 2005 auction brought the first, described as "a 'common' variety in a very uncommon state of preservation." The virtually brilliant Superb Gem hailed from the famous Eliasberg Collection. The second appearance came at FUN 2009, when the Dale Friend Collection contained another Superb Gem; this coin, rather than brilliant, had attractive blue and green-gold toning across each side.

The present piece exhibits similar colors, albeit in a different pattern, and it cannot be the Dale Friend piece, since that coin was certified with a blue-label, pedigreed insert, whereas this example is housed in an old green label holder. Like its fellows, it is immensely lustrous beneath the patina. Though the strike is slightly soft on Liberty's head and the stars, the overall eye appeal is exceptionally rewarding. For the Registry collector who missed the Eliasberg and Friend coins, this is a rare second chance at a second chance. (#6509)

Exceptional 1917-S Obverse Gem Half Dollar

2560 1917-S Obverse MS65 NGC. The 1917 half dollar with the S mintmark on the obverse, coming from a mintage of less that 1 million pieces, is difficult to locate through near-Gem. Gems are rare and finer pieces are nearly unobtainable. Indeed, NGC and PCGS have each graded two MS66s and PCGS has seen one MS67.

Attractive luster exudes from the satiny surfaces of this Gem that display a veneer of light champagne-gold with soft bluish-violet accents, being slightly deeper in shade on the reverse. Liberty's branch hand is well defined, the thumb completely separated from the branch. The usual weakness shows in the eagle's trailing leg. This piece is especially exceptional in that it is devoid of notable marks; the '17-S Obverse is one of the most challenging issues to locate with relatively smooth surfaces.(#6572)

Important 1919-D Select Half Dollar

2561 1919-D MS63 PCGS. The 1919-D is a leading strike and condition rarity in the Walking Liberty half dollar series. Mint State coins are difficult to come by, and in addition to its usual weak strike, the luster quality is often inferior.

MS63 specimens such as the example in this lot are a significant find. Its above average luster enlivens both sides, each of which displays soft beige-gold and violet patina. The design elements exhibit the typical weakness in the centers, though a modicum of definition shows in the branch hand. Fewer and less severe marks are apparent than what might be expected for the Select grade level.(#6578)

Elusive 1919-D Half Dollar, MS63

2562 1919-D MS63 PCGS. CAC. One of the most elusive issues in the Walking Liberty series in high grade, the 1919-D was not well-struck at its inception, and most examples seem to have circulated widely. The present example is attractive, with powder-gray surfaces and good luster. The strike is better than average for the issue, although it is still noticeably soft on the high points of each side. All of the peripheral elements are well-detailed, and the head and breast have a fair strike. The only singular abrasion is a horizontal tick at Liberty's knee. Population: 51 in 63, 79 finer (12/09).(#6578)

Bold Superb Gem 1945-S Walker

2563 1945-S MS67 PCGS. The 1945-S Walking Liberty is probably a somewhat overlooked issue in the series, since it suffers from comparisons with more illustrious dates such as the 1941-S and 1942-S. But at the Superb Gem level of the present piece it is nearly as rare as those coins, and it is much more elusive than the 1943-S. For example, PCGS has certified this piece as one of only four in MS67, with none finer, while the 1943-S has 25 at that level. (The 1941-S and 1942-S have six and one, respectively, in MS67.)

This coin is untoned silver-white, with pristine, reflective surfaces. Although a fully struck 1945-S likely does not exist, this piece shows at least some separation at the thumb, and a good if not full strike elsewhere. Some fuzzy marks on the reverse slab are *not* on the coin. Population: 4 in 67, 0 finer (12/09).(#6626)

PROOF FRANKLIN HALF DOLLARS

Intense 1954 Franklin Half Dollar
PR68 Deep Cameo

2564 1954 PR68 Deep Cameo PCGS. Analysis of certified population data reveals the extreme importance of this coin. While PCGS has certified more than 4,200 proof 1954 Franklin half dollars, only 71 of those coins have received the Deep Cameo designation. Numerically, that service has graded 113 examples in PR68 or better, but just four of those are certified as PR68 Deep Cameo, and only one coin has been called PR69 (11/09).

This piece has fully brilliant silver surfaces with seemingly endless mirrored fields and intense mint frost on the devices. There is no evidence of toning on either side without the use of strong magnification. A remarkable coin that will add many points to the Set Registry collection of proof Franklin half dollars.(#96695)

2565 No lot.

Extremely Rare 1959 Franklin Half Dollar
PR67 Deep Cameo

2566 1959 PR67 Deep Cameo PCGS. This lovely Cameo proof is housed in an older green-label holder and has fully brilliant silver surfaces and no evidence of toning aside from a hint of gold on the raised rims. The surfaces are essentially flawless. Deep Cameo proof 1959 Franklin half dollars are among the greatest rarities in the series. Only the 1950 has a lower total population in Deep Cameo proof. In all grades PCGS has certified six Deep Cameo proofs of 1950, and just 17 each of 1952 and 1959. Following those are the 1951 and 1953 proofs with 38 each carrying the Deep Cameo designation. Population: 6 in 67 Deep Cameo, 2 finer (11/09).(#96700)

Ultimate 1960 Franklin Half Dollar
PR69 Deep Cameo

2567 1960 PR69 Deep Cameo PCGS. Until such time as NGC or PCGS certifies a Franklin half dollar as PR70, the PR69 Deep Cameo is the ultimate coin in the series. PCGS has certified 75 such pieces across the entire series, including 39 dated 1956, 11 dated 1962, and 16 dated 1963. That leaves just nine coins for all other dates combined.

This amazing coin is housed in an older green-label PCGS holder and exhibits stunning mint frost on the devices, with unfathomably deep mirrored fields on each side. The surfaces show incredible proof brilliance with "black and white" contrast.(#96701)

EARLY DOLLARS

Pleasing 1795 B-5, BB-27 Dollar, AU50

2568 1795 Flowing Hair, Three Leaves AU50 NGC. B-5, BB-27, R.1. The diagonal bar in the upper left obverse field is plainly visible on this piece. The reverse has a short extension from the left stem end, similar to a die crack but seemingly constant on all observed pieces. While rather weakly defined at the centers, the peripheral definition is strong. Both sides have satiny silver-gray luster with traces of pale gold and light blue toning. Numerous tiny surface marks are evident on each side, but none are significant. The obverse has a tiny rim bump at 7 o'clock that is partly hidden by a tab from the holder.(#6852)

Splendid 1795 B-7, BB-18 Three Leaves Dollar, AU50

2569 1795 Flowing Hair, Three Leaves AU50 PCGS. B-7, BB-18, R.3. Although a slightly scarcer variety, this is one of three AU examples of the same die marriage in the present sale, certainly providing collectors with a choice of quality. This piece is housed in a green-label PCGS holder and it features light silver-gray surfaces, with deeper steel toning around the devices. The obverse and reverse surfaces have moderate handling marks, yet it is still a splendid piece for the grade. Minor adjustment marks on the reverse are visible outside the wreath, concentrated near TE of STATES and before the first A in AMERICA.

From The Chandler Collection, Part Two.(#6852)

Familiar B-5, BB-27 1795 Flowing Hair Dollar, AU53

2570 1795 Flowing Hair, Three Leaves AU53 PCGS. B-5, BB-27, R.1. Bowers-Borckardt Die State III. Blue-green and russet shades overlie the slate-gray obverse. The reverse has rich mottled cobalt-blue and stone-gray patina. Mint-caused adjustment marks cross the central obverse and make a peripheral appearance near the date and the L in LIBERTY. However, both sides are nearly unabraded save for a faint mark beneath star 8 and an inconspicuous pinscratch aligned with the contour of Liberty's neck. Luster shimmers from the hair, stars, wreath, and legends. The familiar Bolender-5 variety is readily identified by a diagonal die line behind Liberty's highest hair curl. (#6852)

Marvelous 1795 Flowing Hair, Three Leaves Silver Dollar, B-7, BB-18, AU55

2571 1795 Flowing Hair, Three Leaves AU55 PCGS. B-7, BB-18, R.3. Die State I. On this Three Leaves variety with the Head of 1794, there is a pair of berries below the first S in STATES, and star 15 points well below the bust tip. This variety is generally found in the lower grades. Bowers' *Silver Dollar Encyclopedia* estimates that 500 to 800 examples exist in all grades.

This is a marvelous example, with original, problem-free grayish-gold surfaces on both sides. Only a light whisper of wear touches the surfaces, and the only relevant mark is a nick well-hidden in Liberty's rear hair curls. Some planchet adjustment marks appear in the central reverse.

This appears to be the third-finest B-7, BB-18 that we have ever offered since we began maintaining our Permanent Auction Archives, behind the Eliasberg MS64 specimen and the AU58 PCGS coin in this sale. For all Three Leaves varieties, PCGS has certified 45 in this grade, with 63 finer—and it is a sure bet most of them are the R.1 B-5, BB-27. Since PCGS began attributing varieties, the finest B-7, BB-18 dollar they have certified is a single AU50.(#6852)

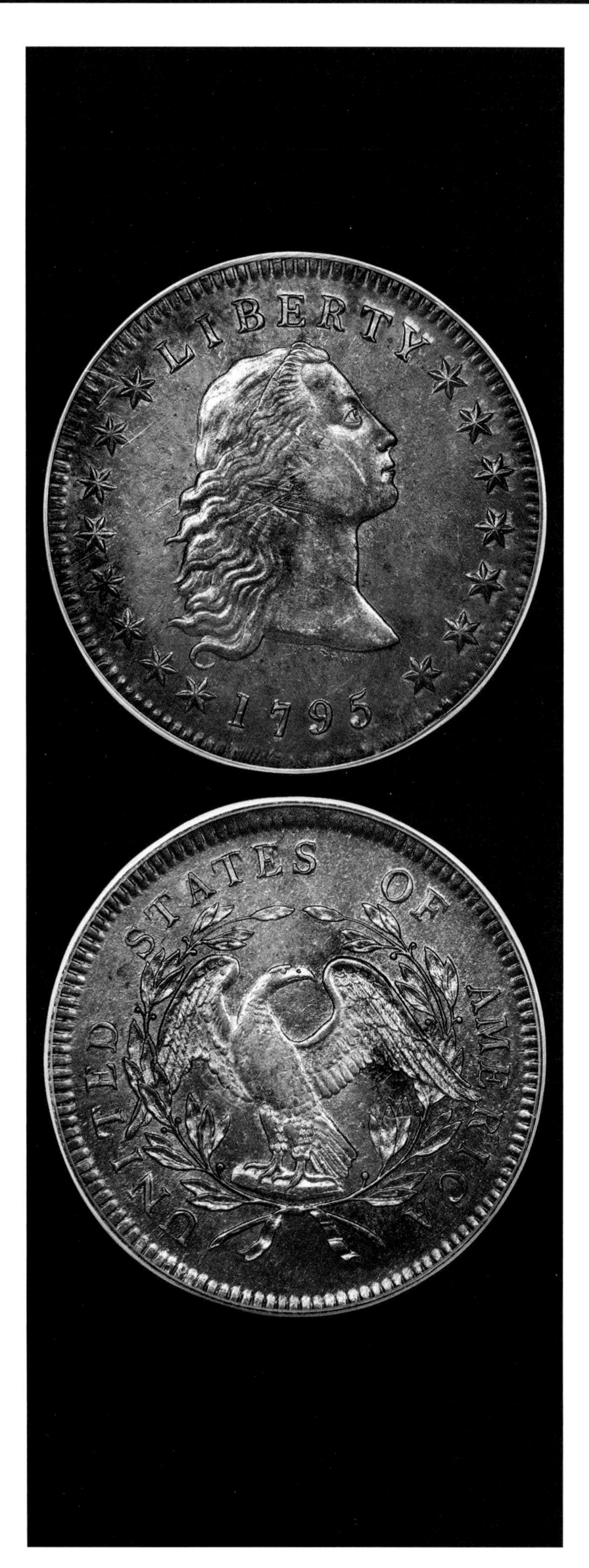

1795 Flowing Hair Dollar, AU58
Three Leaves, B-5, BB-27
Pleasing Original Surfaces

2572 1795 Flowing Hair, Three Leaves AU58 PCGS. B-5, BB-27, R.1. Records indicate the Flowing Hair obverse design was retired on October 10, 1795, after a large mintage of 160,295 pieces. Fifteen different Flowing Hair die varieties are known for the date, and two more of the Draped Bust type. The present coin is an example of the Bolender-5 variety, the most available of the Flowing Hair type. Flowing Hair dollars were only struck for two years, and as the 1794 is a famous rarity, type collectors are obligated to select 1795 examples for their sets.

The first work on early silver dollar die varieties was the Haseltine *Type Table* (John W. Haseltine, 11/1881). The work was actually an auction catalog of Haseltine's personal collection, including attribution guides for all known die varieties. Lot 82 was the Bolender-5 coin:

> "1795; No. 5; wide date; the lower curl is more perfect than in any of the preceding and is not near the stars, but above them; the hair terminates in 6 points; the third and fourth points are close together; rev., heavy wreath; 6 berries on right and 7 on left; there are 3 leaves under each wing of the eagle (there being only 2 in any of the preceding); the eagle's right wing passes behind a cluster of 5 leaves; strictly uncirculated; sharp and boldly struck; mint lustre; very rare in this condition."

Today, early dollar specialists know to look for a bar behind the uppermost hair lock, which provides ready attribution for the familiar variety.

This coin is a pleasing early dollar specimen. Mint luster glows under the moderately toned surfaces. A soft mix of antique-gold and steel-gray deepens toward the margins. A small patch of crisscrossing adjustment marks is present on the portrait, but the surfaces are pleasing otherwise. Unlike most survivors of the type, there are no rim bruises. The patina appears consistent and original. Population: 44 in 58, 19 finer (11/09).(#6852)

Gorgeous 1795 B-7, BB-18 Dollar, AU58

2573 1795 Flowing Hair, Three Leaves AU58 PCGS. B-7, BB-18, R.3. The date is widely spaced. The lowest curl is small and perfect, touching the innermost point of star 1. The reverse is the only Three Leaves reverse with 14 berries, seven on each branch half. There is only one berry on the left branch half between the eagle's wing and the bow.

This piece is housed in an older green-label holder from before the era when PCGS began offering variety attributions. The obverse die was used to strike BB-16, 17, and 18 (B-20, B-18, and B-7, respectively) and the reverse die was used to strike BB-18 and BB-19 (B-7 and B-19). All the other varieties are extreme rarities, so the B-7, BB-18 silver dollar represents the only opportunity to acquire representatives of both dies. A complete set of 19 Flowing Hair dollars of 1795 includes nine that are either R.7 or R.8. However, a collection of dollars representative of all the different obverse and reverse dies can be accomplished with 13 coins and only six that are considered R.7 or R.8.

This exquisite near-Mint example is slightly soft at the centers, including the hair behind the ear and the eagle's breast, but with ample detail everywhere else. The flowing locks are fully separated and the stars exhibit complete details. The eagle's head, wing, and tail elements are bold, and the leaves in the wreath are fully delineated. The strike is nicely centered with complete borders on both sides. The surfaces are frosty and lustrous with light silver-gray color, deeper gray on the high points, and gold and iridescent toning in the fields. A few trivial marks in the left obverse field are the only imperfections on otherwise wonderful surfaces. Population: 44 in 58, 19 finer (12/09).

From The Chandler Collection, Part Two.(#6852)

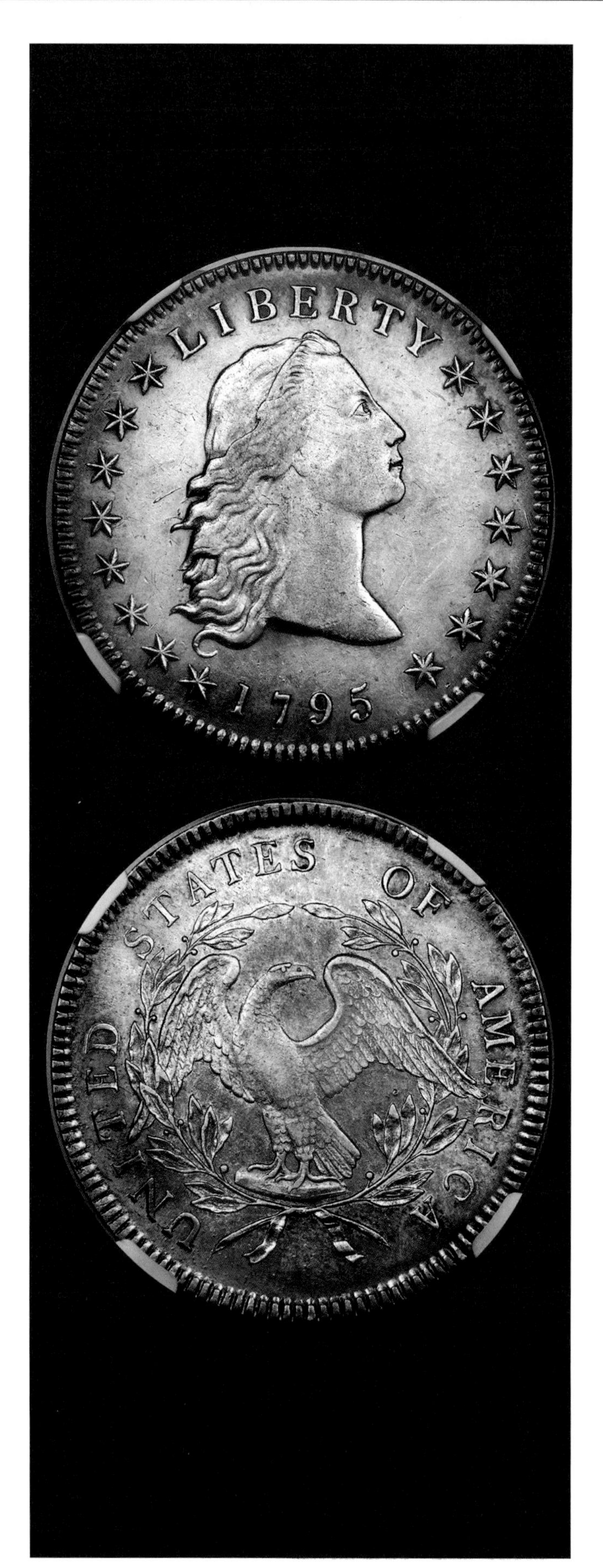

Lovely 1795 B-5, BB-27 Dollar, AU58

2574 1795 Flowing Hair, Three Leaves AU58 NGC. B-5, BB-27, R.1. Bowers-Borckardt Die State III. The B-5, BB-27 is the most available early dollar variety. Specialists in the series, and even some more-casual collectors, know to look for the telltale extra tine or bar of metal behind Liberty's upper lock in back of her head. There are six rear hair curls, with the third and fourth quite close, and the lowest curl is distant from star 1. The figure of Liberty is deeply punched into the die, producing a higher relief on the coin than the other 1795 Flowing Hair varieties. Because of the high relief, examples wore faster on the hair.

The Three Leaves reverse has 13 berries arranged seven left, six right, and there are four leaves below the first S in STATES. The reverse die was also used to produce the BB-25 and BB-26, but the die state for BB-25 has only three leaves under the S of STATES (presumed to be a clogged die that prevented one leaf from striking). On this BB-27 (as on many examples and the BB-25), a crack joins the left stem end and the border, according to the BB reference; that feature is clearly visible on this piece. It is possible that the "crack" is actually a die scratch, as it seems to be constant on most observed specimens. The absence of the crack on BB-26 indicates those coins were produced first. The reverse has numerous raised die pits over much of its surface.

The present piece is somewhat lightly struck at the centers, as nearly always for the variety. Wispy abrasions are consistent with the grade. This lovely example has pleasing light silver-gray at the centers, framed by peripheral iridescence. Faint champagne toning highlights the central design elements.(#6852)

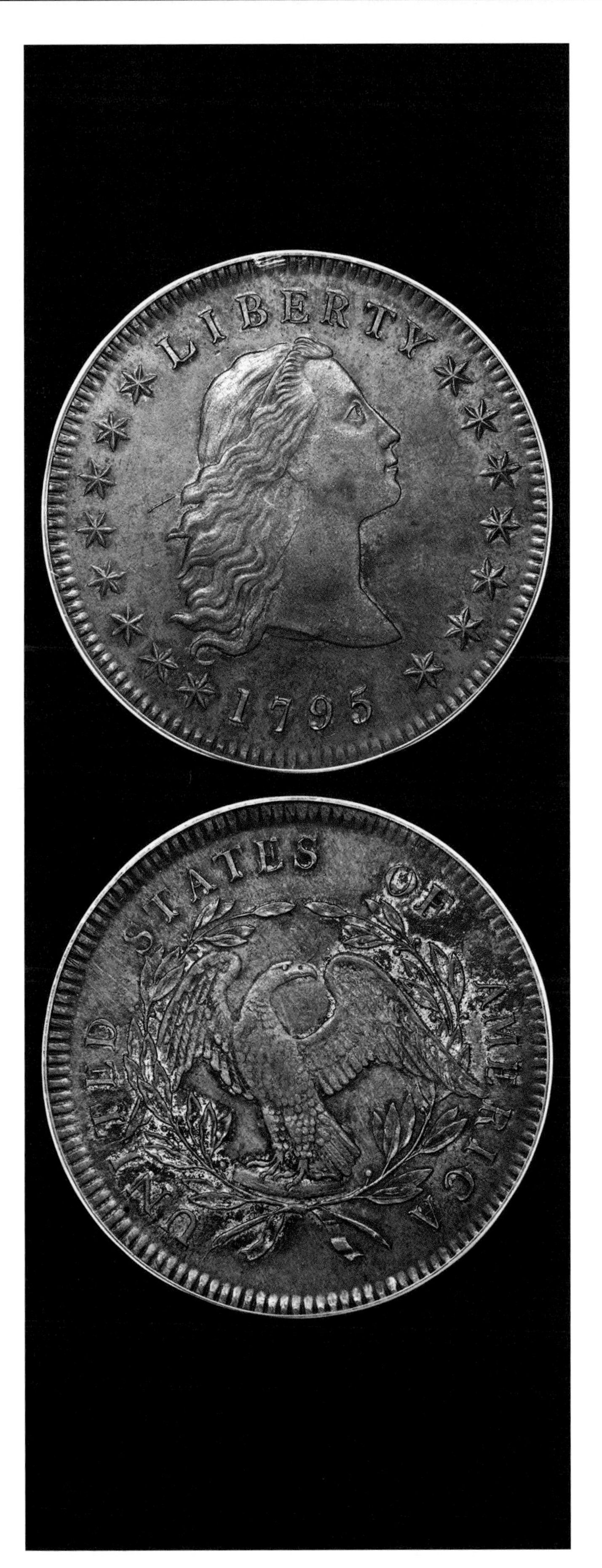

1795 Early Dollar, MS62
Flowing Hair, Three Leaves, B-5, BB-27
Popular Type Coin

2575 1795 Flowing Hair, Three Leaves MS62 PCGS. B-5, BB-27, R.1. Only 1,758 silver dollars were minted in 1794, due to inadequate facilities for coining such large silver coins. A larger screw press had to be designed to provide sufficient striking pressure to fully bring up the design details. Once the new press was installed, Mint officials felt they had to make up for lost time. Accordingly, a large mintage of 160,295 Flowing Hair dollars was achieved by October, followed by 42,738 more dollars of the Draped Bust type before year's end. A total of 17 different die marriages are known for 1795, with 15 Flowing Hair varieties and two of the Draped Bust design. The coin offered here is a representative of the BB-27 variety, characterized by the presence of a 2 mm "bar" near the uppermost curl, pointing diagonally to star 5. The popular BB-27 variety is the most available die marriage of the Flowing Hair type. Type collectors compete avidly with series specialists to obtain an example of this early dollar issue.

Knowledge of early dollar die varieties was widespread after John W. Haseltine published his *Type Table* in 1881. Although catalogers did not always attribute early dollars by Haseltine numbers, many made some effort to differentiate between the more obvious varieties. An interesting example of BB-27 was described in lot 2678 of the George Earle Collection (Henry Chapman, 6/1912):

> "1795 Head in center of field. Curl free of stars. Small cut in the die back of the head. Small scratch before eagle. Three leaves under each wing of eagle. Uncirculated. Brilliant mint lustre. Milling around edge not struck up on half of the circumference; also shows some of the planchet file marks. Very rare in such a mint condition. *Plate.*"

Chapman was correct about the issue's rarity in Mint State. The date is rare at the MS62 level, as PCGS has certified only four coins in this grade, with 11 finer (11/09).

The present coin is deeply toned in shades of steel-gray and light brown, with occasional glimpses of blue. Mint luster shines through the toning in protected areas, particularly near the wreath. Striking details are sharp, and handling marks are minimal for the grade.(#6852)

Sharp 1795 B-2, BB-20 Dollar, AU Details

2576 1795 Flowing Hair, Two Leaves PCGS Genuine. B-2, BB-20, R.3. The PCGS number ending in .94 suggests Altered Surfaces as the reason, or perhaps one of the reasons, that PCGS deemed this coin not gradable. In our opinion, this coin has the details of an AU specimen that has been lightly tooled. The surfaces have mottled blue and subdued gold toning intermingled with lighter gray. The B-2, BB-20 variety is immediately recognized by the short diagonal bar inside star 4. The obverse die was also used for B-19, BB-19, a R.8 variety, but that variety has a Three Leaves reverse.(#6853)

Handsome AU53 1795 Flowing Hair Dollar Two Leaves, B-1, BB-21

2577 1795 Flowing Hair, Two Leaves AU53 PCGS. B-1, BB-21, R.2. Golden-brown overall with electric-blue, olive-green, sun-gold, and ruby-red hues near the rims. This richly toned type coin displays luster throughout design recesses, and neither side has any remotely relevant marks. The eagle's breast and portions of the right (facing) wing display wear, but considerable plumage detail remains. Obverse wear is limited to the highpoints of the hair and cheek. The typical Flowing Hair dollar grades VF, and attractive AU examples are seldom encountered. Population: 14 in 53, 38 finer (11/09). (#6853)

Important 1795 B-4, BB-14 Silver Dollar Silver Plug, VF20

2578 1795 Flowing Hair, Silver Plug VF20 PCGS. B-4, BB-14, R.3. As seen here, the B-4, BB-14 die combination is known with mint inserted silver plugs, and one example is known that was struck over an existing 1794 silver dollar. That combination, along with the existence of a 1794 silver pluigged dollar, suggests that the silver plug experiment took place early in 1795, and may be an additional clue toward development of a conclusive emission sequence for these coins.

This specimen has pleasing pewter-gray surfaces with traces of pale gold patina. The silver plug is bold and complete on both sides, although lacks most of the obverse design detail. A highly important study piece representing early Mint technology.(#6854)

Certified 1795 Silver Plug Dollar B-7, BB-18, VF35

2579 1795 Flowing Hair, Silver Plug VF35 NGC. B-7, BB-18, R.3. Medium gray surfaces exhibit hints of lilac and blue, with lighter reddish-tan on the devices, and a splash of lighter silver color at the lower left obverse. Both sides have the usual minor handling marks that are expected for a coin of this grade and age. Wavy marks across Liberty's neck and jaw suggest the irregular outline of a mint inserted silver plug, intended to adjust the weight of the planchet to the standards of the time. The absence of readily visible adjustment marks suggest that the planchet was initially underweight, and that the silver plug served to bring the planchet up to standard weight. (#6854)

Fabulous 1795 Draped Bust Dollar, MS64
First Year of Design, B-15, BB-52

2580 1795 Draped Bust, Centered MS64 NGC. B-15, BB-52, R.2. The present coin is a magnificent example of this early date silver dollar, with a combination of high technical grade and aesthetic appeal that is seldom equaled. Certain to be a highlight of any collection of early dollars or advanced type set. Writing in 1993, Q. David Bowers estimated a surviving population of 12-18 examples of this date at the Choice Mint State level. Allowing for resubmissions, Bowers evaluation coincides well with current population data. Only 17 coins have been certified in higher numeric grades at both NGC and PCGS combined (6/09).

The year 1795 saw the introduction of the appealing Draped Bust design on the silver dollar. Modeled after a sketch by prominent portraitist Gilbert Stuart, the draped bust was an artistic improvement on the sturdy flowing hair design of the previous year. Stuart's model was the beautiful Philadelphia socialite Anne Willing Bingham. Official records indicate an initial mintage of 42,738 Draped Bust dollars in 1798, small by silver dollar standards. Only two die varieties are known for the date, with the coin offered here representing the less available BB-52 variety.

Early collectors prized the Draped Bust dollars, and the study of die varieties began at an early date. The BB-52 variety was first described in Haseltine's Type Table Sale (Haseltine, 11/1881), lot 91. Haseltine's description reads, "1795 No. 15; fillet head; head well centered; curl not touching the star; the date closer to the lower star on the left; rev., wreath has 6 berries; fine." The lot realized $2.52. Haseltine's auction catalog became the standard reference for attributing early dollars until Bolender's treatise superseded it 70 years later.

The present coin is fully struck throughout, with fine detail on all design elements. The strong devices are complemented by reflective fields. The surfaces are enhanced by lovely tones of golden-brown, with accents of lilac over the central devices. A few horizontal adjustment marks are seen across the eagle's legs. Overall visual appeal is magnificent.(#6858)

Lustrous 1795 B-14, BB-51 Dollar, AU50

2581 1795 Draped Bust, Off Center AU50 PCGS. B-14, BB-51, R.2. Neither of the two 1795 Draped Bust varieties are especially rare, but they are seldom encountered in higher grades. The bust was entered into the die right of center, translating to a bust that is left of center on the struck coin. Slight high point wear is present on this pleasing piece, but the overall appearance is delightful, with attractive champagne and pale gray toning on both sides. Housed in a green-label PCGS holder, this piece retains considerable mint luster on both sides.

From The Chandler Collection, Part Two.(#96858)

Lustrous 1796 B-2, BB-63 Dollar, AU55

2582 1796 Small Date, Small Letters AU55 PCGS. B-2, BB-63, R.4. Six die varieties are known for 1796 silver dollars, and two of the six are exceedingly rare. The other four are each scarce. The six varieties are distributed across three major categories.

The 1796 Small Date, Large Letters dollars are B-4, BB-61 and B-6, BB-64, the latter variety currently listed as R.8.

The 1796 Small Date, Small Letters dollars are B-3, BB-62, B-2, BB-63, and B-1, BB-66, the first variety currently considered R.8.

The 1796 Large Date, Small Letters dollars are B-5, BB-65, and they are instantly recognized by the large die chip at IC of AMERICA.

This piece is a remarkably fine example of the variety with sharp design details, satiny luster, and only a trace of rub on the high points. Both sides have light gold and iridescent toning to heighten its eye appeal.(#6859)

Elusive, Popular XF45 1797 9x7 Stars Silver Dollar, Small Letters, B-2, BB-72

2583 1797 9x7 Stars, Small Letters XF45 PCGS. B-2, BB-72, R.4. The highest wave of hair on Liberty's head is lightly impressed in the die, and a heavy lump appears in the obverse field below star 9. The reverse shows a berry directly under A of STATES. The reported mintage of 7,776 silver dollars struck for the year is certainly too small, and the likelihood is that many thousands of examples were struck in 1798 using 1797-dated dies. As Bowers points out in his *Silver Dollar Encyclopedia,* each of the three known varieties of the year is a distinct subtype: 1797 9x7 Stars, Large Letters (B-1, BB-73); 1797 9x7 Stars, Small Letters (B-2, BB-72); and 1797 10x6 Stars, Large Letters (B-3, BB-71). Each is also listed in the *Guide Book,* further increasing their popularity among the many collectors who attempt to assemble variety sets using that reference.

This is an elusive variety, although due to the confusion regarding mintage figures its rarity has been overstated in the past. The current rarity rating we assign, R.4, reflects a "very scarce" variety rather than an extremely rare one. This piece has medium dove-gray surfaces with good eye appeal despite a few small, darker charcoal areas on each side. The reverse shows the central softness and lapped denticulation typical of the variety, but there are no visible adjustment marks or singular abrasions. A pleasing example of this perennial collector favorite.(#6866)

Spectacular 1798 B-13, BB-108 Dollar, MS61

2584 1798 Large Eagle, 10 Arrows MS61 NGC. B-13, BB-108, R.3. The obverse is easily identified by a die flaw between the bust and star 13, and there is a die crack from the rim to the lower right serif of the L in LIBERTY. Only 10 arrowheads are visible on the reverse, a telltale diagnostic for this die. After striking BB-107 the reverse die was lapped, and the five small berries now have faint or nonexistent stems. Although this variety is relatively available in grades through XF, the Bowers-Borckardt reference states that it is "exceedingly rare" in Mint State. Their list of notable specimens, while not quite a Condition Census, features only three Uncirculated examples, two of which grade MS60.

Hints of gold and rose around the margins accent the mostly medium gray surfaces of this exquisitely preserved representative. There are prominent adjustment marks in the center reverse, with a corresponding area of weakness on Liberty's hair. Plenty of luster radiates throughout the fields and enhances the eye appeal. This is a Die State IV piece, with a die crack from the rim below the 17 in the date that progresses through the first five stars. A spectacular representative from the first year of the Heraldic Eagle reverse. (#6876)

Appealing 1799 B-8, BB-165 Silver Dollar, MS60

2585 1799 7x6 Stars MS60 NGC. B-8, BB-165, R.3. Die State I, with the flaw at the final S visible, but not reverse die cracks. In practice, this variety is usually recognized by the small die flaws at the top of the S. The B-8, BB-165 die combination is relatively plentiful, although far from a common variety. Only a few Mint State pieces are known, including five that were listed in the Notable Specimens section of Dave Bowers' *Silver Dollar Encyclopedia*. This masterpiece has deep blue and iridescent toning over satiny, reflective surfaces. It is sharply struck, even at the centers, with exceptional eye appeal.(#6878)

Important 1799 B-5, BB-157 Dollar, MS61

2586 1799 7x6 Stars MS61 PCGS. B-5, BB-157, R.2. Die State III, with reverse die cracks. The reverse die is defective with the upper left serif of the U in UNITED missing, and that same feature is seen on two other reverse dies used to produce six varieties. BB-157 has the right edge of the upright of the E in STATES over the space between two clouds, BB-158 through 161 have the E in STATES centered over a cloud space, and BB-168 has the cloud space right of center below the E, along with a horizontal crack across the entire reverse die.

This lustrous Mint State piece has splendid ivory and gold color over satiny silver surfaces with excellent eye appeal. NGC certified the Eliasberg specimen as MS64, a coin that we offered four years ago. The next best example of B-5 in our auction archives is AU58. Only a handful of Mint State pieces are actually known, perhaps a dozen in all grades, including the present piece. An excellent opportunity.(#6878)

Important 1799/8 B-1, BB-142 Dollar, MS61

2587 1799/8 13 Stars Reverse MS61 NGC. B-1, BB-142, R.4. Bowers-Borckardt Die State III, the most common, with significant crumbling of the reverse die at the I of AMERICA. Both the B-1 and B-2 varieties are very scarce, and since the 1799/8, 13 Stars Reverse type merits its own listing in the *Guide Book*, the collector going by that reference must acquire an example of both varieties. This Mint State representative of the former has soft, pleasing luster beneath dappled green-gold and lavender-violet patina. A few faint field marks near the chin appear only when viewed from exotic angles. Great overall eye appeal.(#6884)

Shimmering 1799 B-15, BB-152 Dollar, MS63

2588 1799 Irregular Date, 13 Stars Reverse MS63 PCGS. B-15, BB-152, R.3. Bowers Die State IV. The Irregular Date variety with 13 Stars on the reverse is an important major Guide Book variety, and this die combination, struck from a reverse that was previously used in 1798, is the only one of its kind for 1799. The latest die states with extensive cracks on both sides is the most commonly encountered die state of the variety. The present example is extraordinary for its quality, and ranks among the finest known. Dave Bowers wrote in 1993: "Most examples of 1799 BB-152 are in lower grades. Any coin grading AU or better is especially notable. Only a few Mint State coins are known."

In the Bowers -Borckardt reference, one notable specimen was called MS60, another was called AU55, and three others were called AU50. The Cardinal Collection contained an MS64 PCGS example, and that coin was called "the finest known example by a considerable margin." That coin is the MS60 piece from the Notable Specimens list, and now resides in the Hesselgesser Collection. It seems that the present example is the second finest known, and nearly equal to the other Mint State piece.

This piece has shimmering, satiny luster beneath deep steel toning with traces of lilac and gold. Slight weakness is noted on the high points, but the remaining design elements are boldly defined. It is a thoroughly pleasing and attractive example, and ranks among the major early dollar offerings of the past several years.(#6880)

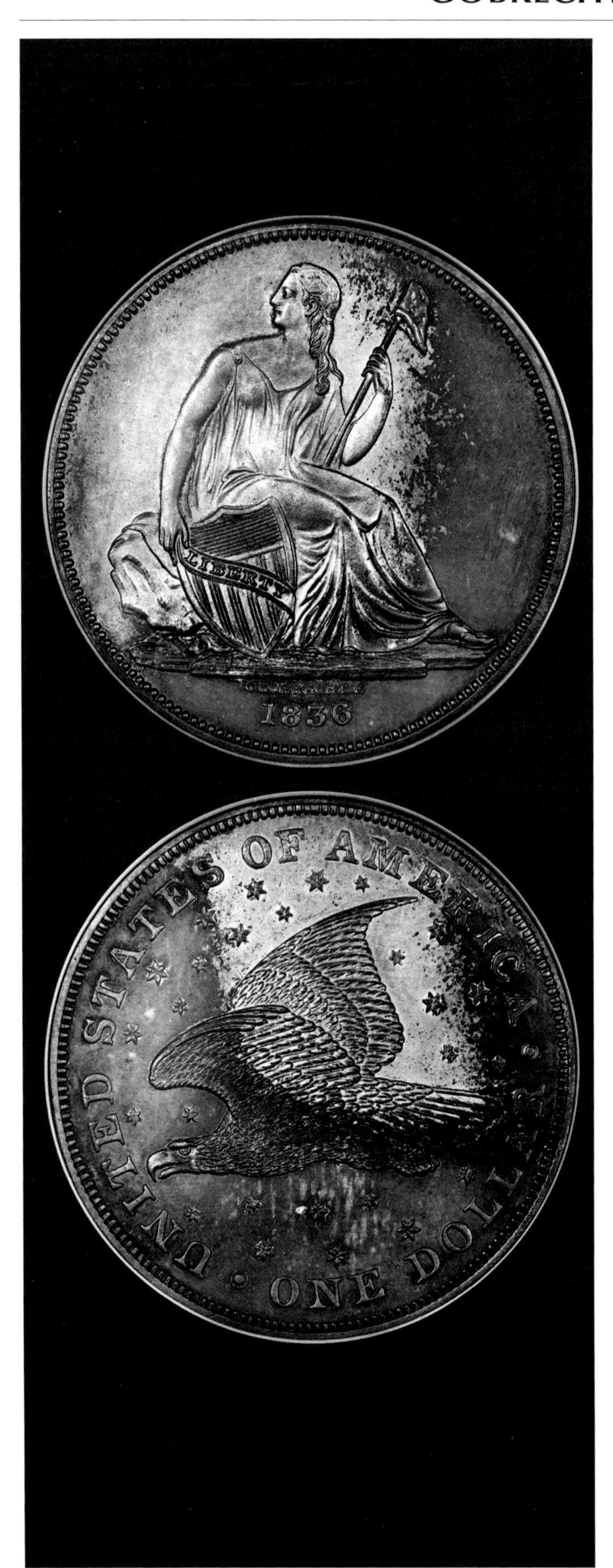

1836 Name Below Base Gobrecht Dollar
PR64 Die Alignment IV, Judd-58 Restrike
One of the Classics of U.S. Coinage

2589 1836 Name Below Base, Judd-58 Restrike, Pollock-61, R.6(?), PR64 NGC. Silver. Plain Edge. Die Alignment IV (center of Liberty's head opposite right side of F in OF). The Name Below Base Gobrecht dollar first acquired its legendary status from Edward Cogan in 1867, when he claimed only 18 pieces had been struck. There is no documentary evidence to support this low figure, and based on the number of observed specimens, it is generally believed that today fewer than 60 examples are known.

One of the curious features of the Name Below Base dollars was recently discovered by John Dannreuther. The Name Below Base dollars are actually struck from a die that had C. GOBRECHT F. effaced from the base! The die is from the same name-removed hub as the 1838 and 1839 dies. This places the striking period not in 1836, as the coin would indicate, but rather in a later restriking period. The non-appearance of an 1836 Name Below Base in the Roper Sale (1851) is significant as it further underlines these pieces were not available until several years later.

The Die Alignment IV Name Below Base dollars are significantly scarcer than their Die Alignment III counterparts. The reverse die cracks through NITED STATE and OLLA are much fainter than the same cracks seen on Die Alignment III coins. It is generally believed the Die Alignment IV coins were made in the late 1850s, rather than one of the later striking periods when Henry Linderman was mint director.

The fields on this piece have glass-like mirrored reflectivity, a finish that is certainly more consistent with a late-1850s proof striking than the finish seen on Original 1836 dollars. Much silvery-white brilliance is seen on each side next to a wide crescent of rich russet toning. Two tiny planchet flakes in the left obverse field are the only pedigree identifiers (other than the distinctive toning) that can reasonably be used to track the provenance of this piece.

The Name Below Base Gobrecht dollar is one of the classics in American numismatics, and this is one of the finest examples we have seen in recent years.(#11217)

Lightly Handled 1836 Gobrecht Dollar
Die Alignment I, Judd-60, PR58

2590 1836 Name on Base, Judd-60 Original, Pollock-65, R.1, PR58 ICG. Silver. Plain Edge. Die Alignment I (the center of Liberty's head is opposite the DO in DOLLAR). 413 grains. The straight-line die clash mark above the eagle's wing is plainly evident, an indication of this piece's striking period in late December 1836. This piece is an excellent example of the curious nature of Gobrecht dollars. The 1836 pieces were struck in proof format, but were intended for distribution in the channels of commerce. This piece was only lightly handled before it was pulled and set aside. The fields show the reflectivity one would expect from a coin struck on specially prepared planchets, and each side has medium gray-blue variegated toning. The surfaces are remarkably unaffected by handling marks and the most apparent surface defect is a tiny planchet flaw on the left facing, upper arm of Liberty.(#11225)

Brightly Mirrored 1836 Gobrecht Dollar
PR62, Judd-60, Die Alignment I

2591 1836 Name on Base, Judd-60 Original, Pollock-65, R.1, PR62 PCGS. Silver. Plain Edge. Die Alignment I (the center of Liberty's head is opposite the DO in DOLLAR). The diagonal, straight die clash mark above the eagle's wing is plain, and identifies the coin as a later December striking. Although noticeably hairlined, the fields show much deeper reflectivity than usually seen. Also, the striking details are absolutely full in all areas, including the head of Liberty, the toes, and center of the eagle's breast. Each side is generally brilliant, but there is a light accent of golden patina around the margins.
From The Chandler Collection, Part Two.(#11225)

1836 Judd-60 Restrike Gobrecht Dollar, PR40

2592 1836 Name on Base, Judd-60 Restrike, Pollock-65, R.5, PR40 NGC. Silver. Die Alignment IV (center of Liberty's head opposite the right side of F in OF). These pieces were struck for regular circulation in March, 1837, but were coined in medallic alignment. Because of the time spent in circulation, the normally seen die cracks are not apparent on this coin. The surfaces show lovely, multicolored toning in shades of lilac and rose with a gray undertone. The high points shows even wear with no singularly mentionable marks on either side. An attractive, problem-free Gobrecht dollar. (#11227)

1839 Gobrecht Dollar, Die Alignment IV Judd-104 Restrike, Proof, AU Details

2593 1839 Name Omitted, Judd-104 Restrike, Pollock-116, R.3—Reverse Spot Removed—NGC. Proof. AU Details. Silver. Reeded Edge. Die Alignment IV (center of Liberty's head opposite the right side of the F in OF). Reported to weigh 411.3 grains according to the Gardner catalog. Die Alignment IV 1839 dollars are found in two variants. Those with no cracks are believed to have actually been struck in 1839, while those with microscopic cracks through MERI and other reverse letters are believed to be later restrikes done between 1857 and 1859. The cracks on the reverse of this piece are extremely faint. The surfaces show handling marks that are consistent with and AU Details net grade. On the reverse, there are two tiny planchet voids above the eagle. A much larger one is in the field below the eagle, and pinscratching is seen within that planchet flaw. That is how the Stack's cataloger saw the coin in 2005 also. Apparently NGC believes this area to be an area where a spot was removed. That's a mighty large spot to remove. Each side has gray-golden centers that deepen to russet and blue around the margins. The striking details are strong throughout.

Ex: Laurence H. Gardner Collection (Stack's, 3/2005), lot 86.(#11446)

1839 Restrike Gobrecht Dollar, PR60
Judd-104 Restrike, Die Alignment IV
A Bright, Lightly Toned Example

2594 1839 Name Omitted, Judd-104 Restrike, Pollock-116, R.3, PR60 PCGS. Silver. Reeded Edge. Die Alignment IV (center of Liberty's head opposite the right side of the F in OF). The usually seen die cracks on the reverse that characterize restrikes are extremely faint on this coin. So much so one might question their existence altogether. However, strong magnification does show some faint micro-cracking between E and R, but we do not see it anywhere else. The surfaces are obviously cleaned, but the fields still retain surprising reflectivity for the grade. Each side is light gray overall with noticeable dabs of light rose and pale blue color also present.
From The Chandler Collection, Part Two.(#11446)

1839 Gobrecht Dollar, PR64
Judd-104 Restrike
Rarely Seen Die Alignment III

2595 1839 Name Omitted, Judd-104 Restrike, Pollock-116, R.3, PR64 NGC. Silver. Reeded Edge. Die Alignment III (coin turn, center of Liberty's head opposite the N in ONE). The consignor has owned this coin for decades, and while its weight is not stated on the insert, he stated it weighs 412.35 grains. The majority of 1839 dollars are found in Die Alignment IV (center of Liberty's head opposite right side of F in OF). The Die Alignment III pieces, such as this coin, are believed to have been made in very limited numbers, perhaps 18-20 pieces are believed known today. It is reasonable to assume that the Die Alignment III 1839 dollars were struck at the same time as the Die Alignment III 1836 dollars, a time period believed by Gobrecht experts Jim Gray and Mike Carboneau to be in the late 1860s (or perhaps even later).

To further underscore the above assumptions about Die Alignment III 1839 dollars, it is worth noting that most are found today in high grade—probably PR63 as an average. This is an absolutely splendid example of this Gobrecht rarity. The fields are deeply reflective and display a finish that is consistent with proof coins produced in the 1860s and 1870s. Each side has even golden-rose toning, and there are occasional dabs of cobalt-blue around the obverse rim. By way of identifying marks, there is a patch of hairlining in the right obverse field, and on the reverse two milling marks are located in the field beneath the first T in STATES.

Our auction records reveal that we have only offered seven examples of this die alignment out of the 30 total 1839 Gobrecht dollars we have offered at public auction over the past nine years. An obvious opportunity for the advanced specialist.(#11446)

SEATED DOLLARS

Desirable 1846-O Seated Dollar, MS63

2596 1846-O MS63 PCGS. CAC. The 1846-O Seated Liberty dollar is the first silver dollar coined at any of the branch mints. A small mintage of 59,000 pieces was accomplished, and the coins circulated extensively in the Mississippi Valley. The issue is available in circulated grades today, but Mint State coins are rare. Q. David Bowers comments, "A top grade 1846-O is an object of desirability. In MS-63 or better grade it is a prime rarity."

The present coin has bright, semiprooflike fields, as often seen on Seated dollars. The reflective surfaces are overlaid with attractive layers of original toning. Pale shades of lilac and rose predominate, with occasional highlights of deeper blue. All design elements are sharply defined, and the surfaces are free of obvious defects. Population: 8 in 63, 1 finer (11/09).(#6933)

1853 Seated Liberty Dollar, MS64
Scarce Heavily Exported Date

2597 1853 MS64 PCGS. Only 46,110 Seated Liberty silver dollars were coined in 1853, a typical mintage for the 1850s, when silver dollars failed to circulate, except in foreign trade. Virtually all 1853 silver dollars were coined on private account, and the small mintages are a reflection of the limited amount of bullion deposited at the Mint.

The Seated Liberty dollars of the 1850s were seldom encountered in everyday commerce, and the Mint did not start widespread production of proofs until 1857. As a result, collectors were forced to depend on coin dealers and bullion brokers to secure specimens for their collections. An early auction appearance of the 1853 was in the J.N.T. Levick Collection (Edward Cogan, 12/1859), lot 28, "1853 Dollar, fine; no proofs coined." Several auction catalogs of the era mention the lack of proofs in 1853, however, demand was great enough that restrikes of the issue were coined at a later time, along with the famous 1851 and 1852 dates.

The present coin is a lovely near-Gem example, with brilliant fields and strong eye appeal. Striking details are sharp on the centers, with just a touch of peripheral softness seen on the stars. A few wispy abrasions in the fields and a couple of tiny carbon spots on each side are all that prevent a Gem grade for this specimen. Population: 15 in 64, 3 finer (12/09).(#6941)

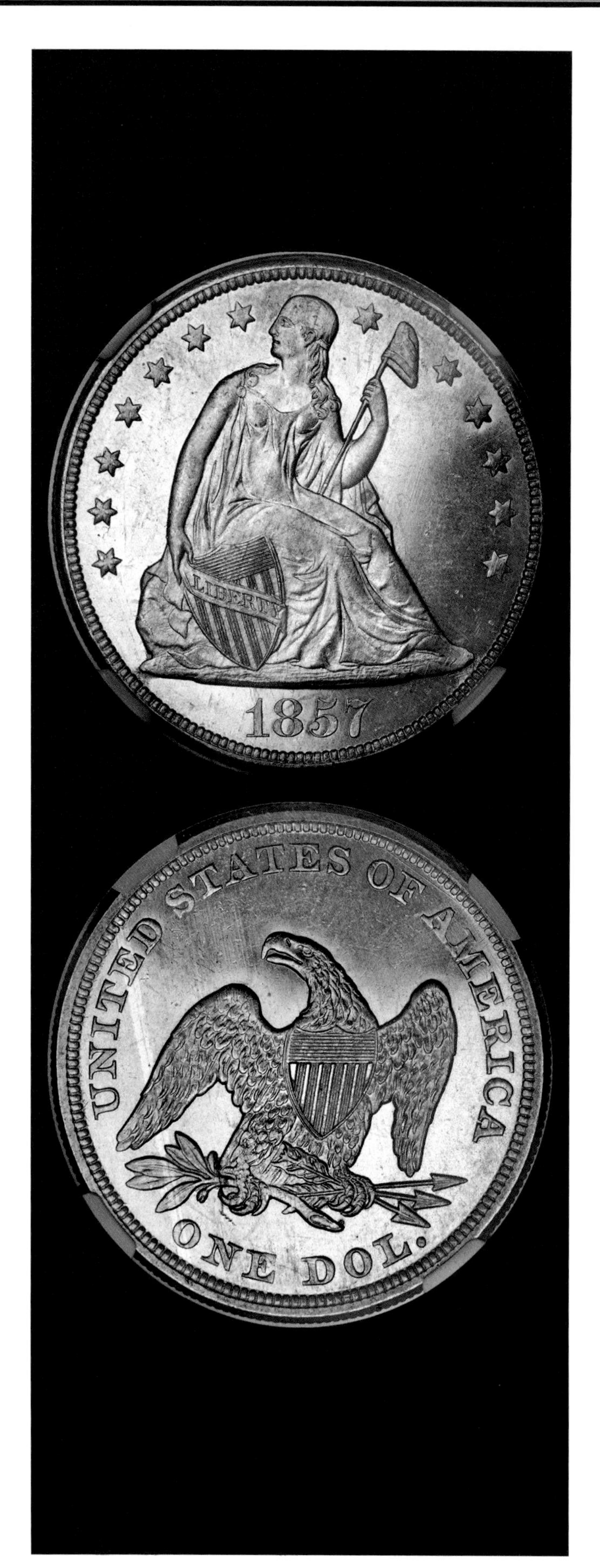

1857 Seated Liberty Dollar, MS65 Prooflike Rare Date, Most Examples Exported Only Two Coins Certified Finer

2598 1857 MS65 Prooflike NGC. While the Mint's official *1857 Annual Report* and the *Guide Book* both list the mintage of the 1857 Seated Liberty dollar as 94,000 pieces, research by R.W. Julian indicates a delivery of 490 pieces on May 29, 1857 was mistakenly omitted from the total. Q. David Bowers speculates the small delivery may have been a special striking for unknown purposes. Because the silver dollar contained a $1.046 melt-down value in silver, the coins rarely circulated domestically. Most examples were used in the China trade, and ultimately melted in the Orient, with the result that the issue is much rarer than generally supposed today. Bowers estimates a few hundred coins may still exist in circulated grades, with Mint State examples "quite rare." At the MS65 level, PCGS has certified two specimens, with none finer; while NGC has seen no coins in this grade, but has graded two examples finer (11/09).

Most early auction appearances of the 1857 dollar were as part of silver proof sets, which seems to be the way most collectors obtained an example of the date. One early offering of a business-strike 1857 was in a fixed price list issued by Augustus B. Sage in June 1859. Sage was asking $1.50 for a very fine example, quite a markup for a circulated coin that was only two years old at the time.

The present coin is a magnificent example, perhaps finer than the coin in Jack Lee's fabled collection. All silver dollars of 1857 were produced with prooflike surfaces. Even coins in circulated grades as low as XF show this feature. The fields of the coin offered here are nicely mirrored, with modestly contrasted devices. The surfaces are mostly brilliant, but there is a slight overlay of pale reddish patina on both sides. Pedigree markers include two tiny marks in the right obverse field and a mark below E in UNITED.(#6945)

Lustrous 1859-S Seated Dollar, MS62

2599 1859-S MS62 PCGS. With a skimpy mintage of 20,000 examples, the 1859-S is an issue that is seldom encountered in the higher Mint State grades. The 1859 Seated Liberty dollars from all three mints were intended for export to China, and the available evidence suggests that most did indeed make their way there, only to be promptly melted down into bullion.

The present piece is one of a half-dozen so graded at PCGS, with another half-dozen pieces in MS62 at NGC (12/07). There are only another dozen pieces at both services graded finer, as always discounting the possibility of duplication in these data. Both sides of this example show a touch of champagne-gold patina over the frosty silver surfaces. While there are a few light contact marks consistent with the grade, none of them are bothersome or individually severe. Population: 6 in 62, 7 finer (11/09).(#6948)

Low Mintage 1863 Seated Liberty Dollar, MS65 Attractively Toned Example Prooflike Fields

2600 1863 MS65 PCGS. Only 27,200 business-strike Seated Liberty dollars were minted in 1863, along with 460 proof examples. Civil War hoarding caused the government to suspend specie payments, and most of the small mintage was struck on private account for depositors of silver bullion. Banks, bullion dealers, and merchants also purchased coins at a premium, for use in foreign trade. Walter Breen stated most silver dollars of the era were "exported to Latin American and East Indian ports."

The combination of low mintage and high exportation rate resulted in a minuscule supply of 1863 dollars available for numismatic purposes. The date is scarce in all grades today, and Mint State examples are rare. Q. David Bowers estimates perhaps 275-400 coins survive in circulated grades, with approximately 50-90 specimens extant in Mint State. At the Gem level, Bowers believes only 8-12 pieces are known. We believe those estimates significantly higher than the actual survival rate. Currently, NGC has certified two examples in MS65, with only two finer; while PCGS has graded two specimens at the Gem level, with four finer (11/09).

As a date, 1863 Seated dollars were popular with collectors almost immediately. However, most examples offered in early auction catalogs were proofs, as that format was more available to collectors of the 19th century than regular-issue coins of the era. The trend continues today, because the proof mintage had a relatively high survival rate, and proofs are definitely more available than their Mint State counterparts. Many business strike 1863 dollars feature prooflike fields, including the coin offered here.

The present coin features brightly reflective fields, under delightful iridescent toning, reminiscent of a toned proof. Both sides have rich multi-layered purple, gray, and lilac centers, surrounded by blue at the margins. The striking details are full, and some light, diagonal die striations are evident in the fields. A small field mark by star 12 prevents an even higher grade.(#6953)

Rarely Seen 1864 Seated Dollar in Gem Condition

2601 1864 MS65 NGC. This Civil War-issue Seated dollar is a scarce one to find in full Gem condition. The mintage was a minuscule 30,700 business strikes, compared to later issues in the six- or seven-digit range. Even with that meager production, most of the coins were exported, and they failed to circulate domestically. Today, there are only a few hundred survivors. Even that estimate may be too ambitious, as less than 200 examples have been certified by NGC and PCGS combined in all grades, a figure that undoubtedly includes numerous duplications (11/09).

This piece is sharply struck throughout, with strong curls on Liberty. The eagle and claws are boldly defined, areas that are weakly struck on many Seated dollars. Liberty's head and all of the obverse stars are likewise sharply, if not fully struck. This excellence of overall detail is quite unusual for the type, and doubtless helps explain the rare Gem grade assessment by NGC. The coin is toned with a blush of light gold over champagne-gray coloration. The fulsome mint luster that shimmers over both sides is of a beautiful, satiny texture. We note a long thin line down the right obverse field, close to the inside stars, and a similar but much shorter faint line just below the stem on the reverse. Fine die lines, as struck, appear around the upper and upper left obverse stars. Census: 8 in 65, 0 finer (11/09).

Ex: Heritage (1/2005), lot 30279, which realized $21,850. (#6954)

XF Details 1873-CC Seated Dollar

2602 1873-CC—Scratched—NCS. XF Details. The last of only four Seated dollar issues struck at Carson City, the 1873-CC was produced for only two or possibly three months before the Coinage Act (also known as the "Crime of '73") deleted the silver dollar from the roster of minted denominations. Examples in any condition are prized. While this well-defined example shows numerous scattered abrasions, as well as reed marks in the right obverse field and a scratch on the eagle's neck and shield, the overall eye appeal holds strong. Light gray surfaces show glimpses of luster in the protected areas.(#6972)

Attractive 1840 Seated Dollar, PR63

2603 1840 PR63 NGC. Two different reverse dies were used to strike the small number of 1840 silver dollar proofs, both of them sharing the same obverse. This reverse is the same one used for proofs of 1842-52, plainly showing two tiny defects on the right side of the last A in AMERICA. The eagle's claws are unjoined and the arrowheads are disconnected, and the third line of the first shield stripe and the first line of the sixth stripe extend far upward into the horizontal shield lines. Breen's *Proof Encyclopedia* notes that some of these pieces may have been struck after 1840. This piece displays attractive silver-gray surfaces lightly tinged with gold on both sides. An interesting, fairly thick die crack runs from the field into star 12. Census: 9 in 63, 10 finer (11/09).(#6981)

Rare, Early Proof 1844 Seated Dollar, PR64

2604 1844 PR64 NGC. As one would expect, the 1844 Seated dollar is a rare coin in proof format. Mintage estimates vary between 15 and 30 pieces with Bowers coming down (as usual) on the higher end of this range. Many, if not most, Seated dollars produced for circulation from the 1840s were usually struck with a semiprooflike finish in the fields. Usually there is little confusion between business strikes and proofs, but in case there is a question about the status of any 1844 dollar, it can be quickly determined. Business strikes of this date have four elements in the vertical stripes on the obverse shield, whereas proofs display three lines. In the November 1977 *Gobrecht Journal* there was a report of almost two dozen three-element 1844 dollars, all grading Fine or less. This, of course, brings up the question of whether these pieces may have been circulated proofs. This report has not been confirmed since.

One does not need to count the number of elements on the obverse shield to know that this is an unquestioned proof. The fields display the deep reflectivity that only a proof coin possesses. Additionally, the design shows pinpoint striking definition in all areas. Close examination shows light hairlining, but the effects are greatly minimized by the rich golden-brown and blue toning seen on both obverse and reverse. A very rare opportunity to acquire an early proof Seated dollar. Census: 2 in 64, 1 finer (11/09).(#6985)

1864 Seated Liberty Dollar, PR65 Cameo Prized Civil War Issue

2605 1864 PR65 Cameo NGC. Only 470 proof Seated Liberty dollars were minted in 1864, but the date is more available than the small mintage suggests. The issue may owe its high survival rate to the difficulty collectors experienced when ordering proofs from the Mint during the Civil War, when the government suspended specie payments. Collectors probably prized the coins because they had to go to so much trouble to obtain, and preserved them accordingly. Few examples have received the coveted Cameo designation. Currently, NGC has certified four coins in PR65 Cameo, with three finer; while PCGS has graded only one example at this level, with none finer (11/09).

The present coin is an attractive example, with strong mirrored reflectivity in the fields. Each side has pleasing golden-rose color that deepens slightly around the margins, with a thin line of cobalt-blue at the peripheries. The devices show noticeable mint frost under the toning, providing the element of contrast.(#87007)

Pleasing 1867 Gem Proof Dollar

2606 1867 PR65 PCGS. CAC. The 1867 is not the rarest of Seated Liberty dollar proofs, but does come under pressure from date collectors owing to the relatively low 49,900 circulation strike mintage. Proofs can be located with minimal difficulty through near-Gem. Gems, however, are quite scarce and finer examples are nearly unavailable.

Frosty devices appear to float over the deep watery fields of this PR65 offering. The essentially untoned surfaces exhibit sharply struck design elements. This nicely preserved coin reveals just a couple of lint marks. Encapsulated in a green insert holder. Population: 16 in 65, 1 finer (11/09).(#7015)

Splendid PR66 1868 Silver Dollar

2607 1868 PR66 PCGS. The present piece last appeared in a Heritage auction on August 23, 1990, as lot 1612 in our Seattle ANA Signature. It realized $35,200, and since the coin remains in the same older generation green label holder of its last public emergence, we expect another remarkable bid to be required to secure ownership.

One of 600 proofs struck, this Reconstruction Seated dollar exhibits apple-green, ocean-blue, autumn-gold, and lilac patina. The strike is absolutely full, down to the each knuckle on the eagle's claws and each strand of hair on Liberty's head. No contact marks or hairlines are evident beneath the rich blanket of original multi-color toning. Population: 2 in 66, 1 finer (11/09).(#7016)

Splendid 1868 Seated Dollar, PR67 ★ Cameo

2608 1868 PR67 ★ Cameo NGC. While the post-Civil War Seated dollar mintage of 1868 business strikes surged from 1867's 46,900 pieces to 162,100 coins, the number of proof coins actually decreased a bit, from 625 to 600. This piece shows minor recutting on the flag and base of the 1 in the date, and the lower inside loop of the second 8 is repunched. Bowers writes in his *Silver Dollar Encyclopedia* that "double punching is evident on early strikes, fading on later impressions. The more obvious the repunching, the rarer." This splendid coin is well-deserving of the Star rating for its over-the-top eye appeal. Original patina on the obverse blends ocean-blue with violet and pinkish-gold, with more lilac hues prevailing on the reverse. The strike is just short of full, despite light roller marks in the center obverse. Generous luster radiates beneath the moderate toning. Census: 2 in 67 ★ Cameo, 0 finer (11/09).(#87016)

TRADE DOLLARS

Impressive 1876-CC Trade Dollar
Doubled Die Reverse, MS61

2609 1876-CC Doubled Die Reverse MS61 PCGS. FS-801, formerly FS-014. Type One Obverse and Reverse. Among the more exotic doubled dies to make it into the *Guide Book,* and the only such variety listed in that source for Trade dollars. The dramatic spread on the olive branch, the eagle's claws, and the nearby lettering is bold and certainly worthy of collector attention. Beyond the variety, this is an attractive MS61 coin for the variety, lustrous silver-white with dots of peripheral golden-tan and charcoal toning. Several abrasions and shallow marks in the fields, particularly on either side of Liberty, preclude a finer designation. For the variety, Population: 3 in 61, 3 finer (12/09).(#97042)

1878-CC Trade Dollar, AU58
Fully Struck and Lightly Abraded

2610 1878-CC AU58 PCGS. Breen-5822, reverse of 1877. The first C in the mintmark is low on this variety. The 1878-CC Trade dollar boasts the lowest business-strike mintage of the series at 97,000 pieces. Q. David Bowers calls the issue "the most popular rarity among business strike Trade dollars." The rarity of the issue was realized as early as the New Jersey Collection (Frossard, 3/1898), lot 308, where the cataloger singled out the date for its rarity.

The present specimen is fully struck, with just the slightest friction evident on the high points of the devices. The surfaces are darkly toned in shades of russet and charcoal-gray on both sides. The fields are free of noticeable abrasions. Population: 12 in 58, 24 finer (12/09). (#7047)

PROOF TRADE DOLLAR

Dazzling AU58 1878-CC Trade Dollar

2611 1878-CC AU58 NGC. Breen-5822. Normal 8 and CC, first C low. The large mintage of 1878-CC Morgan dollars—2.2 million coins—was supported by John Sherman, Treasury secretary who also was a bitter foe of the Trade dollar. A directive limiting Trade dollar payouts for bullion deposits resulted in the melting of 44,148 pieces of the 97,000 made, leaving a net production of 52,852 examples, according to the Bowers silver dollar reference. Business strike Trade dollars of this issue are the rarest of the series. This piece is quite close to Mint State, with just a whisper of rub on the high points of Liberty's thigh, breast, and shoulder. Dazzling patina features daubs of apricot and saffron. Census: 10 in 58, 25 finer (11/09). (#7047)

1882 Trade Dollar, PR67 ★ Cameo Proof-Only Date

2612 1882 PR67 ★ Cameo NGC. CAC. In the 1882 edition of *An Illustrated History of the U.S. Mint,* author and coin dealer A.M. Smith wrote, "Trade dollars of 1879, 1880, 1881 and 1882 are very rare as only a few hundred of each as Proofs for collectors were struck, and command a premium." Today numismatists know 1,097 Trade dollars were minted in 1882, all in proof format, as Smith noted. Examples are relatively easy to locate, unlike as in Smith's day, and the issue is popular because of the overall low production figure.

The present coin is a stunning example, with deeply reflective fields that contrast starkly with the frosty devices. The obverse is lightly toned in shades of pale blue and deep rose, with cobalt-blue at the bottom margin of the obverse. The brightly reflective fields shine through the fragile toning. The reverse is mostly brilliant, with accents of gold around the borders. Overall eye appeal is superb, attested by the CAC sticker. NGC has certified four coins in PR67 Cameo, with two finer; while PCGS has graded only one example at this exalted level, with one finer (11/09).(#87062)

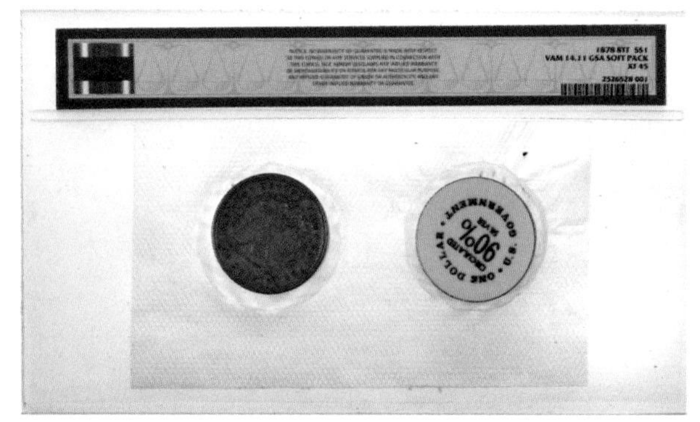

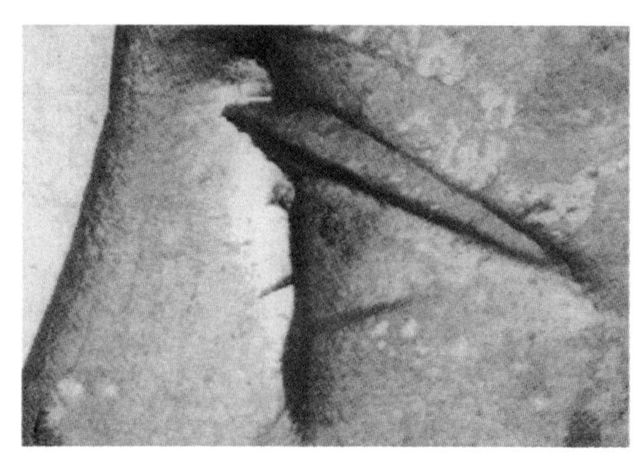

VAM-14.11 Top 100 'Wild Eye Spikes'
Housed in a GSA Soft Pack Holder
1878 Eight Tailfeathers Dollar XF45

2613 1878 8TF Wild Eye Spikes XF45 NGC. VAM-14.11, R.7. A Top 100 Variety. The "Wild Eye Spikes" or VAM-14.11 variety shows prominent doubling of the eyelid, described in Van Allen and Mallis as a "short, thick and blunt spike just below eyelid plus a long thin spike angled downward in front of lower part of eye." Another diagnostic is a dot of raised metal within the upper loop of the first 8 in the date. This lightly worn example of the rare VAM-14.11 is made all the more special by its presence in a GSA soft pack holder, which has since been sealed inside a special NGC holder. The whole is housed in a custom frame proclaiming: "The Sole Top 100 GSA 1878 8TF *ultra rare* VAM 14.11 / 'Wild Eye Spikes'" above. Below is this coin's known pedigree.

Ex: Tom Kern, 2008; Michael S. Fey, Ph.D., 2009.

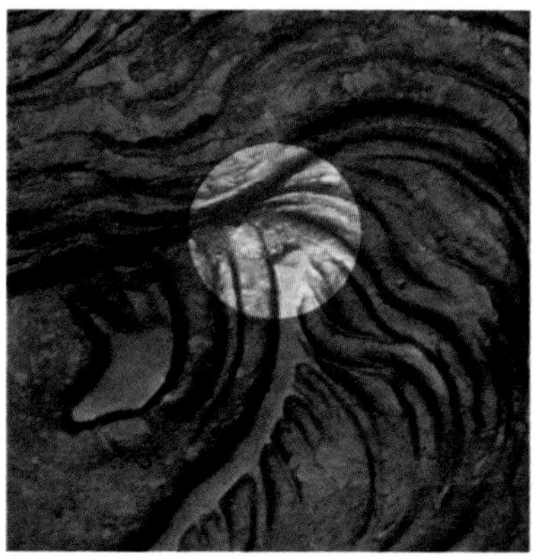

'Ultra-Rare' 1878 8TF Dollar, VAM 14.7
'Flake on Ear,' MS63 Prooflike

2614 1878 8TF MS63 Prooflike PCGS. Flake on Ear, VAM-14.7. A Hit List 40 Variety. www.VAMWorld.com lists this variety as "ultra-rare." The key diagnostic is a tiny flake on the back of the ear, with a tiny die line that connects to a strand of hair. Several of the obverse stars show doubling, and the date shows minor doubling as well. A couple of heavy die cracks appear on the obverse, including a branching one near the date. On the reverse the letters in UNITED are strongly doubled. This piece is silver-white with excellent reflectivity, and only a few minor ticks consistent with the Select grade. The VAMWorld.com site says that only seven specimens are confirmed.(#7073)

Impressive 1878-CC Morgan Dollar MS66, Housed in GSA Holder

2615 1878-CC MS66 NGC. The first Carson City Morgan dollars were struck in 1878, and that initial issue has the second-highest mintage among CC-mint Morgan issues, behind only the 1890-CC. Still, MS66 pieces are elusive and anything finer is a condition rarity. This is an attractive Premium Gem representative, frosty over the devices with reflective (though not strictly Prooflike) fields. Light gray toning overall shows a hint of gold, and though a few small digs are present on the eagle, the obverse is wonderfully preserved. Band-certified in the black GSA holder of issue with outer box, but no certificate; it is the single finest non-Prooflike 1878-CC GSA dollar so certified in a hard case (11/09).
From The Classic Collection.(#7080)

Reflective Gem 1879-CC Morgan Dollar

2616 1879-CC MS65 PCGS. CAC. Perfect Mintmark. The first in the run of difficult mintmarked (and some without mintmark) issues in this hugely popular series, and the first in the great trio of CC-mint rarities. This piece at the Gem level is essentially unimprovable, as NGC and PCGS combined have certified a *maximum* of three pieces finer (12/09). This coin actually has considerable prooflikeness, although undesignated as such by PCGS. The silver-white surfaces lack any suggestion of color, but the reflective fields and thickly frosted devices set up marvelous contrast. Liberty's cheek is remarkably pristine, and abrasions elsewhere are insignificant. A fine coin for a top-notch Morgan dollar collection.(#7086)

Flashy 1883-CC Morgan Dollar
MS67 Deep Mirror Prooflike

2617 1883-CC MS67 Deep Mirror Prooflike NGC. This amazing silver-white coin could easily be mistaken for a true proof, so intense are its reflectivity and lack of noticeable abrasions. The strike is uniformly bold, with minor die clashing evident on each side. Prolonged examination will reveal a couple of marginal ticks in the obverse field before the nose, and a loupe shows a couple of faint abrasions on Liberty's lower cheek and chin, away from the prime focal areas. But no amount of quibbling will diminish the immense appeal, and the CC mintmark only enhances it further. Census: 5 in 67 Deep Mirror Prooflike, 0 finer (11/09).(#97145)

1884-S Morgan Dollar, MS63
Important Condition Rarity

2618 1884-S MS63 PCGS. Brilliant and lustrous with sharp design features and soft, frosty surfaces. Only slight traces of gold toning are visible on each side. This piece is typical of the few surviving Mint State examples of the date, with frosty luster and sharp details. In fact, these are keys to collecting and should always be present on true Mint State pieces. Many near-Mint coins exist with less than full details and with rather dull luster.

The '84-S is a rarity in Mint State grades, although the reasons are not entirely known. While it is certain that there were few, if any, examples among the Treasury silver dollar disbursement of the early 1960s, it is not known how many pieces entered circulation at the time of issue, nor how many may have been melted under the Pittman Act of 1918 or at other times. The preponderance of circulated examples that have survived today clearly indicates that some portion of the original mintage saw use in commerce.

The actual rarity of this date was not widely recognized until at least the 1930s. Before that time, there were relatively few collectors of U.S. coinage, and most were interested in the older types. While some collectors kept up to date by purchasing proofs as they were issued, or pulled a single example from circulation if proofs were not coined, few made an active study of these modern coins. The coin market expanded considerably in the 1930s, influenced by extensive commemorative coinage issues, and it was at that time that the rarity of this issue was first recognized. But it was not until well after the Treasury release of the early 1960s that this date took its place as one of the prime rarities in the Morgan dollar series. Dave Bowers noted: "In the years after 1964, as the framework of the Morgan dollar was built, it was realized that the 1884-S dollar was basically rare in Mint State in relation to the demand, and those that did exist were in lower grades." Population: 37 in 63, 16 finer .

From The Big Sky Montana Collection.(#7156)

Stunning 1888 Dollar, MS67 Deep Mirror Prooflike

2619 1888 MS67 Deep Mirror Prooflike NGC. The 1888 Morgan dollar, with a mintage approaching 20 million circulation strikes, is common through the MS65 level. Even Premium Gems can be located with minimal difficulty. Prooflike examples are also available in the better Mint State grades. Deep Mirror Prooflike specimens in the lofty grade of MS67, such as the current offering, are another matter entirely. Both sides yield stunning field-motif contrast, extremely unusual for '88 Prooflike pieces. A powerful strike leaves strong detail on the design elements, and the only color is a hint of gold-tan on Liberty's cheek. Nicely preserved throughout. Census: 2 in 67 Deep Mirror Prooflike, 0 finer (11/09).(#97183)

Excellent 1889-CC Morgan Dollar, AU58

2620 1889-CC AU58 PCGS. CAC. The 1889-CC needs no introduction as the key-date Morgan dollar from the Carson City Mint. It is on more collector want lists than any other date in the series, except for the 1893-S and the proof-only 1895. This lovely piece has frosty mint luster beneath natural grayish-gold toning, with pleasing blue and yellow peripheries. It is sharply struck and presents excellent eye appeal. Faint traces of rub over the ear on the obverse, and on the eagle's breast on the reverse are nearly invisible without strong magnification.(#7190)

Key Date 1889-CC Morgan Dollar, MS62

2621 1889-CC MS62 PCGS. The 1889-CC is one of the major keys in the Morgan dollar series, and is by far the most elusive Carson City issue. Rusty Goe writes in his book *The Mint On Carson Street* that, for unknown reasons, approximately 250,000 to 325,000 '89-CC dollars of its already small 350,000 mintage were melted. David Bowers, in his 1993 *Silver Dollars* reference, opines that when Carson City silver dollars were being paid out from the Cash room at the treasury Department in Washington, thousands of all issues 1878 to 1893 were distributed *except* 1889-CC.

Most 1889-CC dollars on the market today are in circulated or lower Mint State grades. The issue becomes very difficult in MS63, extremely challenging in near-Gem and virtually unobtainable any finer. We present in this offering a rather pleasing MS62 example. Its satiny silver-gray surfaces exhibit sharply struck design motifs, including strong detail in the hair over Liberty's ear and on the eagle's breast feathers. A few minute marks barely preclude the attainment of the next highest grade level.

From The Big Sky Montana Collection.(#7190)

Lustrous Near-Mint 1892-S Dollar

2622 1892-S AU58 PCGS. CAC. The 1892-S is a coin whose price/grade curve assumes quite a sharp trajectory at and near the Mint State level, and as such this near-Mint State piece might form a wonderful acquisition for some forthright bidder needing to fill that gaping hole in a set without paying a Mint State price. This piece is just a whisper away from Mint State, with nearly full luster clinging to silver-white surfaces on both sides. The reverse is fairly prooflike, the obverse a bit less so. A few minor ticks and scrapes are consistent with a short spate in circulation, but the eye appeal is outstanding. (#7218)

Toned MS65 1892-S Dollar
One of the Keys to the Morgan Dollar Series

2623 1892-S MS65 PCGS. VAM-1. When key-date Morgan dollars are discussed, the 1893-S is usually mentioned first, as it is a rare and important issue in all grades. The proof-only 1895 is usually mentioned next, and beyond that, numerous condition rarities are talked about. The 1892-S is one of those condition rarities, from a mintage of 1.2 million coins, and nearly always available in low to middle circulated grades at a modest price. Other condition rarities include such dates as the 1884-S, 1886-O, 1895-O, and 1901. Each date is relatively common in circulated grades, but rare in Mint State. At Gem or finer grades, there are many other dates that also qualify as condition rarities. Among them, the 1892-S is one of the most important.

For many years, this date was less desirable than most others in Mint State grades, despite being at least equal in rarity. The reason was that many AU coins exist, and those pieces were often sold as Mint State at a discount from prevailing Mint State price levels. However, today, condition is one of the prime factors in the rare coin market. The present amazing Gem is clearly destined for one of the finest Set Registry collections.

In *A Guide Book of Morgan Silver Dollars,* Dave Bowers explains:

> "I am not aware of any bags of Mint State 1892-S dollars released after the 1930s, although now and again a few pieces would be found mixed with other coins. For a long time the 1892-S, although rare in Mint State, was not greatly desired. In 1982, Wayne Miller noted that a half dozen or so Uncirculated coins had come to light in recent years, and that 'probably fewer than 200 specimens exist in choice BU [MS-63] or better condition.'
>
> "Miller also noted that 'most' investment advisory letters stated that the 1892-S dollar 'is one of the few key date Morgans which is not instantly saleable in choice BU condition.' In 1992, Maurice Rosen suggested that the lack of demand was probably because many AU coins were offered as 'Uncirculated,' although true Uncirculated coins were rare. Philosophies change, and today a gem would, indeed, find a ready market."

Unlike the 1893-S that is known in just one die combination, the Van Allen-Mallis reference lists seven different VAM varieties for the 1892-S dollar, and VAM-1 is simply called the "Normal Die" variety and may consist of more than one individual marriage. It might be interesting for some patient researcher to examine all of the 1892-S VAM-1 dollars for distinguishing characteristics. For example, this piece has short, diagonal die lines in the field inside the ribbon bow.

The present piece, a stunning and vibrant Gem, is deeply and colorfully toned with pale greenish-yellow, light blue, violet, and steel patina. Only slight weakness is evident over Liberty's ear, as usual, and the overall strike is excellent, with bold design features on both sides. Population: 5 in 65, 9 finer (11/09).

From The Big Sky Montana Collection.(#7218)

Elusive 1893-CC MS64 Prooflike Dollar

2624 1893-CC MS64 Prooflike NGC. The 1893-CC dollar is a popular, desirable issue owing to it being the last of the Carson City dollars. Fortunately for collectors, NGC/PCGS population reports indicate a large supply through the Select level. Prooflike examples are very elusive, however, especially in MS63 and finer.

The devices on this near-Gem Prooflike offering yield a degree of contrast with the fields over both sides. The design motifs are typically struck in that the centers are soft. Nearly untoned save for an occasional wisp of barely discernible gold color. Some scattered marks and grazes are far fewer and much less severe than typically found on the issue. Indeed, this date is nearly unobtainable above MS63 because most survivors exhibit excessive marks. Census: 1 in 64 Prooflike, 0 finer (11/09).(#7223)

Brilliant 1893-S Morgan Dollar, AU50

2625 1893-S AU50 NGC. The acknowledged key to the Morgan dollar series, the 1893-S comes from a series-low business-strike mintage of 100,000 pieces. The coins were released into circulation at an early date, and served their intended purpose in the regional economy. Today, most examples seen are in VF grades, with other circulated grades underrepresented in population totals, and Mint State coins seldom encountered. AU examples are scarce in absolute terms, and rare in the context of the series.

The present coin is an attractive, untoned specimen, with slight traces of wear on the high points, such as the hair over Liberty's ear. Mint luster is evident in the protected areas of the surfaces, near the devices. The surfaces show fewer abrasions than expected for the grade.

From The Big Sky Montana Collection.(#7226)

Attractive 1893-S Key Date Dollar, AU50

2626 1893-S AU50 NGC. The 1893-S has the lowest mintage of any regular issue Morgan dollar, making it the key date of the series. Paul Gilkes, in an article titled "1893-S Morgans Hot Market Commodity" published in the September 5, 2005 *Coin World*, writes that this low mintage resulted from several factors: the Panic of 1893, an oversupply of silver dollars in Treasury vaults, repeal of the 1890 law requiring massive monthly silver purchases, and the increasing opposition to silver interests.

The present AU offering displays whispers of golden-gray patina, being somewhat more extensive and deeper on the reverse. Traces of luster reside in the recessed areas of well defined design motifs, and both sides reveal a minimum of undisturbing circulation marks. A highly attractive survivor of this important key date.(#7226)

Remarkable MS63 Prooflike 1894-O Dollar

2627 1894-O MS63 Prooflike PCGS. CAC. This is a remarkable coin on several counts. Most Mint State coins are less than attractive, with multiple abrasions, a poor strike, and/or lackluster surfaces. The present coin ends all generalizations, however, with fully prooflike silver-white surfaces, a moderate strike, minimal abrasions, and intense eye appeal emanating from both sides. Were it not for a couple of small marks on Liberty's cheek that are nonetheless undistracting, we would believe this piece deserving of an even finer grade. This is the single finest Prooflike example certified at PCGS; indeed, it is one of only two Prooflikes of the entire issue at PCGS, with the other an MS61. Population: 1 in 63 Prooflike, 0 finer (11/09). (#7231)

Exceptional MS61 1895-O Dollar

2628 1895-O MS61 PCGS. The 1895-O Morgan dollar is readily available in circulated grades, including Extremely Fine and About Uncirculated. Mint State pieces are much more difficult to locate, and when found are apt to be MS63 and below. Moreover, regardless of grade, "... most are casually if not lightly struck and have dull, insipid luster (David Bowers, *A Guide Book of Morgan Silver Dollars*).

The present MS61 offering is an exceptional piece in the above regards. Its strike is well above average, evidenced by the near-full detail in the hair above Liberty's ear. The eagle's breast feathers, though more incomplete than the obverse center, also show good detail. The luster is nearly complete on both sides, and though not dazzling, is certainly not "insipid." Finally, while we notice a few small marks on its essentially untoned surfaces, the coin is far from being "beaten up" as is the case for most MS60 and MS61 pieces. All in all, a nice piece for the designated grade.(#7236)

Richly Toned 1895-O Dollar, MS62 Rarely Seen in Uncirculated Grades

2629 1895-O MS62 PCGS. In 1895, silver dollars were definitely not needed or wanted by the American public. The provisions of the Sherman Silver Purchase Act of July 14, 1890 required the government to produce a vast quantity of these unnecessary coins every month. The thankless task of coining these unwanted coins fell heavily on the staff of the New Orleans Mint during much of the 1890s.

Probably because the coiners knew the majority of these coins would be stored in vaults, far from critical eyes, the staff took no special pains with quality control. In fact, their main concern was to turn out as many coins as possible, in the shortest time possible. In an effort to lessen die wear and prevent breakage, with the resulting delays, the coiners set the dies farther apart than usual, resulting in poor striking quality on almost all specimens coined. Muted mint luster was also a consequence of this casual approach to coinage.

The recorded mintage for the 1895-O Morgan dollar was an anemic 450,000 pieces. Though most of these were stored away, perhaps 100,000 pieces were released into circulation at the time of issue. Coins continued to be released sporadically over the years, until the supply was gone. Apparently, there were no 1895-O coins left in storage by the time of the Treasury releases in the 1960s. Q. David Bowers has stated, "The rarity and importance of the 1895-O in Mint State cannot be overemphasized."

The present coin has a better than average strike for this date, with much detail discernable on Liberty's hair and the eagle's breast. The luster is subdued, as usually seen on this date. Mottled gray and lilac toning accent the fields, and handling marks are consistent with the grade. This offering is an important opportunity to acquire this historic coin in Mint State.

From The Big Sky Montana Collection.(#7236)

Important MS64 1901 Morgan Dollar

2630 1901 MS64 PCGS. 2 Olive C4/C3 Reverse. The 1901 Morgan dollar is on the short list of the most elusive Morgan dollars in the higher Mint State grades, a list that would include other Mint State rarities such as the 1896-O and 1886-O. While the 1893-S is a foundational rarity—rare in all grades—the 1901, 1886-O, and 1896-O are conditional rarities, common in most circulated grades and worth little premium. The 1901 also suffered in the past from the common misperception that P-mint coins, given their generally higher mintages, are less rare than branch mint coinage. The truth is far more complex, however. Most 1901s likely circulated when they were issued, and those that did not were probably melted around 1918 under terms of the Pittman Act. In addition, many past offerings for Uncirculated coins were for pieces that today we would call AU at best. As a result of all those factors, it was only the 1960s and afterward that true Mint State 1901s began to receive the recognition they were due.

This silver-white near-Gem displays coruscating cartwheel luster on both sides, with no suggestion of color. A couple of stray reeding marks on the cheek account for the grade, but abrasions overall are few in number and minor in importance. As one of the most elusive business strike Morgans in high grade, this piece has enormous importance for the legions of series collectors. Population: 20 in 64, 3 finer (11/09).(#7272)

PROOF MORGAN DOLLARS

1894 Morgan Dollar, PR67 Cameo
A Brilliant, Deeply Reflective Example

2631 1894 PR67 Cameo NGC. The business-strike mintage of 110,000 Philadelphia Mint Morgan dollars in 1894 is the second lowest of the series, putting serious pressure on the proof production of 972 pieces. The present coin is a Superb Proof Cameo, with brilliant reflective fields and dramatically frosted devices. The flash of white-on-black contrast is arresting. The striking details are full, with exquisite detail on all design elements. Q. David Bowers notes that examples with good cameo contrast offer good value in today's market. Currently, including resubmissions and crossovers, NGC has certified 28 specimens in PR67 Cameo, with eight finer; while PCGS has graded only two coins at this level, with none finer (11/09). (#87329)

Toned PR63 1895 Morgan Dollar
Mintage: 880 Proofs

2632 1895 PR63 PCGS. For sheer unpredictability, few U.S. coinage series can match the Morgan dollar, with its often topsy-turvy relationship between original mintages and actual rarity. As Paul M. Green wrote for his article "Who doesn't love a Morgan dollar story?" that was published in the November 13, 2007 edition of *Numismatic News,* "When you study Morgan dollars, you quickly learn to appreciate that Morgan dollars are one of the few issues where the unexpected and unusual is basically the norm."

Regarding "the unexpected and unusual," Green further notes that "the 1895 is a perfect example ... it's one of so many Morgan dollar stories where, despite seemingly good information, the facts are sometimes very difficult to find." Ironically, the conclusion he reaches in-between—"that the business strike mintage recorded was a mistake and that the 1895 was only produced as a proof"—has itself been disputed and strongly, even among those who believe that the 1895 business strikes never existed. Of course, both the mystery and the debate surrounding the business strikes and what fate (if any) they met has served to focus attention on the 1895 Philadelphia Morgans that are available: the proofs.

The proof fields on this piece are deeply mirrored, although somewhat muted by the smoky-gray toning that covers each side. Magnification reveals light hairlining, but the most obvious "flaws" are a couple of streaky interruptions in the toning on the left side of the obverse.

From The Big Sky Montana Collection.(#7330)

Superb Proof 1895 Dollar With Speckled, Multicolored Toning Over Each Side

2633 1895 PR67 NGC. Both silver and gold U.S. coins have experienced singular extinction events that cast doubt on the reliability of mintage figures as guides to rarity. The gold recall of 1933 and the subsequent melting of millions of those coins have figured prominently in American numismatics. Just as dramatic, but somewhat less talked-about and understood, was the Pittman Act destruction of 1918, wherein more than a quarter of a *billion* Morgan dollars were reduced to bullion. Paul M. Green, in an article published in the November 13, 2007 edition of *Numismatic News,* wrote with understatement: "That Pittman Act melting ... really stirred the pot of confusion when it comes to Morgan dollars. When you destroy close to half of all the coins ever made of a certain type, as the Pittman Act did with Morgans, but have no record of what dates were involved, it can cause significant confusion."

Among the issues most confused by the Pittman Act melting was the 1895 Philadelphia Morgan dollar. Official records state that the mintage was 12,000 pieces. For multiple generations, until the Treasury releases of the 1960s, collectors wondered whether the business strike 1895 Morgans were waiting to be discovered. None turned up, and numismatists entertained the possibility that perhaps none had ever existed. Thanks to the Pittman Act meltings, whether business strikes were ever produced remains essentially an unanswerable question. What is undoubtable, however, is the existence of the year's proofs and their enduring desirability.

This is a magnificent example that is virtually perfect from a technical standpoint. Both sides display deep, speckled reddish-golden color, generally in the centers, with rich cobalt-blue around margins (again, generally). The depth of mirrored reflectivity in the fields shines brightly through the toning on each side. An outstanding, high grade example of this proof-only issue. Census: 11 in 67, 3 finer (11/09).(#7330)

Imposing 1897 Dollar, PR67

2634 1897 PR67 NGC. CAC. The year 1897 saw a mintage of 731 proof Morgan dollars. According to NGC/PCGS population data, a goodly number of these have survived through the near-Gem level. The Gem and Premium Gem population declines somewhat, and higher-grade coins are elusive.

The bright untoned surfaces of this PR67 example exhibit a degree of field-motif contrast at various levels. A well executed strike leaves sharp definition on the design elements, thought the hair over Liberty's ear reveals just a touch of softness. Immaculate preservation characterizes both sides, and Liberty's cheek and neck are remarkably smooth. This piece exudes imposing eye appeal and will undoubtedly elicit spirited bidding. Census: 14 in 67, 4 finer (11/09). (#7332)

1901 Morgan Dollar, PR68 Cameo
Wayne Miller Plate Coin
Called 'Finest Known'

2635 1901 PR68 Cameo NGC. Ex: Miller Plate/Everest. Quality Mint State 1901 Morgan dollars are extremely difficult to locate. Most of the mintage was either released into circulation at the time of issue or melted under the provisions of the Pittman Act in 1918. Very few business-strike 1901 dollars were saved by collectors, and the date was not represented in the Treasury releases of the 1960s. Today, most examples seen are in circulated grades, and coins that are technically Uncirculated are usually dull and unattractive. The issue is a prime condition rarity in the series, more challenging at the Gem level than any other date from the Philadelphia Mint, except the apocryphal 1895.

The paucity of high grade business strikes has always put significant pressure on the tiny proof mintage of 813 coins. When the present coin was offered as lot 1396 of the Hoagy Carmichael and Wayne Miller Collections (Superior, 1/1986), the catalogers noted:

> "Without question the Finest Known for this date. Fully gem coins of this date are very rare. Most pieces are hairlined. Because of the extreme rarity of the business strike 1901-P Dollar in gem condition, many Silver Dollar collections contain a Proof rather than a regular issue for this date. Consequently, the 1901 has always commanded a premium over most other Proof Morgans."

Silver dollar specialist Wayne Miller featured the coin offered here as the plate coin in his *Morgan and Peace Dollar Textbook,* and called this example "far and away the finest known specimen of this date." The coin is virtually perfect from a technical point of view. Both sides exhibit brilliant, deeply mirrored fields, with rich, frosty devices. The element of contrast is particularly strong. While NGC has graded one other example in PR68 Cameo (11/09), it is difficult to believe any specimen can match the present coin's extraordinary quality.

Ex: Essex Coins; acquired by Wayne Miller in January 1978; The Hoagy Carmichael and Wayne Miller Collections (Superior, 1/1986), lot 1396.(#87336)

COMMEMORATIVE SILVER

Immaculate, Richly Toned 1900 Lafayette Dollar, MS67

2636 1900 Lafayette Dollar MS67 NGC. DuVall 2-C. The Lafayette dollar, design by Charles Barber, synthesized a variety of influences, both acknowledged and unacknowledged. Houdon's bust of Washington and Caunois' 1824 commemorative medal depicting Lafayette are the sources most often named for the portraits, though Q. David Bowers (1991) credits Arlie Slabaugh with noting the unmistakable similarity between the conjoined portraits on Barber's design and "the obverse of the Yorktown Centennial medal of 1881, made from dies engraved by Peter L. Krider." The reverse is after Paul Wayland Bartlett, designer of the statue depicted on the reverse. Barber gave that artist ample credit. (Though Barber's usual monogram is missing, Bartlett's last name is spelled out on the base of the statue.)

Quality control was far from the minds of Mint personnel on December 14, 1899, the day the Lafayette dollars were coined. The press was an old one, long out of regular service and used mostly for traveling exhibits and promotional strikings. After the coins were struck, they fell into a hopper and mixed together, and many examples sustained significant abrasions before they ever left the Mint. Yet a handful of exemplary survivors exist today, coins such as this Superb Gem. Each side possesses warm, radiant luster. On the obverse, amber-russet toning with a touch of red covers much of the periphery, while the center is predominantly silver-gray with small, scattered flecks of golden-tan. The reverse rims have similar wheat patina, though the interior is mostly blue-green with a zone of rose-tinged gray above the horse. A simply exquisite piece that is sure to appeal to the commemorative collector. NGC has certified eight Superb Gems, and PCGS has graded five, with none finer (11/09).(#9222)

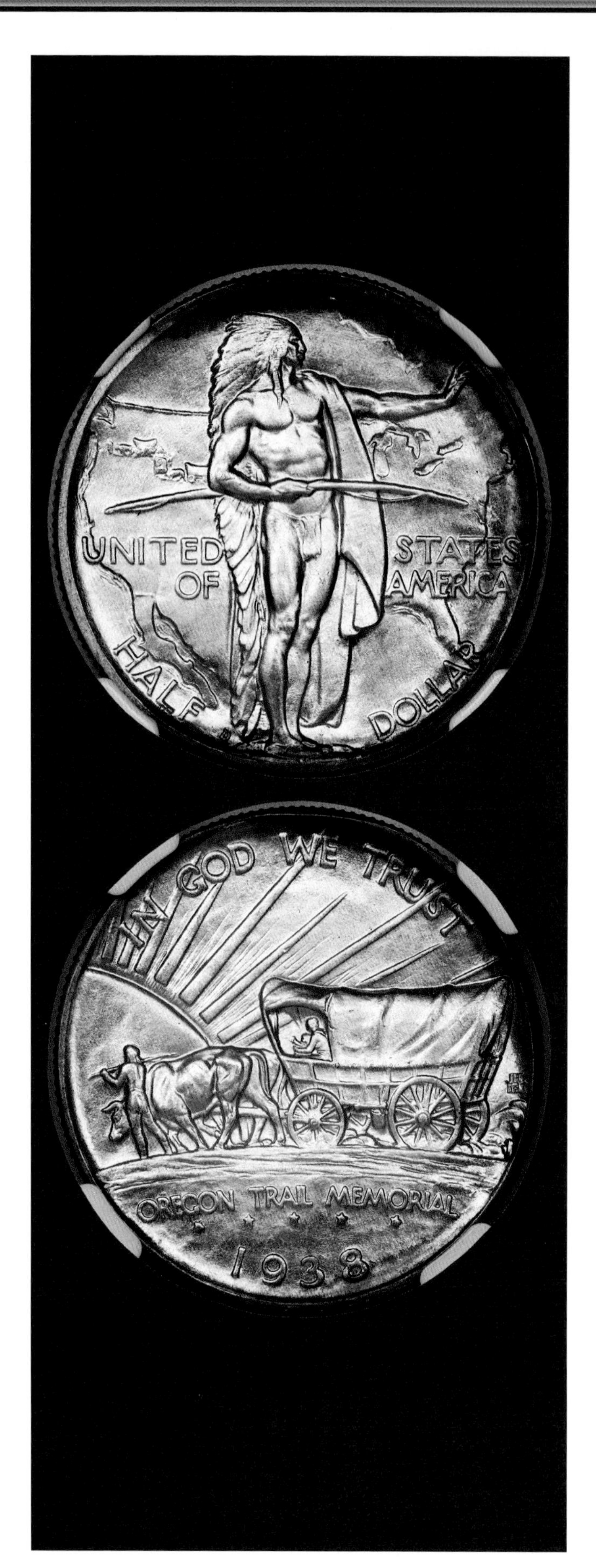

Astounding 1938-D Oregon Half, MS69 ★

2637 1938-D Oregon MS69 ★ NGC. Four auction appearances in our Permanent Auction Archives record Oregon half dollars in MS69, although there are just two different coins, a 1937-D that appeared twice in 2005, and a 1938-D that was sold in July 2002 and August 2004. Three Oregon trails carry an NGC MS69 grade. The 1937-D has no designation, while the two 1938-D half dollars are both graded MS69 ★.

The Oregon Trail Memorial half dollar issue spanned more years than any other type, beginning in 1926 and concluding in 1939. The half dollars also really didn't commemorate anything. The intent of the original legislation was fundraising to erect monuments along the route, which began in Independence, Missouri, and ended at Fort Vancouver, Washington. The true purpose of the issue was greed. Members of the Oregon Trail Memorial Association, including Ezra Meeker who journeyed the trail in 1851, were hoping to line their own pockets with silver.

According to www.coinsite.com, "the obvious abuses, profiteering, and behind-the-scenes political maneuvering didn't sit well with collectors of the day, but the relatively low mintages of the later issues kept sales brisk."

Many original Oregon Trail half dollars exhibit "tab-toning" that duplicates the tabs holding the coins in their original holders. The present piece is slightly different, exhibiting album toning that is the result of this amazing piece being housed in a coin album containing sulphur. Most of the obverse and reverse surfaces of this amazing piece have satiny pearl-gray color, with vibrant peripheral iridescence. It is an incredible Superb Gem, essentially the finest in existence. Census: 2 in 69★, 0 finer (11/09).(#9349)

Gorgeously Toned 1915-S Panama-Pacific Half, MS67 With Repunched Mintmark

2638 1915-S Panama-Pacific MS67 PCGS. CAC. The 1915-S Panama-Pacific half dollar is the only silver commemorative coin celebrating the famous exposition, as the other four associated issues are all gold. An interesting provision in the enabling legislation allowed for the actual production of the half dollars on Mint equipment at the exposition, with as many as needed to be remelted in order to provide an educational demonstration and continuous coinage. The net distribution of only 27,134 pieces was far less than the 200,000 authorized maximum. With an obverse design by Charles E. Barber and reverse by George T. Morgan, the pieces also neatly encapsulate the artistry of the Mint's chief engraver and his more-talented assistant, at a period shortly before Barber's death in 1917.

This gorgeous Superb Gem further enhances the lovely design through its original toning, blending pinkish-gold centers with tinges of ice-blue near the rims on each side, more generously on the reverse. An extra bonus is the nifty mintmark, plainly repunched north. Population: 76 in 67, 2 finer (11/09).(#9357)

Key 1935 Old Spanish Trail Half Dollar, MS68 Tied for Finest Certified

2639 1935 Spanish Trail MS68 NGC. Acknowledged as one of the three keys to the silver commemorative half dollar set, the 1935 Old Spanish Trail half dollar boasts a tiny mintage of 10,008 pieces. The issue was carefully produced and most examples were handled with care, but the issue is particularly susceptible to handling marks because of the expansive, open fields. The present coin is an exception to the rule, as absolutely no marks are visible to the naked eye. Both sides are toned in an even mixture of lilac and rose with strong underlying mint luster. Overall visual appeal is stunning. Currently, NGC has certified six coins in MS68, with none finer; while PCGS has graded only two examples in MS68, with none finer (11/09). (#9376)

The Finest Certified Texas Half Dollar 1936 MS69

2640 1936 Texas MS69 NGC. This is the only MS69 Texas half dollar that NGC has certified, regardless of issue, and the present offering is the first time we have handled the coin. PCGS has never graded a Texas finer than MS68, so this single coin is the finest certified example of the series. A complete set of Texas half dollars includes 13 coins, beginning with 1934, and including three coins of 1935, 1936, 1937, and 1938, struck at the three different mints. Every other issue in the series is available in MS68, and the complete collection would make an incredible display.

The Texas Centennial half dollars were struck to commemorate the 100th anniversary of Texas Independence, bearing the phrase Remember the Alamo. Although the series began in 1934, this 1936 issue is the true 100th anniversary coin of the 1836 Independence, following the Texas War of Independence that culminated in the Battle of San Jacinto. General Sam Houston and his army achieved victory at San Jacinto in just 18 minutes against General Santa Anna and the Mexican Army. The half dollar series continued long enough that "many hobbyists were quite prepared to forget the Alamo," according to www.coinsite.com.

This specimen is sensational. With a strong glass we are unable to find any marks on either side. Both sides are highly lustrous with soft, frosty surfaces. Rich cherry-red and lemon-gold toning provide plenty of eye appeal to this sharply struck Superb Gem. Census: 1 in 69, 0 finer (11/09).(#9386)

COMMEMORATIVE GOLD

1905 Lewis and Clark Dollar Pristine Premium Gem

2641 1905 Lewis and Clark MS66 PCGS. The 1905 Lewis and Clark gold dollar in the highest Mint State grades is much more elusive than its 1904-dated counterpart. A comparison reveals that while PCGS has certified 14 examples of the 1904 in MS67 and one piece in MS68, PCGS has graded only two examples of the 1905 finer than the present piece (11/09).

This Premium Gem boasts rich canary-gold color. While being two-faced is usually a bad thing, on this coin it is a good thing, as both faces, Lewis and Clark, are remarkably free of the pesky little abrasions on the cheek that so frequently plague this design.(#7448)

Important 1905 Lewis and Clark Gold Dollar, MS66

2642 1905 Lewis and Clark MS66 PCGS. Ex: Benson. With just five numerically finer pieces in the combined certified population (12/09), the 1905 Lewis and Clark gold dollar is extremely rare any finer than this Premium Gem, as well as very scarce at the MS66 level. The present coin has strong lemon-yellow color in the centers with pale straw-gold elements closer to the rims. The central definition is excellent, particularly on the often-lost details of the portraits' hair and clothing, while the fields are smooth and essentially untouched. An incredibly appealing piece for the classic gold commemorative connoisseur.(#7448)

Lower-Mintage Round 1915-S Panama-Pacific Fifty Dollar, MS62

2643 1915-S Panama-Pacific 50 Dollar Round MS62 PCGS. The famous numismatist and promoter Farran Zerbe was able to get himself put in charge of the Panama-Pacific Exposition's Coin and Medal Department, which was to strike and issue the commemoratives, souvenir medals, and award medals. He also displayed over 20,000 pieces from his collection in an immensely popular exhibit titled *Zerbe's Money of the World.* Anthony Swiatek and Walter Breen (1990) write that "Zerbe's efforts did more than anyone else's for decades to put coin collecting on the map."

The Act of Congress that authorized these commemoratives specified that 1,500 examples of each of the Octagonal and Round fifties could be issued. That number, plus an additional nine Octagonal and 10 Round pieces for assay purposes, were struck during the course of the Exhibition. Despite Zerbe's efforts, however, the high issue price of these pieces prevented many from selling. The cost of one $50 piece was listed at $100 (although it apparently included a half dollar, dollar, and quarter eagle at no additional cost), a complete five-piece set sold for $200, and a mounted double set (to display obverse and reverse) was priced at $400.

In the May 1916 issue of *The Numismatist,* Zerbe reported that sales would conclude on May 15, at which point the remaining stock of Panama-Pacific commemoratives would be destroyed. However, he appears to have overestimated the distribution of these pieces, and a significant number were left unsold. Ultimately, 855 Octagonal and 1,017 Round fifties were melted.

Nonetheless, Zerbe reports that "the sale of this series, as a revenue producer for the Exposition, has been very successful. The purpose of souvenir coins is not to sell the most coins, but to produce the greatest net revenue, and while the number of these coins distributed may to some be less than anticipated, profits show that the prices established and maintained produced a greater revenue than would have come from a much larger sale at any less price that would have shown a profit ..."

All of the unsold coins were melted on or before October 30, 1916, according to a final report from Zerbe that appeared in the January 1918 issue of *The Numismatist.* He was unduly critical of the $50 gold pieces and offers the peculiar assessment that "originality was lacking" because "coin emblems of ancient days and the graver's work of the medieval period were depicted."

Many of the fifties were sold as part of complete sets, of which about 300 were distributed, "including 60 of the specially certified sets." This accounts for more than about two-thirds of the Round pieces and about one-half of the Octagonals. Garrett and Guth (2003) note that "at one time, a complete set of Panama Pacific coins in their original frame or box was one of the most desirable items in United States numismatics." The vast majority of these sets have since been broken up. The fifties, however, remain highly popular among collectors, and were ranked 26 in the *100 Greatest U.S. Coins.*

This is one of the scarcer Round examples and it is well-matched in appearance with the MS62 Octagonal (below), which come from the same collection. The surfaces display rich, even orange-gold color and only minor (shallow) marks. Excellent mint luster makes this piece appear finer than the stated grade.(#7451)

The Ever-Popular Octagonal 1915-S Panama-Pacific Fifty Dollar, MS62

2644 1915-S Panama-Pacific 50 Dollar Octagonal MS62 PCGS. The recent auction of the Louis Bassano collection (Heritage, July 2009) highlighted the continuing popularity of United States commemoratives. While there are a number of interesting and desirable classic commemoratives, none match the appeal of the 1915 Panama-Pacific $50 gold pieces. Their unique denomination and large size, coupled with the artistic mastery of Robert Aitken, made them greatly anticipated by collectors of the day. Much like today, few could afford an example, although virtually all wanted one.

An interesting article titled "Panama-Pacific Commemorative Coins" in the June 1915 issue of *The Numismatist* not only indicates the public's excitement ahead of their issue, but also provides some useful information about the manufacture and distribution of the fifty dollar gold pieces:

> "A special hydraulic press used for medal stamping at the Philadelphia mint was received at the San Francisco mint during the month. This press, which weighs fourteen tons and has a striking power of 450 tons, is for use in striking the three thousand $50 gold pieces, and is to be returned to the Philadelphia mint just as soon as the coinage has been completed.
>
> "It is expected that the striking of the first $50 piece ever authorized by our Government will be an occasion of some special event at the San Francisco mint. This will be the first special issue to be struck at a branch mint, and the mint mark, 'S', is to appear on all the coins ...
>
> "Designs for the $50 gold pieces are by Mr. Robert Aitken of New York and San Francisco. We understand the same designs with modifications to correspond to shape, round, and octagonal, have been adopted for this denomination. Governed by Mr. Aitken's sculpture and medallic work of the past, and that they will be struck in a medal press with attending slow and careful process, it is a fair speculation that 'high art' and high relief will be notable ...
>
> "Considering that the limited issue of the fifty dollar gold pieces would not produce more than 750 complete double sets, mounted to display obverse and reverse, as they are being purchased by banks, a successful distribution is anticipated ...
>
> "Each complete set and each fifty-dollar gold piece will be delivered in a leather case without additional cost."

The distribution was not as successful as expected, and all of the unsold examples were eventually melted. Consequently, although the original mintage comprised 1,509 Octagonal and 1,510 Round pieces, the actual distribution was significantly smaller with just 645 and 483 examples issued, respectively. While these coins can still be located with patience, the astute collector will note their ever-increasing demand and value. This piece displays rich, even orange-gold color and has a well-balanced appearance from side to side. Only minimal marks are seen on each side with the aid of a loupe, the sole exception a diagonal abrasion in the area of the owl's neck. (#7452)

Impressive MS62 1915-S Panama-Pacific Fifty Dollar Octagonal With Box

2645 1915-S Panama-Pacific 50 Dollar Octagonal MS62 PCGS. Although their round counterparts are slightly rarer, the fifty dollar octagonal Panama-Pacific commemoratives are more prominent to nonspecialists. There is no other issue like it in the American commemorative series, classic or modern; only the fifty dollar round pieces match the octagonal coins' sheer size, and there is no substitute for their singular eight-sided shape.

It is unsurprising that the fifty dollar octagonal coins should be sought-after today, just as they were almost a century ago, despite a selling price that was double an already considerable face value. The fifty dollar octagonal coins had their share of popularity, but the number of individuals who could afford them was small. As Q. David Bowers noted in *Commemorative Coins of the United States: A Complete Encyclopedia:* "Sales were not up to expectations, and after November 1916 a quantity amounting to 855 octagonal pieces went to the melting pot, leaving a net issuance of 645 pieces."

This MS62 representative has warm butter-yellow luster with occasional green-gold accents. The strike is pleasing, if a trifle soft on Minerva's helmet, and there are no singularly mentionable abrasions; rather, a number of wispy marks, some in the fields and others on the central devices, combine to preclude Select status. Still, this coin's considerable eye appeal is not to be denied. A readily collectible example of an important and memorable classic gold commemorative.

An original single coin black box with purple velvet interior accompanies this lot. The box has minor scratches on the lid, and the information card is inscribed in ink: "Property of Mary Rowland, 1926," providing an early provenance.(#7452)

COINS OF HAWAII

Extremely Rare 1847 Medcalf 2CC-6 Hawaiian Cent, MS65 Brown

2646 1847 Hawaii Cent MS65 Brown PCGS. Medcalf 2CC-6. Plain 4 with 15 berries arranged seven left and eight right, considered the rarest variety. In *Hawaiian Money,* Donald Medcalf records six varieties of the 1847 Hawaiian cent, including examples with a Plain 4 or a Crosslet 4 in the date, combined with six different reverse dies. A brief, informal survey of 115 pieces that have appeared in Heritage Signature sales over the past decade indicates that we have handled three examples of 2CC-1, 80 examples of 2CC-2, seven of 2CC-3, five of 2CC-4, 18 of 2CC-5, and only two appearances of this 2CC-6 variety, those two coins both graded AU50. The present specimen is far and away the finest example of the variety that we have seen or handled, and it is sure to find an appreciative new owner in the Hawaiian specialist. Population: 6 in 65 Brown, 0 finer (12/09).(#10965)

End of Platinum Night – Session 2

Heritage Auction Galleries Staff

Steve Ivy - Co-Chairman and CEO
Steve Ivy began collecting and studying rare coins as a youth, and as a teenager began advertising coins for sale in national publications in 1963. Seven years later, at the age of 20, he opened for business in downtown Dallas, and in 1976, incorporated as an auction company. Steve managed the business as well as serving as chief buyer, buying and selling hundreds of millions of dollars of coins during the 1970s and early 1980s. In early 1983, James Halperin became a full partner, and the name of the corporation was changed to Heritage Auctions. Steve's primary responsibilities now include management of the marketing and selling efforts of the company, the formation of corporate policy for long-term growth, and corporate relations with financial institutions. He remains intimately involved in all the various categories Heritage Auctions deals in today. Steve engages in daily discourse with industry leaders on all aspects of the fine art and collectibles business, and his views on market trends and developments are respected throughout the industry. He previously served on both the Board of Directors of the Professional Numismatists Guild (past president), and The Industry Council for Tangible Assets (past Chairman). Steve's keen appreciation of history is reflected in his active participation in other organizations, including past board positions on the Texas Historical Foundation and the Dallas Historical Society (where he also served as Exhibits Chairman). Steve is an avid collector of Texas books, manuscripts, and national currency, and he owns one of the largest and finest collections in private hands. He is also a past Board Chair of Dallas Challenge, and is currently the Finance Chair of the Phoenix House of Texas.

James Halperin - Co-Chairman
Born in Boston in 1952, Jim formed a part-time rare coin business at age 15 after discovering he had a knack (along with a nearly photographic memory) for coins. Jim scored a perfect 800 on his math SATs and received early acceptance to Harvard College, but after attending three semesters took a permanent leave of absence to pursue his full-time numismatic career. In 1975, Jim supervised the protocols for the first mainframe computer system in the numismatic business, which would catapult New England Rare Coin Galleries to the top of the industry in less than four years. In 1982, Jim's business merged with that of his friend and former archrival Steve Ivy. Their partnership has become Heritage Auctions, the third-largest auction house in the world. Jim is also a well-known futurist, an active collector of EC comics and early 20th-century American art (visit www.jhalpe.com), venture capital investor, philanthropist (he endows a multimillion-dollar health education foundation), and part-time novelist. His first fiction book, *The Truth Machine*, was published in 1996, became an international science fiction bestseller, and was optioned for movie development by Warner Brothers and Lions Gate. Jim's second novel, *The First Immortal*, was published in early 1998 and immediately optioned as a Hallmark Hall of Fame television miniseries.

Greg Rohan - President
At the age of eight, Greg Rohan started collecting coins as well as buying them for resale to his schoolmates. By 1971, at the age of 10, he was already buying and selling coins from a dealer's table at trade shows in his hometown of Seattle. His business grew rapidly, and by 1985 he had offices in both Seattle and Minneapolis. He joined Heritage in 1987 as Executive Vice-President. Today, as a partner and as President of Heritage, his responsibilities include overseeing the firm's private client group and working with top collectors in every field in which Heritage is active. Greg has been involved with many of the rarest items and most important collections handled by the firm, including the purchase and/or sale of the Ed Trompeter Collection (the world's largest numismatic purchase according to the Guinness Book of World Records). During his career, Greg has handled more than $1 billion of rare coins, collectibles and art. He has provided expert testimony for the United States Attorneys in San Francisco, Dallas, and Philadelphia, and for the Federal Trade Commission (FTC). He has worked with collectors, consignors, and their advisors regarding significant collections of books, manuscripts, comics, currency, jewelry, vintage movie posters, sports and entertainment memorabilia, decorative arts, and fine art. Greg is a past Chapter Chairman for North Texas of the Young Presidents' Organization (YPO), and is an active supporter of the arts. Greg co-authored "The Collectors Estate Handbook," winner of the NLG's Robert Friedberg Award for numismatic book of the year. He previously served on the seven-person Advisory Board to the Federal Reserve Bank of Dallas, in his second appointed term.

Paul Minshull - Chief Operating Officer
As Chief Operating Officer, Paul Minshull's managerial responsibilities include integrating sales, personnel, inventory, security and MIS for Heritage. His major accomplishments include overseeing the hardware migration from mainframe to PC, the software migration of all inventory and sales systems, and implementation of a major Internet presence. Heritage's successful employee-suggestion program has generated 200 or more ideas each month since 1995, and has helped increase employee productivity, expand business, and improve employee retention. Paul oversees the company's highly-regarded IT department, and has been the driving force behind Heritage's Web development, now a significant portion of Heritage's future plans. As the first auction house that combined traditional floor bidding with active Internet bidding, the totally interactive system has catapulted Heritage to the top collectible and Fine Art website (Forbes Magazine's "Best of the Web"). Paul came to Heritage in 1984. Since 1987, he has been Chief Operating Officer for all Heritage companies and affiliates.

Todd Imhof - Executive Vice President
Unlike most of his contemporaries, Todd Imhof did not start collecting in his teens. Shortly after graduating college, Todd declined offers from prestigious Wall Street banks to join a former classmate at a small rare coin firm in the Seattle area. In the mid-1980s, the rare coin industry was rapidly changing, with the advent of third-party grading and growing computer technologies. As a newcomer, Todd more easily embraced these new dynamics and quickly emerged as a highly respected dealer. In 1991, he co-founded Pinnacle Rarities, a firm specialized in servicing the savviest and most preeminent collectors in numismatics. At only 25, he was accepted into the PNG, and currently serves on its Consumer Protection Committee and its Legislation/Taxation Issues Committee. In 1992, he was invited to join the Board of Directors for the Industry Council for Tangible Assets, later serving as its Chairman (2002-2005). Since joining Heritage in 2006, Todd continues to advise most of Heritage's largest and most prominent clients.

Leo Frese - Vice President
Leo has been involved in numismatics for nearly 40 years, a professional numismatist since 1971, and has been with Heritage for more than 20 years. He literally worked his way up the Heritage "ladder," working with Bob Merrill for nearly 15 years, then becoming Director of Consignments. Leo has been actively involved in assisting clients sell nearly $500,000,000 in numismatic material. Leo was recently accepted as a member of PNG, is a life member of the ANA, and holds membership in FUN, CSNS, and other numismatic organizations.

Jim Stoutjesdyk - Vice President
Jim Stoutjesdyk was named Vice President of Heritage Rare Coin Galleries in 2004. He was named ANA's Outstanding Young Numismatist of the Year in 1987. A University of Michigan graduate, he was first employed by Superior Galleries, eventually becoming their Director of Collector Sales. Since joining Heritage in 1993, Jim has served in many capacities. Jim's duties now include buying and selling, pricing all new purchases, assisting with auction estimates and reserves, and overseeing the daily operations of the rare coin department.

Norma L. Gonzalez - VP of Auction Operations
Norma Gonzalez joined the U.S. Navy in August of 1993 and received her Bachelor's Degree in Resource Management. She joined Heritage in 1998 and was promoted to Vice President in 2003. She currently manages the operations departments, including Coins, Currency, World & Ancient Coins, Sportscards & Memorabilia, Comics, Movie Posters, Pop Culture and Political Memorabilia.

Debbie Rexing - VP - Marketing
Debbie Rexing joined the Heritage team in 2001 and her marketing credentials include degrees in Business Administration and Human Resources from The Ohio State University. Debbie has worked across many categories within the company leading to her comprehensive and integrative approach to the job. She guides all aspects of Heritage's print marketing strategies – advertisements, brochures, direct mail campaigns, coordination of print buying, catalog design and production, The Heritage Magazine, and media and press relations.

Ron Brackemyre - Vice President
Ron Brackemyre began his career at Heritage Auction Galleries in 1998 as the Manager of the Shipping Department, was promoted to Consignment Operations Manager for Numismatics in 2004 and in 2009 added oversight of the entire photography operation at Heritage, wherein his department coordinates all photography, scanning and photoshopping. He is also responsible for the security of all of Heritage's coin and currency consignments, both at the Dallas world headquarters and at shows, as well as cataloging of coins for upcoming auctions, coordination of auction planning, security and transportation logistics, lot-view, auction prep and oversight for the entire shipping department.

Marti Korver - Manager - Credit/Collections
Marti Korver was recruited out of the banking profession by Jim Ruddy, and she worked with Paul Rynearson, Karl Stephens, and Judy Cahn on ancients and world coins at Bowers & Ruddy Galleries, in Hollywood, CA. She migrated into the coin auction business, and represented bidders as agent at B&R auctions for 10 years. She also worked as a research assistant for Q. David Bowers for several years.

Mark Prendergast - Director, Trusts & Estates
Mark Prendergast earned his degree in Art History from Vanderbilt University and began his career in the arts working with a national dealer in private sales of 20th Century American Art. Joining Christie's in 1998 and advancing during a 10 year tenure to the position of Vice President, he was instrumental in bringing to market many important and prominent works of art, collections and estates. Having established a Houston office for Heritage, he serves as Director of Business Development, Trusts & Estates, providing assistance to fiduciary professionals and private clients with appraisals, collection assessments and auction consignments in all areas of art and collectibles.

Coin Department

David Mayfield - Vice President, Numismatics
David Mayfield has been collecting and trading rare coins and currency for over 35 years. A chance encounter with his father's coin collection at the age of nine led to his lifetime interest. David has been buying and selling at coin shows since the age of 10. He became a full time coin and currency dealer in the mid-1980s. David's main collecting interest is in all things Texas, specializing in currency and documents from the Republic of Texas.

Jim Jelinski - Consignment Director & Senior Numismatist
Jim Jelinski has been involved in numismatics for more than five decades as a collector, dealer and educator. He started as Buyer for Paramount International Coin Corporation in 1972, opened Essex Numismatic Properties in 1975 in New Hampshire and has held numerous executive positions at M.B. Simmons & Associates of Narberth, Pennsylvania. He works at Heritage as a Senior Numismatist and Consignment Coordinator.

Bob Marino - Consignment Director & Senior Numismatist
Bob Marino joined Heritage in 1999, managing and developing Internet coin sales, and building Heritage's client base through eBay and other Internet auction Web sites. He has successfully concluded more than 40,000 transactions on eBay. He is now a Consignment Director, assisting consignors in placing their coins and collectibles in the best of the many Heritage venues.

Sam Foose - Consignment Director and Auctioneer
Sam Foose joined Heritage Numismatic Auctions, Inc., in 1993 as an Auction Coordinator. He rose to Assistant Auction Director in 1998, and began calling auctions. After a stint serving as a Senior Manager and Consignment Director in other collectible fields, he returned to Heritage in 2002 as a Consignment Director to help Heritage's expansion into other collectibles fields. Besides calling auctions as one of Heritage's primary auctioneers, he travels the nation assisting clients who wish to liquidate their collections of coins, paper money, decorative arts, and sports collectibles.

Katherine Kurachek - Consignment Director
Katherine Kurachek graduated from the University of Mississippi in 1993 as an art major. She came to Heritage in January 2003, working alongside Leo Frese for several years, learning the numismatic wholesale trade. Katherine frequently travels to coin shows to represent Heritage and service her dealer accounts along with her wide ranging duties as Consignment Director.

Shaunda Fry - Consignment Director
Shaunda Fry ran her own textile company for 22 years before meeting Leo Frese while co-coordinating a local school auction. She followed his suggestion to add auctioneering to her list of talents and, after training, worked part-time at Heritage auctions and began to call. She became a Consignment Director and now travels to shows as part of the "Wholesale Dealers Team."

Mike Sadler - Consignment Director
Mike Sadler joined the Heritage team in September 2003. He attended the United States Air Force Academy, flew jets for the military and is a longtime pilot with American Airlines. Before coming to Heritage, his unlimited access to air travel enabled Mike to attend coin shows around the nation, and to build a world class collection that was auctioned by Heritage in 2004. He is known for his tremendous knowledge of rare coins, making him a trusted colleague to many of today's most active collectors.

Chris Dykstra - Consignment Director
Chris Dykstra joined Heritage October 2006. He has held a number of jobs at Heritage including a stint in Wholesale Sales assisting Heritage's dealer clients in locating specific coins and travelling to shows to work the Heritage booth. In August 2008 Chris was promoted into the US Coin Consignments department as a Consignment Director where he now assists consignors in bringing their collections to auction.

Jason Friedman - Consignment Director
Jason's interest in rare coins, which began at 12 and expanded into his own numismatic business, allowed him to pay for most of his college tuition at the University of North Texas, from which he graduated in 2005. He joined Heritage soon after. He is a member of the American Numismatic Association (ANA) and Florida United Numismatists (FUN).

Bert DeLaGarza - Consignment Director
Bert DeLaGarza joined Heritage in 2008, capitalizing on a longtime passion for, and expertise in rare coins from a very young age. Prior to Heritage, Bert spent over 25 years in Landscape Construction and Estate Management having achieved the Texas Master Nurseryman certification. A member of the ANA, Bert is known for his strong knowledge of U.S. coins and an eye for rare U.S. stamps.

Win Callender - Consignment Director & Senior Numismatist
Win Callender has joined Heritage Auction Galleries as a professional numismatist and consignment director. A lifelong numismatist - he found a 1770 Russian 5 Kopek when he was just 5 years old - Callender parlayed his hobby into a fulltime business when he was in his mid-30s, starting his own business in Broken Arrow, Okla., in 1993. He subsequently worked for Carter Numismatics and David Lawrence Rare Coins, working his way up to Vice President in both firms.

Jessica Aylmer - Consignment Director
Jessica joined the Heritage staff as a Consignment Coordinator in 2007, shortly after graduating with a Bachelor's in Art History from the University of North Texas. She was moved up to Consignment Director in 2009, where her main focus is now on working as part of the Heritage dealer consignment team. Jessica has become a familiar face to the numismatic community, attending coin shows and expositions across the country on a weekly basis. Jessica is a member of the American Numismatic Association, Florida United Numismatists and Women In Numismatics.

Diedre Buchmoyer - Consignment Director
Diedre has worked full-time in the numismatic arena for the past eight years buying and selling rare coins, and assisted in several prestigious auctions including the John J. Ford, Jr. Collection. An honors graduate from Hood College in Frederick, Maryland, Diedre received her BA in Art History with a concentration in Archaeology and a double minor in Business Management and Studio Art. She is a member of the American Numismatic Association, Florida United Numismatics, Women in Numismatics and the Industry Council for Tangible Assets.

Mark Van Winkle - Chief Cataloger
Mark has worked for Heritage, and Steve Ivy, since 1979. He has been Chief Cataloger since 1990, and has handled some of the premier numismatic rarities sold at public auction. Mark was editor of Legacy magazine, won the 1989 NLG award for Best U.S. Commercial Magazine, and has won numerous awards for his writing, including the 1990 NLG award for Best Article for his *Interview With John Ford*, the 1996 NLG Best Numismatic Article for *Changing Concepts of Liberty*. He has published extensively and written articles for *Coin World, Numismatic News* and has contributed to editions of the *Red Book, United States Patterns and Related Issues*, and *The Guide Book of Double Eagle Gold Coins.*

Mark Borckardt - Senior Cataloger
Mark started attending coin shows and conventions as a dealer in 1970, and has been a full-time professional numismatist since 1980. He received the Early American Coppers Literary Award, and the Numismatic Literary Guild's Book of the Year Award, for the *Encyclopedia of Early United States Cents, 1793-1814*, published in 2000. He serves as a contributor to *A Guide Book of United States Coins,* and has contributed to many references, including the Harry W. Bass, Jr. Sylloge, and the *Encyclopedia of Silver Dollars and Trade Dollars of the United States.* Most recently, he was Senior Numismatist with Bowers and Merena Galleries. Mark is a life member of the A. N. A., and an active member of numerous organizations.

Brian Koller - Cataloger & Catalog Production Manager
Brian Koller has been a Heritage cataloger since 2001, before that working as a telecom software engineer for 16 years. He is a graduate of Iowa State University with a Bachelor's degree in Computer Engineering, and is an avid collector of U.S. gold coins. His attention to detail ensures that every catalog, printed and on-line, is as error free as technology and human activity allows. In addition to his coin cataloging duties, he also helps with consignor promises and client service issues.

Dr. Jon Amato - Cataloger
Jon Amato has been with Heritage since 2004. He earned his Ph. D. from the University of Toronto, and was previously a Program Manager in the NY State Dept. of Economic Development, and an Adjunct Professor at the State University of New York at Albany. He is currently writing a monograph on the draped bust, small eagle half dollars of 1796-1797. He has published numerous articles in prestigious numismatic publications and belongs to many numismatic organizations, including the ANA, ANS, John Reich Collectors Society, and the Liberty Seated Collectors Club, and has made several presentations at ANA Numismatic Theaters.

John Dale Beety - Cataloger
John Dale Beety served an internship at Heritage during the summer of 2004 and started full-time as a cataloger in 2006, immediately after graduating from Rose-Hulman Institute of Technology. In addition to catalog writing and editing, he creates the Coin Monday posts that appear weekly on the official Heritage Auction Galleries blog, heritageauctions.blogspot.com.

Cataloged by: Mark Van Winkle, Chief Cataloger
Mark Borckardt, Senior Numismatist; Jon Amato, John Beety, George Huber, Brian Koller, Dave Stone
Edited by: Mark Van Winkle, John Beety, George Huber, Stewart Huckaby, Bob Korver
Operations Support by: Christina Gonzales, San Juana Gonzalez, Manuela Bueno, Christina Ibarra, Ira Reynolds, Cynthia Pina, Daisy Manhard, Maria Flores, Jose Martinez
Catalog and Internet Imaging by: Travis Awalt, Maribel Cazares, Joel Gonzalez, Colleen McInerney, Sharon Johnson, Nancy Ramos, Jason Young, Tony Webb, Donna Rusnak
Production and Design by: Katie Brown, Mark Masat, Mary Hermann, Debbie Rexing

Auctioneer and Auction:

1. This Auction is presented by Heritage Auction Galleries, a d/b/a/ of Heritage Auctions, Inc., or its affiliates Heritage Numismatic Auctions, Inc., or Heritage Vintage Sports Auctions, Inc., or Currency Auctions of America, Inc., as identified with the applicable licensing information on the title page of the catalog or on the HA.com Internet site (the "Auctioneer"). The Auction is conducted under these Terms and Conditions of Auction and applicable state and local law. Announcements and corrections from the podium and those made through the Terms and Conditions of Auctions appearing on the Internet at HA.com supersede those in the printed catalog.

Buyer's Premium:

2. On bids placed through Auctioneer, a Buyer's Premium of fifteen percent (15%) will be added to the successful hammer price bid on lots in Coin, Currency, and Philatelic auctions or nineteen and one-half percent (19.5%) on lots in all other auctions. There is a minimum Buyer's Premium of $14.00 per lot. In Gallery Auctions (sealed bid auctions of mostly bulk numismatic material), the Buyer's Premium is 19.5%.

Auction Venues:

3. The following Auctions are conducted solely on the Internet: Heritage Weekly Internet Auctions (Coin, Currency, Comics, and Vintage Movie Poster); Heritage Monthly Internet Auctions (Sports, and Stamps). Signature® Auctions and Grand Format Auctions accept bids from the Internet, telephone, fax, or mail first, followed by a floor bidding session; Heritage Live and real-time telephone bidding are available to registered clients during these auctions.

Bidders:

4. Any person participating or registering for the Auction agrees to be bound by and accepts these Terms and Conditions of Auction ("Bidder(s)").
5. All Bidders must meet Auctioneer's qualifications to bid. Any Bidder who is not a client in good standing of the Auctioneer may be disqualified at Auctioneer's sole option and will not be awarded lots. Such determination may be made by Auctioneer in its sole and unlimited discretion, at any time prior to, during, or even after the close of the Auction. Auctioneer reserves the right to exclude any person from the auction.
6. If an entity places a bid, then the person executing the bid on behalf of the entity agrees to personally guarantee payment for any successful bid.

Credit:

7. Bidders who have not established credit with the Auctioneer must either furnish satisfactory credit information (including two collectibles-related business references) well in advance of the Auction or supply valid credit card information. Bids placed through our Interactive Internet program will only be accepted from pre-registered Bidders; Bidders who are not members of HA.com or affiliates should pre-register at least 48 hours before the start of the first session (exclusive of holidays or weekends) to allow adequate time to contact references. Credit may be granted at the discretion of Auctioneer. Additionally Bidders who have not previously established credit or who wish to bid in excess of their established credit history may be required to provide their social security number or the last four digits thereof to us so a credit check may be performed prior to Auctioneer's acceptance of a bid.

Bidding Options:

8. Bids in Signature. Auctions or Grand Format Auctions may be placed as set forth in the printed catalog section entitled "Choose your bidding method." For auctions held solely on the Internet, see the alternatives on HA.com. Review at HA.com/common/howtobid.php.
9. Presentment of Bids: Non-Internet bids (including but not limited to podium, fax, phone and mail bids) are treated similar to floor bids in that they must be on-increment or at a half increment (called a cut bid). Any podium, fax, phone, or mail bids that do not conform to a full or half increment will be rounded up or down to the nearest full or half increment and this revised amount will be considered your high bid.
10. Auctioneer's Execution of Certain Bids. Auctioneer cannot be responsible for your errors in bidding, so carefully check that every bid is entered correctly. When identical mail or FAX bids are submitted, preference is given to the first received. To ensure the greatest accuracy, your written bids should be entered on the standard printed bid sheet and be received at Auctioneer's place of business at least two business days before the Auction start. Auctioneer is not responsible for executing mail bids or FAX bids received on or after the day the first lot is sold, nor Internet bids submitted after the published closing time; nor is Auctioneer responsible for proper execution of bids submitted by telephone, mail, FAX, e-mail, Internet, or in person once the Auction begins. Internet bids may not be withdrawn until your written request is received and acknowledged by Auctioneer (FAX: 214-4438425); such requests must state the reason, and may constitute grounds for withdrawal of bidding privileges. Lots won by mail Bidders will not be delivered at the Auction unless prearranged.
11. Caveat as to Bid Increments. Bid increments (over the current bid level) determine the lowest amount you may bid on a particular lot. Bids greater than one increment over the current bid can be any whole dollar amount. It is possible under several circumstances for winning bids to be between increments, sometimes only $1 above the previous increment. Please see: "How can I lose by less than an increment?" on our website. Bids will be accepted in whole dollar amounts only. No "buy" or "unlimited" bids will be accepted.

The following chart governs current bidding increments.

Current Bid	Bid Increment	Current Bid	Bid Increment
<$10	$1	$20,000 - $29,999	$2,000
$10 - $29	$2	$30,000 - $49,999	$2,500
$30 - $49	$3	$50,000 - $99,999	$5,000
$50 - $99	$5	$100,000 - $199,999	$10,000
$100 - $199	$10	$200,000 - $299,999	$20,000
$200 - $299	$20	$300,000 - $499,999	$25,000
$300 - $499	$25	$500,000 - $999,999	$50,000
$500 - $999	$50	$1,000,000 - $1,999,999	$100,000
$1,000 - $1,999	$100	$2,000,000 - $2,999,999	$200,000
$2,000 - $2,999	$200	$3,000,000 - $4,999,999	$250,000
$3,000 - $4,999	$250	$5,000,000 - $9,999,999	$500,000
$5,000 - $9,999	$500	>$10,000,000	$1,000,000
$10,000 - $19,999	$1,000		

12. If Auctioneer calls for a full increment, a bidder may request Auctioneer to accept a bid at half of the increment ("Cut Bid") only once per lot. After offering a Cut Bid, bidders may continue to participate only at full increments. Off-increment bids may be accepted by the Auctioneer at Signature® Auctions and Grand Format Auctions. If the Auctioneer solicits bids other than the expected increment, these bids will not be considered Cut Bids.

Conducting the Auction:

13. Notice of the consignor's liberty to place bids on his lots in the Auction is hereby made in accordance with Article 2 of the Texas Business and Commercial Code. A "Minimum Bid" is an amount below which the lot will not sell. THE CONSIGNOR OF PROPERTY MAY PLACE WRITTEN "Minimum Bids" ON HIS LOTS IN ADVANCE OF THE AUCTION; ON SUCH LOTS, IF THE HAMMER PRICE DOES NOT MEET THE "Minimum Bid", THE CONSIGNOR MAY PAY A REDUCED COMMISSION ON THOSE LOTS. "Minimum Bids" are generally posted online several days prior to the Auction closing. For any successful bid placed by a consignor on his Property on the Auction floor, or by any means during the live session, or after the "Minimum Bid" for an Auction have been posted, we will require the consignor to pay full Buyer's Premium and Seller's Commissions on such lot.
14. The highest qualified Bidder recognized by the Auctioneer shall be the buyer. In the event of any dispute between any Bidders at an Auction, Auctioneer may at his sole discretion reoffer the lot. Auctioneer's decision and declaration of the winning Bidder shall be final and binding upon all Bidders. Bids properly offered, whether by floor Bidder or other means of bidding, may on occasion be missed or go unrecognized; in such cases, the Auctioneer may declare the recognized bid accepted as the winning bid, regardless of whether a competing bid may have been higher.
15. Auctioneer reserves the right to refuse to honor any bid or to limit the amount of any bid, in its sole discretion. A bid is considered not made in "Good Faith" when made by an insolvent or irresponsible person, a person under the age of eighteen, or is not supported by satisfactory credit, collectibles references, or otherwise. Regardless of the disclosure of his identity, any bid by a consignor or his agent on a lot consigned by him is deemed to be made in "Good Faith." Any person apparently appearing on the OFAC list is not eligible to bid.
16. Nominal Bids. The Auctioneer in its sole discretion may reject nominal bids, small opening bids, or very nominal advances. If a lot bearing estimates fails to open for 40–60% of the low estimate, the Auctioneer may pass the item or may place a protective bid on behalf of the consignor.
17. Lots bearing bidding estimates shall open at Auctioneer's discretion (approximately 50%-60% of the low estimate). In the event that no bid meets or exceeds that opening amount, the lot shall pass as unsold.
18. All items are to be purchased per lot as numerically indicated and no lots will be broken. Auctioneer reserves the right to withdraw, prior to the close, any lots from the Auction.
19. Auctioneer reserves the right to rescind the sale in the event of nonpayment, breach of a warranty, disputed ownership, auctioneer's clerical error or omission in exercising bids and reserves, or for any other reason and in Auctioneer's sole discretion. In cases of nonpayment, Auctioneer's election to void a sale does not relieve the Bidder from their obligation to pay Auctioneer its fees (seller's and buyer's premium) and any other damages or expenses pertaining to the lot.
20. Auctioneer occasionally experiences Internet and/or Server service outages, and Auctioneer periodically schedules system downtime for maintenance and other purposes, during which Bidders cannot participate or place bids. If such outages occur, we may at our discretion extend bidding for the Auction. Bidders unable to place their Bids through the Internet are directed to contact Client Services at 1-800-872-6467.
21. The Auctioneer or its affiliates may consign items to be sold in the Auction, and may bid on those lots or any other lots. Auctioneer or affiliates expressly reserve the right to modify any such bids at any time prior to the hammer based upon data made known to the Auctioneer or its affiliates. The Auctioneer may extend advances, guarantees, or loans to certain consignors, and may extend financing or other credits at varying rates to certain Bidders in the auction.
22. The Auctioneer has the right to sell certain unsold items after the close of the Auction. Such lots shall be considered sold during the Auction and all these Terms and Conditions shall apply to such sales including but not limited to the Buyer's Premium, return rights, and disclaimers.

Payment:

23. All sales are strictly for cash in United States dollars (including U.S. currency, bank wire, cashier checks, travelers checks, eChecks, and bank money orders, all subject to reporting requirements). All are subject to clearing and funds being received In Auctioneer's account before delivery of the purchases. Auctioneer reserves the right to determine if a check constitutes "good funds" when drawn on a U.S. bank for ten days, and thirty days when drawn on an international bank. Credit Card (Visa or Master Card only) and PayPal payments may be accepted up to $10,000 from non-dealers at the sole discretion of the Auctioneer, subject to the following limitations: a) sales are only to the cardholder, b) purchases are shipped to the cardholder's registered and verified address, c) Auctioneer may pre-approve the cardholder's credit line, d) a credit card transaction may not be used in conjunction with any other financing or extended terms offered by the Auctioneer, and must transact immediately upon invoice presentation, e) rights of return are governed by these Terms and Conditions, which supersede those conditions promulgated by the card issuer, f) floor Bidders must present their card.
24. Payment is due upon closing of the Auction session, or upon presentment of an invoice. Auctioneer reserves the right to void an invoice if payment in full is not received within 7 days after the close of the Auction. In cases of nonpayment, Auctioneer's election to void a sale does not relieve the Bidder from their obligation to pay Auctioneer its fees (seller's and buyer's premium) on the lot and any other damages pertaining to the lot.
25. Lots delivered to you, or your representative in the States of Texas, California, **New York**, or other states where the Auction may be held, are subject to all applicable state and local taxes, unless appropriate permits are on file with Auctioneer. Bidder agrees to pay Auctioneer the actual amount of tax due in the event that sales tax is not properly collected due to: 1) an expired, inaccurate, inappropriate tax certificate or declaration, 2) an incorrect interpretation of the applicable statute, 3) or any other reason. The appropriate form or certificate must be on file at and verified by Auctioneer five days prior to Auction or tax must be paid; only if such form or certificate is received by Auctioneer within 4 days after the Auction can a refund of tax paid be made. Lots from different Auctions may not be aggregated for sales tax purposes.
26. In the event that a Bidder's payment is dishonored upon presentment(s), Bidder shall pay the maximum statutory processing fee set by applicable state law. If you attempt to pay via eCheck and your financial institution denies this transfer from your bank account, or the payment cannot be completed using the selected funding source, you agree to complete payment using your credit card on file.
27. If any Auction invoice submitted by Auctioneer is not paid in full when due, the unpaid balance will bear interest at the highest rate permitted by law from the date of invoice until paid. Any invoice not paid when due will bear a three percent (3%) late fee on the invoice amount or three percent (3%) of any installment that is past due. If the Auctioneer refers any invoice to an attorney for collection, the buyer agrees to pay attorney's fees, court costs, and other collection costs incurred by Auctioneer. If Auctioneer assigns collection to its in-house legal staff, such attorney's time expended on the matter shall be compensated at a rate comparable to the hourly rate of independent attorneys.
28. In the event a successful Bidder fails to pay any amounts due, Auctioneer reserves the right to sell the lot(s) securing the invoice to any underbidders in the Auction that the lot(s) appeared, or at subsequent private or public sale, or relist the lot(s) in a future auction conducted by Auctioneer. A defaulting Bidder agrees to pay for the reasonable costs of resale (including a 10% seller's commission, if consigned to an auction conducted by Auctioneer). The defaulting Bidder is liable to pay any difference between his total original invoice for the lot(s), plus any applicable interest, and the net proceeds for the lot(s) if sold at private sale or the subsequent hammer price of the lot(s) less the 10% seller's commissions, if sold at an Auctioneer's auction.

29. Auctioneer reserves the right to require payment in full in good funds before delivery of the merchandise.
30. Auctioneer shall have a lien against the merchandise purchased by the buyer to secure payment of the Auction invoice. Auctioneer is further granted a lien and the right to retain possession of any other property of the buyer then held by the Auctioneer or its affiliates to secure payment of any Auction invoice or any other amounts due the Auctioneer or affiliates from the buyer. With respect to these lien rights, Auctioneer shall have all the rights of a secured creditor under Article 9 of the Texas Uniform Commercial Code, including but not limited to the right of sale. In addition, with respect to payment of the Auction invoice(s), the buyer waives any and all rights of offset he might otherwise have against the Auctioneer and the consignor of the merchandise included on the invoice. If a Bidder owes Auctioneer or its affiliates on any account, Auctioneer and its affiliates shall have the right to offset such unpaid account by any credit balance due Bidder, and it may secure by possessory lien any unpaid amount by any of the Bidder's property in their possession.
31. Title shall not pass to the successful Bidder until all invoices are paid in full. It is the responsibility of the buyer to provide adequate insurance coverage for the items once they have been delivered to a common carrier or third-party shipper.

Delivery; Shipping; and Handling Charges:

32. Buyer is liable for shipping and handling. Please refer to Auctioneer's website www.HA.com/common/shipping.php for the latest charges or call Auctioneer. Auctioneer is unable to combine purchases from other auctions or affiliates into one package for shipping purposes. Lots won will be shipped in a commercially reasonable time after payment in good funds for the merchandise and the shipping fees is received or credit extended, except when third-party shipment occurs.
33. Successful international Bidders shall provide written shipping instructions, including specified customs declarations, to the Auctioneer for any lots to be delivered outside of the United States. NOTE: Declaration value shall be the item'(s) hammer price together with its buyer's premium and Auctioneer shall use the correct harmonized code for the lot. Domestic Buyers on lots designated for third-party shipment must designate the common carrier, accept risk of loss, and prepay shipping costs.
34. All shipping charges will be borne by the successful Bidder. Any risk of loss during shipment will be borne by the buyer following Auctioneer's delivery to the designated common carrier or third-party shipper, regardless of domestic or foreign shipment.
35. Due to the nature of some items sold, it shall be the responsibility for the successful bidder to arrange pick-up and shipping through third-parties; as to such items Auctioneer shall have no liability. Failure to pick-up or arrange shipping in a timely fashion (within ten days) shall subject Lots to storage and moving charges, including a $100 administration fee plus $10 daily storage for larger items and $5.00 daily for smaller items (storage fee per item) after 35 days. In the event the Lot is not removed within ninety days, the Lot may be offered for sale to recover any past due storage or moving fees, including a 10% Seller's Commission.
36. The laws of various countries regulate the import or export of certain plant and animal properties, including (but not limited to) items made of (or including) ivory, whalebone, turtleshell, coral, crocodile, or other wildlife. Transport of such lots may require special licenses for export, import, or both. Bidder is responsible for: 1) obtaining all information on such restricted items for both export and import; 2) obtaining all such licenses and/or permits. Delay or failure to obtain any such license or permit does not relieve the buyer of timely compliance with standard payment terms. For further information, please contact Ron Brackemyre at 800-872-6467 ext. 1312.
37. Any request for shipping verification for undelivered packages must be made within 30 days of shipment by Auctioneer.

Cataloging, Warranties and Disclaimers:

38. NO WARRANTY, WHETHER EXPRESSED OR IMPLIED, IS MADE WITH RESPECT TO ANY DESCRIPTION CONTAINED IN THIS AUCTION OR ANY SECOND OPINE. Any description of the items or second opine contained in this Auction is for the sole purpose of identifying the items for those Bidders who do not have the opportunity to view the lots prior to bidding, and no description of items has been made part of the basis of the bargain or has created any express warranty that the goods would conform to any description made by Auctioneer. Color variations can be expected in any electronic or printed imaging, and are not grounds for the return of any lot. NOTE: Auctioneer, in specified auction venues, for example, Fine Art, may have express written warranties and you are referred to those specific terms and conditions. .
39. Auctioneer is selling only such right or title to the items being sold as Auctioneer may have by virtue of consignment agreements on the date of auction and disclaims any warranty of title to the Property. Auctioneer disclaims any warranty of merchantability or fitness for any particular purposes. All images, descriptions, sales data, and archival records are the exclusive property of Auctioneer, and may be used by Auctioneer for advertising, promotion, archival records, and any other uses deemed appropriate.
40. Translations of foreign language documents may be provided as a convenience to interested parties. Auctioneer makes no representation as to the accuracy of those translations and will not be held responsible for errors in bidding arising from inaccuracies in translation.
41. Auctioneer disclaims all liability for damages, consequential or otherwise, arising out of or in connection with the sale of any Property by Auctioneer to Bidder. No third party may rely on any benefit of these Terms and Conditions and any rights, if any, established hereunder are personal to the Bidder and may not be assigned. Any statement made by the Auctioneer is an opinion and does not constitute a warranty or representation. No employee of Auctioneer may alter these Terms and Conditions, and, unless signed by a principal of Auctioneer, any such alteration is null and void.
42. Auctioneer shall not be liable for breakage of glass or damage to frames (patent or latent); such defects, in any event, shall not be a basis for any claim for return or reduction in purchase price.

Release:

43. In consideration of participation in the Auction and the placing of a bid, Bidder expressly releases Auctioneer, its officers, directors and employees, its affiliates, and its outside experts that provide second opines, from any and all claims, cause of action, chose of action, whether at law or equity or any arbitration or mediation rights existing under the rules of any professional society or affiliation based upon the assigned description, or a derivative theory, breach of warranty express or implied, representation or other matter set forth within these Terms and Conditions of Auction or otherwise. In the event of a claim, Bidder agrees that such rights and privileges conferred therein are strictly construed as specifically declared herein; e.g., authenticity, typographical error, etc. and are the exclusive remedy. Bidder, by non-compliance to these express terms of a granted remedy, shall waive any claim against Auctioneer.
44. Notice: Some Property sold by Auctioneer are inherently dangerous e.g. firearms, cannons, and small items that may be swallowed or ingested or may have latent defects all of which may cause harm to a person. Purchaser accepts all risk of loss or damage from its purchase of these items and Auctioneer disclaims any liability whether under contract or tort for damages and losses, direct or inconsequential, and expressly disclaims any warranty as to safety or usage of any lot sold.

Dispute Resolution and Arbitration Provision:

45. By placing a bid or otherwise participating in the auction, Bidder accepts these Terms and Conditions of Auction, and specifically agrees to the dispute resolution provided herein. Consumer disputes shall be resolved through court litigation which has an exclusive Dallas, Texas venue clause and jury waiver. Non-consumer dispute shall be determined in binding arbitration which arbitration replaces the right to go to court, including the right to a jury trial.
46. Auctioneer in no event shall be responsible for consequential damages, incidental damages, compensatory damages, or any other damages arising or claimed to be arising from the auction of any lot. In the event that Auctioneer cannot deliver the lot or subsequently it is established that the lot lacks title, or other transfer or condition issue is claimed, In such cases the sole remedy shall be limited to rescission of sale and refund of the amount paid by Bidder; in no case shall Auctioneer's maximum liability exceed the high bid on that lot, which bid shall be deemed for all purposes the value of the lot. After one year has elapsed, Auctioneer's maximum liability shall be limited to any commissions and fees Auctioneer earned on that lot.
47. In the event of an attribution error, Auctioneer may at its sole discretion, correct the error on the Internet, or, if discovered at a later date, to refund the buyer's purchase price without further obligation.
48. Dispute Resolution for Consumers and Non-Consumers: Any claim, dispute, or controversy in connection with, relating to and /or arising out of the Auction, participation in the Auction. Award of lots, damages of claims to lots, descriptions, condition reports, provenance, estimates, return and warranty rights, any interpretation of these Terms and Conditions, any alleged verbal modification of these Terms and Conditions and/or any purported settlement whether asserted in contract, tort, under Federal or State statute or regulation shall or any other matter: a) if presented by a consumer, be exclusively heard by, and the parties consent to, exclusive in personam jurisdiction in the State District Courts of Dallas County, Texas. THE PARTIES EXPRESSLY WAIVE ANY RIGHT TO TRIAL BY JURY. Any appeals shall be solely pursued in the appellate courts of the State of Texas; or b) for any claimant other than a consumer, the claim shall be presented in confidential binding arbitration before a single arbitrator, that the parties may agree upon, selected from the JAMS list of Texas arbitrators. The case is not to be administrated by JAMS; however, if the parties cannot agree on an arbitrator, then JAMS shall appoint the arbitrator and it shall be conducted under JAMS rules. The locale shall be Dallas Texas. The arbitrator's award may be enforced in any court of competent jurisdiction. Any party on any claim involving the purchase or sale of numismatic or related items may elect arbitration through binding PNG arbitration. Any claim must be brought within one (1) year of the alleged breach, default or misrepresentation or the claim is waived. This agreement and any claims shall be determined and construed under Texas law. The prevailing party (party that is awarded substantial and material relief on its claim or defense) may be awarded its reasonable attorneys' fees and costs.
49. No claims of any kind can be considered after the settlements have been made with the consignors. Any dispute after the settlement date is strictly between the Bidder and consignor without involvement or responsibility of the Auctioneer.
50. In consideration of their participation in or application for the Auction, a person or entity (whether the successful Bidder, a Bidder, a purchaser and/or other Auction participant or registrant) agrees that all disputes in any way relating to, arising under, connected with, or incidental to these Terms and Conditions and purchases, or default in payment thereof, shall be arbitrated pursuant to the arbitration provision. In the event that any matter including actions to compel arbitration, construe the agreement, actions in aid or arbitration or otherwise needs to be litigated, such litigation shall be exclusively in the Courts of the State of Texas, in Dallas County, Texas, and if necessary the corresponding appellate courts. For such actions, the successful Bidder, purchaser, or Auction participant also expressly submits himself to the personal jurisdiction of the State of Texas.
51. These Terms & Conditions provide specific remedies for occurrences in the auction and delivery process. Where such remedies are afforded, they shall be interpreted strictly. Bidder agrees that any claim shall utilize such remedies; Bidder making a claim in excess of those remedies provided in these Terms and Conditions agrees that in no case whatsoever shall Auctioneer's maximum liability exceed the high bid on that lot, which bid shall be deemed for all purposes the value of the lot.

Miscellaneous:

52. Agreements between Bidders and consignors to effectuate a non-sale of an item at Auction, inhibit bidding on a consigned item to enter into a private sale agreement for said item, or to utilize the Auctioneer's Auction to obtain sales for non-selling consigned items subsequent to the Auction, are strictly prohibited. If a subsequent sale of a previously consigned item occurs in violation of this provision, Auctioneer reserves the right to charge Bidder the applicable Buyer's Premium and consignor a Seller's Commission as determined for each auction venue and by the terms of the seller's agreement.
53. Acceptance of these Terms and Conditions qualifies Bidder as a client who has consented to be contacted by Heritage in the future. In conformity with "do-not-call" regulations promulgated by the Federal or State regulatory agencies, participation by the Bidder is affirmative consent to being contacted at the phone number shown in his application and this consent shall remain in effect until it is revoked in writing. Heritage may from time to time contact Bidder concerning sale, purchase, and auction opportunities available through Heritage and its affiliates and subsidiaries.
54. Rules of Construction: Auctioneer presents properties in a number of collectible fields, and as such, specific venues have promulgated supplemental Terms and Conditions. Nothing herein shall be construed to waive the general Terms and Conditions of Auction by these additional rules and shall be construed to give force and effect to the rules in their entirety.

State Notices:

Notice as to an Auction in California. Auctioneer has in compliance with Title 2.95 of the California Civil Code as amended October 11, 1993 Sec. 1812.600, posted with the California Secretary of State its bonds for it and its employees, and the auction is being conducted in compliance with Sec. 2338 of the Commercial Code and Sec. 535 of the Penal Code.

Notice as to an Auction in New York City. These Terms and Conditions are designed to conform to the applicable sections of the New York City Department of Consumer Affairs Rules and Regulations as Amended. This is a Public Auction Sale conducted by Auctioneer. The New York City licensed Auctioneers are Harvey Bennett, No. 0924050, and Samuel W. Foose, No.0952360, who will conduct the Auction on behalf of Heritage Auctions, Inc. ("Auctioneer"). All lots are subject to: the consignor's right to bid thereon in accord with these Terms and Conditions of Auction, consignor's option to receive advances on their consignments, and Auctioneer, in its sole discretion, may offer limited extended financing to registered bidders, in accord with Auctioneer's internal credit standards. A registered bidder may inquire whether a lot is subject to an advance or reserve. Auctioneer has made advances to various consignors in this sale.

Notice as to an Auction in Texas. In compliance with TDLR rule 67.100(c)(1), notice is hereby provided that this auction is covered by a Recovery Fund administered by the Texas Department of Licensing and Regulation, P.O. Box 12157, Austin, Texas 78711 (512) 463-6599. Any complaints may be directed to the same address.

Notice as to an Auction in Ohio: Auction firm and Auctioneer are licensed by the Dept. of Agriculture, and either the licensee is bonded in favor of the state or an aggrieved person may initiate a claim against the auction recovery fund created in Section 4707.25 of the Revised Code as a result of the licensee's actions, whichever is applicable.

Rev. 10-20-09

Additional Terms & Conditions:
COINS & CURRENCY

COINS and CURRENCY TERM A: Signature. Auctions are not on approval. No certified material may be returned because of possible differences of opinion with respect to the grade offered by any third-party organization, dealer, or service. No guarantee of grade is offered for uncertified Property sold and subsequently submitted to a third-party grading service. There are absolutely no exceptions to this policy. Under extremely limited circumstances, (e.g. gross cataloging error) a purchaser, who did not bid from the floor, may request Auctioneer to evaluate voiding a sale: such request must be made in writing detailing the alleged gross error; submission of the lot to the Auctioneer must be pre-approved by the Auctioneer; and bidder must notify Ron Brackemyre (1-800-8726467 Ext. 1312) in writing of such request within three (3) days of the non-floor bidder's receipt of the lot. Any lot that is to be evaluated must be in our offices within 30 days after Auction. Grading or method of manufacture do not qualify for this evaluation process nor do such complaints constitute a basis to challenge the authenticity of a lot. AFTER THAT 30-DAY PERIOD, NO LOTS MAY BE RETURNED FOR REASONS OTHER THAN AUTHENTICITY. Lots returned must be housed intact in their original holder. No lots purchased by floor Bidders may be returned (including those Bidders acting as agents for others) except for authenticity. Late remittance for purchases may be considered just cause to revoke all return privileges.

COINS and CURRENCY TERM B: Auctions conducted solely on the Internet THREE (3) DAY RETURN POLICY: Certified Coin and Uncertified and Certified Currency lots paid for within seven days of the Auction closing are sold with a three (3) day return privilege. You may return lots under the following conditions: Within three days of receipt of the lot, you must first notify Auctioneer by contacting Client Service by phone (1-800-872-6467) or e-mail (Bid@HA.com), and immediately ship the lot(s) fully insured to the attention of Returns, Heritage, 3500 Maple Avenue, 17th Floor, Dallas TX 75219-3941. Lots must be housed intact in their original holder and condition. You are responsible for the insured, safe delivery of any lots. A non-negotiable return fee of 5% of the purchase price ($10 per lot minimum) will be deducted from the refund for each returned lot or billed directly. Postage and handling fees are not refunded. After the three-day period (from receipt), no items may be returned for any reason. Late remittance for purchases revokes these Return privileges.

COINS and CURRENCY TERM C: Bidders who have inspected the lots prior to any Auction, or attended the Auction, or bid through an Agent, will not be granted any return privileges, except for reasons of authenticity.

COINS and CURRENCY TERM D: Coins sold referencing a third-party grading service are sold "as is" without any express or implied warranty, except for a guarantee by Auctioneer that they are genuine. Certain warranties may be available from the grading services and the Bidder is referred to them for further details: Numismatic Guaranty Corporation (NGC), P.O. Box 4776, Sarasota, FL 34230; Professional Coin Grading Service (PCGS), PO Box 9458, Newport Beach, CA 92658; ANACS, 6555 S. Kenton St. Ste. 303, Englewood, CO 80111; and Independent Coin Grading Co. (ICG), 7901 East Belleview Ave., Suite 50, Englewood, CO 80111.

COINS and CURRENCY TERM E: Notes sold referencing a third-party grading service are sold "as is" without any express or implied warranty, except for guarantee by Auctioneer that they are genuine. Grading, condition or other attributes of any lot may have a material effect on its value, and the opinion of others, including third-party grading services such as PCGS Currency, PMG, and CGA may differ with that of Auctioneer. Auctioneer shall not be bound by any prior or subsequent opinion, determination, or certification by any grading service. Bidder specifically waives any claim to right of return of any item because of the opinion, determination, or certification, or lack thereof, by any grading service. Certain warranties may be available from the grading services and the Bidder is referred to them for further details: Paper Money Guaranty (PMG), PO Box 4711, Sarasota FL 34230; PCGS Currency, PO Box 9458, Newport Beach, CA 92658; Currency Grading & Authentication (CGA), PO Box 418, Three Bridges, NJ 08887. Third party graded notes are not returnable for any reason whatsoever.

COINS and CURRENCY TERM F: Since we cannot examine encapsulated coins or notes, they are sold "as is" without our grading opinion, and may not be returned for any reason. Auctioneer shall not be liable for any patent or latent defect or controversy pertaining to or arising from any encapsulated collectible. In any such instance, purchaser's remedy, if any, shall be solely against the service certifying the collectible.

COINS and CURRENCY TERM G: Due to changing grading standards over time, differing interpretations, and to possible mishandling of items by subsequent owners, Auctioneer reserves the right to grade items differently than shown on certificates from any grading service that accompany the items. Auctioneer also reserves the right to grade items differently than the grades shown in the prior catalog should such items be reconsigned to any future auction.

COINS and CURRENCY TERM H: Although consensus grading is employed by most grading services, it should be noted as aforesaid that grading is not an exact science. In fact, it is entirely possible that if a lot is broken out of a plastic holder and resubmitted to another grading service or even to the same service, the lot could come back with a different grade assigned.

COINS and CURRENCY TERM I: Certification does not guarantee protection against the normal risks associated with potentially volatile markets. The degree of liquidity for certified coins and collectibles will vary according to general market conditions and the particular lot involved. For some lots there may be no active market at all at certain points in time.

COINS and CURRENCY TERM J: All non-certified coins and currency are guaranteed genuine, but are not guaranteed as to grade, since grading is a matter of opinion, an art and not a science, and therefore the opinion rendered by the Auctioneer or any third party grading service may not agree with the opinion of others (including trained experts), and the same expert may not grade the same item with the same grade at two different times. Auctioneer has graded the non-certified numismatic items, in the Auctioneer's opinion, to their current interpretation of the American Numismatic Association's standards as of the date the catalog was prepared. There is no guarantee or warranty implied or expressed that the grading standards utilized by the Auctioneer will meet the standards of any grading service at any time in the future.

COINS and CURRENCY TERM K: Storage of purchased coins and currency: Purchasers are advised that certain types of plastic may react with a coin's metal or transfer plasticizer to notes and may cause damage. Caution should be used to avoid storage in materials that are not inert.

COINS and CURRENCY TERM L: Storage of purchased coins and currency: Purchasers are advised that certain types of plastic may react with a coin's metal or transfer plasticizer to notes and may cause damage. Caution should be used to avoid storage in materials that are not inert.

COINS and CURRENCY TERM M: NOTE: Purchasers of rare coins or currency through Heritage have available the option of arbitration by the Professional Numismatists Guild (PNG); if an election is not made within ten (10) days of an unresolved dispute, Auctioneer may elect either PNG or A.A.A. Arbitration.

COINS and CURRENCY TERM N: For more information regarding Canadian lots attributed to the Charlton reference guides, please contact: Charlton International, PO Box 820, Station Willowdale B, North York, Ontario M2K 2R1 Canada.

WIRING INSTRUCTIONS:

BANK INFORMATION:
Wells Fargo Bank
420 Montgomery Street
San Francisco, CA 94104-1207

ACCOUNT NAME: Heritage Auction Galleries

ABA NUMBER: 121000248

ACCOUNT NUMBER: 4121930028

SWIFT CODE: WFBIUS6S

Rev. 7-24-09

Your five most effective bidding techniques:

1 Interactive Internet™ Proxy Bidding

(leave your maximum Bid at HA.com before the auction starts)

Heritage's exclusive Interactive Internet™ system is fun and easy! Before you start, you must register online at HA.com and obtain your Username and Password.

1. Login to the HA.com website, using your Username and Password.
2. Chose the specialty you're interested in at the top of the homepage (i.e. coins, currency, comics, movie posters, fine art, etc.).
3. Search or browse for the lots that interest you. Every auction has search features and a 'drop-down' menu list.
4. Select a lot by clicking on the link or the photo icon. Read the description, and view the full-color photography. Note that clicking on the image will enlarge the photo with amazing detail.
5. View the current opening bid. Below the lot description, note the historic pricing information to help you establish price levels. Clicking on a link will take you directly to our Permanent Auction Archives for more information and images.
6. If the current price is within your range, Bid! At the top of the lot page is a box containing the Current Bid and an entry box for your "Secret Maximum Bid" – the maximum amount you are willing to pay for the item before the Buyer's Premium is added. Click the button marked "Place Bid" (if you are not logged in, a login box will open first so you can enter your username (or e-mail address) and password.
7. After you are satisfied that all the information is correct, confirm your "Secret Maximum Bid" by clicking on the "Confirm Absentee Bid" button. You will receive immediate notification letting you know if you are now the top bidder, or if another bidder had previously bid higher than your amount. If you bid your maximum amount and someone has already bid higher, you will immediately know so you can concentrate on other lots.
8. Before the auction, if another bidder surpasses your "Secret Maximum Bid", you will be notified automatically by e-mail containing a link to review the lot and possibly bid higher.
9. Interactive Internet™ bidding closes at 10 P.M. Central Time the night before the session is offered in a floor event. Interactive Internet™ bidding closes two hours before live sessions where there is no floor bidding.
10. The Interactive Internet™ system generally opens the lot at the next increment above the second highest bid. As the high bidder, your "Secret Maximum Bid" will compete for you during the floor auction. Of course, it is possible in a Signature® or Grand Format live auction that you may be outbid on the floor or by a Heritage Live bidder after Internet bidding closes. Bid early, as the earliest bird wins in the event of a tie bid. For more information about bidding and bid increments, please see the section labeled "Bidding Options" found in the Terms & Conditions of this catalog.
11. After the auction, you will be notified of your success. It's that easy!

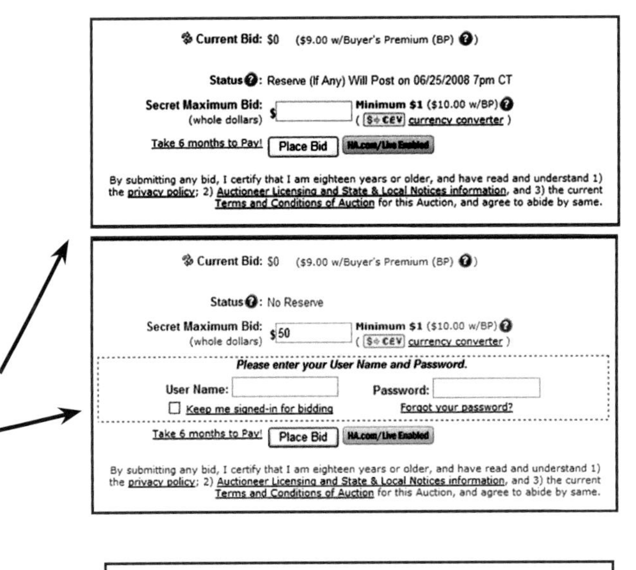

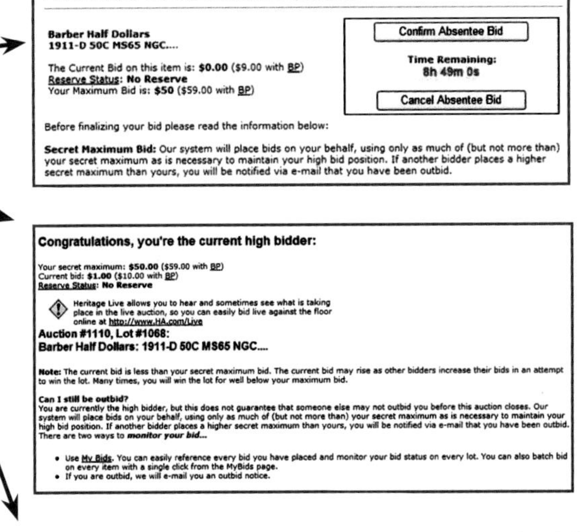

Your secret maximum bid of $36.00 on Lot #1315 in Auction #1110 has been outbid.
Morgan Dollars: 1881 $1 MS65 NGC....

Item Information

Auction: 2008 June West Palm Beach, FL (Summer FUN) Signature Coin Auction

Place Bid

Next Bid: $42.00 ($51.00 with BP)

Secret Maximum Bid: $ .00

② HERITAGE Live!™ Bidding

(participate in the Live auction via the Internet)

1. Look on each auction's homepage to verify whether that auction is "HA.com/Live Enabled." All Signature® and Grand Format auctions use the HERITAGE Live!™ system, and many feature live audio and/or video. Determine your lots of interest and maximum bids.
2. Note on the auction's homepage the session dates and times (and especially time zones!) so you can plan your participation. You actually have two methods of using HERITAGE Live!™: a) you can leave a proxy bid through this system, much like the Interactive Internet™ (we recommend you do this before the session starts), or b) you can sit in front of your computer much as the audience is sitting in the auction room during the actual auction.
3. Login at HA.com/Live.
4. Until you become experienced (and this happens quickly!) you will want to login well before your lot comes up so you can watch the activity on other lots. It is as intuitive as participating in a live auction.
5. When your lot hits the auction block, you can continue to bid live against the floor and other live bidders by simply clicking the "Bid" button; the amount you are bidding is clearly displayed on the console.

③ Mail Bidding

(deposit your maximum Bid with the U.S.P.S. well before the auction starts)

Mail bidding at auction is fun and easy, but by eliminating the interactivity of our online systems, some of your bids may be outbid before you lick the stamp, and you will have no idea of your overall chances until the auction is over!

1. Look through the printed catalog, and determine your lots of interest.
2. Research their market value by checking price lists and other price guidelines.
3. Fill out your bid sheet, entering your maximum bid on each lot. Bid using whole dollar amounts only. Verify your bids, because you are responsible for any errors you make! Please consult the Bidding Increments chart in the Terms & Conditions.
4. Please fill out your bid sheet completely! We also need: a) Your name and complete address for mailing invoices and lots; b) Your telephone number if any problems or changes arise; c) Your references; if you have not established credit with Heritage, you must send a 25% deposit, or list dealers with whom you have credit established; d) Total your bid sheet; add up all bids and list that total in the box; e) Sign your bid sheet, thereby agreeing to abide by the Terms & Conditions of Auction printed in the catalog.
5. Mail early, because preference is given to the first bid received in case of a tie.
6. When bidding by mail, you frequently purchase items at less than your maximum bid. Bidding generally opens at the next published increment above the second highest mail or Internet bid previously received; if additional floor, phone, or HERITAGE Live!™ bids are made, we act as your agent, bidding in increments over any additional bid until you win the lot or are outbid. For example, if you submitted a bid of $750, and the second highest bid was $375, bidding would start at $400; if no other bids were placed, you would purchase the lot for $400.
7. You can also Fax your Bid Sheet if time is short. Use our exclusive Fax Hotline: 214-443-8425.

MAIL/FAX BID SHEET — HERITAGE
Heritage Auction Galleries
1-800-872-6467
HA.com
3500 Maple Avenue, 17th Floor
Dallas, Texas 75219-3941

NAME William Stark — CUSTOMER # #123456
ADDRESS 4739 - B Bradford Drive — E-MAIL ADDRESS wstark@stark.com
CITY/STATE/ZIP Dallas, TX 75219
DAYTIME PHONE (A/C) 214-558-8109 — EVENING PHONE (A/C) 214-528-3500

Dealer References: XYZ Auction Company; ABC Collectibles, Inc.

(Bid in whole dollar amounts only.)

LOT NO.	AMOUNT	LOT NO.	AMOUNT
143	200	3210	325
221	75		
1621	125		
2416	625		
3189	475		

SUBTOTAL 1,825
TOTAL BID 1,825

FAX HOTLINE: 214-443-8425

④ Telephone Bidding (when you are traveling, or do not have access to HERITAGE Live!™)

1. To participate in an auction by telephone, you must make preliminary arrangements with Client Services (Toll Free 866-835-3243) at least three days before the auction.
2. We strongly recommend that you place preliminary bids by mail or Internet if you intend to participate by telephone. On many occasions, this dual approach has reduced disappointments due to telephone (cell) problems, unexpected travel, late night sessions, and time zone differences. Keep a list of your preliminary bids, and we will help you avoid bidding against yourself.

⑤ Attend in Person (whenever possible)

Auctions are fun, and we encourage you to attend as many as possible – although our HERITAGE Live!™ system brings all of the action right to your computer screen. Auction dates and session times are printed on the title page of each catalog, and appear on the homepage of each auction at HA.com. Join us if you can!

We're collectors too, and we understand that on occasion there is more to buy than there is cash. Consider Heritage's Extended Payment Plan [EPP] for your purchases totaling $2,500 or more.

Extended Payment Plan [EPP] Conditions

- Minimum invoice total is $2,500.
- Minimum Down Payment is 25% of the total invoice.
- A signed and returned EPP Agreement is required.
- The EPP is subject to a 3% *fully refundable* Set-up Fee (based on the total invoice amount) payable as part of the first monthly payment.
- The 3% Set-up Fee is refundable provided all monthly payments are made by eCheck, bank draft, personal check drawn on good funds, or cash; and if all such payments are made according to the EPP schedule.
- Monthly payments can be automatically processed with an eCheck, Visa, or MasterCard.
- You may take up to four equal monthly payments to pay the balance.
- Interest is calculated at only 1% per month on the unpaid balance.
- Your EPP must be kept current or additional interest may apply.
- There is no penalty for paying off early.
- Shipment will be made when final payment is received.
- All traditional auction and sales policies still apply.

There is no return privilege once you have confirmed your sale, and penalties can be incurred on cancelled invoices. To avoid additional fees, you must make your down payment within 14 days of the auction. All material purchased under the EPP will be physically secured by Heritage until paid in full.

To exercise the EPP option, please notify **Eric Thomas** at **214.409.1241** or email at **EricT@HA.com** upon receipt of your invoice.

We appreciate your business and wish you good luck with your bidding.

BEVERLY
HILLS

HERITAGE HA.com
Auction Galleries

1.

2.

3.

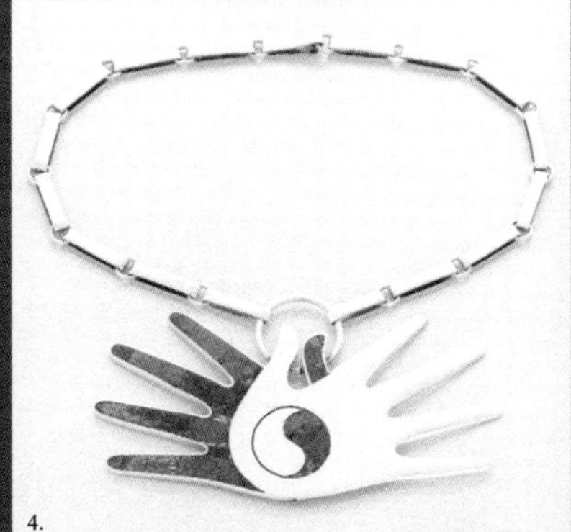

4.

5.

6.

7.

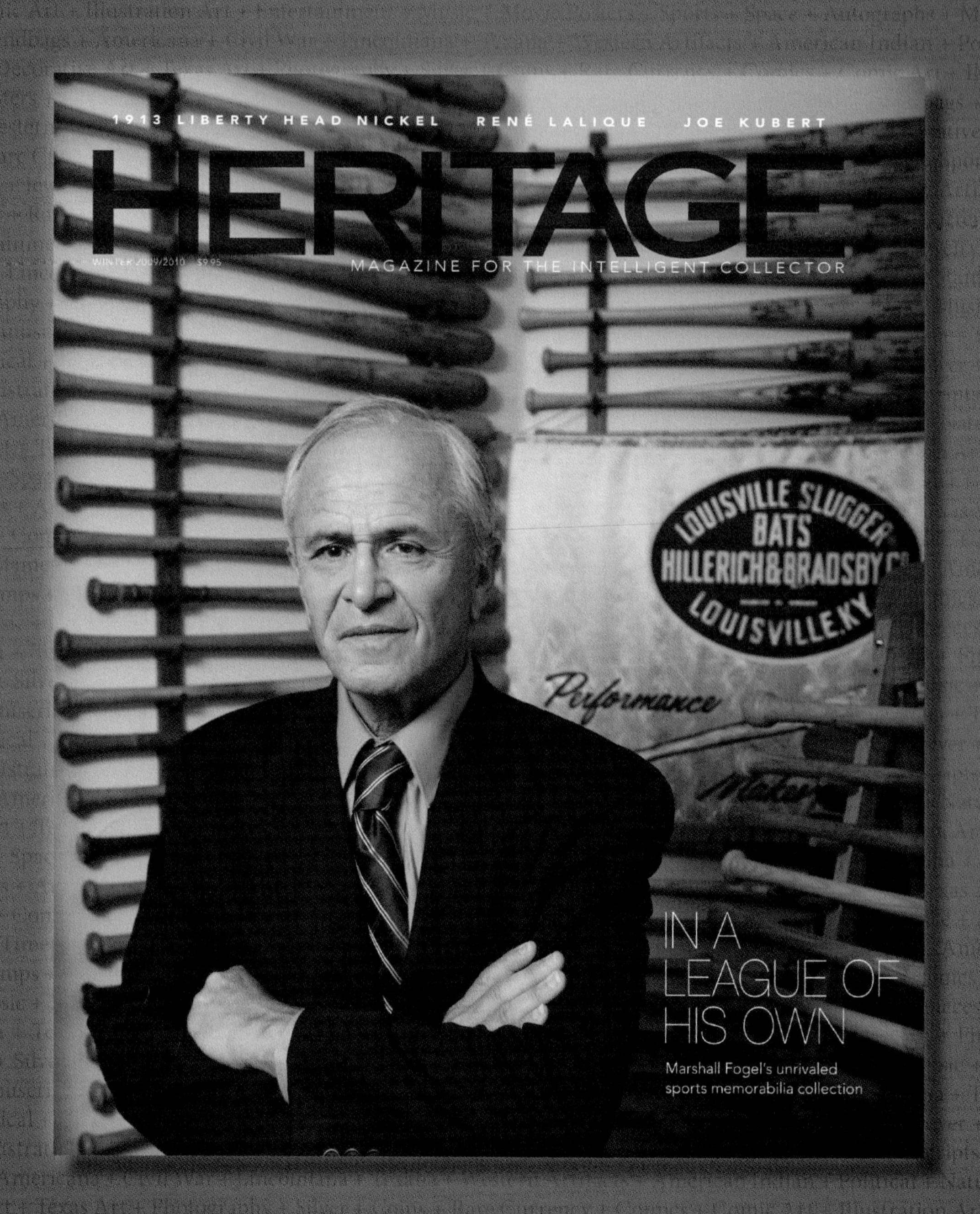
1913 LIBERTY HEAD NICKEL
RENÉ LALIQUE
JOE KUBERT
HERITAGE
WINTER 2009/2010 $9.95
MAGAZINE FOR THE INTELLIGENT COLLECTOR
LOUISVILLE SLUGGER
BATS
HILLERICH&BRADSBY CO
LOUISVILLE.KY
Performance
IN A LEAGUE OF HIS OWN
Marshall Fogel's unrivaled sports memorabilia collection

HERITAGE

OUR MISSION

To be the world's most trusted and efficient marketplace and information resource for owners of fine art, collectibles, and other objects of enduring value

OUR VALUES

INTEGRITY

Honesty and fairness must define every facet of our business

TRANSPARENCY

We embrace clarity and freedom of information, enabling clients, partners and coworkers to make informed, confident decisions

TEAMWORK

We collaborate unselfishly, sharing credit for our accomplishments

EFFICIENCY

We seek to help clients, partners and coworkers save valuable time and resources

EXPERTISE

We never stop studying and learning, because our success depends upon providing our clients with the best possible advice

INNOVATION

We continually make our services more accessible and useful to clients, often rendering our own products obsolete by creating better ones

LONG-TERM OUTLOOK

We strive to carefully construct win-win agreements with clients and partners